Psychology of Personality

McGRAW-HILL SERIES IN PSYCHOLOGY

HARRY F. HARLOW, *Consulting Editor*

BEACH, HEBB, MORGAN, AND NISSEN · The Neuropsychology of Lashley

VON BÉKÉSY · Experiments in Hearing

BERKOWITZ · Aggression: A Social Psychological Analysis

BERLYNE · Conflict, Arousal, and Curiosity

BLUM · Psychoanalytic Theories of Personality

BROWN · The Motivation of Behavior

BROWN · The Psychodynamics of Abnormal Behavior

BROWN AND GHISELLI · Scientific Method in Psychology

BUCKNER AND McGRATH · Vigilance: A Symposium

COFER · Verbal Learning and Verbal Behavior

COFER AND MUSGRAVE · Verbal Behavior and Learning: Problems and Processes

CRAFTS, SCHNEIRLA, ROBINSON, AND GILBERT · Recent Experiments in Psychology

DAVITZ · The Communication of Emotional Meaning

DEESE · The Psychology of Learning

DOLLARD AND MILLER · Personality and Psychotherapy

DORCUS AND JONES · Handbook of Employee Selection

ELLIS · Handbook of Mental Deficiency

FERGUSON · Personality Measurement

FERGUSON · Statistical Analysis in Psychology and Education

GHISELLI · Theory of Psychological Measurement

GHISELLI AND BROWN · Personnel and Industrial Psychology

GILMER · Industrial Psychology

GRAY · Psychology Applied to Human Affairs

GUILFORD · Fundamental Statistics in Psychology and Education

GUILFORD · Personality

GUILFORD · Psychometric Methods

GUION · Personnel Testing

HAIRE · Psychology in Management

HIRSH · The Measurement of Hearing

HURLOCK · Adolescent Development

HURLOCK · Child Development

HURLOCK · Developmental Psychology

KARN AND GILMER · Readings in Industrial and Business Psychology

KRECH AND CRUTCHFIELD · Theory and Problems of Social Psychology

LAZARUS · Adjustment and Personality

LEWIN · A Dynamic Theory of Personality

LEWIN · Principles of Topological Psychology

LEWIS · Quantitative Methods in Psychology

MAIER AND SCHNEIRLA · Principles of Animal Psychology

MARX AND HILLIX · Systems and Theories in Psychology

MESSICK AND BRAYFIELD · Decision and Choice: Contributions of Sidney Siegel

MILLER · Language and Communication

MISIAK AND STAUDT · Catholics in Psychology: A Historical Survey

MORGAN AND STELLAR · Physiological Psychology

PAGE · Abnormal Psychology

RETHLINGSHAFER · Motivation as Related to Personality

REYMERT · Feelings and Emotions

SCHERER AND WERTHEIMER · A Psycholinguistic Experiment on Foreign-Language Teaching

SEASHORE · Psychology of Music

SHAFFER AND LAZARUS · Fundamental Concepts in Clinical Psychology

SIEGEL · Nonparametric Statistics: For the Behavioral Sciences

STAGNER · Psychology of Personality

TOWNSEND · Introduction to Experimental Method

VINACKE · The Psychology of Thinking

WALLEN · Clinical Psychology: The Study of Persons

WARREN AND AKERT · The Frontal Granular Cortex and Behavior

WATERS, RETHLINGSHAFER, AND CALDWELL · Principles of Comparative Psychology

WINER · Statistical Principles in Experimental Design

ZUBEK AND SOLBERG · Human Development

John F. Dashiell was Consulting Editor of this series from its inception in 1931 until January 1, 1950. Clifford T. Morgan was Consulting Editor of this series from January 1, 1950 until January 1, 1959.

PSYCHOLOGY OF
PERSONALITY

Ross Stagner

PROFESSOR OF PSYCHOLOGY
CHAIRMAN, DEPARTMENT OF PSYCHOLOGY
WAYNE STATE UNIVERSITY

THIRD EDITION

McGRAW-HILL BOOK COMPANY, INC.
New York   San Francisco   Toronto   London

PSYCHOLOGY OF PERSONALITY

TO
M. W. S.

Preface

In the Preface to the first edition of this book, written in 1937, I made the following statement: "The material which may legitimately be included in a treatment of the psychology of personality has grown too large to be brought within the compass of a single volume of reasonable size." Over the intervening decades this problem has been magnified tremendously. The psychologist trying to increase his understanding of personality now faces the dilemma once propounded by Lewis Carroll: "To stay where you are, you have to run as fast as you can. To get ahead, you must run twice as fast as that." New theoretical analyses, as well as the flood of empirical research, may well lead to utter confusion for the student.

Necessarily, therefore, I have been severely selective in policies of including or excluding points of view and research investigations in this volume. I have regretfully deleted from the final manuscript many passages discussing differences in point of view among psychologists, and similarly I have found it necessary to cut references to a large number of interesting research studies. In the Bibliography at the end of the volume I have included many of these items, with a reference to the page on which they would have been incorporated had space been available. By this means students interested in exploring a given topic more intensively, or in checking my conclusions against more investigations, can do so fairly easily.

In being so selective I have been guided by several principles. One is that the student has a right to learn of the major differences among psychologists which produce variations in the interpretation of certain data about personality. A second is that these divergencies should not become the center of attention, so that one sees all trees and no forest. In applying this principle I have deliberately emphasized my own conception of personality development and organization, built around homeostasis and the process of perceiving; I have tried to indicate some weaknesses of this formulation, however, and to do modest justice to competing viewpoints. A third principle has been that of avoiding certain technical controversies which are of great interest to professional psychologists. but which might appear quite unimportant to a student just entering this area. Instructors may wish to expand on such points in terms of their own backgrounds and research interests.

Developments in personality study over this period of time have been exciting. Many topics, treated with considerable assurance in the first edition, receive quite a different interpretation in this version. Some sections are totally new; and, naturally, some sections of earlier editions are now missing. The major purpose of the first edition, however, remains unchanged: to provide the student with an introduction to our knowledge of the normal personality. References to pathological personalities have actually been diminished somewhat.

I am indebted to many teachers who have used earlier editions for criticisms and suggestions; to the numerous publishers who have granted permission for reproduction of copyrighted materials; and most of all to my students, whose persistent questioning makes it impossible for me to relax with the contented assurance that I have a sound solution for all problems. I hope that they, and their fellows, will continue to disturb my equilibrium, and that of the instructors who use this book, so that we shall be stimulated to continue searching for new insights into that fascinating phenomenon, the human personality.

Ross Stagner

Contents

358

Preface ix

Section I. Introduction 1

   1. The Scientific Study of Personality 3
   2. Methods: Ratings and Observations 27
   3. Methods: Inventories and Projective Tests 42

Section II. Development 67

   4. Basic Principles 69
   5. Emotional Foundations 87
   6. Frustration, Stress, and Conflict 111

Section III. Description 135

   7. Personality Style 137
   8. Traits 157
   9. The Self 182
   10. Character 214
   11. Attitudes and Values 237
   12. Type Theories of Personality 264

Section IV. Dynamics 287

   13. Biological Approaches 289
   14. Psychoanalytic Theories of Motivation 308
   15. Motivation as Goal Seeking 332

Section V. Determinants 361

   16. Biological Factors 363
   17. The Family: Childhood 397
   18. The Family: Maturity 426
   19. The School System 450
   20. Economic Factors 485
   21. Personality and Social Values 516

Bibliography and Author Index 535

Index 577

INTRODUCTION

The human personality is almost certainly the most complex phenomenon studied by science. It is, simultaneously, the most fascinating, at least to many of us. This is not entirely because we egotistically see ourselves mirrored in the intricate architecture of another person's individuality. It is also because, in our daily lives, we must continually meet, recognize, and deal with other personalities, anticipate their actions, understand their feelings.

The scientific study of personality seems at times to devitalize and even to dehydrate the vivid quality of the unique person. But this is only a preliminary step toward a more intensive exploration and a deeper insight.

Personality has been defined in many ways by different observers. Each such definition has something to offer by way of emphasis upon a particular facet of the complicated whole. And each such definition is likely to imply certain methods, certain techniques of scientific investigation. By way of introducing the student to the problem, we deal first with definitions and methods in the study of the human personality.

CHAPTER 1

The Scientific Study of Personality

Everyone is fascinated by the study of personality. Not only is this illustrated by the huge enrollments in classes that promise a new and brighter face which you can present to the world; it also underlies the perennial popularity of gossip over the back fence or in the little "confidential" magazines. Babies watch adults intently and seem to learn much about the personalities important in their lives. We adults focus our attention on a Roosevelt, a Churchill, or an Eisenhower—we are attracted by inside information about the personalities of the figures that loom large over our own world.

The study of personality is indeed important to us. Marriage is an aspect of life which is of the greatest significance; and what is more decisive for happy or unhappy marriage than the personalities of the two individuals so bound together? Occupations demand different personality patterns; a study of those successfully following a given profession gives the young man a cue as to whether this would be a wise choice for him.

Culture and personality are intimately related. We need not accept the stereotype of an innate Latin temperament to concede that Southern Europeans are generally more expressive, less reticent about their feelings, as compared to Americans or Northern Europeans. The Russian social system, even more than the Russian climate, molds certain kinds of personality patterns. And it is likely that the human personality, plastic though it may be, carries enough inherent drive to modify an entire culture if given time. Great leaders are successful in inducing change if their proposals appeal to the frustrated needs of the group members. Thus, the psychology of personality promises insights and understandings which range all the way from knowing yourself (and persons face to face with you) to better comprehension of politics, history, and culture change.

The Importance of Scientific Study. This chapter has been entitled "The Scientific Study of Personality." It is important that we put the emphasis here on the word "scientific." Casual observations are intriguing, gossipy anecdotes are entertaining, romanticized biographies are exciting. But these are not dependable sources of knowledge. Insights so obtained are likely to be spurious and misleading.

To arrive at a valid understanding of the psychology of personality, we need a precise definition of what it is we wish to study; we need observations which are not influenced by chance or accident; and we need interpretations of these facts which are not biased by personal prejudice. To meet such standards is not exactly easy. Let us take a look at each of them in turn.

DEFINITIONS OF PERSONALITY

There are a number of popular "definitions" of personality, in the sense that there are several different meanings attached to the word as it is used conversationally. Perhaps the commonest of these may be reduced to the formula, "Personality is your effect upon other people." When one hears it said that "Miss Smith has a lot of personality," he knows that people who meet Miss Smith do not forget her easily. She has a high stimulus value.

Another popular view of personality identifies it with the characteristic of aggressiveness. "Jimmy has a weak personality" is interpreted to mean that he is easily imposed upon or that he is lacking in forcefulness. This tendency to identify personalities in terms of a single characteristic is, of course, a common feature of unscientific thinking.

"Personality" is also used colloquially to imply personal attractiveness, the ability to withstand hardships ("character" is commoner here), and other specific qualities. Although occasionally it is used to identify a general integration of responses, an individual style of life, or a unique point of view, such sophisticated interpretations are relatively rare.

Some Scientific Definitions. The scientific conception of personality has been worked out to some extent by trial and error. It may be helpful to the student if we summarize briefly some of the meanings attached to this term by earlier psychologists. Since these definitions show a trend in thinking, following them may quickly orient the student to the value of the final definition which will be the keynote of this book.

Kempf (1919)[1] has defined personality as "the habitual mode of adjustment which the organism effects between its own egocentric drives and the exigencies of the environment." As phrased, this would include practically all of human behavior, since the vast majority of our responses do consist of just such habitual ways of adjusting.

According to Morton Prince (1924), "Personality is the sum total of all the biological innate dispositions, impulses, tendencies, appetites, and instincts of the individual, and the acquired dispositions and tendencies." This defini-

---

[1] Bibliographical references will be identified by inserting the publication date after the author's name. The complete reference is given in the bibliography at the end of the volume.

tion places a potentially useful emphasis on the *inner* aspect of personality. Like Kempf's, however, it seems to cover virtually all of psychology, rather than to delimit a particular field.

Floyd Allport (1924) states that "personality traits may be considered as so many important dimensions in which people may be found to differ." This seems much too inclusive. For example, it includes physical dimensions, which are only indirectly of importance for personality. Elsewhere he offers a more useful formulation, "Personality is the individual's characteristic reactions to social stimuli and the quality of his adaptation to the social features of his environment."

Watson (1924) has called attention to the fact that character is part of personality. He says, "Personality includes not only these [character-conventional] reactions, but also the more individual personal adjustments and capacities as well as their life history. Popularly speaking, we would say that a liar and a profligate had no character, but he may have an exceedingly interesting personality."

Symonds (1928) has defined personality as "the portrait or landscape of the organism working together in all its phases," and May (1929) speaks of "the social stimulus value of the individual."

Definitions in Terms of Stimulus and of Response. If we now examine these definitions and compare them with some examples from popular usage, we find a fairly sharp differentiation into two groups: those which consider personality in terms of its *stimulus value* (the effect one has on others) and those which consider it in terms of *responses* (what the person actually does). There is no necessary contradiction between the two. John's stimulus value for others is necessarily a function of John's behavior. There are, however, important differences between the two, and one or both may be found unsuitable for a sound scientific approach.

Personality as Stimulus. Not only the man in the street, but also many psychologists, would define personality in terms of stimulus value. This is a natural consequence of everyday situations in which the concept is particularly useful, such as picking prospective employees, describing friends, or grading school children. Applicants for jobs are often chosen on the basis of their "personality" as it appears to the personnel interviewer; and this is justifiable, at least in the sense that an applicant who impresses the interviewer unpleasantly might affect customers similarly.

An attempt to use scientifically a definition of personality as stimulus leads to immediate difficulty. This is especially true if we are looking for increased logical precision and quantitative measurements of personality traits. Rigid application of this definition creates the bizarre situation in which each individual has virtually an unlimited number of personalities—one for each of his acquaintances, because he has for each a different stimulus value. He will not be evaluated in the same way by his mother, his wife, his employer, his secretary, his rival for a promotion, and the man he has beaten at golf. Definition of personality as stimulus makes precision impossible, because *two* personalities are interacting in every instance. When Mary reports that Sally is "a malicious gossip," this may give us more information about Mary than about Sally.

Personality as Response. In an attempt to get away from the difficulties which result from defining personality in stimulus terms, many psychologists have shifted to the definition of personality as response. It is plausible, for example, that if Susan has a charming personality (and not merely a pretty face), this is a function of her behavior. It should be possible, then, for methodical study to reveal the particular pattern of responses evoking the judgment "charming."

This is a distinct improvement over the popular approach, in that the personality is now tied down to certain objective manifestations which can be studied by the techniques of scientific psychology. Such definitions as that of Floyd Allport fall in this group. To some extent there is a danger that the definition will be too comprehensive and cover more territory than can be handled in practice; for instance, Watson's definition amounts to saying that personality is "everything you do." The problems created by an attempt to use such a definition in research are obvious.

Guthrie (1944) has defined personality as "those habits and habit systems of social importance that are stable and resistant to change." While this is more precise than the formulations of Kempf, Prince, and Watson, it still raises numerous questions. What about habits which are not of social importance? Some people like to pose before a mirror when they are alone—a habit that may not be "of social importance," although it is certainly a significant clue to personality. Does habit cover the whole of our subject matter? To many the concept of habit will seem strained if it is stretched so widely.

Guthrie's intent, of course, is to combine the definitions of personality as stimulus and as response. His phrase "of social importance" is presumably equivalent to "which determine the impression we make on others." Thus Guthrie would retain the practical advantage of the popular definition, while reaping the scientific benefits of an approach tied to behavior which can be subjected to methodical investigation.

Even Guthrie's definition encounters some problems. When faced with the same stimulus, a person will not always act in the same way. Moreover, two persons may act in an apparently identical fashion for quite different reasons. The inconstancy of individual responses in some cases and the similarity of response by obviously different personalities suggest the need for still further refinement of our definition.

Personality—Mask or Substance? Numerous writers have objected to an approach limited to either stimulus value or response pattern, on the basis that each of these is likely to emphasize superficial aspects of the personality.

It is suggested that we should distinguish between personality as a *mask,* or front, assumed in many instances merely for its effect on others, and personality as *substance,* the "real" or inner personality.

Clearly there is some validity in this proposal. Most of us do modify our behavior to fit our social setting. This indicates that many of our responses are still part of the "mask" of social participation.

More difficult is the implicit assumption that there is a "real" personality underlying the various "mask" manifestations. Naturally one tends to think of a basic reality behind changing appearances. But what is the *real* personality? If, when I am with an attractive young woman, I behave differently from the way in which I act when with a group of men, is this not still a "real" facet of my personality? Difference in behavior need not mean a change in personality. Rather, the behavior exemplifies how my personality responds *to the situation as I see it.*

Personality as Intervening Variable. A synthesis of these approaches may be developed by following out the suggestion just made. It is now a truism in psychology that a stimulus does not immediately and automatically elicit a response. A stimulus affects the organism as a whole, and the ultimate response is a function of both the stimulus and the organism. (When a child is hungry, an ice-cream cone elicits one reaction; when he is satiated, the response is quite different.) There are certain *intervening variables* between the stimulus and the response which affect the nature of the final behavior pattern. Such variables are the person's intelligence, his motives at the moment, his past experience with the stimulus, and his attitude toward the situation in which the stimulus appears. Thus if the stimulus is an invitation to a dance, variables influencing the final response might be the young man's past mishaps at dances, his expectation of meeting a certain girl who attracts him, his financial status, his need to study for an examination during the evening of the dance, and so on. The decision he reaches will be a function of these forces (of which he is not necessarily conscious). Another man may reach the same conclusion, but for entirely different reasons.

Gordon Allport, after an extensive analysis of the possible definitions of personality, has found a definition in terms of intervening variables to be essential. His proposed formulation is as follows: *"Personality is the dynamic organization within the individual of those psychophysical systems that determine his unique adjustments to his environment."* [2]

It will be noted that this definition covers most of the difficulties mentioned above. It recognizes the changing nature of personality (a *dynamic* organization); it focuses on the *inner* aspect rather than on superficial manifestations; but it establishes the basis for the social stimulus value of personality (*unique* adjustments to the environment). While it is not possible to study

[2] G. W. Allport. *Personality: a psychological interpretation,* p. 48. Copyright, 1937, by Henry Holt and Company, Inc.

directly a "dynamic organization within the individual," this definition is compatible with a thoroughgoing scientific approach based upon appropriate research techniques.

It might be possible to improve in minor ways on Allport's definition, but on the whole it meets adequately all the requirements of a scientific psychology of personality. We shall therefore adopt it as a standard for the purposes of the present volume.[3]

Allport makes no attempt to incorporate in his definition any characterization of the kind of psychophysical systems he mentions. This is perhaps good judgment, inasmuch as such a listing, once started, ought to be inclusive, and we do not know how many different systems must be included. It does seem worthwhile, however, to point out the importance of one such system: *our pattern of beliefs and expectancies.*

When John meets a snarling dog, he cries and runs away. His younger brother, Ted, is unperturbed. He scolds the dog and reassures his playmates. This is an important personality difference, which can best be described as a difference in belief or expectancy regarding the harmful potentialities of the dog. Similarly, a man who avoids women is thereby revealing his beliefs about the opposite sex. A boy who feels inferior to his playmates will show characteristic behavior patterns.

The definition of personality as an *inner system* of beliefs, expectancies, desires, and values has numerous advantages. From the viewpoint of research it provides a focus of investigation—less convenient than a definition in response terms, but less confusing than a definition in stimulus terms. On logical grounds it appears to unite successfully these two divergent approaches. One has no difficulty in thinking of an inner structure which determines responses, which in turn influence the judgments of others about us. Furthermore, it resolves certain problems raised by the facts of variable behavior in different social environments and of similar responses which require dissimilar interpretations.

Personality as a Scientific Abstraction. Regardless of our choice among these three approaches to personality, personality remains an abstraction, not a directly observed phenomenon. This occurs in both popular and scientific thought; when you watch your friend in action, you feel sure that there is an underlying unity behind his acts. "I know him; what he is really working for is power; he wants to be the big boss." Thus we confidently assert our theories about the personalities of others.

The scientist, too, is concerned to develop a theory of personality. This may be a generalized theory, intended to cover all sorts of people; or it may be a

---

[3] It is interesting to note that psychologists writing on personality in recent years have tended to avoid giving a formal definition of the term. No statement comparable to that of Allport, cited above, can be found in Murphy (1947), Dollard and Miller (1950), or Diamond (1957). Careful reading of these volumes indicates that the definition quoted above would cover most of what the authors mean by "personality."

special theory, a conception of Sam Wilson, what he is "really" like. In clinical work particularly, the psychologist tries to develop a picture of the "true" personality, the inner unity which coordinates and integrates all the specific actions and fantasies of the individual.

Such a conception of the scientist's efforts is disturbing to some readers. It is a widespread belief that science deals only with what is "real." But the reality may be highly abstract. No one has ever seen an electron; but the scientist has a theory, according to which, if electrons have certain properties, certain effects will follow. Experiment then is designed to observe the effects; the "real" electron is only an abstraction, not an object of experience. In the same way, the "real" personality is an abstraction from many observations and from a theory of personality. The value of a theory is based on its success in helping us to understand, or to predict, what the individual will do.

Consensual Validation. Another way to decide upon the value of a theory is to see if it leads to results which can be observed by others. The psychotic individual reports experiences which are uniquely his own; he may see pink elephants or ask for protection from the millions of little blue cockroaches following him around. In this case his inner organization—his pattern of perception and emotion—leads to a belief about reality. *For him, these experiences are real.* But other observers claim that they are not real. Granting that the majority is often wrong (cf. Christopher Columbus), we can still say that a personality theory which leads to results which look unreal to qualified observers is of doubtful value. Philosophers call this "the criterion of consensual validation," meaning that we can define reality by the agreement of these observers.

The foregoing examples suggest that *personality is a way of looking at reality.* The paranoid person may have a theory that he is being persecuted by the Masons, the Kiwanis, and the Elks. His way of looking at the world is distorted. His behavior will be peculiar because he is responding to his world, not to our world. Within his world, his behavior may be perfectly logical. This is another reason why it is important to find out what is behind a person's responses, not confine ourselves to a study of his behavior. The normal personality is one whose view of the world agrees fairly well with that of people around him. A man is perceived as "queer" if he acts on the basis of a queer theory about reality.

Similarly, psychologists agree about certain fundamentals in the field of personality. This is not to deny that there are vigorous differences on theory. But certain kinds of "theories" are automatically judged to be useless. If someone tries to explain deviations in personality as due to possession by devils, he is treated as mentally unbalanced and certainly incompetent to study personality.

In this book we shall concentrate on those phases of personality research which are agreed upon by most psychologists. It will be necessary, occasionally, to note that schools of psychology diverge on specific points. Even in these cases there is usually an accepted body of observed facts; the variation comes from differences in interpretation. Before we can reasonably consider these interpretations, we must find out what the agreed facts are. The best way to approach this question is to look at the problem of personality description.

ANALYSIS OF PERSONALITY

Every personality is unique. No two of us are exactly alike. Such a view, however, does not lend itself to scientific investigation; we may be led to the conclusion that we can only admire personality, but not study it.

Actually, in the preceding pages, we have implied that it is permissible to analyze personality into different components: the person as seen by others; the person as a pattern of behavior; and the person as a pattern of inner organization, including his ways of looking at people and things, his emotions, desires, and anxieties.

Psychologists, however, continue further with this process of analysis. To illustrate ways of defining specific aspects of personality for more detailed study, we offer a concrete description of a personality—or rather, for reasons which will become clear, a comparative description of two personalities, as certain scientific methods reveal them.

Two Personalities. Sam Wilson is a quiet, reserved youngster who talks freely only about impersonal matters and answers direct personal questions with reticence and apparent resistance. Don Young, by contrast, is jolly, somewhat noisy, and talkative. He discusses the most personal matters with no apparent embarrassment or concern.[4]

Sam is rated "seclusive, closed, unfriendly, lacking in a sense of humor" by his acquaintances. Don is considered to be "sociable, open, friendly, with a good sense of humor."

When asked to look at a series of pictures and imagine stories for which each picture could be an illustration, Sam falls into the mood of the instructions quickly and makes up tales elaborate in detail and full of incisive, somewhat barbed comments about people. Most of his stories are tragic in import and the central figure in each story suffers, or is about to suffer, the loss of something that he values highly. Don, on the other hand, finds difficulty in making up stories and, when he does so, gives brief, conventional plots leading to the ever-popular "happy ending."

The two boys are asked to fill out a widely used questionnaire scale for personality traits. Sam makes a high score on "introversion" and "self-sufficiency," a moderately high score on "neurotic tendency," and a moderately low score on

---

[4] These two "cases" are synthetic; i.e., they are composites prepared from the records of several individuals, because data from the wide variety of techniques mentioned were not available for the same persons. The two personalities have been constructed, however, to maintain the relationships found in relevant investigations.

"dominance." Don makes a very high score on "dominance," medium on "self-sufficiency," and low scores on "introversion" and "neurotic tendency."

Both make the same score, roughly, on an intelligence test and a test of speed in reading. When asked to predict how fast he could read a similar passage on a second test in reading, however, Sam guesses that he can do it much faster, while Don thinks that he would do only a little better the second time. Sam also reveals in other ways that he sets very high standards for himself, while Don's feeling is, "I could make higher grades if I studied, but I guess I like playing around too much."

In a laboratory experiment both boys are interrupted in various things that they have been asked to do. Sam fidgets around until he can get back to the table and finish his uncompleted work. Don sits on the table and begins telling the experimenter about his vacation. When the experimenter leaves the room, Don idly completes one task, ignoring the others. In a test involving quick shifts from one kind of mental work to another, Sam becomes somewhat nervous and mutters a good deal; Don seems completely unperturbed.

On another questionnaire, Sam indicates that he places high value on scientific (theoretical), aesthetic, and social (humanitarian) pursuits. Don reveals a decided tendency to value more highly the practical, economic, and political (power) aspects of situations. Both are a little below average on religious evaluations.

Aspects of Personality. According to any usage of the term, these two boys are different in "personality." It is apparent that they differ not only in their impression upon their friends (stimulus value), but also as they are studied by interview, by laboratory experiment, and by various kinds of standard tests of personality. Personality, then, is something which shows up in our relations to people around us, in our answers to an interviewer (or to a set of printed questions), in our overt behavior, and in our verbal constructions, e.g., imaginative productions. It is, in fact, difficult for a person to engage in *any* activity which does not reflect some facet of his personality.

Many different techniques have been worked out for the study of the human personality. That there is no single *best* way to do this is suggested by the diversity of facts outlined above, each based on a different method of investigation. The psychologist who would study personality must be ready to employ all these and other techniques. This is necessary because even the simplest human personality is very complex. No single key will unlock all its doors.

The Value of Contrasts. It is easier to describe Sam Wilson by contrasting him with Don Young. Varying aspects of personality are brought more sharply into focus by this method. As a matter of fact, this is the basic technique by which we learn most of our judgments about our environment. To the young child, "cold" takes on meaning as it is contrasted with "hot." Color becomes identified as a variable aspect of the environment most readily when attention is called to objects similar except for contrasting color.

Most studies of personality have found it expedient to derive descriptions in terms of pairs of polar opposites, such as sociable-seclusive, optimistic-pessimistic, introversive-extratensive, or dominant-submissive. There is less danger of confusion and misunderstanding in working with this method than is the case when single terms are used to identify specific manifestations of personality.

Is Analysis Legitimate? It may seem strange, but many psychologists object vigorously to attempts to analyze personality into traits for special investigation. This objection is based on the ground that personality is an organized whole and that any form of analysis changes the qualities of the whole. The objection is invalid, since it is based on a false analogy. Psychological traits are not substances, such as water, which can be analyzed into its components, hydrogen and oxygen, only by destroying the material analyzed.

A more realistic approach would be to state that methods of analysis must be appropriate to the material studied and to the ends sought. Water can be studied with regard to such variables as temperature, color, rate of flow, volume, or pressure without destroying it. If proper units of analysis are employed, personality can also be analyzed without doing violence to its unique totality.

To describe Don Young and Sam Wilson, we found it necessary to go beyond a mere statement that each is unique and could not be duplicated anywhere else in the human race. Such a statement would be of no help to anyone. It is true that something very complex, called "total personality," is unique to each of these boys. But for the sake of meaningful description, comparison, and study, it was found desirable to indicate precise *ways* in which they differ. It was then shown that they varied with respect to certain characteristics, such as introversion, level of aspiration, self-esteem, and sociability.

Inasmuch as these are true functional characteristics of the human organism, they seem to be proper units for analysis. They are not, however, physical in character. It would be quite improper to think of traits as if they represented some physiological structure—as if Sam had six units and Don only three units of some organic stuff determining a personality tendency.[5]

The task of describing personalities, then, is not a simple one. It is decidedly easier if we can agree upon a set of terms and their meanings, so that we can picture the typical behavior to be expected of an individual who is characterized by such terms. Comparisons, and the prediction of future behavior, become still more successful when made in numerical form. If Sam is less talkative than Don, we immediately wonder how much less. When comparisons reach the precision of saying that one falls in the 10th percentile of college men, the other in the 75th percentile, we have made a substantial advance in description. And such clear numerical labels can be used for counsel-

---

[5] This is not to say that we may not some day discover such organic determinants—glandular secretions, autonomic nervous-system functions, or something else. These will, however, be discovered by *physiological* analysis and will be related to traits, which are products of *psychological* analysis.

ing and employment procedures with much greater confidence than simple verbal descriptions.

The Range of Individual Differences. The point of view just stated is based on the judgment that analysis of the unique personality into specific traits is defensible and indeed necessary. What is important is that analysis must utilize appropriate units. When we study a phenomenon such as a river, we cannot analyze the water itself without destroying it; but we can analyze such aspects as volume and rate of flow. Similarly, if we analyze personality down to little details like smiling, talking, or finger movements, the total picture is destroyed; but if we use traits such as those described for Don and Sam, we are using units appropriate to the problem.

We also note that such comparisons of traits should be, wherever possible, on a numerical basis. Just as we do not classify rivers into two groups, fast and slow, but apply a numerical measure of speed, so we attempt to use numerical estimates of personality traits. We want to know how often or how consistently this trait description applies to this person. We also want to know how he compares with his fellows on such measures.

When we use this procedure, we find that personality trait differences are usually distributed according to the bell-shaped curve so familiar in studies of intelligence, motor ability, and mechanical aptitude. This means that a few persons are extreme with respect to the trait under investigation; but as we identify manifestations of the same kind which are moderate in degree, more people fall into the middle classes. In most studies, the middle position (not deviating noticeably toward either extreme of the trait continuum) is found to be the most heavily populated. Figure 1.1, which shows the distribution of scores of a college population on a measure of rhathymia (carefree,

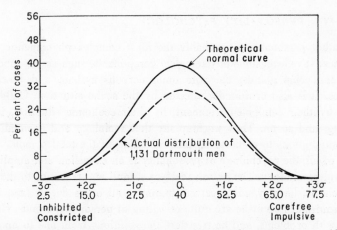

Fig. 1.1 Distribution of scores on a typical personality-trait measure (Guilford's rhathymia scale). Individual differences in personality tend to be distributed according to the normal curve.

happy-go-lucky tendency), illustrates this point. Nobody makes the highest possible score at either extreme of the scale. As we move in toward the neutral point, we find more and more people, with the largest number scoring almost on the center of the scale. Most people are balanced rather than one-sided with respect to this trait.

In this volume we shall be concerned with at least three fundamental problems in the psychology of personality. (1) We shall study the *personality as a whole*—the unique pattern which identifies each person as different from his fellows; (2) we shall study the *traits* into which the total personality can be analyzed in a meaningful manner; and (3) we shall study *individual differences* with regard to these traits.

Looking at our subject matter in a different light, we can say that the psychology of personality is concerned with certain *universals* in human development (motives, emotions, learning) as they determine personality; with certain *unique* phenomena, such as may appear only in a single person; and with certain *group factors* common to those individuals who have had certain experiences, e.g., living in Western European civilization, or being exposed to certain kinds of family patterns.

The study of the unique personality of each individual is extraordinarily difficult. If carried out logically, it might imply writing a separate book about each person studied. It is practical, however, in many cases to consider the unique person as merely a special instance following the same orderly principles as those found in the examination of group factors. Most of the discussion in this text, therefore, will center around trends which can be cross-checked against different individuals. Certain generalizations which develop in the process may then be applied to the case of the unique total personality.

BASES FOR PERSONALITY PSYCHOLOGY

The adult personality is probably the most complex phenomenon studied by science. It reflects some physiological components, such as the functioning of the endocrine glands, the autonomic nervous system, and biochemical processes. It is also profoundly affected by the social situation. Children are molded by their family environment, by their economic situation, by their schooling, and so on. Thus we may say that sociology and economics have their contributions to make to an understanding of the total person.

Most of all, the psychology of personality is an extension and amplification of general psychology. The person receives stimuli and responds to them. Like the psychotic, he may misperceive situations; all of us do, in fact, and the kinds of mistakes we make are quite revealing of personality trends. He learns to deal with problems, and he transfers the solutions from one to another. If he overgeneralizes (tries to apply solutions where they are inappropriate), or if he fails to recognize similarities, these reflect his personality. In short, all the classical categories of general psychology apply to personality. General psychology seeks principles which are universal, applicable to everyone; the psychology of personality seeks principles which explain the *patterns of difference between persons.*

Perception and Response. The classical units for the analysis of human behavior were stimulus and response. The stimulus was treated as an energy change (light waves, sound, heat, pressure, etc.) in the environment, and the response as a muscular or glandular reaction to this physical stimulus. A more sophisticated look at this pattern indicates that adults rarely respond to a simple physical stimulus. A round patch of red, suspended above a street, is not treated as equivalent to a round patch of red in a fruit bowl. The associated sensory experiences, prior responses, and consequent stimulation are all integrated with the present stimulus to form a *percept.* For purposes of personality study, it makes far better sense to study percepts and responses than to study stimuli and responses.

Both percept and response in any stage past infancy are likely to be complex. A percept of a particular person is usually much more than awareness of his identity; it carries feeling tones of pleasure and unpleasantness, anticipation of assistance or frustration, and the like. Even with a stranger, one experiences such overtones as a result of his similarity to persons known earlier. Thus perception is normally a composite of cognitive data (knowledge of the physical properties of the object perceived) and affective material (feelings, emotions, and motivational possibilities). Differences in personality can be related to differences especially on the affective side of this structure; thus, the physical properties of a Picasso painting are the same for all of us, but its affective evaluation varies widely. This is the kind of phenomenon which identifies differences in personality.

The response likewise must be considered to be complex. Psychologists no longer think in terms of simple muscle twitches or even of single reflex units. A response will involve many muscles, excitatory and inhibitory components, in an ordered sequence. We may say, "His response to the insult was to start a fight." But obviously this is no simple unitary response; it may involve all sorts of muscular and glandular components.

Like the percept, the response also should be treated as having a dual significance. Most responses can be viewed as having both an *adaptive* and an *expressive* component. The adaptive portion corresponds to the cognitive element of the perceived situation; it is the efficient way of dealing with the environment. The expressive component parallels the affective aspect; it communicates to others our feelings, or perhaps merely expresses inner emotional states. One person speaks slowly, cautiously, indecisively; another may communicate the same meaning, but by vigorous and rapid speech, he reveals a totally different feeling—and gives us a cue to his personality.

Throughout this book we shall be considering the processes of perceiving

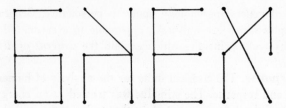

Fig. 1.2 Differing patterns derived from identical starting points. Individuals receiving the same scores on specific traits may yet be unique as regards the patterning of these traits.

and responding, as they throw light upon the personality. Some theorists stress one side, some the other, but it appears that a complete view requires consideration of both perception and response.

The Question of the Unique Person. It may appear that, in thus asserting the continuity of general psychology and the psychology of personality, we are abandoning the principle that each person is a unique individual. Not so. We are committed to the view that uniqueness is a real phenomenon; that it can be observed by a person's friends and also by a trained psychologist.

Some critics have objected that the conception of a unique individual must imply the existence of unique laws which hold for this person and no other. This objection appears completely unfounded. Modern physics accepts the uniqueness of specific events while asserting the applicability of universal laws. Furthermore, a given occurrence may involve the interaction of a number of laws. Bodies in a vacuum fall at a uniformly accelerated rate, but bodies in everyday life fall at varying rates and with different attendant phenomena because of friction, surface area, air currents, and so on. In psychology the number of interacting influences may become very large. Thus, the deviation of specific examples from the general law may be substantial.

This amounts to saying that the unique personality is subject to (and a product of) *general laws* of behavior. Uniqueness derives in part from the particular *combination* of effects wrapped up in one organism. Another source of uniqueness is in the *pattern* of relations among the parts. Five identical points, related in varying ways, can evoke the different visual patterns shown in Figure 1.2, and many others. Six points would generate an even greater variety of impressions; and we can only imagine the number of patterns which could be derived from a set of 100 points. Thus, even with a limited number of values for specific measures of intelligence, coordination, emotional sensitivity, flexibility of response, and so on, there are many possible combinations. Uniqueness need not present any kind of conceptual problem.

THINKING SCIENTIFICALLY ABOUT PERSONALITY

Before the specific techniques utilized in the scientific study of personality are taken up, it seems desirable to state certain general principles of thinking which are involved in this approach. These principles are not specific to the problems of personality, but are sufficiently in contrast with what might be called the common-sense approach to human behavior that special discussion of them is needed.

Animistic versus Realistic Thinking. A substantial proportion of the average man's thinking about psychology, and especially about such complex psychological problems as personality, is *animistic* in character. By this we mean that descriptive generalizations are used as if they were *forces* explaining behavior; that abstractions are often, erroneously, given the attributes of life.

Primitive man "explains" a storm by invoking the presence of a living force, a deity of sorts. Civilized man thinks realistically about storms, in terms of atmospheric pressures, temperature, and humidity. Progress from animistic to realistic thinking in the field of physics and chemistry has virtually been completed.

Animistic thinking in the field of human behavior, on the other hand, continues to be more common than is realistic thinking. Many of us still believe that personality can be changed by magical invocations (swearing at one's roommate, for example) or by human sacrifices, as in the case of mothers, whose sacrifices for their children may do more harm than good. Public opinion on crime and punishment, likewise, shows animistic tendencies. Few people think as realistically about criminals as they do about machines. If an automobile engine breaks down, we look for the cause (defective lubrication, bad fuel, improper ignition) and *correct these conditions* of the engine's behavior. We should not dream of putting the engine in jail for a year and expecting that it would, upon release, decide to perform properly. Yet human beings are still handled on this animistic basis, despite the evidence of thousands of years proving its futility.

A related and equally complicating factor is the virtually universal tendency to classify human behavior as "good" or "evil." A chemist who considered a red litmus reaction good, and pronounced the blue, wicked, would be ridiculous. He must study the behavior of his chemicals dispassionately. But much of what passes for popular psychology gets hopelessly entangled in moralistic judgments. It is not enough to characterize a fascist dictator as a "mad dog." *Who bit the dog, and why is he so mad?* Only through unemotional study of what the person does and of the preceding conditions which led to this response, can psychology progress. We cannot allow our energies to be dissipated in mere moral condemnation. The knowledge so acquired may, later, be applied to "improve" human behavior; that, indeed, is a task explicitly discussed later in this volume. The investigation of personality, however, must be free from judgments of good and evil.[6]

---

[6] It is further significant to note that the most effective systems of psychotherapy (cf. Freud, 1920; Rogers, 1942) emphasize the fact that the psychologist must at all times

Cause and Effect Relationships. The realistic approach suggests that we must have a *deterministic* point of view about ourselves and others. You personally should realize the implications of this view for yourself. You can read because you have been taught; your morals are a product of training; your self-confidence, emotionality, and impulsiveness are results of your specific experiences. To a very substantial extent, *what you will do tomorrow is already determined by what you are today.* This is neither an argument for an attitude of reckless irresponsibility nor an assertion of the unchanging character of human nature. All organisms, but especially the human, have the capacity for seeking out certain kinds of stimulation. By deliberate choice you can expose yourself to stimulus conditions which will result in changing your personality; but it is extremely unlikely that you can produce a change merely by *verbal resolution* to reform.

Genetic Continuity. The preceding formulation leads logically to the principle of the continuity of the personality from conception, through birth, infancy, childhood, and maturity, to old age. Continuity does not mean unchanging rigidity. A river has continuity, but it is constantly changing. In an adult personality we can still locate infantile characteristics, but these have been overlaid by many intervening experiences. The fusion of the male and female germ cells determines certain hereditary potentialities of the individual. From that point on, environmental pressures modify, suppress, or channel these possibilities.

From infancy onward, the individual's reaction to a present stimulus is a function, in the main, of his reactions to past stimuli. Characteristics develop or change little by little over a period of time, with few exceptions. Even in the case of catastrophic changes in personality, it is usually possible to show how the person's past training prepared him to respond in his characteristic way to a crisis situation.

It is apparent that, if we accept this view, we must also accept the view of *multiple causation.* No stimulus ever acts in isolation. While we may successfully identify the immediate cause of a person's behavior, background events played their part as remote causes in determining the response which occurred. It is not, therefore, practical to search for specific one-to-one relationships between experiences and personality traits.

Finally, it seems clear that genetic continuity means that *personality is a process.* In the study of the individual we must necessarily take static cross sections and examine them; but the real, live individual is constantly changing to maintain adjustment to his environment. This will be particularly clear

---

avoid praise, criticism, moralizing, and scolding. His task is to help the patient acquire insight into the real conditions determining his actions and ideas, following which the patient himself can manipulate the environment and his own acts to achieve a better adjustment.

as we examine the extent to which the person, impelled by inner drives and expectations, modifies his environment and is in turn modified.

The Unitary Personality. The personality is a psychophysiological unit, integrated with a specific physical organism. Changes on the biological and biochemical levels affect the manifestations ordinarily called psychological, and changes of a mental character have biological repercussions. It is not correct to speak of these as body influencing mind or vice versa. These changes are simply *personality events*. Nothing but confusion is achieved by ascribing a glandular change to the physical realm and an emotional upheaval to a mental category.

The personality is also a psychosocial unit, being inextricably bound up with a culture and its various subgroups. No one ever escapes completely from the cultural background of his early development. Since the personality is coextensive with a single biological organism, however, it is possible to make an objective distinction between happenings within the individual and stimuli presented by the culture to which he must adapt himself. The psychosocial unity of personality is thus less apparent to the casual observer than is the psychophysiological unity.

HOMEOSTASIS: A KEY PRINCIPLE

Thinking scientifically about the complex phenomena of personality will be facilitated if some unifying principle, some common thread running through a variety of phenomena, can be identified. Such unifying concepts have been suggested by many authors. We propose to use, as a common denominator which will point out similarities in a wide diversity of phenomena, the concept of *homeostasis*. The term will be used in this book primarily to underscore, for the student, certain uniformities in the different manifestations of personality.

The term "homeostasis" is currently used in physiology and psychology to refer to a phenomenon which seems universal in these fields: namely, that the organism takes action to protect or to restore certain favorable steady states. Such homeostatic actions will be pointed out in various aspects of personality function.

Physiological Level of Homeostasis. The concept can best be illustrated on the physiological level. Many bodily functions tend toward constancy, and any disturbance leads to active effort aimed at restoring the steady state. Temperature is a good example. The body temperature tends to remain steady at about 98.6°F. This is not an exact figure, however, and we must think of an upper and a lower threshold value, variation being tolerated within these limits (see Figure 1.3). So, a rise in temperature to 98.7° may have no perceptible effect. However, a rise to 99° is likely to set off corrective actions:

sweating, relaxation of skin blood vessels, reduced metabolic activity, and so on. These generally lead to restoration of the temperature within normal limits. Conversely, if the figure falls to 98°, the skin will pale as blood-vessel constriction occurs, shivering may cause heat production through muscle contraction, etc.

It is not correct to say that the temperature is restored by homeostasis. Properly we say that the protection and restoration of steady temperature is an *example* of homeostasis. In other words, homeostasis is a general principle, not a mysterious force.

Similar examples could be offered for the oxygen–carbon dioxide balance in the blood stream, the glucose level in the blood, its osmotic pressure, and so on. The steady states which are essential to tissue survival, and so to the life of the organism, are generally geared to sensory mechanisms which report when a value has exceeded the threshold, and in turn trigger corrective action.

These mechanisms are often referred to as the *atomistic* level of homeostasis. They are atomistic because they get down to the very lowest unit of living matter, the cell. But observations at this level do not help us much in the understanding of an adult personality. You will not learn much about a man's profession, his politics, religion, social adjustment, or ambitions by studying his blood circulation, breathing, or digestion. The simple manifestations of homeostasis only provide us a *foundation* for the study of personality.

Atomistic versus Holistic Homeostasis. To clarify the point, we may distinguish between atomistic (tissue-level) homeostatic activities, and holistic (total organism) activities. The important features of adult behavior include protecting one's family against economic and other threats, protecting one's feeling of self-respect against attack, protecting the status of one's profession or social group, and so on. It is easy to see that such actions are homeostatic in the sense that the individual has achieved a favorable steady state and acts to defend it, just as he did at the tissue level as regards temperature, water, and food. However, it seems to be a long and hazardous logical leap from atomistic to holistic homeostasis.

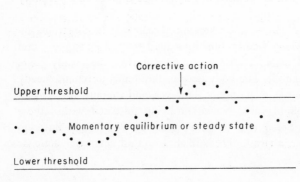

Fig. 1.3 A schematic diagram for homeostasis. Any steady state may vary within certain limits, but a variation outside the upper or lower threshold sets off some kind of corrective action which will return the value within these limits. Corrective action is initiated when the threshold is crossed; however, some time is usually required before restoration of normality is achieved.

Actually, analysis indicates that the problem is not so difficult. Suppose we consider the function of anticipating a disturbance at the atomistic level. The expectancy of such danger can set off holistic (total organism) action. Ordinarily we do not wait for emergencies before taking homeostatic action. One builds a house to forestall winter chills; he may add air conditioning to protect against excessive heat. He is building a *constant environment* to protect the biological steady states. And he will struggle—fight, if necessary—to maintain his home and property, just as he will fight for food or water and other items essential to the biological constancies. It is these holistic activities, these operations of the entire individual, which become distinctive features of personality. Nevertheless, the theory is incomplete if we ignore the atomistic level of homeostasis, and indeed, it seems obvious that these holistic processes are learned consequences of disturbances on the more elementary levels.

The psychologists who have applied homeostatic theory to personality have also assumed that new equilibria are established and defended at the holistic level. Just as a person comes to value his home, his clothing, or his wealth as devices for protecting his physiological steady states, so he may also come to value his mother, his family, his social standing, his professional status. A threat to any one of these "steady states" will evoke energy mobilization and vigorous effort to maintain a favorable situation.

The view set forth in this book, consequently, is that homeostasis provides a convenient framework within which we can view the manifestations of personality. When we say that rationalization is a process of defending a certain constancy (the ego) against criticism, we are pointing to a similarity with simpler processes. When we say that identification with a group is a protective device, we are again indicating a kind of uniformity. This technique is intended to develop a schema, a frame of reference, so that different aspects of personality can be understood in relation to each other.

An Ultimate Explanation? Critics of homeostatic theory often complain that homeostasis doesn't explain anything. This is irrelevant. The concept does not pretend to explain; it only groups together, classifies, so that relationships become visible. Newton never claimed that gravitation "explained" the fall of an object. Rather, he asserted that the principle of gravitation focused on similarities in falling apples, the motion of the earth around the sun, and molecular attraction. Such a principle is valuable if it calls attention to fundamental similarities, regardless of any ultimate explanation.

In fact, scientists have abandoned the search for an "ultimate explanation." Scientists are now satisfied if they can arrive at (1) a historical explanation; or (2) an explanation based on events at a different level; or (3) a "field" explanation.

(1) One may "explain" the baby's agitation when his mother goes away by referring to past occasions when absence of the mother was associated with hunger, discomfort, and the like. This is a historical account; it is not "ulti-

mate," since we should need to explain why the mother went away, why the baby remembered, and so on. Such a series never ends. (2) Or, along another line, we may "explain" the baby's disturbance in terms of the reactions o the heart, blood vessels, digestive apparatus, etc.; we have moved to a different level of discourse to describe what is going on. (3) In the case of an older child, we may move to the "social field" and use as explanation the presence of other children, the smell of food on the stove, and other factors in the surrounding field which influence his behavior. These likewise are not ultimate, since each requires further explanation.

Personality is most often explained by referring to a sequence of historical events. The individual's past frustrations, loves, hates, and anxieties are present in his personality now. We cannot speak Chinese if we have never learned; we cannot deal calmly with emergencies if we have never learned. A major task of personality research is to identify the learning sequences by which a person comes to recognize threats to his valued steady states and to defend these values against disturbance.

A second major phase of personality theory calls for explaining personality in terms of different levels of reality. Thus, Freeman (1948) proposes to reduce all personality traits to events at the level of nerves, muscles, and glands. This may help us to understand certain personality manifestations, but of course the explanation is not ultimate; we may reduce muscle action to chemistry, and finally to electrons and protons; but why do they act as they do? Similarly, Mead (1935) may explain personality in terms of culture; we move to a different level of reality, this time, social. But if we say that Joseph Stalin's personality was merely an individual expression of certain Russian culture patterns, we have only described; why was Russian culture like that? The ultimate still eludes us. An ultimate explanation is based on faith; inherently, it is not open to empirical proof.

Our use of homeostasis, therefore, will be limited to descriptive purposes. We shall be concerned with the values a person tries to defend, the objects he perceives as helpful to these values, the threats he seeks to ward off (and the actions by which he does so). We shall start with very simple phenomena and trace similarities at more complex levels.

Physiological homeostasis is taken as a model for clarity of presentation, but little of personality is directly attributable to events at this level. We can do more in the way of predicting what a given person will do if we know his social background and aspirations than if we know his blood-sugar level and autonomic balance. In daily life, the major steady states are social in character, and the major threats to be parried are likewise social. Hence more space will be devoted to social than to physiological determinants of personality.

Homeostasis and Personality Change. A final point is of particular importance. Some psychologists have objected to homeostatic theory on the ground that they think it implies a static, unchanging personality. This, of course, is quite untrue. As noted above, the individual changes his behavior to protect himself against a threat to a valued steady state or to restore one which has been disturbed. He may develop new skills, new tactics in dealing with people, and even new ways of thinking as a result of such pressures.

This means, for example, that a child who has been striving to achieve his goals by violent aggression may, as a result of repeated punishments and failures, come to understand the inadequacy of this technique. He may come to anticipate the anxiety which will follow his aggressive outburst, and to inhibit the violent act before it reaches expression. If his anxiety is intense, he may even inhibit justifiable aggressive responses, and so develop the extremely meek, submissive exterior with deep hostility which the Freudians have called "reaction formation." He is protecting a valued steady state (most probably his relationship to his parents) by this new mode of behavior.

Homeostatic theory would suggest, therefore, that personality growth and development stem primarily from frustration and conflict. Such frustrations may depend on maturation of the physical mechanism—e.g., the child moves from sucking to acceptance of solid food as his metabolic needs require more, and more varied, substances. Even so, pressure from the mother is often necessary. He abandons infantile games for adolescent pursuits partly under ridicule from older playmates. The pressure of marriage, and of paternity, induces more mature and serious modes of adjustment in most men.

Personality change can also result from anticipated frustrations; the processes of education and therapy attempt to help the individual foresee threats and adopt a new course in order to avoid them. Imagination may enable the youth to picture future difficulties and use such cues to guide adjustive reactions. In brief, there is nothing about homeostasis which argues against the possibility of change; but it is true, of course, that most people resist personality change with surprising stubbornness. The saying that a man's personality is irrevocably shaped by the time he is six years old (variously attributed to the behaviorists, the psychoanalysts, and the Catholic Church) points to the fact that personality tends toward constancy. And that is of course the essence of the homeostatic approach.

Personality as Molder of Culture. The relation of person to society is not a one-way street. Personality is molded by social pressures, threats, rewards, and reference groups—true. But the homeostatic principle asserts that the individual will attempt to defend himself against these social variables; one such defense is to modify the culture itself.

Historians are divided over the issue of whether a great man makes great events or is made by them. But certainly there is at least minimum evidence indicating that the personality of an individual sometimes plays a crucial role in large social trends. If we think of Adolf Hitler and F. D. Roosevelt in the year 1933, faced with somewhat similar social crises, yet effecting sharply different outcomes, the idea may become clearer.

In any event, it seems appropriate to include in this book a discussion of the role of the personality in molding culture. It is unjustifiably pessimistic to view man as merely a creature of his glands or a helpless victim of his social milieu. The unique individual plays his role, too, in shaping his social surroundings. Thus he seeks to forestall threats which might arise, and to ensure the survival of a way of life which seems very dear to him. In today's threatening world, the creativity of the unique personality may be our only defense against annihilation.

PREVIEW

The foregoing pages have stated certain general principles which underlie our treatment of the psychology of personality. It is now in order to plan an approach to this very complex material.

It seems desirable, at the beginning, to consider the major techniques by which psychologists have studied personalities. These techniques differ according to the definition of personality accepted: e.g., methods for studying the stimulus value of personality, methods of identifying the consistent responses of the individual, and ways of inferring with some precision the inner systems which constitute the deeper level of personality. The two chapters immediately following will present these techniques in sufficient detail so that the student can feel some familiarity with the operations utilized by experts in gathering data. The treatment will not, however, make the student a skilled technician in any respect. Only the study of more advanced texts and considerable practice under skillful guidance will accomplish that.

With a little background in methodology, we shall concern ourselves with a comprehensive description of personality. This will be first longitudinal and then cross-sectional in character; i.e., there will be an attempt to describe the processes by which the infantile personality evolves to maturity (Chapters 5 and 6), and, later, a description of some uniformities of personality common to Western culture (Chapters 7 and 8). This will be followed by a chapter on the ego, or self, as a central feature of the adult personality (Chapter 9). Concluding this section will be discussions of such topics as character, attitudes and values, and type theories of personality.

Our material on descriptive psychology attempts to limit itself to processes which can be observed directly or to which inference is fairly direct. This is less easy when we come to consider the problems of dynamics—the question of the motivating impulses which push the developing personality along its path. Admittedly it is highly arbitrary to separate in this manner two aspects of personality which are so intricately interwoven; it is, on the other hand, impossible to study everything of importance simultaneously. The section on dynamics will therefore backtrack and consider some of the same topics presented in the descriptive section, with the aim of exposing underlying motivation. This will include the biological drives (hunger, thirst, pain, etc.) in Chapter 13; some of the more sophisticated motivational constructs, such as those of the Freudians in Chapter 14, and finally a discussion of motivation in terms of goal seeking in Chapter 15.

The discussions of personality on the descriptive and the dynamic level may seem somewhat artificial, in that mention of the role of the environment is kept at a minimum. In a final section we shall try to integrate the motivational analysis with a consideration of the effects of specific environmental situations, to give the best possible "explanation" of the traits described earlier. Principles of explanation must necessarily concern both inner needs and external blockages of these needs; the dynamic character of the organism and the molding effect of the environment. This external shaping starts with parent-child relationships and extends to the complexities of social philosophy. Social conditions at all levels between these extremes play their part in patterning the developing individual. But here we must also recognize a reciprocal relationship; the mature individual is likely also to shape his environment. One who is hungry does not necessarily eat food as he finds it; he may process and improve it. Similarly, we are not doomed passively to accept the social milieu which shapes our personalities; we can react upon and modify it (Chapter 21).

Our first concern will be with getting a reasonably objective picture of how personality develops, and of the major descriptive aspects of personality as seen by the psychologist. We have observed that there are many hazards in this attempt. To rule out some of these dangers, and to maximize the objectivity of our descriptions of personality, psychologists have developed a wide variety of methods for the study of personality. To provide a background for understanding the results of these descriptive studies, the following two chapters will sketch the methods commonly used in the scientific study of personality.

SUMMARY

The scientific study of personality begins with the popular conception of personality as social stimulus value, but immediately begins to refine and tighten this formulation. One's stimulus value for others clearly depends upon the responses he makes, and these in turn depend upon his inner pattern of motives, emotions, and perceptions.

The study of personality is so complex that some unifying concept is needed to highlight similarities among phenomena which will seem quite diverse. This book uses the concept of homeostasis to provide a unifying thread. In an oversimplified way, we can say that personality is a pattern of steady states valued by the person, with the unique ways of protecting these states which he has developed.

The personality thus formed can be described by analyzing it into traits, or it can be treated as a unique whole. The latter is difficult, and although it is accepted as a legitimate phase of the psychology of personality, more attention will be focused on how psychologists study traits, how traits develop, the role of physiological and social factors in forming traits, and so on. Because the person does maintain uniqueness and individuality, he may even modify the environment as a way of protecting an inner state.

We must abandon verbal magic and animistic concepts to achieve a thoroughly scientific approach to our problems. Mind and body must not be separated; the personality is a unity. The scientist need not abandon his moral values, but he must learn to keep them out of his observations if he wishes to achieve understanding. Knowledge, once validly established, can later be drawn into the service of moral values.

SUGGESTIONS FOR READING

An excellent treatment of the normal personality is Gordon W. Allport's *Personality: a psychological interpretation.* A later statement of Allport's views, in highly compressed form, is *Becoming: basic considerations for a psychology of personality.* Another major contribution is Gardner Murphy's *Personality: a biosocial approach to origins and structure.* A novel and difficult but stimulating treatment is that by R. B. Cattell: *Personality: a systematic theoretical and factual study.* Diamond's *Personality and temperament* covers a somewhat more limited field, but in an interesting manner.

The popular aspect of the psychology of personality deals with problems of self-improvement, making friends, and influencing people. The literature in this area, of course, knows no end, but very little of it is based on realistic analysis of the factors affecting personality. Shaffer and Shoben have an excellent discussion of *The psychology of adjustment,* and Fred McKinney has applied some basic principles to student problems in his *Counseling for personality adjustment in schools and colleges.*

CHAPTER 2

Methods: Ratings and Observations

Since there are so many different definitions of personality, inevitably there must be diverse approaches to the study of personality. Some methods stress the personality as stimulus for others; some stress patterns of response. If a psychologist conceives of the personality as "the organism as a whole" in all its functioning, then obviously almost any total organismic function can be treated as a method for studying personality—and this has been done.

The formal statement of principles and procedures for measuring personality by scientific devices is a recent development; but the practical study and estimation of personality traits dates far back into human history. The customs of primitive tribes today reveal practices which have the status of pragmatic tests of personality. Before a boy is accepted into the status of manhood, he must have proved his fortitude, his emotional control, and other traits, to the satisfaction of the elders of the tribe. The history of early religions and other movements indicates that great stress was laid on the personality qualifications of new initiates and that they were required to pass strenuous tests before being accepted into full membership.

The tests employed in these rites were not tests as we shall use the term. They were actual situations. We ordinarily speak of a test when the subject goes through some brief performance which enables us to infer some related quality or ability. In those days the procedure was simpler. Daniel's courage was tested by his being tossed into a den of lions. Adolescent boys are tested in many primitive cultures, even today, by painful skin lacerations. Reactions to such situations are not mere token manifestations of traits, but heroic, full-scale performances.

From some points of view, perhaps, it is to be regretted that such methods are not permissible in our culture. Certainly it is a more valid procedure to test a man's honesty or courage in these ways than simply to ask him questions. On the other hand, psychologists would have great difficulty in getting experimental subjects after the first one escaped!

Scientific Method and Personality Theory. These primitive devices for eliciting evidence about personality were based upon the crude theory of some shrewd individual. Today we have developed far more extensive and precise statements about the presumed fundamentals of personality; yet, for some reason, there is relatively little attempt to devise methods of investigation which derive directly from these theories. Even such valuable books on personality measurement as those of Ferguson (1952) and Allen (1958) classify techniques by form rather than by theoretical inspiration.

In the following pages we shall take an intermediate course between a tight theoretical classification of methods and a simple practical arrangement. This compromise is in part necessitated by the fact that much of the work done in this field is still based on the philosophy of "Let's try this and see how it works." Systematic thinking, however, is emerging as new methods are developed, and we shall call attention to these in their proper places.

Nature of the Recording Instrument. One of the significant problems which faces every scientist is that of deciding what recording instrument is to be employed. The chemist may use colorimeters, balances, radiation meters, and other instruments. The psychologist does not have so extensive an array of technical devices, although gadgetry in the field is increasing rapidly. In Figure 2.1 we have represented, in a way generally approved by research psychologists, some of the relationships between the object being studied and the conception, the comprehension, which is sought.

The object of study is some human being who is engaged in a course of action. John Jones may be observing and responding to "natural" stimuli (not under the control of the experimenter); more often, he is receiving and reacting to standard stimuli, since this makes possible a more rigorous analysis of the observed behavior. The diagram suggests that there are basically four different kinds of "recording instruments" used to make this material available for scientific analysis and theorizing.

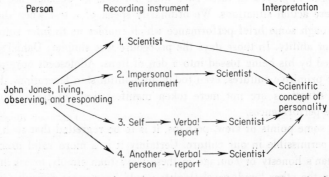

Fig. 2.1 A scheme for gathering data relevant to personality. The scientist's understanding of a specific personality, or of personalities in general, may be derived from a variety of clues. (Modified from McClelland, 1951, p. 57, after Mowrer and Kluckhohn, 1944.)

1. *The Scientist Himself.* A psychologist may directly observe John's actions; or he may make photographs or tape recordings; he may obtain graphs showing pulse rate, blood pressure, galvanic skin response, brain waves, and the like. All these data are then subject to analysis and integration to produce a concept, a theory about personality.

2. *The Impersonal Environment.* John also leaves traces of his personality on the environment and these can be studied. Literary critics infer personality characteristics of an author from his productions, and to some extent this is feasible also for artists and musicians. Indeed, it is now becoming common practice for the scientist to ask his subject to produce something (e.g., a painting) which can then be analyzed according to certain rules to elicit inferences about personality.

3. *The Self.* John may be asked to explain why he did something, to describe "what the situation looked like to him." He may report moods, fantasies, impulses which are completely inaccessible to the scientist. Whether or not these reports correspond to "reality" as others see it, they constitute important data about the person.

4. *Another Person.* Sometimes it is equally important to ascertain how John is perceived by Mary or by Tom. None of us has the gift "to see ourselves as others see us," partly because the personality of the other becomes a component of what he sees. Nevertheless, the scientist can often arrive at valuable inferences about the inner personality of John from the verbal reports made about him by his friends and associates.

The Nature of the Conceptualization Sought. It has already been noted that the scientist is looking for comprehension of a hidden phenomenon, the "inner personality," not accessible to direct study. Further, this inner personality can be conceptualized in terms of social stimulus value, or in terms of response patterns, or in terms of intervening variables, patterns of perception, and belief. The choice among the recording instruments described above will be influenced by the theoretical preference of the psychologist for one or another conceptualization of personality.

The *behavioristic* psychologist will prefer to make his own observations, generally using equipment which reduces his own judgment and personal bias to a minimum. Thus he may count the number of times a child initiates a conversation with others, or record the response of blood pressure to a pistol shot, or determine the visual threshold for accurate report of emotionally charged words. Whereas his personal interests determine both the kinds of stimuli he presents and the kinds of responses he records, the observations themselves acquire greater objectivity than if he simply watched and made notes. The instrumental data can later be examined by investigators with different prejudices, if this seems important in order to rule out any effect of his theoretical preconceptions.

Less has been done with the analysis of traces on the environment. Some work is now being done with paintings, and social psychologists have begun analyzing documents to get at insights regarding public figures. In industry, there is speculation about the study of organizational events to reveal the personality of the leader, although this obviously gets very complicated.

Most extensive use has been made of the "self" as a source of data. Many important events occur in a fashion which renders them inaccessible to recording otherwise; there is probably much visceral activity of significance which we cannot study by instrumentation, and there are tremendously complex perceptual and imaginative processes, regarding which we have not the slightest idea as to physical methods of recording. Hence, much of the personality research going on today utilizes the person's own verbal report to obtain data for analysis. These methods are used extensively by psychoanalysts and by psychologists who are looking for a conception of personality in terms of intervening variables.

Finally, the use of "other persons" as recording instruments is directly tied to the conception of personality as social stimulus value. If we wish to know John's effect on Mary, there is virtually no method of study which does not involve using Mary as the recording instrument. Generally, we obtain the verbal report of the second person as to the perceived qualities of the first. These reports can then be processed to obtain insight into the social stimulus value of the subject person. This class of methods will be examined first.

PERSONALITY AS STIMULUS

When we speak of the personality in terms of its social stimulus value, we imply that the appropriate "recording instrument" to be used in research will be another person. The psychologist may himself watch and record what he perceives to be the personality of the subject; or he may induce others to record their perceptions and provide him with these records for analysis (cf. Figure 2.1).

Since our perceptions of others are notoriously in error, at least a fair share of the time, the problem of method here is that of devising ways of recording observations which will minimize these errors. This is a crucial problem, of course, in all research: how to minimize errors of observation.

Since the specific devices to be mentioned here are subject to certain errors in common, we shall simply describe the techniques which have been employed and then discuss the problem of reducing error in relation to all of them.

The Personality as a Whole. The purpose of the psychologist may be to get an over-all impression of a given subject, with no special effort to analyze the percept into attributes. This is particularly true when interest is focused on comparison of various members of a group, such as a school class or a bomber crew.

The Guess Who Test. Hartshorne and May (1928) asked school children to give their impressions of each other in an ingenious way. A description was read to the class, such as "a boy who gets into fights a lot on the playground"; they were asked to write down the name of the boy. Obviously this gets at an aspect of social stimulus value; unfortunately, sometimes it only produces an indication of dislike, not of the specific kind of personality described.

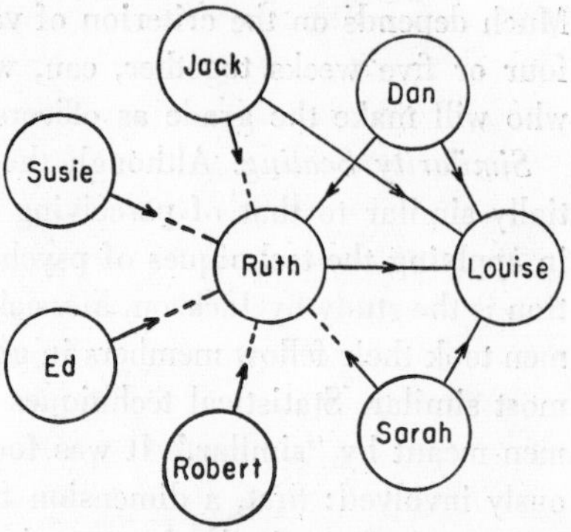

A more sophisticated use of the Guess Who technique is described by Mitchell (1955). In this case, resort to factor analysis [1] makes possible a rather precise determination of the attributes which influenced the children making the judgments.

Fig. 2.2 Social atom (after F. B. Moreno, 1942). Solid lines indicate choice as playmate, dashed lines indicate rejection. Arrow shows direction in which contact was initiated. Ruth, chosen by all, plays only with Louise and Dan; Louise also accepts Jack and Sarah. Susie, Ed, and Robert are temporarily isolated. (Reproduced by permission from *Sociometry*, **5**, p. 408.)

Sociometry. Moreno (1934) suggested that it would be possible to measure an individual's social status by a somewhat similar method. Nursery school children may be asked, "Whom do you like to play with?" (see Figure 2.2). Air Force cadets have been asked, "What men do you think will make the best officers?" Fraternity men have been asked to choose prospective roommates, study partners, buddies for a beer party, and so on. Where members of the group have had a good chance to become acquainted, this method has obvious values in terms of the recording of social stimulus value.

The number of times a person is chosen for a particular role indicates his positive or attraction value; a person who gets many choices obviously has some attribute which causes him to be perceptually distinctive. As noted above, this may not be the attribute defined by the instructions. Some studies (e.g., Mouton, Blake, and Fruchter, 1955) have found sociometric judgments to have substantial validity; other studies have found that they do not.

---

[1] Factor analysis is a special mathematical technique by which underlying dimensions can be identified. A very simple case is that of taking measurements on a large number of boxes of different sizes and shapes. Factor analysis reveals that the relationships among these measures can be accounted for by three dimensions: length, width, and depth. This agrees with common knowledge; but when we deal with judgments of personality we do not know in advance the nature of the basic dimensions. Factor analysis is thus a useful tool for psychologists, and frequent references will be made in this book to studies relying on this method. The student can appropriately think of it as a technique for identifying the dimensions which may underlie observed aspects of personality (see p. 158).

Much depends on the criterion of validity employed. Apparently cadets, after four or five weeks together, can, with considerable accuracy, pick the men who will make the grade as officers.

Similarity Scaling. Although the problem of perceiving persons is essentially similar to that of perceiving objects, surprisingly little has been done in applying the techniques of psychophysical scaling in this area. One exception is the study by Jackson, Messick, and Solley (1957a), in which fraternity men took their fellow members in groups of three and chose the two who were most similar. Statistical techniques were then applied to determine what the men meant by "similar." It was found that two sets of standards were obviously involved: first, a dimension from "intelligent-studious" to the opposite (some men were similar because they were close together on this dimension); second, a dimension of general liking. The intelligence dimension might, of course, be replaced by some other or others, if a college context were not involved. One can imagine, for example, that in a factory group, a dimension might be skill, or attitude to the union, or even conflict with the foreman. Unfortunately, the scaling technique does not automatically identify these dimensions; their identification depends on the ingenuity of the investigator.

Identification of Attributes. A second broad category of devices for studying social stimulus value seeks to determine the extent to which a person manifests given attributes. Mostly these are called "rating scales," and a rating scale is simply a device for recording the extent to which a person is perceived as possessing the defined attribute.

Each of us finds it necessary at times to make judgments about the extent to which a friend possesses some quality. In occupational, political, and social situations we are not necessarily interested in his all-around "goodness"; we want to know if he is vigorous, or shy, or practical in his judgments. The psychologist needs the same kind of evaluation, for the same reasons. He differs from the amateur chiefly in the controls that he imposes on the task. He *defines* more precisely the characteristics that he wants to study; he uses a *standard scale* for recording his impressions; and he sets up *uniform conditions* in an attempt to reduce the effect of irrelevant factors. Further, he introduces *statistical checks,* to determine the freedom from prejudice, and from inconsistency, of his judgments. Let us see how some of these apply.

Graphic Scales. Much effort has gone into the development of forms which will facilitate the recording of impressions in an accurate manner. An exam-

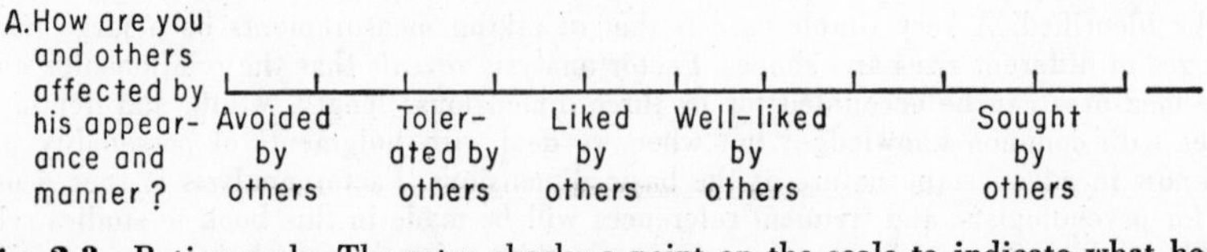

Fig. 2.3 Rating scale. The rater checks a point on the scale to indicate what he perceives. The dash on the end means "no opportunity to observe."

ple is shown in Figure 2.3. The attribute to be observed here is not defined by a single word, such as "appearance," but a question is asked which defines more precisely what to look for. The response is made by checking along a linear scale; it is believed that this induces in the rater an attitude of measuring differences. The *degrees* of possession of this characteristic are defined by a series of phrases below the line; this means that different judges, using the same scale, will be more likely to have the same meaning in mind.

Graphic scales are extensively used in personnel work, e.g., by interviewers who wish to record their impressions of an applicant, by supervisors making merit appraisals of workers under their supervision, and so on. They are also used widely by the armed services and by civil service.

Numerical Scales. Instead of checking on a line, the rater may be asked to assign a number between 1 and 10, or between 0 and 100, to indicate the degree of a certain attribute. These scales do not differ in principle from the graphic scale. Whereas there is a spurious appearance of greater precision in a scale of 100 points, numerous studies have demonstrated that the average observer cannot use effectively more than 11 steps on such a scale, and this only after training. For untrained raters, 5 or 7 steps would be the maximum usable.

Sources of Error: Reliability. The problem of methodology is the problem of reducing error. Everyone makes judgments of personality; the task of the psychologist is to develop techniques which are more consistent and more dependable, in short, which accomplish the purposes for which they are made. The discussion of these sources of error traditionally centers around two concepts: reliability and validity.[2]

One source of error is revealed when we find that the same person, evaluated by the same rater on two occasions, gets quite a different rating. Let us suppose that on one instance the rater was suffering from indigestion, had not slept on the train the night before, and was in a strange office. On the second occasion he felt well, was fresh and rested, and was in familiar surroundings. The influence of these irrelevant factors upsets the consistency of the ratings. *Chance errors,* then, represent a problem in making judgments of persons.[3]

The term "reliability" refers to freedom from chance errors, and in a positive sense means that a measuring device renders substantially similar results when applied to the same person. A yardstick made of rubber would be an

---

[2] A detailed discussion of the problems involved in rating of attributes will be found in Symonds (1931). For some reason, more recent works on measurement have treated the problem rather sketchily. Ferguson (1952) takes up rating problems in personnel, and Allen (1958) hardly mentions ratings.

[3] Such factors may be within the person making the judgments, or in the external situation, or they may be variations of the person being judged. These last are not always classed as coming under the rubric of reliability, since they imply that the person has actually changed. However, they will show up in measures of reliability of the ratings.

excellent example of an unreliable measuring device. While physics does not use such instruments, the importance of increasing reliability by ruling out chance errors is stressed in all physics research. In quantitative chemical analysis, it is standard practice to take 10 readings of the microbalance to reduce these chance errors.[4] Psychologists could profit by this example.

Reliability is commonly divided into two aspects, *consistency* and *stability*. Consistency of an estimate may be determined by splitting our observations in half, and correlating one against the other set.[5] Thus if we observe Johnny for two minutes each day, for ten days, we may add all the odd-numbered days together, add the even-numbered days together, and so determine whether the attribute we are recording is consistent. Or we may have two judges observe Johnny and correlate their ratings to show consistency.

"Stability" refers to consistency over time. Johnny's behavior in January may be related to his behavior in June. Reliability in this case means high predictability from one time to another. (It is obvious that stability figures will tend to be lower than consistency figures; some real change in Johnny, besides chance factors affecting the judgment, may occur in six months.) Stability figures based on the same judge, however, may be spuriously high; the judge may recall his rating on the second occasion.

Even among skilled judges the range of reliability measures may be very great. Stern, Stein, and Bloom (1956) report on a study of school children in which pairs of clinicians gave reliabilities ranging from $-.48$ to $+.73$, after very careful study of the children. We suspect that the negative correlation was an accident, since even untrained judges rarely disagree that much, but it is obvious that ratings are often unreliable. Such interviewers as those in industrial personnel offices are likely to give reliabilities around $+.50$, which would mean that many chance errors are affecting the results.

Validity of Ratings. It is clear that unreliability of a rating will also affect its validity—i.e., the success with which it identifies the person "really" possessing a given attribute. However, reliability is often high and yet validity is low. For example, ratings of the intelligence of a beautiful woman, made by male observers, might all agree (hence, meet the standard of reliability), yet be grossly in error when checked against her score on an objective test of mental ability.

Such errors are endemic in all sorts of judgments of personality. It should

---

[4] Some interesting data on the reliability of quantitative chemical analyses, which make psychological work look fairly precise by comparison, will be found in Belk and Sunderman (1947). A study of diagnosis by X-ray photographs, showing marked unreliability, is that of Birkels et al. (1947).

[5] A correlation is a numerical index of the degree of agreement of two sets of measurements. A correlation of $+1.00$ means perfect agreement; knowing one set of figures, we could predict the others without error. A correlation of $.00$ means pure chance agreement; given the first measure, we could predict the second no more accurately than we would by guessing. A correlation of $+.50$, then, means that there is some agreement between the two measures, but that accuracy of prediction is only modest.

be remembered, as was outlined in Chapter 1, that personality is always inferred. Certain cues come from the person being observed; the judge takes these in, compares them with his mental yardsticks (frames of reference), and arrives at a percept. Since these frames of reference will never be identical from one judge to another, differences in rating will ensue. Analysis indicates some sources of difference, and appropriate steps for their reduction.

Errors of Definition. Judgments of personality must be made in terms of trait names, but not all people use the same terms and, even when two individuals use the same descriptive adjective, they may not have the same meaning in mind. Nervousness to one judge is primarily a physical phenomenon, including trembling, jumpiness, tics, and stammering; whereas a second interprets it in terms of mood, depression, worries, and other emotional upsets. The defect can be remedied by providing a uniform list of all terms for all judges, preparing detailed operational definitions for these terms, or having conferences at which the judges agree on definitions. Murray (1938) reports that many lengthy debates were held before his group of experts came to use trait names in a uniform fashion.

Errors of Distribution. Judges are often found to differ on their concepts of high, low, and average for a given trait. One may be lenient, putting all his judgments above the theoretical neutral point, while another is severe. One judge uses extreme ratings often, while a second avoids extreme marks. Either deviation will introduce inaccuracies into the ratings.

A statistical technique for correcting this difficulty involves converting ratings to standard scores.[6] It is arbitrarily assumed that each judge should come out with the same average and the same scatter of ratings. The standard score method enforces this requirement. Thus it avoids errors in validity of the type described.

Errors Due to Unequal Units. Ratings are made on the assumption that units of judgment are equal—that the jump from 2 to 4 on the scale is as large as that from 4 to 6. Some judges do not, for one reason or another, stick to this rule. A very conservative judge, for example, will be unable to distinguish units on the radical end of the scale. Socialists, communists, and Trotskyites may all look alike to him.

There is some evidence (cf. Murray, 1938) that this is a general problem in judging human nature. Men generally rate most accurately the personalities of those most resembling themselves; judgment of those markedly different is less accurate. It is difficult to correct such a basic distortion; we can only suggest (1) that judges should be carefully selected to exclude extremists, particularly in the field being studied; and (2) that the individual who is often called upon to make judgments of personality ought to cultivate a

---

[6] The technique of preparing standard scores from ratings, test scores, or other raw figures will be found in elementary textbooks on statistics. Limitations of space do not permit inclusion of detailed instructions in this volume.

middle-of-the-road position and make a special attempt to understand people who are quite different from himself.

Halo Effect. Perhaps the most persistent and most annoying of all errors in personal judgment is the *halo effect.* This term relates to the following type of mistake. Because Sam is excellent in schoolwork, his teacher rates him high on character. Because Dick is rebellious and disobedient, she rates him low on general intelligence. The term "halo" means that from some central fact—friendship, high intelligence, beauty, or some other trait of importance to the judge—an influence radiates out to change the ratings on other traits.

The halo effect has so far proved to be the most troublesome of all problems in rating. It is particularly operative when a judge is asked to estimate several different traits of the same person in succession. The perception of personality tends toward a *gestalt,* an integrated pattern. It thus becomes difficult to make independent judgments about specific aspects of an individual. This may explain the fact that long acquaintance does not automatically make for valid judgments. We may simply become more and more confirmed in our *incorrect* judgments of a person.

The principle of perceptual closure, regarding which we shall say a great deal more in later chapters, may operate to interfere with accurate ratings. As Luft (1950) and Dailey (1952) have demonstrated, if the observer arrives at a premature hypothesis as to "what this person is really like," this hypothesis may interfere with the use of additional information about the personality being studied.

Stereotypes. Another type of error results from the fact that the judge identifies the person being observed as a member of a certain group, and then imputes to the individual those attributes which he believes pertain to the group. In its extreme form this kind of error is manifested in the stereotype of a racial, national, or religious minority. A person who sees all Negroes as lazy, ignorant, and dirty can scarcely give an accurate evaluation of a Negro who has earned a Ph.D. degree in nuclear physics. The judge sees only his mental picture, not the real person.

Gage and Cronbach (1955) have shown that the stereotyping phenomenon is almost ubiquitous; the example given is only one instance of it. They found that their observers, making judgments of grade school and high school students, were actually employing stereotyped beliefs of the form, "All ten-year-old boys are . . . ." Differences in accuracy of judgment of specific children, surprisingly enough, turned out to be due in large part to differences in the accuracy of these stereotypes. Their results suggest that all perception of other persons may utilize this process, and that the training of judges is in part a matter of giving them a larger number of categories (e.g., in clinical psychology the student must study many different kinds of abnormal personalities) and of teaching sensitivity to the cues identifying these groups. Obviously it is also helpful for the judge to be aware of his own stereotypes and to watch for signs that the individual in question deviates from the stereotype. Further research on the problem of minority group stereotypes will be summarized in Chapter 11.

It should perhaps be noted in conclusion that there is a semantic problem of considerable size involved in validity studies of social stimulus value. This problem arises because only the judge can report on his own perceptions. If he says, "Mary looks lazy to me," no one can challenge this. His percept of Mary is a uniquely private event. But if he says, "Mary is lazy," he is committing himself to a judgment which is open to consensual validation by other observers. It is only in this latter sense that we can speak of validity of ratings. But, after all, the overwhelming majority of judgments of others are framed in exactly this fashion.[7]

PERSONALITY AS RESPONSE

We have already suggested that, while the psychologist starts with the notion of personality as the social stimulus value one individual has for another, he soon shifts to an interest in the responses which give rise to this stimulus value. After all, a percept does not arise without cues. The person being observed must give off information which, received by the judge, elicits in him the awareness of certain attributes. (His awareness, as noted above, may be in "error" in the sense of not agreeing with other observers, but within his own phenomenal field it is an unquestionable fact.) The primary mode of emitting information which serves as a basis for such judgments is, of course, behavior. Gestures, words, vocal inflections, facial expressions—not to mention the organized activities of the individual—give clues to the observer as to "what manner of man is this?"

As Cattell (1957) has noted, progress in the study of personality seems to be correlated with a gradual shift from an interest in over-all judgments of attributes to a more precise determination of units of behavior, through questionnaires and through experiments. For systematic reasons we defer the consideration of questionnaires to the following chapter. The other points will be taken up here.

Behavior Ratings. Cattell (1950) has particularly favored a mode of investigation which he calls "behavior rating" to distinguish it from attribute rating. He notes however, that the making of such ratings for personality studies is a somewhat tricky proposition. First of all, the behavior should be very carefully defined: "Thus the judges are not asked to rate 'sociability'

---

[7] It is also worth noting that the rating reflects certain aspects of the personality of the judge, since any percept is an interaction of present cues with traces existing within the observer, and these latter inevitably get mixed up with his "personality." Brunswik (1947) has argued that a rating task, using standard stimuli, is a good method for eliciting information about the judge. Cline (1955) used a rating set-up in this fashion; his main interest was in determining the attributes of the judges who gave the most valid ratings.

but, 'How often does the person speak to a fellow worker spontaneously, without practical need?' 'Does he speak to strangers first?' and so on" [p. 49]. Secondly, the judges must be trained in observing these units of behavior. Often there is a marked increase in reliability after the judge has practiced making these observations.

On the other hand, it must be noted that these behavior ratings encounter their own characteristic difficulties. For example, a young man may not speak to his fellow workers because his work place is too noisy. The interest may be present, but the opportunity to manifest the specific behavior is not. Hence Cattell must use a number of behavior ratings, all of which bear upon the attribute in which he is interested, and count on probabilities to rule out these interfering effects.[8]

Time Sampling. An extension of the same idea is found in the sampling of observed behavior for specific time units. Time sampling has been used especially often with young children, for whom verbal report is likely to be quite unsatisfactory anyway; their significant behaviors are likely to occur in the open, in play groups, and easily observed interactions. This has led to sample studies of thumb-sucking, fighting, competition and rivalry, and similar behavior. A particular exponent of the sampling technique is Roger Barker, who has gone to the extreme of following a specific child throughout an entire day, sampling all of his interactions with significant people and social roles (see, for example, Barker and Wright, 1951; Barker and Wright, 1954).

Many early time-sampling studies deteriorated into trivia of counting without meaning. Barker and Wright (1954) avoid this criticism by dealing with what they call "behavior episodes," recognizable by the observer as a unified piece of action by the subject, directed toward a certain end. Thus, when a boy spies an old crate, works it free from entanglements, and drags it across to a preferred play spot, this is clearly identifiable as an episode which is unified as far as the boy is concerned. Such behavior sampling enables the researcher to deal with meaningful units, and makes possible significant generalizations about the personality under observation.

Problems with Behavior Sampling. Behavior sampling generally attains a much higher reliability than the judgments of attributes described earlier. Reliabilities as high as +.90 have been reported in well-planned studies; this means that the records are about as accurate as any but the most refined physical measurements.

Validity is, of course, more difficult to ascertain. In a sense one can say

---

[8] Because of these difficulties, psychologists insist on observing a number of persons, or the same person many times. By chance Cattell might get one observation indicating that the young man is shy when he really is not. If he takes 20 observations, we assume that the law of probabilities will give a majority of ratings which correspond to the "true personality" of the person being studied. Likewise personality tests often ask the same question with slight changes of wording—this is an effort to control chance variations in a person's way of responding.

that if a person executed a certain kind of act six times in a specified number of opportunities, this is a valid fact in itself. However, the psychologist always has more in mind than a simple census of behavior. He wants to know what further inferences can be made about the personality from this behavior sample (cf. Figure 2.1). Cattell (1957) reports that in many instances he gets loadings as high as $+.70$ for a particular behavior rating on a "source trait" or common factor in a set of data. However, it is not yet clear that this figure really indicates ability to make valid predictions about any significant aspect of the personality; a factor loading tells how well the behavior rating agrees with the entire factor, but this need not mean agreement with an observable and significant attribute of the personality being studied.

Laboratory Situations. Behavior rating and behavior sampling are attempts to get significant material about the person within a normal environment. (There is some doubt that this holds perfectly; certainly an observer, following a child all day long, is bound to have some significant effects in modifying the latter's actions. In general, however, the total context of behavior is reasonably normal.) Behavior sampling in a laboratory situation is inevitably artificial, since the subject may be responding out of curiosity, or to do the examiner a favor, rather than as an expression of his normal impulses.

Laboratory situations, on the other hand, may be so devised that the results are of value regardless of these factors. One method, of course, is to make the laboratory a part of the life situation; Voas, Bair, and Ambler (1956) put Air Force cadets into a decompression chamber, representing it as a simulated "high altitude" test, and noted the evidences of anxiety shown by each cadet. A later check of men washed out of flight training for psychiatric reasons showed that most of them could have been predicted ahead of time by these records. Hence, whatever underlying personality attribute caused the psychiatric failure was rather well-sampled by this laboratory test.

The foregoing example illustrates what has been called the "miniature-situation" approach to testing. In the Office of Strategic Services' work on assessment of agents during World War II (see OSS Staff, 1948) miniature situations were used extensively. For instance, the candidate was told to build a small wooden structure; he was assigned two helpers (members of the assessment team). One of the "helpers" was incredibly clumsy; the other, critical and sarcastic. Observers rated the candidate on how he tolerated and dealt with these helpers.

Crutchfield's Conformity Test. It is possible to miniaturize the situation even more, and thus get more complete control of all possible variables. One must assume, for example, that the two frustrating assistants did not perform in exactly identical fashion at all times, hence some candidates got more stress than others.

Crutchfield (1951) has developed an artificial group situation which gives the experimenter complete control over the stimuli which apparently emanate from the members of the group.[9] This makes it possible for him to study differences in conformity tendencies. Each S has a panel of lights, the flashing of which purports to show judgments made by other members of the group. For example, he may be asked to judge the relative sizes of rectangles; he is told that the lights show which rectangle is judged longest by each of the group members. Actually, the experimenter feeds the same cues to all members, but records the judgments made by each. At a critical point S is given "information" that everyone else considers a rectangle largest which, he can plainly see, is not. He is then under pressure to agree with the group. Yielding to a "majority" judgment which opposes his own views shows conforming behavior on the part of S.

Another version of this technique uses tape recordings, with each S wearing earphones (cf. Blake, Helson, and Mouton, 1957). S believes that he is hearing the voices of his fellow subjects, giving their judgments in a certain order, his own coming last. Thus all subjects are under the same pressure to conform. Results of these studies will be noted in Chapter 7. We mention here only that these kinds of controlled situations offer exciting promise for advance in personality study and may ultimately provide high validity diagnoses of underlying trends on truly significant variables.

The reliability of these procedures varies with the kind of task presented. Blake, Helson, and Mouton (1957) report that reliabilities on specific tasks ranged from +.68 to +.78 and the reliability of conforming tendency, measured across three tasks, was +.87. This latter is quite satisfactory.

Expressive Movements. Finally, we may mention another category of responses which are revealing of personality. Gestures and expressive movements have been objects of interest to psychologists for many years. The manner of executing a perfectly ordinary task may be very useful as an index of underlying trends. In speaking, for example, two men may use the same words to deliver messages which are identical in intellectual content, yet by their manner they may convey quite different impressions. Speed, hesitation, change of tone, accenting words, and other cues are involved.

Handwriting, too, is often expressive. Not only letter form, but linkages of letters, spacing, curved or angular style, and similar bits of information may be relevant. The results of scientific research on handwriting are far less exciting than the often fantastic claims of commercial graphologists, but it is clear that some information can be gotten from a study of handwriting. Reliabilities of specific data about script are high, but the reported validities, when these are checked against ratings or tests of personality, are rather low. More will be said on this problem in Chapter 7.

---

[9] It should be noted that Festinger had earlier devised methods of intercepting messages within his groups and substituting those prepared by the experimenter, thus obtaining control of stimulus values. However, he was rarely interested in personality as such, but rather in group variables.

SUMMARY

Everyone studies personality. As opposed to popular devices, the scientific study of personality is distinguished by consideration of reliability, validity, and objectivity. In accordance with the three approaches to a definition of personality outlined in Chapter 1, techniques can be divided into three groups. Two of these have been considered in the present chapter.

Personality as stimulus is investigated chiefly by the rating technique. Ratings are useful, but subject to numerous errors. Both reliability and validity of ratings can be appreciably increased by due consideration of (1) characteristics of the rater, and (2) technique of making and summarizing ratings.

Personality as response may be studied by behavior samples and miniature situations. The miniature-situation technique is hopeful, although it is difficult to find such tests which will adequately predict the individual's behavior in life situations. Behavior samples are useful in young children, and samples of functions such as gesture and handwriting may yet be found useful in the analysis of the adult personality.

SUGGESTIONS FOR READING

The best recent books in this area are by Allen: *Personality assessment procedures*, and by Ferguson: *Personality measurement*. An older book, quite good on interview, observation, and ratings, is Symonds's *Diagnosing personality and conduct*.

CHAPTER 3

Methods: Inventories and Projective Tests

We seek greater precision in our estimates of a person's social stimulus value by developing better rating scales. We may also sharpen our understanding of an individual by obtaining samples of his behavior under standardized conditions. But our long-run purpose is to get a more satisfactory method for studying his inner personality, the structure of perceptions, expectancies, desires, and ideals, which accounts both for his behavior and for his stimulus value.

There are, broadly speaking, two classes of devices which have become preeminent in studying personality as an intervening variable. One class includes the personality questionnaires and inventories which have multiplied so rapidly in the United States and are now proliferating in other parts of the world. Essentially, these devices assume that we can infer the nature of the person's inner organization from his answers to questions—not directly, in many cases, since what he will give us is his "mask" or the picture he wants us to have of him. Indirectly, however, we should be able to make inferences from combinations of items and by including correction factors of various kinds.

The second broad category of methods relevant here includes the so-called "projective tests." Essentially these tests involve facing the subject with an ambiguous stimulus and requiring him to respond. Since he cannot figure out what the examiner wants, he must "project" his own meanings into the situation and behave accordingly. Obviously it should be necessary for him to reveal something of his concealed self in this operation.

The research publications dealing with these techniques—inventories and projectives—fill several volumes annually. The following treatment can do no more than identify some examples and try to outline the key problems relevant to their application in the study of personality.

INVENTORIES AND QUESTIONNAIRES

The first questionnaire designed to obtain a self-description of personality seems to have been that devised by Woodworth (see Hollingworth, 1920).

Table 3.1

Questions Intended to Test "Emotional Instability"

1. Do you usually feel well and strong? (no)
2. Do you usually sleep well? (no)
3. Are you frightened in the middle of the night? (yes)
4. Are you troubled with dreams about your work? (yes)
5. Do you have nightmares? (yes)
6. Do you have too many sexual dreams? (yes)
7. Do you ever walk in your sleep? (yes)
8. Do you ever have the sensation of falling when going to sleep? (yes)
9. Does your heart ever thump in your ears so that you cannot sleep? (yes)

SOURCE: Hollingworth (1920).

This was used with draftees in World War I, in an effort to locate psychiatric risks before they broke down under stress of combat. The items, samples of which are shown in Table 3.1, were essentially symptoms taken from psychiatric notes on patients. It was assumed that if a soldier reported more than some minimum number of these symptoms, there was a high probability that he possessed a "neurotic personality" and would be incapable of functioning under combat conditions.

In the period between the two wars, psychologists in the United States produced a wide variety of inventories and questionnaires calculated to measure many different aspects of personality. Important contributions are associated with the names of Bernreuter, Cattell, Guilford, Bell, and Thurstone. A good summary of developments in this area can be obtained from Ferguson (1952).

Assumptions of the Inventory Technique. Any technique which purports to measure some aspect of personality starts from certain assumptions about the relation of this aspect to an observable act. Thus, inventories depend upon assumptions about the relation of the postulated underlying "trait" of personality to the act of answering questions about oneself.

Common Traits. All inventories, and indeed, all measurement techniques which can be used to make quantitative comparisons between individuals, assume the existence of common traits. Although this point will be elaborated in Chapter 8, we note here that common traits are assumed to be essentially similar structures in all personalities, scalable in the same units. (Height, for example, is a common physical trait; it can be measured in the same units for all individuals.) Thus, it is assumed that sociability, emotional stability, self-sufficiency, manifest anxiety, and other traits are common to the population being studied; one may therefore make numerical comparisons within this population.

Quantitative Nature of Traits. It is further assumed by most inventories that traits can be estimated quantitatively by simply adding the number of indicators. For example, a given scale may include 55 items (the Minnesota Multiphasic Personality Inventory—MMPI—scale for hypochondriasis, described below). John answers 11 of these in a "hypochondriacal" manner, and Sam also gets a score of 11. The test user holds that John and Sam are equally characterized as average on this aspect of personality, even though the 11 items scored for John are not the same as the 11 scored for Sam. This approach assumes that the trait is simply a kind of quantitative sum of specific acts, and that these are equally diagnostic for the trait. Critics of the questionnaire approach reject this view; however, one has difficulty in avoiding it, even when dealing with the more subtle projective tests (see page 59).

Relation to Inner Pattern. Finally, developers of these tests assume that there is some kind of dependable relation between the act of answering the questions and the existence of some unknown inner pattern (the "real" trait). This does not necessarily mean that the person is assumed to be giving an accurate description of himself in the ordinary sense. Such an item as "I would never tell a lie under any circumstances" is not interpreted as meaning that this individual possesses a truthful personality. Rather, it is scored in terms of a desire to make a good impression, to deny the presence of disapproved attributes. Thus, psychologists assume a predictable relationship of a response to some inner pattern, but not necessarily the one manifestly involved in the item content.

The Minnesota Multiphasic Personality Inventory. Only one example of a personality inventory can be analyzed carefully in our limited space. The Minnesota Multiphasic Personality Inventory (MMPI) has been chosen for this purpose because of its wide use in clinical and research work by psychologists.

Hathaway and McKinley (1940) set out to develop an inventory which could be used for estimating the extent to which a person showed a variety of personality traits. Their procedures will be listed in some detail, since these same steps have been followed in most scale construction of this type.

(1) The authors collected about one thousand items of a self-descriptive form, such as "I often feel as if things about me are not real." These items were collected from earlier tests, from clinical case histories, from autobiographies, and from conversations with patients. (2) Ambiguous and duplicate items were eliminated; thus the total number was cut down to 504. (3) These items were administered to various groups of persons, selected in some fashion to exemplify the extreme of some alleged personality pattern; e.g., to a group of hypochondriacs (persons who show an "abnormal, psychoneurotic concern over bodily health"). The answers to all 504 items were tabulated for the 50 patients who showed a fairly pure kind of hypochondriacal reaction pattern, and for normal control subjects. (4) By statistical means, 55 items were selected which differentiated the hypochondriacs from

the normals at a suitable level of significance. These 55 items thus constituted the MMPI scale for *hypochondriasis*.

The procedure thus far is similar to that used by various other investigators. Hathaway and McKinley, however, took steps to avoid one criticism leveled at such standardization. This criticism is: The hypochondriacs used to select the item key were also psychiatric patients; isn't your "trait" confused with sheer abnormality without any specific pattern? To avert this possibility, the MMPI was administered to a large group of patients who were not hypochondriacs, and a "correction key" was prepared. This key shows the typical answers of abnormals who are not hypochondriacal. In use, the hypochondriasis score is determined, and this correction score is subtracted from it to give the final trait score.

The MMPI has such a large reservoir of items, many of which are still unscored, that investigators regularly choose new groups and set up new scoring keys. Keys are now widely used for schizophrenic tendency, mania, "psychopathic deviation," paranoid tendency, anxiety, depression, "ego strength," and an assortment of other variables. The test is used extensively in clinical practice, and also in research when an investigator wishes to select subjects who can be presumed to be extreme on a specific personality trait.

Special Validating Scales. Hathaway and McKinley have also attempted to build into the test some safeguards against criticisms of inventories in general. These safeguards take the form of three special validating scores which can be used to decide how far a given person's diagnostic scores should be trusted.

1. The *question score* is simply the number of times he has checked "cannot say" instead of giving a "yes" or "no" answer. A question score above 30 casts doubt on the subject's scores, since it is assumed that he is being excessively evasive.

2. The *lie score* represents the person's tendency to give socially desirable answers even if they are untrue. The items scored are of such an ideal character that very few of us can truthfully give an affirmative answer; the individual who feels that he must make a good impression on the examiner, however, will give such answers.

3. The *validity score* is composed of 64 items which are very rarely answered in a given manner by normal subjects. Hathaway and McKinley allege that a high score on these items indicates that the items were marked carelessly or that the person could not understand what he was doing.

These three validation scores undoubtedly represent a significant methodological improvement over previous questionnaire construction, in that they attempt to forestall certain kinds of criticisms. However, the authors have given us little evidence to support their claim that these three scores actually serve the purpose claimed for them.

Reliability. On a test-retest basis, the reliabilities of the various subscales of MMPI run from $+.46$ to $+.93$. Repeated retesting of a small group indicates that though specific scores change, the profile (relatively strong and weak points in an individual's pattern) remains rather constant. The reliabilities are probably satisfactory, particularly for the more widely used scales such as the Manifest Anxiety Scale.

Validity. Studies of validity of the psychiatric scales have given widely varying results. Some investigators find that the scales select patients and predict their diagnostic categories with marked accuracy. Others are more critical. Apparently psychiatrists differ markedly in their use of certain diagnostic terms, so that a test which is valid in Minnesota may not work so well in California. This raises the problem of choosing a validating criterion for any kind of personality measure; we shall return to it at the close of this chapter.

Cattell's 16 PF Scales. The MMPI has been attacked on other grounds. One is that its basis is purely empirical; there is no rationale behind the various scores, except that a criterion group could be found which was presumably extreme on some dimension. A second is that the scales are not independent of one another; many items are scored for more than one trait. Thus, a person taking the inventory who receives a valid high score on one trait may get an unjustified high score on another because of these questions which are scored for both.

One attempt to deal with these problems is that offered by Cattell (1957) with his 16 PF test. This test evolved out of a long series of researches. Starting with behavior ratings (cf. Chapter 2), Cattell identified 131 clusters of ratings, which were then reduced to 50 "nuclear clusters." These 50, in turn, were arranged to identify 20 "sectors of the personality sphere," independent traits which rather thoroughly covered the social stimulus aspects of personality.

In a later study Cattell attempted to develop inventory items which would measure these 20 aspects by self-description. Using the method of factor analysis, he succeeded in locating 16 groups of items which could be paired modestly well with the earlier data. The procedure of factor-analyzing the relationships among items assures the unity and independence of the 16 scales; and the general procedure gives some theoretical groundwork for this grouping, although there is no way of being sure that the entire "personality sphere" is being covered.

Grygier's Dynamic Personality Inventory. A few attempts have recently been made to construct personality scales based directly on some theory of personality. Sigmund Freud suggested, many years ago, the importance of studying personality in developmental terms (cf. Chapter 5). The child, he said, goes through oral, anal, phallic, and genital stages, and the adult personality usually bears the marks of fixations and frustrations at each of these stages. Krout and Tabin (1954) prepared an inventory (PPS) based on this theory. Grygier (1957) started with their test, but greatly expanded it. He also took the step of intercorrelating and factor-analyzing his items, thus assuring unity and independence of his various scores. His Dynamic Personality Inventory looks promising, but is too new for any substantial evidence to have accumulated as to its value.

Edwards's Personal Preference Schedule. Edwards (1954) likewise attempted to develop an inventory based on a theory: in this case, Murray's theory of needs, such as the need for achievement, the need for change, the need for affiliation, heterosexual needs, and other impulses.

Edwards made use of another recent development in test methodology, the *forced-choice* technique. The subject is presented with two items, and must say which is more descriptive of himself. Edwards experimented with items worded in different ways, and matched his pairs of items for "social desirability," i.e., each member of the pair sounded just as good as the other. It is now generally conceded that social desirability of items must be controlled, and that the Edwards procedure is probably superior to the "validity scores" developed for the MMPI. The forced-choice procedure is also considered desirable for many kinds of personality measurement tasks.

The Semantic Differential. Although it does not take the form of a questionnaire, the semantic differential developed by Osgood (see Osgood, Suci, and Tannenbaum, 1957) is basically a way of asking questions and getting quick responses. The form used is a graphic rating scale similar to that shown in Figure 3.1. The subject responds by making a check mark somewhere along the line to indicate how he perceives the concept presented.

The differential so far has been used to provide two kinds of data. Obviously, it gives the qualitative attributes of the percepts held by this particular person. A woman, for example, may describe father, husband, boss, and other male figures as weak, dirty, small, etc. This provides highly significant information about her orientation toward males.

Secondly, the differential makes possible a unique determination of organization for this person. A young man may cluster his responses in such a way that father, God, power, and security are all close together in his "semantic space," i.e., his meaning structure; whereas another cluster includes mother, sin, fraud, and sickness. Although it cannot be assumed, without further evidence, that these data are valid representations of his personality organiza-

Fig. 3.1 Form of Osgood's semantic differential. The person puts a check on each line to show how he judges the concept at left for this attribute (defined by the polarized adjectives).

tion, it does seem highly probable that he has problems in relation to his mother.

The simple format of the differential makes it easy to introduce new concepts which may be significant for a specific person. This is in contrast to structured inventories such as MMPI, where new items cannot be introduced. On the other hand, if an investigator wishes to classify subjects as hypochondriacal, paranoid, manic, etc., the MMPI would be much more useful than the differential.

What Is a Good Personality Inventory? What are the characteristics which identify a personality inventory as good or poor? The criteria most often stressed are *reliability* and *validity*.

Reliability. We have noted earlier, in connection with ratings, that an unreliable measure is one which fluctuates in an unpredictable sort of way, and hence is of little value for any kind of research. Specifically, a personality inventory on which chance is a major determinant of scores will not be very useful in diagnosing anyone's personality.

Reliability is usually broken down into two components: consistency and stability. *Consistency* refers to the degree of agreement inside the measuring device; for example, all of the inventories described above have been tested for internal consistency. Half the items are scored and compared with the other half, to show that the person's score agrees fairly well on the two halves. *Stability* refers to reliability measured over time; thus, a person tested at six-month intervals should presumably get comparable scores on successive tests. This assumes, on the other hand, that personality does not change, and we know that it does. Hence, psychologists do not demand that reliability over time be as high as reliability (consistency) at a point in time. Although any figure chosen is arbitrary and subject to criticism, a common opinion among psychologists is that consistency should be not less than .80 and stability around .70, for a test to be useful.

Validity. A more difficult question is that of validity. A test is said to be valid if it "measures what it is supposed to measure." This means, inevitably, that any single test may have high validity, low validity, or no validity at all, depending on how it is being used. For example, a test of "neurotic tendency" may successfully pick out people who worry and experience a lot of emotional disturbance, but it may not pick out people who make nervous movements. Is the test valid or not? Much depends on what is claimed for it, or what the test user is trying to accomplish.

Validity is also affected by the circumstances under which the test is administered. Some personality tests have proved useful in counseling and guidance situations, in helping young people choose the type of work they want; but if such tests are used in a personnel office, in selecting applicants for that same kind of job, they are not valid (cf. Heron, 1956). Why? The reason seems to be that in the guidance center respondents are more likely to tell the truth;

in the employment office they are more likely to say what they think the employer wants.

Cross-validation. One way of determining validity is simply to repeat the procedure used in the original validation. Hathaway and McKinley, for example, developed their hypochondriasis key; then they gave the MMPI to a new set of hypochondriacs, and demonstrated that the key assigned scores to this group which were significantly above those obtained by a group of normals. If a test is developed around a group chosen by such an external criterion, a new group of the same kind can be chosen for cross-validation.

Predictive Validity. An even more severe test of validity is that of showing that the test can predict future personality developments. The original inventories were devised in an attempt to preselect soldiers likely to become psychiatric casualties in wartime. During World War II several such tests were administered to military personnel, and later follow-ups were conducted to see if the scores were valid. For example, Jennings (1948) studied MMPI profiles of 516 Air Force officers. Of these, 33 had psychiatric breakdowns in service. When they were compared with those who completed tours of duty without breakdown, highly significant differences appeared. Thus the MMPI seems valid when tested for predicting breakdown under stress. By contrast, it has proved invalid for predicting failure in flight training (a relatively less stressful situation).

There are several reasons why such tests of validity encounter difficulties:

1. If an individual is trying to get into a desired situation (employment, the Air Force, officers' training school, etc.), he will be tempted to distort his answers, wherever possible, in the direction he believes to be acceptable. Thus, many of the military studies may have failed because the individual falsified the inventory—from the best of motives, of course.

2. Another difficulty lies in the fallibility of the criterion. If psychiatric breakdown is used, we assume that the judgment of a military psychiatrist is a safe criterion. But numerous studies [1] indicate that psychiatrists often disagree with each other, that a given psychiatrist changes his mind about a specific patient, and so on. Hence the low validity of the test may be an artifact produced by a poor criterion.

Peer Ratings. In the preceding chapter behavior ratings and attribute ratings by peer groups were described as ways of identifying certain kinds of personalities. Obviously, then, these can be used as criteria for inventories. Questionnaires for children have often been related to judgments by class-

---

[1] For example, Masserman and Carmichael (1938) followed up patients after one year and found that 41 per cent had to be reclassified. See also Cameron (1941) and Raines and Rohrer (1955). Otis (1954) reports on some military research regarding men who had been patients at the mental hygiene clinics at Yale and Harvard, and finds evidence of marked unreliability in the judgments of service psychiatrists; also, many men judged unfit for service achieved fine records, and many men judged acceptable had breakdowns. Thus the criterion may itself lack validity.

mates of each other, using either defined scales, sociometric choices, or the Guess Who technique. The assumption here is that an inventory should be able to differentiate among children who are perceptibly different from their classmates. If this is verified, then the psychologist can use the test in dealing with children for whom such ratings are not available; and he may be able to ascertain ways in which the child's personality can be modified to improve his acceptability or to reduce the amount of friction he has in his group.

Self-ratings. Finally, we may mention efforts to demonstrate the validity of a test by checking it against self-ratings of the corresponding trait. Since, it may be argued, no one knows this person better than he knows himself, agreement with a self-rating should be good evidence of validity. There are two sound objections to this; one is that many people do not know themselves; indeed, they avoid observing their own weak points (see Chapter 6). Secondly, people are notoriously gullible about descriptions of their own personalities. The author has often used a set of glittering generalities, collected by Forer (1949), to demonstrate this fallacy. Persons who have taken a personality inventory are handed a sheet with these glowing statements checked in such a way as to make it appear that the sheet is different for each person. They are asked to report how valid the description is. About 90 per cent of a college student or businessman's group (Stagner, 1958) will check either "amazingly accurate" or "fairly good." Since everyone received identical "diagnoses," it is clear that the average person cannot be trusted to judge whether a given test score is an accurate reflection of his inner make-up.

A Survey of Validity Studies. The problems involved in arriving at an overall assessment of the validity of inventories can be illustrated by reference to the survey by Ellis (1953). A critic of the inventory approach, Ellis shows that of 499 articles published between 1946 and 1951, 290 reported significant evidence of test validity, while 209 did not (see Table 3.2). This looks rather poor for the inventories. What Ellis does not do, however, is very important. (1) He does not eliminate studies in which no theory would have predicted a difference; indeed, in some cases it could be argued that the groups compared should *not* differ, e.g., age, sex, and socioeconomic groups. And he includes some studies for which no rationale is apparent; for example, *should* inventories reveal differences in extrasensory perception when the phenomenon itself is still of dubious reliability? (2) He does not differentiate between inventories, some of which give more satisfactory results than others. (3) He fails to consider the fallibility of the criteria used (see our discussion above). These criticisms do not justify reversing Ellis's conclusion and deciding that inventories are valid; rather, they suggest that *some inventories are valid some of the time,* and we should be selective about inventories and also about the criteria we expect them to meet.

Table 3.2

Summary by Ellis of Validity Studies on Inventories, 1946-1951

Type of validation	Studies in which significant differences were found	Studies in which no significant differences were found	Total
Inventory scores vs. diagnostic examinations (psychiatric, therapeutic, delinquent)	114	52	166
Inventory scores vs. ratings (by associates, instructors, etc.)	13	13	26
Inventory scores vs. behavioral characteristics (usually objectively measured)	53	41	94
Inventory scores vs. vocational and academic test and performance results	45	56	101
Inventory scores vs. group differences (age, sex, socioeconomic, etc.)	65	47	112
Total	290	209	499

SOURCE: Ellis (1953), Table 1, p. 40. By permission of the American Psychological Association, Inc.

Criterion Validity versus Construct Validity. The foregoing discussion assumes the existence of an external criterion for the trait or a criterion performance which the inventory seeks to predict. In such a case one can compute a validity coefficient, a correlation showing the degree of confidence we can adopt with respect to the test as a predictor. Such validity coefficients are widely used in connection with aptitude and ability tests, where it is fairly easy to obtain a criterion performance or criterion group to use as a standard of success.

In the field of personality measurement, on the other hand, it is often difficult to locate a suitable external criterion. Suppose we postulate that there is a personality variable called "anxiety," which refers not to a momentary state but to a recurrent pattern. Criterion groups may be located by psychiatric judgment, or by peer judgment, or by self-evaluation, but in each case we may question whether the basis of selection is satisfactory.

The developer of a test for anxiety, then, may fall back on evidence that the test picks people who behave as they would be expected to in terms of a theory. Thus, the Manifest Anxiety Scale (Taylor, 1953) has been shown to relate to amount of palmar sweating in stress situations, to loss of efficiency of problem solving under shock threat, and so on. Since these are "reasonable" predictions in terms of a hypothesized trait of anxiety proneness, the test may be said to have validity even though no criterion group was tested.

This kind of validation is referred to as "construct validity." It means that a personality measure may be judged valid if its relations with other variables fit a theory in which the assumed personality trait is a "hypothetical construct." The trait cannot be defined observationally but the theory holds that such a trait must exist in order to explain behavior which is observable. Validating criterion groups cannot be identified in such cases. Consequently, much work is now being done using construct validity as the logical basis for justifying the value of the test. This holds also for projective devices, to which we now turn.

PROJECTIVE METHODS

As formal procedures for studying personality, the so-called "projective" techniques are about as old as the questionnaire; Rorschach published his

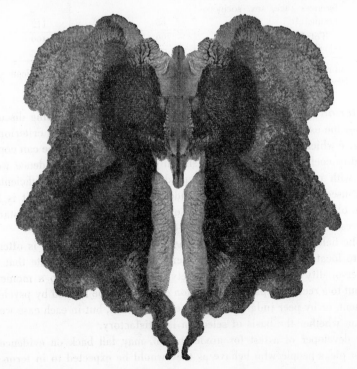

Fig. 3.2 Ink blot. This is similar to those used by Rorschach. How many "things" can you see in this one? Outlines, shading, etc., may give suggestions.

Psychodiagnostik, the first systematic use of ink blots, in 1921. While similar devices had been used earlier, their value as approaches to personality was not perceived.

The term "projective tests" has come to be applied to all methods facing the person with an "unstructured" situation, in which his responses are not determined by the outer stimulus and hence must depend upon inner conditions. Rorschach asked his subjects to look at an ink blot (similar to that shown in Figure 3.2) and tell "what it might be." Murray (1938) presented rather vague pictures and asked for stories to which the pictures might serve as illustrations. Shneidmann (1948) carried this idea a step further by handing his subject a picture of a background (living room, street corner) and asking him to choose a human figure, place it in the scene, and make up a story. Ambiguous auditory stimuli, colored tiles for mosaics, and other devices have been employed. All have in common the fact that the organization of the material must be supplied by the subject; "meaning" must be projected into the situation, hence the individual's personality must to some extent be revealed.

With increasing acceptance of the notion that personality is at its base a perceptual organization, the projective tests have seemed especially appropriate, and their number has multiplied amazingly. In this chapter we shall describe two: the Rorschach and the Thematic Apperception Test (TAT). We are more concerned with the general attributes of projectives than with the specific kinds which are available to the psychologist.

The projective devices have one great advantage over inventories and questionnaires. Since S does not know the meaning and does not know what will make a good impression on the experimenter, he has more difficulty in presenting only his mask; there is a greater likelihood that the projective test will pick up what is behind the mask. Another way of saying this is that projectives tap unconscious material. Conscious censorship can limit what the person reveals on an inventory; it is relatively difficult to censor the projectives. This fact raises an ethical question: to what extent and under what conditions is the psychologist justified in thus inducing the person to reveal what he might wish to conceal? Obviously professional controls are important here.

THE RORSCHACH TEST

"Structured" test situations interfere with the free expression of personality trends, because each of us has learned to do things in the correct and proper way. Verbal material has a strong tendency to set off logical definitions or culturally approved stereotypes which do not truly represent the inner personality structure. Rorschach therefore sought a device to stimulate associations of ideas which would be relatively free from such cultural influences.

His use of ink blots would appear to have been a happy solution to the problem.

Each ink blot (cf. Figure 3.2) is symmetrical, irregular in outline, varied in shading, and susceptible to a number of interpretations. Out of several hundred blots, Rorschach selected 10 which gave a rich variety of responses; most of the enormous Rorschach literature has been based on these 10 ink blots.

Administration. The subject should be relaxed and at ease as far as possible. The idea of a "test" should be dispelled by emphasizing the absence of right and wrong responses.

Instructions are intended to favor complete freedom for each individual to handle the cards in his own way. Klopfer and Kelley suggest the following: "People see all sorts of things in these ink-blot pictures; now tell me what *you* see, what it might be for you, what it makes you think of." [2] The examiner attempts to record the subject's exact words, time between responses, and significant gestures.

After the responses have been completed, it is necessary to run through the cards again for an *inquiry* into factors influencing the responses: the *location* on the card of each item seen and the *determinants* of the response, especially color, shading, and form.

Interpretation. After the responses have been tabulated and scored, [3] an interpretation is prepared. Some of the major factors presented for interpretation are the location of responses, the use of form, the reaction to color and shading, and the perception of movement. Relatively less attention is paid to the actual content (animals, objects, landscapes, etc.) reported.

Location. It is alleged that a preference for using the whole blot (W); a large, obvious detail (D); or a tiny detail (d) can be interpreted as a manifestation of a general personality tendency. "A relatively high number of W, according to the tradition of the Rorschach literature," write Klopfer and Kelley, "represents an emphasis on the abstract forms of thinking and the higher forms of mental activity." [4] This encouraging promise of a new approach to intelligence testing is slightly dashed by the comment, on the same page, that W responses are also likely to indicate certain kinds of mental defect, such as severe brain injury.

The extensive use of D (large detail) responses is said to indicate attention to the routine problems of daily life; a concentration upon d (tiny details) is related to a critical attitude or an overconcern with trivialities.

---

[2] Klopfer and Kelley (1942), p. 32. Reprinted by permission of World Book Company, publishers.

[3] Scoring the Rorschach requires considerable technical training. We shall not even attempt to outline the method here.

[4] Klopfer and Kelley (1942), p. 259. Reprinted by permission of World Book Company, publishers.

Movement. Many subjects perceive a kinesthetic quality, a feeling of action, in the blots: "two clowns playing pat-a-cake," "kicking feet," "two bears climbing." These movement (*M*) percepts are said to be indicative of richness of inner life, imagination, and creativeness. Animals in motion (*FM*) are considered to represent a more infantile level of fantasy, which has not been brought into an adult relationship with external reality.

Color. Cards II and III contain colors in addition to the black-gray outlines of the other blots; and VIII, IX, and X are entirely chromatic. Great stress is laid on differences in reaction to these as compared with the achromatic cards.

Generally speaking, *C* (color) responses are related to the outer world, in contrast to *M* which is identified with inner strivings. Thus the *M:C* ratio is employed as an introvert-extravert indicator. Persons with a marked excess of *C* over *M* are said to be *extratensive*, controlled chiefly by outer stimuli; they are impulsive in response to external stimulation. An excess of *M* indicates responsiveness to inner impulses. A decided lack of *C* responses is considered an indication of avoidance of emotional stimulation, often even a fear of becoming emotionally aroused.

Relations among Determinants. Some overenthusiastic Rorschach advocates offer sweeping statements regarding the significance of a definite sign. Well-considered writings emphasize a kind of check-and-balance system in interpreting the test: the significance is thus and so, unless something else is present. While this point of view is eminently realistic, it is sometimes discouraging to the student trying to learn precisely what the test is measuring.

Reliability. Because of the insistence by most Rorschach experts on the interpretation of the record as a gestalt, in which single scores cannot legitimately be isolated for statistical analysis, most of the studies of reliability of the test have been made by its critics. This raises problems, in that the investigators may have unconsciously stacked the cards against the test. However, the studies deserve careful consideration. A gestalt is not independent of its component parts; a square in which one side varies in a random manner quickly ceases to be a square.

Studies of the reliability of specific components in the Rorschach, such as the *M* score, the sum *C* score, and others, are very discouraging. Vernon (1933) reported split-half reliabilities based on 90 subjects; these were very low; the highest was .62 for *M*. Hertz (1934), on the other hand, studied 100 subjects; she correlated the five odd-numbered cards with the even-numbered cards, and got coefficients ranging from .67 to .92. Most of these were high enough to be quite acceptable to psychometricians.

Other investigators have studied the reliability of ratings prepared from Rorschach records. (After all, the scores themselves are of no value until they have been interpreted by an expert in the technique.) Grant, Ives, and Ranzoni (1952) presented the Rorschach protocols of 71 boys and 75 girls, all 18 years old, to three Rorschach "experts." The ratings prepared by the judges were then intercorrelated. The average agreement on boys was $+.70$ and on girls, $+.66$. Although these coefficients are statistically significant, they are low enough to indicate that the kind of interpretation one gets from a Rorschach depends very much on who does the interpreting. The same conclusion is reached by Baughman (1951).

Validity. The least that can be said regarding the validation studies on the Rorschach is that they are in violent disagreement. Clinicians, by and large, praise it highly. They believe that its use in dealing with patients gives quick insights into many fundamental aspects of personality. Psychologists with a more experimental or statistical bias have been less enthusiastic.

As with reliability, part of the difficulty revolves around the tendency of the statisticians to pull out specific scores for analysis, while the clinicians rely more on a global, over-all view of the test record. Rorschach himself, of course, started out with a consideration of specific scores; for example, he wrote (1942):

As many protocols as possible from as widely diversified clinical material as available were obtained and the results analysed according to the individual factors (C, M, FC, etc.). Thus it was discovered that those subjects giving the most primary color answers were exclusively epileptics, manics, . . . or notoriously hot-headed and hyper-aggressive and irresponsible "normals." From this it was concluded that C answers have a "symptom value," that is they represent the common trait of all these cases, namely, the tendency to impulsive emotional discharge [p. 33].

Even if we leave out of consideration the somewhat dubious validation procedure of considering normals who were "notoriously hotheaded" as a criterion group, it is obvious that Rorschach first identified the significance of his response categories by referring to differences between groups on a specific response type. It is argued by current Rorschach devotees, of course, that a specific Rorschach score has meaning only in relation to the pattern of other scores; this is a needed refinement, just as it is needed for the refinement of questionnaires and other devices.

Efforts to validate specific scores on the Rorschach have concentrated on experimental procedures. For example, Baker and Harris (1949) related changes in speech performance under stress to certain Rorschach items alleged to indicate control. Some of the results were significantly positive. Similarly, Williams (1947) got results indicating that the control measures on the Rorschach predicted ability to work efficiently under stress; on the other hand, Carlson and Lazarus (1953) repeated Williams's study with a negative outcome. Contradictory findings have also been reported on other Rorschach measures by various investigators.

Symonds (1955) was interested in the question of whether interpretations based on the determinants (form, color, etc.) were superior to interpretation based on the symbolic meaning of the responses given. He submitted a detailed Rorschach record to seven experts, asked for interpretative statements about the personality, and asked if the statement were based on determinants or on content. The judges got 65 per cent of their items correct, as compared with detailed therapy records; 44 per cent were said to be based on determinants, 56 per cent on content. Of those related to determinants, 59 per cent proved correct; of those based on content, 74 per cent were correct. Symonds is critical of the Rorschach on the basis of low over-all accuracy, but these figures do not seem excessively discouraging.

Validation of Total Diagnosis. Proponents of the Rorschach, again, would argue that the appropriate validation is to be based on an interpretation of the whole record, not on fragments pulled from it. However, the published studies which have used this method do not greatly strengthen the case for the Rorschach. Grant, Ives, and Ranzoni (1952) had three Rorschach experts analyze the protocols of 71 boys and 75 girls and correlated the results with ratings prepared by caseworkers who had been studying the 146 youngsters over a period of several years. The results were most discouraging. Of 144 correlations computed between personality ratings by Rorschachers and caseworkers, only six were large enough to be significant at the 5 per cent level of confidence.[5]

There seems little doubt that the Rorschach distinguishes satisfactorily between groups having different degrees of psychiatric impairment (cf. Allen, 1958). Classification of patients into subordinate diagnostic groups has occasionally been fairly successful, in other cases less so.

Some studies have indicated that experts looking at a Rorschach record can match it with a detailed personality sketch very accurately (cf. Vernon, 1935). "Blind analyses" (reports written by a Rorschach specialist without any contact with the subject) have been tried by several investigators. The results seem to differ, studies made by critics being negative, those by proponents of the test, positive. Krugman (1942) found very high success when his judges were asked to match descriptions written from Rorschach records with descriptions of problem children written by clinical psychologists without the Rorschach.

The controversy over the validity of the Rorschach has been exacerbated by the excessive claims made by proponents of the test. At the outbreak of World War II the test was urged as a screening device for aviators; later evidence indicated that it was quite useless. Harrower mentions the following observation: "The records of thirty aviators who had been decorated and

[5] If one were simply to roll dice to obtain "Rorschach scores" and "caseworker ratings," he would occasionally get a set which agreed closely enough to suggest that the two were measuring the same trait. Consequently, psychologists are not impressed by an occasional high correlation. In the study cited, 6 high correlations out of 144 could easily have occurred by chance.

had completed over thirty missions successfully were contrasted with those who had failed to complete more than five missions. No differences on any of the Rorschach findings or significant ratios were discovered. Moreover, among this group of highly decorated individuals were records that in the normal course of evaluation would have been termed those of frankly unstable or psychopathic personalities." [6]

Another kind of claim has been that the Rorschach would select executives, e.g., sales managers. Kurtz (1948) conducted a study which is a methodological classic in examining this claim. From one group of life insurance sales managers a key was developed which scored as positive those responses given by successful managers and as negative those given by poorer managers. When this key was applied to a new group of managers, the correlation of the scoring key with judged success was .02. In other words, the Rorschach, even with a key specially developed for this group, could not predict success. These studies indicate, at least, that the test should not be applied to military and vocational selection.

THE THEMATIC APPERCEPTION TEST

Perhaps as widely used as the Rorschach, today, is a rather different kind of projective test, the Thematic Apperception Test (TAT). This test, developed by Murray (1938), is somewhat more structured than the Rorschach; most of the pictures have recognizable human figures of different age and sex categories. For instance, there is a picture of a young woman and an old woman (Figure 3.3). The instructions call for *S* to make up a story about the picture. Usually he is asked to tell what led up to this situation, what the characters in it are thinking and feeling, and how it will work out. Thus he may say that the daughter went out with a boy against her mother's wishes; now she is being scolded, but she will be forgiven and will not hold a grudge. Obviously all this must be projected by *S*, since there are cues in the pictures to justify almost any interpretation.

Administration. The administration of TAT is less standardized than that of the Rorschach. Everyone agrees that the atmosphere should be relaxed and should not suggest a test situation. The examinee is asked to make up a story about each card, but it is common to permit him to reject a card when it appears that he will be disturbed by the emotions it evokes within him.

At present (third revision) the TAT consists of 30 pictures plus a blank card. Some are used for boys under 14, others for girls under 14, for adult males, and for adult females. The usual administration involves 20 pictures for a given person. Commonly 10 pictures are presented, with either a short rest or a full day elapsing before the second set of 10.

The instructions likewise tend to vary. As noted above, most examiners

[6] Harrower (1950), pp. 173–174. Reprinted by permission of Alfred A. Knopf, Inc.

ask for a statement of what is happening, how it arose, the thoughts and emotions of the characters, the probable outcome. Usually five minutes are allowed for each card, though a person who indicates that he has completed all his associations to one is allowed to go on to the next, and he is not shut off if he is still going at the end of five minutes. Allen (1958) recommends the use of a tape recorder, because it leaves the examiner free to notice gestures, flushing, and other signs of emotion; the tape also preserves a record of vocal changes, pauses, irrelevant noises, and similar cues. These often indicate that the topic being mentioned is emotionally significant to the examinee. A great deal of research work using TAT has allowed subjects to write their own stories. Under these circumstances, of course, the kinds of cues just mentioned are lost.

Scoring. Scoring, likewise, is much less standardized than for the Rorschach. Some psychologists have developed fairly complex formal systems for analyzing the TAT material; others prefer a kind of free-wheeling intuitive judgment in which the psychologist tries to identify significant themes, needs felt by the subject, and emotional attitudes toward parents and other figures. Bellak (1948) uses a check list on which he records the perceived characteristics of the hero (or heroine) of the story; the attitudes to parental figures (grateful, submissive, respectful, aggressive, fearful, etc.); attribution of

Fig. 3.3 TAT picture. (Reproduced by permission of Harvard University Press.)

blame; significant conflicts (superego-id, achievement-pleasure, etc.) ; signs of inhibition when discussing sex or aggression; happy or unhappy outcome; and other details. As we shall see later, the results of research cast some doubt on the appropriateness of this kind of analysis.

Reliability. Since the scoring procedures are not uniform, reliability of TAT is difficult to ascertain. The use of any instrument for detecting alleged trends in personality assumes (cf. page 32) that the test will yield consistent trends from one part to another and also that the trends revealed will be stable over reasonable periods of time. Sen (1953) reports on assessments made by the same judge with a nine-month interval between; the average correlation for various traits was $+.59$, which is at least minimally satisfactory. Lindzey and Herman (1955) report split-half (consistency) coefficients which were significant, but very low; it must be noted that they did not use the full-length test. Harrison and Rotter (1945) tested for agreement between two judges of the same protocols, and report 74 per cent agreement, which they consider satisfactory.

Undoubtedly reliability is affected by the kind of scoring system employed. If an attempt is made to estimate a number of details rather precisely, the apparent reliability goes down; if the examiner is content with rough estimates of a few outstanding items, the reliability seems higher. The selection of pictures and devising of a specific focus for scoring also improves reliability. McClelland et al. (1953) have used the TAT technique for estimating the intensity of need for achievement and have reported satisfactory reliability.

Validity. The more serious challenges to TAT come on the score of validity. We find here, in even more serious form, the difficulties noted above for the Rorschach. Clinically sensitive examiners, using the TAT as an aid to interview, feel that it gives them quick insight into deep and relatively unconscious aspects of the personality. Statistics-minded researchers, looking for findings at a more objective level, have often been disappointed. Further, the lack of standardization of administration and scoring means that the test may have validity in one context or for one examiner, and not elsewhere. It is even possible (see page 62) that the test may have validity for some subjects and not for others.

Identifying psychiatric patients as to diagnostic grouping has been successful for some observers (Harrison, 1940) but not for others (Eron, 1950). Henry (1956) indicates that his TAT analyses have been validated by various independent types of data; he has also reported (1949) satisfactory differentiation of successful and unsuccessful business executives from TAT protocols. Friedman (1957) found that the "heroes" in TAT stories told by normal subjects were judged to be more adequate, more optimistic, and closer to the person's "ideal self," as compared with heroes of stories by psychoneurotics and by paranoid schizophrenics. And Purcell (1956) found evidence favoring validity of TAT as a means of identifying soldiers with a tendency toward antisocial aggression. Many such studies support the claims for validity of TAT.

On the other hand, many authors have been very critical of TAT. For example, Child, Frank, and Storm (1956) presented to male college students a questionnaire, using self-ratings, about various characteristics, such as achievement, dominance, and isolation; the same subjects on another occasion wrote TAT stories which were analyzed for the same traits. Their report states that the self-ratings "yielded measures of very satisfactory reliability and, for three variables for which a pertinent criterion was available, substantial validity. A group TAT . . . yielded measures of generally very low reliability, of no validity (by the same criterion applied to the questionnaire), and of no apparent relation to the corresponding measures obtained from the questionnaire" [p. 113].

Another study questions a fundamental assumption of TAT, namely, that the fantasies elicited by the TAT pictures have a close connection with the individual's inner percepts of major persons or events in his life. Meyer and Tolman (1955) analyzed the diagnostic test records of persons who had been through psychotherapy (in the course of which one must necessarily reveal in detail his feelings, e.g., about his parents). They found that the images of the parents reported during the therapeutic sessions did not correspond to those described in TAT stories. Such results are, to say the least, discouraging. They seem to deny a basic assumption of projective tests.

Other Projective Devices. Many other methods have been employed to induce the person to reveal inner tendencies. Rosenzweig (1945) uses cartoons showing common frustrating situations. The words of one person are given as a stimulus; the subject must write in an answer for the other person pictured. Rotter and others have used an "incomplete-sentence" method; the subject must write in something to finish the statement. For example, if the test blank offers the item: "Professors are . . . ," and the subject writes in "dull," he is revealing an unfavorable perception of professors.

The variety of such devices is too great for us to review them here. Good accounts are offered in Abt and Bellak (1950) and Anderson and Anderson (1951).

Validity of Projective Devices. A critical review of all the studies on projectives would be impossibly long and confusing. We summarize, therefore, by giving what seems the most tenable conclusion today: under favorable conditions, and in the hands of some examiners, projective tests reveal significant information, which often extends to unconsciously held beliefs or percepts. However, the conditions of testing and the nature of the examiner-examinee relationship can be crucial. Some examiners can create an atmosphere which elicits useful responses; others may cause the subject to conceal sensitive areas. An unfavorable environmental situation can also induce a response set in the person of withholding information. Putting the matter differently, we can say that, under appropriate circumstances, projective devices serve as cues to elicit from *S* information which helps the examiner to develop an accurate estimate of some personality attribute. The information so elicited, however, often lacks generality.

A crucial problem in regard to the validity of all projective tests results from questions about their objectivity. If the bias of the examiner enters into the interpretation, validity is necessarily reduced. There is a strong suspicion that such effects do operate to a significant degree. Hammer and Piotrowski (1953) estimated the hostility tendencies of six clinicians, and then tallied the amount of hostility "seen" by these clinicians in projective material from a series of child patients. The correlation of the two measures was $+.94$; in other words, the clinician's hostility was a major factor in determining what he found in the records. Masling (1957) had two girls memorize identical answers to the Rotter Sentence Completion Test. Each was tested by a class of psychology trainees. One girl acted interested, friendly, and helpful in her examinations; the other was critical, cold, and distant. Although the words used in their answers were identical, the former was unanimously adjudged to be a better-adjusted personality! In ordinary clinical practice, of course, a psychologist is perfectly justified in using these direct perceptions as a guide in his judgment. The study indicates, however, that the test device is being distorted to fit in with these impressions; i.e., the test is lacking in objectivity.

Another problem to which little consideration has been given is the possibility that each *S* may respond to the projective test in his own unique way. By this we mean that the same determinant on the Rorschach, the same thema on TAT, does not necessarily have the same meaning for different subjects. On a questionnaire, the same response by different persons may have widely different significance. Some individuals may conceal themselves successfully from either Rorschach or TAT probing. And some may have revealed aspects which were unsuspected because the examiner had too firmly established a stereotype regarding the meaning of a given story. If this interpretation is correct, it would perhaps help us to understand why some examiners are so enthusiastic about these tests and others are not. It may also explain why efforts to establish rigorous scoring and interpretative rules have been resisted. Perhaps these methods have optimal utility only when they are used by an examiner as a stimulus, when the real instrument is the sensitive recording device of the examiner's perceptual apparatus.

ON THE "MEASUREMENT" OF PERSONALITY

Inventories and projective devices make up the major tools used by psychologists in "measuring" personality. Although we have described only a few of the great number of inventories, and only two of the common projective techniques, this sketch should serve to indicate the lines along which research proceeds in an effort to improve our estimates.

The results, as sketched above, have not been highly encouraging. That this does not reflect a personal bias of the author can be seen from the results of a questionnaire by Kornhauser (1945) which was distributed to a wide sample of psychologists (see Table 3.3). Although this study was done in 1945, it is likely that the same conclusion would be reached today, namely, that the validity of both inventories and the Rorschach can best be categorized as "doubtfully satisfactory."

Testing and Perception. Allen (1958) has suggested that it is fruitful to consider the four desirable attributes of a personality test (validity, reliability, objectivity, and standardization) in terms of the errors they are intended to avoid. Putting this in perceptual terms, we can say that tests are devised to improve the perception by the examiner of a particular person (cf. Figure 2.1). Specifically, the development of a personality test is calculated to reduce certain perceptual errors.

1. *Validity* focuses on the elimination of *constant* errors. If a questionnaire uses complicated words, it may be an intelligence test but not a valid measure of personality. If an ink blot evoked the same responses from everyone, it would not be a valid device.

Table 3.3

Opinions of Psychological Test Experts Regarding Certain Tests

In the field of personality testing, how satisfactory or helpful for present practical use do you consider:

    (*a*) Personality inventories and questionnaires (such as those of Bernreuter, Bell, Humm-Wadsworth)?

    (*b*) The Rorschach test?

	Inventories, per cent	Rorschach, per cent
Highly satisfactory	1.5	0.0
Moderately satisfactory	13.5	20.0
Doubtfully satisfactory	36.0	29.0
Rather unsatisfactory	33.0	22.0
Highly unsatisfactory	16.0	29.0
Total	100.0	100.0
Number of psychologists	67	59

SOURCE: Kornhauser (1945). Reprinted by permission from *Educ. psychol. Measmt*, 5, 3–15.

2. *Reliability* refers to freedom from *chance* errors. The results of the measurement should not vary randomly but should be stable and consistent.

3. *Objectivity* is sought to eliminate the prejudices of the examiner. As noted above, the attributes of the examiner affect notably the outcome of projective tests. Research on scoring methods is directed (so far not too successfully) to the elimination of these observational errors.

4. *Standardization* attempts to reduce sampling errors by providing a wide range of data for comparison. The beginner, especially with projectives, often exaggerates the significance of certain responses. As he gets a wider range of observations, he perceives more accurately the relevance of specific items.

In short, we suggest that the purpose of personality measuring devices—experiments, projectives, questionnaires—is to provide perceptual aids to the psychologist. His task is to identify the "real" attributes of a person under conditions such that the same attributes will be observed by another competent psychologist.[7] All of us suffer from some degree of perceptual distortion. In a sense, then, we may say that most of this research is ultimately devoted to a study of the personality-as-stimulus, but it is focused on the person as observed with the aid of special devices by an observer trained for the job.

SUMMARY

Personality inventories provide lists of specific acts, feelings, percepts, and the like, which are presumed to have value as defining attributes of personality. The inventory may be composed exclusively of one category or item—i.e., all items are assumed to be symptomatic for a single trait or attribute. Other inventories are omnibus affairs with many items, some of which may be scored for more than one trait.

Psychologists do not assume that a self-report of a given action is a valid indicator that a person has carried out or will carry out the action defined. Often the person sees only a distorted picture of himself, and he exaggerates his favorable attributes. Much caution is therefore required in the use of such inventories.

Projective tests present ambiguous stimuli to which the subject is required to respond. Essentially the stimulus is meaningless, but the person has to try to find some basis for a response. What he finds and reports is therefore a projection of his own personality.

Inventories have fairly high reliabilities but only modest validities for most purposes. Projectives have only fair reliabilities and, partly as a result of this fact, their validities are still rather controversial. In some clinical situations they seem quite useful. Both inventories and projectives are widely

[7] We do not suggest that these tests must be so constructed as to be usable by laymen. The chemist, the physicist, and the biologist all use observational techniques which require training. The goal is to devise techniques which will minimize perceptual deviations among trained personnel.

used in work with personality problems, and to some extent in employment, in school guidance work, and in other similar situations.

SUGGESTIONS FOR READING

The best volumes on the problems discussed in this chapter are probably Allen's *Personality assessment procedures* and Ferguson's *Personality measurement*. On projectives good commentaries will be found in Anderson and Anderson, *Introduction to projective techniques*, and Abt and Bellak, *Projective psychology*. Articles in these two references provide bibliographies on specific tests such as Rorschach and TAT.

DEVELOPMENT

The individual is born with certain potentialities for personality. He has a perceptual system, a response system, and an organizing system. Infants at birth show few of the characteristics we have indicated in the preceding chapters as attributes of personality. There is a long process of development ahead for each child.

Every adult personality is unique, but in some respects all human beings are alike. This paradox need not concern us seriously. The universal aspects of human nature are chiefly our inherited features, those we share with other members of the animal kingdom. The distinctively human personality is a more complex and later development.

It is this process of development which we must now examine. We shall give some slight attention to the hereditary fundamentals, and then take up the processes of learning and maturation, conflict resolution, and socialization. By these processes each individual acquires his characteristic patterns of belief and response. The prima donna and the clown, the worrier and the optimist, the grouch and the philosopher have similar beginnings but develop along different paths to reach their ultimate destinations. Let us see what fundamental processes are involved in these developmental sequences.

CHAPTER 4

Basic Principles

The methods for investigating differences in personality, which have been described in the preceding chapters, serve to give concrete form to the definitions of personality we have mentioned. A consideration of these methods can also point to some of the problems which must be faced as we deal with the development of personality. All babies are cute; but they diverge rapidly in social stimulus value from that time on. All babies have a certain limited repertoire of responses, which are very similar from one child to another; but at maturity they differ greatly. We cannot speak with authority of the inner organization of the infant personality, but it probably is subject to the same rule. Our problem, then, is to spell out the processes which govern personality development from infancy to maturity.

We cannot study directly the development of social stimulus value, since that depends upon the qualities of the observer as well as of the person observed. We can examine the growth of response systems, particularly gestures and facial expressions, which are revelatory of inner patterns. Our greatest interest, though, will be in the development of perceptual patterns. We want to know how some people become optimists and others pessimists, some shy and others friendly, some dominant and others submissive. For the most part, the answers will be found in the way in which a given individual perceives himself and his environment.

The account offered will mention some observations which have been stressed by the psychoanalysts, others cited by the behaviorists, by gestalt psychologists, and so on. No effort will be wasted on a debate as to which of these theories is "the right theory." Theories are useful in various ways, and a theory which is best for one purpose or in one context might not be so valuable in another. The following pages will therefore try to lay out a framework for the student, a way of thinking about how personality develops, without seeking tight logical consistency or final answers.

HOMEOSTASIS AS A UNIFYING CONCEPT

In looking for this framework we should begin with the principles of general psychology. The laws of behavior and experience which hold for human beings in general must also be valid for the unique individual. Therefore, an analysis of personality development must be firmly grounded on broad general principles. Further, there is an advantage, in terms of finding similarities among diverse phenomena, in stressing generalizations of wide applicability.

The principle of homeostasis has much to commend it in this respect. As we have noted (page 19), it holds for many varieties of human behavior. It is cited by psychoanalysts, behaviorists, and phenomenologists as being compatible with their theories of personality.[1] And it provides a link between the very simple and the most complex levels of individuality. For this reason it will be used as a kind of continuing thread in this discussion, in an effort to point out underlying similarities in what may seem, superficially, to be quite different happenings.

Homeostasis, we have observed, is a principle which relates to the maintenance and restoration of favorable steady states under a variety of conditions. In Chapter 1 we sketched the notion that an external stimulus, such as a drop in temperature, can disturb an inner equilibrium. Energy is then mobilized by the organism to restore the condition which is favorable to life. Such effort may first take the form of reflex, automatic changes such as blood-vessel constriction, increased heat production, shivering, and so on. If these are unsuccessful, holistic (total organism) activities, such as putting on heavy clothing, firing the furnace, etc., will be tried.

In that connection it was also suggested that man comes to value other than purely physiological states. So he may come to protect his toys and scream for their return; or he may be upset by the lack of a "hot rod" (and constitute a threat to the equilibrium of the parents until he obtains one); he may place a high value on a gang, protect it, fight when the gang is threatened, and so on. These examples are cited to foretell some of the extensions of the concept of homeostasis which will be offered and to explain the trend of some analyses of perception and learning.

PERCEPTION: THE KEY PROCESS

The principle of homeostasis is primarily a dynamic concept, that is, it offers a way of thinking about how the child gets pushed along, how energy is mobilized, how effort becomes channeled into learning and development. A second key concept is that of perception. This is the process which gets structured, organized, and modified as the individual matures. Our stress on perception is based on the view that *perception determines response.* Thus, the young man who avoids women whenever possible, and is rude or aggressive toward them when he cannot escape, is revealing the fact that he per-

[1] See, for example, Freeman (1948), Menninger (1954), Allport (1955), and Snygg and Combs (1949). Critical comments on the homeostatic approach will be found in Weber (1949) and Toch and Hastorf (1955).

ceives women as threatening. The significant learning was learning to see women in this fashion, not learning to make certain movements. Emphasis in the following pages will consequently be on how the child comes to perceive himself, his parents, other adults, and the roles acted out by different people. From this analysis it is possible to derive a picture of how personality takes on its particular attributes.

Homeostasis and Perceiving. How do these two key concepts relate to each other? As might be expected, there is a complex interaction. When an inner equilibrium is disturbed (e.g., when the child becomes hungry), perception functions as an essential tool for the restoration of favorable conditions. This is no less true for the infant than for older children; in the infant, of course, very little learning is necessary to perceive the touch of the nipple against lips or cheek as a cue for sucking. In later years the individual must locate a suitable goal object and devise ways of obtaining it before he can relax and be comfortable again. Furthermore, perception determines what goal objects are acceptable. To most Americans, grilled earthworms or dragonflies fried in palm oil would not be perceived as goal objects unless hunger was truly extreme, and even then they would not look attractive, whereas to people of some other cultures they appear quite desirable. An important aspect of personality derives from the fact that individuals come to perceive different goals as attractive—in members of the opposite sex, in social activities, in vocational choice, and in other aspects of life.

Perception also plays an essential role in upsetting some equilibria. If I should happen to see a lion approaching, I would experience marked disturbance and tension. Considerable energy would be expended to remove me from the vicinity of this threatening stimulus. I would not be particularly upset by a yapping cocker spaniel; some individuals, however, respond with real terror to such an animal. Hence another source of personality difference is found in the percepts which cue off disturbances of equilibrium.

Essentially, this view says that we can treat the process of personality formation as a process of learning to perceive objects, persons, and situations as attractive or threatening. For the quality of being attractive we shall say that the object possesses *positive valence;* objects which are threatening will be described as having *negative valence* (Figure 4.1). It goes without saying that the same physical object may have positive valence for one person, negative for another.

Tension, Satiation, and Valence. The term valence refers primarily to a phenomenal attribute, viz., the attraction or repulsion value of an object, but it also has homeostatic significance. Whenever an equilibrium is disturbed, the organism must search for objects which will restore stability. It appears that, under these conditions, tension increases and relevant valences are also heightened. To take a simple example, a very hungry man may perceive a hamburger as an intensely desirable object, whereas under normal circumstances he would find it neutral or even somewhat negative. Soldiers on duty in remote parts of the world find women looking very beautiful, who, a few months earlier, would not have seemed attractive at all.

It must be noted that the range of stimulus generalization is important here. If the new (formerly unattractive) object is too remote from the normal source of gratification, it may not even be perceived as a possible satisfaction. The starving man may not consider human flesh as even conceivably a source of food, hence it does not tempt him. But within the range of objects perceived as potential satisfiers, valence is markedly affected by tension.

Satiation, meaning the satisfaction of a need and restoration of equilibrium, reduces relevant valences. Little Johnny may find one ice-cream cone very attractive, a second nice, a third mildly interesting, but the fourth or fifth is likely to have little appeal, and he soon reaches a point at which the valence is negative.

There is some evidence, based especially on experiments with animal infants, to suggest that repeated intensification of a valence early in life causes it permanently to be exaggerated in importance; and vice versa, one which has been chronically satiated in infancy never seems as urgent to this individual as to others. So the child who has had little affection in infancy may be very demanding, constantly seeking a show of affection from his wife, his friends, or his boss, in what has the net effect of being an annoying manner. The child who has always had many toys feels relatively little concern about physical possessions. We may put this in terms of expectancy of gratification. If the child feels quite certain that his need will be taken care of, he is only moderately concerned about a disturbance; if, on the other hand, his expectancy is of deprivation and continued discomfort, he may become very anxious and search vigorously for an object which, to others, appears of little significance.

The Phenomenal Field. It will be remembered that personality, for purposes of this volume, has been related to Allport's definition of "the dynamic organization within the individual of those psychophysical systems that determine his unique adjustments to his environment." When we cited this defini-

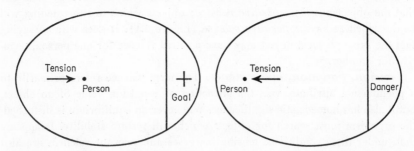

Fig. 4.1 Relation of valence and tension. When a person is faced with a positive valence, he feels tension pressing him toward it; with a negative valence, tension pushing him from it.

tion on page 7, we noted that both perceptual and response systems might be among those included by Allport. Stress has been placed on the perceptual side as being the point at which the adjustment is determined. This point is stated even more vigorously by Snygg and Combs (1949) in their treatment of personality. They say: *"All behavior, without exception, is completely determined by and pertinent to the phenomenal field of the behaving organism"* [p. 15].

Snygg and Combs define the phenomenal field as "the entire universe, including himself, as it is experienced by the individual at the instant of action" [p. 15]. This simply says, as has been indicated above, that a person reacts not to the object of physics, but to the object as he sees it. Children play with live hand grenades (sometimes fatally) because they do not perceive such an object as dangerous. A person who sees tomatoes as poisonous fruit refuses to eat them (naturally) and so never learns of his error. The phenomenal field, then, is composed of various perceived objects, with their positive or negative valences and other attributes.

How does this bear on Allport's definition of personality? It appears that the phenomenal field is determined to some extent by cues from outside (the object of physics) and to some extent by factors within the organism. It is this internal component in which we are interested.

The phenomenal field, however, includes all behavior of the person, whereas Allport limits his definition to the person's *unique* adjustments. We can, therefore, rule out the kinds of actions which are uniform to all mankind: reflexes, walking, talking, digesting, breathing. If, however, a person has a unique gait, or pattern of speech, etc., this can be taken in under the rubric of personality.

Furthermore, personality is *organized*. The phenomenal field is organized at a moment in time, but personality is organized across time. A man tends to retain his individuality over long periods, with very slow change. Our study, then, will be focused on those features of an individual's phenomenal fields which persist, which recur, which are systematically and dynamically organized.

Homeostasis and Dynamics. We have indicated that needs to protect and restore favorable constancies affect perception. Objects which promise need satisfaction acquire positive valence. Objects which threaten disruption of comfort have negative valence. Further, it should be noted that certain important positive valences come to be perceived as valuable steady states in themselves, and hence, to be protected whenever they are threatened. Thus the mother, originally valued only as a means to physiological equilibrium, later becomes an object to be defended against threats even at the cost of physical comfort.

Personality, then, can be considered as a set of organized ways of perceiving the environment, including the self, which determine the individual's unique ways of adjusting to the environment.[2] These will include such items as: the objects perceived as having positive or negative valence, the particular steady states which he perceives as most important, and the courses of action which he perceives as most likely to protect equilibrium or restore it. On the response side we shall be especially interested in the person's unique ways of dealing with certain valences or of executing certain kinds of adjustments.

PRINCIPLES OF PERCEIVING

This book cannot deal extensively with major issues in the psychology of perception. Our concern is solely with the process of perceiving as it becomes identical with, or a major component of, the process of personality development; just as we are concerned with percepts in so far as they help us to understand a given personality.

Naïvely, one might hold that we see things in a certain way because they are that way. The untruth of this view is readily established by such simple items as the Müller-Lyer illusion (Figure 4.2) and the numer-

Fig. 4.2 Müller-Lyer illusion. The two horizontal lines are really of equal length, but appear unequal because of the context (arrowheads).

ous others of its kind; it is well known that we must regularly distinguish between "what a thing looks like" and "what it really is." Actually, perceiving always involves an interaction between external cues and the organism; a red apple does not look that way to a color-blind man.

We shall take a somewhat simplified stand in answer to the question, "What is the *real* object?" Is the apple really red? If a number of normal observers agree that it is, we shall use this as a standard and examine the perceptual deviations of our subject from it. (There are other standards, such as the laws of physics; but since these always reduce to observations by independent observers, we may as well simply define "reality" as the agreement of the apparently normal majority of the group.) Reality, then, depends on *consensual validation;* in our approach to personality, we shall be interested particularly in the circumstances in which the reported object is *not* perceived by the majority.

Consider for a moment the Müller-Lyer illusion shown in Figure 4.2. Why do the two lines look unequal? The immediate answer is: because of the context. The additional lines in the one case seem to extend, in the other case to limit, the central lines. The percept is modified by the context.

This context need not be consciously perceived. It is possible in a tachistoscope, by showing the central lines continuously, but flashing the additional

---

[2] A closely similar statement about personality as a pattern of unique ways of viewing the world will be found in Kelly (1955, vol. 1). This is not to imply that the present formulation duplicates that of Kelly, or that we are in agreement with all of his deductions; the premises, however, are closely parallel.

lines at intervals too brief for conscious recognition, to make one line look longer than the other without any apparent context.[3] Further, the context can be provided by memory; in observing any object, one may unconsciously be affected by past contacts with it, and these modify the present percept. Experience and training can also change the effect of a present context; people can learn to perceive the Müller-Lyer illusion differently and judge accurately the real length of the central lines.

We shall be particularly concerned with variations in perceiving which are related to experience, because they especially illuminate the study of personality. The development of personality will be represented here as a process of developing distinctive ways of perceiving and dealing with objects.

Some Basic Principles. As a setting for the discussion to follow, here is a summary of certain key principles relevant to the process of perceiving:

1. The organism is constantly being bombarded with stimuli. Some of these "get through" to the central nervous system; others are blocked out. We may say that the individual becomes conscious of some, not of others. This state of affairs is unavoidable; one would be paralyzed and overwhelmed by a "blooming, buzzing confusion" if he were really made aware of all the cues potentially influencing his sense organs at a typical moment. Peception thus depends on a process of *sampling* the environment. We see some of the visible objects, hear some of the sounds, are aware of some of the inner bodily processes of which we might be conscious.

2. Samples which occur together tend to become associated. The round, red shape of an apple gets associated with its taste. Mother's soothing voice gets tied in with feelings of visceral comfort, cutaneous pleasure, and so on. These experiences tend spontaneously to become organized into wholes, or configurations. The gestalt psychologists (e.g., Köhler, 1948) place a great deal of emphasis on heredity as regards the patterning of these percepts. Hebb (1949) offers an explanation in terms of learning. Since these features of perceiving with which we are concerned depend on experience, we emphasize the learning approach here.

3. The recurrence of a sample (one cue, or a set of cues) tends to evoke the complete organized percept to which it is appropriate. Mother's voice evokes an image of her face, memories of comforting experiences, etc. The crying infant is quieted by hearing the mother's voice even before she has done anything to restore it to a comfortable status. The important point to be recognized here is that *every percept is determined in part by the perceiving organism.* Something is "added to" the immediately present stimulation. This something derives from the person's past contact with this or similar cues. When, in the process of sampling the environment, one receives information indicating

[3] There is a technical controversy as to whether the context (the arrowheads) presented in these experiments was really below the visual threshold. All observers seem to agree, however, that the subjects could not report having seen the additional lines; hence, we can assert that one's behavior may be affected by cues of which he is not aware.

that a certain object is "out there," the total percept of that object tends to be reinstated. Thus, to a person who has been painfully bitten by a dog, a mere bark (without visual cue) may set off the whole pattern of pain, fright, and running away.

4. The organism scans the inputs from the various sensory modalities, but individuals differ in their reliance upon specific kinds of sensory cues. Some seem to make much greater use of interoceptive stimulation, while others are focused on what is coming from outside the body. An "inward-oriented" individual will have a phenomenal field more profoundly modified by the feedback from visceral responses; he is less interested in the auditory qualities of the dog's bark than in his inner experience of upset.

Perception and "Reality." It should be noted that, to the person involved, the bark is really a signal of danger. And the dog (even if others know him to be playful and harmless) is a menace. *To each individual his own percepts are real.*

From principles 1, 2, and 4 above, it would appear inevitable that each individual lives in a "real world" which is somewhat different from that of anyone else. Each of us receives a somewhat different sample of physical stimuli. Further, we will build up different patterns, based on the chance probabilities that certain cues will occur together in one person's experience and not in others. Thus it is literally true that each person lives in his own private world; I can never know exactly how things appear to you, but it is easy to prove that in some respects things appear differently.

This does not lead to the conclusion that our percepts are in complete disagreement. Obviously we can usually agree on the properties of a chair, a table, or a bar of iron. The patterns of cues emitted are highly stable, and the probable consequences of dealing with them are quite uniform from one person to another. There are, however, occasional personalities who see even physical objects in quite a unique manner. A young woman who reported that she could see cute little babies cuddling in the branches of a tree outside her bedroom window, like the man who claimed that he was being pursued by millions of little red caterpillars, was clearly psychotic. Such perceptual distortions indicate a truly abnormal personality.

The ease with which normal persons reach agreement on the perceived attributes of physical objects vanishes when we turn to social perception. Human beings do not emit cues which are neat and uniform, in the manner of sticks and stones; on the contrary, they vary from time to time in a most vexing fashion. Father is sometimes indulgent, sometimes punishing. He may help you or block you. He may be a source of pleasure or of painful stimulation. Thus, the image of "father" developed by a given child will depend on what samples of father's behavior he encounters, and particularly on what combinations of samples he gets. Two brothers not infrequently have diametrically different pictures of their father. Again we note two points: (1) the "real" father for each boy is the one he perceives (regardless of what others agree [4] about the father); and (2) such differences in perception are deeply embedded components of the personalities of the sons.

The Concept of Schema. We must now go one step beyond the development of a percept. The position so far has been that, if the child encounters a specific object, he builds up a percept of that object which is a function of the present physical cues and the past cues represented in the form of memory traces. We must now consider the situation when the child encounters an object of the same class but differing in some respects: e.g., a small dog versus a large one, an overstuffed chair versus a wooden chair, and so on. As the child learns that these objects are, by adult criteria, "the same" (in a limited sense which we do not communicate very clearly to children), he must cancel out some components of the earlier percept so that it does not conflict with the new one. This process of combining two or more percepts to form a skeletonized "class percept" or concept we shall call "schematizing," and the outcome is a *schema*. (This term avoids an argument as to whether the new formation is properly a percept or a concept. It is of perceptual origin, but is one step removed from direct experience.)

The schema is important for several reasons. First, we note that a great deal of behavior is guided simply by the class category of the stimulus object; if all dogs are seen as dangerous, classifying a new animal as a dog determines the person's behavior. The same holds if a person is hostile to all authority figures, and so on. Second, it appears that one may respond to certain attributes of a schema before becoming consciously aware of the specific percept. For example, evidence indicates that observers can correctly categorize words as pleasant or unpleasant, at exposure speeds so fast the word cannot be named. Third, one's behavior toward a particular person may depend on the class category in which he has been placed, without the observer being conscious of the fact that he has so classified this individual. In other words, schemata are capable of setting off actions (discriminatory, affectionate, submissive, etc.) even when the behaving person does not know what feature of the stimulus person is affecting him. The schema, in these instances, produces its effect by modifying the phenomenal quality of the percept specifically in view at the moment; i.e., I may observe a woman, and on the basis of certain cues classify her as overaggressive and masculine; I may then behave as if she actually has these attributes, in the absence of valid evidence. In my phenomenal field, she *has* these attributes because of the way I have categorized her.

[4] We have introduced the concept of "consensual validation," or agreement by a majority, as a criterion of "what is real." This serves certain useful purposes, e.g., in connection with ratings of a person or judgments of a situation. But the individual's behavior is governed by his phenomenal reality, i.e., reality as he sees it. He may sometimes yield to pressure from a majority and modify his percept accordingly; see Chap. 7 for experiments on this phenomenon.

Schemata, therefore, are the "implicit personality theories" (see page 9) which guide much of our daily behavior. It would literally be impossible to function without them; we could not possibly explore every new object, every new person, to catalogue all relevant attributes. Schema formation is a short cut which is indispensable for efficiency; but it is also a source of perceptual distortion.

The Concept of Adaptation Level. If you place your left hand in hot water, and your right in cold, and then immerse both in the same pan of lukewarm water, the left hand reports that the water is cool, while the right reports warmth. This, in an oversimplified way, defines what is meant by adaptation level. Every sensory input is estimated as to intensity, duration, and other variables in terms of a comparison with past experience with this class of objects.

Thus, we judge a man to be tall if he appears taller than the average of our acquaintances; learned, if he seems to have exceptional knowledge; talkative, if he emits more words than other men known to us.

This means that all the estimates of personality considered in Chapter 2 must be understood as judgments relative to the experience of the observer. If his adaptation level has been affected by contact with very energetic individuals, he may attribute "laziness" to someone who in fact is average on energy level. A Malayan youth in an American university pointed up the problem when he was asked to describe himself as short or tall. "In my country," he commented, "I am tall, but here I am short." Differences between nations and cultural groups have profound effects on judgments of personality for the same reason.

Adaptation level thus provides a key to understanding differences between judges (cf. problems of reliability, Chapters 2 and 3). It also helps us to appreciate some of the differences between people in responding to inventories and projective tests. An item asks: "Have you worried a great deal about sex?" One person, who has friends who worry more than he does, answers "no"; another, whose friends never indicate any such worries, may answer "yes." Yet a time sample might show them to worry the same amount.

Each class of objects or persons has to be judged against a suitable standard. A "large" wire-haired terrier would be a "small" Airedale. Behavior which is noisy and out of place in church would not be noticed in a beer parlor. Thus the concepts of schema and adaptation level go hand in hand. As schemata are developed to cover the various objects, persons, roles, and social situations the child encounters, he also begins building up a base line for judgments in terms of adaptation level.

Frame of Reference. Even a specific physical cue is subject to modification in terms of a context brought to it by the perceiver. Whether a given weight is judged "heavy" or "light" depends on the recently experienced weights with which comparison is automatically made. Helson (1947) has shown that the frame of reference within which we view a stimulus depends on the established adaptation level. A little patch of green in early spring "looks different" as compared with early summer.

These effects are even more pronounced as regards perception of persons. A person who feels rather conservative in Greenwich Village may find himself pretty radical when he gets in with a group of Vermont Republicans. Many Englishmen find Americans somewhat noisy because of the contrast with the behavior they normally encounter in their home country. Our perceptions of ourselves and of others are profoundly affected by our frames of reference; thus we shall find it important to consider how frames of reference get organized and applied in given classes of situations.

Adaptation level is determined by the frequency, intensity and range of previous stimulation by objects of a certain kind. That is, if we have frequently encountered persons who gesture a great deal, our frame of reference will be modified in that direction, and a person of restrained movement will look "frozen" or constricted. Experience with a wide range of values broadens the frame of reference; the study of cultural anthropology helps us to see our own culture as only a narrow selection from the possible range of human behavior. Parents advocate that young people date a variety of persons of the opposite sex before marriage, so that evaluation of attractive and unattractive individuals is not distorted by a narrow range of observation.

The Role of "Feedback." When an equilibrium is disturbed, either by changes inside the organism or by external stimulation, certain responses occur. In hunger, for example, there are changes in stomach contractions, tensing of striped muscles, and probably numerous other effector activities.

Every response provides a pattern of stimulation to the central nervous system. Thus, the sampling of cues from the external environment is immediately followed, or at least has a substantial probability of being followed, by sensory inputs from the muscles and viscera (cf. Mandler, Mandler, and Uviller, 1958). The tightening of the stomach in the case of fear and the pounding of the heart in anger become integral portions of the percept. When, on a later occasion, the individual encounters the object which has set off this emotional state, he experiences the inner upset as well as awareness of the object itself. The "phenomenal field," in short, is modified by afferent impulses deriving from responses.[5]

The term "feedback" can of course be extended beyond this immediate application to sensory consequences within the body. When we respond to a person, the person typically responds in turn. That is, there is some feedback in terms of how he perceives our action. Much important social learning depends on this mechanism. The child learns the meaning of "tact"—the neces-

---

[5] Positive feedback occurs when the feedback intensifies the response; e.g., a child is taught, "You should be ashamed of being afraid." So, when he is frightened, these visceral cues set off fear of scolding or ridicule; thus his original fear is exaggerated. Negative feedback occurs when the feedback weakens the response.

sity of avoiding certain topics of conversation, the dangers of being too frank
—as he comes to identify the responses he gets from them. Some individuals
seem relatively incapable of such learning; they go through life insensitive
to the impact of their behavior on their friends and associates.

In connection with the problem of judging other people's personalities we
noted the importance of perceptual sensitivity. This is not merely a matter of
noting the occurrence of facial expressions, vocal changes, and gestures; it
involves also an awareness of what is behind these responses, what they are
signaling of the internal process. It is only as we come to sense anger, fear,
affection, jealousy, and similar states that we can judge others with reasonable accuracy.

Whenever a homeostatic disturbance occurs, responses follow and feedback
in turn affects the phenomenal field. It seems likely, therefore, that differences
in the frequency and intensity of such disturbances will affect the individual's
perception of his world and thus will modify his personality.

Internal and External Stimulation. This view of the development of
percepts calls attention to the fact that almost any experience is likely to have
both exteroceptive and interoceptive components. The percept of an apple
integrates aspects which are visual and olfactory with others, such as taste,
texture, and crunchiness (kinesthetic), which derive from within the body.
Similarly, our awareness of another person is not limited to the visual and
auditory cues received from him; it incorporates also visceral feedback from
prior emotional experiences, and perhaps kinesthetic feedback from remembered activities shared with this individual.

We have noted earlier (page 76) that *scanning* is a feature of the organism's information-getting procedures. Not all sensory modalities are represented in awareness all the time. There seems, however, to be some kind of
process by which samples are taken from the various sensory channels more
or less in rotation. When we say we are "paying attention" to a particular
input, we are sampling more from that channel, less from others.

It follows from this that one source of personality differences will be
found in relative tendency to rely on exteroceptive and interoceptive input.

Fig. 4.3 Figures used
in the study of perceptual
organization. Some chil-
dren were rewarded when
Clem was seen, others
when Jake appeared. When
the test figure was pre-
sented, each group re-
ported seeing only the rewarded figure. (From Sol-
ley and Sommer, 1957, Fig.
1, p. 5, by permission of
the Journal Press, publishers.)

Clem   Jake   Test

Observant judges of people have for a long time noted that some of us respond quickly to changes in the outer world, while others seem to be wrapped up rather completely in happenings inside the skin. There is some evidence (cf. Bieri and Blacker, 1956) that the "introversion-extraversion" dimension of personality differences is tied to this difference in scanning of external stimuli and internal stimuli. This point will be elaborated later (Chapters 9 and 12).

Figure-Ground Organization. All perception apparently tends spontaneously to be organized in the phenomenal field, of which the parts are figure and ground. The figure is relatively clear, more detailed, brighter; the ground is vague, rather undifferentiated, almost unconscious. Ground includes the influences earlier referred to as context; it is well known that changes in the ground can modify the figure, and indeed that the figure may shift, as another portion of the field becomes clearer.

Learning can modify the figure-ground relationship, too. Solley and Sommer (1957) made use of an ambiguous figure (Figure 4.3), which can be divided along the wavy line into two "faces." In the study children were shown one or the other "face," labeled respectively "Clem" or "Jake." For some subjects Clem was always associated with the receipt of money; for others, Jake was the reward symbol. After learning trials, the children were shown the ambiguous figure (full circle). The rewarded figure was reported to be brighter, nearer, and of more sharply defined contour. In work with older subjects, Solley and Long (1960) asked that stories be made up about Clem and Jake, in the fashion of the TAT. These can be illustrated by the following from a girl who lost money when Clem appeared, but lost nothing when Jake was shown: "Clem looks like a sourpuss. He doesn't smile very often and he doesn't have many friends. He has a sour disposition and all he needs is a smile." About Jake: "This could be a happy-go-lucky fellow. Most people like him. He looks like he likes to whistle." [6]

Such observations, along with those of the children, provide strong evidence that the figure-ground organization is modified by reward and punishment, or by association with pleasant and unpleasant stimuli. The effects seem clearly to be on the perceptual side, not on responses. Clarity of boundary, relative brightness, and other attributes are affected. In addition, such direct attributions of personality characteristics as are illustrated in the preceding paragraph can be produced. The importance of such phenomena in understanding how it happens that we perceive strangers as likable or hostile, or how we distort the expressions of friends and acquaintances, hardly needs emphasizing.

Focusing. Concentration upon the figure in a field is fostered by increased tension, if this figure is associated with tension reduction. A man with a strong

[6] This study would suggest that the TAT may have higher validity than was indicated in Chap. 3. It will become apparent in later chapters that TAT and Rorschach data, in combination with other sources of evidence, are often valuable. Our position simply is that projective tests should be viewed with caution, not that they should be rejected.

sex drive may focus his attention so completely upon an attractive woman that he is literally unconscious of many important aspects of his environment.[7] In later chapters we shall have a great deal to say about learning to emphasize certain objects and ignore others. Let us note here only that this principle is important in relation to Rorschach and TAT responses. A certain area of a Rorschach ink blot may cue off a percept which is so important to the individual that he talks only about it and ignores many other possibilities. A certain kind of person or object in a TAT picture often determines the response to the entire picture, apparently blocking out any awareness of other details which might have cued off a different story.

Perceptual Constancies. Particularly interesting to us, for many reasons, are the perceptual constancies. It is a familiar fact of everyday life that a person walking toward you does not seem to be growing larger, although the retinal image is rapidly increasing in size. We speak of "size constancy" to refer to this fact. Familiar objects tend to maintain the same apparent size despite marked changes in the retinal image. (This particular constancy is difficult to demonstrate with sensory modalities other than vision.)

Shape constancy is another example. If you look at a coin from an angle, it continues to look circular, although the retinal image is now an ellipse. A rectangle such as a door or window, seen from one side, gives a retinal image of a trapezoid, but continues to look rectangular. This phenomenon holds also for color (under illumination of changing wave length) and for brightness. The organism tends to maintain perceptual properties of the figure constant, despite changes in the ground.

This is ascribed to the relative importance of the "memory" component of perception as opposed to the immediate sensory component. If we perceived objects solely in terms of immediately present cues, a man standing 100 yards away would be seen as an infant or a doll. However, his mode of dress, proportions, etc., identify him as a man, and associated experiences take over to determine the apparent size of his body. Size constancy is also supported by the characteristics of the ground; a 6-foot actor can be made to look like a child by putting him in children's clothing and then surrounding him with furniture built on a gigantic scale.

Ambiguity and Threat. We survive by responding to real size, not to apparent size. Constancies, even though superficially distortions of perception, have survival value. An automobile at a distance of 200 yards has the retinal image size of a toy; but it behooves us to behave as if it were full

---

[7] We shall not concern ourselves with the neurological basis of these phenomena. In most cases what is known about the functioning of the nervous system fits with the observations of behavior and perception cited. For example, with respect to the "focusing" phenomenon, it has been demonstrated (Hernandez-Péon et al., 1955) that when an animal is highly attentive to one stimulus (a cat sniffing at a mouse) other sensory impulses are blocked before they get to the cortex. Thus the nervous system is organized to focus on one major stimulus at a time.

sized. A tiger seen under unusual illumination seems to have changed his color; but it is adaptive to assume that he has not changed in any significant respects.

The development of a stable, predictable environment thus becomes the first order of business for the infant beginning to have working contacts with the world. Ambiguous situations are potentially dangerous. Children have a great deal of curiosity, and establish expectancies about objects, animals, and persons very quickly. The baby may object bitterly to the loss of a familiar toy, and not infrequently he responds with distress to presentation of a new one which does not resemble any prior possession.

Children differ with respect to the degree of upset or unease shown in ambiguous situations. It will appear in later discussions that this aspect of personality has extensive ramifications into complex phases of behavior.

Constancy of Persons. The phenomenon of constancy in the perception of persons is particularly important. A girl may experience her mother as very strict and unsympathetic. Perhaps the mother really had been this way, but over the years she has become more relaxed and understanding. The daughter, unfortunately, continues to perceive the mother as having the attributes which belong to her earliest perceptions rather than noticing the modification.[8]

Closure and Constancy. An important determinant of constancy is the tendency toward *closure*. This simply means that if one receives cues which are adequate to define part of a familiar percept, the remainder tends to be supplied by memory, and the individual perceives the total. Experimentally we study this by showing that the person often adds parts to an incomplete figure (cf. Moffitt and Stagner, 1955). Thus the daughter, in the example above, sees the mother as physically the same person and "adds in" the familiar behavior pattern even though it has been substantially modified. Closure, then, tends to interfere with awareness of changing reality. Furthermore, as Dailey (1952) has shown, closure may prevent us from being receptive to new cues about a person. Jumping to a premature conclusion, we feel that we know this individual, and so block out new information which might show that he is quite different.

EQUILIBRIUM AND CONSTANCY

We suggested earlier that objects of perception, means to restoration of valued steady states, become values in themselves and are protected in a similar manner. A way of representing this process is shown in Figure 4.4. It is proposed that physical objects (food, clothing, house, and similar property)

[8] For reasons such as this, Korzybski (1933) advocated that we should learn to think of persons with an index number attached. In the example cited, mother$_{1910}$ might be quite different from mother$_{1925}$, but because of the operation of the constancy principle, the daughter fails to perceive the difference.

are first perceived as useful in protecting and restoring physical comfort. Later, the person comes to perceive these as equilibria to be defended, and he may fight, risk physical pain, to maintain his property. The property, according to this view, has the function of an envelope protecting the physiological equilibria; but now a threat to the environmental constancy is responded to by mobilization of energy and vigorous action. This reaches its most clear-cut form in the case of people who react violently to proposals for tearing down old landmarks, modifying traditional institutions such as the San Francisco cable cars, or chopping down an old, familiar tree.

The next outer circle in the diagram represents the establishment of a constant social environment. Mother is valued first for her contribution to physical comfort; later the presence of mother is desirable in itself, and if she goes away, great disturbance occurs. Similarly, people become positively oriented to a home town, to a peer-group gang, to an employer, or to a labor union. In each case the original valence was the food, comfort, physical security, or economic protection provided. With time and repetition, however, these social groups become valued in themselves and they too will be protected with surprising energy. Here again we point to the operation of constancy both in the sense of seeing things as they may have been years ago, when perhaps they were of greater value, and secondly, in the sense of an active demand by the individual that these remain constant, that they be *not disturbed* (by legislation or other external threat).

The outermost circle in the diagram represents an "envelope" of ideologies which the individual may later develop and strive to maintain. Religious beliefs, faith in certain economic institutions, or political values may fall in this category. Not all persons show this phenomenon. Perhaps it is a question of whether ideological matters have ever been clearly enough perceived to become significant features of the environment. Certainly for some people

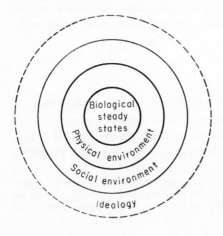

Fig. 4.4 Valued steady states. In infancy the only constancies protected are biological. Later the person develops successive "envelopes" which protect the organism's integrity, and these too become valued and defended.

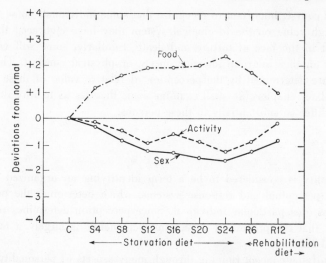

Fig. 4.5 Hierarchy of need states. When a basic biological steady state is threatened (as in long-continued hunger), other goals, such as sex and freedom of activity, are seen as less important. The data are self-ratings on strength of various desires. (From Keys, et al., 1950, by permission of University of Minnesota Press.)

the defense of capitalism, or Catholicism, or communism, may become an overriding value.

Generally these envelopes peel off, under stress, in the reverse order of formation. To avoid torture or persecution, people first make compromises in their religious or political beliefs; the number of persons who resisted the Nazis in the 1933–1939 period on purely ideological issues was quite small. In this country many individuals abandoned liberal ideas in the heyday of "McCarthyism" to avoid the threatened discomforts. Next, people abandon their friends, social groups, even their families, to avoid hardships and punishment. Some men will rush into a fire to save their children, it is true; but it is also true that a great many abandon their children and wives to get away from relatively lesser discomforts. Finally, the individual gives up even his wealth under threat of injury or death. When the chips are down, the biological constancies are usually the ones protected to the last.

The predominance of basic biological equilibria over other steady states valued by the individual can be illustrated by a World War II study of semi-starvation. Twenty young men (conscientious objectors) volunteered for an experiment on the effects of prolonged malnutrition. As Figure 4.5 shows, the hunger drive soon began to dominate their thoughts and dreams; sex and other desired goals seemed far less important to them. Most observers of wartime behavior agree that the majority of human beings will abandon ideals, friends, and property simply to stay alive.

It is, of course, important to recognize that some individuals come to place such a high value on the ideological system they have embraced that they cling to it in the face of torture and death. Similarly, some will value the family or another in-group above property or physical comfort. These differences are determined by the perception of relative value of these various goals. In later chapters we shall examine some theories as to why these perceptions differ so substantially in these persons.

SUMMARY

Personality is considered to be a term identifying an organized process, including perceptual and response systems, which determines the perceived uniqueness of a particular individual. Since perception determines response, it is held that the process of developing personality is largely a matter of perceptual learning.

As a unifying concept running through many aspects of personality formation, the principle of homeostasis is given special emphasis. Homeostasis affects perception in that the individual comes to identify certain cues as signals of objects which restore a valued equilibrium (positive valence), and others as signals of impending disturbance of equilibrium (negative valence).

Partly as a result of the phenomenon of perceptual constancy, the individual comes to protect and defend positively valent objects in somewhat the same fashion as he protects and defends his biological steady states which are essential to life. Thus he learns to value and defend property and physical possessions, family and social groups of which he is a member, and finally, ideologies to which he feels loyal.

The study of personality then becomes a study of the particular steady states which are valued by a given person, the objects he cherishes as means to these favorable conditions, and the pathways of action he perceives as appropriate to the defense and restoration of his valued equilibria. Likewise, the analysis of personality development becomes the process of ascertaining how these unique systems get organized. This will be the topic of the immediately following chapters.

SUGGESTIONS FOR READING

Much of the material presented in this chapter will not be found in current books on personality. Hans Selye's *The stress of life* describes his work related to the concept of homeostasis, and may illuminate some of the ideas offered here. The importance of perception as an approach to the conceptualization of personality is ably set forth in various chapters of the volume edited by Blake and Ramsey: *Perception: an approach to personality.* Bellak's "Psychoanalytic theory of personality" in the volume edited by McCary, *Psychology of personality,* also gives some interesting applications of perception to personality.

CHAPTER 5

Emotional Foundations

We have started with the general principle that personality is a genetic phenomenon, that it is a continuous developmental process and can be understood only in the light of its history. We have also outlined a theoretical framework within which this development is conceived as taking place. It is now appropriate to consider the developmental process itself.

In this and the succeeding chapters, a picture will be presented of the evolving personality. This picture is highly schematic and is intended to cover general principles only. These are derived from diverse case studies and statistical analyses; they present that which is common to all growing personalities. The principles, however, are believed to be adequate to the explanation of deviations and of abnormal personalities, as well as of the normal trend. In Section 4 of this volume data will be presented regarding the impact of variations in environment upon the person. At present, only the typical situation will be examined.

Has the Infant a Personality? We have defined personality as the individual's inner pattern of emotions, ideas, beliefs, and expectancies regarding himself and his environment. Can the newborn infant be said to have a personality in this sense?

The answer seems clearly to be "Yes." The distinction between self and environment probably becomes sharply defined much later—perhaps, on an average, during the third year of life. On purely logical grounds, however, the personality must be intimately related to the physical organism and, thus, may be said to have some sort of existence from conception onward. Because of the painful character of the birth process, the newborn must be assumed to have a generalized expectancy that his environment is going to be unpleasant.[1] This anticipation is, of course, subject to rapid modification. Gesell mentions a newborn infant who cried upon being picked up; a few days later, he cried upon being laid back in his crib.

---

[1] Compare the interesting but somewhat imaginative treatment by Otto Rank, *The trauma of birth*, which seems to trace all adult personality disorders back to this early shock, especially to the separation from the mother.

From birth onward, individual differences in personality begin to be noticeable. Children vary in amount of crying, smiling, and motor activity. They also differ in the kinds of stimuli which set off such activities. They follow the principle of homeostasis, but each is likely to do so in his own unique way. It is now important to trace the beginnings of these differences in personality.

FEELINGS AND HOMEOSTASIS

The infant at birth possesses a biological mechanism, and this responds to disturbance of essential steady states, such as the blood-sugar level, temperature, water content, and other inner constancies, in the ways we have already described. The hungry infant cries, threshes around, flushes, and probably has contractions of the muscles in the stomach. When food is supplied, he relaxes, both as to skeletal and as to visceral muscles.

Homeostatic processes in the older child and the adult are inextricably related to the affective processes we call feelings, and students of infant psychology are in general agreed that we are justified in assuming the inheritance of at least two feelings, pleasantness and unpleasantness. There is some evidence favoring inheritance of two more, excitement and depression.

The process of personality development begins as feelings become associated with objects and with persons. The rich affective life of the adult, with his numerous preferences, enthusiasms, aversions, and prejudices begins at this point. Let us examine some of the evidence more closely.

Pleasantness. Chronologically it may be true that pain is our first sensation and unpleasantness our first feeling, as birth takes place. Perhaps this accounts for the common view that "life is just a vale of tears." Logically, however, there are good grounds for beginning with a consideration of pleasantness.

Observers are agreed that sweet tastes, moderately warm temperatures, gentle stroking of sensitive skin areas, and similar stimulations elicit in the child a kind of behavior that can appropriately be called pleasure. Further, this pattern appears under circumstances of restoration or protection of essential steady states—feeding, restoration of skin comfort, and so on. It seems plausible to assert that pleasantness is the phenomenal sign that homeostatic processes are going smoothly.[2]

The types of stimuli which can evoke pleasant feelings in the infant are strictly limited by these biological requirements. The kind of food which will sustain life during the first days is warm, sweet liquid. The range of body

---

[2] This does not necessitate the assumption that the infant inherits a desire for pleasure. Rather, this view emphasizes the inherent need for stable biological conditions and suggests that pleasant feelings merely serve a signal function for these; later, of course, the craving for pleasure may come into conflict with biogenic needs.

temperatures that can be tolerated is rather small, and so on. With increasing physical maturity, food tolerance increases, and cultural differences in food preferences can be trained in. Tolerance for variations in water intake, temperature, and skin stimulation permits a wider range of environmental conditions. By the age of three, children of different cultures enjoy quite divergent patterns of stimulation. Both physical maturation and learning play a part in this change; but maturation functions chiefly to make variation possible—learning is the process which builds in these personality differences.

Unpleasantness. Homeostatic disturbances in infants are accompanied by crying and vigorous muscular action. Phenomenally, they are undoubtedly accompanied by a feeling of unpleasantness. This may be acute and definitely localized, in which case it is referred to as pain; but in many cases it seems to pertain to no particular organ and can best be called a feeling. It seems better to treat pain and unpleasantness as a single phenomenon; criteria for trying to distinguish between them usually encounter snags, and we obtain some logical advantages by keeping them together.

Cutaneous pain seems invariably to refer to some kind of threat to the integrity of the skin, with potential damage to the organism. Visceral pain is most commonly found with digestive upset. Illness induces a feeling of diffuse malaise and sometimes localized pain. Thus it seems safe to say that unpleasantness is the phenomenal sign of a threat to homeostatic equilibrium.

The kinds of exteroceptive stimulation which evoke unpleasant feeling are distinctly limited for the infant. Loud sounds, hot and cold skin stimulation, pinpricks, and blows are examples. However, it has been clearly demonstrated that many stimuli alleged to be inherently unpleasant lack such properties. Snakes, fire, the dark, and other stimulating conditions which are often said to be universally frightening have no impact on the infant.

Again, we note that both maturation and learning influence the affective development of the child. With maturation the possibility of perceiving certain distinctive stimulus qualities may result in changed behavior. Hebb (1949), for example, has shown that chimpanzees isolated from birth show no fear of snakes in early life, but later they show such fear under circumstances which rule out learning. For the most part, however, it seems that unpleasantness has the sign function for threats of disturbance, just as pleasantness is a signal that homeostasis is operating normally.

Valence and Feelings. We have defined valence as a perceived attribute of an object. If an object is seen as attractive, we say it has positive valence; if it is seen as threatening, it is said to have negative valence. We can now merge these definitions for most purposes, and say that, in the normal course of events, pleasant situations have positive valence, while unpleasant situations have negative valence.[3]

[3] The kind of situation which constitutes an apparent exception will be discussed in Chap. 6. In this case the individual shows behaviorally that he is attracted to an object,

Physiological Basis of Feelings. Important recent developments have given us valuable insights into the neurological structures which are associated with feelings. Olds and Milner (1954) demonstrated the existence of a center in the rat's brain which might well be called a "pleasure center." The experimenters implanted an electrode in this region, in the septal area, and arranged a circuit such that the animal could give himself a weak electrical stimulation by pressing a bar. The rats would, if permitted, keep this up to the point of ignoring hunger and thirst. Recent unpublished work on human beings suggests that there is no question that such stimulation gives rise to feelings of pleasure.

Correspondingly, Delgado, Roberts, and Miller (1954) have reported the existence of an "unpleasantness center." In this case electrodes were implanted in a cat's brain, in a region adjacent to that studied by Olds and Milner. The experimenters found that stimulation of this area elicited behavior similar to fear or anger, but that when it was paired with an external stimulus, the cat learned to avoid this external cue. Phenomenally we would judge that the cat feared the consequences of this stimulus.

Visceral Feedback. In discussing perception (Chapter 4), the point was stressed that every percept, except possibly the very first contact with some kind of stimulation by an infant, is modified by the interoceptive cues associated with prior responses to that object. This point is particularly important in connection with feelings. As suggested in Figure 5.1, we must think of the homeostatic mechanism as a complete circuit; when a threatening stimulus appears, efferent impulses go out to muscles and glands, and as responses occur, afferent impulses pour back into the central nervous system. These, plus the feeling tone of unpleasantness, become incorporated in the percept and will be rearoused whenever this object is encountered in the future.

Although the visceral consequences of pleasant stimuli are less pronounced than those observed with unpleasant events, there are definite muscular, visceral, and circulatory patterns involved. Here again the organized percept of the object incorporates the "warm feeling" of the inner state as well as the conscious pleasure experienced.

Excitement and Depression. Agreement that pleasantness and unpleasantness are inherent and require only an appropriate stimulus to elicit them is virtually universal among psychologists. Whether there are more innate feelings is a matter of considerable controversy. It has been argued (Harlow and Stagner, 1932) that observation of human infants leads also to support for postulating two additional feelings, excitement and depression.

Homeostatically we would relate excitement to the increased bodily activity, tension, and arousal associated with efforts to avoid threat, to restore

---

but he may assert that consciously he feels it to be unpleasant. The crucial difference, then, is that valence refers to a behavioral tendency which is usually but not invariably pleasant.

equilibrium, or to approach a positively valent object. For the most part this increase in bodily activity goes along with unpleasantness; however, in adults excitement and unpleasantness are phenomenally quite different, and as we watch children, we can usually distinguish the two.

Child psychologists report marked differences in the activity level of infants prior to any opportunity for learning. This suggests that excitement, rather than depending on a specific brain region as seems to be true for pleasantness and unpleasantness, may be chiefly an awareness of bodily response. If some babies are so constituted by heredity as to react vigorously and often, the flow back to the brain from these processes may be experienced as excitement and so they tend to experience this feeling more than do other children. Sheldon's work (page 275) on body types would suggest such a theory, and his data seem to give support to an assumption of differences in reactive vigor.

Depression. The evidence for an innate feeling of depression is not so satisfactory as for the three others we have cited. Depression is often not observed in a young infant, although some observers have reported seeing it. It is harder to identify with a particular reaction pattern, since even as adults we have no uniform way of expressing depressed feelings. Further, the kind of stimulus situation which evokes depression varies rather more than for the other feelings. The nearest to a definite behavior pattern seems to be a kind of inhibition of movement (as contrasted with excitement, where all movements tend to become exaggerated); or perhaps better, a lowering of response level.

The reaction of very young children to separation from the mother, and

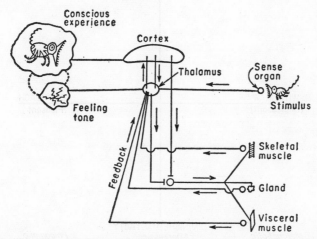

Fig. 5.1 Stimulus, behavior, and feedback in homeostatic process. The stimulus ("frightful object") is shown at the right. Efferent impulses go to muscles and glands, which send afferent (sensory) impulses back to cortex. The percept is modified by the sensory feedback and feeling tone aroused. (Modified from Harlow and Stagner, 1932.)

placement in an institution where a minimum of attention is given the infant, has been treated by Spitz (1945) as a form of depression. Extreme physical apathy, loss of appetite, poor circulatory reaction, and other signs of interference with bodily function are noted. All these are compatible with adult behavior when depressed.

Feelings Basic to Personality. The central place of feelings in the development of personality should be apparent. The frequency with which an individual experiences pleasantness, unpleasantness, excitement, or depression will certainly be a distinctive feature. The intensity of his feelings, the kinds of stimuli that elicit them, and the kinds of responses they set off are also crucial components of his personality. These, then, are the foundations, the simplest and most nearly hereditary elements out of which personality develops.

It is possible to relate these to the traditional "types of temperament." Galen, the earliest observer to describe these types, said that men could be classified into four groups: the sanguine, the phlegmatic, the melancholic, and the choleric. (These types were assumed to be related to the excess or deficiency of certain body fluids, respectively, the blood, the phlegm, the "black bile," and the "yellow bile.") The sanguine individual has a surplus of pleasant feelings and excitement; the phlegmatic person is low on activity, with some excess of depression, but not predominantly an unpleasant tone; the melancholic personality shows surpluses of unpleasantness and depres-

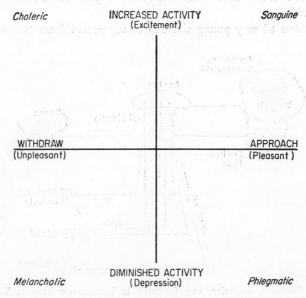

Fig. 5.2 Feeling tone, activity level, and temperament. (Suggested by Diamond, 1957.)

sion; and the choleric individual has a bad temper (unpleasant and excited). The pattern of relationships is diagramed in Figure 5.2.

EMOTIONS

Emotions are more complex than feelings and appear to be products of learning more than of heredity. When we examine an emotion critically, we usually find that it can be analyzed into a feeling or feelings, plus certain expectancies about the object of the emotion. Suppose we examine a few examples from this point of view.

Watson (1924) held that his observations revealed three innate emotions in infants: love, fear, and rage. As stimulus patterns for each he reported the following: for love, stroking of sensitive skin areas; for fear, loud sounds and sudden loss of support; and for rage, interference with freedom of movement. Attempts to repeat Watson's studies (Sherman, 1927) indicated that the disturbed behavior induced by loud sounds, by loss of support, by restraint of movement, by mild pain, and by hunger could not be distinguished by nurses, by mothers, or by psychologists, when they did not know what stimulus had been applied to the baby. This supports the view that excitement rather than a specific emotion (fear, rage) is involved.

Incidentally, the gross visceral changes associated with fear and with anger in adults are very similar. It is only with rather careful measures and with methodical statistical analysis that investigators (cf. Ax, 1953) have been able to demonstrate physiological differences between these two emotions.

It thus seems plausible to hold that fear and anger develop out of excitement and unpleasantness by a process of learning certain expectancies. Fear is the simpler instance; in this case the emotion is no more than an awareness of a stimulus object plus an expectancy that contact with it will result in pain or unpleasant feeling. Watson (1924), for example, tells of his experiment with a baby and a white rat. On first exposure to the rat, the baby reached for the animal with every sign of pleasure. A loud noise was then produced, and the child began to cry. Later the rat and the noise were again presented, and so for three or four repetitions. At the end of this series the baby cried as soon as the rat was shown. We can say, then, that a new expectancy has been established; for the child, there is a high probability that the appearance of the rat will be followed by a very unpleasant feeling. We may now assert that the child fears the rat.

It is also defensible to treat love in the same manner. The infant at birth cannot possibly love his mother; he has no awareness of her existence. After a number of repetitions of the sequence discomfort → mother → comfort, however, he will develop an expectancy that mother means pleasure, restoration of comfort, relaxation, security. When he begins to react to the mother with evidences of pleasure before she has done anything, this expectancy is well established. At this point we can say that some degree of "love" has developed. According to Stewart et al. (1954), this is observable by about the age of six weeks. Prior to this time the child does not distinguish among different adults.[4]

Dependency and Emotional Learning. The foregoing description sounds as though the child were largely a passive creature, something molded by his environment. To a very substantial extent this is exactly true. The crucial fact about the human infant is that he is completely helpless, dependent upon a social environment for survival. His homeostatic mechanisms are utterly inadequate to maintain life. His efforts—in so far as he experiences them in the form of feedback from his responses—are associated with very little change in his inner comfort. The presence of an adult, on the other hand, has a high probability of association with comfort and pleasure.

When we speak of the child's dependency needs, or his need for security, therefore, we do not imply that he has any inborn tendency of this kind. McDougall, Cattell, and others have assumed the existence of some such innate impulse, but the evidence is scanty and the assumption seems unwarranted.

The compulsion to relate to the external world is rather innately determined in a different sense. First of all, the child has receptors, and he must therefore sense his environment. He need not be endowed with an instinct to see; he sees because his eyes are stimulated by cues in the form of visible light. He must hear, touch, taste, and smell because he is so constituted. Secondly, he must relate to his environment in order to survive. The maintenance of essential bodily constancies cannot be achieved without help from adults. Hence he cannot avoid establishing expectancies about adults and their significance for him.

Security. It follows from this that the child must necessarily learn that the cues associated with adults "mean"—i.e., will probably be followed by— pleasure or unpleasantness. If the child is in a normal situation, adults will generally be sources of pleasant stimulation; his needs will be taken care of, painful objects will be removed, food will be supplied. He thus establishes expectancies with respect to these gratifications.

But since the same adult may very well take care of all his needs (or since he may not be able to perceive differences among adults), he also generalizes. He does not learn that this sound means food, a certain odor means relief from pain, or such specific connections. Rather, it seems that he learns a generalized expectancy about life; he feels *secure*, he feels that his needs will be taken care of, that the environment is predominantly pleasant. In

---

[4] The ingenious experiments of Harlow (1958) indicate that feeding alone does not produce the "love" reaction in infant monkeys. Stimulus qualities which human beings would call pleasant also are necessary.

terms of long-run personality trends, we may say that he acquires *optimism.*[5]

By contrast, the baby who gets only meager care, with considerable fretting and scolding, with rough treatment and little caressing, may very well develop an expectancy that life is harsh and cruel, that terrible things are about to happen. In such cases we speak of the child's feelings of insecurity, and we anticipate that in later years he will be decidedly pessimistic.

Looking at either of these examples, we can see the importance of the child's dependency. Each child must necessarily and inevitably learn the importance of adults, the dangers of aloneness, his own helplessness in the face of a terrifying world. The chief difference seems to be that if a child grows up in an atmosphere of security, he is not overwhelmed by this; because he is basically convinced that everything will come out right in the end, he is free to try to do things for himself. The very insecure child, by contrast, is so sure disaster is just around the corner that he dares not do anything which might precipitate it. Thus he has great difficulty in getting away from the dependency relationship, even though for him it is less satisfying than for a secure youngster.

Experimental Studies. We cannot, of course, experiment with children's emotional security in a manner which is likely to prove harmful. But we do have those observations of children placed in institutions, cited by Spitz (1945) as evidence that neglect sets off depression, to indicate that early infantile deprivation in this area retards emotional maturity.

It is permissible to experiment with animals on such phenomena, and although the transfer of knowledge to human subjects is somewhat speculative, the data indicate clearly that isolation from normal contacts is extremely detrimental. Melzack (1954) describes the rearing of nine puppies in isolated cages where they could see no animals (apparently, not even the men who took care of them) to the age of maturity. These puppies, when released and for weeks afterward, showed great diffuse excitement, but seemed incapable of avoiding pain or of acting aggressively when frustrated. Even a year later, the experimental dogs were clearly handicapped, as regards emotional adjustment, when compared to their littermate controls.

Other studies (e.g., Levine, Chevalier, and Korchin, 1956) have shown that hunger, electrical shock, and other traumatic experiences in infancy leave permanent traces in the emotional repertoire of the adult animal. Early expectancies seem to dominate the organism's approach to the world, so that painful experiences during the first period of life determine perceptions out

---

[5] Stewart et al. (1954) studied 18 infants intensively during their first six months. According to Brody (1956), "In the first month of life the crying of all eighteen infants generally persisted until their needs were met. After about 6 weeks, the infants who cried least stopped crying in the presence of the adult who usually satisfied their needs, whereas those in the excessive-crying group stopped crying only after the need itself had been satisfied . . . the authors deduced that infants who are in general less adequately cared for may not develop an expectation of being satisfied . . ." [p. 91].

of all proportion to their number. (Compare this with the notion of imprinting, page 399.) Apparently all early infantile experiences have this effect of slanting the individual toward a certain kind of personality and can be canceled only with the greatest of difficulty.

Rating Studies. The process of emotional development can hardly be studied experimentally (certainly not by such drastic methods) in human infants. We can, however, use the method of behavior rating (cf. page 37) to obtain data on the development of consistent patterns of emotion.

One investigation of particular interest in the present context is that of Burt (1948), dealing with observers' ratings of emotional behavior in young children. If the point of view sketched in the preceding pages is correct, there should be some consistent pattern of relations among actions which involve components of pleasantness, unpleasantness, excitement, and depression. Burt sought for this pattern by computing correlations among the observers' judgments and applying factor analysis (see page 158) to the resulting table. He first found a general factor of high and low responsiveness —some children were consistently high on all varieties of emotion, others uniformly low. After the effects of this variable were extracted, he found two more which are of special interest to us (Figure 5.3). The factor labeled II in the diagram seems to resemble the increased activity–decreased activity axis of Figure 5.2; and factor III seems to involve a pleasant-unpleasant dimension. Certainly it cannot be maintained that Burt's data fit perfectly

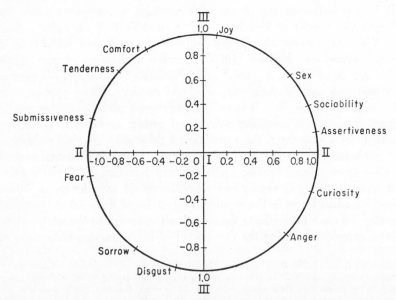

Fig. 5.3 Relations among ratings of emotional behavior in children. While this chart does not match point by point with Fig. 5.2, the clustering of pleasant, unpleasant, active, and quiet tendencies is clear. (From Burt, 1948, by permission of the publisher.)

the theoretical scheme of Figure 5.2, but on the whole, they seem to support the idea that emotional aspects of temperament develop out of the four basic feelings.

GENERALIZATION AND DIFFERENTIATION

All psychologists are in agreement that the more complex and subtle emotional states develop as the child matures and learns. At first, it seems, he simply acquires expectancies of pleasure or pain, and develops reaction patterns of excited activity or inhibition. He will manifest specific emotions, such as love for his mother, fear of harsh authority figures, anxiety when in an unpredictable situation, and so on. The child's personality, however, includes far more than the specific reactions to persons with whom he has had contact. He may show hostility to adults in general, or distrust of a man he has never met before, or enthusiasm for an activity even when his first efforts are failures. How do we explain such phenomena?

Generalization and Positive Transfer. The most important principle in explaining these phenomena is that of stimulus generalization. Experiments show that an expectancy, once established for a given object, tends to generalize to a class of objects. If the child loves his mother, he is likely to be favorable to women in general. If he is bitten by a dog, this may generalize to all sorts of four-legged animals. Generalization may extend to the point of a broad expectancy, such as "Life is good" or "People can't be trusted" (cf. the concept of schema, page 77).

The transfer of an expectancy or response to a different object of a class, however, may be only partial. Grant and Schiller (1953) presented a rectangle 1 by 12 inches to their subjects, and shocked them to produce a galvanic skin response (GSR). After this response was well established, they presented rectangles varying in height from 9 to 15 inches. Generally speaking, the greater the difference from the 12-inch original, the less the GSR. However, all these transfer stimuli obviously elicited some expectation of being shocked.

Differentiation. The child does not simply transfer blindly from one stimulus pattern to another. He learns early to *differentiate*, to discriminate between objects having certain points in common. One of the earliest differentiations probably is that between adult males and females, as the child learns that mother is different from father both in immediate stimulus properties and in the aftereffects of being cared for. Later he learns to differentiate among women and among men.

Social Situations and Social Roles. One of the most difficult classes of differentiation is that which requires that the child learn to identify differences between social roles, in which the same adult may function as a different stimulus according to the situation. Mother, for example, must be treated differently when company is present; church represents a different kind of expectancy; and so forth.

As he grows older, the child must learn to expect different consequences from Mr. Jones as neighbor and Mr. Jones as policeman, from Miss Smith as teacher and Miss Smith on a picnic. The differentiation of these roles is made more complex by the fact that clear-cut cues are often unavailable. Roles with distinctive features (the policeman's uniform, for example) are differentiated easily. Others are more subtle.

An important component of the child's personality growth is his increasing sensitivity to cues indicating a shift in roles. Some adults seem never to acquire this sensitivity, and "do the wrong thing" because they misperceive the role of the other person. The argument about friendships between officers and men in military service stems from exactly this problem. If the soldier perceives Lt. Smith as a buddy and a joker, does this set up conflicts when the situation demands that he perceive Lt. Smith as an authority figure? Enough soldiers have difficulty with such shifts to provide some realism to the policy of forbidding much social contact outside the military role.

LEARNING

Our discussions, both in this and in the preceding chapter, have assumed that learning plays a predominant role in the process of personality development. We have talked so far mostly about the formation of expectancies, i.e., the simple learning that A is probably followed by B. There are some other points that merit observation with regard to the learning process as it is relevant here.

Classical Conditioning. Expectancy formation corresponds to what is usually called "classical conditioning," classical in the sense that it fits the pattern set by Pavlov and his followers some forty years ago. In this design the animal is passive and something happens to it; for example, a bell rings and food follows, a metronome clicks and shock follows, etc. The early theorists treated this as evidence of the formation of a "conditioned response"; the bell became a stimulus for the activation of the salivary glands, in the food experiment. There is some reason to suspect that what is formed is not a stimulus-response connection, but an expectancy. (When Watson's baby subject grew older, he ran away from the white rat, but obviously this was not a conditioned response, because he was incapable of running when the learning took place.) For the most part, the student can handle the personality implications of learning by considering these experiments as evidence for a process either of conditioning certain responses, or of establishing expectancies. While the treatment in this volume obviously favors the latter view, the conditioned-response view can be adapted to the data to be presented.

Instrumental Conditioning. Classical conditioning resembles the situation facing the infant, in that the animal is passive and helpless to avoid the food or shock presented. Another type of learning experiment, called the "instrumental conditioning" experiment, resembles more the situation of the older child who has some freedom to vary his behavior.

The difference between the two kinds of situations can be illustrated as follows: suppose a rat is running down an alley and comes to a metal grid in the floor. As he steps on it, an electrical circuit is closed; he receives a shock, leaps forward, and runs rapidly away from the grid. Now, in terms of simple classical conditioning, he ought, the next day, to approach the grid, leap, and run down the alley. Actually he does no such thing. He slows down as he comes to the grid, and may completely refuse to cross it, or he may vacillate and then rush across. He is responding to the perceived quality of the grid (as associated with painful stimulation) rather than giving a simple stimulus-response association. Culler (1938) has pointed out the change in response as the animal learns what he can do. In this instance the dog hears a bell, then gets a shock to the paw. At first the response includes yelping, thrashing around, biting at the harness, etc. Later the dog learns that lifting his paw avoids the shock; then all these excess movements drop out, and only the act which is instrumental in avoiding the unpleasant stimulus remains.

We must expect, therefore, that the development of personality will show many instances of both classical conditioning and instrumental conditioning; or, put otherwise, examples of learning to perceive an object or person differently, versus learning to modify a response as a result of environmental pressure.

Reinforcement. The phenomenon of instrumental learning raises the problem of reinforcement as an aspect of learning. The animal modifies his behavior because he gets food or avoids shock. Empirically there is no question that reward and punishment are effective in modifying behavior, if properly used. However, there are some difficult theoretical problems which we must at least mention.[6]

Reward and reinforcement are usually defined in a circular fashion; i.e., an animal is given a substance at the conclusion of an act, and if this leads to increased probability that the act will occur again, it is said to be a reward or a reinforcement. Generally we can say that food, water, a member of the opposite sex, etc., are likely to function as rewards, but the only way to be certain is to try it out. (If the animal is satiated for food, water, or sex, the reward value disappears.)

[6] Dollard and Miller (1950) offer a treatment of personality which stresses reinforcement as a factor in learning, but they too admit the difficulty of defining reinforcement (see pp. 39–47 of their book).

On the other hand, "satisfaction" is a term which customarily refers to human experience. I may feel satisfied after a good meal, or after I have finished a task I had set myself. For human beings, satisfactions are usually also rewards, and vice versa. Prediction of satisfaction (or reward) value, however, is difficult for human beings. The event must be looked at from the point of view of the person involved. A boy may get satisfaction out of provoking his mother, even though he encounters painful stimulation afterward. As a broad generalization it would be correct to say that pleasant stimuli are satisfying and have reward value, but such exceptions as the one just mentioned warn us of problems. We must define pleasant, satisfying, and rewarding in terms of the perceptions of the person being studied.

Secondary reinforcement occurs when a stimulus, ordinarily neutral, acquires reward properties. Thus Zimmerman (1957) trained animals to press a lever for a sip of water when thirsty. A clicking sound accompanied the operation of the device delivering the water. After some practice, the animals would work just to hear the clicking sound, even though it often did not signal water. The sound could now be used to reinforce new habits. Animal trainers use this method; dogs are given food rewards for correct performance, and also given verbal praise. Soon the dog responds as well for praise as for food.

Young (1955) has demonstrated a somewhat similar effect with animals. Rats will work, and learn, for a "reward" which is only a drop of saccharine solution. Since saccharine tastes sweet, we assume that it has "satisfying" properties for the animal even though we cannot possibly know how the rat feels. Certainly it does not have any food value. (Since it tastes like some foods, it may function as a symbolic reward for the rat.)

These observations lead to the following general conclusion: human beings (and animals) learn to accept many kinds of stimuli as secondary reinforcers. For human beings, verbal reinforcers are especially significant. Since children go through so many common experiences, we can expect certain words, smiles, tones of voice, etc., to acquire this reward value. We must, however, always be prepared for the child who does not value these stimuli, does not find them pleasant, will not be influenced by them. Thus, personality differences are revealed by the kinds of rewards which are effective with a given person.

Fromm-Reichmann (1950) describes a striking incident to illustrate this. The patient, a young woman, told her psychiatrist that she had decided to attend a party that evening; since this would indicate real improvement in her adjustment, the psychiatrist said, "Fine." At her next interview she explained that she had not gone to the party after all; when asked for a reason, she said that her mother, when disapproving of some intended action of the patient, used to say "Fine" in just that way. In this case the patient was conscious of the origin of her emotion; in far more instances, the historical explanation has been lost, but the individual's behavior is still molded by the emotional coloring lent by a particular cue. The reward value of words of praise and similar symbolic stimuli will depend on the way they are perceived by the recipient.

Effectiveness of Verbal Reinforcement. Everyday observation leaves little question that verbal reward for an action does increase the probability that a person will repeat it, but psychologists have been interested in determining the range and limits of the phenomenon. Verplanck (1955) has described various studies in which verbal reinforcement was effective in modifying behavior without conscious awareness on the part of the subject. For example, in a word-association procedure the experimenter would say "Uh-huh" whenever a plural response was given, but would say nothing to singular responses. There was a steady increase in the rate of emitting plurals. In a similar study Nuthmann (1957) presented items from a personality inventory one at a time, and asked each subject to say whether or not the item was applicable to himself. She said "Good" whenever S accepted a certain category of statement, and within a short time the average number accepted within this category had doubled. Many similar studies could be cited to show the effectiveness of the method.

The limits of the technique seem to be set by the strength of the tendency to a response other than the one being reinforced. For example, in an unpublished study of labor union attitudes, the experimenters said "Good" when subjects accepted an item in a given category (prounion for some subjects, antiunion for others). On the average, no increase in frequency of the rewarded response was found. Interviews with the subjects indicated that preexisting feelings about unions probably overruled any effect of the verbal reward. This limitation presumably would be of little significance in work with children.

Shaping Responses: the "Mask." We have commented elsewhere that the child learns to put on a mask of socially approved gestures and verbalizations even though these may run counter to his private feelings. Reinforcement, especially verbal reinforcement, is the tool used by parents and other adults in inducing these response modifications. The process of socialization is largely a process of praise for some behavior, scolding (and other punishment) for disapproved acts. The child is rewarded for saying those things which are approved by his parents, which means, in general, by society; he learns to express the "nice" emotions, to admit to having wishes and fears which are acceptable. He learns not to mention—and probably becomes incapable of recognizing—the presence within himself of impulses to violence, to sex, to "improper" pleasures. The process of blocking out these unacceptable experiences from the possibility of verbal report is more complex than is implied by simple approval or disapproval; but it would appear that this is an essential element in the sequence.

The Process of Psychotherapy. Although we are not concerned in this book with the clinical applications of personality theory, it is interesting to speculate on the relationship of verbal reinforcement to psychotherapy. In this relationship the therapist requires the client to discuss all sorts of personal topics. However, he usually makes it clear that he considers it a waste of time for the client to talk about his profession, his hobbies, or other aspects of daily life. He may reward the client only for talking about sex, or about his early relations with his parents, or about rivalries with his siblings. The client, not unnaturally, finds it easier and easier to talk about these topics and to ignore the others. Thus we have such amusing findings as that of Heine (1953), regarding therapists of different theoretical schools. Clients reported that these therapists actually used very similar methods, regardless of the theory preferred; but they also reported very different "fundamental causes" for their personality disorders, and these fundamental causes fitted perfectly with the theoretical biases of the therapist.[7]

Partial Reinforcement. Before leaving the subject of reinforcement, we may note one other experimental finding which is relevant to personality. Normally in an experiment an animal is rewarded every time he performs the required act. In human affairs, however, reward is likely to be somewhat inconsistent. We may ask, from the point of view of personality development, is it better for parents to seek to reward *every* occurrence of a desired response, or is this unnecessary?

The answer can best be derived from experiments on *partial reinforcement*, such as those described by Skinner (1953). In these experiments, rats learned that if they pressed a bar, a pellet of food would drop into a feeding cup. At first every bar press was rewarded. Later the schedule was changed so that only every third or fifth act led to food. With practice the rat learned to continue for rather long periods (14 pressures to get one pellet, for example). We would say that the animal has learned an expectancy which might be verbalized as "I will be successful if I keep trying."

The most important outcome of these experiments on partial reinforcement is the finding that habits set up under such conditions are far more resistant to experimental extinction than those in which the animal is rewarded for every act. This means that if the experimenter shuts off the food supply,

---

[7] Some cynics have interpreted this to mean that the therapist does not discharge the client as cured until he has finally yielded and accepted the diagnosis appropriate to the therapist's school. A more plausible view may be that the chief benefits of therapy have to do with the reorientation of percepts, behavior, and emotions, and that the "diagnosis" is a relatively minor point. That is, the individual may need a new way of perceiving himself, his mother, his wife, and his children; whether this is alleged to be due to an unresolved Oedipus complex, to infantile dependency, to birth trauma, or to sibling rivalry may be quite incidental.

the animal will continue to press the bar for long periods of time. Under 100 per cent reinforcement, the rat will stop shortly after the food stops. It is apparent, then, that expectancies which are developed in a partial reinforcement situation will hold up for a longer time.

Applying this to the problem of personality development, we can suggest that, once the child has acquired an expectancy of pleasant stimuli being associated with adults, it is possible to begin a gradual shift to less indulgence. He must and can learn that adults may also be restrictive, and even punitive, without losing his basic belief that adults are kind and gratifying. The prediction can be offered with high confidence that the child thus gradually induced to expect some deprivation and frustration will be more resistant to adversity in adulthood than one who has been indulged up to a certain point and then suddenly faced with the realities of failure, loss, and punishment.

THE HIERARCHY OF VALUES

In the preceding chapter we noted that the individual builds around himself a series of constant states: a physical environment, including wealth and property, which he values and seeks to protect; a social environment, including affectionate relations with his family and friends, likewise valuable to him; and in some cases, an ideological environment, consisting of the beliefs he holds dear and will defend. In earlier pages of this chapter we have tried to spell out in more detail just how this happens; the individual experiences pleasantness in connection with parents, with property, and with institutions and social roles, so that the perceived signs of these will in the future arouse pleasant feelings. Likewise he has various unpleasant experiences which lead him to expect unpleasantness in the future when given stimuli are contacted.

These experiences do not go into storage as isolated, independent units. Rather, the individual builds up a schema or generalized perception of a class of persons, objects, or situations (stimulus generalization) and segregates one category from another (differentiation). As this process continues, he develops frames of reference for the evaluation of items in this category.

Consider the question of objects of food. The child can be nourished by many substances, but he soon develops decided preferences. Typically he places sweets at the top of the list, meats in the middle, and leafy vegetables at the bottom. Variations in these can be induced by homeostatic need (e.g., vitamin deficiency), but after a scale of preference has been well established, the person may continue to strive for objects he does not need and ignore those which would be "good for him." Babies will choose a diet which meets their needs, but adults, because of this learned set of evaluations, may not.

Similarly, the person develops standards for evaluating the attractiveness of members of the opposite sex, the threatening quality of different physical dangers, the desirability of different housing arrangements, occupations, churches, political programs. In a rough way we may say that he will have as many frames of reference as he has discriminated different categories of significant objects. Within a given frame of reference he will choose on the basis of relative valence among objects available to him.

Choices across Frames of Reference. The person develops also a hierarchy which cuts across frames of reference. Maslow (1954) suggests that the average individual reveals a series of needs; those at the top of the hierarchy (commonly called the "basic" needs!) will dominate behavior until they are relieved, after which less demanding needs may achieve expression. His hierarchy looks like this:

- ✓ Physiological needs (hunger, thirst, etc.)
- ✓ Safety needs (pain, fear, etc.)
- ✓ Belongingness and love needs
- ✓ Esteem needs
- ✓ Self-actualization needs

According to this view, when any situation involves the physiological needs, it will tend to make objects in that group especially attractive (valence is increased) until the disturbance is removed. After these are satisfied, the safety needs predominate, and objects of protection and defense look very attractive. When these are taken care of, the desire to be loved and to belong to a friendly group will dominate the phenomenal field; and so on through the list.

This sequence obviously looks very much like the series of "envelopes" around the ego, which we described earlier (page 84). In effect, this theory says that objects will be perceived as more attractive, if they appeal to an unsatisfied need which is more "basic"; and as these fundamental states are taken care of, objects which offer gratification to the "higher" desires will appear more attractive.

Individual personalities, then, will differ in two respects, according to this analysis. (1) Within a given need category the kind of object considered most attractive will vary; so we may identify a person in terms of his preference for particular foods, drinks, recreations, etc. (2) Across need categories this system of dominance of values will vary. Some individuals develop little interest in property (cf. the Freudian theory of development, below). Some are concerned primarily with being loved, being looked up to or admired. Others may channel a lot of energy into their ideals, and the situations which elicit the most intense effort are challenges to their church, their political beliefs, or their aesthetic values. These frames of reference become the bases for traits of temperament (Chapter 8), for character (Chapter 10), and for systems of attitudes and values (Chapter 11).

In molding these frames of reference, infantile experiences carry great weight. "Mother's food is best." The acts for which we have been rewarded seem right, others seem wrong. If safety needs have always been satisfied, the person unconsciously expects no frustrations in this area; he is said to have high confidence that he will be able to escape any dangers that arise. If he has been successful in getting what he wants by acting aggressively, he will see this as the proper course for the future.

Present Field versus Past Experience. There is another point which should be emphasized here. Many able psychologists, e.g., Lewin (1943), have insisted that behavior is determined by "the field at that given time." In a sense, of course, this is merely a platitude; obviously, what I do must be determined by conditions existing right now. But this only means that the past experience is represented by expectancies within the organism. For example, two children try to put a puzzle together; both fail. When given another chance, one tries, the other refuses. Now the field is, in a physical sense, identical for the two. But it is perceived differently. To one child it is still a field in which success is possible; to the other, it is a hopeless situation to be avoided.

Looking back at the partial reinforcement experiments, we see that the first child has established an expectancy that one failure is not final; there is still a probability of succeeding. For the second child, this probability is nonexistent. As he sees it, failure is inevitable, so why try?

Unquestionably Lewin's statement is true. Theoretically, behavior is always determined by the field at the present moment. But if we want to understand *why* the field is so perceived—or if we want to manipulate the child's field—we must take into account his developmental history. The past exists in the present as a pattern of memories. The perceptual process includes scanning these memories as well as the physically present stimuli. If these stimuli evoke only memories of pain, of discomfort, and of humiliation, the present field will necessarily be perceived as threatening, something to be avoided.

The Difficulty of Changing Personality. These considerations are relevant to the problem of changing personality. The individual carries with him what has well been called his "apperceptive mass," the meanings and emotional significances of objects, persons, and situations. This is truly a mass, in the psychological sense of being inert and heavy to move. Primacy tends to favor early memories which may be unpleasant. Partial reinforcement may have strengthened the unpleasant rather than the pleasant expectations. Ambiguous experiences may then be perceived as unpleasant, not pleasant. Thus the person's subjective probabilities are heavily loaded in favor of his belief that people are bad, that society is unjust, that he will be mistreated.

These are not the only reasons why it is difficult to change a personality once it is molded. They indicate, nonetheless, some of the factors involved. They should lead to awareness that one does not reform by an act of will, and that sudden restructuring of personality is the exception, if it ever occurs. Modification of any personality after early childhood is a difficult, tedious procedure. Months and even years may be required.

FREUDIAN THEORY OF PERSONALITY DEVELOPMENT

The foregoing pages stress the notion that infancy and early childhood play a decisive role in shaping the adult personality. This view is generally accepted, but its implications are not understood. A necessary consequence of these facts is that the adult is not free to have any kind of personality he wants; he has been shaped, bound, and delivered with certain infantile characteristics built in, and it is extremely difficult to get rid of them.

The most thorough study of the relations between infantile and adult personalities is that constantly being carried on by the psychoanalysts. Their observations have been crystallized in a formulation of the developmental process which we here summarize in very brief form.

Stages of Development. According to the Freudian conception, the infant develops through a series of stages in which he successively seeks pleasure, primarily through different mechanisms or relations to his environment. It is generally implied that heredity and maturation play a greater role in this sequence than does learning, but it is equally possible to assume that learning plays an important part in the process.

The Infantile Passive Stage. Since the baby at birth is helpless, it is not surprising that the earliest stage identified is the passive attitude of lying around waiting for good things to happen. The pleasures most sought after at this time are assumed to be warmth, physical relaxation, and the like. Krout and Tabin (1954) suggest that vestiges of this stage may be such items as liking to swim in warm water (prenatal enjoyment?), swinging in a hammock, and drinking warm, sweet liquids.

The Oral Sucking Stage. Very shortly the child's pleasure seeking gets focused on the pleasures of sucking; indeed, some psychoanalytic writers merge the passive into the early oral phase (e.g., Munroe, 1955). In this stage the baby delights in putting everything into his mouth, sucking his thumb, mouthing his blanket, and so on. There is some evidence that children who do little sucking to get their food (milk flows easily from the nipple) suck more than others; this leads to the argument that the child must get a certain amount of sucking pleasure before he is ready to abandon this activity. In opposition to this there is evidence that long-continued practice in sucking causes the child to enjoy sucking even more; it does not induce him to stop.

More interest attaches to vestiges of this stage likely to be carried over to adult life. Special interest attaches to the age of weaning, the point at which pleasures obtained through sucking are diminished very sharply. Although the research data are by no means in complete agreement, a study by Goldman-Eisler (1951) seems to typify the most careful investigations. She found that her subjects who had been weaned prior to the age of four months showed adult characteristics of pessimism, passivity, and aloofness: characteristics which, we might speculate, reflect an expectancy that "good things will be taken away; I cannot count on people to be sources of pleasure." Studies by anthropologists of the child-rearing practices of different cultures lend some support to the notion that a person's outlook on life may be affected by age at weaning and abruptness of the process.

The Oral Sadistic Stage. The child continues to be largely passive during the early oral or sucking stage. But with the development of teeth, during the second half-year, he begins to take a more active role, biting into things and exploring them more aggressively. (Part of this development may simply be a matter of muscular strength and perceptual maturation.) He also learns that he can affect others by biting them, and perhaps even at this age he becomes able to express aggression. Certainly in later life "biting remarks" become ways of expressing hostility in a somewhat approved fashion.

The Anal Stages. At a slightly later stage the child shows pleasure in bowel movements, in stimulation of the anal region, and in playing with his excretions. Freud centered attention especially on the presumed pleasure from the anal area, because it showed up in the free associations of many of his patients. Further, he found that this phase is particularly important in terms of the child's acquiring mastery of his own impulses. For the first time, the baby is at a point where he can act on an impulse, or not; i.e., he is in this respect not purely passive but active. (Although self-initiated activity occurs in the biting stage, there is not the clearly defined internal impulse which characterizes defecation.) And, as many a mother intent upon toilet training is aware, the baby can be very capricious when he realizes his capacity to inhibit or release these movements!

If pleasure is obtained mostly by retention and refusal to give up movements on parental request, the theory says the individual tends toward a miserly, retentive adult personality. He places a high value on property and ownership. If, on the other hand, pleasure comes primarily from expulsion, the person may become profligate and spendthrift. The evidence on these points is somewhat less than satisfactory although it is suggestively favorable to the theory.

The Phallic Phase. Infants show pleasurable reactions to stroking of the sex organs, but special interest in this area seems to follow the anal phase. Somewhere around the fourth year of life (these ages vary widely), pleasure seeking seems to focus on the genitals. At this point, however, there is little clear awareness of relations with a person of the opposite sex, hence Freud referred to this phase as phallic rather than genital. In boys this phase is marked by a certain exhibitionism, by interest in the sex organs of others, and by fear of castration. In girls an envy of boys is likely to be a characteristic feature.

The Oedipus Complex. An event which is essentially part of the phallic phase demands special mention. This is the development of the Oedipus complex, in which the child focuses his pleasure seeking on the parent of the opposite sex, hostility and aggression on the parent of the same sex.[8] It is easy to see, for boys, how this happens. The mother is the source of food, of comfort, of many of the pleasures characteristic of the oral and anal stages. Without knowing anything very clearly about the sexual relationship, he can understand the idea of having possession of the mother for his own pleasure, of throwing the father out. As he begins to express such attitudes openly, he runs into vigorous disapproval from both parents. Also, he may fear the father, who is bigger, stronger, and wiser (castration anxiety is especially marked about this time). Often the result is repression (see page 123) of his desire for the mother, and instead identification with the father.

Similarly, the girl is at first devoted to the mother. Hostility to the mother, however, is also present because of toilet training and other restrictions (present likewise for boys, but felt more keenly by girls, for reasons not quite clear). As the girl accepts her status as a female, she may express the wish to marry her father, often coupling this with the hope that the mother will die or go away. Social disapproval causes this wish to be inhibited as in the boy's situation.[9]

The Latency Phase. At the resolution of the Oedipus conflict, the child normally goes into a "latency" stage in which little interest is revealed in the opposite sex. This perhaps is based on the "burnt child dreads the fire" axiom; avoiding members of the opposite sex may seem to be the safest way of staying out of trouble.

The Genital Phase. The final stage, which all of us would reach if we developed truly mature personalities, is the genital phase. Here a major source of pleasure is found in bringing pleasure to a member of the opposite sex, with the emotions of tenderness and protectiveness appropriate to the relationship. The individual has by this time presumably worked out his passive dependency desires, his tendency to bite aggressively, his dogged refusal to yield to the wishes of others, and similar infantile characteristics. Actually, of course, each of us reveals some traces of these infantile phases; it is only in extreme cases (see Chapter 12) that an adult personality is dominated by these infantilisms.[10]

[8] Freud used the term "Oedipus complex" for boys and "Electra complex" for the girl's fixation on her father with hostility to the mother. Current usage tends to apply "Oedipus" to both sexes.

[9] In both instances we are likely to find that the frame of reference for evaluating marital partners is profoundly influenced by developments at this stage. If the Oedipus is successfully disentangled, the boy will tend to find women resembling his mother sexually attractive; the daughter will be attracted to men resembling her father.

[10] The foregoing paragraphs summarize the stages of personality development as classi-

Validity Studies on the Theory. A theory as complex and inclusive as this one is necessarily difficult to validate. There have been many studies using observations of children, questionnaires, projective tests, and experiments. Some of these have led to negative results, whereas others seem to support the theory. The importance of the castration and Oedipus complexes, for example, is quite generally accepted. Greatest doubt is expressed with regard to such topics as the necessity of all stages occurring in the life of any specific child, the sequence of these stages, and the tracing of adult personality characteristics to residues of particular stages. (The question of whether personality "types" are formed as a result of frustration or overgratification at one of these stages will be discussed in Chapter 12.)

It appears that a considerable number of children manifest characteristics at successive ages which resemble those postulated by Freud. The explanatory principle, however, may be simply learning to expect certain kinds of pleasures and discomforts in association with parents and other significant figures; the theory proposes a kind of mystical attachment of libido to objects in an automatic manner without learning. This part of the theory is looked upon with marked skepticism by American psychologists.

Explaining Developmental Progress. This matter of why the child moves on from lower to higher phases of development is a problem not only for Freudian theory but also for homeostatic views of personality. Critics of Freud object to the notion of an inherited pattern which unfolds in an automatic fashion. Critics of homeostasis inquire: Why, if the child is comfortable and happy at a certain stage, does he abandon this equilibrium to move on to another?

Actually, of course, the child does not move on spontaneously. Usually he is pushed. His comfortable equilibrium is disturbed by forces either inside or outside his body. Freud thought the changing body structure caused one area to become less pleasure giving, and another more so. Thus old gratifications would seem less interesting, new ones more attractive.

But the social factor is obviously important. With the development of teeth, the baby may bite his mother and bring on weaning. Social expectations impose toilet-training requirements. At a slightly later stage he may be ridiculed for behaving in a "babyish" manner, and of course, he is likely to be punished for some forms of sex play.

It seems probable, therefore, that the child abandons one pleasant equilibrium and goes through the discomfort of developing another, not voluntarily, but under pressure. Perhaps, if he lives in a very permissive culture, he may spontaneously abandon sucking, may toilet-train himself, etc., because of his changing pleasures and interests. But it would seem that the equi-

---

fied by "orthodox" followers of Freud. Other psychoanalysts have modified these schematic stages in varying ways; a particularly interesting formulation is that of Erickson (1950). Space limitations prevent inclusion of this and other theories here.

librium is usually disrupted by adults, and the development of new patterns occurs under pressure.

Basic Role of Conflict. Freudian theory, consequently, points to the basic role of conflict in personality growth. Each of us desires pleasure; we develop certain mechanisms for obtaining this gratification. But negative valences, threats, scolding, punishment, may be interposed by the adult world. We must then adapt to this situation by working out solutions to the conflicts presented. The following chapter will be devoted primarily to an analysis of techniques by which the individual resolves these conflicts.

SUMMARY

The innate components of personality include the feelings of pleasantness, unpleasantness, excitement, and depression. These feelings are logically related to homeostatic processes, and they apparently come to function as signs of restoration of equilibrium or of threats to equilibrium. Feelings become integrated into percepts of persons and objects which are related to satisfaction of these biological needs.

By the process of stimulus generalization, percepts of mother and father may transfer to all adults or to persons perceived as similar. Differentiation occurs as the child learns to discriminate among other persons, and associates feeling tones only with those persons who resemble the parents in some essential fashion. The child also learns to recognize social roles and to behave differently in situations which adults define as socially distinctive.

Learning is not purely perceptual. Rewards make it possible to induce changes in response, and punishments can inhibit responses. The child learns to behave in ways that are socially approved, to put on a mask of conventional verbalizations, and to suppress tendencies which are disapproved. The split thus induced between perception and action may have serious repercussions, as will be noted later.

The child's quest for pleasure is a varied one. To try to bring some order into it, we have presented the Freudian theory, according to which the individual develops through a series of stages, each characterized by a predominance of pleasure seeking through a specific bodily mechanism. A satisfactory equilibrium is normally established at each phase, but it is disrupted by pressures, usually interposed by adults. How the child learns to deal with such conflicts thus becomes our next problem.

SUGGESTIONS FOR READING

The material of this chapter is typically discussed in a wide variety of texts. Murphy's *Personality: a biosocial approach to origins and structure* has several chapters covering ideas summarized rather sketchily here. Diamond's *Personality and temperament* also has useful treatments of some of these concepts.

CHAPTER 6

Frustration, Stress, and Conflict

In the preceding chapter some account was given of the child's search for pleasure, or, to use more formal terminology, his behavior directed toward positive valences. That statement was somewhat arbitrarily simplified for the sake of clarity. It is now appropriate to explore some of the complications which get involved in this developmental sequence.

First of all, it should be noted that the child is often blocked in his quest for a given goal object. This gives rise to a variety of affective responses, the most commonly observed of which is anger. The tension level usually goes up markedly, and the amount of energy discharged increases likewise.

The blockage may not be a simple barrier; it may take the form of a negative valence: punishment, or loss of some other valued goal. In this case we speak of conflict rather than frustration, although it is clear that the two phenomena may merge in some situations. Major elements of personality development involve the acquisition of ways for dealing with conflict. These are likely to be acquired by imitation of adults, from suggestions given by adults, and by trial and error.

Finally it is to be noted that both frustration and conflict involve the notion of *stress*. This term, so freely bandied about nowadays, lacks a precise definition; even Selye (1956), whose researches on stress have won wide acclaim, defines it more by example than by logical categorization. Nevertheless, the way in which the person responds to stress plays a crucial role in his personality organization. Frustration, conflict, and stress, then, will be the topics of this chapter.

FRUSTRATION

In psychological writings the term "frustration" has been used to cover several different kinds of events. Some distinctions will have to be made in order to deal effectively with frustration as a factor in personality development.

1. Frustration has been said to occur when any behavior sequence is blocked. For example, a child is playing with an attractive toy; the toy is taken and placed behind a screen so that he can no longer touch it.

2. Frustration has been used to describe the situation in which a person wants two incompatible goals; he is said to be frustrated because he cannot both eat his cake and have it. For such events the term *conflict* will be used.

3. Frustration is used to identify events in which an individual anticipates a given outcome and is disappointed. Thus a young man takes a job in a research laboratory and may have certain expectancies as to how he will be treated; if the situation proves otherwise, he may be "frustrated" by this lack of conformity to his expectations.

Frustration, then, has been considered to occur when a behavior pattern is blocked (1) by a physical obstacle or by the action of some other person; (2) by a conflicting pattern within the person; or (3) by the *absence* of environmental objects which were anticipated for the fulfillment of the behavior pattern. Category 2 seems distinctively different from the others, since it places the source of blockage plainly within the person himself. The other two, although differing in obvious respects, have a definite similarity. We shall therefore continue to call each of them "frustration."

Immediate Consequences of Frustration. In infants and young children, the most probable response to frustration seems to be attacking behavior, an effort to remove the obstacle (Figure 6.1). Thus it is associated with the experience of anger, and most psychologists believe that anger is always a product of some frustration. Watson (1924), it will be remembered, proposed the view that rage, induced by blocking bodily movement of the neonate, was an innate emotion. While some babies merely go to sleep when confined tightly, it is obvious that somewhat older children react violently to severe restrictions on their freedom of movement.

Freud (1924) proposed that aggression should be explained on the basis of a "death instinct" or instinct of hostility. Even among the psychoanalysts this view seems to have faded into obscurity. Most of Freud's concrete material bearing on this problem appeared to involve some frustration of pleasure-seeking behavior, and for this reason the trend today is to hold that aggression is a secondary phenomenon rather than an innate impulse. This has certain implications for personality theory; for example, it would suggest that hostile, aggressive personalities are more adequately explained as resulting from accumulated frustrations. The "death instinct" theory would at least imply that some persons are born with a strong destructive impulse and that not much could be done about them. Since Freud himself clearly rejected this consequence

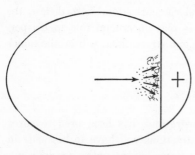

Fig. 6.1 Frustration and aggression. When the person is blocked from attaining a desired goal, the immediate consequence usually is anger and attacking behavior.

of his theory, it seems preferable to concentrate our attention on reactions to frustration.

The Intensity of Aggression. The frustration-aggression hypothesis (Dollard et al., 1939) suggests that the intensity of the aggressive emotion generated by a given frustration will be a function of three variables: (1) the strength of the motive being blocked (positive valence); (2) the degree of interference with the desired response; and (3) the frequency with which this interference occurs.

Most of these are self-evident; it is obvious that a man will become more angry if something blocks him from keeping a date with a beautiful woman than if he is prevented from keeping an appointment with the dentist. Crimes of violence occur only when very powerful positive valences (sex and money, most often) are involved.

The extent and frequency of blockage are also relevant. Sometimes an interference is relatively minor and can be pushed aside. But repeated minor blockages can cause a burst of rage. Let us note that the occurrence and intensity of aggressive acts will also be related to (1) the perceived probability of getting what one wants, the positive valence, by aggression; and (2) the perceived probability of punishment and the relative intensity of the negative valence involved. Some individuals fail to develop ability to judge such consequences, and so frequently commit acts which subject them to punishment.

In addition to the foregoing points, Pastore (1952) has noted that the perceived *arbitrariness* of the frustration is relevant. If a blockage appears reasonable and proper, we react with less anger than if it is apparently someone's whim. And finally, Cohen (1955) has shown that frustration by a person of equal status evokes more aggression than frustration by an authority figure (perhaps this would also suggest that frustration by a perceived inferior would be even more irritating; cf. the reaction of many businessmen to union action by their employees).

The Expression of Aggression. Young children respond to frustration particularly with overt violence, although sulking and withdrawal into fantasy are also common. With increased maturity, the child may express hostility verbally, or by attempting to frustrate the other person, and (occasionally) by trying to understand and remove the frustration.

Freud has suggested that his "death instinct" might be directed outwards, against others, or turned inward upon the self. Depression and guilt feelings are illustrations of the latter. The proponents of the frustration-aggression theory have taken over this notion, and Rosenzweig (1944a) has suggested that outward aggression be called "extrapunitive," and aggression against the self, "intropunitive."

Extrapunitive aggression seems naturally more satisfying; indeed, intropunitive aggression means self-punishment, and is automatically painful. However, it may be less painful than the anticipated punishment if one attacks an authority figure. Hence, if anger is directed toward a parent, and if the parent is punitive, the child is especially likely to show intropunitive reactions.

Displacement. Sometimes aggression is vented, not upon the immediate frustrating agent, but upon some substitute. This is particularly likely if the frustrator (1) is not available or (2) is in a position to inflict severe punishment if attacked. This is assumed to follow the principle of stimulus generalization; i.e., if the frustrator has certain attributes, the "scapegoat" is likely to be chosen because of these attributes. Miller (1948a) and Bush and Whiting (1953) have attempted to spell out precisely the circumstances under which displacement occurs.

We are interested here especially in the fact that these expressions of aggression, including displacement, may become systematic, repeatedly manifested aspects of a specific personality. This can happen as a result of several processes:

1. After several frustrations, the child may develop a kind of "generalized expectancy" of being frustrated. This means that a wide range of stimulus situations will look to him as if they are going to be frustrating.

2. Aggressive responses may become habitual. If certain persons or objects repeatedly play a frustrating role, the conditioning process may operate and aggressive behavior may come to the fore even before frustration takes place. This is particularly true if the aggressive behavior has been rewarded by reaching the desired goal.

3. Aggression evokes counteraggression. If the child has a "low boiling point," bursts into a temper tantrum on slight provocation, he is likely to be punished. Since this may also be perceived as frustrating, a tendency to act aggressively may be exaggerated by a positive feedback mechanism.

Habit versus Catharsis. Some authors have called attention to the fact that frustration builds up tension, and that the occurrence of physical activity, especially aggression, relieves the tense state. This relief is known as catharsis. From this the deduction has sometimes been made that overt expression of hostility should be encouraged in order to reduce the tension level. Counter to this is the view that aggressive acts, if repeated and especially if rewarded, become habitual aspects of the personality.

There can be little doubt that, for some very tense, severely frustrated children, the value of catharsis is real. In play therapy, the child may be encouraged to smash dolls which symbolize frustrating people and in other ways to vent some of his pent-up hostility. But the child is not permitted to attack persons, and an effort is made (after the tension is released) to help him understand his situation. If children are permitted to express their aggression in physical violence against real people, the result is likely to be the development of a belligerent personality.

Especially important in this connection is the continuance of frustration. If the frustrating situation continues, any benefit obtained from catharsis is strictly temporary. Any long-range plan for helping aggressive personalities, then, must look to the questions: What are the chronic frustrations which keep piling up tension for this person? Why has he built up so much hostility? As a clever observer wrote about the European political situation in 1938, "If there are 'mad dogs' abroad, it is not enough to cry for guns and chains. Who bit the dog, and why is he so mad?" An intelligent approach to personality problems calls for a look at the underlying frustrations related to aggressive behavior.

ANXIETY

In a sense, the emotion of anxiety is rather like aggression. Yet its ramifications through the personality are even more extensive, and the complications in which it becomes enmeshed are even more involved. Anxiety is a major factor in virtually every form of personality breakdown and is a significant component of the "normal" personality as well.

The significance of anxiety arises, of course, from its role in the process of *socialization*. The infant has certain demands for food, for comfort, for sexual (or love) gratification, for aggression, etc. In the first few months these may be allowed rather free expression. But soon the parents begin to impose limits and to apply punishments for violations. These punishments need not be physical; with the older child they may take the form more often of denial of love and privilege. But this may arouse intense fear. In any event, we must recognize that discipline must be somewhat unpleasant, and that negative valences will be involved. The child fears (or experiences anxiety about) the punishment which follows certain acts.[1] Thus a typical behavior sequence would be: disturbance of equilibrium → impulse to act in a certain way → memory of former punishment → anxiety → inhibition of action tendency.

It is clear from this analysis that the problem of anxiety and the problem of conflict cannot be handled separately. Let us pause for a moment and examine the phenomenon of conflict.

Three Types of Conflict. It is logical, if there are two kinds of valences, that the individual can encounter three types of conflict situations, as diagramed in Figure 6.2. He may find himself drawn in opposite directions by two positive valences; he may be between two negative valences, so that as he tries to escape one, he gets threatened by the other; and, most perplexing of all, he may find an object which is both positive and negative (or he may see

---

[1] Typically we distinguish fear from anxiety by saying that fear relates to a specific object, whereas anxiety often seems quite diffuse and nonspecific. The person may say that he feels afraid but does not know why.

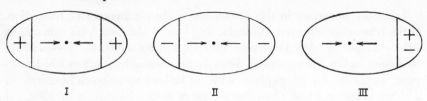

Fig. 6.2 Three types of conflict. The person may find himself between two positive valences, drawn toward both; or between two negative valences, repelled by both; or he may be attracted and repelled by the same object or situation.

negative valences blocking his way to the positive goal, in a situation somewhat resembling frustration).

The type I conflict ($++$) rarely has significance for personality. If a child is torn between his desire for a comic book and for an ice-cream cone, he usually compares them mentally and decides which is more attractive. Or he may, as Adams (1954) suggests, find some larger goal (such as recreation) and see that he is attaining this goal by either pathway. The only situation in which such conflicts appear to have major significance is that in which the abandonment of either positive valence is seen as a serious loss. In this case we are really dealing with a positive-negative conflict (see below).

Anxiety enters the picture when we consider the conflicts which involve negative valences. We may note, first of all, that fear (cf. Chapter 5) is simply the anticipation of unpleasantness if a certain situation is encountered. We fear biting dogs because of physical pain; we fear parental scoldings because of diffuse unpleasantness. Such situations, which we seek to avoid, are said to possess negative valence.

Double Avoidance Conflicts. If the child is afraid of a lion, he has no conflict; he expresses his fear frankly and openly. But if he is afraid of the dark, he may hesitate to say so because he encounters parental disapproval. The boy who attempts to escape from his arithmetic lesson faces the prospect of punishment. The soldier who would like to get away from danger in combat faces the probability of charges of cowardice, not to mention punishment.

It is characteristic of this type of conflict (cf. Figure 6.2) that the individual may tend to take off in a direction which avoids both negative valences; the schoolboy runs away if precautions are not taken, and soldiers have been known to do the same. This type of behavior comes under the general heading of delinquency, or socially disapproved action; and we shall have more to say about it in Chapter 10.

Approach-Avoidance Conflicts. The category of conflict which has most extensive implications for personality development is that in which the same goal is seen to have positive and negative valence, or in which a negative valence must be accepted in order to reach the positive goal (see Figure 6.2). Perhaps the commonest instance is that of sex. The child cannot escape the biological factors which make sex attractive; but usually he has been taught to fear sexual contacts as "bad" or immoral. If this conflict becomes severe, it can precipitate a personality breakdown.

It is in this category of conflicts that anxiety becomes most acute. Often the individual cannot say of what he is afraid. He experiences fear without being able to relate it to an external cause. The reason for this can be stated in very simple form, although many complications will be pointed out later. Anxiety generally develops in situations in which the immediate stimulus comes from within the person. Thus, in the case of conflicts about sex, the precipitating stimulus is the bodily state of sexual arousal; since this is only vaguely perceived at best, and is a taboo subject as far as conversation is concerned anyway, the person may say that he feels frightened but without any cause. Perceptual defense (page 121) and repression (page 123) may also have operated to make it even more difficult for him to label the source of his anxiety.

Pleasure Principle and Reality Principle. Let us return now to a consideration of the child's development. He experiences an impulse to act in a certain way, but the impulse cues off anxiety. He is thus in an approach-avoidance conflict. This point in his development marks his transition from what Freud called the *pleasure principle* to the *reality principle*. Briefly put, the pleasure principle simply says that the child tries to attain a maximum of impulse gratification; to restore valued equilibria, regardless of the effect on others and perhaps on himself. The immediate gratification dominates the phenomenal field.

The reality principle states that, with increasing maturity, the child seeks the maximum of gratification *in the long run*. In other words, the perceptual field is no longer dominated by the immediate positive valence; the threatening punishment or loss is also perceived.

We can diagram this task which the child faces as in Figure 6.3. A relatively small reward, close up, may look much bigger than the future punishment. The child must learn to anticipate the remote threat, to bring it up into the psychological present, to evaluate it realistically in comparison with the proposed pleasure. This is all that the reality principle means.

Obviously the example can be reversed. Some children are so distressed by an immediately present negative valence (e.g., the discomfort of doing home-

Fig. 6.3 Punishment-reward relations. In socialization the child learns that he must accept small discomforts to achieve larger rewards. However, he may attend so closely to the pain that he remains unaware of the greater reward and thus loses it.

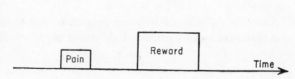

work) that they do not see the larger reward in the future. (College students occasionally have this difficulty. The negative valence sets off responses of avoiding and postponing.) The reality principle says that mature personalities can correctly perceive the greater value of the future reward and be guided by it rather than by the minor immediate discomfort. The so-called "psychopathic personality" is one in which the pleasure principle still dominates; these individuals childishly grasp immediate pleasures without thought of the future pain certain to follow.

Anxiety and Phobia. It follows from what has just been said that a certain amount of anxiety is normal and necessary. The child should and must experience some conflict when he is tempted to perform acts disapproved by his parents or by the community. However, some training procedures elevate anxiety levels excessively. This is particularly true when the child does not get a clear picture [2] of what it is that he may be punished for—as when his acts transgress moral taboos which the parents enforce but do not explain to him. And of course some of the impulses involved, particularly sex and aggression, are very powerful, so that the temptation to carry out the forbidden act is intense.

Displacement. Again we note the operation of displacement, or substitute stimuli, as in the case of aggression. Clinical psychologists often encounter cases of phobias, irrational fears of marked intensity, in which the object feared is manifestly inappropriate but serves as a substitute for the originally feared situation. A fairly common case is that of the married woman who develops a fear of going on the street alone. She can go with her husband, or with her child, but if alone, she panics and must return to her home. Generally this turns out to be a sexual conflict; she has been attracted romantically by a man other than her husband, would like to go to him, but feels that this would be immoral, unfair to her husband, against her standards of behavior. In this case she is really afraid of her own impulses; but she does not want even to admit to herself that she has such "sinful" desires, and so displaces the fear onto an irrelevant association, going away from home. (The expression of such fears is often revealingly symbolic; she may say that she is afraid of "falling," or of being contaminated in some way.)

Stimulus Generalization. Symbolism usually appears also with regard to the objects which elicit anxiety; a long, pointed object, such as a knife, may symbolize the male genital by an obvious physical similarity; however, a knife may also symbolize aggression, and the two ideas may become fused, as for example, in the case of a woman who is hostile to her husband because of the way he has treated her sexually.

Since the parents are frequent sources of punishment, it is not surprising that they may also be perceived as having negative valence, despite the strong

---

[2] Compare our discussion of the child's need for a stable, clear-cut, predictable world around him (p. 83).

positive valences involved. We noted in connection with the Oedipus complex (Chapter 5) that a boy may perceive his father as both protecting and threatening, helpful and punishing. Similarly the girl may be torn in conflict between her positive and negative feelings for her mother.

In these situations a fascinating phenomenon, which has been called "splitting the parent image," may occur. Let us say that the boy has built up a picture of his father as friendly, a wise adviser, a protector in time of trouble. But he also has a picture of the father as restrictive and punitive, as one who takes possession of the beloved mother and shoves out the son, etc. It appears to be possible for these two pictures to be separated; despite the fact that the physical father is the same in both cases, the percepts are segregated. Now the "bad father" image may get displaced onto robbers, or leaders of an enemy nation, or some other threatening figure, thus making it possible for the boy to see his father as definitely positive.

Intolerance of Ambiguity. The kind of situation in which the child perceives the parent as both positive and negative can be called an "ambivalent" or "ambiguous" situation. It is easy to see that this must be uncomfortable for the child. Not only does he want to express positive attitudes, but he is anxious about the negative attitudes—since expressing them would almost certainly lead to parental scolding. Thus splitting off the "bad image" and attaching it to someone outside the family circle must have considerable value in relieving tension.

In the homeostatic frame of reference, we can readily see that any ambiguous situation is somewhat tension-arousing. One needs to know whether a given object is a goal object or a threat. If the attributes of the object are not clearly discernible, tension seems to build up until a clear-cut percept is formed. It is interesting to note that youngsters who are especially disturbed by ambiguous situations are also those who appear to be insecure in their relations with their parents (cf. Chapter 7).

Since successful adjustment requires the ability to perceive the environment realistically, it follows that the child who resolves his conflict by splitting the image of the parent and disposing of part of it elsewhere is well on the way to personality difficulty. The better-adjusted child, by and large, is the one who can love his parents even though he sees that sometimes they must frustrate and punish him.

In the earliest stages, the child's perception of his parents is based solely on their behavior in restoring his physical equilibrium. Later he may come to perceive other mothers (or fathers), and their attributes provide a kind of ground against which his own mother is seen as a figure. He develops a frame of reference by which he evaluates her as "better" or "worse" than others. In relatively simple societies, this produces no problems because all mothers behave in pretty uniform fashion; in our complex Western world, the child finds many models of maternal behavior, many of which may look more gratifying than his own. At a still later age, his fantasies about mothers, his reading, movies, and TV will modify still more his frame of reference for determining what mothers should be like.

Memory Distortion. Since perception always involves some contribution from the perceiver, it follows that such modifications in the child's frame of reference change the context he brings to any awareness of his mother. This can extend even to his memories of past situations. If he focuses all of his "good mother" pictures on a fantasied fairy godmother and perceives his real mother only as restrictive and scolding, then he will distort his memories of her past behavior to fit this picture. This is one of the reasons why personality research gets so difficult; one cannot study the development of a particular pattern simply by getting the person's memories of how he was treated. More often than not his memories do not agree with those of independent observers.

DEVELOPMENT OF CONFLICT SOLUTIONS

In trying to clarify the significance of anxiety for personality formation, we described one way in which the child may resolve a conflict. He may achieve this by splitting his picture of a parent, and attaching one aspect (either positive or negative) to some real or fantasied person outside the home. There are, however, many other conflict solutions. Let us examine them a little more systematically.

Perceptual Vigilance and Perceptual Defense. It is obvious that the boy who displaced his hostility toward his father onto Joseph Stalin (and so got rid of his "bad father" image) utilized certain perceptual processes which have already been described. He focused on certain cues (favorable acts by the father) and failed to observe others. Popular psychology assumes that much of the time we see only what we wish to see. To what extent does scientific research support this notion?

The term "perceptual vigilance" has been used to identify a presumed tendency among people to exaggerate cues which are related to the satisfaction of needs, or to sample more extensively the cues which set off positive valence. There is ample evidence to indicate that some such phenomenon occurs, although its exact extent and limits are matters of controversy.

We have already noted that figures associated with reward are described as brighter, clearer, etc. (Solley and Sommer, 1957). Ansbacher (1937) showed that the value of postage stamps affected estimates of their number; when the same numbers of two-cent and three-cent stamps were exposed briefly, observers thought there were more of the three-cent items. Bruner and Goodman (1947) reported that children overestimated the sizes of coins as compared with gray discs, and poor children exaggerated more than those from well-to-do homes. Dukes and Bevan (1952a) found that children overestimated the sizes of jars filled with candy as compared to jars filled with sand. In a second study (1952b) these investigators had college students engage in a kind of gambling game in which winning money was associated with certain rectangular cards. The subjects consistently overestimated the sizes of cards associated with winning. Michael (1955) reported that symbols associated with winning money appeared "clearer" when presented at a speed too fast for identification.[3]

As noted above, results from this kind of experiment are not entirely consistent, although the trend is clear. One factor which may complicate the results has been identified by Klein, Salomon, and Smith (1959). They arranged to feed subjects a very salty meal which induced marked thirst; before allowing anyone to drink, they got size estimates on pictures of thirst-related objects. Similar estimates were obtained under conditions of water satiation. There were no differences when the entire group was treated as a unit. However, they separated the subjects into those who showed interference on a simple perceptual task and those who showed no interference. The former group *underestimated* the thirst symbols, and this tendency was exaggerated when thirsty; the second group *overestimated* the same symbols, and likewise exaggerated their errors when thirsty.[4] Thus it appears that some people illustrate something which might be called perceptual vigilance (and perhaps everyone does under appropriate conditions), but we are not sure about the conditions. It is possible, for example, that the symbols used by Klein, Salomon, and Smith only irritated some subjects, who did not like to be reminded of their annoying thirst. Perhaps these were the people who had cultivated habits of control, as indicated in the perceptual interference task.

The foregoing experiments (only a sample of the literature in this area) suggest that there are at least two kinds of perceptual exaggeration: relatively permanent changes in the apparent size and clarity of objects associated with pleasant events (including satisfaction of need); and a temporary increase in these attributes for items associated with probable gratification of a need being experienced at the moment; presumably the former is a kind of crystallized residue of the latter. Each of these may vary to an unknown extent from one person to another, depending on intrapersonal variables not yet identified.

Perceptual Defense. It is also suggested that people can easily become "blind" to objects they prefer not to know about. The term "perceptual defense" refers to the blocking of perception under conditions usually involving some kind of threat to the person.

---

[3] For other ingenious experiments indicating that pleasant experiences can modify percepts in the direction of greater size or clarity, see Smith (1952), Filer (1952), and Simpson (1956).

[4] The effect of some immediate need in producing perceptual exaggeration of relevant objects has been studied by many investigators: cf. Sanford (1937), Gilchrist and Nesberg (1952), McClelland and Atkinson (1948), Lazarus, Yousem, and Arenberg (1953), and others.

Dulany (1957) obtained measures of the relative clarity of geometrical figures at very brief exposures. He then subjected two groups to different training: one group would receive shock whenever a given figure (e.g., triangle) was flashed, at subliminal speed (too fast for recognition); the other group was shocked when any figure except the triangle came up in this series. Later the clarity was redetermined. For the first group, the triangle was now considerably less clear; for the second group, the triangle had gained in clarity. Rather similar experiments and results have been reported by Reece (1954), Rosen (1954), and Raskin (1954). As Figure 6.4 shows, such a perceptual change often facilitates conflict solution.

Eriksen and Browne (1956) showed that even if frequency and recency of experience with words are controlled, it is still possible to demonstrate perceptual defense by attaching anxiety to some of the words. This type of experiment is somewhat more convincing than research using words which have "naturally" acquired anxiety value, because it is so difficult to learn all about the history of this acquisition. It appears (DeLucia and Stagner, 1954) that words having strong emotional significance for a patient may elicit either vigilance or defense. One hypothesis is that words symbolizing an *external* threat will elicit vigilance (since it would be adjustive to detect such threats quickly); whereas words symbolizing *inner* states which might set off acts leading to punishment would evoke perceptual defense (on an unconscious theory that if the person refuses to recognize this state within himself, he won't be tempted to act on it). This hypothesis cannot be said to be well supported as yet.

Mechanisms Involved. As noted above, perceptual vigilance seems to be associated with excessive sampling from certain sets of cues which are associated with a current need or with satisfaction of past needs. This probably means failure to sample other stimuli, but this cannot alone explain perceptual defense, since defense can be demonstrated when the person is not discernibly concentrating on anything.

Since it has been shown (Asher and Ort, 1951) that abnormal eye move-

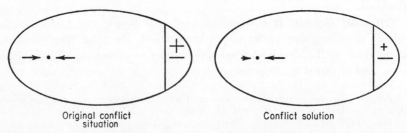

Original conflict
situation

Conflict solution

Fig. 6.4 Perceptual defense as conflict solution. As long as the two competing valences are perceived as equal, conflict persists; but if defense operates to make one valence appear smaller, the person moves in the direction of the stronger tension and so solves his conflict (temporarily, at least).

ments occur when the individual looks at emotionally disturbing words, and also at certain parts of Rorschach blots (Blake, 1948), it might seem that perceptual defense is no more than looking away from distressing stimuli. But the matter is not so simple. How does the person know when to look away? Clearly he must have recognized, in some vague way, the nature of the object. Further, this would not explain auditory phenomena, in which defensive blocking of unpleasant material has also been demonstrated (Simpson, 1956).

The best explanation seems to be based on sampling, but quite different from that suggested for vigilance. If the individual receives some sample of cues from the environment, this immediately evokes associated memories of past percepts, including records of internal sensations and feelings. These may be intense enough to interfere with further sampling of the external object. Hochberg et al. (1955) showed that a buzzer did not interfere with visual recognition speed for nonsense syllables; but when certain subjects received shock paired with the buzzer, and later the buzzer alone was sounded as the syllables were shown, interference was substantial. The sound of the buzzer now "demands" attention, thus reducing the sampling of the visual environment.

Anxiety and Closure. A similar conclusion is supported by other studies in which anxiety has been related to perception. Moffitt and Stagner (1955) have reported on a study in which anxious subjects showed a stronger tendency to complete an incomplete design, shown for very brief intervals, as compared with relaxed subjects.[5] It was inferred that sampling of the visual environment, which would have revealed the breaks in the design, was interfered with by the scanning of other modalities, particularly visceral.

Clinicians have long noted that anxiety patients have a great capacity for focusing on certain cues to the exclusion of others. This may be a combination of vigilance and defense, i.e., the person "oversamples" from one object and ignores the presence of others. Defense is particularly obvious when the threat is plain to other observers but the person himself denies that it exists.

Repression. Closely allied to perceptual defense, and perhaps nothing more than the same mechanism operating more extensively, is the phenomenon of repression. This, as originally proposed by Freud, meant the forcing of certain ideas out of consciousness by anxiety. The child feared punishment, or loss of parental love, or other dire consequences if he mentioned a certain topic; indeed, he must not even think about it. This has resulted in instances of memories being buried so thoroughly that only months of patient questioning and exploration of related topics can bring them to light.

In recent years the term *repression* has been used somewhat more flexibly, and often applies to the forgetting of unpleasant experiences even though no serious anxiety is involved. On the average, persons memorizing lists of pleasant and unpleasant words will forget the latter more rapidly. When failure or threat to the person's ego is introduced, the effect is stronger. Frequently the

[5] See also Korchin and Basowitz (1954).

subject is given a number of tasks to perform, each of which is fairly simple. However, he is arbitrarily stopped before completion on some items, with the information that the average individual would already have finished. If he perceived this as a blow to his self-esteem, he tends to forget those tasks on which this happened. (Some subjects show no memory differences; inquiry usually indicates that they did not believe the experimenter when he gave them spurious information of comparative performance.)

Repression, then, may be extended to include the notion that the individual protects certain kinds of equilibria by forgetting experiences which would be upsetting. Its similarity to perceptual defense is thus clear. If my comfortable feeling of intellectual superiority is disturbed by failing on a task, one simple way of dealing with the disturbance is to erase it from memory.

Both perceptual defense and repression are markedly unsatisfactory devices for adjustment in one important respect: by shutting out certain aspects of reality, they deprive the person of information which may be needed for later behavior. If Americans prefer to protect a stereotype of national scientific superiority by repressing memory of Russian achievements, this tends to block out information needed for effective adaptation to the situation.[6]

Rationalization. Vigilance may aid the individual in protecting himself against a conflict situation. In the failure example cited above, he may seize upon some detail, as many people do in the Rorschach ink blots, and exaggerate its importance. Thus he failed because the instructions were not clear, or because his pencil was defective, or because the task was silly anyway. Psychologists label such excuses as *rationalizations*.

Essentially, therefore, the rationalization solves the conflict by redefining the situation. Remember that our behavior is guided by perception. If the individual can misperceive his problems suitably, he can make them disappear. Thus the famous "sour grapes" mechanism is a way of saying "The grapes were not valuable, and I didn't really want them." A young man who has just lost his girl friend is especially likely to indulge in this device. While the technique may be adopted at first for the benefit of his friends, he will very shortly believe his own rationalizations.

There are many varieties of excuses which may be developed in this fashion, and there is no point in cataloguing them here. Like repression and perceptual defense, rationalizing involves a necessary distortion of reality. Consequently, it interferes with later adjustments. While a little rationalizing does no one serious harm, the habit readily grows and becomes maladaptive. In extreme forms rationalizations expand into delusions of grandeur and delusions of persecution.

---

[6] Psychoanalysts object to classifying these memory failures, which are readily corrected, with "true" repression. They argue that repression applies only to powerful inhibition of awareness due to intense anxiety. In the absence of quantitative measures, it is difficult to draw a line here. Even "true" repression can be overcome with time and effort; the difference seems to be one of degree only.

Introjection and Projection. Perceptual vigilance and defense underlie other mechanisms for dealing with conflict situations. Two which are quite important are *introjection* and *projection.*

Psychologists speak of introjection as the process of "taking in" external objects and situations, treating them as if they were really a part of the personality. Thus the child may focus on certain aspects of "my school," "my country," etc., and behave as if these were really extensions of himself. He is selectively exaggerating the connections to himself and ignoring the facts which should remind him that these are really external phenomena.

Projection, as the name implies, is just the opposite of introjection. In this case, the person takes an inner state, such as an emotion, and projects it onto the outside world, denying any connection with himself. Consider the very hostile, destructive person, for example. He experiences powerful surges of anger. But he refuses to recognize these as part of himself; instead he says others are behaving aggressively, are trying to start a fight with him. (Usually he then considers himself justified in fighting, since the other man really started it.) Projection, then, implies defensive refusal to be aware of inner states, with a parallel vigilance to pick up the slightest cue from outside which indicates the presence of this emotion in others.

Normally, introjection and projection develop together. The child learns to understand others by introjection, i.e., by assuming that they feel what he feels. Similarly he learns to "see himself as others see him" by projection. But the normal personality requires a neat balance of the two; i.e., an excessive introjection of another person may amount to a loss of "self" in the personality of the other; whereas excessive projection means complete inability to see others realistically.

Introjection solves conflicts by providing the child with attributes he craves but does not possess; he can be strong, wealthy, and wise by introjecting these attributes from others. Obviously, if this helps him to continue working to acquire these traits realistically, the mechanism is a good one. If he simply relaxes parasitically on the accomplishments of others, the result is undesirable. Similarly, projection helps the child avoid self-punishment; he says, "It is not I who have bad sexual and aggressive impulses, but somebody else." Again, as a temporary safety valve, this may be of little significance; but practiced regularly it distorts reality to a dangerous extent.[7]

LEARNING AND CONFLICT ADJUSTMENT

We have shown how some of the commoner forms of conflict adjustment derive from perceptual processes which selectively magnify some aspects of

---

[7] These discussions of mechanisms of conflict solution are intended only to show how certain operations contribute to the development of generalized personality patterns. We have not attempted a catalogue of all adjustment devices, such as sublimation, reaction

the environment (and the self), block out others, and distort still others. It is likely that such techniques could be evolved by the child without help; i.e., if faced with a conflict, even without adults to use as models, he would manifest such processes as vigilance and defense. It seems clear, however, that the development of personality is molded by interaction with adults, so that the particular mechanisms developed are by no means matters of chance.

Imitation. Children modify responses to conform to the behavior of adults. They acquire techniques of dealing with physical problems, and also with social conflicts, by observing and modeling themselves on parents and friends.

Psychologists long believed that imitation was a human *instinct,* that the child possessed an inherent tendency to copy the actions of others like himself. Today it is generally held that imitation is a form of learning, in which the child learns to shape his own responses in accordance with cues based on actions of others.

Specific skills, such as handling a hammer, are learned more promptly if the child has someone to imitate. Speech is obviously a matter of imitating; Southern children develop Southern accents, whereas those born in New England do not. If the child can observe an adult's response, either visually or auditorily, he can then vary his muscular activity until he gets feedback that he recognizes as similar. Facial expressions, gestures, and similar movements are also handed down from parent to child by imitation.

Matched-dependent Behavior. In the preceding paragraphs we implied that the child copied a specific response, using the same muscles in much the same way as the model. Actually, much imitative behavior is more appropriately called "matched-dependent behavior" (Miller and Dollard, 1941), in which the follower uses the leader as a cue, but without focusing on specific acts. For example, a boy four years old may recognize the sounds of his father coming home, and run toward the door; the two-year-old may roll toward the door on his tricycle, even though he is not sure what is about to happen.

Most matched-dependent behavior, of course, is that of the child modeling himself on an adult. This is homeostatically adaptive, since adults know how to reach many goals which are beyond the child's scope. Thus matched-dependent behavior is frequently rewarded. Unfortunately, the lesson often learned from this is to be submissive, to yield to adults, never to trust one's own judgment. This is especially probable if the parents ridicule or scold the child when he acts independently and gets into trouble.

Suggestion. Like imitation, suggestion has often been considered to be instinctive in origin. Today it is considered to be exclusively a function of learning. Indeed, it differs from imitation in only one respect; whereas the child imitates by copying acts directly from a model, he is guided by sug-

---

formation, etc. For a good treatment of these see Shaffer and Shoben (1956), Sappenfield (1954), and Shaw and Ort (1953).

gestions through symbolic channels. This means that he has to develop some understanding of language before he can be influenced by suggestion.

Suggestion and command are very closely allied in the life of early childhood; and indeed, with some parents it is always difficult to tell the difference between command and suggestion. Operationally, we may say that a command carries with it the promise of immediate reward or punishment, whereas suggestion only hints at such consequences or may ignore them completely.

Once the child has learned to respond to the suggestions of others, it is possible for him to make suggestions to himself. A child may be heard saying to himself, "You mustn't take any of that candy." As adults we think through problems and suggest possible courses of action. If we think of our own parents or other models and say, "What would his advice be?" we are combining introjection and suggestion as guides to action.

Suggestibility. As a result of the rewards he gets for accepting suggestions, and the punishments encountered when he rejects them, the child may develop a submissive attitude toward suggestions from adults; and he may even act on what he believes to be a suggestion emanating from an adult, when the adult does not intend it. Employers, political leaders, and other authority figures find this person very compliant and cooperative; his great defect as a follower may be that he is helpless when he has no leader to lean on.

Selection of Adult Models. Who will be perceived as a model suitable for imitation? Parents, obviously, are in a preferred position in this respect. The parents are not only sources of gratification; they are also *power figures*, persons who can grant or withhold many kinds of satisfaction, or impose pain and frustration. Because of the intimate relationship between goal orientation and perception, it is inevitable that such power figures shall be observed carefully. It is also probable (unless the power figure deals out too much pain) that the child will begin to imitate the behavior of the adult. Such imitation may have two sources: (1) The child may have a kind of implicit assumption that "if I imitate father, I will have some of his power." (2) By chance the child imitates his father and is rewarded, so he tends to repeat such acts and eventually develops what Miller and Dollard labeled "matched-dependent behavior." If these are accompanied by introjection of the father's characteristics, we usually speak of *identification* of the son with his father.

The child may, moreover, perceive other power figures and acceptable models in his environment. Lippitt et al. (1952) studied the emergence of leadership and imitation of leaders in a group of child campers. They noted that a boy might get a power status primarily because of some athletic skill, but that this might rapidly generalize to other roles, so that his judgments would have high cue value for the other children in almost all situations. Further, the followers soon began to imitate the boys who achieved leadership status, presumably for the two reasons cited in the preceding paragraph.

With increasing maturity and scope of experience, the individual may find models among teachers, employers, political leaders, or even in literary creations having no independent existence. However, all these later patterns must be superimposed upon an existing percept, which is usually that of the parent. Thus there is normally a dilution of effect, and many important patterns of perception are never modified from childhood on. In later chapters we shall consider some empirical investigations indicating the importance of such perceptual models in molding specific aspects of personality.

Acquisition of Social Norms. Through the processes outlined above, the child acquires a set of social norms. He learns the limits within which impulse gratification is permitted, and beyond which punishment will result. He learns the kinds of responses which are appropriate to certain contexts and social roles. Essentially this is a process of developing a picture of the world. It may be a rigid picture with everything depicted either black or white; as in Nazi Germany, "Everything which is not compulsory is forbidden." On the other hand, it may be less clear-cut, with ambiguities and shades of gray blurring much of the picture.

Hammond and O'Kelly (1955) have argued that the acquisition of social norms is essentially no different from the development of physical norms. The child must learn to perceive sizes and distances with reasonable accuracy; if he fails, he is "punished" by failing to achieve the results he desires. He must develop an appropriate frame of reference for machines, in order to judge what he can safely do and what is unsafe. Equally, he must acquire a social frame of reference which enables him to judge what is "good" and what is "bad," what will further his own satisfactions and what will evoke anxiety.

The process of "socialization" includes many interactions, such as those of affectionate care, punishment, guidance, and suggestion; on the child's side it includes the formation of expectancies about the consequences of certain actions. In becoming socialized the child learns to inhibit certain impulses and to release them only within situations defined by society as appropriate—toilet training is only a particularly obvious illustration. Sex and aggression are the impulses most subject to inhibition and control; but even hunger encounters some taboos. The desire to dominate others must be curbed, and even the wish to lean on others. Socialization, then, is a process of learning what negative valences to anticipate, and what kinds of behavior patterns can be exercised which will achieve some degree of positive gratification, some approach to the equilibrium being sought, without too much punishment or discomfort.

The differentiation of social roles is an important part of this process. Acts are permitted to a person in one role which are punished in another role. A man may carry a loaded revolver if he is a bank guard, but not on the grounds that he is being persecuted by the Kiwanis clubs. The child is therefore faced constantly with the necessity for learning to differentiate between situations.

As he acquires these discriminations, he has at least the capacity for personal maturity.

STRESS

A common thread running through this chapter has been the fact that the child's impulses, his efforts to protect an equilibrium against disturbance or to restore one, may encounter either blockage or a negative valence eliciting anxiety. We have observed that such situations uniformly involve a mobilizing of energy, an increase of tension. This tension has extensive physiological repercussions which are important for personality. We may say that they represent the organism's reaction to *stress*.

Stress, unfortunately, is not a clearly defined entity. Selye avoids a precise definition of the term. He says rather that the stress reaction is the body's nonspecific way of dealing with certain kinds of internal and external agents: fatigue, cold, microbes, acid, and anxiety are among his examples. "No one can live without experiencing some degree of stress all the time," he writes. "The soldier who sustains wounds in battle, the mother who worries about her soldier son, the gambler who watches the races, the horse and the jockey he bet on: they are all under stress." [8]

The stress reaction includes particularly changes in the adrenals, thymus, and stomach, according to Selye; however, he also mentions changes in the blood concentration and other variables. He coined the term "general adaptation syndrome" (GAS) to identify the pattern of physiological changes which seemed to occur together, regardless of what kind of noxious stimulus he applied to the organism.

It became apparent early in his work that there was some connection between this "alarm reaction" on the part of the body, which mobilized resources to deal with a damaging stimulus, and Cannon's conception of homeostasis. Selye noted, however, that Cannon had been concerned primarily with the *specific* homeostatic action for dealing with a given disturbance of equilibrium; for instance, cold sets off changes in the circulatory and muscular systems adapted to raise the body temperature. The GAS, by contrast, is composed of *nonspecific* responses, i.e., responses which are the same for excessive cold, extreme heat, acid on the skin, and other injurious factors. Thus, disturbances of steady states are all stressors, but the term "stress" focuses attention on the *general* bodily adaptation, not upon the specific devices adopted for dealing with the particular disturbance.

Stress Tolerance. One of the most important consequences of Selye's work, for psychology at least, is the idea of stress tolerance. After the generalized alarm reaction to a threat, the organism typically goes into a "stage of re-

[8] Selye (1956), p. 4. Reprinted by permission of McGraw-Hill Book Company, Inc.

sistance" in which it can take substantially greater stress without damage than was true initially. The occurrence of moderate damage, so to speak, builds up immunity, and the organism can now tolerate an injury which would formerly have been fatal.

This generalized, nonspecific ability to deal with stressful situations without physiological damage is a significant feature of personality. It is unquestionably tied, in some way, to such other phenomena as the ability to keep trying in the face of disappointment (see the discussion of partial reinforcement, above) and also to frustration tolerance. This term is used to refer to the fact that an individual can build up a "tolerance" for frustration, and will not flare into open aggression. Much depends on his learning to perceive the blockage as a problem to be solved, rather than an obstacle to be knocked down. The study by Thetford (1952) on patients undergoing psychotherapy indicated that their viscera react less intensely to stress stimuli after treatment. Perhaps the development of frustration tolerance and stress tolerance go hand in hand. Certainly as the individual acquires these attributes, his personality becomes more mature and less distressing to others.

Disturbance of homeostatic equilibrium, then, will set off the specific kinds of adjustment previously discussed, and will also set off the GAS. And the ability to deal with such disturbances will improve in two ways: the knowledge of specific techniques, such as building a fire to keep warm; and the change in general stress tolerance.

Homeostatic protective and corrective actions play a key role in personality development; for example, the child learns to use adults as protections against certain dangers, or he retreats into a world of fantasy to get away from them. Similarly, stress tolerance becomes important; whether a child will become demoralized, panic-stricken, or psychosomatically ill under stress probably depends on the development of stress tolerance. Both concepts are useful, and they are related, but not to be confused.

Physiology of Frustration and Anxiety. Both frustration and anxiety qualify as stresses, and each tends to set off the GAS. However, each also has certain unique physiological effects. And both are in opposition to pleasantness, which has largely antagonistic physiological correlates.

Both anger and fear activate the sympathetic division of the autonomic nervous system, giving rise to increased heart rate, interference with digestive action, heightened blood pressure, etc. It was only by rather detailed manipulations of various measures of visceral processes that Ax (1953) was able to prove that fear and anger involve different patterns. And there is some reason to believe that these may vary from person to person. It may be that the child learns some aspect even of these unconscious, involuntary response patterns.

The modern view of psychosomatic disease suggests that gastric ulcers, asthma, chronic hypertension, and other disorders may be due to persistent emotional stress. It seems probable, for example, that an individual beset by conflicts involving inhibition of strong aggression may develop arterial hypertension. Either the blood-vessel reaction has become habitual, or permanent damage has been done by the stress reaction. Similarly, chronic anxiety is sometimes associated with gastric ulcers.

The Sympathetic-Parasympathetic Antagonism. The effects of innervating the sympathetic nervous system are largely antagonistic to those of the parasympathetic. The latter, for example, usually slows the heart rate, relaxes the arteries, and facilitates digestive peristalsis.

The existence of these antagonistic mechanisms is of more than academic importance. We have noted that situations which phenomenally give rise to fear or anxiety will, on the behavioral side, set off responses of digestive, circulatory, and respiratory mechanisms. These visceral activities will in turn feed back to the central nervous system a flood of afferent impulses, giving rise to sensations which maintain and strengthen the anxiety felt by the person.

Any attempt to "control" this anxiety by voluntary effort or "will power" is doomed to failure. The visceral responses are automatic and involuntary. There is, however, a method for canceling them out. This is to activate the parasympathetic system. Thus, if potent stimuli known to arouse parasympathetic patterns are applied to the individual, it becomes possible to lower the tension level and then to deal with a problem when the individual is not confused by his felt anxiety.

While mothers have known this fact for thousands of years, it has only recently been explored in the laboratory. Jones (1924) showed that food could be used with children to eliminate fears, by repeated presentation of the threatening stimulus (at a distance) while the child was happily eating. Gantt (1942) reports that anxiety symptoms in male dogs can be made to disappear by presenting a sexually receptive female. Davitz and Mason (1955) found that they could reduce conditioned fears in rats by placing them with other rats who had not learned to fear the conditioned stimulus.

Individuals may, through trial and error or by the other means listed above, develop techniques for relieving anxiety and stress. Some of the commoner devices are listed in Table 6.1. Other methods, such as psychotherapy, require the assistance of another person.

There is some evidence that as psychotherapy progresses, the parasympathetic kind of reaction begins to predominate over the sympathetic. Persons who have successfully completed therapy show reduced physiological upset under stress (Thetford, 1952). The importance of the positive transference (affection of the client for the therapist) so often observed in therapy may lie in this effect. Certainly the ability to handle conflicts is essential to avoiding serious stress effects under conditions of modern living.

Table 6.1

Devices Commonly Used to Reduce Tension Level

Restoration of infantile equilibria:
  Contact with soft, warm materials, eating sweets, sound of soft voices, retreat into
    passivity, sleep, appeal to adults
Catharsis:
  Muscular activity, swearing, laughing, crying
"Self-control":
  Voluntary inhibition of muscular activity; rigidity
Perceptual defense:
  Refusal to see conflict situation, repression of memories, splitting of ambivalent
    images
Fantasy:
  Daydreaming of pleasure
Active effort:
  Planning an escape from real conflict, working to bring about a modification of the
    environment

THE QUEST FOR NEW EQUILIBRIA

So far we have talked about frustration, conflict, and anxiety as if these
set off only efforts to restore a previously existing equilibrium. Let us now
consider a constructive alternative.

It was noted in Chapter 5 that, according to Freud's theory of psychosexual development, the child moved away from one comfortable equilibrium
and struggled to achieve another only when he was pushed. In other words,
our normal tendency is to achieve a steady state and then try to maintain it;
it is only as a result of pressures that efforts are initiated to achieve some
new kind of balance, some new pattern for dealing with desires and conflicts.

The model for a new equilibrium is often based upon the parents or older
children. The child abandons sucking when he is weaned, but the parents
help him develop new techniques for satisfying needs. He must abandon
dependency on his mother when a new baby is born into the family, or when
he is pushed to become independent. Ridicule for "acting like a baby" can
be a threat, and the model for "acting like a man" is held up by parents and
others. Imitation and suggestion, introjection and identification may give
models for new modes of adjustment.

Fantasy and Reasoning. The individual can also create for himself a
new model of what he wants to be. Perhaps, strictly speaking, this always
involves elements of what he has learned from others, but he may recombine
these to constitute a novel invention as far as he personally is concerned.

Fantasy, of course, may be only a means of protecting an existing equilibrium. Faced with a conflict, such as that produced when the parents threaten
punishment if he indulges in some forbidden pleasure, the boy may daydream of having wealth and power so that he can enjoy himself without

stint; he may even dream sadly of the death of his parents, thus removing the obstacle to his gratification.

Fantasy, however, grades over into reasoning and logical thinking. Rather than indulging in pure wishful thinking, the boy may deal with thoughts of the real environment, and figure out a way of obtaining his gratification under circumstances to which his parents will not object. He may, for example, realize that if he gets a job and earns some money, a major portion of the opposition will be overcome.

Reasoning, of course, can go considerably further than this. A man frustrated and upset by the labor of rowing a boat can visualize the possibility of putting an engine to doing this work. He can then utilize various sources of information to develop an outboard motor. A person who is upset by seeing children working in factories at the age of six may fantasy a world in which this is illegal, and then go out and lobby for such legislation. In other words, technological and social advance derives from conflict solutions arrived at by people who were not willing to put up with the existing equilibria.

The same principle holds with respect to new goals and aspirations for the individual himself. A poor boy of immigrant parents may have a *modus vivendi*, but he can picture himself getting a college education and becoming a lawyer. He may actually undergo greater discomfort—he may abandon existing sources of pleasure and deliberately face many unpleasant situations —in order to construct this new steady state where he will have greater satisfaction and security.

Homeostasis and Personality Change. It may be argued, then, that the picture of personality development which we have constructed, using homeostasis as a unifying principle, is compatible with the abandonment of pleasure and equilibrium in favor of a search for a new steady state. It is only in the infantile stage of personality that one seeks immediate gratification and restoration of a disturbed balance. As maturity is acquired, the child learns to tolerate frustration, to sustain tension, in order that he may maximize the long-run satisfactions. At the moment, the end in view may be that of restoring a preexisting equilibrium which appears very attractive. But it may happen that in the course of this detour behavior, new skills may be developed and new percepts acquired which make the old way of life look childish. The individual may then picture himself in a new role—as artist, as philosopher, as religious leader—and set forth to build a new equilibrium. Essential to this is his picture of himself as he wants to be—his ego ideal. We shall pick up and utilize this concept further in Chapter 9.

SUMMARY

As the child develops, he encounters frustrations and threats, which tend to elicit aggression, anxiety, and stress. Conflicts between positive and negative valences raise the tension level and cause diffuse physiological disturbances, as well as interference with psychological processes.

The intensity of the stress is largely a function of the intensities of the positive and negative valences. The physiological tension can be discharged temporarily by catharsis, but this does not relieve the conflict. Conflicts may be alleviated by perceptual defense (refusal to perceive all or part of the conflict situation), by rationalization, introjection, and so on. However, longrange solutions depend on finding socially acceptable ways either to bypass the negative valence or to substitute another positive valence which is less anxiety-arousing.

In working out these conflicts the child makes use of his parents (and others) as models for imitation; he is also influenced by suggestion, direct and indirect. He acquires a picture of the social norms which determine punishment, and can thus plan a course of action within this framework which will minimize discomfort.

Homeostasis need not mean that the individual only devises techniques to restore a preexisting equilibrium after it has been upset by frustration or conflict. Instead, the person may develop a picture of a new equilibrium, a new ideal for himself, toward which he directs his efforts. In this case he reveals personal maturity by accepting present discomfort to obtain greater long-run gratification.

SUGGESTIONS FOR READING

On the topic of stress, Hans Selye: *The stress of life* is a simple and informative book. Much of the material on defense mechanisms is treated more extensively in books such as Shaffer and Shoben, *The psychology of adjustment*. Valuable comments from other points of view are given in Allport's *Personality: a psychological interpretation* and Murphy's *Personality: a biosocial approach to origins and structure*.

DESCRIPTION

The foregoing chapters have given only a minimal sketch of the processes of personality development. Emphasis has been laid on the development of expectancies, with regard to people, objects, and social roles. The child learns to anticipate certain rewards and certain punishments. His behavior is guided by the relative probability (as he perceives it) of occurrence of these positive and negative valences.

Conflict arises when the individual encounters valences which tend to induce incompatible modes of response. Under these conditions the person evolves defense mechanisms, techniques for resolving the conflict. Some such mechanisms are primarily perceptual in character; i.e., they operate by distorting the perceived attributes of the person or situation involved. Others are behavioral; they are manifested in distinctive action patterns.

The valences perceived by the person, as well as the defense mechanisms he adopts in dealing with them, are profoundly influenced by his social context. By suggestion and imitation he acquires from persons around him overvaluations and undervaluations, evasions and rationalizations, and a scale of relative values. His superego or conscience is primarily the organization of these into a pattern which is meaningful to him.

We come now to the consideration of the adult personality as an outcome of these developmental processes. What are the enduring features of personality? To what extent are these values consistent? Are they completely dominated by the immediate situation? Does an individual use the same defense mechanism over and over, or does he change randomly from one to another? What, if any, steady states does he mobilize most energy to defend? And what are the unifying influences which tie all these diverse aspects into a single, functioning whole?

These are the questions to which we now turn.

CHAPTER 7

Personality Style

The child's personality develops as he acquires stereotyped pictures of himself and of his parents, of significant figures, groups, and institutions in his environment. He perceives certain goals as attractive, others as threatening. He devises responses calculated to attain these goals. He finds himself in conflict and develops characteristic defense mechanisms. This description, realistic though it is, makes personality sound like a patchwork quilt, like a chance series of percepts and responses cemented together, but inherently unrelated. Such a picture of personality is patently inaccurate. What are the sources of internal consistency and unity, of uniqueness and individuality appearing in a wide variety of contexts?

Some sources of unity have already been identified. R. B. Cattell (1950) has suggested that psychology has its equivalent of Newton's first law of motion in that a percept, once established, tends to resist change. Thus a person who has acquired a certain percept will behave consistently when this percept is evoked by a cue in the environment. And stimulus generalization accounts for consistency in similar situations. But this is still a very inadequate view of the unity and consistency of personality.

Such an approach can best be described as atomistic and universal. It tends to imply that personality can be understood by grasping a large number of specific facts about the person's development; and further, it suggests that all personalities develop according to a uniform pattern. How can we harmonize this kind of information with the uniqueness and organized consistency of the individual?

One concept which helps to bridge this gap is the concept of *personal style*. This refers to the fact that, entirely aside from specific percepts or specific responses, the person may show a characteristic *pattern of perceiving* or of responding. The origin of these styles is at present indeterminate; some may be inherited, others based on very early experience. The purpose of the present chapter will be to show some of the evidence for particular perceptual styles and response styles, and then to indicate how they help us comprehend the organized unity of the individual personality. The general theme will be that all children go through learning sequences more or less resembling those described in the preceding chapters; but the outcomes will not be standardized because what the child learns will be applied differently in terms of his particular personality style.

PERCEPTUAL STYLES

Individual differences in ways of perceiving (as distinct from what is perceived) have been objects of study for a long time. However, early psychologists tended to discard such observations as indications of error in their experiments; they assumed that human beings would obey laws as exact as those of the physical sciences, and hence they had little tolerance for these differences among individuals. There were, however, early researches in which temperament was related to variations in perception (Heymans, 1908; Wiersma, 1906); and more recently, Thurstone (1951) found that variations in certain perceptual measures seemed to identify personality attributes. There has been a great upsurge of interest in this field since World War II, and we shall concentrate our treatment on the perceptual studies reported during this period.

Credit for highlighting the importance of perceptual style for personality probably goes to George S. Klein, who has done extensive research and writing in this field. As we have done in the preceding chapters, Klein recognizes both universal and unique aspects of personality: "The organism continually wrestles with and seeks equilibrium between two sources of tension, its inner strivings and the demands of reality. . . . Perception lends itself to this [use] by virtue of its 'adaptive properties.' But these properties, common to all perceivers, are employed idiosyncratically; the personal styles in using them for reality appraisal, I have called *perceptual attitudes.*" [1] The term "attitude" is somewhat dubious here, because of its association with social attitudes (cf. Chapter 11). We have therefore adopted the term "perceptual style," but we are using it as Klein employs "perceptual attitude."

Klein's work shows that individuals develop characteristic ways of dealing with material presented to the senses, irrespective of content and sensory modality. This perceptual style is apparently an important source of unity and consistency within the personality; it cuts across specific expectancies, specific defense mechanisms, and complexes. It is consequently a factor making for a characteristic way of dealing with the environment which comes to be an identifying feature of the unique personality.

Leveling and Sharpening. We have referred earlier to the fact of stimulus generalization. One rarely encounters exactly the same stimulus

---

[1] George S. Klein. The personal world through perception. In Robert R. Blake and Glenn V. Ramsey (Eds.), *Perception: an approach to personality*. New York: The Ronald Press Company, 1951. P. 335.

object on successive occasions; he meets not the same but a similar dog, not the same but a similar woman. He tends to *generalize,* to emit the same response when he perceives a new stimulus as substantially equivalent to an earlier one. This has been a commonplace of general psychology for a long time. Its significance for personality differences, however, had not been explored.

In an early experiment (Holzman and Klein, 1956) subjects were presented with square designs and asked to judge each for size. At first only squares 2 to 6 inches on a side were presented. Later the 2-inch drawing was omitted, and a 7-inch square substituted. After a few more judgments, the 3-inch square was replaced by one which was 8 inches on a side, and so on. Thus without his knowledge, *S* was being required to deal with gradually changing groups of stimuli. The results were surprising. Some subjects held closely to the actual sizes presented; they were realistic and accurate. Others got set for a given size and continued to repeat this judgment when it was no longer appropriate. The extent of this lag can be shown by the fact that some subjects toward the end of the experiment were judging a 13-inch square to be only 4 inches on a side.

Klein proposes a dimension of perceptual functioning which he calls "leveling-sharpening" to describe this difference among individuals. Levelers tend to ignore changes in the stimulus, to deny differences, to give a response which was appropriate in the past where it no longer is appropriate. Sharpeners, by contrast, are alert to changes; in one connection Klein speaks of them as having a tendency to "respond excessively to fine nuances and small differences, to exaggerate change." The levelers had difficulty finding a simple figure embedded in a complex design (Figure 7.1), the so-called "Gottschaldt figures." They were also inferior in finding hidden faces in puzzle pictures, and they reported less contrast (of figures differing in brightness). Thus there seems substantial ground for asserting that these individuals have a perceptual style which characterizes them in many situations.[2]

How could this affect broader aspects of personality? We think at once of the probability that the levelers will overgeneralize from past experiences to new events; they will "see" father and mother in adults they meet, will find it difficult to judge new persons and events independently of similarities to past encounters. It is interesting to note that therapists, describing patients in the leveling group, used terms such as "passive, dependent, self-abasement, exaggerated need for nurture and succor." Ultimately we may find that this perceptual style gets established as a result of child-mother interaction. At present any such generalization would be premature.

Rigidity. Klein's leveling-sharpening dimension looks very much like a variable which other psychologists have called rigidity. Pullen (1952) used

[2] Deutscher (1955) has also verified the consistent nature of the leveling-sharpening dimension.

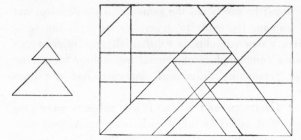

Fig. 7.1 The embedded-figures task. This task, devised by Gottschaldt, requires that the person locate the simple figure at left in the complex figure at right. A test using many of these has been employed in studies of perceptual style.

tests involving awareness of changes in color and in shape which gave results paralleling those reported by Klein. Luchins (1951) describes studies in which the *Einstellung* test has been used in personality research. In this test the *S* is given a series of problems which can be solved only by a given approach; later he gets test problems which can be solved by a much simpler method. Often the person ignores the rather obvious simple technique and continues to use the cumbersome prior method. The resemblance to the Klein variable is clear. Although no appropriate data are available, it seems safe to predict that levelers will show rigidity on the Einstellung test.[3]

Categorizing Attitude. Still another perceptual phenomenon seems to be related to leveling-sharpening. This is the kind of categorizing shown by the person. Gardner (1953) presented his subjects with a large number of miniature objects and asked each person to classify these into groups that belonged together. Some *S*s looked for very broad categories and divided the objects into a few groups. Others tended to stick fairly close to the distinctive features of each object, and thus used a large number of groups or categories. Further tests suggested that those using broad categories were levelers and those using rather specific classifications resembled the sharpeners. Here again we find evidence for a broad, general aspect of personality affecting the person's way of dealing with a variety of emotion-arousing, environmental stimuli. And, as suggested earlier, we suspect that persons in the leveling group are those who fail to observe differences among individuals, who have a few broad categories into which people fit.

Fiedler's Work on Assumed Similarity. A suggestive lead for extension of these studies to perception of other persons comes from the work of Fiedler (1958) on leadership. Fiedler has found that effective leaders differ from ineffective leaders on a measure which he calls "assumed similarity." If we ask a leader to describe his best coworker and his poorest coworker, we get an index of how discriminating the leader is. If he describes these two as

[3] The underlying factor which seems to run through these measures of perceptual style is a difference between scanning the immediately present cues and scanning the memory trace of prior experience. The person who shows leveling in Klein's sense, or rigidity in Pullen's sense, is continuing to be dominated by the first, or at least the early, items in the series. When the physical stimulus changes, he does not become aware of the change because his percept derives its attributes primarily from the memory image.

very much alike, he shows high "assumed similarity of opposites." If he differentiates them sharply, his assumed-similarity score is low. Interestingly enough, the effective leader seems to be the one who makes the discriminatory judgments. We are tempted to assume that these individuals are sharpeners in Klein's terminology; certainly the others, exaggerating similarity and denying differences, behave like the levelers.

Unfortunately, these leads have not yet been explored. Over the next few years we can anticipate studies to show how these perceptual styles relate to the child's picture of himself and of his environment, to his transfer of emotion from an original cue to somewhat similar objects, and to his generalization from persons to groups and institutions. A chronic problem in the psychology of personality arises from the fact that two children may have apparently the same objective traumatic experience, yet one shows widespread disturbance, and the other shows few generalized effects of the occurrence. An important factor here, we suggest, is that levelers will show extensive generalization from a fear or frustration to other situations, while sharpeners restrict the emotion to the original event or keep it within narrow bounds. Careful research is needed, of course, to verify this hypothesis.

Intolerance of Instability and Ambiguity. Klein has described a second perceptual dimension which he has called "resistance to instability." He first encountered it in using the apparent-movement experiment. (Two lights are flashed in succession; most people see the light as moving through space.) Some individuals seem to resist the perception of motion in this situation; they *know* that two cues are involved, and they are unwilling to let them merge into an illusory single moving light. A variety of visual stimuli gave similar differences in resistance to perceiving movement. Klein and Schlesinger (1951) showed that the persons resisting instability in this experiment also resisted opportunities to perceive movement in the Rorschach test. The perceptual attitude is thus general, not limited to the laboratory test situation.

Intolerance of Ambiguity. Frenkel-Brunswik (1951) became interested in the problem of perceptual attitudes as a result of her participation in the work on the "authoritarian personality" (see Chapter 11). In that research it appeared important that some people could consciously admit to having both love and hate for their parents, or could concede that a person might be both good and bad—as contrasted with persons who had to see everything as black or white, all good or all bad. She decided to test for tolerance of ambiguity in a strictly perceptual sense by presenting pictures in series which gradually changed from one percept to another (e.g., cat to dog). The *Ss* who were classed as "intolerant of ambiguity" were those who held onto the original percept for a considerable time, then switched to the other (were unwilling to admit that the picture might be either object). These individuals were found to overidealize their parents, but gave distinct suggestions of hidden hostility in indirect ways. Frenkel-Brunswik held that these person-

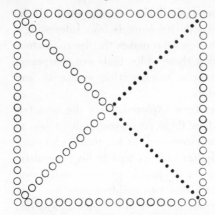

Fig. 7.2 Closure-test figure. S was first shown the entire figure (cross within square); later, at very fast exposures, figures with one or more lines missing, e.g., the two right-hand diagonals. Closure was indicated if S drew a figure indicating that he "saw" the missing lines.

alities tend toward extremes in their emotional reactions as well as in their perceptual style. For them it was more important to have a clear picture than a correct one, if correct meant accepting a confused, fuzzy, uncertain state.

Anxiety and Closure. These observations lead appropriately to a consideration of the phenomenon of closure. This term refers to the fact that when a cue indicative of part of a familiar percept is presented, we unconsciously tend to fill it out and "see" the entire object. Moffitt (1953) showed that, under anxiety stress, Ss manifest closure to a significantly heightened degree. For example, in one of his tests students were shown a design such as a cross inside a square (Figure 7.2).

In subsequent exposures they saw at brief exposures designs which might be complete or might have some lines omitted. Those tested under anxiety filled in more of the missing lines. This effect has been confirmed by Korchin and Basowitz (1954) and other investigators.[4]

If we now suppose that children with conflicts of feeling about their parents suffer more from anxiety than other children, we might speculate that they would show the tendency found by Frenkel-Brunswik, i.e., to modify an ambiguous figure to make it fit something familiar. The anxious person passing a cemetery at midnight may transform a vague blur into a clearly outlined human figure; similarly, in an ambiguous social situation, he may see completely good or completely bad people, thus increasing his own feeling of security. When all the world is made up of black and white, sharp distinctions, decisions are easy; no anxiety is aroused about the danger of making a mistake. Thus it appears that this perceptual style may be effective in avoiding conflicts for the individual.

Figure-Ground Effects in Perception. The third and last of the distinctive perceptual styles to be discussed here may be called field-analytical

---

[4] It is probable that the extreme reactions found in anxiety states may also reflect perception. Kamenetzky (1955) had his subjects make ratings of two ambiguous personality sketches under nonanxiety and anxiety conditions. Persons who were anxious made the same kinds of judgments, but in more extreme form, as compared to the nonanxious subjects. This may be essentially the same as closure—that is, the subject sees only extremes and becomes less aware of intermediate degrees. If a person often experiences anxiety in childhood, then, he may acquire a consistent tendency to see everyone in black and white terms, to make sharp distinctions among people.

versus field-dependent perception. The gestalt psychologists fifty or more years ago called attention to the fact that all perceiving involves structuring of the phenomenal field as figure and ground. And various German psychologists called attention to the fact that some persons seem more analytical in their mode of perceiving, others more "synthetic," more influenced by the background. (An excellent review of these early studies has been published by Granger, 1953.) A major contribution to this aspect of perceptual style was made by Witkin and his coworkers (1954).

The Witkin research led to identification of a dimension of perceptual style varying from "field-analytical" to "field-dependent." The field-analytical mode of perceiving focuses on the figure and resists the influence of the ground. Field-dependent perceiving is markedly modified by variations in the background. Tested individuals vary in their tendency to be field-analytical or field-dependent, but—and this is more important for us—a given individual's perceptual style tends to remain constant over a variety of test situations. In the rod-frame test, S was placed in a dark room where he could see a luminous rod surrounded by a luminous square frame. With the frame tilted out of the vertical, he was asked to set the rod to the true vertical. In some cases this was complicated by seating him in a chair tilted the same way as, or opposite to, the frame. Another task called for a similar judgment of the vertical in a small room tilted off the horizontal. He was also required to set the room to the true vertical. Another test involved the Gottschaldt embedded figures, in which a simple figure is shown and then must be found where it is concealed within a complex figure (see Figure 7.1). The "field-analytical" were not disturbed by the tilted visual framework and could find the embedded figure easily, whereas the "field-dependent" subjects had great difficulty with both tasks.

Witkin points out that a perceptual style of such general applicability as this one must necessarily have extensive implications for personality. It affects the person's percept of himself, his views of others, and his adjustment to situations. Witkin feels that the main difference between his field-analytical and field-dependent cases is the difference between active and passive personalities. In intensive studies of persons with extreme perceptual styles, he finds differences in self-image, in relations with others, and especially in conformity and submission to authority. Reference will be made to these points in subsequent chapters. Our concern here is only to emphasize the role of the perceptual mode. The field-analytical person "keeps his eye on the ball"; he focuses on what is for him the important issue. Thus he is likely to be less distracted by irrelevant stimuli or to diffuse his efforts unnecessarily. Such differences, like those cited earlier for intolerance of ambiguity and for leveling-sharpening, must be expected to show up in many aspects of behavior. Consequently they make major contributions to the unity and consistency of personality.

Consistency in Defense Mechanisms. The term "perceptual style" should probably be limited to such consistencies as have been detected by the procedures described above—consistencies in the way a person relates himself to the world of objects through perception. Perceptual styles, then, would include leveling-sharpening, intolerance of ambiguity, and field-analytical versus field-dependent styles.

It is difficult, however, to separate such uniformities in perceiving from others. We noted, in the preceding chapter, that the term "perceptual defense" has been used to identify the phenomenon of protecting oneself against certain unpleasant stimuli by blocking them out. If now it can be shown that some persons consistently use perceptual defense in a wide variety of situations, we can hardly confine this phenomenon to the category of a defense mechanism (which relates usually to a specific threat or conflict).

Eriksen (1952) and Miller (1954), among others, have demonstrated that people behave consistently in their use of perceptual defense. Some of Miller's subjects uniformly failed to recognize stimuli which had been associated with failure on an assigned task. Others were consistently alert to these failure stimuli. The two groups showed differences in other measures which fitted this observation. DeLucia (1953) also reports data which indicate this tendency to use "defense" in a consistent manner.

It seems likely, therefore, that the category of perceptual style will have to be expanded to include such consistent features of personality as this tendency to block out unpleasant stimuli. Would such a perceptual style influence personality in a significant way? Miller comments, "A person who is relatively unresponsive to stimuli which are unpleasant or dangerous would be apt to behave impulsively and would be unable to foresee possible unfavorable consequences of his actions" [p. 247]. Thus, like the other modes of perceiving we have described, this one too can be expected to account for important personality variables appearing in a wide variety of situations. This point will be developed in later chapters.

RESPONSE STYLE

As the foregoing studies indicate, the individual tends to develop characteristic modes of perceptual functioning, which we have designated "perceptual styles," and which are relatively independent of content. That is, the data indicate that this style affects the manner of perceiving of various categories of events, and is not related to specific preferences, aversions, or emotional states.

Evidence has also been accumulating for the existence of certain kinds of response styles. These include not only fairly obvious kinds of generalized action patterns, such as gestures, but also more subtle consistencies, such as a tendency to agree with statements regardless of content. Let us examine first the evidence regarding the simpler kinds of response consistency.

Stability and Lability of Movement Patterns. Just as the leveling-sharpening dimension indicates that people vary in specificity of perceiving, so Luria (1932) has shown that variations occur in precision of movement control. Figure 7.3 shows an illustration of his data. It is apparent that his "stable type" gives precise, regular responses; his "labile type," on the other hand, responds to stimuli other than the correct one, gives variable strengths of response, and so on.

This is important for the development of styles in behavior. If, as has been suggested, the basic units of personality are such emotional responses as fearing, loving, raging, seeking, etc., then variations, inconsistencies, and irregularities in such emotional responses must contribute to the development of that distinctive pattern which is the unique individual.

Freeman's "Discharge Types." Luria's work was based on the striped muscles and assumed that we can detect personality differences by the manner in which a response is made, even though different persons emit the same response. Freeman (1948) proposed a view which goes further than

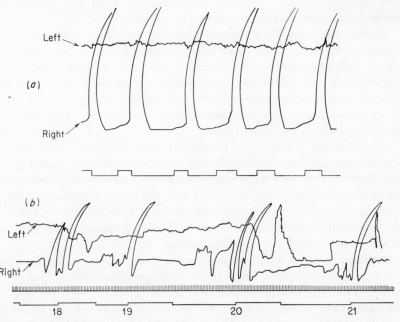

Fig. 7.3 Luria's reactive-stable and reactive-labile types. *a*, record of a stable subject. Left-hand record uniform; right hand gives smooth reactions to stimulus words. *b*, record of a labile subject. Left hand fluctuates in pressure, right hand makes uneven reactions, often when no word presented. Numbers represent time in minutes. (From Luria, 1932.)

this. He suggested that two persons may have the same inner tension (desire, emotion, etc.) but may choose different channels of expression. He defined four "discharge types," which we would call "response styles," which may serve to identify different kinds of personality. Although Freeman's view is not supported by as much data as would be desirable, it does fit with a good deal of evidence on the expression of personality. His studies reveal distinctive differences in the way persons can respond to the same stimulating conditions.

Active-motor Discharge Type. One consistent way of behaving, he says, is characterized by the use of the striped muscles. In an extreme form this would be represented by the individual who uses his fists instead of his brains, or more precisely, by a person who goes into overt action with relatively little thought or verbalization.

Vocal Discharge Type. A second response style is that of using the language mechanism. Such individuals talk a great deal in dealing with problems, striving to attain goals, relieving anxieties and frustrations. In some degree this response style is more favorable to personal adjustment than is the active-motor pattern, since the latter may often lead to acting impulsively without sizing up the situation. If, however, the "vocal type" person talks endlessly and does nothing, adjustment is not improved.

Somatic Discharge Type. Instead of acting or talking, some people stew viscerally; their tensions find an outlet in stomach disturbances, heart, and blood-vessel responses, and the like. Freeman seems to suggest that persons whose active and verbal responses have been punished may block such outlets and hence may respond chiefly with visceral turmoil. He also implies that this response style is associated with the development of psychosomatic ills, such as ulcers and hypertension.

Ideomotor Discharge Type. Finally, Freeman suggests a response style which is characterized chiefly by fantasy and daydreaming. Although he does not clearly say so, this pattern is probably associated to some extent with verbalizing, but under conditions such that the person does not feel free to speak to others; it may also go with the visceral response style, since the inner muscular disturbances may very well cue off thoughts of strong emotional coloring—and vice versa, of course.

It should be noted that Freeman does not imply that these discharge types occur on an all-or-nothing basis. There are degrees from high to low on each of these, and very few persons could properly be called "clear-cut types" in any sense. (For a further discussion of the complications one gets into with a type theory of personality, see Chapter 12.) The same individual may utilize each of these response mechanisms on different occasions. His suggestion simply is that here we find another source of personality organization and consistency. We may ask, Why does each person impress us as having a continuing, unified, unique personality? Perceptual constancy contributes to this;

habit is a concept which helps us understand personality consistency; the notion of response style, cropping up as a characteristic way of doing things under varied circumstances, also helps us in this regard.

Variations in Tension Level. Closely akin to the response style which Freeman called somatic or visceral is the notion of general tension level. Duffy (1957) has reported on several investigations in which the same person undergoes a variety of arousal or frustrating situations. Muscular and physiological data on tension (grip pressure, heart rate, blood pressure, etc.) are collected in each situation. When these data are correlated and factor-analyzed, she finds a strong common factor which is best described as an index of general tension level. Some persons are generally relaxed; if they have to act, they are capable of mobilizing energy promptly, responding, and then calming down again. Others show tension effects in muscles and viscera for some time.[5]

GRAPHIC RESPONSE STYLES

The work of Duffy and Freeman on generalized tension levels suggests that diagnostic information about personality might be obtained through examination of handwriting and drawing, forms of behavior which are quite complex and which seem often to reveal evidence of tension. The results here are tantalizing—not nearly so revealing of personality differences as the graphologists claim, but successful enough to encourage continuing research.

The Allport-Vernon Studies. One of the earliest investigations to use modern precautions in the study of graphic response style is that of Allport and Vernon (1932). In this research, persons were asked to write (using either hand), copy geometrical designs (with pencil, for the hands, and in a sandbox with the toe), and carry on various routine activities, in some cases without knowledge that they were observed. From an analysis of these interrelationships, three "factors" or dimensions of response style were identified.

[5] We are concerned, in this connection, with the uniformities shown by a person in many situations. Interesting facts are also brought out by a study of how tension level may be specific to a given context. Thus Malmo et al. (1953) found that headache-prone patients not only showed higher general tension level, but also developed tension in the neck muscles to a greater extent than other patients. The tendency to channel tension into this specific muscle group seemed to have some connection with the chronic headaches. Another interesting observation, by Malmo et al. (1956), shows that certain ideas may be coupled with certain muscle groups. A divorced woman, age thirty-three, was being interviewed about her problems while electrical action potentials were recorded from different muscle groups. When she was talking chiefly about her hostility to her ex-husband (and other people), the main electrical activity was in the arm muscles; when she was discussing her sexual adjustments, the main activity was localized in leg muscles. We may thus assume that, not only are there broad response styles such as those suggested by Freeman and Duffy, but also there are more specific reponse styles, restricted groups of muscles which are the preferred outlets for specific emotions or desires. The individual personality, then, is characterized to some degree by such unique ways of responding.

1. *Areal Group Factor.* Some persons spread their movements over a large area; others take up little space. This trend showed itself in movements of both arms and also of the legs and feet. It was somewhat negatively related to speed of movement. Presumably it is connected to "expansive" gestures (but not necessarily to the kind of personality often referred to as expansive).

2. *Centrifugal Factor.* A second group factor was identified as "centrifugal" because it involved chiefly movements toward or away from the body. Persons high on this variable tended to overestimate distances from the body, but underestimate distances toward it. They also underestimated weights (these were pulled toward the subject, hence the result is consistent with underestimating distances). Younger subjects seemed to be more "centrifugal" than older ones.

3. *Emphasis Factor.* A third group factor involved pressures, voice intensity, and movement during speech. Allport and Vernon note that pressure alone was not enough to identify this variable: "Mere physical pressure or tension would seem to be significant only as part of a wider and more psychological tendency to make emphatic movements" [p. 115]. Thus it would appear that a response style which might be characterized as vigorous or emphatic is the variable involved here.

Studies of Tempo in Personal Style. Allport and Vernon had anticipated that they would find personalities characterized by distinctive tempo or speed of response—the quick, impulsive pattern versus the slow, cautious, inhibited pattern. As noted above, their data led to a somewhat different conclusion: that speed measures become significant chiefly when related to area or direction of movement. There have, however, been numerous studies which reveal significant consistencies within persons as to tempo of movement. Space limits us to a mention of only a few such researches.

Bieshuevel and Pitt (1955) started with a theory of a balance between primary function (quick, impulsive action) and secondary function (delay, perseveration, inhibition, lag of neural processes). They obtained a large number of measures of motor tempo, as well as some perceptual indexes, from subjects who were observed and rated on a variety of personal attributes. Analysis of the data indicated two factors: freedom from inertia, or speed of closure, which seemed to be mostly a perceptual factor; and motor speed itself. The ratings indicated that, in general, the personality was judged to have characteristics which fitted with the tempo measures.

Rimoldi (1951) repeated many of the measures used by Allport and Vernon, but concentrated particularly on the question of personal tempo. He found little evidence that an individual has one uniform style which is reflected in his speed of making many kinds of movements. Rather his subjects showed a preferred tempo for each of several categories; for example his factor *A* included speed in bending the body, arm movements, and leg movements. Others factors were: preferred tempo for *small* movements; drawing with the foot; drawing with the hands; verbal speed; reaction time to definite stimuli; and some not easily interpreted.

It is interesting to note that Rimoldi confirms the Allport-Vernon observation as regards correlations of hand and foot drawings, and also for tapping with hand and with foot. However, the preferred tempo for *movement* does not agree with the preferred tempo for *stimulation*, e.g., by a metronome.

Graphology. It will be noted that we have said nothing in these pages about the use of handwriting and drawing as devices for revealing "the total personality." Rather we have dealt with graphic movements as indexes of sharply restricted aspects of personality, in the form of "response style."

There are grounds for believing that such activities as handwriting, sketching, and doodling may reflect emotional states and even enduring character trends. Any complex response must be affected by processes going on elsewhere in the organism. This statement, unfortunately, does not get us very far if we do not know what kinds of effects to expect and what kinds of deductions to make from these effects when they occur.

The claims of graphologists to diagnose complex personality patterns have mostly been rejected when tested by modern methods. Eysenck (1948) reports that he gave a set of handwriting samples to a graphologist; some samples came from neurotic patients in a military hospital, the others from surgical cases with no psychiatric problem. The graphologist proved incapable of separating the two groups at better than a chance level. More striking, in some ways, is the anecdote reported by Roback (1957) regarding his correspondence with Sigmund Freud. Roback submitted a sample of Freud's handwriting (without identification) to Robert Saudek, a noted graphologist, who prepared a "personality sketch" based solely on the writing. Roback then sent the sketch to Freud "for validation." Freud, who might be expected to know his own personality fairly well, rejected the whole thing, calling it a "sorry joke." Most graphologists, of course, are skillful at giving glib generalities which offend no one and create an illusion of validity (cf. Stagner, 1958, for an illustration of this illusion).

The Mira "Myokinetic Psychodiagnosis." Trying to bring some control to the studies of graphologists and others working with graphic expression, the Spanish psychologist Mira (1940) developed a standardized series of graphic tasks which he calls "myokinetic psychodiagnosis." This phrase suggests the diagnosis of personality through muscular movement.

The subject sits before a drawing board, blindfolded or shut off by a screen so that he cannot watch his hands. He must keep his wrist off the board, thus giving the arm and shoulder muscles a chance to determine the results. He draws 10 lines, which are to be of a given length, with each hand, in the following ways: from left to right, from right to left, outward from the body, and inward toward the body; then, with the board in a vertical plane, upwards and downwards.

The analysis of results involves finding the center of the first line drawn, and erecting a perpendicular which cuts across the succeeding nine lines. The centers of these lines are located, and distance from the intersection of the perpendicular is measured. Some subjects will keep "center of gravity" pretty close to this line; others show a steady drift above or below. Such a drift indicates a persistent muscular tension in the direction of shift.

On the basis of abnormal cases (manics, depressives, suicidal, and paranoid patterns), Mira believes he can identify certain deep tendencies in the personality. For instance, a marked drift *away* from the body, in the case of lines drawn to and from the body, was associated with aggressive attitudes toward others, while an *inward* drift was associated with self-directed aggression and suicidal trends. Subjects who, when drawing in the vertical plane, moved the center of gravity upward, were pretty consistently found to be elated, manic cases; those whose shift was downward were characteristically depressed.

Mira's observations were based on extreme cases (hospital patients mostly) and were largely impressionistic. A careful investigation using his method is that of Talmadge (1958). Talmadge studied a sizable group of subjects and intercorrelated various measures derived from the test in an attempt to locate response styles. As usual, he found that the graphic measures (pencil pressure, length of line drawn, time, etc.) had only modest reliabilities; the average was $+.62$; the range was from .26 to .82. Thus it appears that people are fairly, but not strikingly, consistent in graphic response style.

Similar consistencies were found when he correlated diverse measures of similar performance. He obtained some evidence for a *personal tempo*, or a normal speed of responding which was a fairly dependable characteristic of a person giving different graphic responses. He likewise confirmed the Allport-Vernon data regarding a *pressure* factor, and (with less certainty) their report of an *area* factor.

In some respects the Allport-Vernon study is more satisfying, in that the response styles were demonstrated to operate across a greater variety of muscle groups than in the Talmadge study. However, it seems reasonable to infer that these three kinds of response style may be found in most subjects. The three seem to be independent of each other; fast tempo does not necessarily correlate with either marked pressure or broad space of movement.

The foregoing studies, ranging from simple observations of stability in movement to complex patterns of handwriting and gesture, throw light upon the personality, particuarly as it is seen by others. We emphasized in Chapter 1 that each personality tends to be distinctive, to be recognized by others as a unique pattern. It is obvious that these styles of overt movement contribute in no small degree to that distinctive appearance.

Gestures are particularly important in social perception because of our training to conceal certain kinds of information about ourselves. Each of us develops his mask or *persona* which he wishes to show to others. The child must learn not to speak the truth about a lady's new hat; later, he learns not to reveal the fact that he is annoyed, frightened, or intensely moved in any way. The strongest taboos relate to revealing one's inner passions—loves and hates, rages and anxieties. Verbal censorship is not too difficult. Gestures, on the other hand, may reveal inner emotions because the response mechanism reflects such disturbances readily. Thus, a conversation between two adults may reveal only a smooth façade, whereas observation of expressive movements and vocal inflections indicates strong personality involvement.

Each of us, therefore, comes to watch the gestures of others as a device for penetrating the culturally imposed mask and ascertaining what is underneath. Many of our "meaningless" movements, as Krout (1935) has shown, do have such significance. Mira's finding that elated people exaggerate upward movements, suicidal individuals overdo movements toward the body, etc., would support the view that we can draw some legitimate inferences from these movement patterns. The good judge of personality may very well be the individual who is sensitive to these cues and adept at interpreting them.

Perhaps a caution should also be inserted here. The cues are ambiguous. The picture is blurred; important elements have been cut out by the effort of the individual to conceal his emotions. Thus it is easy for an observer to misinterpret the inner state underlying the mask. Shyness is often confused with snobbishness, and a loud voice may mistakenly be perceived as evidence of self-confidence. A ready smile and a firm handshake do not provide valid indicators of honesty and integrity; indeed, the confidence man and the high-pressure salesman are adept at providing such cues. One should not attempt to make extended interpretations of personality from these gestural patterns.

COMPLEX RESPONSE STYLES

The foregoing illustrations of response style have used quite simple variables, such as variability, expansiveness, and tempo. Let us now consider two examples of more complex response patterns which seem to throw light on the unity and consistency of personality.

The individual may develop a characteristic style, not only in his gestures, or his way of acting out an emotion, but in the manner of relating to his environment and to other people. Let us first consider what has been called a "response set" of conformity, or a tendency to agree with all sorts of statements and persons.

Acquiescence and Conformity. The existence of a response set toward agreement with positive statements has been noted for a long time, and in early discussions of personality measurement the point was often made that it was desirable to try to balance the number of items calling for "yes" and "no" responses in order to avoid bias on this count. Other students of this problem suggested that, since comparisons were being made only within groups, and since all persons responded to all items, the effect of a tendency to agree would cancel out. What this argument ignores is the obvious point that individuals differ in the consistency with which they acquiesce. Some persons seem to find it very difficult to reject any plausibly phrased item, while others reject large numbers. Since there is reason to suppose that acquiescence may be correlated with a variety of personality traits, failure to consider response bias has introduced error into many inventory measures.

F-scale Studies. Interest in the problem of acquiescence as a response set suddenly rose around 1950 with evidence that this bias did correlate substantially with certain aspects of personality. One of these is conformity behavior, or the tendency to modify one's judgments to agree with an opposing majority. The other is the "authoritarian tendency," an aspect of personality to which we shall pay considerable attention in Chapter 11.

Adorno et al. (1950) reported on extensive personality research, beginning with the problem of prejudice and anti-Semitism, but rapidly fanning out into perceptual and motivational problems. In the course of this work they developed the "F scale," or scale for measuring potential fascist attitudes; it has since been utilized in a truly astounding variety of studies. The F scale is composed of 40 statements having the quality of glittering generalizations, such as, "There are two kinds of people: the strong and the weak." It was not long before several researchers noted that the F scale was heavily loaded with items calling for agreement, and that high scorers might only be people with an acquiescent response set, not necessarily a profascist viewpoint. Useful work along this line has been reported by several investigators, including Cohn (1956) and Jackson, Messick, and Solley (1957b). In the latter study, for example, a reversed F scale was prepared by rewriting all items to give exactly the opposite attitudinal slant. F-scale scores correlated $+.45$ with reversed F-scale scores; this can only be interpreted as evidence that some of the subjects were simply agreeing with everything, paying no attention to meaning. (Although it would be defensible to argue that such persons are easily led to agree with fascist propaganda, such research casts grave doubt on the notion that persons scoring high on the F scale have any distinctive prejudices or stereotypes.)

Conformity Behavior. Asch (1952) picked up and modernized an early line of research into the yielding of subjects to majority pressure. Using physical stimuli (such as lines of obviously different length), he subjected individuals to group pressure to give a judgment contradictory to evidence of the senses. (For a description of the experiment, see page 39.) He found that many people, faced by a unanimous majority of five or more, would yield in such a test. It now appears that the same response set of acquiescence may be a variable in such conformity behavior. Linton (1955) has shown that per-sons high on acquiescence (agreeing with many items irrespective of meaning) tend also to yield readily to the majority. And Blake, Helson, and Mouton (1957) have shown that conformity to group pressure behaves like a trait; i.e., it is revealed in a number of different task situations. The correlation of conforming responses in half of these tasks (against the other half) for a group of 90 college men was .87; in other words, persons who yield to social pressure in one situation are very likely to yield in others. Similarly, Janis and Fields (1956) have shown that persons who are easily persuaded by one type of propaganada are easily influenced by other types of material on other issues.

It would be tempting simply to leave this as a response variable and say that some individuals develop a habit of saying "yes," of accepting suggestions made to them, and so on. However, this offers no hypothesis as to why some persons acquire this response set and others do not. It seems plausible to speculate that parental training may be an important variable. Some parents deride or scold their children for venturing an independent judgment, particularly when it proves unsound. Thus the child learns that it is safest to agree (first with adults and authority figures, later with words in print, textbook authors, newspaper writers, etc.). If this hypothesis is correct, persons with a marked acquiescence tendency should be below average on self-confidence. There is some evidence (page 204) to support this speculation.

Deviant Response Set. A second kind of response style which merits attention in this connection is a kind of mirror image of the first, although this does not mean that one can be predicted from the other. If we take any kind of patterned response, such as word associations, answers to inventories, stories on TAT tests, and percepts reported on the Rorschach, we get certain common or modal responses. These presumably reflect the prevalent determinants operating on this group of subjects: their biological make-up, family background, economic and cultural status, etc. In any group, however, there will be a few subjects who give deviant or atypical responses. If the acquiescent response set accounts for some portion of scores on personality measures, it seems probable that deviant response set also accounts for part of the variance.

Berg (1955) proposed the hypothesis in the following terms: "Deviant response patterns tend to be general; hence those deviant behavior patterns which are significant for abnormality and thus regarded as symptoms, are associated with other deviant patterns which are in noncritical areas of behavior and which are not regarded as symptoms of personality aberration" [p. 62]. In other words, Berg is suggesting that a person who shows some deviant responses (hallucinations, delusions of persecution, or less serious distortions) which are readily recognized symptoms of personality breakdown will also show many deviant responses (choices of food, word usage, little trivia of everyday behavior) not identifiable as evidence of disorder, but nonetheless detectable as varying from the group norm.

Berg's work was quickly extended and clarified by Barnes (1956), who showed that it is necessary to break this response set down into its component parts. On the MMPI he found that some subjects gave relatively more "atypical-true" responses, while others gave more "atypical-false" responses. That is, there are some items which are answered "true, this applies to me" by only two or three persons in 100; and some which are denied, marked false, thus rarely. When he segregated persons with a large number of atypical-true responses (people who accepted as self-relevant many items which were usually rejected), he found that they scored high on the *psychotic* scales, such as mania and schizophrenia. Conversely, those with high atypical-false scores (many items rejected which the average person accepts) scored high on the *neurotic* scales such as hysteria and hypochondria.

Starting only with Berg's observation, we might have concluded that persons who, just by chance, develop a few atypical behavior patterns may become slanted toward abnormality. The data by Barnes tend to contradict such a view; if this were a pure response set, there would be no reason to expect a difference between atypical-true and atypical-false subjects. Since such a difference seems fairly well substantiated, it seems necessary to conclude that the abnormality comes first, and the response set develops afterward. The person who develops a distorted perception of himself or of his environment tends toward abnormality; as he practices doing things which deviate from the norm, he may manifest response generalization by developing abnormal responses in areas which are unrelated to his basic personality problem.

SUMMARY

As the individual tries to maintain homeostatic equilibrium, as he seeks goals and avoids dangers, he must make responses. In the ordinary activities, such as walking, talking, and gesturing, one can observe variations which are due to emotions or other inner states, and these variations provide cues to inner process. Response styles develop, and these supply some of the unity and consistency observed in the adult personality.

Similarly, people show distinctive styles of perceiving. Whether these are likewise related to emotional states is less clear, although it appears that the occurrence of anxiety and insecurity to a marked degree in early childhood does predispose to certain ways of perceiving. These perceptual styles have broad significance for the organization of personality because they determine the extent of generalizing from one emotion-arousing experience to another, readiness to modify goals in the face of changing external situations, ability to focus on defined objectives, and other important personality variables.

Little has been done so far to relate these perceptual styles to the response styles. There is some reason to suspect that field dependency in perceptual style is related to conformity-acquiescence on the response side. Most psycholo-

gists today seem disposed to treat the perceptual variables as more fundamental (in the sense of determining aspects of the total personality), but further research is needed before such a conclusion is justified.

SUGGESTIONS FOR READING

Most of the material summarized here has not yet found its way into book
form. George Klein has described his work in a chapter entitled "Cognitive control
and motivation" in Lindzey's *Assessment of human motives;* and also in "The
personal world through perception" in the volume edited by Blake and Ramsey,
Perception: an approach to personality. Allport and Vernon's *Studies in expressive
movement* is still one of the few books discussing gestures as objects of scientific
study.

CHAPTER 8

Traits

No personality, not even that of the most disorganized schizophrenic, is a mere random assortment of perceptions, emotions, and responses. The preceding chapter has brought together evidence for certain sources of uniformity: consistencies within the individual as regards his habitual ways of perceiving, his gestural style, and his physiological response patterns. Those components of style, however, said nothing about uniformity with respect to classes of stimuli, objects of emotion, goals sought to meet the aspirations of the individual.

We turn now to a consideration of organized patterns within the personality which have definite content. We shall use the term "trait" to refer to a consistent feature of personality which has some emotional or ideational content, in opposition to the term "style," which was relatively pure process without any reference, either external or internal. The term "character trait" (Chapter 10) will identify those generalized patterns of behavior and experience which relate directly to moral and ethical issues. "Attitudes" (Chapter 11) will be used with respect to concepts having political, economic, and similar external reference.

From the point of view of social stimulus value, we can readily show that trait uniformities are recognizable. We speak of John as being "sociable," and this goes considerably beyond any specific response such as talking pleasantly with people. It suggests a way of perceiving, a collection of emotional attitudes, and a high probability of certain kinds of behavior. It is not necessarily erected on any specific perceptual style, although it would appear that "leveling" would foster sociability; the assumption implied is that pleasant experiences with some persons transfer in a relatively undifferentiated manner to most human beings. (As soon as any significant class of persons is differentiated and rejected, the term "sociable" is acceptable only with qualifications and restrictions.)

Trait and Temperament. The concept of trait, as it is used here, will in considerable degree be a subcategory within temperament. We have noted (Chapter 5) that relative frequency and intensity of emotions constitute the temperament of an individual. The emphasis in that context was upon the establishment of emotional expectancies relative to specific persons or objects; i.e., affection for mother, fear of strange situations, and so on. We could, however, see the possibility of different "types" of temperament, based upon one or two of the innate feelings, pleasantness, unpleasantness, excitement, and depression. Diamond (1957) suggests that it is appropriate to select out affiliative tendency (fondness for people and seeking contact with them), aggressiveness, fearfulness, and inhibitory control as major examples of these temperamental tendencies.

Common and Unique Traits. To suggest, however, that all persons will manifest the same traits runs counter to evidence already presented. Each person is unique, not only by virtue of an inherited physiological organism which will not be exactly like that of anyone else, but more importantly, by virtue of his unique pattern of experiences which induces perceptions distinctively his own. It seems probable, therefore, that some traits are special cases for particular people and do not exist in the general population.

In contrast to this position, it must be noted that all of us have certain experiences in common, and that we have perceptual worlds which (for normals at least) are similar enough that we can communicate and transact affairs with one another. Hence it seems safe to assume that certain *common traits* can be identified in a population having a fairly uniform cultural milieu. The restriction is deliberate; it is a safe assumption that traits common to Western civilization may be barely recognizable or nonexistent in a primitive culture.

THE NATURE OF TRAITS

A trait, as described above, would necessarily have to be generalized. In fact, if we look back to our operational bases of estimating traits (Chapters 2 and 3), we see that even the units from which scores are derived have the quality of generalization. Suppose we take the item, "Do you daydream frequently?" This does not say, "Are you daydreaming right now of inheriting a fortune and living a life of ease?" The item as it appears in a test asks about a whole category of experiences which bear the label "daydreams." But this, to yield a trait score, must be related to many other kinds of generalized responses, each of which is called an *indicator*. We concede the existence of a trait only when a number of indicators point in the same direction, for reasons which will be amplified below.

Traits as Functional Unities. One of the major defects of popular and literary psychology is that "traits" are coined right and left with no consideration of logic. So, if someone seems very indifferent to the sufferings of another person, he is said to be "hardhearted." But actually his indifference may have been based on a dislike for the other individual, not on a generalized pattern at all.

The primary consideration in respect to any assumed trait is that it be shown to possess functional unity. This means that there must be different indicators of the trait which vary together, or which are manifested in a consistent manner. It was for this reason that the question of reliability received so much attention in Chapters 2 and 3. Reliability refers either to consistency (different parts of the measuring device give consistent results for this person on this trait) or stability (the person gets the same trait score on repeated measurement). Either offers some evidence of functional unity.

In addition to reliability, one can demonstrate the unity of a trait by converging evidence of different kinds. Thus, if a person is rated "shy" by his peers, describes himself as "seclusive" on an inventory, and tells stories on the TAT which indicate anxiety about being in a group, we have evidence of unity in his inner structure.

Factor Analysis. As was noted earlier (page 31), psychologists today make extensive use of factor analysis as a method for demonstrating the existence of functional unity. It is thus important for us to examine this method in somewhat greater detail.

We start with the fact that two characteristics, *A* and *B*, may be observed to vary together. This is the simple fact of correlation. If *A* and *B* increase together or decrease together, the correlation is positive; if one decreases as the other increases, the correlation is negative.

The concept of a factor, or an underlying dimension, is used to explain a set of correlations. If we correlated the height and weight of college men, we would get a coefficient of about +.60. We can say that this correlation is due to body size. If we included length of arm, length of leg, chest circumference, etc., we would still get evidence of a single factor, body size.

In more complex situations, more than one underlying dimension is necessary to explain the correlations. If college students are compared on course grades, high correlations are found between performances in various courses. If measures of intelligence and time spent studying are included, it can be shown that some of the variation in grades is due mainly to intelligence, some is due mainly to effort. In this case we can say that two factors are necessary to explain the correlations. A factor, then, is an underlying dimension which helps us to understand a series of correlations.

The examples cited are instances in which we knew ahead of time what the major dimensions were. It is, however, possible by the method of factor analysis to determine how many factors are needed to explain a certain network of correlation coefficients, and how much of the variation between persons can be attributed to each factor. Cattell (1950), Diamond (1957), and Guilford (1959), making extensive use of factor-analytic data, have published books on personality.

In later pages we shall often make use of the phrase "factor loading." Essentially this means the extent to which variation in a certain measure can be ascribed to the underlying factor. Thus Cattell (1950) gives the following example: responses to the statement, "I want to spend somewhat more on drinking and smoking than I am now able to do" have a loading of .56 on a narcissism factor [p. 174]. This means that there were a number of items in the instrument which related to self-indulgence, and that narcissism (self-love) emerged as a factor running through these items; further, the item quoted correlated +.56 with this factor, hence a great deal of the variance in responses to the item seems attributable to variation in the underlying narcissistic dimension.

It is not always appropriate to think of factors as causes. We have cited (page 31) Thurstone's study of boxes, which led to three factors, length, width, and depth. A set of correlations among locations on the earth's surface would reveal two factors, latitude and longitude. In such cases it is clear that the factor does not cause the measured relationship; it merely provides the minimum number of measures for defining precisely what we are studying. In other instances the factor may have a causal role. Cattell (1950) holds that with adequate data, factor analysis could reveal the causal effectiveness of different influences upon personality development. In this chapter we shall be concerned with factors mainly in the descriptive sense. An analysis of the interrelations of various inventory scores, or of various behavior ratings, may lead to the identification of variables which go together, or form what we have called a "functional unity." Determining why this particular unity exists may be a matter for much more extensive research.

Traits as Abstractions. It should be clear, then, that we do not directly observe a trait in another person. We observe specific indicators, acts, and verbalizations. From these we generalize. If you see John bossing others on several occasions, you say that one of his traits is dominance. If you see him in several situations lose his temper with slight provocation, you say that he has a trait of irritability. In essence you have observed a correlation, a functional consistency across situations. Mentally we may even engage in a rough kind of factor analysis, abstracting from several patterns a hidden tendency which seems to explain or describe John's behavior.

What is important here is that one does not observe the trait directly. In Chapter 1 we pointed out that personality is not an object open to immediate observation—it is not justified to think of a personality which can be extracted from the body by physical or chemical means, dissected, and analyzed. The word is merely a convenient collective term for certain psychological functions, just as water pressure is a convenient way of identifying certain effects of water, but not something separable from water. We now wish to emphasize the same idea in connection with traits. Too many psychologists write as if a trait were *an effective cause of behavior*. This is quite incorrect and misleading. Jane's trait of dominance does not cause her to order her girl friends to do certain things; but, given the observation that she is characterized by a trait of dominance, we can predict that she will boss others when she finds it possible. The trait, then, should be considered *descriptive*, but not *explanatory*. The causes of human behavior, in so far as we can identify them, are the motives which impel us to act and the environment which shapes our actions.

Traits May Lack Objective Reference. Many of the early studies in this field seemed to disprove the existence of traits. In most such cases, if not all, the difficulty arose from the assumption that the trait had to be consistent in terms of the objective situation. For example, it was supposed that "speed of movement" would be a trait; a person would tend to make finger, hand, arm, and other movements at the same relative tempo. What was ignored was that the consistency of responses depends on their *meaning to the individual.* A girl who writes rapidly may draw slowly. The one is due to her desire to obtain maximum expression of ideas per unit time, the other to her desire to achieve a high level of artistry per unit time. Responses which seem, on objective reference, to be inconsistent may be consistent in an inner frame of reference.

Traits as Higher Order Habits. It is conceivable that we might extend the concept of habit to cover the kind of personality organization which we have designated as a trait. This is the interpretation favored by Guthrie. He illustrates with the orderliness displayed by a typical sailor.

The sailor on a sailing ship, living in cramped quarters and dependent in emergencies on having available and ready the gear of his ship, and living with other sailors, is gradually forced to acquire a large repertoire of acts that keep things ship-shape. He has been punished or admonished in the presence of disorder, unready gear, uncoiled ropes, unsecured hatches, until the sight of disorder motivates him strongly to react, and the reactions that remove the disorder remain as his characteristic behavior in its presence.[1]

Whether disorder can be a stimulus for a habit is a matter about which we might debate. It is certainly far from the kind of specific stimulus-response sequence ordinarily designated by the term "habit"—such as coiling up rope whenever it is seen lying uncoiled. Disorder could set off habits of orderliness only through some process of *abstracting a relationship* in the situation and verbalizing about it to oneself. The essential element of the situation, then, would be subjective, not objective.

What Guthrie's theory really calls for is an objective "identical element" running through the various situations in which the trait is manifest. Suppose that a child were beaten by a red-haired bully, injured by a red automobile, frightened by a woman in a bright red coat, and scolded severely for soiling his mother's red scarf. He might develop a generalized pattern of fearing and avoiding any situation involving red. The trouble with this view is that the

---

[1] Guthrie, in Hunt (1944), p. 61. Reprinted by permission of The Ronald Press Company.

uniformities we find in traits reside not in objective elements, but in subjective meanings.

Traits as Mental Sets. Another interpretation of traits which deserves serious consideration is that the trait is an elaborate mental set—a readiness to respond to any of a variety of situations in a consistent way. An obvious illustration is that of the irritable man, whose anger responses are set to go off on almost no provocation at all. Cason (1930) has shown that there is a generalized tendency for some people to be annoyed easily, others only upon considerable provocation.

Another example would be that of the "professional" patriot, the so-called "100 per cent American." He may react with vigorous resentment to the word "socialism," to the sight of a volume of Marx's writings, to the CIO, to a neighborhood consumer cooperative, and to the suggestion that Americans subject their collective ego to international law. The objective similarity in these situations is nonexistent, but he is mentally set to oppose anything which in his eyes is un-American.

The interpretation of this behavior in terms of set is somewhat difficult, because the response is likely to vary considerably. In one case he may write a letter to the editor; in another, he speaks passionately to people; in a third, he throws the book into the ash can; in a fourth, he merely explodes viscerally. "Mental set" should imply readiness for a particular response.

Traits as Frames of Reference. At various points in previous chapters we have stated the proposition that personality is an organized system of beliefs and expectancies about the environment and the individual's relation to it. In terms of such an approach, it seems plausible to define traits as *organized frames of reference;* otherwise, as established scales for evaluating environmental situations.

Consider again the instance of Guthrie's orderly sailor. Instead of saying that the sailor acquires a habit of picking up loose tools or coiling rope, of mopping up slippery spots on the deck, and of fastening down large movable objects, it would seem simpler to infer the development of a frame of reference. Perhaps the sailor has been punished for leaving a tool in the wrong place. Later he is hurt when the ship rolls and a loose carton slides against his leg. Then he hears another man criticized for failing to coil up rope. These experiences form the basis for *evaluating situations,* on a scale from good to dangerous (anxiety arousing), according to the amount of disorder, size of the objects involved, cutting edges present, and so on. The intensity of his response and the amount of effort that he will expend to restore order will be related to his judgment of danger, not necessarily, of course, to objectively verifiable danger.

The superpatriot has evolved a frame of reference for certain situations, on a scale ranging from good (American) to dangerous (un-American). The standards that he develops through experience and reflection will determine the range of situations judged to be un-American and anxiety-arousing. His responses will be determined partly by the objective situation, but mostly by his judgment of the degree of "un-Americanism" involved.

Finally, let us consider a more generalized trait, such as dominance. We suggest that the individual has certain experiences in which he has achieved happiness when leading, but has had other experiences in which discomfort resulted from submitting to leadership. He gradually evolves a scale for judging situations, ranging from good (his dominance unquestioned) to dangerous or bad (his submission to others required). His behavior then will be related not to the external situation but to his appraisal of it.

We need not necessarily consider the interpretation of traits as frames of reference to exclude either the habit-system or the mental-set interpretation. Each in its own way may help the student to grasp the functional character of traits. The frame-of-reference idea appears, however, more inclusive and less subject to exception than the other interpretations.

The Trait Continuum. It is important to remember that differences between individuals with regard to a given trait are matters of degree rather than of kind. We do not have sharp classifications of people as talkative and taciturn, seclusive and sociable, emotional and unemotional. Rather we have a *continuous gradient* of differences from one extreme to the other (cf. Chapter 1). As an illustration, consider the distribution of cases on the trait of rhathymia (Figure 1.1, page 13). There is a continuous range of scores from 5 (very inhibited) to 79 (very carefree). The largest number of individuals are in the center of the range; they have some tendencies toward each pattern of behavior. The important point, however, is that there is no score anywhere on the scale where we can cut off clearly inhibited cases without being arbitrary; similarly, there is no dividing point for the carefree group. *Trait organization is not an all-or-nothing affair;* it varies by degrees from one extreme to the other.

What Is a Trait Scale? We may, then, define a trait scale as a continuum, or variable, along which (1) we may perceive others as differing (rating method); (2) the individual may perceive himself as differing from others (self-rating or questionnaire approach); or (3) the behavior of individuals may be demonstrated to vary (experimental and projective approaches).

In any case, trait judgments will depend to a marked extent on the trait concept developed by the observer. This is particularly true in rating and self-rating studies, in which an incorrect concept leads to meaningless results. It is true to a lesser extent in questionnaire and projective studies, in which objective demonstration through statistical analysis is sometimes possible (cf. Chapter 3). Even in the laboratory, the experimenter's conception of what to look for often determines whether he will find unity or disunity in personality.

Theoretically we might have as many trait scales as there are paired polar adjectives describing personality differences. In practice these can be restricted to a manageable number, through some of the forms of analysis now to be described.

EMPIRICAL STUDIES OF TRAITS

As was noted in Chapter 3, investigators have assumed the existence of a wide variety of traits and have developed scales which presume to measure these. Naturally the results overlap from study to study, so that it is difficult to select certain traits as common to most persons in our culture. The following sketch of the literature is therefore intended primarily to show what is possible and to offer some suggestive findings.

Surface and Source Traits. Certain traits are readily observable: they appear in interpersonal contacts, in one's way of doing a job, in responses to questionnaires. These may be represented (Figure 8.1) as being close to the surface of the personality. They are likely to be readily modifiable under environmental pressure. It seems appropriate to follow Cattell (1945) in designating them as *surface traits.* Cheerfulness, liveliness, and quarrelsomeness would be apt examples.

Source traits may be thought of as underlying structures, expressed not directly but through the medium of the surface traits. We might, for example, think of a general reactivity to social stimuli, lending unity to the apparent inconsistency of a man who is above average on both friendly and quarrelsome behavior. This might also explain the observation by Murphy (1937) that the children in her group who were most often sympathetic were likewise most often aggressive in their relations to playmates. Source traits, of course, may be either common or unique, as may surface traits.

How many surface traits there are, and how many source traits, cannot be definitely stated. Allport and Odbert counted 17,953 trait names in English, but many of these were synonyms and others represented temporary rather

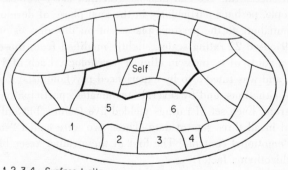

1, 2, 3, 4 – Surface traits
5, 6 – Source traits

Fig. 8.1 Surface and source traits. 1, 2, 3, 4, easily observable attributes such as cheerfulness and sociability; 5, 6, inferred characteristics such as drive level.

than permanent trends. R. B. Cattell (1945), making an exhaustive study of ratings, found a total of 131 "phenomenal clusters," or common traits. These grouped themselves readily into 50 "nuclear clusters" of related traits, which in turn could be arranged in 20 "sectors of the personality sphere." This set of 20 sector names, with a few of the nuclear clusters subsumed to show the general relationships, is reproduced in Table 8.1.

It will be noted that it is often necessary to define both ends of the continuum before a sector or a cluster is clearly understood, and also that a given term may serve as an anchor point for more than one cluster. Placidity, for example, occurs in sector 3 and also in sector 8, but in the first case it is set opposite agitation or melancholy; in the second, opposite high-strung instability. It is clear that placidity is not quite the same quality in the two contexts. The bipolar labeling system is, therefore, desirable (cf. Chapter 1).

Cattell believes that he has effectively covered the personality sphere with these 20 sectors; i.e., he believes that any surface trait will be found to fit snugly into one or another sector. A source trait, however, might underlie several sectors.

Among the major source traits reported by Cattell (1957) are cyclothymia versus schizothymia, ego strength versus proneness to neuroticism, excitability-insecurity, dominance versus submissiveness, surgency (cheerful, energetic, sociable) versus desurgency, superego strength, and several others less clearly defined. The schizothyme end of the cyclothyme-schizothyme factor is characterized by such surface traits as obstructive, cantankerous, rigid, secretive, suspicious, cautious; on the other end, of course, by easygoing, warmhearted, frank, trustful, impulsive. It seems plausible that there is some common thread running through each group of surface traits, which is precisely what Cattell is arguing. He is not sure what this common thread is, but suggests that it may have an innate basis, may involve frustration tolerance (the cyclothymes having more tolerance), and may also relate to ability to abandon habits which are not successful. We can also suggest that early unpleasant experiences with people, perhaps particularly in the anal phase of development (see page 107), contribute to the person's placement on this dimension.

Fiske (1949) used 22 rating scales, slightly modified from those developed by Cattell, in a study of trainees in clinical psychology. Each of 128 trainees rated himself, and was rated also by experienced psychologists observing him in a variety of situations, and by several "teammates" participating in the assessment program. Each set of ratings yielded five factors, but only two were clearly defined in all three sets of data. These two were called "social adaptability" and "emotional control." The first of these rather resembles Cattell's cyclothyme-schizothyme factor.

Guilford (1948) started from an interest in Jung's conception of a personality variable called introversion-extraversion (see pages 272–273). From the intercorrelations of several hundred questionnaire items he successively

Table 8.1

Chart of Principal Surface-trait "Sectors," According to Cattell *

1. Fineness of character	vs. Moral defect, nonpersistence
a. Integrity, altruism	vs. Dishonesty, undependability
b. Conscientious effort	vs. Quitting, incoherence
2. Realism, emotional integration	vs. Neuroticism, evasion, infantilism
a. Realism, reliability	vs. Neuroticism, changeability
b. Practicalness, determination	vs. Daydreaming, evasiveness
c. Neuroticism, self-deception, emotional intemperateness	vs. Opposites of these
d. Infantile, demanding self-centeredness	vs. Emotional maturity, frustration tolerance
3. Balance, frankness, optimism	vs. Melancholy, agitation
a. Agitation, melancholy, obstinacy	vs. Placidity, social interest
b. Balance, frankness, sportsmanship	vs. Pessimism, secretiveness, immoderateness
4. Intelligence, disciplined mind, independence	vs. Foolish, undependable unreflectiveness
a. Emotional maturity, clarity of mind	vs. Infantilism, dependence
b. Gentlemanly, disciplined thoughtfulness	vs. Extraverted, foolish lack of will
c. Creativity, self-determination, intelligence	vs. Narrowness of interests, fogginess
d. Intelligence, penetration, general talent	vs. Lack of general ability
5. Egotism, assertion, stubbornness	vs. Modesty, self-effacement, adaptability
6. Boldness, independence, toughness	vs. Timidity, inhibition, sensitivity
7. Sociability	vs. Timidity, hostility, gloominess
8. General emotionality, high-strungness, instability	vs. Placidity, deliberateness, reserve
9. Gratefulness, friendliness, idealism	vs. Sadism, slanderousness, suspiciousness
10. Liveliness, instability, verbal expressiveness	vs. Reserve, quiescence, naturalness
11. Imaginative intuition, curiosity, carelessness	vs. Thrift, inflexible habits, smugness
12. Bohemian, disorderly	vs. Persevering, pedantic
13. Aesthetic, thoughtfulness, constructiveness	vs. Absence of these
14. Physical strength, endurance, courage	vs. Physical inactivity, avoidance of danger
15. Amorousness, playfulness	vs. Propriety
16. Alcoholism, rebelliousness, carelessness	vs. Piety, reverence, thrift
17. Curiosity, wide interests	vs. Limited interests
18. Hypochondriacal, taciturn retroversion	vs. Eloquence, interest in future
19. Asceticism, eccentricity	vs. Comfort-loving conventionality
20. Inflexibility, wandering	vs. Adaptableness, ease of settling down

* The grouping of these characteristics is based on actual correlations from rating studies. The sectors which are immediately adjacent to each other are, likewise, as a general rule, positively correlated; clusters within a sector show significant positive correlations with each other.

SOURCE: The table is modified from one in Cattell (1945).

isolated single dimensions or factors which got such names as social introversion, thinking introversion, depression, cycloid (fluctuation) disposition,
rhathymia (carefree, impulsive), ascendance, activity, inferiority feeling, and
so on.[2] This looks as if it might lead back toward the 17,953 trait names found
by Allport and Odbert, and it is encouraging to observe that Lovell (1945),
working from Guilford's data, was able to identify four "second-order" factors
which accounted for most of the variance of the 13 primary factors. These
four were labeled "drive-restraint, realism, emotionality, and social adaptability." It is clear that these get down to rather basic dimensions of temperament: impulses and their controls, realistic perception, facile emotional response to stimulation, and affectionate orientation toward people.

Interpersonal Definition of Traits. In contrast to Cattell, Guilford, and
other investigators who have tried to define a trait in terms of consistent responses by a person, Leary (1956) offers an approach which defines a trait
in terms of a consistent pattern of interpersonal relationships.

Leary's system is somewhat like that of Cattell in that he arranges personality patterns in a circle, so that similar actions are spatially near, and actions
of antithetical meaning are at opposite ends of a diameter (Figure 8.2).
Thus, blunt and aggressive behavior is at the opposite pole from cooperative,
overconventional behavior. By this device he seeks to cover all of the observable personality.

Leary speaks of his system as if it were based upon "reflexes" or specific
responses. An examination of the sample items shown in Figure 8.2, however,
will indicate that the *perceived meaning* of an act is essential to its classification. Thus, "ask help, trust" is listed as an "adaptive reflex" under "docile,
dependent." But it is clear that asking help may be integrated into a pattern
quite different from docility-dependence; it would be diagnostic of this trait
or category only if the subject perceives another person as one on whom he
can depend, someone he can trust. It seems probable that some of us grow up
with the expectation that we can trust almost everyone, whereas others acquire
the belief that they must be suspicious at all times. It is variation along this
continuum from trusting to suspicious, rather than behavior, which is crucial
to the personality classification.

So far we have little or no information on how traits identified by Leary's
system will match up with those derived from consistency analysis of individual responses. There is a limited amount of evidence (e.g., LaForge et al.,
1954) that predictions from Leary's diagnosis of personality to such behavior
as selective forgetting can be made successfully.

---

[2] The original work on these 13 factors was substantially duplicated by Guilford and
Zimmerman (1956). However, instead of reducing the number, they found it necessary
to postulate 14 independent factors; most of these resembled closely the original 13. It
is interesting to observe that Cattell finds 16 to be the minimum number of factors needed
at this level, a fairly close agreement with Guilford's work.

The Maladjustment-Neuroticism Dimension. As was noted in Chapter 3, much research on personality measurement has been directed to a search for a device which will identify preneurotics (or prepsychotics) before they actually break down in a stress situation. Woodworth's inventory (page 43) was intended for this purpose, and other instruments, such as those of Thurstone and Thurstone (1930) and Hathaway and McKinley—the MMPI— (page 44)—have focused on related problems. Recent work makes it appear that two dimensions are involved. Eysenck (1953) reports studies on the basis of which he asserts that neurotic and psychotic tendencies are quite independent of each other. This is more or less supported by the MMPI work, in which it is found that neurotic patterns, such as hysteria, hypochondriasis, and depression, vary almost independently of the psychotic patterns, schizo-

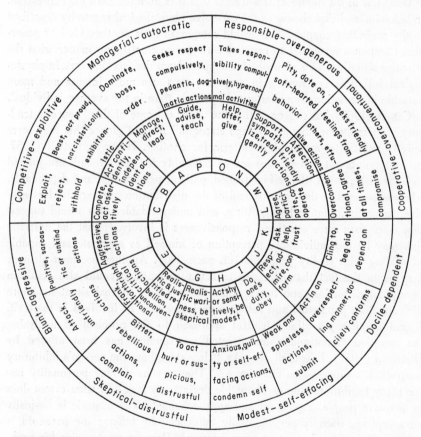

Fig. 8.2 Leary's system of trait classification. Traits are defined in terms of habitual ways of relating to other persons. Note that similar patterns are close together on the circle; opposing patterns are at opposite ends of a diameter. (From Leary and Coffey. 1955, Fig. 1, p. 112, by permission of American Psychological Association, Inc.)

phrenia, paranoia, and mania. And it will be recalled that Barnes (page 154) found differences in response set between neurotics and psychotics. The exact meaning of this difference, however, is not clear. Suggestibility and an excess of negative valences seem to characterize the preneurotics, whereas lack of motor control and failure of realistic perceptions seem to be involved on the psychotic dimension.

The omnibus inventories of "neurotic tendencies," such as that of Thurstone and Thurstone, are internally consistent, having high split-half reliability coefficients. This does not, however, necessarily prove the existence of a functionally unified trait.[3] It may only indicate that the various kinds of symptoms were sufficiently well balanced between the two halves of the test so that a person scoring high on one part would score comparably high on the other.

One view of the nature of this trait is that it is no more than the expression, in behavior and experience, of the excessive physiological reactivity described in the preceding chapter. This would categorize it as another kind of generalized response set—a set to respond with strong emotion no matter what the stimulus situation. This view obtains support from the fact that certain physiological activities (galvanic skin response, etc.) are more intense and more variable in "emotionally maladjusted" persons than in the average individual.

Cattell (1957) has suggested that the upper extreme of this "neurotic tendency" is simply the absence of "ego strength." At first glance this may seem only to substitute one ambiguous term for another. However, Cattell (1957, p. 100) points out that persons scored favorably for ego strength are judged to be realistic about life, self-controlled, patient, persevering, and dependable, whereas persons at the opposite end of the distribution are perceived as evasive, immature, changeable, quitting, and undependable. This would suggest that more than mere emotional responsiveness is involved; that the unifying link may be the individual's perception of himself as adequate and capable of dealing with reality problems (cf. page 200). Another common element may be in the fact that excessive tendency to emotion could also result in perceptual distortion, and hence make the handling of real situations more difficult. Both perceptual and response variables may be involved in the trait.

Still another potentially fruitful approach to the problem of analyzing the so-called "emotionally maladjusted" personality has been offered by Diamond (1957). Essentially he asks, "How strong are the person's inhibitory controls, his superego or conscience?" The "psychasthenic" personality has too many inhibitions, the psychopathic deviate too few. "To what extent does he perceive people as pleasant and approachable?" The hysteric is basically an accepting, friendly person, easily influenced by others; the paranoid is cold, suspicious, and resistant to suggestion. "Does he try to solve his problems by withdrawal or approach?" The hypochondriac is trying to get sympathy from others in his troubles; the schizophrenic retreats from social con-

---

[3] For the logic behind this statement, see White and Saltz (1957).

tacts. This kind of analysis of the broad category of maladjusted personalities is valuable for two reasons: first, because it emphasizes that within this grouping there may be different "types" of emotionally handicapped persons, such as are picked out by the MMPI; and second, because it reminds us that the historical explanation of any trait is to be found in the basic processes of perception, response, emotion, and conflict.

THE ORIGIN OF TRAITS

We have used the term "indicator" to refer to a specific response unit, such as answering an item on an inventory, behaving in a given fashion in an experiment, or reporting some kind of percept in a projective test. It is the accumulation of several of these indicators, in a congruent fashion, which justifies our stating that an individual manifests a given trait. *The trait does not cause the behavior.* The cause, to the extent that we can identify one, is the sequence of learning experiences, from infancy to adolescence, operating on an inherited constitution, which built up this consistent pattern. The trait is merely a convenient way of describing a person who is found to manifest such consistency.

This view of traits is represented diagrammatically in Figure 8.3. According to this view, specific perceptual or response units become organized into patterns which we call traits, if the reference is to an aspect of temperament, or attitudes, if the reference is to some person or institution in the social environment. Generally we say that the trait is stronger if there is a

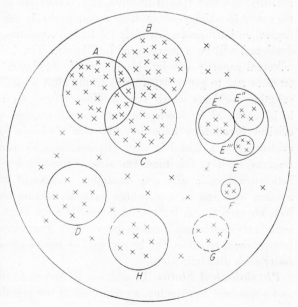

Fig. 8.3 Relationship between indicators, traits, and attitudes. x, specific expectancy, verbalization, habit, or unit of behavior; A, B, C, indicators organized into consistent groupings as traits; D, F, H, more or less specific attitudes; E, relatively generalized attitude (E', E'', E''', relatively independent of each other except as integrated into the generalized attitude) ; G, partially integrated attitude.

high probability that the subject will act in the way defined by the trait; thus, the higher the concentration of items inside the circles of Figure 8.3, the more predictable the subject's behavior and the better organized his traits.

Heredity and Trait Origin. We shall cite additional evidence regarding the role of heredity in Chapters 12 and 16. Let us only note here that certain traits are unquestionably favored, if not actually determined, by hereditary predispositions. Strong feelings and emotions activate the autonomic nervous system (ANS). Persons born with a very reactive ANS will experience more emotions, with stronger feedback, in a wider range of environmental situations. Thus they will establish more, and more intense, emotional expectancies than their fellows. Similarly, the development of inhibitory control may be more difficult for them because of the high level of excitability built into their nervous mechanisms.

Glandular constitution and body build may be other hereditary factors determining traits. It has been established (Chapter 12) that the kind of physique an individual possesses will in some way affect his energy level and his enjoyment of some kinds of stimulation. Very little is known at this time about the role of sensory thresholds in personality development. It may be that a person with a low pain threshold is almost certain to develop as an anxious, fearful individual because of the excess of pain experiences he will encounter. We have, in the preceding chapter, mentioned various kinds of perceptual styles which also play a role in trait formation, but the extent to which they are determined by heredity is unknown.

Importance of Intelligence. Intelligence, which is largely influenced by heredity, deserves special mention here. Traits are generalized patterns, and the extent to which generalization occurs probably depends, to some unknown degree, on intelligence. Certainly the logical consistency of the generalizations developed will be a function of intelligence. The individual of superior intellectual capacity will be able to identify fundamental similarities and differences and to group experiences in the most meaningful manner. Thus, by rejecting incidents which can be differentiated from the class with which he is concerned, he develops a more realistic concept—or a trait which favors efficient functioning in society. To take a simple example, he may detect evidence that a friend is under tension, and so discount fretful or hostile remarks made at this time. On a more complex level, he may discriminate between a woman who acts masculine because of her inner anxieties, and another who acts in a masculine manner because she is self-confident and feels no need to ask for special favors. It must be conceded, of course, that some very intelligent persons prove very insensitive to such nuances of interpersonal relations. On the average, we must suppose that intelligence does foster such discriminations.

Physiological Status. In addition to hereditary differences in glandular and autonomic functioning, we must admit the possibility of trait formation under the influence of temporary conditions within the body. Freeman (1948), for example, has pointed out that some individuals build up substantial residual tension if they experience frustration and have no opportunity to discharge this in some form of action. Under the pressures so generated, the individual's ability to make intelligent discriminations is reduced, his perceptions are modified, and his capacity for learning affected. Weisgerber (1954) has shown that speed of recovery of the ANS from a disturbing stimulus is significantly correlated with a measure of perseverative thinking, which in turn predicts several measures on MMPI.

There is also some evidence to the effect that changes in biochemical functioning, as in metabolizing certain amino acids, may profoundly affect perceptual and emotional life. These changes, so far noted only in psychotics, may occur to minor degrees in normals. Indeed, our understanding of these processes is so limited that we cannot be sure whether the biochemical deficiency precedes or follows the personality breakdown. Some of these studies will be reviewed in Chapter 16.

Many psychologists hope that factor analysis may help in disentangling the twisted threads linking observable facets of personality to these physiological (innate or acquired) determinants. Figure 8.4 represents a hypothesis about such relationships. It would suggest, e.g., that a physiological state (9) may affect cycloid tendency (6), a trend toward variation in mood, which in turn may influence observed cheerfulness (1), sociability (2), and tactfulness (3). Since the intermediate source traits are obviously affected also by environmental pressure (10), the chain of determination may appear complicated.

Environment and Learning. As is suggested by Figure 8.4, most psychologists believe that environmental forces play a role in personality determination equal to or greater than the physiological aspects. We have described (Chapter 5) some of the studies on animals, in which isolation during infancy produced profound emotional disturbances, effects of which were still visible years later. The mechanisms of conditioning, imitation, and suggestion were noted as instances of ways in which the child forms emotional expectancies about himself, his parents, his peer group, and other environmental situations.

The key to trait formation, however, is the process of integrating these independent reaction patterns into generalized, consistent systems. By chance the child will have some pleasant and some unpleasant experiences, respond angrily and again fearfully to the same person. Yet he grows into an adult who is not simply a package of unrelated reactions. He does not reenact all these diverse learnings. Indeed, he does not show much evidence of specific expectancies. Rather, he shows highly generalized anticipations that certain consequences are probable in certain classes of situations. Without such generalization, any discussion of traits would be completely irrelevant.

We have noted some sources of integration in earlier chapters. Stimulus generalization, for example, operates to induce similar percepts, including affective tone, for objects in the same category. Summation of probabilities seems to be another relevant phenomenon; the person seems, as it were, to add up his positive and negative experiences with an object or person, strike an average, and use this as his best prediction of what to expect.

Selective Perception. If the person is faced with an ambiguous situation (and how many of the problems we encounter are equivocal in interpretation!) he may pick out and exaggerate one set of cues, predicting favorable results, or he may select those of negative import. So he increases the number of occasions which support his mental bias, by selectively perceiving only the evidence which supports it. Thus a young woman who feels socially rejected may go to a tea. If nine guests speak pleasantly to her and one snubs her, she is prone to remember, talk about, and become emotional over the one unpleasant item, ignoring the nine pleasant contacts. Edwards (1941) presented a speech to a group of students, with pro- and anti-New-Deal statements exactly balanced. The items noticed and remembered in the speech, however, were those most congruent with the preexisting prejudice of the listener.

This means that people who are cheerful tend to become more so, while those who are leaning toward depressiveness are steadily rendered gloomier. It also means that this established interpretation of situations, based on early experience, spreads to related items of experience and thus increases the degree of congruence between related personality traits.

Selective Forgetting. A second phase of the same process is that of selective forgetting. People tend to repress and forget not merely that which interferes

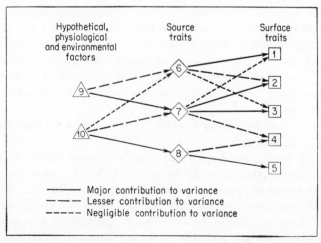

Fig. 8.4 Possible relationships between surface traits, source traits, and determining factors. (Suggested by Tucker, 1940.)

with satisfaction of a need or that which is unpleasant, but also that which does not coincide with previous judgments. Charles Darwin once remarked that, if he encountered any bit of evidence which contradicted his theory of natural selection, he had to write it down immediately; otherwise, it was quickly forgotten. The paranoid personality forgets acts of kindness, but remembers with grim pertinacity all evidences of hostility.

Distortion and Invention. Furthermore, the person may actually distort remembered occurrences to fit into his frame of reference, or he may go so far as to invent incidents which have no foundation in reality. Edwards's subjects, for example, actually took some of his statements and twisted them into complete opposites, so that they would conform to established patterns. Among abnormal personalities, delusions of grandeur or of persecution are likely to be supported by "memories" which are completely fictitious.

Relation of Traits to Personal Styles. In the preceding chapter attention was directed to styles or generalized patterns of perceiving and responding. These styles were considered as being more or less content-free, i.e., rigidity might apply to a person who was either liberal or conservative; focusing might apply to love, to anger, to anxiety; leveling and sharpening might relate to perception of objects, persons, or situations. Nevertheless, it must be assumed that the perceptual styles play a role in the formation of traits conceived as frames of reference, and response style is relevant to the formation of behavioral traits.

Dominance, for example, involves perception of others as available to be bossed around. It is well known, however, that some individuals are quite dominant, even domineering, with persons of inferior status, but are quite submissive with persons of higher status than themselves. On the other hand, some are dominative regardless of status of the other person. We might plausibly assume that the latter group tends towards leveling (i.e., denying differences in perceived objects), whereas the former manifests sharpening, at least on a relative basis.

All children tend to imitate their parents and to model behavior on parental examples. But some show this tendency far more clearly than others. The development of a response set of conformity or acquiescence may well be a mediating step between the simple process of copying specific sequences and the complete mimicking of the parent which is sometimes observed.

We do not, at present, have enough observational data on children to test these hypotheses. Nevertheless, they appear plausible and certainly merit investigation.

Trait Origins and the Normal Curve. We have laid some emphasis upon the point that personality traits, like physical and intellectual traits, tend to follow a curve of normal distribution. This fact does not conflict with our emphasis upon environment or with the statements about increasing consistency which have just been made.

Let us assume that a given personality trait (security feeling) is a function of 10 independent factors, such as kind of inherent autonomic nervous system, glandular balance, type of family, and the first seven experiences with people. We shall also assume that each of these items can vary only as plus or minus, increasing or decreasing the tendency to security. In this case, we have a situation comparable to that of tossing 10 pennies and counting the number of heads and tails each time. If "heads" means a predominance of secure influence, we should find about 1 of 1,000 cases with *all* factors making for security; 10 cases with 9 favoring, 1 opposing; 45 cases with 8 favoring, 2 opposing; and so on. We shall thus obtain the "normal" distribution of security feeling in 1,000 people (see Figure 8.5, curve *a*).

Suppose, on the contrary, that we predetermine the results to some extent by making four pennies show heads continually, tossing only the remaining six (e.g., where family factors all favor security). In that case we should get a distribution with no entries beyond 6T4H and, consequently, no extremely insecure personalities. We should, however, get a great many more secure individuals than in the pure chance situation, although the maximum degree of security is unchanged. The curve would still be normal in shape but narrowed in range and moved toward the upper end of the distribution (see Figure 8.5, curve *b*).

We can also apply this mathematical analogy to the determination of a trait within an individual. Under a pure chance situation he would be most likely to develop an average degree of any particular characteristic. He is not, however, operating under pure chance conditions. Having once become slanted in a certain direction, his mental processes operate to increase the bias; i.e., many "negative" situations no longer affect him, while "positive"

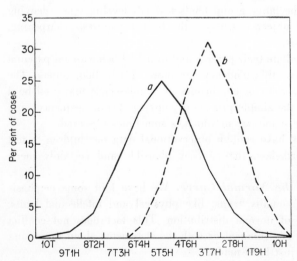

Fig. 8.5 Normal distribution of traits as a probability function: (*a*) distribution that would be obtained if a trait were a product of 10 chance factors (as by heads or tails on 10 coins); (*b*) distribution if four coins are left heads up, and only six coins are tossed (four fixed factors, six chance factors).

situations are noted, rehearsed, and emphasized. He will, therefore, tend toward the upper end of the distribution. Conversely, a child slanted toward insecurity in early life may show the same cumulative effect.

We have suggested (Chapter 1) adherence to the view of *multiple causation* in personality. It should now be apparent that the study of both individuals and groups lends support to such a view. The mechanisms of selectivity in learning, forgetting, and recalling, however, mean that, of the various causal factors impinging on the individual, some will be relatively more effective than others, viz., those which are congruent with trends already established. It should also be noted that, when a group of people face an environment loaded against them, the personality trait distribution will be shifted. Certain undesirable family situations (cf. Chapter 17), for example, will stack the cards in the direction of insecurity, neuroticism, inferiority feelings, and other traits indicative of personality maladjustment.

THE CONSISTENCY OF TRAITS

The position we have taken with regard to traits implies that they will continue in a relatively unchanged form over a period of time. We have, however, stressed the importance of learning, at least in connection with the

Table 8.2

Drop in Trait-score Consistency with Time

Time interval	Retest correlation
5 mo	.77
8 mo	.71
1 yr 8 mo	.69
1 yr 10 mo	.67
2 yr 3 mo	.43
2 yr 8 mo	.60
3 yr 3 mo	.64
3 yr 8 mo	.57
4 yr 6 mo	.47
5 yr 6 mo	.34
6 yr 6 mo	.56

specific manifestations of traits. This suggests that traits will be modified with experience.

The evidence is that trait measurements of any individual are fairly consistent; from year to year they vary within a narrow range, but this range widens as the time span increases. One of the best studies in this area is that of Crook (1941), who retested college students with a neuroticism questionnaire after 6½ years. His results are summarized in Table 8.2.

It appears from this table that there is a fairly steady decrease in the uniformity of the individual's scores as the time between tests increases. There is, nevertheless, a substantial degree of agreement between a person's status as a college freshman and his standing 6½ years later.[4]

A more extended period of time was covered in the research reported by Kelly (1955). In this study couples who had first been tested in their twenties were retested some 16 to 18 years later. The correlations on trait measures such as that used by Crook are comparable with those cited above: for example, the Bernreuter *F1-C* score (emotional inferiority feelings) correlated .61 with the original score, and *F2-S* (sociability) correlated .46. Self-ratings on various traits gave figures somewhat lower than these; they may be due in part to the generally lower reliabilities of such ratings as compared with questionnaire scores. In all cases, however, it is permissible to conclude that personality at the age of 45 can be predicted rather well from observations at the age of 25.

Trait Consistency in Children. Studies of consistency in children are also becoming more numerous, but the problem of getting measures which can be compared across time becomes crucial. Shirley (1933), for example, comments that if we try to compare specific responses, we miss the boat. The fearful child at one year of age screams a great deal; the same child at two is less vocal, but runs away from threatening situations. The consistency is in the perception, not in the overt action.

Neilon (1948) took the detailed personality records accumulated by Shirley in her very careful study of 19 youngsters, and set out to track them down fifteen years later. She located 15 of the 19 and again obtained extensive personality data. Descriptive sketches of the infant personality and of the adolescent personality were prepared independently, and presented to judges who knew none of the children. The judges were asked to match the infant sketch with the corresponding adolescent personality. The matches for the 10 boys were well above chance, and those for the five girls were extraordinarily good. (It is interesting to note here that four of the five girls proved very easy to match, but one girl apparently had changed substantially, since no judge matched her two records successfully. We do not know whether some especially traumatic environment may have been responsible for this degree of change.)

At the earlier ages consistency can be shown with respect to personality style or orientation toward other children. McKinnon (1942) reports on a study in which 16 children who had been observed in detail at the age of three were reviewed at the age of eight years. A fourfold classification of types was employed: conformity, invasiveness, caution, and withdrawal, according to the child's dominant pattern. (None of them adhered exclusively to one

---

[4] Crook found that 82.8 per cent of the questions were answered in an identical manner after 6½ years. This is rather high consistency, considering all the possibilities for change in that time. Furthermore, 62.8 per cent of the changes in response canceled each other—i.e., a person might drop one neurotic response only to pick up another.

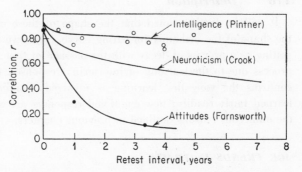

Fig. 8.6 Decline in consistency of various psychological measures with time. Consistency of intelligence test scores decreases only slightly over a period of years. The decline for a personality trait (neuroticism) and for attitudes gives a curve resembling the typical forgetting curve. (From Crook, 1941.)

type of behavior.) After five years, McKinnon found that 10 of the 16 children still fell in the same type class. Most of the changes were from invasive to conforming, a logical outcome of training. A single illustration of consistency is the following: [5]

Randall (3) "pushes and pulls children, grabs their materials, makes shrill piercing sounds and has frequent physical conflicts." (Invasive)

Randall (8) "seeks attention from peers and enjoys showing off. His time is spent in idle chatter. He fights, boasts, teases others, and is inconsiderate and thoughtless. Children say he is silly and that he talks too much. He engages in no constructive or cooperative activities." (Invasive)

Long-term Consistency. Even more impressive than McKinnon's material are investigations tracing the same individuals from childhood to maturity. In these studies individuals admitted to mental hospitals were checked against child-guidance records, and actual notes on the child's behavior were compared with his adult psychotic symptoms. In most cases, congruence was observed between childhood traits and adult symptoms. Birren (1944), for example, reports on 38 children who were examined in a child-guidance clinic and later became psychotic. He finds that their symptoms correspond closely to the pattern of traits observed in childhood. "Personality characteristics of psychotic patients," he concludes, "are stable and evidence continuous development from childhood."

Trait Change and the Curve of Forgetting. Crook (1941) plotted curves showing the rate of decline of measured consistency, based on retest correlations, for intelligence test scores, neuroticism, and attitude test data. The curves (Figure 8.6) show high consistency for intelligence, medium for neuroticism, very little (after one year) for attitudes. These findings are in harmony with what we should expect. Intelligence is determined to a substantial degree by hereditary factors, and hence should show little inconsistency; attitudes are virtually pure effects of environment, and hence are easily modified. Emotional instability is probably dependent upon both heredity and environment.

[5] McKinnon (1942), p. 58. Reprinted by permission.

It will be further noted that the shape of these curves resembles closely the shape of the orthodox forgetting curve. Since we no longer interpret forgetting as a process of decay with the passage of time, but rather as an active process due to the learning of interfering responses, the shape of the curves confirms the view that learning is involved. Conflicting attitudes may be learned fairly readily; new emotional responses are acquired less easily, for the numerous reasons outlined in previous chapters.

AGE TRENDS IN TRAITS

A confusing factor in the study of trait consistency results from the fact that social expectancy as to "proper" personality traits varies with age. As Tryon (1939) has so well demonstrated, the traits which 12-year-old boys approve in each other are identical only in part with those accepted as standards at the age of 15. Even more was such a shift noted in girls from 12 to 15. Such variations probably account for some of the shifts in the adult years which have been summarized by Kuhlen (1945). We do not expect from the middle-aged man the amount of drive, social activity, impulsiveness, and emotionality that he displayed when younger. The conflicts and problems that he faces will also change. (There may, of course, be a "true" change within the individual; his glands slow down, his nervous system is less reactive, and his perspective on events is somewhat wider. He has also learned new social and emotional patterns.)

Kelly (1955) took advantage of the fact that he had retested individuals in early middle age after studying them in early maturity, and prepared comparisons showing age trends. They were less extreme than might have been thought. The following changes were statistically significant:

Religious value (Allport-Vernon scale) went up for both males and females; aesthetic value decreased for both; theoretical value declined for males only.

On Bernreuter's scale, women showed a decline in self-confidence; they had more worries and feelings of insecurity. Neither sex showed a change in sociability.

On the Strong Vocational Interest Blank, both sexes shifted toward more masculine interests.

On self-ratings, both sexes reported a loss in physical energy, less neatness in dress, and narrower interests. They also judged themselves lower on a scale from good-natured to ill-tempered. While it may be that young adults really are more good-natured, Kelly suggests that the ratings made in middle age may have been merely more realistic.

The Question of Age Roles. As Tryon suggested, the expectancy of others may determine what standards we will use as guides at different ages. The "ideal" personality at age 12 is not the same as at 15; and this holds even more for the jump from 15 to 25. There is, however, a long plateau in adulthood, which may be characterized as roughly the period of the parental role. Thus Kelly's data may have minimized the change in traits by his selection of a follow-up date. About the age of 50 many parents find themselves being cast in the role of grandparents, with different duties and different social expectancies. Kelly might therefore expect greater changes in another 10 years than had occurred in the preceding 20.

When we consider all the factors making for change, both within and outside the individual, we find that man shows a surprising tendency to maintain an established trait pattern. Consistency, not change, is the rule.

SEX DIFFERENCES

Whereas sex differences in general intelligence have been found to be quite small, differences in measured personality attributes are often large and significant. Since the differences which have been studied tend, if anything, only to reproduce the popular beliefs about the variation between males and females, an extended sampling of the literature would serve no useful purpose. It is generally agreed that girls are more prone to anxieties, depressions, and other symptoms of conflict and stress than boys (cf. Figure 8.7). Similarly, objective tests indicate that females are more submissive, do not have as strong desires for achievement, and so on. Such differences accord with the popular stereotype; it would thus be easy to gloss them over as being of no importance.

There are, however, some questions which need to be considered here. To what extent, we may ask, is the popular stereotype the cause of the differ-

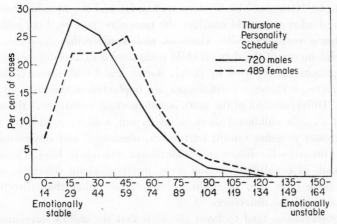

Fig. 8.7 Sex differences in emotionality. Although the difference in average scores is highly significant statistically, there is still a substantial degree of overlap of the two distributions. (Data from Stagner, 1933b.)

ence? As we noted above, people expect boys to act aggressively and may actually reward such behavior, whereas girls are scolded for similar actions. Boys are encouraged to daydream of achievement and success, whereas girls are urged to focus on aspirations for marriage, a nice home, and children. Boys are criticized for crying or showing timidity, whereas girls learn to use these tactics as devices for social control.

On the other hand, it is obvious that hormonal and other physiological differences exist and must be taken into account. Freud assumed that there were innate tendencies for the boy to be attracted to his mother and the girl to her father. The sequence of events as postulated in his theory of psychosexual development (Chapter 5) would predict more emotionality for girls because of the larger number of conflicts encountered.

The data of Goodenough (1931) indicate that outbursts of anger are of approximately equal frequency in boy and girl babies up to almost two years of age. By thirty months, however, girls have declined sharply, while boys show a much less precipitate decrease. One is tempted to interpret this as evidence that the innate tendencies are the same, and that environment and social expectancy bring about the difference; but certainly the evidence is incomplete.

The observations of the cultural anthropologists also give substantial support to the view that social expectancy is the crucial factor. Mead (1935) reported that she found, within a few miles of each other in New Guinea, primitive cultures in which the traditional sex roles were sharply divergent. Among the Tchambuli she found that women were typically calm and dominant; they took over the roles of planning, controlling the society, and so on. The men in this group were described as temperamental, petty, gossipy, artistic, and submissive. Among the Arapesh, Mead found both males and females to be "feminine" by Western standards; and the Mundugumor deviated toward what we would consider the masculine pattern, both males and females being very aggressive, vigorous, and domineering.

A careful survey of the data on child socialization in 110 different cultures (mostly primitive), reported by Barry, Bacon, and Child, supports the view that the more pervasive sex differences are implanted in the child by social training. "Differentiation of the sexes is unimportant in infancy," the authors say, "but . . . in childhood there is, as in our society, a widespread pattern of greater pressure toward nurturance, obedience, and responsibility in girls, and toward self-reliance and achievement striving in boys. There are a few reversals of sex difference, and many instances of no detectable sex difference; these facts tend to confirm the cultural rather than directly biological nature of the differences."[6]

Such observations tend to favor the view that the child's development of

[6] Barry, Bacon, and Child (1957), p. 332. Reprinted by permission of the American Psychological Association, Inc.

specific traits depends on the models he observes and the kinds of behavior for which he is rewarded. There may be an underlying biological difference which loads the dice in favor of a certain masculine or feminine pattern, but the environment evidently can overrule this bias.

SUMMARY

Whether we consider traits to be predominantly perceptual or predominantly patterns of response, it is clear that they grow out of specific experiences and are gradually built up into consistent, organized systems. Traits involve frames of reference for judging the kind of situation a person wants to approach or avoid, the kind of action which characterizes him, and his habitual relations with others. They may involve habits of emotional expression, and ways of behaving in certain categories of situations. Although no trait apparently develops directly out of any specific perceptual style or response style, these underlying generalities seem to foster the development of consistent trait patterns.

Likewise we cannot trace any particular trait to any specific conditioned response, or expectancy, or defense mechanism. The trait is rather a higher-order generalization which may include both positive and negative valences, and the residues of various defensive techniques. (For example, if one has selectively forgotten certain experiences, his surface traits will be modified accordingly.)

Traits are surprisingly consistent over periods of several years. This conforms to the emphasis laid in previous chapters upon the importance of the early years of life in molding a given personality.

Sex differences conform to the popular stereotype of masculine and feminine personalities, and the existence of the stereotype may explain many of the differences. In a society where the expectancies are different, the traits shown by the typical adult male or female are likewise different from the pattern we know in Western civilization.

SUGGESTIONS FOR READING

Important contributions to the study of traits have been made by Raymond Cattell, whose *Personality* and *Personality and motivation structure and measurement* concentrate heavily on his own research programs. Guilford, like Cattell, uses primarily a statistical approach; he has published a book, *Personality*, giving his results and some discussion of others'. Diamond, in his *Personality and temperament*, deals with some of the problems raised in this chapter. Allport's *Personality: a psychological interpretation* is both a historical landmark and a currently valuable contribution to trait theory. *The structure of human personality*, by Hans Eysenck, is the most mature and thoughtfully prepared report on the research of this prolific English investigator. From a methodological point of view William Stephenson's *The study of behavior* also merits study.

CHAPTER 9

The Self

In the preceding chapters we have built up successively the important elements for a comprehensive description of personality. Any given individual may be described in terms of his specific emotional and affective responses, such as a phobia for high places or a fondness for brunettes. He may also be characterized in terms of broad temperamental patterns, such as optimism or excitability. A good description should include his customary mechanisms for adjustment when important equilibria are threatened, e.g., his use of vigilance or defense. It is also helpful to know about his style of perceiving and responding, and the traits on which he is distinctively different from or similar to the average of his group.

While this may seem like a fairly heavy assignment, the task of developing a satisfactory personality description has just begun. We come now to the central concept, the core around which all these other elements are organized. This has variously been referred to as the "self," the "ego," the "self concept" and the "self-image."

Concepts such as the self or soul were widely used in discussing human personality up to the end of the nineteenth century. With the rise of behavioristic psychology, these notions were judged too mystical to be of value in a scientific study. It is only recently, perhaps since the publication of Allport's (1937) volume on personality, that the self has again become respectable.

The need for some such concept is apparent if one rereads some of the earlier passages in this volume. We have spoken of "how the person sees things" as a crucial problem. Who is this "person"? How do we represent the total individual in our calculations? The various traits and adjustment mechanisms get systematized and coordinated; how? There must be a unifying component, a factor which integrates all of these percepts and responses. This place is filled by the concept of the self.

Can the Self Be Known? Philosophers often enjoy debating such questions as, How can the self know the self? How can that which is examined be that which is examining?

We shall have to content ourselves with answering this question on a fairly naïve level (with the parenthetical thought that deeper answers may not be answers at all). The position adopted here is that introspectively we can distinguish readily between two types of experiences: those which have ego reference, and those which do not. Washington crossed the Delaware; *I* crossed the Connecticut. *My* home, *my* school, *my* writings are items in memory which have a unique quality, the quality of self-reference, which is not found in memories of things that I have read about or acquired in some impersonal fashion. Further, each of us is aware of the *continuity of experience;* I am the same person who did this twenty years ago, and there is no possibility in my mind that it could have been anyone else.[1]

Koffka (1935) has suggested that we can locate the self spatially as the point which divides "in front of" from "in back of," as well as "left" from "right." Temporally it is at the point separating the future from the past. One can think of incidents which have already occurred and can imagine similar happenings yet to come; the felt self-reference is different in the two instances.

Not all of our experiences involve awareness of self, and in some cases it seems difficult to link the memory to the self. For example, a man may in a fit of anger speak obscenely to his wife. Later he says, "I don't know why I did it; I was not myself." The action, as recalled, does not seem compatible with his image of himself. Studies of amnesia indicate that a severe blow may cause a loss of self-reference without loss of consciousness; the person may act in a normal manner, yet be unable at a later time to recall his actions following the injury. Physiologically we might say that self-awareness is the most complex function of the cerebral cortex, and that emotion or physical shock may upset this function without blocking apparently normal operation of verbal and manual habits.

How Does the Self Become Known? Ever since William James, it has been customary to speak of the infant's consciousness as a "big, blooming, buzzing confusion." The accuracy of this description may forever remain indeterminate. It seems pretty certain, nonetheless, that the infant's consciousness includes no awareness of himself as an individual. As far as we can judge from observation of young children, their mental states can be described as "It hurts!" rather than "I have a pain!"

Self-awareness develops gradually as the individual recognizes the distinction between self and not-self, between his body and the remainder of the visible environment. It seems probable that awareness of his body furnishes a common core, about which self-reference becomes organized, although later one can distinguish self from the physical body. The child sees portions

---

[1] This is, of course, limited to normal personalities. Confusion of identity is a feature of various mental abnormalities, and is perhaps the most striking symptom of personality breakdown to the average observer.

of his physique as common factors in all his experiences; he has muscular and organic sensations as part of all his activities; and his feelings of pleasure and pain, especially in the early years, are associated with definite bodily sensations.

Self-awareness is fostered by the fact that the child is given a name, and this name becomes a repetitive element in many memories. He is presented with toys and clothing, and adults treat such items in a distinctive way, trying to point out their special relationship to himself. At first, possessions have no meaning to him. Later he may pass through a stage in which injury to them may be treated like an injury to his body. He is identified with a family, and he similarly may behave as if the family were an extension of his body.

The consciousness of self comes to full focus, however, as the individual experiences himself as a continuing unity in a *changing* environment. The self is best understood by contrasting it with the not-self, the outer world. Constant change in the outer environment emphasizes the stable self. Children who are moved often from one neighborhood to another are more sharply aware of themselves as persons. Primitives who live always in the same village, with the same neighbors, commonly show practically no self-awareness. Even civilized adults become self-conscious in a strange situation.

Factors Delaying Self-awareness. Why is the child so slow in developing an awareness of self as differentiated from others? Why is the nucleus of self-feeling detectable only after the second or even the third birthday? Three contributing factors deserve mention.

1. The infant has a very poor memory. Learning is possible during the first postnatal week, or even prior to birth, but only very simple learning seems possible and several repetitions are required. Since the idea of self is essentially an abstraction of a common factor from all one's personal memories, it must necessarily wait until the memory function is better developed.

2. Even if the memory process were more efficient, the young child simply does not have the *background of experience* to distinguish self from environment. When things happen, he does not have the necessary data to evaluate their importance *to him*. He cannot separate mother from himself (mentally, that is) until there have been some vivid occurrences involving physical separation. He must build up some idea of the differences between himself and others. Even with an excellent memory, it would take the child some time to accumulate the data requisite to evolving the concept of self.

3. Another factor is the child's deficiency in language. Numerous experiments indicate that discriminations are much easier when distinctive responses can be made to each discriminable stimulus. The discrimination of self from environment calls for some kind of differential response; the most available type is verbal. Although self-awareness could probably be developed without language, it would almost certainly be of a diffuse type, which

would merge the individual's conception of himself with his personal possessions and his nearby environment.

It is impossible to present any position with regard to the concepts of
ego and self which corresponds to a consensus among psychologists, for the
simple reason that there is no consensus. Some reject the concepts entirely;
Dollard and Miller (1950) make it rather plain that they are willing to deal
with perception, learning, and labeling, but not with ego or self. Freud
(1920) has used the term "ego" in a highly restricted sense as a portion of
the self, the executive or acting component, without making clear what the
self might be. His pupil, Alfred Adler, on the other hand, evolved a theory
of the self as a highly personalized subjective system, with a characteristic
"life style" which the self actively sought to enhance. Sullivan (1953), like
Freud, reduces the self to a "self system," a set of techniques for dealing
with anxiety. And Murphy (1947) defines the self as the person's perceptions
and concept of himself as a totality—what is referred to below as the self-
image. Many other diverse views could be cited, but these will serve to illustrate the lack of agreement in this area. Despite this disagreement, most
psychologists hold that some central unifying concept is essential to the psychology of personality. In the remainder of this chapter we shall employ
two: the self, and the self-image.

The Self-image. Social psychologists, especially those with a strong
sociological orientation, have emphasized the "looking-glass" theory of the
self (cf. Cooley, 1902; Mead, 1934). According to this view, the child does
not spontaneously become aware of himself as an object, but learns that
others perceive him as an object with certain attributes. Since he acquires
his knowledge of the attributes of nonhuman objects from his parents and
others in his environment, he comes also to accept the image of himself, as
reflected in the evaluations of those around him. This view, like that of
Murphy cited above, identifies self with self-image.

Self versus Self-image. Perhaps the existentialists (cf. May et al., 1958)
have been most vigorous in asserting that there is a distinction between the
self and self-image, but Allport (1955) also has spoken out firmly for this
view. There seems to be some justification for separating the two conceptually, although it is obvious that in experience they are intertwined.

The status of the self as an object of perception can best be stated somewhat as follows: Every child has experiences in which he is aware of himself
running, talking, lying down; he experiences himself happy, hungry, tired,
excited; he sees himself doing certain things successfully, others ineptly,
and so on. This situation is one which is favorable to the emergence of an
awareness of self as something which is common to all these contexts, and by
that very fact independent of them; "I am what I am" is the succinct Biblical
assertion that selfhood cannot be further defined but must be experienced.

This awareness of the self can be distinguished from the self-image. The self-image always implies the attribution of traits, such as, for example, intelligent, beautiful, clumsy, naughty. As we have suggested above, the child's self-image reflects the opinions others hold of him; he accepts their characterizations of him to no inconsiderable degree, as the sociologists have so often emphasized. Even when the child judges himself, he must use the norms he has acquired from his social environment; thus the self-image inevitably has a strong social coloration. The self, on the other hand, is a kind of primitive experience about which communication is virtually impossible. Just as we can point to a red object and talk about the experience of red, but can never define it, so one can experience the self but this experience must be uniquely personal. In this respect the term "self" as used here is very much like what the existentialists have called "Being."

The self is thus at the very nucleus of what we have called the unique personality. If we seek to describe a person in terms of common traits, such as those mentioned in the preceding chapter, we necessarily pick out aspects in which the individual resembles others; in a large population, there will be many who make the same score he does on sociability, optimism, depression, constriction, need achievement, or any other trait measurable by objective or projective tests. Nevertheless, the person says, "I am I; I am something other than the listing of these traits; I am a unique individual; only part of me is covered by these measures." We have already conceded that uniqueness is virtually impossible to describe; we now simply conclude that this uniqueness is tied to the experience of self, also impossible to describe. This may not result in much clarification, but at least we have only one unknown instead of two.

Ego, Self, and Perception. The self-image clearly is a perceptual phenomenon, an organized percept constructed out of personal experiences and labels ascribed by others. The self, as defined above, is also a percept, having an elemental quality which can be pointed out but not defined. The ego, as defined by Freud (1924), also is predominantly a perceptual organization: "It seems to me that the ego obtains this influence (over the id) in virtue of its intimate connections with the perceptual system—connections which, as we know, *constitute its essence* and provide the basis of its differentiation from the id" [p. 21]. These views indicate that we are operating at the level of intervening variables, rather than dealing with any kind of response system.

For the sake of simplicity, we shall concentrate our attention now on the concept of the self-image. As we have shown, many psychologists reduce the self or ego to this concept, and even among those who do not, the distinction does not seem to have important implications. Let us turn, therefore, to the origin and constitution of the self-image.

The Body Image. The self-image is first and above all a body image. As we have suggested above, the child experiences sensory inputs from his own muscular actions, his own viscera, his own bumps and falls. It seems likely that the distinction between "me" and "you," between "I am running" and "he is running," develops on the basis of somesthetic sensitivity. "My" actions are accompanied by sensations of effort; "your"' actions may look the same but do not feel the same. Thus these internal sensory sources may provide the nucleus for the self.

In determining the body image, certain parts of the body seem to have more importance than others. Horowitz (1935) tells of asking very young children the question, "Is this you?" as he pointed to parts of their bodies. One little girl located her self in the mouth region, another in the abdomen, a third in the head. Freud (1924) commented that "the ego is first and foremost a body ego; it is not merely a surface entity but it is itself the projection of a surface."

Fisher and Cleveland (1955, 1956) have published a series of researches on the body image. They utilize projective tests, free associations, and other indirect ways of getting at what may well be an unconscious percept. A major finding is that some persons perceive their body as surrounded by a hard, protective armor, whereas others see themselves as open and soft. The authors have been particularly concerned with demonstrating that arthritis, skin cancer, stomach ulcers, and other ailments are systematically related to these body-image types; our interest, however, is in the relation of body image to the self-image generally. It seems highly probable that persons having the "armored" body image also behave in a hard-boiled, unsentimental fashion and think of themselves accordingly; whether this tough exterior is a defense against excessive emotionality is a question which need not concern us here.

Social Influences on Body Image. The child's body image will certainly be influenced by his "real" characteristics, size, speed of running, muscular coordination, etc. But even these depend on social norms (in part, on the performances of those around him) and the evaluation of "good" or "bad" will be distinctively social. Thus a boy from the slums may be praised by adults for being a good fighter, whereas the upper middle-class youngster is scolded for fighting. At any rate, the child's percept of self as *adequate* in physical and mental performances enters into his self-image.

It is plausible to predict from this that the individual's body image will be significantly related to his self-evaluation. This prediction has been confirmed by an ingenious series of studies by Jourard and Secord (1955a, b). For example, college students were asked to indicate the dimensions of different portions of their bodies, and to rate their feelings of satisfactions with these segments. In general, those who were satisfied with their bodies were also found to be fairly secure and self-confident, free from feelings of inferiority, etc.

The importance of social norms is neatly illustrated in the Jourard and Secord study. They found that for males, a large body was conducive to self-satisfaction; for females, on the other hand, a body somewhat smaller than the norm led to greater feelings of satisfaction with the self—with one exception: bust measurement. The relation of this observation to current social norms of feminine beauty needs no amplification.

Obviously other aspects of the self-image can give rise to satisfaction or frustration; intelligence, for example, or beauty, verbal facility, or artistic talent. The general principle which must be recognized is this: The individual's evaluation of self, his sense of personal worth, is directly related to his evaluation of various specific components, such as physique, agility, clumsiness. With increasing age the emphasis shifts from simple muscular aptitude to verbal, musical, scientific, or some other ability. The child's satisfaction with himself will depend on how well he measures up to the norms which appear to be relevant—those held up to him by his parents or by his peer group.

Reference Groups. Not only with respect to the body image, but also with reference to other perceived attributes of the self, including the traits described in Chapter 8, is it important to know what social norms the person uses in evaluating himself. These are, in the earliest instance, determined by the social groups of which he is a member.

Family Influences. The self-image will be molded by the attribution of traits within the family. A boy who has grown up surrounded by an admiring family may grossly overvalue his intelligence, attractiveness, and skill. He may have been protected from testing his qualities in real situations, and instead has accepted the beautiful picture held before his eyes.

Conversely, great damage can be done to a child by derogatory descriptions handed down by adults. Parents may induce a youngster to perceive himself as clumsy, stupid, or untrustworthy by ill-considered criticism. "My parents are very wise; if they say I'm a bad boy, it must be so." He is then likely to act in terms of this characterization. Jourard and Remy (1955) have demonstrated the extent to which the child's self-image is modified by his understanding of his parents' appraisal of him. (It is important to note, in this connection, that the "real" appraisal by the parents is not crucial. The child's percept of his parents' evaluations becomes incorporated into his percept of self.)

It is true, as has been noted earlier, that children are often surprisingly acute at detecting concealed emotional states in adults. Thus it is conceivable that a boy's belief about his father's evaluation of him may be closer to the truth than what the father says openly. It is not, however, necessary to assume this. The boy's percept is what guides his own behavior.

Comparison Groups and Reference Groups. The child's self-image will be enhanced if he is compared with people less able than himself, and depreciated if he is compared with a superior norm. These comparisons may be with specific individuals (an average child with a brilliant older sibling perceives himself as dull), but more often the comparison is to a group. The child may feel poor, to an objectively unjustified degree, if his parents associate with people of higher income level. In school, the youngster may wish to join a certain club or clique and may try to acquire the attributes of persons already members. If he is accepted, he will tend to take on attributes of the group (Manis, 1955). This does not necessarily hold if he is a member of a group but does not care about being accepted by it. We use the term "reference group" to identify desired groups; the others are merely comparison groups. Mannheim (1957) showed that college men incorporated into their self-images the traits attributed to them by certain groups only if the men expressed a desire to be accepted into that group. Early childhood comparisons, of course, may be effective regardless of the desire to join the group.

This "interactionist" view of the development of the self-image suggests that an important aspect may be organized around the person's feeling of belonging or not belonging in any group. The sociologists have spoken of "anomie," or the condition of not having any norms to live by, as a cause of profound personal disturbance, including suicide. This is closely related to the feeling of being isolated from groups which might provide norms, a situation for which Davids (1955) has suggested the term "alienation." His definition would incorporate within the alienation syndrome such traits as egocentricity, distrust, pessimism, anxiety, and resentment. His investigation indicated that persons can be ranked on an alienation scale, and that this ranking predicts with considerable accuracy their selective perception of ambiguous auditory material, their selective memory for alienation phrases, and their responses to word-association and sentence-completion tasks. It is, in other words, a pervasive influence on the person's manner of adjusting to his environment. Nettler (1957) has a different measure of alienation, but the personality correlates resemble those reported by Davids.

Inner Aspirations. If a child acquires, usually from his parents or other adults, the aspiration to achieve a certain social role, he is likely to distort his self-image in the direction of the appropriate attributes. He may actually succeed in developing these characteristics. Thus a boy who reads books of military heroes may aspire to such a status and may cultivate mannerisms and habits of thought appropriate to it.

In the long run, it seems that the self-image is molded by social influences. The individual, however, has some opportunity to pick and choose; or, more precisely, as he learns to view one adult or group favorably, he accepts their attributions more readily, rejecting influences emanating from groups he dislikes.

Studying the Self-image. In a sense, of course, the personality inventories and self-rating devices described in Chapters 3 and 8 give data on the self-image. The only point to be noted is that our attention heretofore has been focused chiefly on getting an estimate of a specific trait, whereas we now are interested in trying to obtain a kind of portrait of the total personality.

Profile Methods. The self must be presumed to incorporate all the individual's traits. It thus follows that one approach to the self-image would be simply to plot a profile showing his comparative standing on a number of common traits. This method has been used by Cattell (1950), by users of the MMPI (cf. Hathaway and Meehl, 1951), and many others. It is a device for getting at organization or internal relationships, as opposed to point scores. So far these profiles can best be described as promising; their applications, in many instances, seem to boil down to looking for high and low scores, which could be done without plotting a profile at all.

The Q Sort. A method which seems more truly to get at the total portrait of the individual is what Stephenson (1953) has christened the Q sort. This technique requires that a person sort a set of statements to indicate how well they describe him. Typically around a hundred statements are used; he will be asked to put, say, 7 in the "most typical" pile, 14 in the next, and so on, so that the largest number will be in the middle of the series. He is thus forced to pick out the aspects of his personality which he considers most and least characteristic. Now, if two persons make these Q sorts, the distribution of items can be correlated, and the result is a direct index of the degree of similarity in their self-images. Clusters may be located by grouping together people who correlate relatively well; these will usually be found to be similar in respect to some aspect, such as intelligence, economic status, or psychiatric category. Q sorts describing the person can also be done by observers (e.g., a therapist may describe his patient, or the patient may describe the therapist). The method thus is flexible and useful for studying certain problems which cannot readily be reduced to dimensions.

The Ideal Self. Earlier in this volume we have referred to the "ego ideal," or the ideal acquired by the child, usually from his parents, as to a pattern of behavior which he should follow. Put in terms of a pattern of ideal traits, this becomes the ideal self, or more aptly, the ideal self-image. A number of investigators have compared the person's self-image with his ideal self-image, with interesting results.

Perhaps this point can best be developed by reporting a specific set of figures. Nunnally (1955) gives the correlation of various Q sorts made under varying instructions by a young woman ("Miss Sun") undergoing psychotherapy. She was required to sort into piles, labeled from "most characteristic" to "most uncharacteristic" of herself, statements such as the following:

"1. I am very self-conscious about sex. I become embarrassed when sexual matters are discussed among my friends.

"2. I guess I would be called soft-hearted. Tears come to my eyes rather easily.

"3. I am calm and placid most of the time."

Sixty such statements had to be classified into nine groups, with the largest number in the center or neutral position.

When Miss Sun's self-descriptions were intercorrelated and factor-analyzed, a general factor was found which seemed to represent her generalized self-image. The relation of this factor to specific Q sorts is given as follows:

As I am generally	.85
As I was from 16 to 18	.77
As I was from 9 to 16	.60
As my father regards me	.51
As my father wants me to be	−.45
As my friends in general regard me	.04
As I would like to be	−.21

It will be noted (1) that her present self-image agrees rather well with her memory of herself from the past, but with increasing distance in time, the similarity declines; (2) that her self-image agrees moderately well with what she perceives to be her father's image of her, but is reversed from what she thinks her father wants her to be; and (3) her present self-image is also in some respects opposite to what she would like to be.

The finding of a negative correlation between self-image and ideal self-image has been reported a number of times, and has been associated chiefly with persons showing emotional maladjustment or undergoing treatment for personality disturbance. It seems plausible that the individual who is aware of a discrepancy of this kind would be troubled by it, would exert effort to correct the discrepancy, and would show symptoms of emotional disturbance. However, because of the important effects of repression and perceptual defense in blocking awareness of such facts, severely abnormal personalities may not show this discrepancy. Friedman (1955) reports that normals show a high positive correlation of reported self-image and ideal self-image, neurotics show little agreement of the two reports, while schizophrenics show agreement almost as high as the normals. This last finding is interpreted as evidence that the schizophrenic is not aware of his own characteristics (does not perceive himself accurately), and hence can easily believe that he resembles his ideal. Indeed, it can even be argued that he is increasing his feeling of subjective comfort by so doing, since it eliminates the unpleasantness which would derive from recognizing his failures [2] (see also Chodorkoff, 1954).

---

[2] There is considerable support for the above view. It must be noted, however, that Levy (1956) has data which cast some doubt on it. Levy asked people to rate themselves for self and ideal; then he asked them to rate "your home town" as it really is, and as you would like it to be. The discrepancy for self correlated +.70 with discrepancy for the town. Levy concludes that some persons constantly see discrepancies of reality from what things should be like; he would consider this a response set rather than a basic source of personality disturbance. It can be argued, on the other hand, that anyone who has this jaundiced view of reality—as being far from ideal—must have problems and these may lie chiefly in his own failure to measure up to his ideals.

Projective Methods. The self-image may be studied indirectly by projective tests. Friedman, in the study just cited, had his subjects tell TAT stories; he then took the central character in these stories, assumed that they represented the person telling the story, and made a Q sort describing what this person would be like if this assumption were correct. He called this the "projected" self. Friedman's findings indicate that the normals and neurotics agree fairly well as to real and projected self-images; the schizophrenics, however, show no relationship of real self to projected self.

Basically similar in theory, though quite different in technique, is the work of Wolff (1943). Wolff had people judge personality traits from samples of recorded voices, mirror images of handwriting, etc. Without their knowledge, samples of their own products were included. Under these conditions, he got evidence of the unconscious self-image. His outstanding finding was that people tend grossly to exaggerate their good points under these conditions; to a lesser degree, at least, some persons also exaggerated their weaknesses. More will be said on this point later.

Organization within the Self-image. Relevant to the foregoing paragraphs is the problem of the internal organization of the self-image. The importance of this issue can be brought out by reference to the work of McQuitty (1949, 1950). McQuitty introduces one of his papers with the hypothetical example of a person who responds to two items on an inventory:

"1. My dearest friend just died.

"2. I'm the happiest person on earth."

It is obvious that a person can plausibly answer "no" to both of these, or he can answer "yes" to one and "no" to the other. If, however, he answers "yes" to both, something is wrong. What is missing here is the element of integration or consistency. A person so disintegrated as to answer positively both of the items cited would almost certainly be psychotic.

There are, however, degrees of integration of the self, just as there are degrees of the other attributes we have discussd. McQuitty proposes a statistical technique, pattern analysis, for dealing with the question of integration within the individual. His method provides a way of identifying combinations, patterns of answers, characteristic of normal people. He has provided data to show that patients in mental hospitals are distinguished more clearly by lack of these patterns than by deviation from normal answers to single questions. The abnormal personality, he concludes, lacks organization, or the organization is of a variety distinctly different from that of the average citizen. He would argue that the presence of conflicting subsystems within the self (e.g., realistic percepts and hallucinations existing side by side) indicates a failure of personal integration. Even the normal person, of course, has some inconsistencies of habits and percepts. Not much is known about the extent to which inconsistency and disintegration can be tolerated within a given personality. Perhaps (cf. Chapters 12 and 16) some individuals have a higher tolerance level than others.

Some of the circumstances which give rise to conflicting percepts or habits have already been traced (see Chapters 5 and 6). A set of experiences with siblings and peers, for example, may have built up expectancies of hostility, cruelty, and tension; experiences with adults may have established expectancies of acceptance, kindness, and relaxation. Since both of these sets have the self as a common element, there is an obvious danger of ambiguity, the inability to arrive at a stable self percept. Because the self is such a tremendously important object, ambiguity at this point may be intolerable, and the individual may resolve his problem by refusing to see the two aspects simultaneously. Since this does not solve his basic problem, he continues to manifest symptoms of maladjustment.

Stability. Brownfain (1952) has used another measure of the self-image, which he calls "stability." Probably it would be better called "ambiguity" of the self-image. He asked his subjects to rate themselves on 25 traits, first, "as you really are," second, "the highest you think you are," third, "the lowest you think you are," and fourth, "as others see you." His major interest was in the distance from "highest" to "lowest"; this represents the area of doubt, presumably, on the part of this indvidual as to where he properly falls. As would be expected, large differences were associated with emotional difficulties.

The Brownfain test was used by Funkenstein et al. (1957) in their study of physiological responses to frustration. The "stability" of the self-image was shown to be significantly related to immediate response of the circulatory system to a stress situation. More data are needed, however, before we can infer a physiological basis for an integrated self-image.

Tolor (1955) has devised a test somewhat like Brownfain's, but asking for descriptions of the self now, ten years in the past, and as expected in the future. It seems likely that the basic aspect being measured is the same in both cases: the extent to which the person can be aware of (or is impelled to deny) his inconsistencies. The normal personality would be expected to fall in the center of such a distribution, since he will (1) not have too many inconsistencies, but (2) be capable of recognizing them. The abnormal person is likely either to report an excessive number of conflicting traits or to report none at all (denying his inner difficulties).

TOWARD INNER UNITY

It is obvious, then, that no individual has a completely consistent, unified self-image. Consciously he may perceive all of his various attributes as fitting together amicably into a cooperative whole; but at least some items are rejected and those constitute inconsistencies. The clinician makes use of these in accounting for behavior which deviates from his client's usual pattern; he may, for example, be self-confident in most situations but become exceedingly unsure of himself when the task requires that he work under the supervision of a woman. This probably indicates a self percept ("I'm not the kind of guy to take orders from a woman") which he consciously denies, but which unconsciously affects his dealing with the task and his way of expressing himself.

The evidence, nonetheless, indicates that each of us tends to develop an inner unity, a unified organization of complexes, traits, attitudes, and values, in which one set of beliefs does not induce acts which violate other beliefs. The process involved is very complex; Figure 9.1 does no more than indicate some of the relationships that must be accounted for.

The Quest for Consistency. The development of the self-image is intimately tied to the need for consistency in behavior. We have stated earlier that the child needs a dependable, consistent environment to carry on homeostatic acts. But he is himself a tool, an integral part of this adjustment process. Thus he too needs to be consistent; or, he needs to perceive himself as consistent. A boy who sees himself as a very good athlete, and who learns that athletes are supposed to be dumb, may slack off in his studies and picture himself as not very bright. If he has identified with his father, who is a quiet professional man, and also hero-worships the latest rock-and-roll singer, who

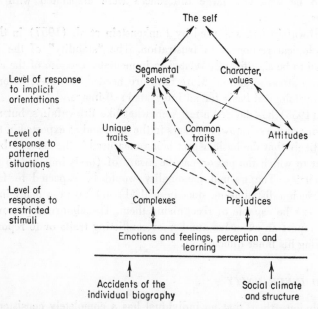

Fig. 9.1 Interaction in the development of complex phases of personality. Arrows indicate the direction of modification; e.g., prejudices may help to determine attitudes, and in turn be modified by them. Items higher in the chart usually develop from, but in turn dominate, those at lower levels. (Suggested by a different representation in Allport, 1937.)

is very noisy, he must in some way work out a resolution of the inconsistencies involved.

A major function of the self-image, then, is to bring consistency into behavior. The individual has a mental picture of himself and of the actions appropriate to this image. When faced with alternative courses of action, he may say of one, "I would never do a thing like that." His self-image is a guide, a source of inner cues to behavior which makes for consistency. Similarly, he may say, "I was not myself when I did that." He may have succumbed to temptation and taken some money; this is contrary to his self-image and he is literally puzzled as to how he could have done such a thing. The quiet, meek man who lashes out in anger will later have great difficulty in understanding what happened. The very rarity of such occurrences points to the function of the self-image in promoting inner unity and consistency of behavior.

Self-respect. In some cases we can identify "self-respect" as an intervening variable in the maintenance of consistency by the self-image. "I couldn't live with myself if I did that." Such attitudes, of course, must be traced back to prior learning sequences. The child learned first that he would be punished by his parents for acts contrary to a certain standard; later he accepted this standard and punished himself (felt guilty) when he acted against it. This corresponds to what Freud called the "superego." No new concept seems necessary if we keep in mind that guilt feelings occur only when an act is perceived as deviating from a standard. The superego is not a little man somewhere in the head who jabs me with a pitchfork when I violate social norms. I myself observe the violation, feel anxious, and scold myself for this unaccustomed act. It is also important to note that one may punish himself for acts which have nothing to do with social taboos—e.g., a researcher who commits a statistical blunder and feels depressed for days afterward. If his self-image had not included any belief in his statistical competence, he would not have reacted so strongly. He does not feel badly, for example, when he blunders at bridge.

Self-respect appears to be chiefly our introjected conception of the respect of others. We respect in ourselves what our parents praised and rewarded in us (Jourard and Remy, 1955) or what was approved by our friends (Manis, 1955). Thus it is an aspect of what Mead and Cooley have called "the looking-glass self," i.e., the self as reflected back to us by adults and peers.

Self-respect also shows a hierarchy of values analogous to that described in Chapter 4 (page 84). There will be certain aspects of the self-image which will be maintained and defended at all costs; others will be abandoned if they come into conflict with these "higher" aspects. Thus a Southern youth who places a high value on humanitarianism may come North and find that those associates whom he respects for this value are also prointegration. In this case he finds it necessary to abandon a lower-level prejudice in order to maintain his self-respect, i.e., the higher aspect of his self-image. And it must be understood that "higher" is defined by the individual's scale of values, not necessarily those of society.

Segmental Selves. A reference group may determine a whole pattern of traits rather than a single characteristic. This kind of organization we have called "segmental selves" in deference to the comment of William James that a man has as many selves as there are separate groups about whose opinions he cares. Many men have a business self and a home-family self which are different in a number of respects. He may also have a self for the gang with which he plays poker or for other special groups. It seems clear that the individual can maintain a few integrated, extensive patterns like this, if they are related to distinct environments. But if the situations overlap, then ambiguity develops and the individual has to choose; he must have a clear percept of himself and of how he will act. The number of segmental selves, then, is severely limited.

The Fantasied Self. The child does not, in every case, put forth energy to bring about conformity of the self-image with the ego ideal. In some instances nothing more tangible than fantasy results. Daydreams of being a charming conversationalist, an enchanting dancer, or a gifted artist may provide small, temporary gratifications which relieve the tension and no work is done.

Under special conditions, such as fatigue, severe frustration, or shock, the person may repress the normal self-image and begin to behave in terms of the fantasied image. This apparently is what happens in such cases of "multiple personality" as was described so graphically in *The Three Faces of Eve.* Thigpen and Cleckley (1957) indicate that "Eve Black" and "Eve White" may have arisen out of a splitting of the self-image early in life, somewhat as we suggested for the parent image (see page 119). Eve White became a good, quiet, inhibited girl; but she may have had daydreams of being a bold, sexy, gay flirt. At some point of considerable strain in her adult life she began acting out this hitherto repressed self-image.

Generally the search for unity continues. It is impossible for either self in such a split personality to achieve a gratifying and stable equilibrium. The individual usually needs professional help, in the form of psychotherapy, to reintegrate these conflicting patterns.

SECURITY AND SELF-ESTEEM

The self can best be understood by relating it to the surrounding environment, just as, in any percept, the figure must be seen against a background. And in many cases, as has been stressed in previous passages, the quality of the individual (how he perceives himself) can best be inferred from how he perceives his environment. The new development known as "existentialist analysis," a kind of therapy which involves ascertaining in what kind of world the patient lives, emphasizes the necessity of such an approach.

Our discussion of homeostasis led to the conclusion that the individual must try to maintain constancies. But the kind of equilibria he constructs and defends will depend on the kind of world he inhabits. If this is a world of soft voices and slow change, of kindly people and stable objects, the person needs no elaborate defenses and he can accept new experiences without feeling overwhelmed. But if the individual sees around him a world of harshness, where people are cruel and no relationship can be trusted, he must develop a defensive structure and maintain it at all costs. And where the first of these two hypothetical cases may have a self-image with attributes of openness and flexibility, friendliness, and confidence in others, the second will manifest a self-image of quite a different sort: closed off from others, armored against chance happenings, secretive, and distrustful. The point simply is that the self-image and the imaged environment are reciprocally related; sometimes it is best to try to understand a person by one path, sometimes by the other. For the pattern which includes an evaluation of the environment as warm and friendly, we shall use the term "security." For a feeling of ego adequacy, of ability to overpower the environment, we shall use the term "self-esteem." Obviously the two concepts are related.

Security. In Chapter 5 we laid considerable stress on the point that the young child begins to develop a generalized picture of the environment from the time of birth, and that the chief axis of variation between individuals was with reference to the favorable or threatening quality of the external world. As the child encounters a majority of pleasant experiences, he tends to evolve a picture of himself in a warm, friendly environment, where he is loved and cared for. By contrast, the child who experiences a great deal of frustration, pain, discomfort, and uncertainty may be described as developing a picture of himself surrounded by dangers, threats, and impending catastrophe. The two extremes of this dimension are called security and insecurity, respectively. Whenever attempts have been made to measure these features of the self-image (cf. Maslow et al., 1945), it has been found that most people fall between the extremes: they have some security and some insecurity feelings. This is logical, in view of the fact that every child is likely to encounter some pleasant and some painful experiences; to find that some adults are kind, others harsh to him; and to succeed in some, fail in other goal-directed activities.

A high level of security seems associated with a high degree of frustration tolerance. Since the individual perceives his environment as basically friendly, he can take a considerable number of shocks before his equilibrium is disturbed. The insecure individual, by contrast, cannot appreciate good fortune; the world is to him intrinsically hostile, and he will not believe in evidences of good faith. He is, nonetheless, likely to make exaggerated demands upon his friends for manifestations of affection and to treat every microscopic slight as proof of deep ill will. Secure personalities are generally characterized by patience and tolerance, qualities which are relatively lacking in the insecure person.[3]

Acceptance of Self and of Others. The concept of security inevitably involves the relationship between the individual's evaluation of himself and his judgments of other people. Generally they lead to the conclusion suggested above, viz., that persons who really like themselves also like others, and vice versa. By the process of stimulus generalization, similar attributes should be perceived in the self and in others. The evidence may, however, become confused because of the effects of repression and of modesty.

Fey (1955) tested 58 medical school students with a series of inventories. One involved self-judgments, and gave a score for self-acceptance; another estimated how much the person accepted others, and the third, how much he believed other people accepted him. The correlations were all positive; self-acceptance agreed with acceptance of others (+.71). Other investigators (McIntyre, 1952; Crandall and Bellugi, 1954) have reported similar observations. It thus appears that the person who approves of his own attributes also approves of other people. We cannot, however, be sure which percept is the original, the self or the other. It could very easily happen that the child first learns to like others, and transfers this attitude to himself; or it could be that he perceives undesirable attributes in himself, and projects them onto others. The data do not show which comes first.

Insight. Presumably an accurate or realistic self-image would be one which agrees with the consensus of detached observers (consensual validation). The agreement of the individual's self-ratings with ratings by a group of close associates has often been used as a measure of insight. Fey found that his subjects could not predict with any better than chance accuracy whether they would be accepted by others. Norman (1953) compared people's ratings of themselves with ratings made by close acquaintances to get a more direct measure of insight. His findings suggest that individuals somewhat satisfied with themselves, but not too high on self-esteem, came closest to predicting how others would rate them. This is plausible, in the sense that raters would probably assume that everyone has a few failings (and would not repress them, as the individual might do regarding his own weak points).

Problems in the study of insight are numerous. Everyone has a tendency to overvalue himself, but some are much more egocentric than others. Everyone has some undesirable traits, but some repress more than others. In evaluating others (an essential part of the operation), one may like people similar to himself and overstate their good points; or, finding a person like himself, he may project his weaknesses onto this apt figure. At best we can say that insight is important, and that it seems to be more characteristic of persons who are judged emotionally well adjusted than of those who have emotional disturbances.

[3] Cf. Frenkel-Brunswik and Sanford (1945) on anti-Semitism.

Self-esteem. Since conceit (egotism, or self-esteem) constitutes an aspect of personality which can scarcely be overlooked, it has long been studied and discussed by psychologists. The conceited individual perceives himself as being superior to others in one, many, or all respects. All people in Western culture are subject to pressure for overestimation of self, but also to a degree of modesty in direct expression. Persons who are overtly egotistical are thus likely to be infantile, inadequately socialized, and unpopular. If the excess of self-esteem is compensatory in character (developed to cover an inner feeling of inferiority), this failure to achieve popularity forces the individual to act even more blatantly, just as the behavior of the insecure individual often increases his insecurity.

Both very low and very high self-esteem are likely to be associated with inadequately integrated self concepts. The individual whose self-image includes many derogatory self-evaluations finds it difficult to live with and accept this image. An exaggerated sense of self-importance is likely to occur only in a rather infantile person who has failed to develop an accurate perspective on his status in society. Moderate self-esteem is correlated with better adjustment than either extreme.

The Ascendance-Submission Test developed by G. W. and F. H. Allport (1928) includes some measure of self-esteem, although it was intended primarily as a measure of socially assertive behavior. Persons with low self-esteem tend to project their ideas onto others and to assume that others have low opinions of them. They then avoid being in a forward or conspicuous role, to allay this anxiety.

Bernreuter (1933a) included in his Personality Inventory a measure derived from the A-S test, but he labeled this trait "dominance" and found it to be negatively related to introversion and emotional instability. Stagner (1937) prepared a scale with a set of questions alleged to measure persistence, but upon interviewing his subjects concluded that persons rating themselves high on persistence were really conceited. Order was brought into this area by the work of Maslow (1939), who pointed out the necessity of separating *dominance behavior* from *dominance feeling*, and concluded that dominance feeling was virtually identical with self-esteem.

Relations between Security and Self-esteem. Curiously enough, there does not seem to be any very close correlation between security and self-esteem. There is a general tendency for persons who feel insecure to evaluate themselves poorly, but there are a great many exceptions, mostly of a compensatory type.

Maslow, who has done some of the best work in this area, proposes that the interrelations of security and self-esteem can best be understood if we examine the extreme combinations. Four, he points out, are possible: (1) High security, high self-esteem; this person has strength, and also affection for his fellow man; he behaves in a kindly, protective fashion. (2) Low security, high self-esteem; this individual has strength, but feels hostility and fear of others, and is likely to behave in a ruthless, sadistic manner. (3) Low security, low self-esteem; this is the masochist, or "bootlicker." (4) High security, low self-esteem; this is the quiet, sweet, dependent personality. While these characterizations are wholly applicable only to a few individuals in any group, they are suggestive of the importance that these two facets of the self-image have in determining total behavior.

EGO STRENGTH AND EGO AUTONOMY

The concept of ego strength relates to this question of self-esteem and emotional adjustment. Clinical psychologists have for a long time spoken of the ego as the system of habits by which one adjusts to reality; a weak ego was one which was easily influenced by environmental stimulation, the strong one had clear and realistic percepts of self and of the external world. Barron (1953) isolated from MMPI a set of questions measuring what he called ego strength; these involved freedom from worry, self-confidence, tolerance. On the Rorschach, accurate form perception, good ability to organize the ink blots, the constructive combination of form and color, etc., are said to indicate ego strength.[4] On the TAT, estimates of ego strength are commonly based on the kinds of heroes described in the imaginative productions (possession of desirable qualities, adequacy of performance, ability to control the environment and his own impulses, etc.). Cattell (1957) considers ego strength to be largely describable as the absence of emotional infantilisms, excessive worries, anxiety and depression, unrealistic thinking, and inaccurate perceptions. It will be noted that in all these approaches there are suggestions that the strong ego (or self) is one which can view the environment realistically, evaluate inner impulses correctly, and deal constructively with both sets of factors.

Indicators of Ego Strength. Symonds (1951) proposes six criteria of ego strength. These may be considered indicators of the relative strength of the ego (or self) or the efficiency of the personality in dealing with internal and external disturbances of equilibrium.

1. *Toleration of External Threat.* The ability to accept disappointment, to bear physical discomfort, and to function efficiently while subject to fear of physical injury is a good criterion of a strong ego. Note, in this connection, the identity with stress tolerance and frustration tolerance (page 129).

---

[4] Eriksen (1954a), for example, derived a measure of "ego strength" from the Rorschach blots. He defined ego strength as "the individual's capacity for appraising the reasonable limits in his interpretations and perceptions of the environment." Pointing to a certain area on a Rorschach blot, he would ask, "Could this be a . . .?" Answers which were accepted by a majority of a normal group were scored as reasonable. If the subject accepted many "unreasonable" suggestions, he was considered to show ego weakness.

2. *Dealing with Guilt Feelings.* The strong ego is one which can work out compromises in behavior so that needs are satisfied without excessive guilt; and if the person does feel guilty, he is not overwhelmed by this emotion.

3. *Capacity for Effective Repression.* Some inhibition of antisocial impulses is necessary; but the person should be able to recognize that he has such impulses without being horrified at this unlovely feature of his self-image. (The use of the term "repression" is questionable here.)

4. *Balance of Rigidity and Flexibility.* As we noted in Chapter 7, individuals vary in rigidity of perception and of motor responses. The person who is too flexible, who is affected by every environmental change, is unable to maintain a course of action; but if he is too rigid, he cannot profit by new opportunities in the environment. In this case, ego adequacy goes with a moderate degree of rigidity-flexibility.

5. *Planning and Control.* The strong ego, says Symonds, is one which can make plans and then maintain a course of action to execute the plan. This implies a high degree of symbolic control of motor activity; it also suggests, as in the preceding paragraph, that some modest degree of rigidity is indispensable to avoid being shipwrecked by every little breeze.

6. *Self-esteem.* Finally, it is possible to assert that, in general, the individual who genuinely perceives himself as worthwhile has a stronger ego than one with feelings of inferiority. Care must be exercised here, since the person's conscious report of self-esteem may be coupled with unconscious self-depreciation (see above, page 193).

An examination of these six criteria for ego strength indicates that all of them derive from the basic processes of personality development which have been described in the preceding chapters. If the individual has experienced external and internal threats and dealt successfully with them, he acquires confidence in his adequacy and develops a strong ego. This almost amounts to saying that if one has a strong ego, he has a strong ego. In less circular fashion, we can emphasize the role of the environment. If the child does not have the misfortune to encounter extraordinarily strong threats, and if he is given good advice and good models by adults, he will develop these adequate techniques for adjusting. Perceiving himself as adequate, he will develop a self-image which includes self-control, frustration tolerance, and freedom from panic. If his family gives him a feeling of security, external threats will not appear excessively threatening; and if adults give him love and respect, he will perceive himself as meriting such emotions. Thus ego strength depends on the socialization process.[5]

A concept of "ego strength" as the measure of the person's freedom from

---

[5] Freud's theoretical formulation of this relationship is sketched in Chap. 14. Note particularly Fig. 14.4, p. 317, in which it is indicated that an individual may develop a strong ego in some areas but show scattered (or extensive) weaknesses elsewhere.

perceptual distortions is endorsed by Bellak (1956), a psychoanalyst who has become interested in the clarifications of analytic theory obtainable by using a perceptual framework: "Many, if not all, phenomena of ego weakness can be shown to be primarily characterized by perceptual disturbance, specifically a disturbance of the differentiation of past apperceptions from contemporary ones" [p. 30]. This approach would fit very comfortably with that outlined in Chapter 4, where it was noted that persons may be expected to differ as regards the weighting of past residues as opposed to immediately present cues. Bellak, of course, uses the term "disturbance," which seems to imply that the differentiation had once been established and later disturbed; however, it seems likely that he could accept an alternative statement, namely, that unfavorable early experiences may predispose a child to overemphasize past components of a percept and hence to fail in adjusting to the realistic contemporary situation. Such a sequence, if continued for some time, would certainly result in the "ego weakness" he mentions.

Efficient Functioning and Self-value. One way to sum up these views is to say that perceived self-value, or ego strength, is an index of the efficiency with which a person has been functioning. An illustration can be taken from the work of Solley (1954). Solley had his subjects describe themselves, using the Osgood semantic differential. They were then randomly assigned to experimental conditions, as follows: (1) all received six fairly easy anagrams to be solved; (2) upon finishing these six, group I received five insoluble anagrams, group II received three, and group III received no insoluble anagrams; (3) all were immediately given six new soluble anagrams. As expected, efficiency on the anagrams in stage 3 was sharply reduced for those encountering frustration from the insoluble anagrams. Most important for our present concern are the findings as regards the role of self-image. Correlations were computed between perception of the self as "valuable" and speed of solving the first anagram in stage 3. For the no-frustration group, this correlation was negative; for the mild-frustration group it tended to be positive but small; for the high-frustration group it was positive and very large. Solley interprets this in homeostatic terms: "It is believed that perception of 'value' of self is an index of homeostatic efficiency of behavior in that it indicates ability of the individual to compensate efficiently for delay in goal-reaching" [p. 134]. Genetically, he assumed that the person who had successfully dealt with barriers came to perceive attributes of effectiveness in the self, and so to value the self as a tool for dealing with problems.[6]

The Relevance of Perceptual Style. Since ego strength is, by general consent, involved in accurate perception of the self and the environment, it

---

[6] An interesting incidental finding was that those who perceived self as valuable made remarks about the task, commenting on the "crazy words" (insoluble anagrams), whereas those with low valuation of self made deprecatory remarks about themselves and expressed the desire to get out of the situation.

is natural to expect that the perceptual styles described in Chapter 7 are relevant. The data support this expectation. It appears, for example, that the development of a "rigidity" pattern will favor the perpetuation of infantile self-attributes, since rigidity is associated especially with overweighting cues from the past relative to those based on the present stimulus.

The most important of the perceptual styles, however, as we consider the role of the self in personality, is that which revolves around the figure-ground phenomenon. It will be recalled that some individuals were "analytic" in orientation; they held on to the figure and blocked out irrelevant changes in ground. Others were more "holistic" in perceiving; they modified the figure as changes (even irrelevant ones) occurred in the ground.

The work of Witkin (1954) has offered clear evidence that significant attributes of personality are associated with the extremes of this dimension. Thus he reports that his "field-dependent" subjects tended to be somewhat passive, to feel helpless in the face of environmental pressures, to lack self-assertiveness, and to be somewhat afraid of their own sex and aggression impulses—in short, to show signs of ego weakness.

Rudin (1955) continued Witkin's work, using social stimuli. He showed that persons who were strongly affected by the background in the physical perception tasks were also induced to change their ratings of themselves or of others by changes in social context. Thus "field dependence" and "field independence" were generalized characteristics which carried over from physical to social perception.

Ego Autonomy. Rudin and Stagner (1958) suggested that it might be more appropriate to speak of ego autonomy [7] than of ego strength in this connection. The autonomous ego, they proposed, is one which is relatively independent of field forces, whether these derive from contextual cues in physical perception or from suggestion in a social context. The autonomous ego is one which maintains a constant self-image despite variations in the situation; this would resemble Brownfain's "stability" index. The field-analytical person may perceive himself as figure with society (or at least, nearby persons) as ground. Since he habitually focuses on the figure and ignores the ground, he will be less affected by the attitudes and expectancies of others; he will be aware of, and attempt to gratify, his own impulses; he will learn realistically to observe and obey social controls, but will not be afraid of or overwhelmed by them. The field-dependent subject, by contrast, may never sharply differentiate himself from his social milieu, may have grave doubts about his own adaptive attributes, and may be overimpressed by the power of the surrounding social group to control his behavior. The authors suggest the term "ego autonomy" to identify this dimension from sharply defined self-awareness to the poorly delimited self so readily modified by the milieu.

---

[7] The term "ego autonomy" seems first to have been used by Hartmann (1939), who started from a psychoanalytic rather than a perceptual basis.

This interpretation would explain why studies of persons with decided tendencies to conform in the Asch-Crutchfield type of experiment have shown them to be somewhat anxious and submissive. If the individual does not have a clearly defined self-image, he may well be uncertain as to what he can accomplish and hence more anxious, more willing to subordinate himself to others. But even if we treat the conforming-acquiescent response pattern as an independent factor, it is clear that the tendency to conform must have the same result; i.e., the individual pictures himself not as one with constant, unchanging self-attributes, but as one who often changes to fit the environment.[8] Regardless of the correct explanation of the relationship, it should be obvious that the individual's perception of self will be affected by the same variables which influence his perceptions of parents, friends, institutions, and social roles.

The concept of autonomy would help to make plausible the data of Funkenstein et al. (1957) regarding self-image, anger, and circulatory response. Whether a strong ego is one which directs anger outward is uncertain. But an autonomous ego would most probably be one which inhibited direct expression of aggression in a test situation; the individual would maintain independence, not allow himself to be dominated by the stimulus. (In so doing he might well incur a large circulatory response.) Whether ego autonomy should be identified with ego strength in general is another matter. The persons identified by Witkin and by Rudin as field-independent would be those who made high ego-strength scores on the Rorschach, but might not fit the criteria proposed by TAT and by Barron's questionnaire. It is possible that ego strength and ego autonomy are partly independent.

Self-evaluation, Self-reward, and Ego Autonomy. It has been implicit in all of our preceding discussions (cf. Chapters 5 and 6) that the child acquires his images or generalized conceptions of "good" and "bad" behavior from adults. Furthermore, he learns that he is rewarded for one kind of behavior and punished for the other. The initial steps of an action evoke a memory of punishment, with concomitant anxiety, and the act is inhibited. Conversely, rewarded acts acquire positive valence and are repeated.

This process is far more complex than a mere automatic establishment of specific responses. The child who is punished for taking cookies quickly

---

[8] We could infer from this line of reasoning that, when a person is faced with a group of peers whose opinions sharply diverge from his, he will suffer a decline in self-confidence. This prediction was confirmed by Hochbaum (1954). Using the method of faked reports of group voting, he led some subjects to believe that they were a minority of one in a group of five or six. Under such conditions, reported self-confidence in opinions declined sharply. No such experiments, of course, have tried to reduce a person's self-confidence *in general*; such a procedure, if successful, would be rather dangerous. However, it seems from Hochbaum's results that this would be possible, and that perception of self as isolated from the majority would lead to a decided decline in self-esteem for the typical American youth. Such influences have been used by the Chinese Communists, especially in brainwashing their fellow citizens.

learns that this applies also to candy, to books, and to toys. It appears that much of this is a process of learning to see the situation as the significant adults see it; in novel surroundings the child must ask himself, "Is this what my parents would consider good?" Gradually he comes (in the normal course of events) to build up his own norms and to view actions as good or bad accordingly.

This leads to the possibility, according to Whiting and Child (1953), that the child can *reward himself* in the absence of parental reward, at least with praise and symbolic approval; and he can *punish himself* in symbolic and even in physical ways. This, of course, is a main goal of parental training; we wish the child to follow approved norms even when he is not under supervision.

But this leads also to a potential conflict. As soon as the child has reached the stage of having his own norms, and of providing his own rewards and punishments, the possibility arises of a divergence between parental norms and child norms. This difference is exaggerated as the child's percepts are modified by experience in school, on the playground, and at the movies. Then the child, acting on his own norms, may go counter to his parents' preferences. His self-reward (self-approval) becomes more important to him than the rewards and punishments from the parents.

Importance of the Self-image. We do not know much about the determinants of this phenomenon. However, many parents will attest to its occurrence. It seems likely that one major factor is the child's self-evaluation. If he perceives himself as capable of making wise decisions, then he will have more confidence in himself, and his self-rewards will presumably have high motivating value for him. There is some evidence that, in the Asch conformity experiments (see page 152), individuals with high self-esteem and self-confidence yield less often to pressure from a majority.

Ego Autonomy. Similarly it would appear that the ability to differentiate central from peripheral stimuli, the ability to cling to a percept in the face of distracting cues, may be a relevant consideration. The child may come to disagree with his parents without hostility if he feels that his percept is accurate, and that he does not have to take account of their emotional reaction. Perhaps the ability to distinguish between parental love, which is central, and parental disapproval of this act, which is peripheral, is also involved.

At any rate, as psychologists see the problem today, the development of the independent thinker is a matter of combining the perceptual style which we have called "field-analytical" or autonomous with a self-image which involves a high evaluation of the self. Under these circumstances the child becomes capable of making independent decisions and adhering to them in the face of pressure from parents or from peers.

As ego autonomy (in this sense of self-guidance) increases, we may also predict an increase in integrity, or unwillingness to act against one's own principles (cf. Chapter 10). The person who has a sharply defined image of his own norms of behavior, differentiating these from the views held by others, will be relatively less likely to show inconsistencies based on temporary pressures, the persuasion of friends, and similar influences which would, if he yielded to them, make him appear to be lacking in integrity.

This analysis has a bearing on another intricate problem upon which we have touched in other connections. We have noted (page 86) the problem which arises from the fact that some individuals become martyrs—they will tolerate even pain and death on behalf of an ideal—or, in less extreme form, will sacrifice personal comfort for a friend, a group, or a tradition.

It is obvious that the phenomenon of ego autonomy is somehow related to this question of unique motivation. Most people will abandon ideals and even friends to preserve life. The person who is capable of standing up against brainwashing, tortures, and threats of death must possess to a remarkable degree the capacity to hold to a way of perceiving an issue or a belief regardless of the extraneous stimuli brought to bear upon him. We would tentatively suggest, therefore, that ego autonomy may be a key concept in understanding why some individuals show such behavior and others do not. The perception of the situation and the channeling of motivation are inextricably intertwined.

Self-actualizing Behavior. Kurt Goldstein (1947, p. 228) refers to self-actualization as "the tendency to achieve the optimal performance of the total organism" and considers it the key concept for the understanding of personality. Maslow (1954), following Goldstein, has written extensively of "self-actualizing people" as the most psychologically healthy personalities, and those who most fully express themselves. Unfortunately, he does not give us any criteria by which we can identify such persons, except to indicate that they are pretty individualistic and do what they please, regardless of the opinions of others. Obviously such a person may be sufficiently mature that he can decide rationally to ignore social customs, or he may simply be a spoiled brat who "self-actualizes" at the expense of everyone around him.

Maslow suggests that the individual who can be a painter "must" be a painter, i.e., there is an inner need to express his potentiality. By the same token, one speculates, the gangster has an inner potentiality and "must" be a gangster. Maslow would argue that the gangster is reflecting frustration rather than true self-actualization, but he is extremely vague about the criteria by which we can distinguish healthy self-actualizing behavior from egocentric infantilism or aggression. There is a need for better analysis of this aspect of the self.

Mention has been made earlier (see page 205) of the difference between the child who actively resolves his difficulties and the one who passively waits for adults to solve them. Phenomenally, the experience of active solution would contain a strong kinesthetic component, an awareness of one's own effort in striving against obstacles. It is now feasible to relate this observation to the discussion of ego autonomy. The work of Witkin and Rudin has indicated that the autonomous personality must be guided by bodily cues to a greater extent than by visual cues, when these are pitted against one another in laboratory tests. Rudin showed that these individuals perceive themselves as changing less under environmental pressures, and there is some evidence to suggest that they actually do yield less to group influence. Such persons would be (relatively, at least) more capable than their fellows of self-actualizing, i.e., of converting ideas into actions. Particularly, they would be able to carry on courses of action which were nonconformist, and both Maslow and Goldstein seem to consider this diagnostic of the self-actualizing person. However, even this formulation would not exclude the bully, the dictator, or the sadist from the self-actualizing category. We must, therefore, reserve judgment on the view that the self-actualizing person is the healthiest, most fully developed personality.

LEVEL OF ASPIRATION

A crucial consideration in regard to self-actualizing behavior, as well as the ego ideal and other aspects of self-evaluation, lies in what we may call the *level of aspiration* phenomenon. It is a matter of common knowledge that some individuals are ambitious, perceive themselves as qualified for lofty goals, and seek to achieve them. Others aspire to little more than a biologically comfortable existence. We shall have more to say in Chapter 14 regarding Adler's theory of an inborn "will to power." At this point we wish to consider the experimental evidence on the phenomenon of aspiration level and relate it to the self-image.

Here, as in so many instances, psychologists encounter grave difficulties in trying to take personality into the laboratory. It is easy enough to devise an experiment which asks a person to indicate how much success he hopes to achieve; but it is not necessarily true that the person reveals the same inner pattern which guides him in his quest for goals in the economic, political, scientific, or artistic realms. A young man may be intensely motivated toward high achievement in writing, but when asked to throw darts at a target or cancel printed letters, he may perceive these as trivial tasks and show a low level of aspiration. For the same reason, in other parts of this book, an effort has been made to verify laboratory findings against clinical observations. Obviously the experimental method has advantages, but it also fails us in some of the crucial aspects of personality research.

With this caution, let us consider some of the investigations on level of aspiration. The standard procedure for an experiment on this phenomenon calls for presenting an individual with some task of moderate difficulty, in which he is not skilled—e.g., dart throwing, tossing pennies, or canceling letters. He is given one trial and told his score. He is then asked to predict his performance on the next trial. "What will you do next time?" is a commonly used form for this question.[9]

It is presumed that the individual's need to impute only the characteristics of success to his self-image will impel him to set his goal higher than his performance. Frank (1935) argues that the difference between past-performance score and expressed-aspiration score will be a function of varying tendencies: the need to keep aspiration level high, the need to make aspiration level conform to reality, and the need to avoid failure. In the actual experiment, it appears that these specific needs may function in radically different fashion within different personalities. One boy may define failure as doing less than he predicted; another may define it in terms of a concealed standard far below his expressed aspiration.

Even more confusing, from the point of view of interpreting aspiration scores, is the fact that the same person does not always show similar aspirations in different tests. Gould (1939), in a careful study, used six measures: synonyms, steadiness, speed in addition, digit substitution, cancellation of letters, and a target test (sliding metal disks onto a bull's-eye). She found that the difference scores (amount by which prediction differed from performance) in these six tests did not agree very closely. The 15 intercorrelations ranged from .04 to .44, with a median at .29. This means that a man with high aspiration on one test might be very low on a second and average on a third—the aspiration level was not constant. Thus there may be not a level of aspiration in general, but only specific levels for each task set.

Gould's interviews with her subjects indicated, however, that different estimates of performance might serve the same ego-protective function. Thus a person might take a certain pride in setting a high goal, even though he never achieved it; a second individual would take pride in always achieving his estimate; and a third might be proud of uniformly doing better than his estimate! A study of rationalizations indicated that the same difference score might mean different mental processes in varying subjects.

Group Standards. We have already indicated that frames of reference are profoundly influenced, if not absolutely determined, by the standards of the group within which a personality develops. Similarly, level of aspiration is markedly determined by the group with which the person compares himself. Festinger (1942) informed his subjects that they were doing better (or worse) than some specified group: high school, college, or graduate students. Aspirations were affected particularly by the subjects' being told they were below college students (their peers). His subjects were not much motivated by being either above or below high school students (inferior standard) and

---

[9] We cannot explain why such an ambiguous question has been so widely used. As recent experiments have shown, the wording of the question leaves the subject free to state what he really *expects* to do, what he would *like* to do, or what he is *afraid* that he may do.

were satisfied to be either above or below graduate students (superior standard). Preston and Bayton (1941) studied Negro college men. Midway in the experiment the subject was informed that he was doing as well as white (or Negro) men in other colleges. The group compared with whites tended to a lower aspiration level, especially as defined by estimates of the lowest score that they might make. This is interpreted as indicating the demoralizing effect of comparing a subordinate to a dominant group. Performance much inferior to the whites was now perceived as a reasonable possibility.

Maladjustment. Gruen (1945) has shown that level of aspiration is related to emotional maladjustment. Students who rated themselves as emotionally unstable (Rogers test) tended to make either very high aspiration estimates, or estimates below actual performance. The well-adjusted group consistently gave estimates just a little above average performance.

We have referred to the fact that ego strength is associated with close agreement of self-image and ideal self-image. In a sense this is a case in which the person's level of aspiration (ideal) is not too far from his present level. Ego weakness is associated with a wide discrepancy between perceived self and ideal self. On this reasoning Cohen (1954) predicted that persons showing self-rejection (disapproval of self-attributes) would reveal this in their behavior in the level-of-aspiration experiment. His actual findings resemble those of Gruen, i.e., persons showing self-rejection showed either very high or very low aspirations. Setting a low aspiration is, obviously, a way of protecting oneself against failure. Those using very high aspirations may have been very unrealistic in their perception of what was probable (perceptual defense), or they may have been using the high aspiration as a kind of substitute gratification in itself. The well-balanced individual is one who can realistically assess himself and his task; thus his aspirations are only modestly beyond his actual attainment.

Since people vary as regards aspiration level on different tasks, we cannot expect the foregoing generalizations to apply uniformly. Probably the person reveals his preferred style for defending against failure most clearly when the task presented is central, closely related to his self-image—in other words, is important to him. Under such circumstances level of aspiration may be a valuable clue revealing the inner personality.

UNCONSCIOUS SELF-JUDGMENTS

It has been necessary several times in this chapter to refer to "unconscious self-judgments." These are derived from indirect materials, e.g., by making deductions from the stories told in response to TAT pictures, from human figures seen in the Rorschach blots, etc. Manifestly it is important to get a somewhat more dependable method of identifying the attributes of a person's unconscious self-image.

The problems here are not simplified by the difficulties of getting the conscious self-image. Even at the conscious level we must bypass the tendency to conceal inferiorities, the culturally imposed need to appear modest, and a certain anxiety about what the experimenter is going to do with this highly sensitive information. At the unconscious level the problem is complicated by the person's lack of knowledge of his repressed experiences, and by the necessity of using verbal responses which seem likely to make these evaluations conscious and hence run head on into the force behind repression.

The most successful technique for resolving these difficulties to date is that proposed by Wolff (1943). The method is striking in its simplicity. Without the knowledge of his subjects, Wolff obtained photographs of their clasped hands, of facial silhouettes, and other features not likely to be immediately or certainly identified; samples of their handwriting, and of their voices; movies showing the person walking or performing a simple routine, disguised to prevent definite recognition. For verbal materials, all subjects used the same words, so that S could not recall what he had said in the recording situation.

Some weeks, or even months, later, the subjects were asked to participate in an experiment which involved judging personality traits from hands, from profiles, from voices, etc. Ss did not know that their own records were included, and virtually none recognized themselves (recognitions were discarded, since they did not meet the criterion of unconscious judgment). Under these conditions, S was shown to be revealing his secret judgment of himself when, in response to his own voice, he attributed certain traits to the person whose voice he was hearing. Wolff noted that people sometimes became quite excited under these conditions, although they firmly denied recognizing the samples as their own.

A replication of Wolff's work by Huntley (1940) used a larger number of subjects but confirms his findings in most respects. The outstanding observation is the tendency of S to make *extreme* judgments when responding to his own voice, handwriting, etc. (Figure 9.2). The number of very strongly positive evaluations is significantly above chance, and the number at the neutral point significantly below chance. Wolff also found a marked increase in very unfavorable ratings, which he interpreted as evidence that some Ss have repressed perceptions of themselves as ugly, cruel, dishonest, etc. Huntley found a slight but not significant increase in these unfavorable judgments, and Epstein (1955) obtained very few in his study.[10]

Diller's Study of Induced Failure. The findings of Huntley and Epstein suggest that Wolff's technique only strips the façade of modesty from infantile self-esteem. Wolff's original report, however, has received experimental sup-

---

[10] Exaggerated boasting and merciless self-deprecation can, of course, be observed also under sodium pentothal, moderate alcoholic intoxication, etc. The Wolff technique is superior because of the experimental control possible.

port from a study by Diller (1954), who used the technique of assigning a task and arbitrarily allowing some Ss to succeed, others to fail, without their knowledge that he was manipulating the situation. Under these conditions, Diller argued, there should be different effects on conscious and unconscious self-evaluations. This prediction was confirmed. Success on the task led to a better opinion of self as expressed both on conscious self-ratings and in the Wolff measures. Failure on the task did not lower self-value as reported consciously; but on the Wolff measures, those who failed showed a significant lowering of self-value. It would appear, therefore, that a person who fails a task may bolster his ego consciously and deny any lowered opinion of his capabilities (perceptual defense); but this failure is effective at a level not consciously recognized, or at least not consciously admitted, and the indirect techniques devised by Wolff are sensitive enough to detect this change.

Such observations are compatible with the notion of a threshold effect in personality breakdown. An individual may encounter a number of successive failures without consciously revealing demoralization. At this unverbalized level, however, tension has been accumulating, the self-image is undermined, he begins to perceive himself as essentially incapable of coping with his environment. At some point the surrounding threats are perceived as too great for him to deal with, and he "suddenly" goes to pieces. The accumulating changes might be traced by indirect methods; reliance on direct conscious report would be unwise in such instances.

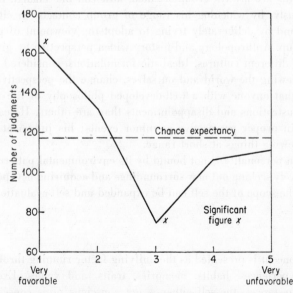

Fig. 9.2 Distribution of unconscious self-judgments. Note the great excess of highly favorable judgments of self, as compared with chance expectancy, and the relative scarcity of neutral evaluations. (Modified from Huntley, 1940.)

PERSPECTIVE

Objects which loom large when viewed at close range seem smaller at a distance. An out-of-focus perception distorts the real relationships of things in the environment. Adequate perspective allows us to get large and small troubles into their proper proportions.

The good judge of personality is capable of detachment from his social milieu; he can achieve psychological distance from people and judge them without feeling a close involvement. Adequate self-judgment apparently requires a similar detachment from the self. It is desirable to achieve proper perspective on ourselves and our traits in relation to our social environment.

There probably is no such thing as a judgment made without a frame of reference, and our evaluations of personality—including self-evaluations—are made within a frame of reference determined by our experiences. To use a fairly simple example, a person may judge himself to be a radical if his reference standard is a group of Vermont Republicans, whereas if he associated for a time with Greenwich Village Communists, he might rate himself rather conservative. The same holds for more intimate personal characteristics. An individual's evaluation of himself as dominant or submissive, emotional or calm, sociable or seclusive, will be dependent to some extent upon the group with which unconsciously he compares himself.

If judgments are always group-oriented, how can one change his perspective? Obviously, by widening his range of group contacts, in either reality or fantasy, and by deliberately trying to adopt the viewpoint of people in a different group. Anthropology and history widen perspective by giving us the standards of different cultures. Idealistic formulations, considered as vantage points for viewing the world and ourselves, change the perspective. It is for this reason that anyone with a well-developed philosophy of life is less perturbed by frustrations and disappointments than are others. He can see such happenings in proper perspective as minor events; his judgment is not obscured by viewing things at short range.

The human personality is not bound by its environmental patterns. It is capable of actively seeking out new surroundings and acquiring new perspectives. In this way the scope of the self can be expanded and self-evaluation clarified.

SUMMARY

The self concept is presented as the unifying factor running through all our emotional experiences, habits, memories, traits, and values. Except under special circumstances, the self either is not conscious or is conscious in the form of the self-image, an abstraction of one's perceptions of his real physique, intellect, habits, and emotions; of his conception of how others see him; and of fantasied qualities and accomplishments.

In Western culture the self seems to acquire through social pressure an upward tendency, a need to be evaluated highly. This need can be demonstrated to some extent in the level-of-aspiration experiment and very well in Wolff's technique for unconscious self-judgment.

The self-image always evolves relative to a social group; and in highly stable, small groups, such as primitive tribes, there may be little awareness of self as opposed to others. An individual with high security feeling has little self-consciousness. Persons shifted often from group to group will develop a clearly differentiated self concept. If this shifting involves a loss of affection and a feeling that the environment is full of dangers and threats, the person is said to feel insecure. The security-insecurity dimension is a fundamental aspect of the self-image.

Self-esteem is the positive expression in consciousness of the upward tendency of the self. Young children show exaggerated self-esteem. As we become socialized, we learn to put on a show of modesty, which may be penetrated by special methods or may be sloughed off in personality breakdowns.

Insight is the ability objectively to evaluate the self. Lack of insight is associated with projection, rationalization, and other maladjustive practices. Adequate insight into the self and its shortcomings is fostered by the attainment of perspective.

SUGGESTIONS FOR READING

The most stimulating and provocative treatment of problems relating to a psychology of the self is to be found in Gordon Allport's *Becoming: basic considerations for a psychology of personality*. Various chapters in Murphy's *Personality: a biosocial approach to origins and structure* also deal at a sophisticated level with this area. *Self-consistency: a theory of personality*, by Prescott Lecky, has been influential with American psychologists. Symonds discusses some of the empirical and clinical research in his *The ego and the self*.

CHAPTER 10

Character

The term "character" has almost as extensive a variety of meanings as does the term "personality." We shall confine our attention to two of these, which cover all the important phenomena which are relevant to our topic.

Character, first of all, refers to the individual's behavior in so far as it conforms to local mores or ethical standards. Thus, one is said to have a good character if he executes those acts which are expected by his society and refrains from those which are forbidden in the society. To some extent this tends to reduce to the common saying that a man of good character is one who has never been arrested, although most of us are inclined to go a little further than this. Character may be thought of as behaving in accordance with social expectancies.

There is, however, another group of responses, aspects of the total personality, to which the term "character" is frequently applied. An individual who shows ability to persevere in a course of action despite distractions, to keep focused on a long-term goal rather than seeking immediate pleasure, to sustain tensions rather than releasing them in impulsive behavior is often described as having a "strong character." (It is interesting that even popular speech recognizes some distinction between these two facets of character, applying the adjective "good" to the first and "strong" to the second.)

Research on both aspects of character has been somewhat limited. If we seem to dismiss the character problem in much less space than seems appropriate (in the light of its broad implications for society), this should be interpreted only as indicating the lack of dependable data. It is to be hoped that future research will clarify more of the problems in this area.

CHARACTER AS MORAL BEHAVIOR

Let us turn first to the commoner consideration, of character as a collective term for the moral habits of the person. It is clear that this component can be divided into perceptual, response, and dynamic aspects, as has been true in our analysis of other personality patterns. We may, in other words, study how the individual *perceives* actions in the frame of reference of social mores; how he *responds*, whether he behaves in accordance with the mores; and what he *desires*, that is, the motivating influences which relate perception to behavior.

The process of perceiving is important here, as in all our discussions of personality, but in a somewhat different way from that developed in the preceding chapters. We must distinguish between the individual's percept of an act as something honest (or dishonest) and as something he wishes to do. In Chapter 8 we spoke of sociability as a tendency to see other people as attractive stimuli to be approached. We assumed that no conflict existed; if the person wished to approach others, he would generally do so.

For character traits the situation is different. The world is full of attractive objects which we are forbidden to touch (property rights). We may encounter many persons who set off aggressive impulses, but we are forbidden to attack (person taboos). In at least one sense, the kind of character a person has depends on how he responds to conflict situations. If he is deficient in inhibition (response to negative valences), then he is likely to have a "weak" or "bad" character. He steals, for example, even though he knows it is forbidden.

It should be noted here that inadequate characters (psychopaths, delinquents, criminals) are not distinguished by misperceiving acts as "right" which society considers "wrong." Often such a person will claim that he thought his action was justified, but on tests of moral knowledge, delinquents as a group do not differ from nondelinquents nor do adult criminals differ from noncriminals. The difference in *character* derives from the fact that the criminal, desiring some goal which is forbidden, devises rationalizations to excuse his resolution of the conflict by breaking the law.

This view of character holds that character is a system of habitual patterns of behavior organized around goals designated by society as permissible or forbidden. Contrary to other traits of personality, which seemed to be better described as perceptual organizations, this aspect may be better described in response terms.

The Character Education Inquiry. A very important series of investigations into the problem of character is that published under the general title of the Character Education Inquiry (CEI).[1] Starting with the definition of character as behavior (as sketched above), the researchers devised a number of ingenious behavioral tests of "good" character. Thus, a child might be sent on an errand in the course of which he received more than the correct change. He had an opportunity to turn the money in or to pocket it. He had chances to cheat on school tests when apparently unobserved, and to cheat in party games. Other tests involved willingness to sacrifice personal advantage (e.g., winning a monetary prize) in favor of some other person or group. Clearly,

---

[1] The major publications resulting from CEI were Hartshorne and May (1928), Hartshorne, May, and Maller (1929), and Hartshorne, May, and Shuttleworth (1930).

these are operational samples of the kind of response we would commonly label "character."

In addition, CEI included measures of moral knowledge, attitudes and opinions, and measures of character reputation. The latter used Guess Who tests in which both teachers and classmates nominated children who showed high or low character traits.

The Generality-Specificity Question. The major theoretical problem involved in the CEI data is that of generality versus specificity of character traits. Is honesty, for example, a general trait or is it simply a label for a variety of unrelated responses? The CEI investigators concluded that character in their data was primarily *specific;* correlations between tests intended to measure the same "trait" were low. A child who cheated with money might not cheat on examinations or in games. Tests within the same environment tended to agree better; two or three classroom measures were likely to correlate fairly well. But on the whole, the results pointed to the conclusion: Children learn specific habits, they do not learn generalized traits such as honesty or integrity.

Opposing Views. This interpretation of the findings has not gone unchallenged. Gordon Allport (1935), after an examination of the CEI volumes, notes that the results were ambiguous and that the sampling of such attributes as honesty and self-sacrifice was quite restricted. A different approach might have led to different conclusions: [2]

It has been objected . . . that a high degree of generality must not be expected in young children, and that in the older children, the Inquiry did indeed find greater evidence of consistency. It has been objected that the moral habits studied are too few and too distantly related to give a reasonable opportunity for generality to emerge in the results. It has been objected that ethical rather than psychological conceptions were used, and that, although children may not be consistent in character, *socially defined,* they may be quite consistent in their own *personal* attitudes and traits. It has been pointed out that, although general moral attitudes have not been developed under our piece-meal method of education, there is no proof that such general attitudes cannot under proper conditions of instruction be produced. It has been objected, furthermore, that the theory of specificity rests upon an arbitrary interpretation of equivocal results.

Allport (1937) elaborated on his suggestion that consistency might be found in uniquely personal traits, rather than in character traits. Figure 10.1 shows his approach. The CEI data showed that lying and stealing were virtually unrelated (correlation of only +.13, which means just about no agreement between the two kinds of behavior). Allport suggests that, for a particular child, stealing may have been integrated into a pattern of showing off to prove to other kids that he was not inferior, perhaps by skill in avoiding detection.

Conversely, lying may be a protective mechanism, by which he defends himself against criticism by the teacher; and perhaps he thinks he will gain

[2] From *Handbook of social psychology,* ed. by C. Murchison, p. 811. Used by permission of Clark University Press, publishers, 1935.

influence over her and so be able to dominate the other children. This view assumes that the child's social-emotional traits (Chapter 8) and self-image (Chapter 9) provide major determinants of his character behavior. Such a view can hardly be questioned; the possibility that generalized traits of character may some day be identified must remain open.

A Study of Character Training. Allport's criticisms (and others) led most psychologists to abandon the CEI tests as inadequate for research on character. Not so E. M. Ligon, whose Character Research Project has led to numerous publications in the field of character and religious education. Most of these are remote from the problems we are discussing; but a study by Schwilck (1956) is relevant here. He divided 74 boys (of grades 5 to 8) randomly into an experimental and a control group. The former received direct character education materials relating to the question of sacrifice to help others. The latter studied a vocational problem during this period of time. At the close of the experiment, a battery of tests from the CEI research was administered to both groups. The tests included such items as working for an individual prize versus working for a class prize; voting to use the prize money to help others; giving up a preferred dessert so the money could go to a welfare agency. The tests were presented ingeniously so that there was relatively little probability that the students saw any connection with the training program.

Since the CEI conclusion had favored a specificity theory of character, it might have been predicted that the training would not affect test performance, or would affect some tests but not others. Surprisingly, *every* test showed greater willingness to sacrifice among the experimental groups, to a statistically

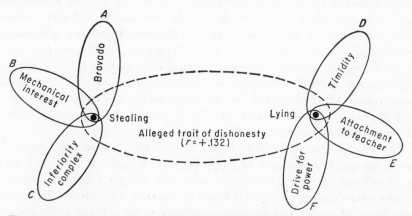

Fig. 10.1 Critique of a statistical study of traits. While the CEI study is correct in concluding that honesty is not a consistent trait (stealing and lying correlate only +.132), there may be other personal traits that were not investigated. In the situations presented to the child, lying may have been related to timidity, protecting status with teacher, etc., whereas stealing was unrelated to these attributes. (From Gordon W. Allport, *Personality: a psychological interpretation*, 1937, p. 251. Reprinted by permission of Henry Holt and Company, Inc., publishers.)

significant extent. Thus the results are compatible with the view that willingness to sacrifice may be a generalized trait.

There may be several reasons for the difference between the CEI and the
Schwilck study. The most obvious distinction is that in the CEI work the
performance of a single child was compared from one test to another. Thus,
differences in the economic status of the parents, the child's motivation, his
attitude toward his teacher, and even whether he had just received his allowance may have affected the consistency of his test performance and thus lowered the obtained correlations. Schwilck canceled out these variables by comparing only groups; his data show that training affected the average level of
sacrificing behavior, but say nothing about whether some children sacrificed
in one test and others in a different test. The Schwilck investigation consequently does not give a definite answer to the generality-specificity problem.

Reputation as a Criterion. The difficulties encountered by the CEI
tests have deterred other investigators from attempting to utilize them. Havighurst and Taba (1949) have this to say: "Good as the tests might be, and
the Character Education Inquiry Tests were good, observation of behavior
in test situations must always be a doubtful substitute for observation of
everyday behavior. The great variety of everyday situations cannot be duplicated in a small number of tests, and there is always the question whether
the test situation is lifelike enough to motivate the subject to behave as
he would in real life" [p. 9].

The solution adopted by Havighurst and Taba (which is also found in many
other studies) is to use character reputation as the criterion. The investigators collected ratings of all the sixteen-year-olds in a small Midwestern
city: ratings by adults, such as teachers, employers, and Scout leaders; Guess
Who, for ratings by age mates on specific character traits such as honesty,
loyalty, and responsibility; Portrait Guess Who scale, which gave a number
of attributes (all plausibly related to a central value such as honesty, responsibility, etc.) and still other devices. These measures provided the criteria
for selecting children high and low on various aspects of character, who were
then studied to obtain clues as to the role of parents, the church, the school,
etc., in character formation.

The General-Specific Problem. In the light of what was said in Chapter 2
about ratings, it should not be surprising that Havighurst and Taba find
more evidence for "generalized" character than did the CEI. The intercorrelations for different instruments aimed at the same attribute are high, running from .46 to .86; and the intercorrelations of the different traits judged
are also high, ranging from .55 to .86. This would tend to support the common belief that people can properly be placed on a dimension running from
"good character" to "bad character."

But there is an obvious weakness in this conclusion. What the Havighurst-
Taba data show is that people *think* in terms of generalized character. Un-

fortunately, we knew that before the investigation started. Thus, we cannot tell from these data whether the adolescents got similar ratings on loyalty, moral courage, honesty, and responsibility because these are intrinsically associated; or whether the ratings were similar because each rater simply had an over-all impression of the youngster as good or bad.

The difficulties of finding a good criterion for research on character, then, are obvious. It is for such reasons that many investigators have focused on the study of juvenile delinquents (or adult criminals) in order to escape the criterion problem. At least, the study of delinquents provides a clear-cut, unambiguous standard. Society defines persons convicted of antisocial behavior by the judicial process. In later pages we shall review some of the research which has utilized delinquents as the criterion group.

Character and Personal Adjustment. Before leaving the Havighurst-Taba study, let us note some of their findings relevant to the relationship between character, as they defined it, and personal adjustment, a trait of personality as set forth in Chapter 8. It will be remembered that in discussing adjustment, we considered the hypothesis that emotional maladjustment reflects a surplus of frustrations and conflicts which have established habits of perceiving and responding in certain ways. Such a hypothesis is also relevant to our analysis of character. We may speculate that the child who has encountered too many frustrations may reject his parents, his society, and the values they represent; or, alternatively, that the aggressive tensions built up by these frustrations bring him into conflict with social rules so that he behaves badly.

The evidence tends to support the expectation outlined. There is a consistent tendency for the children of "good character" to report the kinds of emotional reactions and perceptions which we call "well-adjusted." The correlations are shown in Table 10.1. These correlations receive support from item analyses which indicate that the youngsters in the "poor character" group are more likely to answer "yes" to questions such as: Do you feel that people often treat you rather badly? Do you usually get discouraged when other people disagree with you? Are you considered a failure in many of the things you do? Do you have many problems that cause you a great deal of worry?

These data, of course, do not prove that the frustrations, failures, criticisms, and scoldings are real. They do indicate how the youngster perceives himself and his environment; *these percepts are real for him.* Given the kind of world he lives in, it is not surprising that he fails to conform to the character expectations of society.

Age Changes. One further point about Table 10.1 deserves mention. The correlations are much higher for the ten-year-old group than for the sixteen-year-olds. In the Character Education Inquiry, an apparently opposite finding was reported. The older children showed more "generalized" character, less difference from one test to another. It was argued that this indicated an increasing degree of personality unity or integration.

Unfortunately, Havighurst and Taba have not published the correlations of character traits for their ten-year-old subjects, hence we cannot see if the sixteen-year-olds show more evidence of character integration. The authors, however, point out that there are other possible explanations for the difference between the two age groups in their data. They suggest, for example, that the sixteen-year-old subjects may have been something less than frank

Table 10.1

**Correlations between Personal Adjustment
and Character Ratings**

	Personal adjustment	
	16-year-olds	*10-year-olds*
Honesty	.39	.46
Moral courage	.26	.31
Friendliness	.43	.59
Loyalty	.31	.59
Responsibility	.20	.45

SOURCE: Havighurst and Taba (1949), pp. 293–294. Reprinted by permission of John Wiley & Sons, publishers.

in answering questions about their feelings of inferiority and insecurity. This implies that the correlations would have been higher had such frankness been obtained. A second possibility is that the older group has had longer to learn social rules and regulations (which are taught) but has had no help in achieving better personal adjustment; hence, the correlation of the two variables will be less than at the younger age. No satisfactory answer to this question is available at present.

CHARACTER AS INNER ORGANIZATION

In a study of "social responsibility," Gough, McClosky, and Meehl (1952) cite the following definition of "positive character integration" which was used by an assessment staff at the University of California: "Conscientious, sense of responsibility, strong, internally-determined principles, ethical sensitivity, sources of value internal rather than social. Stability, strength, resourcefulness under stress, and self-reliance."

While reference here is made to the acceptance of socially approved values (ethical sensitivity, sense of responsibility), one notes with interest the emphasis upon inner determination of behavior as opposed to social conformity. We would infer that the assessment staff wanted to differentiate those persons who behave in accordance with ethical standards because they have, as children, accepted these standards and perceive situations accordingly from a contrasting group of persons who may act in an ethically approved manner because of fear of punishment. This distinction is no doubt justified. We stress, however, the fact that such a distinction means abandoning a purely behavioristic or response-pattern view of character—since responses might be the same for the two groups of subjects—in favor of a view of character as an organized way of perceiving social and ethical situations.

Starting from the above definition, Gough, McClosky, and Meehl (1952) developed an inventory to measure feelings of social responsibility. Although this is a purely verbal measure, and as such is open to marked distortion by subjects who may answer so as to appear in a favorable light, the authors report several kinds of evidence supporting their claim that the scores do tend to discriminate responsible from irresponsible high school and college students.

Harris et al. (1955) used the Gough-McClosky-Meehl scale with several hundred children of various ages. One of their findings is that teachers' ratings of responsibility agree only modestly with the child's report on the inventory. This correlation, only +.23 for 10-year-olds, increases to +.34 for 15-year-old cases. This suggests, as did the CEI report, that character integration may increase with age. An alternative interpretation, unfortunately, is that the older children could better understand the meaning of the questions and so felt impelled to give answers more in accord with their knowledge of other people's judgments. As was noted in Chapter 9, the child's self-image is profoundly affected by evaluations he receives from adults. The correlation cited may confirm this assertion.

A Study of Adults. The problem of adult character has been a focus for close observation and detailed analysis over thousands of years, but little material is available which has utilized the framework and methods of scientific psychology. (We shall comment later on some of the studies of the adult criminal.) One interesting research, in the vein of those just cited, is that of Woodworth, Barron, and MacKinnon (1957).

In this investigation 100 Air Force captains were subjected to a lengthy and detailed assessment. One of the aspects of personality considered was labeled "character structure" and was operationally defined as including "integrity in the ethical sense, honesty, responsibility, dependability, lack of guile, absence of deceit, trustworthiness." Officers who were found to be high in this dimension were also said to be free of major internal emotional conflicts, to show insight, and to be low on opportunistic and exhibitionistic tendencies. The key finding was that character structure was the best predictor of success as an Air Force officer. While it is obvious that situational factors have much to do with the success of any individual in a leadership role, we may well believe that a personality located well toward the positive end of this "character" dimension has optimum probabilities as a leader. The reason for this, in terms of how he is perceived by his followers, needs no elaboration. He will provide a stable and dependable guide, a minimum of frustrations and of disappointments; in short, he will aid the follower's quest for equilibrium.

The authors conclude that character, as they have defined it, is a generalized, integrated structure. This tends to lend support to Allport in his hopeful commentary on the CEI data. Perhaps, even though children begin the sequence of character development with specific habits, they tend, on the average, to develop internal consistency and integration as they arrive at maturity.

Some Determinants of Integrity. The positive aspect of character, as indicated by these studies of children and of adults, involves some kind of picture of ideal behavior and an effort to act in accordance with this ideal when physical discomfort, social obstacles, or rival attractions militate against such persistence. We say that a person who thus clings to his path of action shows integrity. Let us now ask: Why would a person seek to maintain his integrity? And what aspects of the process of socialization seem to be involved in its development?

1. *Social Pressure.* Sociologists and anthropologists have pointed to the importance of social expectancies in this regard. Unpredictable, "spontaneous" behavior is frowned upon. The child early learns that consistency is considered a virtue. Furthermore, he is likely to discover that his reputation determines what he will be perceived as doing, irrespective of his overt acts. (The boy who gets a reputation as a delinquent will be "seen" doing forbidden things even when he is innocent. So he is prone to conclude that he might as well act in accordance with these expectancies.)

2. *Personal Expectancy.* Much of one's internal consistency and uniformity, however, is due to the fact that he wants to live up to his own picture of himself. If a boy gets a self percept which includes daring and adventurousness as salient traits, he will accept challenges which secretly he might prefer to evade. He is unwilling to abandon the image of himself which guides his behavior.

At first glance it might seem that this is only the introjection of the social expectancies imposed by his family and other persons around him. But closer study reveals that each of us often feels misunderstood, feels that his "true self" is not that seen by the neighbors. The effort to conform to self-expectancy, therefore, is not simply a response to social pressure.

Perhaps it should be noted once more that such tendencies toward the maintenance of self-constancy are not always conscious and voluntary. Indeed, it is most probable that the individual simply fails to see those alternatives which do not fit his self percept. Phenomenally, the perceptual field may be limited to those acts which are compatible with this determining pattern.

3. *Impulse Control.* Behind these tendencies toward conformity to social pressure and to self-expectancy is a variable about which relatively little is known. We have indicated earlier that the occurrence of a homeostatic disturbance sets up tension, and this tension tends to be discharged in immediate action. Punishment of impulsive acts leads to conditioned inhibition, and the inhibition of a response tendency raises the tension level still higher.

Some people do well at sustaining these tensions without overt response, until the socially approved situation is reached where action is permitted. Others seem relatively less capable of tolerating tension, and they may show either perceptual inefficiency (failure to observe cues, or fantasy of cues which are not realistically present) or behavior ineptitude (doing things clumsily, doing the wrong thing, etc.).

When we speak of integrity in the popular sense of the term, we are usually referring to an individual who stands fairly high on impulse control. When he has embarked upon a course of action, he inhibits and sustains successfully tensions related to other acts. He is not distracted, does not scatter his energies, finishes one task before beginning another.

There may be a physiological basis for impulse control. Freeman (1948) makes such a suggestion, although he is rather vague about its nature. He seems to think that variations in functioning of the frontal lobe of the cerebrum may be involved. Hebb (1949) notes that some central (cortical) organizations are more easily disrupted by incoming stimulation than are others, but most of his discussion focuses on the degree to which the on-going organization has become established. It may be, however, that there are constitutional differences in the stability of these cortical organizations; thus, to a physically identical stimulus, one person may show no disruption effect, while another is quite disorganized. Sheldon (1942) proposes that hereditary differences in body type may be involved. This theory will be considered further in Chapter 12.

4. *Perceptual Differences.* Integrity may also be fostered (or diminished) by variations in perception of the external situation. We have spoken of hierarchies of goals; a person normally seeks a highly valued goal, postponing action on goals which appear less valuable. But to some extent this process for keeping one action sequence going until completion depends on the constancy of goal percepts. A college man may, for example, see the attainment of his professional degree as a dominating goal and push aside other tendencies, such as the desire to get married. However, he may be plagued

by variations in the perceived desirability of these competing goals; on one day, marriage looks more attractive, on another, the career.

We do not know much about the factors determining these fluctuations in perceived attraction, either. It may be that they are identical with those referred to above in connection with impulse control. Perhaps all we mean by impulse control is that the person, having once structured a perceptual field so that one goal is clearly dominant, holds onto that perception. If we adopt this view, we must keep clearly in mind the fact that the consciously perceived goals are not always the decisive ones. A young man may say that his sole goal is to care for his elderly mother, when deeper exploration indicates his desire for dependency upon her and his reluctance to take the risks of living an independent life.

Clearly, then, integrity must be related to the kind of early childhood one experiences. Uniformity and predictability of parental behavior would establish at an early age clearly defined goals and clear behavior expectancies. (Whether these are "good" in either the character sense or the mental-health sense is another matter.) A boy who gets an unconscious image of his father as a powerful, punishing, rigid person may show a high degree of perseverance and resistance to distraction, but at great intrapsychic cost. His dependability is ascribable to the fact that his perception of all sorts of situations is dominated by this image of his father.

Will Power. In a sense, integrity is what is popularly referred to as "will power." Psychologists generally object to the use of this phrase. It suggests that voluntary decisions are made and carried out without regard to external circumstances. This simply is not true.

Integrity implies the ability to adhere to a course of action once it is adopted, even in the face of criticism, discouragement, and discomfort. But there is no mystical source of power which one taps to achieve this. Indeed, one would be stupid to cling to a course of action when a more pressing emergency arises. He reaches a decision on the basis of the perceived importance of the competing goals, including the goal of maintaining social acceptance and his own self-respect. This is probably the only source of additional energy which is drawn in to maintain an action sequence once it has been begun. "Will power" is no electric battery from which extra power can be obtained. Will power refers to these patterns of perseverance and predictability of behavior which we have described under the label of "integrity."

STUDIES OF JUVENILE DELINQUENTS

The problem of the criterion keeps cropping up in studies of character. Teachers' judgments, like those of parents, are notoriously faulty. It is not surprising that many investigators have decided to start with the legal criterion: a delinquent character is one who has been arrested and convicted of antisocial behavior. (To make this even sharper, most studies have concentrated on juveniles with several arrests and convictions; this excludes the casual mischief-maker and the youth who gets innocently involved with a tough gang.)

Perhaps the most studied question is that which was suggested in an earlier passage: What is the relation of character to temperament? Specifically, are delinquents prone to show evidence of emotional maladjustment, neurosis, or psychosis?

Studies Using the MMPI. A considerable number of studies of delinquent and control populations have been published, using one or another personality inventory. Since we have described MMPI at some length in Chapter 3, and since the findings are rather clear-cut, we shall first describe some of the MMPI research.

A Study of Delinquent Girls. One of the better early studies is that of Capwell (1945). She compared 52 delinquent girls with 52 nondelinquent girls of the same age level and matched as to IQ. Several personality tests were employed; the one giving the most clear-cut results was the MMPI. On this inventory, as Table 10.2 shows, there were highly significant differences on six scores. The delinquents were higher on the "psychopathic deviate" scale (*Pd*), indicating a trend to rebel against social controls, to disregard parents and others, etc. They were also higher on the "paranoid" scale (feelings of being treated unfairly). On the other hand, they were less extreme on depression, on psychasthenia (worries, daydreaming, etc.), and on schizoid tendency (withdrawal from people and from reality generally). This study clearly indicates that temperament and character are functionally related;

Table 10.2

Emotional Trends of Delinquent and Nondelinquent Girls of Equal Intelligence

MMPI scale	Percentage of delinquents who reached or exceeded 75th percentile of nondelinquents
Psychopathic deviate	93
Paranoid	84
Manic	63
Schizoid	57
Psychasthenic	57
Depression	55

All of the differences shown are statistically significant. In a normal population, about 25 per cent would reach the stated level.

SOURCE: Capwell (1945).

it raises the possibility that the occurrence of delinquent behavior can be predicted by a study of the child's temperamental trends.

A Predictive Study. As we noted in Chapter 3, the most severe test of the validity of a personality measure is its use in a predictive study. Capwell's work on the MMPI suggested the possibility that delinquent behavior might be predicted before it occurred; and Hathaway and Monachesi (1953) have demonstrated that the MMPI meets this test. These authors arranged to test the entire ninth grade in the Minneapolis public schools, some 4,048 children, with MMPI. Two years later a careful check of the local court records indicated that the test scores did predict, at a level far above chance, the probability that a child would get into trouble with the authorities.

For the more serious categories of delinquent behavior, the following scales gave significant differences between those boys becoming delinquent during the two-year period, and a matched control group of nondelinquents:

1. The psychopathic deviate (*Pd*) scale, which involves items about rebelliousness, conflict with parents, and lack of concern about misbehavior

2. The mania (*Ma*) scale, with items about overactivity, high energy level, inability to stop something under way

3. The masculinity scale (the delinquents asserted more masculinity)

4. The depression scale (delinquents showed less depression)

5. The *F* scale (one of the MMPI validity scales)

6. The social introversion scale (delinquents were slightly more extraverted)

The difference on the *Pd* scale needs no explaining; it is, however, interesting that a simple questionnaire such as this can identify ahead of time so many of the youngsters who will end up having court trouble. If we combine *Pd* with *Ma* (lack of social inhibitions and excess of activity), we get approximately twice as many delinquent boys as could be expected by chance. A similar finding holds for girls. It must be noted, however, that even this procedure predicts correctly for only about 20 per cent of those becoming delinquent over the two-year period, and it would incorrectly predict delinquency for more youngsters than it correctly identified. Hence the most we can say at present is that additional counseling and adult help for young people in these categories having poor prognoses might be of value; but the MMPI certainly does not segregate the sheep from the goats with desirable precision.[3]

Attitude toward Self. Peters (1957) has demonstrated statistically what has been known observationally for a long time, viz., that delinquent adolescents

---

[3] We have suggested earlier that the so-called "psychopath," the individual who continues in delinquent behavior even when punishment is highly certain, has failed to learn to anticipate consequences. It is consequently interesting to note that Warren and Grant (1955) find a learning deficit in persons high on the *Pd* scale. These individuals tend to give conditioned responses to both positive and negative stimuli; this behavior suggests that they have failed to perceive discriminatory cues. Further research on this line would be valuable.

have unfavorable attitudes toward laws and toward work. However, his study goes considerably beyond this unnecessary information. He compared 167 adolescent delinquents with 164 nondelinquents, roughly matched for age, race, sex, education, and urban-rural residence. The delinquents revealed unfavorable attitudes toward themselves, toward their parents, and toward other persons in general, when compared with the nondelinquent group.

This finding not only confirms the observation, in the preceding chapter, that attitudes toward the self and toward others vary together (a person who dislikes himself also dislikes those around him); it also suggests an important psychodynamic factor in delinquent behavior. The delinquent is apparently someone who has a surplus of unpleasant experiences, who lives in a threatening, unpleasant world. His feeling of self-worth has been undermined. He has, therefore, little to lose in terms of being criticized or even jailed for misbehavior. He has no social status to protect; hence, the threat of losing it does not motivate him to make such effort as is required to conform to society's standards. Further—either because he has had so many painful contacts with people, or because he sees them as like himself—he values others very little, and so discounts in advance their opinions of him. This set of perceptions makes it difficult to establish contact with him, in an effort to "reform" him.

Projective Test Data. The best available study on delinquents using the Rorschach test is that reported by Glueck and Glueck (1950) in their study of approximately five hundred delinquent boys and a matched control group. The Rorschach studies were done by E. G. Schachtel and Anna H. Schachtel, both recognized authorities in this field. Their approach tends to emphasize what we have in earlier chapters called acquisition of negative valences or anxiety conditioning; this anxiety is related particularly to figures imposing social controls. Schachtel explains their approach in the following words: "The most important consideration in answering that question (is this boy likely to be a delinquent) was whether or not the boy showed much dependence on, and fear of, authority. The more such fear and dependence had become part of the character structure, and the commands and prohibitions of the significant authoritative adults had been internalized, the more likely it seemed to me that the boy would not become delinquent." [4]

The Rorschach experts were in fact able to differentiate delinquent from nondelinquent boys from their Rorschach records alone, with a surprising degree of accuracy. Using only a "yes" or "no" prediction they correctly labeled over 81 per cent of the delinquents and 71 per cent of nondelinquents, in a population of almost nine hundred boys equally divided between the two groups (Glueck and Glueck, 1950, p. 264). (This is not, of course, prediction as in the Hathaway-Monachesi study; by prediction, Schachtel meant that

---

[4] Glueck and Glueck (1950), p. 217. Reprinted by permission of Harvard University Press.

he did not know in which group a boy belonged, and he was trying to judge from the test record alone.)

A look at the specific traits found to be most differentiating shows substantial agreement with the Hathaway-Monachesi study using MMPI. Of the delinquent boys Glueck and Glueck say, "They are to a much greater degree socially assertive, defiant, and ambivalent to authority; they are more resentful of others, and far more hostile, suspicious, and destructive; the goals of their drives are to a much greater extent receptive (oral) and destructive-sadistic; they are more impulsive and vivacious, and decidedly more extroversive in their behavior trends." [5] These findings certainly support the MMPI results as regard the psychopathic deviate and mania scales. They suggest that youngsters with certain kinds of emotional impulsiveness and lack of control may be "delinquency-prone" because of their personalities.

The Bodily Vigor Hypothesis. Temperament refers to the emotional and dynamic aspects of personality. The findings cited above would suggest that delinquents are different by temperament from nondelinquents; they have more powerful drives, stronger emotions, and especially more hostility than nondelinquents. A hypothesis offered to explain these observations is that the delinquent boy is by heredity more vigorous, more active, and hence more likely to encounter frustrations and become aggressive.

A noted proponent of this theory is W. H. Sheldon. In his research (Sheldon, 1949) the technique of somatotyping (see page 275) was applied to 200 young men in a home for delinquents. The result was quite impressive; as can be seen in Figure 10.2, college men scatter all over the somatotype chart, whereas the delinquents cluster heavily in the muscular, solid, powerful physique area. Men with this type of body build, according to Sheldon's earlier work (1942), have an excess of energy, a liking for vigorous activity, and a strong response to frustration. If these generalizations are true, we can readily see why such youths would be likely to become delinquent. Being active, they encounter more frustrations; being vigorous, they respond to frustration with marked aggression; being strong, they succeed (are rewarded for aggression). Since fighting and property damage are defined in our society as delinquent behavior, these lads are prone to wind up in that classification. (Note how well this view fits with the MMPI and Rorschach data.)

Sheldon concedes that the physical type is not in itself predictive of a delinquent career: "To try and predict such a thing as criminality from the somatotype alone would be like trying to predict where a bullet will strike by describing only the gun and the bullet and powder charge. You still have to deal with such variables as how the gun is aimed." [6]

[5] Glueck and Glueck (1950), p. 240. Reprinted by permission of Harvard University Press.
[6] Sheldon (1949), p. 745. Reprinted by permission of Harper and Brothers.

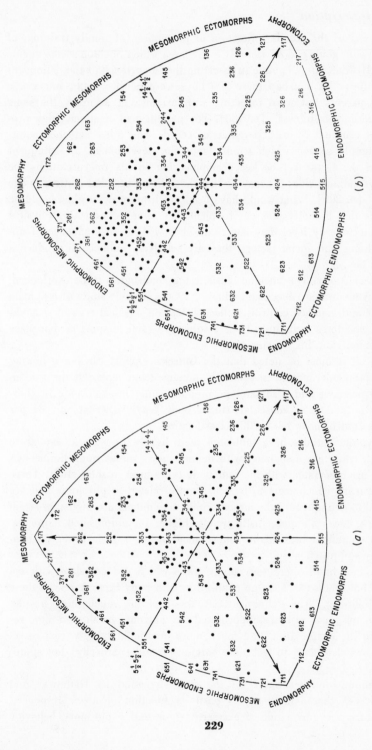

Fig. 10.2 Association of delinquency with somatotype: (*a*) distribution of somatotypes for 4,000 college males (each dot = 20 cases); (*b*) distribution for 200 delinquent boys. Note the heavy concentration toward mesomorphy in (*b*). (From Sheldon, 1949, Figs. 19 and 20, pp. 728, 729, by permission of Harper and Brothers, publishers.)

The aiming of the gun is a function of perception, of family training, of experience with goals and barriers. It is this area which Sheldon seems unable to accept. His data are emphatic in asserting the importance of the delinquent family setting: "As a group these 200 boys were neither better nor worse than their parents but were reflecting with astonishing accuracy the same level of life and usefulness" [p. 780]. The parents had relatively high proportions of criminal records, psychiatric records, and other evidence pointing to a family setting which would favor the development of delinquent patterns in the boys; yet he keeps emphasizing in his interpretations the purely physiological side: "It may be that the delinquency that matters in life is cellular" [p. 800]. What would have been much more defensible would be to conclude that heredity plus environment determine delinquency. Physical structure and energy level may contribute, but without the influence of unfavorable home and social factors, they are relatively unlikely to produce a delinquent boy.

The Glueck Study. The Sheldon thesis is too challenging to be overlooked, and it is fortunate that Glueck and Glueck (1956), in their study of 500 male delinquents and matched controls, collected data on physical type by a modification of Sheldon's technique. Their results give some support to, but place some limitations on, his conclusions.

First of all it must be noted that the Gluecks support Sheldon's finding about the preponderance of mesomorphs among delinquents. Of their delinquents, 60 per cent had a somatotype predominantly mesomorphic in character (this is the stocky, muscular, sturdy body type), whereas only 31 per cent of the control boys fell in this classification.

Secondly, the authors have tabulated their figures in such a way as to show which traits are associated with delinquency (versus nondelinquency) and which are associated with the four body types used in their study. There are several traits which seem to be consistently related to physique, and are also related to delinquency: the mesomorphic delinquents are higher in social assertiveness, lower in masochistic trends, higher on uninhibited motor responses to stimuli, a little higher on acquisitiveness, a little lower on conventionality and practicality.

On the other hand, there were many traits which did correlate with delinquency, but seemed to have no connection with body type. A few of these were the following: The delinquent boy was typically much more hostile, more suspicious, suggestible, stubborn, and adventurous; he showed more resentment in the examination and much more emotional lability (explosiveness); he was also likely to feel more narcissistic and (naturally) not appreciated.

These findings offer support for the view suggested by Hathaway and Monachesi, i.e., that delinquency is partly a function of anger responses, which in turn may arise out of excessive vigor and exploratory behavior which encounters barriers seen by the youngster as arbitrary. Not all of this can be ascribed to physical type.

The role of the family appears to be highly important; despite the careful matching of delinquents and controls, it was found that the delinquent boys' families were more often on public welfare support, were more often broken, moved more often; there was, as in Sheldon's study, a high proportion of parental delinquency (66 per cent of fathers, 45 per cent of mothers)—but, interestingly enough, a good deal also among parents of controls (32 per cent of fathers, 15 per cent of mothers). There was also some evidence of significant effects from the family's handling of the child; for instance, physical punishment was far more common in the delinquent group. (This raises an interesting problem for those who hold that delinquency could be prevented by more vigorous punishment [7] of misbehavior in early childhood.) Thus unfavorable environment has its impact on all boys, regardless of body type.

It is obvious that the Hathaway-Monachesi type of study has the highest potential for revealing important information about delinquency. However, it lacked the extensive data on family patterns which might have explained why 20 per cent of the *Pd + Ma* group (the overactive, rebellious, antiauthority youth) became overtly delinquent and 80 per cent did not. The Glueck study shows that Sheldon's emphasis on inherited body structure was overdone; there are many traits which differentiate delinquents from nondelinquents which are unrelated to body type. Yet the essential compatibility of Sheldon's stress on the mesomorph as the vigorous, adventurous, reckless boy with the Hathaway-Monachesi temperament findings, and with the Glueck statistics, cannot be ignored. As noted above, Sheldon does not argue that mesomorphy causes delinquency; he only maintains that the mesomorph is more likely to bump into barriers, to respond aggressively, *and to succeed in his aggression.* Thus, delinquency, in the sense of aggressively attacking barriers, is maintained as a pattern by the mesomorph, while other boys perhaps try it, fail, and lapse back into more socially approved patterns.

Family Factors and Delinquency. Even though Glueck and Glueck (1950) went to considerable pains to match delinquent and nondelinquent boys as to intelligence, socioeconomic status, age, and ethnic origin, they found great differences within the families of the two groups. We have noted above that there was more "parental delinquency" in the delinquent category. Further, it was observed that the nondelinquent boys were more likely

---

[7] Physical punishment is common in working-class families; however, the Gluecks controlled for class differences. Endorsement of the punitive approach to the correction of delinquency is itself a reflection of personality trends. Weiss and Fine (1955) found that propaganda favoring severe punishment was accepted far more by persons who were themselves high on aggressiveness (TAT) and extrapunitive (Rosenzweig's Picture-frustration Test). In a second study (1956) they showed that frustration increases receptivity to a communication favoring harsh treatment of delinquents.

to be living with their own parents; their fathers manifested more warmth and affection (this was also true for mothers, but to a lesser degree); and the boys showed more emotional ties to father (again, likewise to the mother, but to a lesser degree). Thus it appears that the boy-father relationship is particularly important here. If this is a favorable relationship, and if the father is nondelinquent, there seems to be a high probability that the boy will develop behavior patterns which are socially acceptable.

Such an observation is entirely compatible with the comments offered on personality development (Chapters 5 and 6). If the father is perceived favorably, the son will tend to identify with and imitate him; if the father has a good character pattern, the son will acquire it. The acquisition of an ego ideal (ideal self-image) and of a superego (system of inhibitions on impulse gratification) will be favored by this kind of family setting.

The *methods of control* used by parents would seem to be of importance. Schachtel (see above) stressed the role of "fear of authority" in the Rorschach data as a factor predicting nondelinquent behavior. Similarly, many commentators on contemporary juvenile delinquency espouse a return to vigorous physical punishment for misconduct by youngsters. The study by Glueck and Glueck raises grave doubts about the wisdom of such a policy. As Table 10.3 shows, the parents of the delinquent boys were already using physical punishment to a vastly greater extent than parents of nondelinquents. Even if we make allowances for the possibility that the delinquents

Table 10.3

Methods of Control of Boy by Parents

	Delinquents	Nondelinquents
By mother:		
Physical punishment	55.6%	34.6%
Deprivation of privileges	46.5	45.2
Threatening or scolding	46.9	37.0
Reasoning	16.4	28.2
Appeal to pride	9.7	9.4
By father:		
Physical punishment	67.8	34.7
Deprivation of privileges	24.9	26.2
Threatening or scolding	32.2	31.5
Reasoning	11.3	24.4
Appeal to pride	3.7	6.0

Percentages are based on 482 mothers and 441 fathers of the delinquent boys, 489 mothers and 447 fathers of nondelinquent boys.

SOURCE: Glueck and Glueck (1950), p. 132.

had no doubt provoked the parents, we certainly see no indication that increased physical discomfort would have any perceptible effect in reforming these boys.[8]

Evidence from other kinds of studies (cf. page 406) suggests that physical punishment is effective only if it is given within a context of warmth and affection. We speculate that punishment in a context of affection is perceived by the boy as correction of his behavior; but in an atmosphere of rejection by the parents, he perceives the punishment as simply more evidence of parental hostility. The latter, certainly, will not bring about correction of misbehavior.

THE ADULT CRIMINAL

Less research has been done on adult criminals than on juveniles, and much of what is available has been poorly done. We arbitrarily summarize, therefore, the consensus of those studies which seem to provide dependable results. In the first place, the prison population (which we here define as criminal, using the legal criterion) does not differ significantly from the non-prison "normals" as regards intelligence and other manifest characteristics. Secondly, men in prison do not differ from those outside of the same cultural level as regards judgment of what is "right" and "wrong." Moral knowledge and moral concepts have been acquired. There are, however, evidences of poor impulse inhibition (the inability to foresee future punishment) and low ego strength (tendency to rationalize, to believe what one wishes to believe, to deviate from realistic perceptions).

The importance of the person's relation to authority figures has been stressed earlier as regards the juvenile delinquent. Students of adult criminality have emphasized the same point. R. M. Lindner (1944) wrote an excellent analysis of an adult criminal psychopath under the intriguing title, *Rebel without a Cause*. According to his view, the true criminal is in rebellion against the socialization process and is permeated with hatred for parent figures and anyone who symbolizes the parents. This hostility may be focused on policemen, the courts, persons possessing wealth who do not share it (this is the picture many children have of their parents).

Such criminals undoubtedly occur. However, it is worth noting that the adult criminal often shows a specific character defect rather than a generalized "bad character." The CEI data cited above indicated that children may consistently cheat in one situation and be consistently honest in another. Similarly, criminals often show a highly specific pattern (a good safe-cracker would not deign to stoop to shoplifting) and may be surprisingly dependable in some aspects of human relationships. This line of thought suggests a

[8] The role of severe physical punishment in childhood backgrounds of adult murderers is discussed with dramatic illustrations by Duncan et al. (1958).

restriction on Lindner's view that the criminal is a rebel against authority. Perhaps the average criminal is rebelling against authority in a specific context; or he may simply lack the ability to anticipate punishment and hence to mobilize the anxiety which would block his specific antisocial habits.

Criminal behavior can also be homeostatic, in a real and important sense. Harold Lindner, another specialist in criminal behavior, offers the following analysis: "The understanding and treatment of criminosis—real crime—lies in the proper evaluation of those *predisposing motivants* which predispose one toward criminal behavior, as well as those *precipitating (environmental) factors* which kindle the crime and offer the external media in which it is enacted. Criminosis results when the predisposing motivants are ignited by the precipitating factors. Criminotic behavior is an attempt to alleviate the internal crisis and restore internal balance." [9] This view would hold that the predisposing motivants include an excessive desire for a certain kind of gratification (e.g., money, sex), an exaggerated hostility toward persons who deny the individual some kind of gratification, an excessive fear of seeming weak and unmanly, etc. Given the presence of such an inner state, the precipitating environmental situation merely triggers an explosion; the criminal act then is an attempt to regain equilibrium. Obviously such behavior is shortsighted; the criminal act simply leads to another disturbance of equilibrium, the threat of punishment. We may suggest, then, that criminal behavior is homeostatic in a short-run sense, but that it reveals an inability to perceive the probable consequences of such behavior.

CHARACTER AND EQUILIBRIUM

Seen in the frame of reference developed in preceding chapters, character involves efforts to maintain certain kinds of constancies or equilibria. Delinquent behavior appears as an effort to protect or restore steady states valued by the individual, even if this effort exposes him to the risk of other threats and disturbances (social punishment). To put it succinctly, the delinquent perceives the risk of punishment as either improbable or unimportant. The rewards appear either more certain or more significant. These may include group approval or protection of a self-image (vigorous, daring, independent of authority).

In the same way, the positive aspect of character, the ego ideal of integrity and responsibility, represents a valued state which the individual strives to protect. In Chapter 9 we noted that great energy is mobilized to stabilize the self-image. We now emphasize the idealized aspect of the self-image. The person who has accepted from his parents a picture of himself as conforming to certain standards, stronger than certain temptations, will try hard to

[9] Lindner (1955), p. 286. Reprinted by permission of Charles C Thomas, publisher, and the author.

protect that picture. The delinquent often is doing the same thing, but his loyalty and perseverance are focused on perceived objects disapproved by society.

Obviously there is a continuum of personalities involved here. We do injustice to the facts when we adopt a legalistic frame of reference and view all convicts as completely bad, all citizens without police records as good. The "good" character has occasional weaknesses, and the criminal may show loyalty and adherence to standards in his own fashion. For social purposes it may be necessary to divide people into the "good" and the "bad," but psychological realism denies the validity of such a dichotomy. There are all degrees of good and bad character. They differ as regards the kinds of values they are protecting, but they are the same in seeking to maintain these desired states.

How do these points relate to the role of family factors in delinquency? First, if social ideals are not represented in the home, no desire to conform to such ideals is built into the personality; the maintenance of this aspect of the self-image is never brought into play.[10] (It should be noted that in the delinquents studied by both the Gluecks and Sheldon, the parents tended also to be relatively delinquent, and the child's ideal self presumably reflected this fact.) Second, if the parents preach social ideals but reject and punish the child, he may perceive these "approved" values as alien or threatening. If he perceives no chance of attaining success (love of his parents) by following these ideals, he will reject them. Positive character training, then, must hinge on associating these ideals with good parent figures, with affection, with a strong self-image, and with rewarding experiences. Third, excessive punishment or punishment in an atmosphere of rejection does not teach the child to avoid criminal behavior. It is likely rather to generate hostility directed against authority figures and society in general, which will motivate antisocial acts when opportunity offers.

SUMMARY

Character has an ethical-conventional reference, and thus it is less easy to define than temperament. Character traits are traits which carry a pronounced flavor of social approval or disapproval. Since this implies an evaluative judgment of an individual's behavior, there is a strong argument in favor of defining character traits in terms of responses, whereas we have in preceding chapters treated traits as patterns of perception.

Studies of behavior have led to a controversy as to whether general traits

---

[10] The possibility that the parents hold ideals other than those approved by the majority of society must not be overlooked here. See p. 499 for a discussion of the possibility that social-class differences may account for some of the differences in both character and temperamental traits of working-class as compared to middle-class children.

of character exist; some evidence suggests that we can identify only specific habits. When we deal with character reputation, however, we find that people believe in generalized character traits, and some research has used such social judgments as a criterion of character.

A great deal more work has been done using a legal criterion, i.e., conviction as a criminal or repeated conviction as a juvenile delinquent. By both this and the reputation criterion, delinquents appear to have less ego strength; they have unfavorable self-images, excessive worries, and hostilities. A combination of bodily vigor and poor home environment seems to be exceptionally fertile in producing delinquency. Physical punishment seems, if anything, to strengthen delinquent behavior, not to eliminate it.

Character conceived as integrity, loyalty, and similar inner traits has been studied increasingly in recent years. Persons assessed as high on character in this sense were found to be free of major emotional conflicts, to have favorable self-images, in short, to show what we have called ego strength. Character is therefore intimately integrated with temperamental traits and with the self as described in preceding chapters.

SUGGESTIONS FOR READING

The literature on character is voluminous, but good material containing empirical research is relatively rare. The volumes published by the Character Education Inquiry illustrate the methodological problems encountered in such work: Hartshorne and May, *Studies in deceit;* Hartshorne, May, and Maller, *Studies in service and self-control;* Hartshorne, May, and Shuttleworth, *Studies in the organization of character.* Havighurst and Taba, *Adolescent character and personality,* is probably the best of recent investigations in this area. Using the criterion of juvenile delinquency, Glueck and Glueck have made important contributions to the study of character: *Unraveling juvenile delinquency,* and *Physique and delinquency.*

CHAPTER 11

Attitudes and Values

In the preceding chapter it was suggested that personality can be thought of as being divided into two parts, temperament and character. Unfortunately, this dichotomy leaves some relevant aspects of the individual unaccounted for. Certainly most of us would agree that a man's personality is not completely described until we have paid at least some attention to his religious, political, aesthetic, and other values; and in general, it would also seem important to consider his attitudes on various more specific issues, such as racial segregation, labor unions, and the like. These are, of course, related in some way to character, since they involve the person's perceptions of societal institutions and controversial social issues. The difference from character is found precisely in the fact that traits described under the rubric of character are matters of virtually universal agreement within a society. Almost everyone, even penitentiary inmates, agrees that stealing is "wrong." On the topics we shall now discuss, large groups within our society are in marked disagreement.

Homeostasis, Attitude and Value. It was proposed in Chapter 4 that, as the individual develops, he builds up successive "envelopes" in the form of a stable physical environment, a social environment, and finally an ideological environment. Further, the person tends to mobilize energy to protect these constancies from disturbance in much the same way as he does to defend himself against physical pain and deprivation. This connotation is clearly most relevant to what are commonly called "values." A man with a strong religious value may accept ostracism or even torture rather than abandon his beliefs. To him the ideological envelope is of surpassing importance and he will tolerate disturbance of other equilibria to protect it. (This is not entirely dependable as a criterion separating value from attitude, since a man's attitude favoring labor unions may be so potent that he will similarly face physical brutality rather than give up his views. In general, however, "value" designates a stronger potency and "attitude" a lesser potency of belief.)

The difference between trait, as a generalized pattern of perceiving and behaving, and value or attitude is likewise fuzzy. Traits, it should be observed, have generally a subjective reference, involving the individual's image of himself or of his interactions with others. Attitude and value have relatively objective reference to institutions or organizations of a less immediate nature. As an example, we might say that John has an aggressive personality (trait level) which helps to explain the vigor with which he expresses his political views (level of attitude). This same example can serve to remind us that all of the dissecting of personality presented in these chapters is arbitrary and artificial and is done for clarity only. Defense mechanisms, traits, values, and character systems all exist simultaneously within a single person, and they interact with each other continuously. The clinical psychologist, trying to work with the whole person, must be simultaneously aware of most of these variables.

In the homeostatic process of trying to defend preferred values, the individual makes use of whatever resources he has. Thus a devoted Communist (a kind of fused religious-political-economic value) who perceives himself as an intellectual may try to defend his faith by writing and argument; another, whose self-image is more socially oriented, may utilize face-to-face persuasion more, and so on. His way of responding to attack will also reveal his characteristic defense mechanisms; one man will repress any awareness of defects in communist ideology or practice, another will rationalize, another will project responsibility onto the "bad capitalists." (Need it be added that staunch defenders of capitalism show the same defense mechanisms? It should not be assumed that mental health and sound personalities are all lined up on one side of any controversial issue.)

The Role of Stereotypes. It is important to note that many attitudes, at least, do not represent the kind of value constancy described in the preceding paragraphs. One may develop a hostile attitude toward Jews, or toward organized labor, etc., on a basis similar to that described in Chapter 5 for learning to perceive objects as attractive or threatening. That is, the child may hear the name of a racial, religious, or nationality group coupled with very unpleasant epithets or with atrocity stories; this tends to establish a percept of this group as having undesirable attributes. If, however, this process never becomes associated with strong emotional systems (such as the child's attitudes toward his parents), the prejudice remains superficial and easily modified. We shall discuss later in this chapter some important research which indicates the role (in relation to prejudice) of the child's emotional security with his parents.

Attitudes are generally recognized as having three attributes: (1) an object; (2) a direction; and (3) intensity. This analysis holds up well where stereotypes are involved. Thus one may have an attitude toward Adolf Hitler (object) which is unfavorable (direction) and powerful (intensity).

Osgood (1957) reports several studies which suggest the necessity of breaking down these variables further. Analyzing data collected with the semantic differential (see page 47), he concludes that judgments made of attitude objects are likely to vary along an evaluative (good-bad) dimension, a potency (strong-weak) dimension, and an activity (active-passive) dimension. It should be noted, however, that the occurrence of the last two (activity and potency) seems to depend on the sampling of attitude objects used. All of his analyses show the evaluative factor as the most important, hence it would appear that if we know the object, the direction of evaluation, and the intensity of evaluation, we have the major components of any attitude.

METHODS IN ATTITUDE STUDY

Since the attitude is similar in most respects to a trait, the techniques used for studying attitudes are on the whole similar to those used for traits described in Chapter 3. Perhaps the most widely used is a modified questionnaire or inventory technique known as the opinionaire, or attitude scale. Projective devices have also been employed, and the Osgood semantic differential has recently become popular in attitude research.

Scaling Techniques. Widely used in the construction of attitude scales are the methods associated with the names of Thurstone, Likert, and Guttman. Each method involves collecting a considerable number of statements about the attitude object; for instance, one might clip from newspapers, or invent, statements ranging from enthusiastic support of labor unions to belligerent attacks on unions. From this point on, the methods differ, although in essence they all seek to identify statements which fall on an assumed dimension from favorable to unfavorable. Thurstone (1929) has a number of judges read each statement and assign it a value from 1 (pro) to 11 (anti). If judges disagree, the item is discarded. The remaining statements can then be set up in a scale and given to subjects, who are asked to check only those which represent their feelings about unions; the average of the ratings given by the judges to those items checked determines the person's score.

It is readily apparent that the Thurstone technique allows us to determine, for any subject, the direction (favorable or unfavorable) and intensity of his feeling with respect to the object of the scale. It was thus a simple step for Remmers and his students to develop generalized scales without naming the object of the attitude. Thus one could merely preface the following statements by any object, e.g., monogamous marriage, to obtain scale scores for this attitude: [1]

1. Is perfect in every way.
12. Is valuable in creating ideals.
19. Is improving with the years.
25. Is too conservative for a changing civilization.

[1] Reprinted by permission from Remmers (1933).

38. Is entirely unnecessary.

45. Has positively no value.

This device has proved useful in studies where it is desired to obtain quickly a numerical score representing attitudes of subjects toward one or more social institutions. It does not, of course, tell us anything about the factors contributing to this attitude; Remmers would argue that such information should not be mixed in with the task of measuring the attitude itself.

An approach which resembles that of Remmers in some respects but must be developed separately for each attitude to be measured is that proposed by Guttman (1950). In this "scalogram" technique the step of having statements judged for favorableness, as in the Thurstone and Remmers methods, is eliminated. However, most users prefer to develop the scale on one group of subjects and apply it to another, hence the amount of work is rather similar to that in the Thurstone method. Guttman argues that a true scale should be so arranged that a person will agree with all items up to a certain point, and then reject all beyond that point. (Thus, a person might agree to some statements: that unions are not necessary, and that workers are free to join unions if they wish; but might reject statements approving a union shop contract or a closed shop agreement.) Since the statistical requirements of the Guttman technique are rather strict, he may start with 50 items and wind up with five or 10 in his scale. These are likely to be very obvious, ranging from "I think unions are wonderful" to "I think unions are terrible." The measurement properties are excellent, but the amount of information obtained is limited.

The Likert method is simpler than the others in that the opinion statements are presented to the subjects, who usually answer each item on a 5-step scale from strong agreement to strong disagreement. An arbitrary score is computed for each subject, in terms of the investigator's judgment as to the favorable and unfavorable items,[2] and on this basis, a group of extremely favorable and a group of extremely unfavorable subjects are established. Each item is then tested to see if it agrees with this rough "total score" grouping, and if it fails to do so, it is rejected. The final scale then is composed of items which agree well with the total score for the attitude.

Essentially all of these methods are devices for ensuring the internal consistency or reliability of the scale. They do not guarantee the validity of the scale. Validation depends on some external criterion, such as voting behavior, joining groups devoted to a certain cause, or donating money to such causes.

Qualitative Analysis of Stereotypes. If one starts with a stereotype, such as communism, or Jews, or labor unions, or Republicans, he can develop

---

[2] In his original work Likert (1932) used a very complicated method for determining the values to be attached to the five answers for each opinion. However, he found that attitude scores using these elaborate procedures correlated +.99 with scores obtained simply by assigning weights of 1, 2, 3, 4, and 5 to the steps from strong agreement to strong disagreement.

one of these scales and get a quantitative measure of the exact degree to which a person favors or is hostile to that stereotype. But in many cases we would like to know more than this. We would like to know, for example, the attributes he perceives as inhering in a given stereotype. If the word "Democrat" evokes an image of someone who is dirty, wearing ragged clothes, and using uncouth English, we know much more about the person having such images than simply his score on a scale (although we can infer this easily!).

The semantic differential has been utilized for this purpose. A subject may be asked to judge the same concept, e.g., Russians, on a number of adjective scales. He may indicate that he sees Russians as unfair, cruel, and bestial, but strong and swift. Contrariwise, he may judge the Hungarians as unfair and cruel, but weak and slow. The scale score might be the same for the two stereotypes, but qualitatively there are important differences which should not be lost.[3]

The extent to which the semantic differential picks up meaningful differences can be illustrated by reference to data collected in a study involving 150 community adults in the summer of 1952; they were asked to judge a number of political figures and issues on the differential scales. The data were analyzed in terms of the three factors mentioned earlier (good-bad, strong-weak, and active-passive).[4] The wide divergencies of meaning can be illustrated by citing a few instances: General Douglas MacArthur was judged to be very fair, very strong, and very active by Taft Republicans; he was seen as somewhat fair, moderately strong, and moderately active by Eisenhower Republicans; and by Stevenson voters he was judged to be neither fair nor unfair, and only a little above neutral on the strong scale, but quite active. Since MacArthur was the same stimulus for all, it is clear that attitude is having a major influence on how he is perceived by different observers. To take one more example, "labor unionism" was seen as a little unfair, but strong and active, by Taft supporters; the Eisenhower group agreed, less emphatically; and the Stevenson voters judged this concept slightly on the fair side, but decidedly strong and very active. These findings surprised no one, in the sense that experienced political observers could have predicted all of them; however, the technique permits the uncovering of relationships which could not be detected, or verified, without such a method. For example, it appeared from the data that "socialism" was judged unfavorably by all groups of voters; but it was also judged to be weak and passive, hence, presumably, the failure of propaganda based on an appeal to fear of socialism. One does not fear something which is weak and ineffectual.

[3] For examples of the type of study described, see Stagner and Osgood (1946); Osgood (1957), pp. 189–199.

[4] Cf. Osgood et al. (1957), pp. 104–124. The judgments were actually made on 10 scales, but these were reduced to 3 by combining those having heavy loadings on a given factor.

Projective Studies. Numerous investigations have been published utilizing projective methods for revealing attitudes. Haire (1955) showed a photograph of a man, with brief biographical data, to union officials and company executives. (The same photo was shown to both groups.) When the picture was labeled "secretary-treasurer of his union," the unionists perceived him as conscientious, honest, and responsible, but the managers did not. When his photo was labeled "local manager of a small plant which is a branch of a large manufacturing concern," the company executives described him as having these desirable traits, but the union men could not see them. Similarly, Haire and Morrison (1957) showed a picture of a picket line to several hundred school children. Those from poor neighborhoods described the strikers as "good people, clean, smart, nice." Those from relatively wealthy neighborhoods rejected such descriptive phrases. Thus it is clear that we can learn about attitudes through projective methods.

Relation to Self-image. We may also obtain important information by ascertaining how closely the qualitative attributes of a stereotype agree with attributes the person ascribes to himself. Child and Doob (1943) showed that college students ascribed to preferred nations (our allies in World War II) the traits ascribed to self and liked; they ascribed to enemy nations traits they did not like, and denied possessing themselves. Stagner (1950) found that if men were classified by an attitude scale as prounion or antiunion, their pictures of the stereotyped factory worker and business executive differed sharply. What was especially interesting was that the prounion students projected *their own traits* onto the factory worker, not the business executive; while the antiunion students reversed this. As we have commented many times, each person lives in a reality uniquely his own; the objects to which he is responding have the attributes he ascribes to them. It is hardly surprising that misunderstandings are so common in areas of attitudinal controversy; the "facts" are quite different for people at different points on the attitude scale.

Autobiographical Materials. Actually, almost any kind of freely expressed comments reveal significant aspects of attitude. Consider the following quotations, each written by a college freshman:

I have been raised as an Orthodox Jew. I attended Hebrew school for 7 years, going after-school each day and Sunday morning. I still pray about five mornings a week, using the leather bands on my arms and head. I still feel quite keenly about my religion. I have never eaten anything but kosher food. I feel in deep need of religion, and get consolation out of thinking about my religion. I believe that religion is the greatest thing in a man's life. I cannot understand what atheists live for.

The other writes thus:

Concerning religion, I could write all day, but I will boil down my idea in a few words. I think that all religion, as it is today, is too narrow, too hypocritical, too backward, and is and will retard the advance of the present civilization if the people do not recognize the latent danger in the outworn church policies. The church is one of the many outworn machines of the patriarchal [*sic*] system that must go.

We would have no difficulty in assigning either of these young men to a place on a pro- or antireligious scale; but we learn a great deal more than this from reading their comments.

Various investigators have employed autobiographical materials in attitude research. Stouffer (1931) had students write accounts of their personal experiences relevant to alcohol and the prohibition legislation; judges read these statements and rated them for attitude toward prohibition. The ratings correlated very highly (better than .80) with measures based on a Thurstone type of scale for attitude toward prohibition.

ATTITUDE AND FRAME OF REFERENCE

In many preceding chapters it has been necessary to call attention to the concept of frame of reference. The individual develops a certain set of standards, in terms of which he views new objects as they appear. The professional weight lifter finds a dictionary "light" whereas the watchmaker says it is "heavy." A person who is "boisterous" in Scotland may seem "inhibited" in Italy. The frame of reference is normally internalized and used unconsciously in such evaluations. In effect it means that one's past experiences, systematized and crystallized, provide a context for new events.[5]

The frame of reference is obviously related to the concept of reference group. We assimilate, from groups of which we are members or aspire to be members, certain standards of what is "good" or "bad" and we use these standards in judging. Thus, the aspiring medical student adopts the accepted "line" on socialized medicine; the labor union member incorporates standards of value which are accepted in his group; and the young corporation executive quickly learns what attitudes are safely expressed in the office. We all tend to conform to our social groups, and these views soon become introjected so thoroughly that the individual sees new ideas in the approved frame of reference quite automatically.

The number of dimensions appropriate to a frame of reference has never been satisfactorily decided. In Chapter 4 we suggested that behavior has essentially two dimensions, approach-withdrawal and excitement-depression. It may be that in judging objects, we use essentially the same two: approval-

[5] This and other passages of similar import rely on the demonstration by Helson (1947) that a person's percept, in a specific cue situation, is a function of his previously established adaptation level for that class of stimulus. Our implicit assumption is that traits (perceptions of others and of specific self-attributes), the self-image, and attitudes could all be related to an adaptation-level base. The number of logical steps necessary to fill out this argument disposes us to leave it as speculative at present.

Fig. 11.1 A visual representation of British and American stereotypes. The cartoonist has graphically depicted the role of perceptual distortion in mutual misunderstanding. (By permission of *Time and Tide*, London.)

disapproval, and intensity (cf. the discussion of stereotypes, pages 238 and 241). As already noted, however, Osgood (1957) argues that semantic space, which is what we are talking about, has three dimensions. His analyses indicate that people make judgments about ideas, persons, and objects in terms of (1) evaluation, (2) potency, and (3) activity. This analysis has yet to win widespread acceptance, but it may well be that every frame of reference can be reduced to certain standards by which we make judgments in these independent dimensions. (Thus, two observers might disagree in judging Franklin D. Roosevelt as good or bad—in a political sense—while they agreed in conceding that he was potent in terms of national significance and "active" in terms of his impact on events.)

Perceptual Distortions. Viewing persons and events through these frames of reference, each of us distorts to some extent the attributes perceived. An amusing illustration of this is offered in Figure 11.1; the cartoonist shows how the typical American and the typical Briton misperceive each other. It seems clear that attitudes may involve the same kinds of perceptual errors which have been listed elsewhere. One may *magnify* certain cues (e.g., when a few corrupt union leaders are exaggerated to cover the entire union movement), *repress* certain facts (Americans denounce the Russians for punishing writers who sympathize with the West, but ignore American denunciations of anyone sympathetic to Russia), or *distort* information to fit a preconceived notion (Communists see American troops in Lebanon as imperialist aggressors, but Russian troops in Hungary are befriending the workers).

Attitude and Learning. Numerous studies have shown that such attitudes, once established, can interfere with the acquisition of new information contradicting the attitude. Levine and Murphy (1943) had students memorize passages relating to communism. Those whose attitude scores were relatively favorable to communism learned procommunist material easily, but had trouble with anticommunist passages; the reverse was true of the students whose measured attitudes were anticommunist (see Figure 11.2). Havron and Cofer (1957) have confirmed the Levine-Murphy finding, using paired-associates learning. Edwards (1941) used a related technique to show modification of memory by attitudes. He presented a speech carefully equated to have just as many statements favorable to Franklin D. Roosevelt's New Deal program as were hostile to it. Students who reported attitudes favoring the New Deal could recall, on a memory test, considerably more such items in the speech than could students critical of the New Deal; the latter, in turn, remembered much critical material which had been forgotten by the students friendly to Roosevelt. We must assume, therefore, that, once a frame of reference has been established, it will have a selective effect not only on learning but also on forgetting. Thus we line up evidence to support our prejudices, but resist vigorously any observations which tend to break them down. This, after all, is what should happen in line with our discussion of homeostasis (Chapter 4). Once a comfortable equilibrium has been established, we usually resist factors which would disturb it.

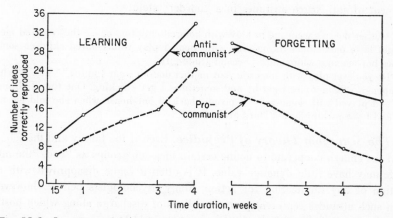

Fig. 11.2 Learning and forgetting of controversial material. People learn more rapidly and forget more slowly material that agrees with their prejudices. The material here was an anticommunist paragraph; Ss were two groups of college students selected for relatively extreme attitudes for or against communism. (From Levine and Murphy, 1943.)

DEVELOPMENT OF ATTITUDES

A specific attitude develops as (1) a percept of an identifiable, distinctive object is formed and (2) a consistent emotional orientation is adopted with respect to this object. If this happens in early childhood, the first observable attitudes are likely to be extreme because of the relative intensity of the child's emotions. Just as the little boy, at the Oedipus complex stage, may express the wish that his father would die, so he may demand the extermination of all Negroes, or capitalists, or Germans, when he adopts a hostile attitude to any such group.

Blake and Dennis studied the development of white children's attitudes toward Negroes. They found that the youngest children showed no prejudice. However, when prejudiced attitudes were first detected, they were quite extreme: [6] "The young white child acquires first of all a generally unfavorable attitude toward the Negro, which makes him unwilling to attribute to the Negro any 'good' traits. With increased age and experience, the child gradually learns to apply the adult stereotypes, a few of which are complimentary." Thus the older children ascribed to Negroes such attributes as "musical" and "good sense of humor," whereas the younger ones had only an all-or-nothing reaction of disapproval.

Importance of Family Group. Relatively few attitudes are acquired, it seems, from direct experience with the object involved. Usually the child acquires a favorable (or unfavorable) definition of a group from his own reference groups, primarily his family. One observational and interview study of considerable interest is that of Horowitz and Horowitz (1938), on the development of anti-Negro attitudes in a "border" state:

"Mother doesn't want me to play with colored children, cause they colored men. Might have pneumonia if you play with them. I play with colored children sometimes but mamma whips me." [Second-grade girl.]

"Do you ever play with someone your mother doesn't want you to?" "Yes." "What happens?" "Sometimes I get by and sometimes I get a licking. One time I slipped off and played with some colored people, back of our house when she told me not to, and I got a whipping." [Third-grade boy.]

The Scapegoat Theory of Prejudice. Even if the family and the school and the church cooperate to define certain ideas or groups as "bad," the attitude may have little dynamic value. It is often a vague disapproval with no notion of any implication for action. Many psychologists believe, however, that such attitudes represent preformed lines of discharge along which hostility, if aroused, is likely to be displaced (cf. page 118).

The most widely cited experiment relevant to this problem is that of Miller

---

[6] Blake and Dennis (1943), p. 531. Reprinted by permission of the American Psychological Association, publishers.

and Bugelski (1948). In this study boys in a CCC camp were given a simple rating scale to show attitudes toward Mexicans and Japanese; then they were subjected to a boring series of tests which were so dragged out that they missed the weekly movie, an important item of recreation for the boys. The attitude tests were repeated at the end of the evening, and it was found that a decided shift in attitude, toward relative hostility, had occurred. The interpretation proposed is that hostility toward the experimenters had been displaced onto the scapegoat groups.

Stagner and Congdon (1955) attempted to repeat the Miller-Bugelski study, using college students and a laboratory frustration. They found no evidence for a scapegoat effect, but the differences in testing conditions prevented direct contradiction of the scapegoat theory. It seemed possible that the Stagner-Congdon subjects blamed themselves rather than the experimenter for their failure, and hence had no surplus of hostility to displace onto the minority groups in the attitude measurement situation.

Importance of Displacement Theory. The importance of the phenomenon of displacement of desire and emotion onto irrelevant objects, in psychological theory, can hardly be exaggerated. We have noted (Chapter 5) that stimuli present along with pain or pleasure can acquire the properties of punishment or reward. Freudian theory holds that the affection or hostility of the child toward his parents becomes displaced to the nation, to authority figures, and to the system of law and order imposed by the parents as agents of society. Some statistical evidence favoring this view has been published (see Krout and Stagner, 1939; Stagner, 1944, 1954). The studies on *The Authoritarian Personality*, to be examined in later pages, also require an assumption of this kind. And of course, in Chapter 10, our discussion of delinquency suggested the relevance of such a theory.

Not all of these are precisely analogous to the scapegoat situation. There are many cues which facilitate identification of the nation and the legal system with the parents. We speak of the "fatherland" and "mother country." Parents reinforce their own authority by more or less veiled references to the police. History books and political speakers stress the role of the nation as a source of protection, nourishment, and security.

It must be noted, however, that some of the same influences favor scapegoating in the sense of providing cues by which the child may come to identify certain groups as suitable objects of aggression. Parents and schools hand down folk tales and traditional distinctions which suggest that foreigners are bad, members of opposing religious groups are bad, members of other races are bad. Thus it seems likely that the typical child has ample opportunity to acquire unfavorable stereotypes of minority groups; he is psychologically prepared to channel hostility against these groups if he is frustrated and the frustrating agent is so powerful he dares not attack it or even fantasy attacking it.

This view holds that social attitudes derive their dynamic force from the personal emotional life of the individual, and that his enthusiasms, prejudices, and institutional loyalties are channels through which emotions become attached to symbols rather than to specific individuals. The person for whom symbols have low reality value will not show this process to any great extent; this may account for the fact that the "ideological envelope" is not an important homeostatic factor in a great many personalities.

Age Differences. The mechanism of selective learning would suggest that people become better integrated and somewhat more extreme in their attitudes as they grow older. This would occur because the individual would "see" the evidence which supported his attitudes, and fail to observe occurrences which contradicted his view.

Fisher (1948) compared college students with their parents on a series of attitude scales. She reports the curious finding that the older generation is more extreme both on radical and on conservative items. This would seem to suggest that the various opinions were held in more extreme form by the parents, but that they had not reflected upon and integrated these items. The over-all comparisons, including moral and religious issues, showed the parents to be unquestionably more conservative than the students.

Similar observations, excluding the extreme endorsement of radical items, have been reported by others. Peterson (1936) compared parents and high school children on several scales. The parents were more conservative on all except items regarding old-age pensions (where endorsement of pensions was scored as liberal). Newcomb and Svehla (1937) found students more liberal on religion than their parents. However, these researches may contain unsuspected pitfalls. Bender (1958) retested 84 Dartmouth College men after 16 years, and found that they had shifted significantly to become more religious and more theoretical in their values, less aesthetic, and less social (humanitarian). This seemed to indicate an important age trend; but when he compared the alumni scores with a current class of Dartmouth men, he found no significant differences! The shift from 1940 to 1956 on the part of the alumni, then, may have been only a reflection of a change in the cultural climate, not a true effect of aging.

Bender's observations fit with those reported by Nelson (1954), using an omnibus questionnaire asking for opinions on a wide variety of issues. Nelson compared scores of over 3,000 students from various kinds of college institutions in 1936; later, in 1950, he obtained retests from a substantial proportion of them. His data are summarized in Table 11.1. At first glance it appears that age has induced a decided shift toward the liberal position, with every group changing in that direction. But when we compare a control group of 1950 students at University B with the 1936 group from that university, it appears that Nelson found a liberal drift in the cultural climate rather than a bona fide change due to aging. The correlations found between the 1936 and

Table 11.1

Shifts in Attitude with Age

	N	1936	1950	p
		Attitude means		
Students at four state universities	190	31.64	30.62	.08
Students at six Lutheran colleges	360	34.15	30.93	.003
Students at six other denomina- tional colleges	351	30.58	29.38	.001
Students at University B	106	34.69		
Control group at University B	405		32.74	.008

SOURCE: Nelson (1954). Reprinted by permission of the American Psychological Association, Inc.

1950 scores of individuals (.52, .50, .63) indicate that each person tended to keep his place in the group, but shifted along with the group.

Why would Nelson find a cultural shift to liberalism while Bender obtains a more conservative pattern for religion? The answer seems to lie in the issues covered by Nelson's inventory. Nelson inquired about attitudes on free trade, race relations, and world organization of nations. On such issues there has been a marked change in majority opinion in the United States. In 1936 the New Deal reforms, moves toward reciprocal trade agreements, and fair employment practices were highly controversial; the nation still held aloof from the League of Nations. In 1950 we were firmly committed to the UN, and had moved far toward the "liberal" position on other issues.

It is difficult, then, to say that age in itself affects attitudes. The process of aging may make for adopting a more extreme stand on an issue already accepted or rejected; this would follow from selective perception and learning. But people also tend to conform to a majority, and during the 1936–1950 period governmental action plus world events brought about majorities decidedly on the "liberal" side of the issues cited. Religion, not being subject to these pressures, could shift in the opposite direction; but as Bender showed, the higher religious values of 1950 also reflected cultural shift, not age change. Presumably age in and of itself does not make people either liberals or conservatives.

THE AUTHORITARIAN PERSONALITY

Perhaps the most important single book in the field of attitude-personality studies is *The Authoritarian Personality* by Adorno, Frenkel-Brunswik, Levinson, and Sanford (1950). The study began as a study of prejudice against Jews and Negroes. However, it soon became apparent that these prejudiced personalities had many other attributes in common. The concept of "fascist attitudes" suggested by Stagner (1936a, 1936b) and developed into "politico-economic conservatism" by Newcomb (1943) was applied and found useful. Projective devices were utilized for evoking significant emotional ties with parents and other authority figures. Ultimately the authors accumulated evidence which pointed—so they felt—to the existence of an integrated syndrome which they called "the authoritarian personality."

The chief components of this personality pattern were said to be the following:

Conventionalism: Rigid adherence to established middle-class values

Authoritarian aggression: Readiness to condemn, reject, and punish anyone who violates these conventional values

Authoritarian submission: Submissive, uncritical acceptance of conventional values

Anti-intraception: Hostility to imaginative or tender-minded attitudes

Superstition and stereotypy: Mystical beliefs; rigid categorized thinking

Power and "toughness": Focusing on weak-strong, leader-follower relations; overemphasis on importance of dominance and power; exaggerated assertions of personal strength and toughness

Destructiveness and cynicism: Considerable hostility, pessimism about worthwhileness of the human race

Projectivity: Belief that the world is wild and dangerous, projecting inner hostility onto external circumstances

Sex: Exaggerated concern with sexuality of others

As one of the steps in the development of a measuring instrument (the F scale) [7] the authors correlated each of these items with every other item. The average of the 435 coefficients was $+.13$, the range from $-.05$ to $+.44$. Thus it appears that these items "hang together" to some degree and support the notion that the antidemocratic syndrome is real. However, there was no tendency for items relating to each of the clusters cited above to agree especially well; hence, there was no justification for treating the clusters as meaningful. The authors simply call attention to some of the kinds of symptoms that were found to make up the authoritarian syndrome.

In addition to this technique, the authors also established the internal consistency of the F scale by showing that each item in the scale distinguishes people in the same direction as the total score on the F scale; hence, all the items have direction in common. As a sequel to this, they interviewed inten-

---

[7] "F scale" refers to an assumed identity of these attitudes with fascist ideology. The regimes of Adolf Hitler and Benito Mussolini embodied many of the above beliefs. However, as is noted on p. 252, other "authoritarian" ideologists exist which were antifascist during the critical years 1930 to 1945.

sively persons scoring high on the F scale, and found evidence that all these individuals did have emotional attributes in common. Finally, it is especially important to note that the F scale did correlate to a satisfactory extent with questions directly related to prejudice against minority groups.

Conclusions from the Adorno Study. Obviously, one major conclusion from the research published in *The Authoritarian Personality* is that social attitudes have an underlying emotional content as opposed to rational content. For example, they noted that Jews are criticized as too clannish, group-centered, shutting out Gentiles, etc., and are also criticized for being too "pushy," trying to force their way into Gentile groups and not staying where they belong. There is an obvious logical contradiction here, but in terms of emotion, the person who feels hostile to a stereotype of Jews can endorse all kinds of critical statements. Thus the two sets of criticisms ("seclusive" and "intrusive") give a correlation of $+.74$.

A second major conclusion is that prejudiced individuals are more alike than unprejudiced individuals. This likeness cuts across a variety of areas, family life, sexual adjustment, social relationships, religion, economics, and politics. "A basically hierarchical, authoritarian, exploitive parent-child relationship is apt to carry over into a power-oriented, exploitively dependent attitude toward one's sex partner and one's God and may well culminate in a political philosophy and social outlook which has no room for anything but a desperate clinging to what appears to be strong and a disdainful rejection of whatever is relegated to the bottom." [8] In contrast, it appears that there are many "types" of democratic, equalitarian, affectionate personalities.

As is implied in the preceding paragraph, a third conclusion relates to parent-child interactions. The prejudiced adults reported that as children they had been subjected to harsher and more rigid discipline; the parents were perceived as distant and forbidding; the goals set for the child by his parents seem to have been quite conventional. The parents were described as impatient and easily displeased. It is interesting to observe that interviews with prejudiced and nonprejudiced children led to similar conclusions (Frenkel-Brunswik, 1948).

While the authors specifically disclaim any concern with ideologies, it is obvious that such investigations have important significance for politics and economics. We shall note some of these implications in Chapter 21.

Criticisms of the Adorno Study. While admitting the great impetus to attitude research given by the Adorno research, many psychologists feel that this work was conducted within a limited frame of reference and hence requires both amplification and restriction. Shils (1954) and Rokeach (1954) have noted that *The Authoritarian Personality* studies began at a time when social scientists were concerned with fascism and anti-Semitism as salient

[8] Adorno et al. (1950), p. 971. Reprinted by permission of Harper and Brothers, publishers.

problems. It was thus easy to concentrate on the authoritarian attitude as one of adherence to the "leader principle" of Hitler and Mussolini, ignoring authoritarian components in the communist ideology, in the Catholic Church organization, and even in areas of science, art, and philosophy. Similarly, the Adorno group thought of intolerant attitudes as prejudices against Jews, Negroes, and minority national groups. Rokeach observed that many people who are free of these prejudices show sharp intolerance of Republicans and Democrats, classical liberals, and anyone else who rejects their belief system.

"Dogmatism." Following up this approach, Rokeach (1954) published research using a "dogmatism" scale, which included items such as "My blood boils whenever a person stubbornly refuses to admit he's wrong." He reported that his dogmatism scale picked out not only those persons high on the *F* scale but also others who were highly intolerant of deviant opinions. Another scale he prepared was called the "Opinionation Scale" and used phrases such as "Only a simple-minded fool would think that . . ." This scale agreed rather well with the dogmatism scale. In some research in England he found that Communists were more dogmatic than adherents of the Conservative, Liberal, or Labour parties. Admitted Communists are hard to find in the United States, but he did find that Catholics tended to be more dogmatic than Protestants or Jews.

Barker (1958) has also demonstrated that "authoritarianism" can occur among conservatives, middle-of-the-roaders, and liberals or leftists. He finds, for example, that a group of dogmatic leftists and dogmatic rightists were similar in their readiness to impose censorship—they simply differed in the persons they wanted to censor. Comparing dogmatic and nondogmatic *S*s, he found the dogmatists different as follows:

 ⟋ Less tolerant of ambiguous situations
 ⟋ More inclined toward stereotyping people
 ⟋ More opinionated
 ⟋ More submissive toward authority
 ⟋ More favorable to censorship of individuals named

(As noted above, the authorities accepted and the individuals to be censored differed within the dogmatic group.)

Judgments of "Authoritarians." DeWit (1955) attempted to study the dimensions of authoritarian attitudes by using Osgood's semantic differential, but instead of applying factor analysis, he determined the extent to which a given person used other adjectives as equivalent to "good" and "bad." Thus, he hypothesized, an individual might use "strong" as equivalent to "good" and "weak" corresponding to "bad," as is suggested by Adorno et al. (1950). From the list of aspects of "authoritarianism" cited above, DeWit selected three possible dimensions for testing: conventionalism, anti-intraception, and power. (As noted above, the "authoritarian personality" has been alleged to be highly conventional, hostile to idealistic or impractical views, and power-oriented.) To test the hypothesis that people use these three dimensions in judging attitude objects, he computed a measure of relationship [9] for the extent to which judgments agreed with each other. Thus for each person he computed a figure showing how well a scale such as "conventional-unconventional" agreed with "good-bad."

The study supported the prediction that three scales for "conventionalism" would agree highly. Evidently this is a meaningful and consistent dimension for judging concepts such as "beer drinking," "atheist," "Harry S. Truman," and "dictator." The anti-intraception or idealistic dimension did not hold up so well. These scales (idealistic-realistic, subjective-objective, intellectual-practical) did not agree well among themselves. Nor did the "power" dimension prove satisfactory. Further, the "conventional" scales agreed only slightly with the anti-intraception and power scales.

DeWit's analysis indicates that people do not make judgments in the manner alleged by the authors of *The Authoritarian Personality*; persons scoring high and low on the F scale do not differ in their use of these scales. Particularly in the case of the adjectives relating to power, there was no evidence that persons high on the F scale tended to consider powerful objects as good, and weak ones as bad. Persons high on the F scale were significantly more inclined to treat "conventional" and "regular" as positive values (suggesting conventionalism) and also "practical." Since the superiority of the businessman over the intellectual is a part of the American cultural climate, it may be that this use of "practical" also reflects a conventional turn of mind. At any rate, it would appear from DeWit's findings that if a high score on the F scale has any bearing on attitudes, it is in the tendency to treat the conventional as the good. As noted below, other evidence suggests that the F scale may be a measure of conformity rather than of power orientation as suggested by its authors.

Response Set and Acquiescence. A different, and perhaps more serious, criticism is that the F scale, which plays such a central role in the "authoritarian personality" research, involves a strong "response-set" bias. All of the items included in the final version of the scale are to be answered in the affirmative to be scored for profascist attitude. (There were three items to be answered in the negative in a preliminary version, but statistical analysis screened them out.)

We have already pointed out (Chapter 7) that acquiescent response set can operate in a wide variety of situations—in true-false examinations, in personality and attitude inventories, in the Asch conformity experiment, and so on. The importance of this variable as regards the F scale is indicated by such studies as those of Jackson, Messick, and Solley (1957b). They prepared

---

[9] The measure developed indicates how well judgments of good-bad agree with judgments on other bipolar scales. To get a more reliable measure of what S considered "good," ratings were pooled for the three scales "good-bad," "valuable-worthless," and "fair-unfair."

reversed statements of F-scale items, so that they had a new scale with opposite content, but couched in the same somewhat vague and pompous style of the original scale. They obtained many positive correlations between the F-scale item and its reverse; this result indicates that many people were simply agreeing with broad generalizations and disregarding the meaning of the items. The F scale and its reverse correlated $+.35$ (Jackson, Messick, and Solley, 1957), whereas the correlation should have been negative according to the Adorno results. Bass (1955) has shown statistically that at least 25 per cent of the variance among people's F scores is due to the response set of acquiescence, instead of to authoritarianism as such. Many psychologists suspect that the 25 per cent figure is low. Cohn (1953) and Ancona (1954) have also published evidence indicating that acquiescence is an important component of F scores. All these authors hold that the error due to response set is so important that it vitiates many of the conclusions reached by the Adorno group relative to the "authoritarian" person.

In opposition to these critics, Gage, Leavitt, and Stone (1957) offer the interesting notion that acquiescence is really an aspect of yielding to authority, and hence it is right and proper that the F scale should mix content (the meaning of the items) and form (the tendency to agree with any conventional statement). They argue, consequently, that the F scale or its successors should continue to use primarily negative or authoritarian items. This argument is compatible with ideas suggested in Chapter 7 (see page 153), but it represents a point of view not widely held by psychologists. Most would prefer to see a measure of authoritarian attitude which was not contaminated by the response set of acquiescence.

Correlation with Intelligence. Still another weakness of the F scale is that a number of studies have shown that it correlates negatively with intelligence to a substantial extent (Cohn, 1953; Davids, 1955). This observation has raised the question, more or less implicit in our discussion of acquiescence, whether the F scale may pick out primarily a rather shallow and superficial trend to agree with conventional-sounding statements. It may well be that intelligent persons make low F scores, not because they are free of authoritarian attitudes, but because they recognize the inadequacies of the clichés so freely utilized in the F scale. Rokeach has asserted that his dogmatism scale is independent of intelligence; since it has not been so widely used as the F scale, this statement is not adequately verified. However, it would seem likely that attitudes of submission to authority, hostility to out-groups, and blind defense of ideology may vary independently of intelligence.

As noted above, these criticisms do not diminish the importance of the Adorno group's contribution. Publication of *The Authoritarian Personality* gave a tremendous impetus to research on the interrelations of temperamental, emotional attributes and social-political attitudes. It is now generally agreed that a man's attitudes are an integral part of his personality, and that such attitudes derive their dynamic power from the emotions channeled into them. If these emotions are infantile, intense, and little subject to conscious scrutiny, the attitude may become a principle guiding the individual in his major activities, distorting his perception in related fields. In such ways arise the fanatic, the ruthless supporter of a group or a belief.

Further Studies of Authoritarianism. The F scale has given rise to a spate of studies seeking to relate inner personality characteristics to social attitudes. Jones (1957) analyzed the "authoritarian" tendency into anxiety, hostility, and rigidity. It is easy to see how a person with such characteristics might become the conservative conformist featured in the F-scale studies; but it is equally obvious that he might become an authoritarian radical, rejecting established values but conforming blindly to an ideology or a party. Such a view would be compatible with the view expressed by Rokeach, and illustrated by his work on dogmatism.

Intolerance of Ambiguity. In Chapter 7 we mentioned, as an example of perceptual style, the phenomenon of "intolerance of ambiguity." Frenkel-Brunswik (1949) showed that children differed with respect to their ability to accept an ambiguous state of affairs, and indicated that prejudiced children sought to read definite meaning into ambiguous stimuli. This work has been extended by Kutner (1958), who found that prejudiced children tend to be "stimulus bound," i.e., to be excessively concrete, incapable of abstracting attributes from the stimulus objects; they were also inclined to "jump to conclusions," to show premature closure, and to perseverate on incorrect hypotheses, thus showing rigidity. An "intolerance of ambiguity" showed up in several tests. These findings are closely parallel to those reported above for adults; since the subjects in Kutner's research were second-grade children, we are led to speculate that the perceptual style favors the development of prejudice.[10] Only a longitudinal study of the same children over a period of time would *prove* that the perceptual style preceded the development of prejudiced attitudes.

Guilt and Hostility. McClosky (1958) speaks of measuring attitudes of liberalism-conservatism and relating these to feelings of guilt and hostility; however, his items are rather similar to those in the F scale. Further, all his items give a conservative score to a "yes" answer, thus conforming to the "acquiescent" pattern noted above. It seems likely, therefore, that his conservatives are much like the "authoritarian" group. Some of his items are shown in Table 11.2. The items were first classed as conservative by judges, then subjects were classified into four groups—extreme liberals, moderate liberals, moderate conservatives, and extreme conservatives—by their scores

---

[10] Contrariwise, it should be observed that some investigators (McCandless and Holloway, 1955; Davids, 1955) report evidence rejecting the theory that intolerance of ambiguity is associated with high F-scale scores. The weight of the evidence at present, however, seems to favor such an association.

Table 11.2

Items Used to Define Liberalism-Conservatism

If something grows up over a long time there is bound to be much wisdom in it.
If you start trying to change things very much, you usually make them worse.
You can usually depend more on a man if he owns property than if he does not.
A man doesn't really get to have much wisdom until he's well along in years.
It's better to stick by what you have than to be trying new things you don't really know
about.

SOURCE: McClosky (1958), p. 31. Reprinted by permission of *American Political Science Review*.

on the entire set of items. Each group included 200 to 300 adults in the Minneapolis area.

McClosky also obtained from his respondents answers to questionnaires constructed to measure temperamental-social traits, such as feelings of hostility, rigidity, contempt for weakness, ego defensiveness, dominance, pessimism, social responsibility, self-confidence, and guilt feelings. The scores of persons in different attitude groups were then tallied for high or low tendencies on the temperamental inventories.

The results are rather astonishing for their consistency. As one reads the tabulations across from liberal to extreme conservative (Table 11.3), there is a steady *increase* in the following: guilt feelings, hostility, paranoid tendency, contempt for weakness, ego defense, rigidity, obsessive traits, and intolerance for human frailty. Conversely, there is a steady *decline* in the qualities of dominance, social responsibility, and self-confidence.

McClosky holds that there is a logical and plausible relationship between the attitudinal and the temperamental measures. "In many ways hostility is a principal component of the conservative personality, as it is a principal component of conservative doctrine," he writes. "It does not seem accidental, considering the data . . . that conservatives prefer to believe in man's wickedness, that they choose to see man as fallen, untrustworthy, lawless, selfish and weak. Expressed as political doctrine, these projections of aggressive personality tendencies take on the respectability of an old and honored philosophical position." [11] As to the lack of self-confidence and dominance, he comments, "Persons who feel inadequate and who for one reason or another dislike themselves are often the quickest to aggress against others and to demand perfection of them" [p. 43]. The argument, thus, is that the frustrations, the insecurities and the inadequate self-image have a primary role; the conservative philosophy is accepted because it fits these strong emotional needs. This is essentially the same as the interpretation offered by the Adorno group for their findings. We

[11] McClosky (1958), p. 41. Reprinted by permission of *American Political Science Review*.

have already indicated that many psychologists criticize the Adorno study as being loaded in a certain direction, i.e., concentrating on the "authoritarian" conservative and ignoring the "authoritarian" radical. McClosky's data must be viewed in the same light. He ignores the probability that some individuals with strong guilt feelings adopt radical philosophies and project their hostilities onto the "bad conservatives," as the conservatives do with the "bad radicals." At most we can conclude with confidence that political attitudes do frequently serve as a channel for the expression of inner emotional tensions, anxieties, and hostilities.

Table 11.3
Personality Traits and Conservative Attitudes

	Liberals	Moderate liberals	Moderate conservatives	Extreme conservatives
Dominance:				
% high *	72	50	29	14
Social responsibility:				
% high	47	31	23	8
Self-confidence:				
% high	46	38	24	20
Guilt:				
% high	16	18	28	47
Hostility:				
% high	18	37	46	71
Paranoid tendencies:				
% high	16	27	37	62
Contempt for weakness:				
% high	8	18	29	55
Need inviolacy (ego defense):				
% high	11	20	38	60
Rigidity:				
% high	18	32	41	60
Obsessive traits:				
% high	24	31	43	55
Intolerance of human frailty:				
% high	8	16	23	54

* % high = percentage of the group scoring in the upper third of the distribution on the personality scale.
SOURCE: McClosky (1958). Table reprinted by permission of *American Political Science Review*.

Conforming Behavior. The experiment on conformity to majority pressure devised by Asch (1952) obviously identifies persons who have something in common with the conforming behavior shown by those scoring high on the *F* scale; and Linton (1955) has shown that high *F* scorers do tend to conform more than others. In a sense, therefore, it is appropriate to refer to conforming behavior as an attitude. Among our acquaintances we readily note those who habitually conform to custom, and those who blatantly disregard common habits as to dress, manners, and other aspects of society. These nonconformists are also likely to endorse opinions which are contrary to majority views. Thus, while the importance of the "response set" on the *F* scale is not to be denied, there still is an aspect of personality here which merits consideration.

One of the most methodical explorations of the personality traits of the conformist is that of Crutchfield (1955). In this investigation 100 Air Force officers (average age, 34) were subjected not only to the conformity experiment but also to a variety of personality assessment procedures. These men, above average in intelligence and all having leadership experience, were nonetheless susceptible to the conformity pressure. Using the procedure described on page 39, Crutchfield presented them with situations in which a "majority" gave an answer which was obviously incorrect. In this conflict situation many yielded to majority opinion. The proportion conforming varied, of course, with situations; on an *obviously* incorrect judgment of size, 46 per cent gave in to group pressure; on ambiguous stimuli, 79 per cent accepted the group answer. When their attitudes were compared under free-response and group-pressure situations, great differences were found. It was possible to increase agreement with such proposals as putting a limitation on freedom of speech from 19 per cent to 58 per cent by this technique.

Crutchfield was especially concerned with the personality traits of men who yielded consistently to group opinion, as contrasted with men who yielded rarely. According to a staff of psychologists who observed all of the men for several days, the conformers were "submissive to authority, narrow of interests, over-controlled, vacillating, confused under stress, lacking in self-insight." On a questionnaire the conformers preferred strict laws, and clear-cut situations. They reported some fear of high places, guilt feelings, and other signs of emotional disturbance significantly more often than did the nonconformists.

In the absence of developmental studies of individuals, one cannot say which came first, the acquiescing-conforming kind of response set or the emotional anxiety about social situations. If the child learned that he got along most smoothly by conforming to adult requirements, then any ambiguous situation (requirements not clear) might make him anxious. Conversely, if he became anxious easily in social situations, he might adjust by learning to imitate others closely and thus reduce his anxiety.

Frenkel-Brunswik (1948), in her studies related to "authoritarianism" and the *F* scale, believed that she had pushed this analysis back to the child's insecurity in the family. She utilized retrospective interviews with college students and also observation and interviews with young children. Her conclusion was that insecurity was primary, that conforming and stereotyped behavior developed afterwards, as a way of reducing anxiety. Logic seems to be on the side of this kind of interpretation as regards social conformity; and we may speculate that the child learns to say "yes" to many statements simply to avoid possible conflict with parents. In the same way, we have noted (Chapter 7) that anxiety facilitates perceptual closure; so the anxious child may develop the "intolerance of perceptual ambiguity" through a sequence in which closure (jumping to a conclusion in an unclear situation) relieves his anxiety and thus is strengthened as a habit.

VALUES

The term "value," we have indicated, is generally employed to designate a relatively generalized attitude, and consequently differs only to a slight extent from the "authoritarian" and "liberal-conservative" viewpoints we have just discussed. In other words, the student should think of a continuum from highly specific attitudes, such as approving of President Eisenhower or opposing birth control, to highly generalized attitudes which we may call religious values, economic values, and the like. Authoritarianism would be between these extremes, but toward the generalized end of the scale.

The Allport-Vernon-Lindzey Scale of Values. An inventory designed to measure values was published by Vernon and Allport (1931). Recently it has been revised and republished—Allport, Vernon, and Lindzey (1951). The revision seeks to improve, but does not basically modify, the original, which sought to measure six values: theoretical (love of truth), economic (practicality), aesthetic (love of beauty), political (love of power), social (humanitarian), and religious. Essentially, it presents forced-choice items which require a choice between two or more of the values listed. Thus, one item in the 1931 edition asked: "Do you think that a good government should aim chiefly at (1) more aid for the poor, sick and old; (2) the development of manufacturing and trade; (3) introducing more ethical principles into its policies and diplomacy; (4) establishing a position of prestige and respect among nations?" Obviously this permits a person to show his relative concern for social, economic, religious, and political considerations. A number of items must be answered consistently, of course, to get a meaningful score on any value.

The scoring of the scale is arbitrarily arranged so that the magnitude of the score obtained on certain series of items gives the relative strength of the corresponding value for this person. Thus a score of 37 on any of the scales is said to show a strong affective reaction toward objects of that particular value. Since the test is so constructed that the subject cannot make high scores on all the scales (in raising his score on one, he lowers it on others), the scores give only relative comparisons within the personality of the strength of these interests or affective responses.

The validity of such a subjective measure as the Study of Values is difficult to demonstrate objectively. The best evidence comes from testing groups who have already, by some decisive action, given an indication of the relative dominance of particular value attitudes. The results of such studies tend in general to confirm the validity of the scale. A group of theological seminary students, for example, made extremely high scores on the religious value, and above average on social; all their other scores were below average. Business-economics students make their highest scores in the economic scale, while science and medicine majors are highest on the theoretical scale.

Since the scales are so standardized that a score of 30 is the hypothetical neutral point for all scores, profiles showing the deviations of individuals above and below this point give a quick indication of major values. In Figure 11.3 is given a composite profile of the members of the psychology faculty of Dartmouth College. The very high scores on theoretical, aesthetic, and social values and very low ranking on political and economic items are logically appropriate in this field, particularly in an academic environment. For comparison, the profiles of a large group of Dartmouth undergraduate men and Wellesley undergraduate women have been drawn in on the same chart. The characteristic sex differences are shown: Men run consistently higher on economic and political, women on aesthetic and religious values.

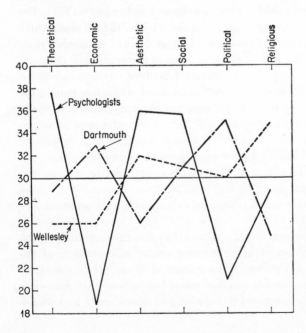

Fig. 11.3 Value profile of a psychology faculty. The heavy line shows the composite profile, on the Allport-Vernon Study of Values, for six professors of psychology. For comparison, composite profiles are also shown for several hundred Dartmouth and Wellesley undergraduates.

Stability of Values. Whereas it might be thought that values, being more highly generalized than attitudes, would be more stable, the evidence is somewhat ambiguous. Bender (1958) retested 84 Dartmouth men after sixteen years, and found substantial correlations. Greatest constancy was found for the aesthetic value (+.61), least for social (+.20). Bender, interestingly, found that there had been a significant rise in religious value over the sixteen-year period, but in general, the increase was proportional for everyone, hence the two sets of scores correlated fairly well (+.49). Bender had rated these men in 1940 for the amount of energy channeled into their value systems (the vigor with which they seemed to pursue these values). He reinterviewed 61 of them in 1956 and found a correlation of +.31 with the earlier ratings; thus it seemed that there was a trend for the more intensely motivated men to continue so, and for those less motivated to remain low on the energy scale. Perhaps one might have anticipated even higher constancy; but over sixteen years, many changes in energy level must be expected.

WAYS OF LIFE

The concept of "value" as used in the Allport-Vernon-Lindzey scale is, even if more general than "attitude," still somewhat specific. The term "value" is also employed rather often to identify a broad value orientation which can be illustrated by referring to the difference between Western Europe and the Orient. When we speak of the value of a life of contemplation versus one of hedonistic enjoyment or one of vigorous activity and manipulation of the environment, we are operating on a level of abstraction beyond that of the AVL scale. The individual has established some very generalized image which guides him in his choices of specific actions, and a search for the sources of consistency in his behavior must lead to this generalized picture.

Since most of the research on values has been done within Western civilization, it is difficult to say whether or not such sources of consistency can be identified. Certainly the philosophers and the historians of culture would assert that such broad cultural orientations can be identified by trained observers. They might not wish to assert that these orientations guide many specific individuals. We are aware of wide differences among Americans with respect to the "values" of Western culture. The differences among Indians, Chinese, or Japanese may be equally extensive.

Nevertheless, the stereotyped beliefs about such cultural values exist, and these can be studied. One of the most ingenious and persistent students of this problem is Charles Morris, whose *Varieties of Human Value* (1956) summarized his observations about major value orientations in the civilized world. From these summaries, he constructed a questionnaire for use in objective studies, which presents 13 "ways of life"; these are obviously derived from the world's great religions and the cultural values which have by tradition become associated with these ideologies. In a recent report (Morris and Jones, 1955), data from hundreds of young men, from all over the world, have been analyzed to throw light on this problem.[12]

Morris and Jones show that people can react intelligently to these "ways of life" and that national choices correspond more or less to stereotyped beliefs. For instance, way 1, preferred by the Indian students, stressed moderation, orderliness, refinement, and control. Way 3, preferred in Norway, emphasized sympathetic concern for other persons. Way 7, most chosen in the United States, includes "the dynamic integration of enjoyment, action and contemplation."

The authors also applied factor analysis to the data and found evidence that similar frames of reference were operating in different cultures. This means that, even though two cultures may make different choices, they are discriminating the same variables within value systems. The five factors isolated are defined as follows: social restraint and self-control; enjoyment in action; withdrawal and self-sufficiency; receptivity and sympathetic concern; and self-indulgence. On the first of these, India was high and the United States low (of five countries surveyed); on the second, China and the United States were high and Japan low; on the third, India and Japan were high, the United States low. Obviously the results look plausible in terms of popular beliefs about the different countries.[13]

Much research is going to be necessary before we know to what extent these value systems actually guide behavior. To some degree people behave as they do because of social pressures and environmental limitations; i.e., if there are no social roles which permit one to live a life of contemplation, the person who might prefer that way of life must perforce adopt another. Further, we may discover that these national differences may not hold for individuals at all; that individual Americans (and Chinese and Norwegians) scatter over a variety of world views, and that it is only average differences which show up in the Morris-Jones data. Such studies, nevertheless, are important, since we are now aware of the desperate urgency which attaches to efforts to understand the values of peoples outside our own country.

[12] Morris concedes that his data do not prove that people live by these value systems. He has only verbal reports of what people say they prefer. It is indeed probable that many individuals behave in ways quite in conflict with their verbal reports.

[13] The problems of cross-cultural study in such areas as this are very difficult. In a review of the book by Morris (1956) reporting in detail on his comparisons of values from various nations, Fearing (1957) comments on the difficulties of translation: "In the Chinese translation of Way Thirteen (the Way widely preferred by Chinese students), the opening sentence had become: 'A person should make himself useful.' In the English original this sentence was: 'A person should let himself be used.' This suggests difficulty that deserves more than a passing reference." Certainly, to Americans, there is a vast difference between "making oneself useful" and "letting oneself be used." Despite these complications, Morris's study is certainly of substantial value, and should be pursued.

SUMMARY

Attitudes and values develop within the personality as one learns to perceive as attractive or repulsive symbols representing organizations, ideologies, and ways of living. Attitudes generally have fairly specific objects, such as labor unions, Jews, censorship, socialism. Generalized attitudes, however, develop as the process of abstraction continues; thus we observe that people can be classified as "liberal" or "conservative" and that this predicts with fair accuracy a number of more specific attitudes. Complex attitudinal systems such as that called "authoritarianism" have also been identified, although this particular syndrome has been called into question by further research.

The significance of attitude and value for personality study lies in the fact that temperamental and dynamic qualities are integrated into these patterns of perceiving and acting. It seems clear, from the available research, that the individual's anxiety and hostility need not be directed against people in his immediate environment; these emotions may be, and often are, focused on symbols such as authority figures, groups, and institutions. This interpretation is, of course, compatible with the research on character reported earlier.

As further investigations are carried out, it is likely that methods will be devised for measuring more successfully these generalized attitudes, values, and ways of life which play such an important role in our perceptions of foreign peoples and governments. Increased understanding of these differences in perceived reality is urgently needed if we are to achieve communication, mutual understanding, and cooperation, instead of mutual extinction.

SUGGESTIONS FOR READING

A major contribution in this area is, of course, *The authoritarian personality* by Adorno, Frenkel-Brunswik, Levinson, and Sanford. Comments and critical studies about this book have been assembled by Christie and Jahoda: *Studies in scope and method of the authoritarian personality.* Companion volume to the Adorno book is *Dynamics of prejudice*, by Bettelheim and Janowitz. Charles Morris discusses some of the larger problems of value systems in his *Varieties of human value.* Methods of measuring attitudes and values are discussed by Ferguson in his *Personality measurement.* Relevance of such measures to a concrete social problem is developed in Stagner: *Psychology of industrial conflict.* Another stimulating treatment will be found in *Opinions and personality* by Smith, Bruner, and White.

CHAPTER 12

Type Theories of Personality

There has been a great deal of controversy over the concept of types in psychology, and this chapter can only summarize some of the different views offered, without providing a satisfactory conclusion. Before considering these different approaches it will help to try to sharpen the distinction between a type theory and the dimensional point of view which has been assumed in Chapters 7 to 11.

In common thinking, the best analogy to a type theory would be the awareness of species differences. We are not, for example, surprised when a dog ignores a worm and digs for a bone, while a bird ignores the bone and digs for a worm. The one "type" is recognized as having different properties from the other. There is no question of comparing the two species on a quantitative scale for worm-seeking behavior. Quantitative comparisons are, of course, permissible on certain dimensions such as length and weight, which ignore the type distinction.

Another way to think about the concept of type is to consider the difference between a triangle, a circle, and a square. The type called a triangle obeys certain laws which simply do not hold for the others; e.g., the sum of the angles equals 180 degrees. For the circle, the area equals pi times r^2, but that rule holds only for figures belonging to this type. Again, we note that it is possible to make quantitative comparisons of triangle and circle as regards area, a dimension which disregards the typological classification.

By analogy, then, we may suggest that a type approach to personality will be defensible if we can demonstrate (1) that certain rules hold for personalities falling into one type, and are simply inapplicable to persons belonging to another type; or (2) what amounts to the same thing, that differences in quality or pattern, not reducible to dimensional scales, can be identified as distinctive of each type. This does not imply that no quantitative scales apply to members of several types. Assuming for the moment that personality types do exist, this would not debar us from applying scales for measuring traits, attitudes, and values to members of these diverse types.

A more important possibility must nevertheless be considered. This is that the significance of a quantitative score varies according to the type within which it occurs. To take a fairly obvious example, a score of 90 on a masculinity-femininity scale does not have the same significance if earned by a girl as it does when earned by a boy. In one case it means a normal boy with interests and activities appropriate to his social role; in the other, it means a girl who is in conflict with social expectancies, probably identifying with her father, and pushing along pathways in which she will encounter an unduly high number of frustrations.[1]

Perceptual Origin of Types. Let us revert, for a moment, to the discussion of general principles in Chapter 1. We observed then that the scientific study of personality begins with the perception of individuals as differing in various respects; the term "personality" came into use to identify, or summarize, these differences which had already been recognized.

"Types of personality" become objects of discussion in the same way. Just as primitive man found that dogs had a distinctive pattern and invented a label for them, to clarify that he was not speaking of cats, burros, or small children, so people may observe persons who seem to "typify" a personality pattern and invent a label to point to this pattern.

Stephenson humorously uses Winston Churchill to illustrate this idea. Churchill, he says, "is widely regarded as typically British, if not, indeed, *the* Britisher par excellence. He is the very essence of all things English, of the hard-living, practical-idealistic, richly enthusiastic type . . . Churchill is *Britannus rubicundus*, very much a person and a specimen of the choicest kind. Another type, *Britannus vacuus* is of a different form: one thinks of the pale, vague, bemonocled, languid Englishman of American caricature, who is rather stupid, you know, but jolly decent." [2]

On this kind of basis we could have virtually an infinite number of types. Any observer, dealing with a variety of personalities, can abstract certain attributes, and classify together those perceived as similar. Thus, Havighurst and Taba (1949) cite certain "basic personality types" among their adolescent group: the "self-directive person"; the "adaptive person"; the "defiant person"; and the "unadjusted person." These categories really correspond to extremes of some attribute; the authors have simply chosen youngsters in whom a certain trait is outstanding, and used this to designate a type. (It will be remembered—Chapter 8—that Allport and Odbert found over seventeen thousand names for personality traits in the English language; we might arrive by this procedure at a similar number of types.) This mode of operation does not seem very fruitful. How can we go about the study of types scientifically?

---

[1] Such a statement should not be read as implying that the girl "should not" do this. It only asserts a prediction with a high degree of probability.

[2] Stephenson (1953), p. 160. Reprinted by permission of the University of Chicago Press.

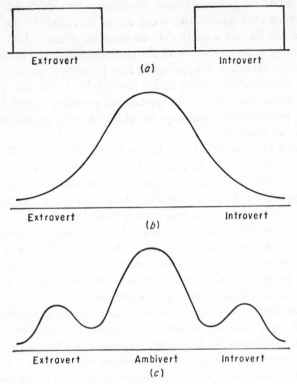

Fig. 12.1   Three conceptions of types.

Psychological Conceptions of Types. Because of this somewhat confused state of affairs, American psychologists have not taken kindly to the type concept. European psychologists, more inclined to armchair theorizing, find the type approach quite congenial. But American attempts to test European theories have generally led to disappointment. Part of this, as we shall attempt to show, has been due to poor logic and failures of communication.

The points of view commonly expressed about types by American psychologists have generally fitted into one of the three patterns illustrated in Figure 12.1. Starting with our analogy of cat and dog, we note that many psychologists hold that if type theories have any validity, then people must be classifiable into neatly discrete pigeonholes (Figure 12.1a). In the realm of biology, such neat categories are the rule if not quite universal (there can be quite an argument, for example, as to whether the shark is a fish). But in personality it is commonly found that most of the population refuses to fit into the proposed types. (We may note that even that well-established male-female typology encounters some cases which cannot be unequivocally typed.)

When type theories have been tested, what is derived often appears to be a one-dimensional trait (Figure 12.1*b*). For instance, Jung (1923) propounded a theory which seemed to say that people could be classified as either introverts or extraverts. When tests were prepared using lists of indicators from Jung's writings, a normal distribution was found. It would be possible to mark off arbitrarily the extreme cases and call them "types" but there would be little logical justification for so doing.

Despite these observations, some psychologists felt that the type concept was worth saving, and suggested that with adequate measures, we would find that certain combinations of symptoms would occur more frequently than others, even though a single dimension appeared to run through all cases. This would give rise to a multimodal distribution curve (Figure 12.1*c*), which would indicate that no simple unified trait was involved.

In recent years thinking about types has taken a different turn. Eysenck (1953) has pointed out that arguments based on the shape of the distribution curve are not on firm ground. The science of personality measurement is not far enough advanced, he asserts, for such evidence to be conclusive. He has also noted that type theories need not necessarily imply discontinuity such as implied by Figure 12.1*a*. Many European theorists have stated explicitly that type distinctions are based on *relative dominance* of a particular pattern and do not imply an all-or-nothing category.

Stephenson's Proposals Regarding Types. In view of the split between American and European psychologists, implied above, as regards types, it is especially appropriate that Stephenson (1953), a British contribution to the United States in this field, has offered some important clarifications to the logic of the matter. Stephenson suggests that we should recognize the following five usages for the term "type" and make clear which type of type we have in mind when we discuss the problem.

1. Types obtained by simply slicing a normal distribution. We speak of idiots, imbeciles, and morons, but know perfectly well we are referring to arbitrary sections of a graduated dimension. If Klein (1951) had referred to his levelers and sharpeners as types, he would have been using this procedure. See also our comments on Havighurst and Taba, above.

2. *Supraordinate types* are those constructed by slicing related distributions. We could, for example, construct a "scholastic type" by choosing persons who fell in the top third on intelligence, in the top half of their class on grades, and in the top quartile on achievement motivation. The variables involved need not be correlated as long as they have common functional effects. On page 92 we noted Diamond's proposal to combine pleasant-unpleasant with excited-depressed to define the four classic temperaments, sanguine, phlegmatic, choleric, and melancholic. If we divided the diagram of Figure 4.1 into sections, we could call persons in one corner the "sanguine type," others the "choleric type," and so on.

3. *Profile types* can be identified by matching people up on strong and

weak points. Figure 11.3 presented the values profile of a group of psychologists. We could define this as a type and identify another person as fitting the type if his profile matched this one (cf. Figure 12.2).

4. *Types based on Q sorts* have much in common with profile types, but are differently determined. In a *Q* sort (cf. Chapter 9), a person describes himself by choosing statements which best describe him; items less descriptive; and so down to those which he regards as the opposite of descriptive for himself. Correlations of such *Q* sorts will be high when the persons involved pick the same statements as highly accurate, doubtful, or inaccurate. It is proper to speak of a type, Stephenson holds, when factor analysis of person correlations reveals a common factor. An individual's "representativeness" for that type is given by his loading on the common factor.

5. Finally, Stephenson leaves a place for *types based on psychological theory*. He reserves this category for theories such as those of Jung (1923) or Spranger (1928), which offer a logical basis for a certain pattern within a personality. Methodologically, however, he makes it clear that such a theory can be supported only by tests such as the *Q*-sort procedure. For our purposes, therefore, we can combine this class with group 4.

Few psychologists can be convinced that any value resides in the usage listed by Stephenson for group 1. The common usage of terms such as idiot and moron tends to impede, not facilitate, psychological understanding. Usages 2, 3, and 4, on the other hand, have real possibilities. Each case implies a patterning of personality attributes; each case involves something more than the single dimension implied by Figure 12.1*b*. In the following pages we shall refer back often to these three concepts.

Eysenck's View on Types. H. J. Eysenck (1953) has also offered a formulation with regard to types. It is best presented by referring to a diagram which he uses to explain it (Figure 12.3). The three lower levels, specific response, habitual response, and trait, correspond to our analysis of traits in Chapter 8. Examples: I observe John talking to a friend (specific response); over time I find that he talks to many people and at considerable length (habitual response); across situations I find that he goes to dances, partici-

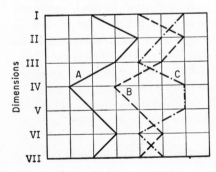

Fig. 12.2 Personality types as determined by profiles or salient trait relations. Persons *A* and *B* would be said to belong to the same type, although their average dimensional scores are quite different. Person *C* belongs to a different type because the pattern does not match.

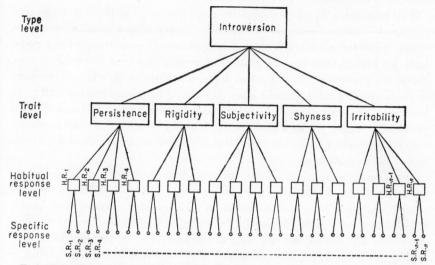

Fig. 12.3 Eysenck's conception of types. In this diagram introversion is represented as a "type" which is identified by determining the common components in a series of related traits: persistence, rigidity, etc. (From Eysenck, 1953, Fig. 2, p. 13, by permission of Methuen and Co.)

pates in bull sessions, plays cards, and seizes all occasions for social interaction; his talking, then, is integrated into a trait of sociability.

Eysenck now proposes that we carry this analysis one step further. If habits form a functional unity (are highly correlated), we say they form a trait. Why not, then, take the position that correlated traits define a type? Thus, in the diagram, significant positive correlations among persistence, rigidity, subjectivity, shyness, and irritability provide justification for a type which he calls introversion.

Such a usage for the concept of type seems to add nothing and to introduce confusion. If introversion and extraversion refer to nothing more than consistent patterns of responses, distributed along a continuum (as in Figure 12.1b), the term "trait" is entirely adequate and appropriate. To incorporate the new term, "type," is merely to bring in confusion.

It may be, on the other hand (Eysenck does not make it clear), that he would consider the operational definition of a personality type to involve high scores on several of the trait measures simultaneously. Thus he may mean that the term "introverted type" should apply only to persons making high scores on persistence, rigidity, subjectivity, shyness, and irritability. In this case we should have a real instance of multivariate determination (Stephenson's case 2) and there would be a meaningful distinction from the individual trait measures.[3]

---

[3] The reference to Stephenson's case 2 is to one of the five meanings of "type" summarized on pp. 267–268.

This conception of type would correspond somewhat to popular usage. The "egghead" (still not quite accepted in this country despite constant assertions of our need for more intellectual accomplishment) would be defined popularly by high intelligence, idealistic rather than practical orientation, emotional sensitivity, etc. In this sense, types obviously exist, since all we need to do is attach a label to those cases discovered as having certain trait combinations. The type concept, however, adds nothing to our understanding of personality if used in this way. More value would be derived if some *necessary* connection could be invoked to explain why high scores on these individual measures are associated.

It appears that Eysenck believes there is some necessary connection among the attributes he groups into a type. In his theory (Eysenck, 1955), certain assumed inhibitory processes in the cerebral cortex play a major role. So far Eysenck has been rather successful in deducing hypotheses for testing from his theory and finding that the data fit his view. The key concept is *reactive inhibition*, which is popularly observed in the fact that most people dislike to continue making a simple response over and over. Eysenck assumes that people differ as regards the speed with which reactive inhibition builds up and dissipates, and that certain consequences of this build-up, in relation to other factors, define the introverted and extraverted personality types. If further data support the theory, it should attain an important place in our understanding of personality.[4]

Types as Qualitative Groupings. A consideration of these points of view suggests that the concept of type will add something to our descriptions of personality only if it is distinct from trait. This means that we will abandon Stephenson's case 1 (persons who are simply extremes of a distribution) and use "type" only to apply to his other four instances, in which a grouping of several attributes is used to define the type. This need not mean that persons of differing types cannot be compared on dimensions; it means only that the type is some kind of patterning which is distinctive and different from other patterns (cf. Figure 12.2).

To revert to our geometrical analogy, both triangles and circles can be arranged on a linear scale for dimensions such as area; and they may even arrange themselves into a normal distribution (Figure 12.1b). Nevertheless, there is an obvious qualitative difference between them, and certain kinds of relationships hold within one group which are utterly irrelevant in the other group.

Within-group Similarity and Type. Logic parallel to that used above is employed by McQuitty (1957) when he defines a personality type as "a category of persons, of such a nature that everyone in the category is in some way

---

[4] A study by Ray (1959) confirms one of Eysenck's deductions but fails to confirm another. Evidently some time will be required to accumulate enough data to evaluate the theory fairly.

more like some other person in the category than he is like anyone not in the category" [p. 213]. Thus, if we were sorting figures, we would have no trouble seeing that all triangles resemble each other in certain respects more than they resemble any circles, squares, or hexagons. If we are categorizing persons, and if type is a useful way of describing persons, then it should be possible to group together persons who resemble each other in some patterned way, regardless of their standing on unidimensional measures.

Operationally, McQuitty has proposed two ways of identifying persons belonging to the same type. In the article just cited, he says, "In terms of co-efficients of correlations between persons, every person in a type would have a higher correlation with some other person in the type than he would with anyone not in the type." In other studies (1950, 1956) he has developed a method called "agreement analysis" which groups persons into similar categories according to the number of attributes they possess in common. A third statistic D^2, developed by Osgood and Suci (1952) and by Cronbach and Gleser (1953), resembles a correlation coefficient and enables us to classify people according to a numerical index of similarity. Finally, the Q sort described by Stephenson (1950) and outlined on page 190 can be utilized to determine similarities among persons. While all these are available for testing theories as to "types" of personalities existing in the population, surprisingly little research has been done on testing the various type theories. By and large, psychologists, at least in the United States, have chosen either to study traits, or to go all the way to a vaguely defined type as in some projective test work, using terms so unclear that testing for the existence of the type is most difficult.

So much for general comments about type theories. Let us now examine some of the more influential views which have been proposed, and see how these generalizations apply to specific cases.

TYPES BASED ON MENTAL FUNCTIONS

Type theories have been erected on a variety of foundations. For the sake of order, we have selected three groups for presentation here: those which emphasize some aspect of mental functioning, sensory, emotional, or organizational; those which involve some physiological basis; and those which depend on experience patterns. While it is impossible to cover all of these or to give any of them an extensive treatment, we shall attempt to present a fair picture of a few samples.

Type theorists have commonly started with some specific experiment or problem in which they were interested, and have used it as a universal standard for personality classification. Thus Külpe found that his subjects in an experiment on perception fell mostly into two classes: those whose reports were influenced most by the color of the stimulus and those whose reports were determined by shape or form. He spoke of these individuals as representing the "material" and the "formal" types, and these groups have been studied by followers of Külpe to locate differences in other psychological functions correlated with the color-form distinction. Similarly, the brothers Jaensch (1930) began with an investigation of eidetic imagery and evolved a complex theory of personality types.

There are several theories which focus on the direction of attention and interest, inward upon the self or outward upon the environment, among them those of Jung, Stern, James, and Rorschach.[5] As an example we shall take that which has been most widely discussed—Jung's theory of introversion-extraversion. According to Jung, the most fundamental distinction in personalities is that of orientation toward objective reality or toward subjective determinants:[6]

> When the orientation to the object and to objective facts is so predominant that the most frequent and essential decisions and actions are determined, not by subjective values but by objective relations, one speaks of an extraverted attitude. When this is habitual, one speaks of an extraverted type. If a man so thinks, feels and acts, in a word, so *lives,* as to correspond *directly* with objective conditions and their claims, whether in a good sense or ill, he is extraverted.
>
> His entire consciousness looks outwards to the world, because the important and decisive determination always comes to him from without. But it comes to him from without, only because that is where he expects it. . . . *Interest* and *attention* follow objective happenings, and primarily, those of the immediate environment. . . .
>
> Introverted consciousness doubtless views the external conditions, but it selects the subjective determinants as the decisive ones. The type is guided, therefore, by that factor of perception and cognition which represents the receiving subjective disposition to the sense stimulus. . . . Whereas the extraverted type refers pre-eminently to that which reaches him from the object, the introvert principally relies upon that which the outer impression constellates in the subject.

It will be noted that, in this quotation at least, Jung considers his "type" introverts and extraverts to be only the extremes of a normal distribution. Introversion and extraversion are types of reaction, and it is only when *one of these is habitual*—i.e., consistently manifest—that he speaks of the personality type. It is, however, difficult to feel sure that Jung rejects the view of types as means of classifying all individuals. He speaks of the difficulty each person has in identifying his own type, and also of the importance of remembering that there are subtypes as well as the two major types.

These subtypes are erected upon a combination of the basic introvert-extravert dichotomy with the four psychological functions of thinking, feeling,

[5] A good summary of a number of type theories will be found in MacKinnon's chapter in Hunt, *Personality and the behavior disorders;* also, in Murphy and Jensen, *Approaches to personality.*

[6] Jung (1923), pp. 417, 472. Reprinted by permission of Harcourt, Brace and Company, Inc., publishers.

sensation, and intuition; there are thus eight subtypes. Each shows a predominance of one of the four functions, oriented inwardly (introvert) or outwardly (extravert). Thus these definitions meet the requirements of Stephenson's case 2; they are selected for high or low status on several attributes simultaneously.

It seems desirable, in this connection, to call attention to a point presented in Chapter 4. The personality is formed as percepts develop around incoming sensory information. Some persons appear to scan more intensively the external channels (sight, hearing), whereas others pay more attention to internal channels (muscular and visceral sensitivity). The parallel to Jung's dimension of extraversion and introversion seems clear; and it may be, as he suggests, that the person may not always be consistent about preferred channels, but may rely on one or another depending on the situation.

Utility of Jung's Theory. While earlier psychologists had called attention to the contrast between personalities with an inward or an outward orientation, Jung made an important contribution to personality study by exploring systematically the various implications which might be drawn from such personality variables; and, as noted in the preceding paragraphs, he took account of the interaction of this basic variable with other important aspects of the individual's functioning. In these respects Jung undoubtedly has helped professional psychologists and psychiatrists to sharpen their thinking with respect to personality.

On the other hand, if we think of utility in terms of facilitating shorthand descriptions of individuals, we must conclude that Jung's contribution has not been important. As noted above, research using Jung's lists of criteria generally has led to the determination of a single dimension, not to the complex type structure he postulated. (Research reported by Stephenson, 1953, runs contrary to this statement, but it does not seem to conform to Jung's predictions either.)

Perhaps the greatest utility in Jung's work is in providing an anchoring point for a frame of reference. All perceptions, we have found, derive some of their attributes from the frame of reference adopted by the observer. A person familiar with Jung's theory will undoubtedly be sensitive to aspects of personalities about him which he might otherwise have missed. And he may very well learn to think in terms of how closely a given individual approaches to one of Jung's ideal type descriptions. It is a commonplace of training for scientific observation that one must have the major variables well in mind before he can do a satisfactory job. We conclude that, for a study of personality, having Jung's standard picture in mind is of value. Most of the time it will be better to think of personalities as varying along a normal distribution from extreme introversion to extreme extraversion, with the majority falling in the central zone.

TYPES RELATED TO PHYSICAL CHARACTERISTICS

Even the Greeks attempted to evolve classifications based upon physical appearance which would also correspond to distinctions in personality. Aristotle is said to have written a treatise on physiognomy (predicting personality pattern from facial appearance) and Hippocrates tried to connect temperamental types with an excess of some bodily fluid. Today physiognomy is accepted only by charlatans, but there is a widespread feeling among psychologists that the over-all physical pattern has some ill-defined relationship to personality.

Kretschmer. As with other problems in personality, a common starting point has been the abnormal individual. The best of the physical typologies, that of Kretschmer, began as a study of two extreme mental disorders, schizophrenia and manic-depressive psychosis. From these he developed the idea of two normal temperamental types, the schizoid and the cycloid, respectively. The schizoid is characterized as unsociable, quiet, serious, reserved, and prone to dissociation (clearly somewhat related to Jung's introverted pattern). The cycloid is described as sociable, good-natured, humorous, impulsive, and prone to marked variations of mood (cf. Jung's extraverted attitude). Kretschmer believed that a normal cycloid would, if he broke down, develop manic-depressive psychosis, while the normal schizoid would develop schizophrenia.

In working on this problem, he became impressed with the correspondence between physical and temperamental type. His cycloids and manic-depressives, he found, were mostly of the "pyknic" build—relatively broad trunk, short arms and legs, inclined to put on weight. His schizoids were mostly narrow and elongated, with long extremities (leptosomes), or athletic (somewhat intermediate between pyknic and leptosome).

The work of Kretschmer has attracted a great deal of attention and many investigations have sought to verify or disprove his claims. At present the preponderance of evidence seems to favor his interpretation as regards psychotics. Studies of normal individuals, however, have failed to confirm Kretschmer's predictions.

Sheldon (see Hunt, 1944) has summarized the status of the Kretschmer typology adequately as follows:[7]

(1) The descriptions of the physical types and the criteria for their recognition were found to be confusing and unsatisfactory. In fact, it was soon made evident that types as such do not exist. (2) Yet in a number of instances where investigators sidestepped this stumbling block, accepting what may possibly be called *the spirit rather than the letter* of Kretschmer's claims, and proceeding to grade physiques according to their manifest general tendencies—in a considerable number of such instances significant positive correlations were found between

[7] Sheldon, in Hunt (1944), p. 533. Reprinted by permission of The Ronald Press Company, publishers.

physical tendency and psychotic tendency. (3) However, no American students, using Kretschmer's technique as he presented it, have been able to demonstrate significant relationships between physical type and temperamental or normal psychological characteristics.

Sheldon's Somatotypes. Influenced by Kretschmer's views, but finding his theoretical approach inadequate, Sheldon (1940, 1942) proposed a typological theory which incorporated bodily and temperamental attributes in a new way. The theory has two major points: (1) there are three major bodily (and temperamental) components; and (2) types are defined by the *relative dominance* of these components. As noted in our brief comment on his theory in Chapter 10, the bodily components are endomorphy, mesomorphy, and ectomorphy; the corresponding temperamental dimensions are viscerotonia, somatotonia, and cerebrotonia.

When *endomorphy* predominates in the individual, he shows massive and highly developed viscera, while his somatic structures (bone, muscle, etc.) are relatively weak and undeveloped. *Mesomorphy*, when predominant, means that the structure is hard, firm, upright, and relatively strong and tough. This is the athletic-appearing individual. *Ectomorphy* is associated with long, slender, poorly muscled extremities, with limited development either of viscera or of somatic structures (Figure 12.4).

Sheldon has developed an elaborate system for determining *somatotypes* in terms of the relative predominance of these three components. He considers that *in the normal population there is a normal distribution* of endomorphy, mesomorphy, and ectomorphy; [8] but that certain combinations of these characteristics may appropriately be called somatotypes. Thus a 7-1-1 would be an extreme endomorph with negligible development of mesomorphic or ectomorphic trends; a 4-4-4 would be a person in whom no component seemed better developed than the others.

Parallel to the three physical components he finds three temperamental components—viscerotonia, somatotonia, and cerebrotonia. Extreme *viscerotonia* is characterized by love of comfort, gluttony, sociability, and affection. *Somatotonia*, when predominant, indicates a craving for muscular activity and vigorous self-assertiveness. Generally it is associated with a lust for power, a certain callous ruthlessness, and a love of risk and chance. *Cerebrotonia*, in extreme form, connotes excessive restraint, inhibition, and shrinking from social contact. There is likely to be repression of somatic and visceral expressiveness.

Sheldon reports amazingly high correlations between his somatotypes and temperamental components: endomorphy with viscerotonia, .79; mesomorphy with somatotonia, .82; and ectomorphy with cerebrotonia, .83 (Table 12.1). However, in accordance with his general orientation, which is essentially

---

[8] Thus Sheldon avoids the conflict with measurement studies which show normal distributions. This device is the same as that adopted by Stephenson, case 2.

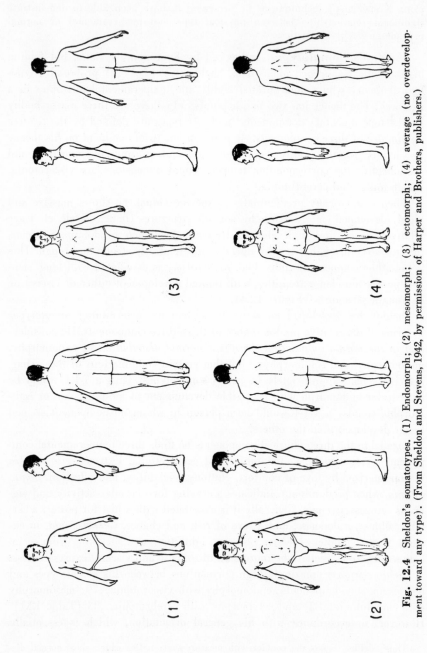

Fig. 12.4 Sheldon's somatotypes. (1) Endomorph; (2) mesomorph; (3) ectomorph; (4) average (no overdevelopment toward any type). (From Sheldon and Stevens, 1942, by permission of Harper and Brothers, publishers.)

Table 12.1

Agreement of Sheldon's Physical
and Temperamental Types *

Dimension of temperament	Dimension of physique		
	Endomorphy	Mesomorphy	Ectomorphy
Viscerotonia:			
Sheldon	+.79	−.23	−.41
Child	+.13	+.13	−.15
Somatotonia:			
Sheldon	−.29	+.82	−.53
Child	+.03	+.38	−.37
Cerebrotonia:			
Sheldon	−.32	−.58	+.83
Child	−.03	−.38	+.27

* It should be noted that the temperament scores in Sheldon's study were based on ratings made by Sheldon after interviewing each subject; hence, the ratings may have been influenced by Sheldon's knowledge of the person's physical type. Child, on the other hand, used a questionnaire constructed from Sheldon's descriptions of the temperamental patterns. His scores thus may reflect the person's inability to give an accurate self-report.

SOURCE: Sheldon (1944); Child (1950).

typological, he prefers to stress the identifying characteristics of each somatotype (e.g., 1-3-6) in terms of its corresponding temperamental pattern. As would be expected from the numerical designations, these grade into one another; i.e., there is only a minute difference between a 1-6-2 and a 2-6-3. Sheldon claims that, while the somatotype and the temperamental type do not always agree perfectly, the instances of any *reversal* of order of dominance in the three components are rare.[9]

We are not especially concerned with the adequacy of Sheldon's way of determining the physical type. It is interesting, nonetheless, to note that Lorr and Fields (1954) were able, by factor analysis, to establish the existence of two basic dimensions of physique which give rise to three distinguishable

[9] This matter of relative order of dominance is of course crucial to any typological theory (Stephenson, cases 3 and 4). A man who is a somatic 2-4-6 has a physique which is chiefly ectomorphic, mildly mesomorphic, weakly endomorphic. If his temperamental rating came out 1-3-5, the relative order of traits would agree perfectly with the somatotype, although the strength would be less than predicted. A reversal would occur if the temperament index came out, say 3-1-5. It is these reversals which, according to Sheldon, are uncommon.

groups of individuals; and these three groups matched the descriptions given by Sheldon very closely.[10]

Empirical Studies of the Theory. In proportion to the debate aroused by Sheldon's theory of physique-temperament relationships, a fairly small amount of research has been published dealing with his views. This may be due to the fact that the determination of somatotypes is rather tedious. Another factor, referred to above, is the skepticism about type theories among American psychologists.

The most thorough application of the Sheldon approach, and probably the most impressive success of his theory so far, is the work on delinquency, summarized in Chapter 10. As was noted there, mesomorphy unquestionably has something to do with a boy's chances of becoming delinquent. As regards his personality theory, which is our main concern, other investigators have not been successful in locating the clean-cut relationships reported by Sheldon (cf. Table 12.1). In Child's research (1950), which is sometimes cited as giving "strong experimental support" to Sheldon, the drops in correlations look like this: from $+.79$ to $+.13$, from $+.82$ to $+.38$, and from $+.83$ to $+.27$. (These are for the three crucial correlations, viscerotonia with endomorphy, somatotonia with mesomorphy, and cerebrotonia with ectomorphy.) Perhaps we can say that Child's data give weak support to Sheldon, but surely not strong support.

A more encouraging study is that of Davidson et al. (1957) on British children. Contrary to the frequent criticism that Sheldon's somatotypes cannot be determined for young children, they found it feasible to type over one hundred seven-year-olds and obtain observers' ratings of personality. Some of their correlations, while not phrased exactly in Sheldon's vocabulary, clearly give support to his theory; for example, ectomorphy and emotional disturbance correlated $+.65$. A finding which is directly related to his formulation is that dominant children fall toward the mesomorph pole and submissive children toward the ectomorph or endomorph pole (Figure 12.5). This should be compared with Figure 10.2, which shows the distribution of a group of aggressive delinquents, who were certainly not submissive.

Sheldon has attracted considerable interest in Europe, where the typological tradition is strong and the work of Kretschmer is favorably regarded. Corman (1954), Barahona Fernandes (1955), and Bergeron and Benoit (1954) provide some confirmation of Sheldon's views. With what we are beginning to consider characteristic French lack of concern with precision, Bergeron and Benoit endorse a casual, impressionistic typing procedure instead of Sheldon's meticulous method, to which they refer as requiring "enormous labor."

---

[10] On the other hand, a critical view of Sheldon's methods is expressed by Humphreys (1957), who holds that some of Sheldon's findings were artifacts produced by his methods. The questions raised are too intricate to develop here.

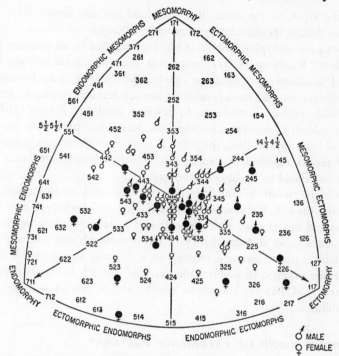

Fig. 12.5 Distribution on Sheldon's somatotype chart of children rated "submissive." (Black circles = submissive; white circles = nonsubmissive.) Note clustering of submissives away from the mesomorph pole. (From Davidson et al., 1957, Fig. 7, p. 59; reproduced by permission of *British Journal of Educational Psychology*.)

Basic Mechanisms. Sheldon is not entirely consistent with regard to the role of heredity and environment in his theory of temperament. At some times he stresses heredity heavily (see page 230); at other times he makes a place for environment. In his comments on delinquency he notes that the mesomorph, with his superior musculature, probably succeeds in fights and therefore learns to be aggressive and dominant.

An interesting hypothesis with regard to the role of sensory feedback in these processes is offered by Barahona Fernandes (1955) who suggests that "the presence and the reference of all psychic acts to a Central Self can be related to the integration of interoceptive sensitivity into the brain mechanisms which are fundamental to the activities of the individual" [p. 617]. He proposes that persons of different physical types have a different feedback pattern which makes for temperamental variation. We can imagine, for example, that the mesomorph may get more intense awareness of muscular action, and that his self-image may become suffused with action images to a vastly greater extent than do others.[11] In either case we imply that Sheldon's tem-

[11] See also McClelland (1951), pp. 329–330.

peramental types, to the extent that they hold up, may derive from experience, even though the somatotype may be hereditary.

Sheldon's somatotyping technique has been applied to an amazing variety of problems. Winthrop (1957) found that endomorphs showed the highest degree of inconsistency (endorsing opinions which were mutually contradictory), with ectomorphs most consistent. We are inclined to suspect an irrelevant variable, perhaps intelligence, in this case. Similarly, Morris (1948) has tried to establish a connection between somatotype and preference for one or another of his "ways of life" (page 261), without much success. Some of the negative results reported by Smith (1949) also relate to attributes hardly likely to be related to Sheldon's patterns.

It would be unfair to Sheldon to expect his typology to explain everything under the sun. We have shown that the physical body type does help us to understand the aggressive delinquent; and in later chapters we shall note that the extra vigor and impulsivity of the mesomorph may account for the fact that he reacts to parental controls in a different way from his ecto- or endomorphic siblings. In a pluralistic universe where behavior is determined by a variety of factors, body type should not be loaded with too heavy responsibilities.

TYPOLOGIES BASED ON EXPERIENCE PATTERNS

Type theory has been notably favorable to an exaggerated emphasis on heredity, even when no explicit assumptions are made regarding the role of environment. With the conception of type as a coherent, tightly organized personality structure, with closely interdependent systems, there would naturally be associated an emphasis on the unchanging character of this organization. Following this argument backward in time, we inevitably arrive at a theory of hereditary determination.

A few writers have, however, propounded type theories which stressed organizations crystallized by experience and henceforward changeable only by major outside intervention, e.g., psychoanalysis. The most important of these, and the only one we shall discuss here, is the psychoanalytic theory of anal-erotic, oral-erotic, and genital types.

Psychoanalytic Theory of Personality Types. The theory of personality formation developed by Freud and his followers is inclined to emphasize environment somewhat more than heredity. While much of the Freudian material on psychosexual development [12] reads like an account of the unfolding of a complicated hereditary pattern, it is usually clear that the implications for personality are closely related to environmental gratifications and frustrations. We thus feel that it is legitimate to classify the Freudian types as based on experience patterns.

[12] For a summary of this material, see pp. 106–110.

The Anal-erotic Type. Freud (1924, Vol. II) first noted a triad of characteristics which occurred as a pattern, and designated them as making up the "obsessional character"; these traits were orderliness (often, overfussiness about details and pedantry), parsimony (often to the point of miserliness), and obstinacy. Upon closer study of several cases who showed this fussy, stingy, stubborn personality to extreme, he concluded that the basic phenomenon was the fixation of the libido (basic motivation) upon anal mechanisms. Other studies by Ernest Jones and Karl Abraham seem to confirm this general association.[13]

Some of the discussions of the anal type suggest that there is a constitutional predisposition to become fixated at this level of development. In general, however, the opinion seems to be that an anal-type character is produced by such phenomena as toilet training of an extremely rigid and severe kind or by circumstances such that the child finds that he can get special pleasures by control of his excretory functions. These pleasures may include special attention from the parent at toilet time, concern if excretory functions become irregular, a great deal of praise for cleanliness; conversely, if the child feels hostility and resentment toward the parents, soiling his clothing may be pleasant as an expression of aggression.

The evidence that the orderliness-parsimony-obstinacy triad is related to anal sexuality is too complex and would take us too far afield to be summarized here. There does seem to be fairly convincing proof that, at least in extreme cases, the connection is present.

The Oral-erotic Type. While some psychoanalysts distinguish two anal-erotic types, these overlap sufficiently that the single description given above seems satisfactory. It is generally agreed, however, that there are two oral types, the passive, or "sucking," type and the active, or "biting," type.

The oral-passive type is the dependent, optimistic, immature individual who thinks the world owes him a living. He longs to continue as an infant, cared for by his parents; while he may have ambition, he is unwilling to exert the effort or to endure the discomfort necessary to achieve anything. The analysts consider this type produced by a fixation at the nursing, sucking stage of infancy.

The oral-sadistic individual presumably owes his characteristics to a frustration of nursing activity and to a fixation on such functions as biting and chewing. His basic outlook is one of pessimism and an anticipation of malice. Like the oral-passive type, he thinks the world owes him a living, but suspects that he is going to be thwarted. He is likely to be sarcastic and bitter in conversation, if not actively sadistic in his treatment of others.

The Genital Types. If the child succeeds in developing normally past

---

[13] A purely statistical study of questionnaire data by Stagner and Krout (1940) also lends some support to the stated association, although not necessarily to the typological theory.

the oral and anal stages, he may become fixated at the phallic stage, instead of progressing to the normal genital level of mature adjustment. The phallic type is described as narcissistic and overambitious, an exhibitionist and braggart. He must always be the center of attention and reacts very poorly to any kind of thwarting. His difficulty arises from traumatic factors operating in early adolescence, at the stage when a transition to a normal adjustment to members of the opposite sex should begin.

Beyond the phallic type we find the complete maturity of normal genital sexuality. This can hardly be referred to as a type, since it comprises a rather large segment of the population and is presumably the norm at which the others aimed but which they failed to reach. It involves an adequate balance of selfishness and altruism, dependency and independence, ambition and restraint. It thus incorporates material from the oral, anal, and phallic stages into a well-rounded personality.

Studies of Freudian Type Theory. The psychoanalytic theory of types grew in a rather uncoordinated fashion, and neither Freud nor any of his followers ever prepared what could be considered a definitive statement of it. Nevertheless, Krout and Tabin (1954) felt that they could identify specific symptoms which ought to be associated with successive stages (a considerably finer breakdown than sketched above) and prepared an inventory to measure these. That some degree of functional unity, corresponding roughly to several of the postulated stages, exists in responses of college students to this inventory was demonstrated by factor analysis (Stagner, Lawson, and Moffitt, 1955). However, this demonstrates only that the questions "hang together" in the ways proposed by Krout and Tabin; it does not verify a typological categorization of persons.

Applying the logic that persons within a type must resemble each other more than they resemble persons of other types, and using the technique of profile correlation, Stagner and Moffitt (1956) tested for the grouping of persons into types. The results were uniformly negative; persons of the "oral-passive" type did not resemble each other any more than they resembled "anal-retentive," "phallic," or other types.

It cannot, of course, be asserted that this demolishes psychoanalytic type theory. The Krout-Tabin inventory may not be adequate; expansions and presumed improvements upon it have been reported by Grygier (1957). Some Freudians would argue that types can be diagnosed only by taking into account unconscious material, i.e., by close observation by a trained analyst. Nevertheless, the data do seem to cast considerable doubt on the notion that these "types" will be useful for description of persons. Even J. F. Brown, a psychologist with a strong analytic orientation, offers the following warning with respect to looking for individuals who fit these descriptions: [14]

---

[14] Brown (1940), p. 396. Reprinted by permission. The italics are ours.

We seldom find pure character disorders of the types of which we have spoken. Usually there are present in the same individual strong orally determined personality character disorders with less striking anal- and phallic-determined ones, or strong anally determined character defects with the others less striking. *The transition* to perversion or mental illness, on the one hand, and to complete normality, on the other, *is also a gradual one.*

It is further apparent that this theory is compatible with a bias in favor of learning. While there is some suggestion of the thought that an individual frustrated on a certain level must inevitably develop certain traits, most analysts recognize the role of environment in implanting these specific trends. At the most, the dynamic factors sensitize the person so that he picks up certain attitudes and rejects others. Thus the overconcern of the anal character with money is traced to a symbolic relationship between money and feces, mediated by the conceptions of value which the child acquires from adults.

Finally, it would appear that few of the exponents of this theory would use it as a basis for classifying personalities in general. The types are conceived more as special cases, which illuminate milder trends in the general population—not as a comprehensive scheme of classification within which all or most individuals can be included.

IS TYPE THEORY USEFUL?

It seems worthwhile, before closing this discussion of type theories, to raise the question: Is type theory useful? Perhaps a better form of question would be: Under what conditions is it useful?

Determination of Parts by the Whole. Type theory has served a useful purpose by emphasizing the extent to which the parts (specific emotions, prejudices, traits, and attitudes) of personality are determined by the whole. The gestalt school of psychology, as Murphy and Jensen (1932) have shown so well, lays an excellent basis for a typological approach to personality. All the data on configuration, figure-ground relations, and closure are harmonious with a theory in which a total organization, once established, imposes strict limitations upon the variability of parts within the system. In their attempt to put this case as favorably as possible, however, we suspect that Murphy and Jensen become too poetical when they assert that "the present is as much determined by the future as it is by the past, but of course it is not determined by either. It is rather an aspect of a total which is itself an aspect of a still larger pattern in reality." [15] This business of patterns being part of larger patterns, which are parts of still larger patterns, begins to sound suspiciously like the verse which goes

> Great fleas have little fleas upon their backs to bite 'em,
> And little fleas have lesser fleas, and so *ad infinitum.*

[15] Murphy and Jensen (1932), p. 24.

It is possible to argue, not only that the whole determines the parts, but that the parts determine the whole. The personality is a product of its historical development, a function of the interaction between a physiological organism and the environment. Traumatic experiences, religious conversion, psychoanalysis—such factors can be associated with definite changes in the whole personality.

There is actually a danger, when one insists upon the importance of the whole in determining the parts, of exaggerating the unity of personality. All observers agree that there is also a substantial degree of disunity and inconsistency—at least, within most of us. Thus the type theory is not unlikely to encourage a spurious assumption of unity when only limited unity is present.

The determination of parts by the whole personality is not exclusively accounted for by type theory. The learning theory set forth in Chapters 5 to 9 proposes that, as larger integrations are established, they modify certain more specific tendencies to achieve conformity; and they establish broad mental sets, within which future developments are normally limited. This view seems to cover the verifiable facts about the part-whole relationship in personality.

The Hypothetical Pure Case. Another defense of type theory, which seems more plausible, evades many of the criticisms that we have presented for various theories. Granted that pure types may be rare and that random variations may obscure relationships, as far as the average person is concerned, may it not still be true that an isolated, special case may be more informative to the psychologist than the general run of the population? Lewin (1935) has presented the view that scientific laws may be better based upon the pure case than upon the average of many observations. This view, of course, would militate in favor of type theories and against the impressiveness of statistical evidence for the opposed view.

Let us take a single example from physics. If we measured the rate of fall of rocks, wood, feathers, silk, and other substances through a vacuum, through air, and through water, the resulting average figure or the resulting distribution of speeds would not enable us to derive the basic equation for the rate of fall of physical objects. The extreme case, that of falling through a vacuum, furnishes the best approach to the true law, although in "real life" such a case might never occur. We must assume that all falling bodies obey this physical law, hence it does not matter that the fall through the vacuum is a special case; it is really interpreted as a case in which confusing factors are eliminated.

In the same way, one may agree with Lewin that, even though a pure personality type does not occur, it may still be the hypothetical pure case which gives the most illuminating insight and the most basic formulation of personality. In everyday behavior, responses to real situations are confused by the interpolation of various matters which are not really relevant to the personality trait that we should like to test. One of the difficulties with scoring traits on the basis of questions answered is that the same answer may be diagnostic, now of one trait, now of another. Behavior is not "pure"; it is confused by the interaction of numerous determiners. Thus the hypothetical case, by eliminating these irrelevant factors, may give a more accurate view of the total personality.

If the other type theories are viewed from this angle, they may be seen to contribute something to psychological analysis, even if they do not reveal existent separations of human beings into pigeonholes. Jung's conceptions of introversion and extraversion, for example, help toward understanding the behavior of some individuals, even though with others they may be useless or misleading. Freud's oral-erotic and anal-erotic types are rare; yet an awareness of these organizational patterns may be of value in understanding a personality which is not nearly so extreme as the type description.

Types as Anchoring Points. All observations of personality result in judgments, and these judgments are oriented to a certain frame of reference. Every reference scale must have certain anchoring points—extreme instances within which minor variations can be discriminated. A man who moves to an area where the physical appearance of the people is markedly different from his usual associates—e.g., a European going to Central Africa —has difficulty judging height, recognizing faces, and making similar discriminations until he establishes a new reference scale. For this to be possible, new anchoring points must be established and degrees of difference marked off mentally.

It seems that the greatest single value of type descriptions is as anchoring points for reference frames regarding personalities. Careful study of such type theories as those of Jung, Kretschmer, Spranger, Sheldon, Jaensch, Adler, and Freud will provide the psychologist with certain landmarks or reference points. He can then orient himself, in his study of any given individual, by comparing this personality to the standard types, noting certain aspects which call to mind the introvert, the cerebrotonic, or the oral-sadist. He can thus achieve, in his own mind, a fuller and more complete description of the personality than would be possible without such reference points. He may, however, find that none of the type theories help toward understanding the origin of the personality structure, or in planning advice or therapy.

SUMMARY

If types are conceived in terms of the relative dominance of certain characteristics within the individual, it is possible to harmonize type theory with the fact of normal distribution of measured traits. It is possible, consequently, that Jung's introverted and extraverted types, Kretschmer's cycloid and schizoid, or Freud's oral-erotic and anal-erotic types can be identified by the study of dominant features within the individual personality.

The very multiplicity of type theories, however, belies their general applicability. Were there any universal system of typing which would fit a substantial number of cases or throw special light upon personality organization, it would be espoused by a greater number of psychologists than at present. Each type theory represents the special interest of its inventor.

Type theories have certain values for psychology, in that they emphasize the importance of conceiving the personality as a gestalt, a pattern in which the parts are to some extent determined by the whole. Types are also valuable in the sense that certain experiments in physical science are valuable; they call attention to certain processes in relatively pure form, uncontaminated by accidental and confusing factors. Finally, types are especially useful in providing reference points for the psychologist as he attempts to comprehend and understand an individual personality under investigation. Care is necessary, chiefly to avoid the common error of attempting to classify everyone into types; because the average person, it would seem, does not fit any of these type descriptions.

SUGGESTIONS FOR READING

An old but still valuable treatment of type theories will be found in Murphy and Jensen's *Approaches to personality*. Stephenson's logic, with some supporting data, is presented in his *Study of behavior*. Eysenck offers his approach in his *Structure of human personality*. The best source on Jung is his *Psychological types*; an American exponent is found in Wickes's *The inner world of man*. Sheldon's views are given in his *Varieties of temperament* and neatly summarized in Hall and Lindzey, *Theories of personality*, chap. 9. Freud's personality typology is briefly summarized in Blum's *Psychoanalytic theories of personality*, chap. 8.

DYNAMICS

In earlier chapters a deliberate effort was made to evade questions relating to motivation. The development of personality was described, as it were, from the outside. Although some mention of positive goal seeking, as in love, ambition, or patriotism, and of negative tendencies, as in anxiety and aggression, proved necessary, it was kept to a minimum.

Personality is, however, a dynamic entity. The most characteristic feature of a friend may be the goals he seeks or the dangers he fears. No analysis of personality is complete without an exploration of psychodynamics.

Unfortunately, scientific psychology is inadequately developed in this area. Motive, necessarily, is an intervening variable. Stimuli can be observed and catalogued with considerable precision. Responses, even those hidden from external observation, can be recorded and the results analyzed statistically. Motive, on the other hand, stays concealed. Hence we have numerous theories of motivation, each of which is likely to have some virtues. The following chapters therefore will stress theory. To some extent they will pick up the facts set forth about personality description and will ask how adequately this or that theory of motivation explains the facts.

There are sound reasons for starting with an examination of motivation from the biological side. It can be argued, nonetheless, that biogenic drives reflect more the animal side than the human aspect of personality. Consequently, later chapters will present theories of motivation which reflect more adequately the rich variety of mature adult personalities. Suggestions are offered as to the relations existing between these theories and the data on personality traits, attitudes, and values.

CHAPTER 13

Biological Approaches

The baby at birth is a biological entity, but he lacks many of the attributes distinctive of human beings. He has no speech, no culture, no traits, no attitudes. Nevertheless, out of this little squirming mass of protoplasm develops the complex adult personality. In Chapters 4 to 6 some views on how this developmental process occurs were summarized. We are now concerned with the dynamics of personality, and once again it seems necessary to start at this simple physiological level.

The problem of motivation is the problem of energy mobilization. Each person differs, from time to time, in the amount of energy he manifests, and individuals differ from each other in their habitual energy levels. Such differences are important aspects of personality. As we have stressed ways of perceiving and responding, so we must now emphasize the energizing component of any trait or attitude.

It is a matter of common observation that one man may exert his maximum energy in pursuit of the opposite sex, another is most highly motivated toward economic gain, another toward ambition, power, or prestige. The same individual, at different times, seeks food, water, rest, a mate, status in his group of friends, and so on. How do these differences at the adult level arise? How are they related to the structures and functions observable in the newborn infant?

INSTINCT THEORIES

With the rise of Darwinism and a biological view of man's fundamental nature, instinct theories of motivation achieved prominence. Prior to this time the problem of human energy had either been ignored or been imputed to mystical concepts such as "the soul" or "will power." Instinct theory consequently represented a dramatic step toward dealing with personality as an object open to scientific study.

This approach can be well illustrated by the work of McDougall (1908), who postulated the existence of some 28 inherited needs or tendencies. These ranged from the very simple and obviously innate needs such as hunger

289

and sex to complex "tendencies" such as constructiveness and gregariousness.

Although the instinct theory had its origins in observations of allegedly universal behaviors of man, it has obvious implications for personality. Differences among individuals in the intensity of the gregarious need, for example, would account for variations in a trait such as sociability, while different experiences would explain the fact that one individual enjoyed noisy companions and another preferred quiet conversation. In essence, the theory proposed that the most important differences in energy mobilization should be explained on a hereditary basis.

The reasons for the decline of instinct theory are numerous and we need not consider them here. Most important was the fact that it proved difficult to find observable behavior which was clearly related to the assumed "instincts"; it was likewise difficult to identify stimulus conditions setting off these innate energizing tendencies; and it was virtually impossible to locate any physiological bases for many "instincts." From the viewpoint of personality research, instinct theory had the grave defect of stressing heredity excessively and hence of hampering research on motivational variables. However, there are ways of avoiding this obstacle; Freud, for example, simplified McDougall's formulation down to an assumption of two or three instinctive needs, and then emphasized learning of instinct-goal relationships (cf. Chapter 14). Other psychologists have, in recent years, proposed a revival of instinct theory, as will be indicated in later pages.

BIOGENIC DRIVES

Under the influence of John B. Watson and K. S. Lashley, American psychologists broke away from instinct theory in the early twentieth century and turned to a concept of motivation based largely on peripheral biological states. Hunger was assumed to be based on stomach contractions, thirst on dryness of mucous membranes, sex on distention of genital tissues, and so on. Today it is clear that these drives are not simple instances of energy being mobilized in response to such peripheral changes; central mechanisms are involved, and hormones as well as neural process play a part. Such problems are beyond the scope of this volume. We are interested only in the fact that many modern psychologists consider such drives to be the necessary and sufficient constituents of human energy mobilization.

Motivating conditions such as hunger, thirst, and pain are observable in the infant and also in the adult. These terms relate to highly predictable energy mobilizations, occurring under conditions which can be specified with a considerable degree of precision. Since these conditions relate to survival of the organism, the term *biogenic drives* (drives arising out of the nature of life) has come to be widely applied to them.

Students of introductory psychology will remember the familiar cycle involved in these drives. An inner or outer stimulus activates a *need* (e.g., metabolism burns up glucose, and more is needed to maintain the organism); the need sets off restless activity as energy is mobilized (drive) to deal with the need state; search leads to contact with the stimulus needed to restore equilibrium; the drive is reduced as equilibrium is regained. This consequently is identical with the concept of homeostasis developed earlier in this volume (pages 19 and 84).

Deprivation and Satiation. The key concepts in the homeostatic cycle described above are deprivation and satiation. The major biogenic drives (for food, water, oxygen, etc.) are triggered by deprivation, since the metabolic processes go on continuously and regular access to these needed substances is essential. As we noted in Chapter 4, the organism tends to build up environmental constancies, secure supplies of these items, in order to protect life. By the same token, it is difficult to use the biogenic drives as explanatory concepts in dealing with the adult personality because, in Western society at any rate, such deprivations are not common. The social system has built in protections against deprivation to a substantial degree.

In a different situation, the biogenic drives almost certainly play an important role in personality. Holmberg (1950) has described a primitive tribe, the Siriono, living on the ragged edge of starvation, in which the need for food dominates the individual's behavior constantly. In this society dominative behavior, appealing behavior, cooperative behavior, etc., may develop as the individual strives to obtain food. American theorists wishing to explain personality in biogenic terms have assumed that the fear of these basic deprivations underlies much of personality. It is difficult to obtain much evidence to support this assumption.

Satiation. As deprivation increases tension, satiation reduces it. Eating when hungry and drinking when thirsty lead to a lowering of the activity level. The significance of satiation for personality theory resides primarily in its function as reward or reinforcement (cf. page 99).

Tension. Any personality theory which leans heavily on the biogenic drives must make considerable use of tension as an important variable. The prototype of tension is the cramping of stomach muscles during hunger. Most theories of this sort have assumed that some kind of physiological tension is set off by deprivation. In the earlier forms this tension was considered to be actually muscular in character; as we have noted (page 80), there is some value in assuming that heightened drive level is associated with an increased input of visceral sense impressions to the central nervous system, thus affecting our sampling of cues from the environment. It is clear, however, that a large number of motives cannot be directly related to tension; and it would be an extraordinary kind of muscle tension indeed which could persist for years, as in the case of professional ambition, enduring love, hatred, and so on.

Faced with this problem, recent theorists (Morgan, 1957) have switched to a kind of tension of the central nervous system; and Hebb (1949) has also utilized a concept of a central nervous "cell assembly" as the physiological process underlying tension. Space does not permit us to explore these theories, since they are not directly relevant to our concern. In so far as the questions raised below are pertinent, both Morgan and Hebb could phrase their theories in such a way as to provide answers, but these answers at present must remain speculative.[1]

Variety of Biogenic Needs. Textbooks in general psychology customarily list a number of biological needs which apparently can motivate behavior. These include not only calories (food as ordinarily considered), but specific foods such as vitamins and minerals. (It can be shown, for example, that a vitamin-deprived animal will mobilize more energy and learn more efficiently for a reward containing the needed material.) Some of these needs, however, do not seem to function as drives, and it is assumed that in these cases no sensory function exists by which the animal can become aware of the deprivation or of the reward value of satiation. Such observations suggest that it is not deprivation, but *awareness of deprivation* which sets off tension; and similarly it is not satiation, but *awareness of satiation* which constitutes a reward.

The exact number of biogenic needs has never been determined. It may be equal to the number of indispensable elements in protoplasm. Since we are biochemically complex, we probably have a large number of such deficit motives, or biogenic drives. It is not, however, clear that most of these have any particular significance for personality.

Sources of Drive Variation. Drives become effective in bringing about differences in personality when there are differences in the intensity of the drive or in the mode of its gratification. Let us see what the possibilities are in this connection:

1. *Heredity.* Children obviously differ in many respects as a consequence of hereditary patterning. Differences which might be expected to bring about significant variations in personality are the following: (*a*) differences in the arousal mechanism, such that one child consistently mobilizes more energy than another, regardless of the specific deficit involved; and (*b*) differences in the threshold for particular needs, so that one child is strongly affected by deficits which hardly influence another. The first of these is supported by considerable data; observations of infants reveal a wide range of activity levels, and some psychologists hold that these differences persist for many years, giving a flavor to the entire personality (Freeman, 1948). With regard to the

---

[1] Other theorists, notably Lewin (1935) and Snygg and Combs (1949), have used the concept of tension in a purely phenomenal sense, i.e., the individual experiences tension. Since this point of view gets very far from our physiological emphasis, it will not be examined further here.

second possibility, that of differences in arousal by specific needs, the situation is less clear. Sheldon (1942), as was noted in the preceding chapter, certainly would claim that his endomorphic type would be vigorously motivated by hunger and similar "visceral" or comfort needs, in contrast to both his mesomorphic and ectomorphic groups. This assertion, however, is based on observation of adults; we know next to nothing about such differences in the newborn.

2. *Environment.* Alternatively, these deficit states may have differential motivating effects because of the results of past experience. These have already been described, in a different context, in Chapter 5. (*a*) *Frustration* of a particular drive may cause relevant goal objects to be overvalued. The child who never quite receives enough food, or receives it irregularly, may quickly come to exaggerate grossly the importance of food. The deadly character of quarrels over water rights in the American West stemmed from this kind of insecurity about important drives. (*b*) Dependable *gratification* of a drive may cause the relevant goal to be undervalued. No one thinks of oxygen as an important goal in life, but we would die in a few minutes without it. In ordinary life, we hardly give water a thought; but when water is scarce, it is highly valued.

Probability of goal attainment, then, is a significant determinant of the energy aroused by a specific need. If the person sees the probability of gratification as very high, he mobilizes little energy; he is sure not much effort is required (Figure 13.1). If the probability is seen as moderately low, great effort is expended. On the other hand, if the probability approaches zero, effort again drops off; why struggle, when there is no chance of success? An excellent analysis of the process of demoralization, and consequent lack of motivation, in workers such as Negroes (last to be hired, first to be laid off) has been given by Davis (1946). As the Negro worker gradually comes to perceive success as unattainable (in the sense of job security, status, and

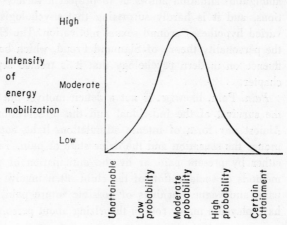

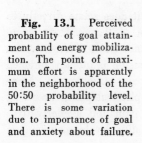

Fig. 13.1 Perceived probability of goal attainment and energy mobilization. The point of maximum effort is apparently in the neighborhood of the 50:50 probability level. There is some variation due to importance of goal and anxiety about failure.

prestige), he channels all his energy into the quest for food, liquor, and sex. These basic biological satisfactions, once enjoyed, cannot be snatched away by the whims of an economic system, whereas savings, job status, and the like may be painfully won, only to be wiped out at the will of the employer.

Nondeficit Drives. The foregoing paragraphs have related particularly to the deficit motives such as hunger and thirst. But we must also recognize the importance of biogenic drives such as sex and pain, neither of which is characterized by correcting a deficit of a needed substance. Each of these is of course capable of evoking tension, of mobilizing energy, and of maintaining action until some kind of gratification is attained.

Sex. It is well established that sexual gratification is not essential in the life of the individual, although it seems likely that the evolutionary process would somehow have built into the structure of the individual a need which would ensure the perpetuation of the species. Animal research indicates that this is accomplished by the secretion of hormones: a surplus of estrogen in the female, or of androgen in the male, leads to heightened sex drive. There is some reason to believe that these hormones not only increase restless activity, but also modify the perception of an individual of the opposite sex: the positive valence is increased tremendously under these conditions. Thus, instead of being a deficit motive, sex is more aptly a surplus motive, a drive induced by a surplus of the relevant hormone.

This would suggest that relative masculinity or femininity of personality might be a function of the proportion of androgen or estrogen in the blood stream. Unfortunately, in human beings, the traits and attitudes characteristic of sex differences are so profoundly affected by experience that clear-cut differences are hard to find. We can assert that the sex hormones do affect sexual motivation, and they do also affect mannerisms, interests, and ways of looking at situations. The relationships, however, are complex, and the evidence often contradictory. As we have commented in discussing projective tests, an ambiguous situation allows us to project a variety of theories or interpretations, and it is hardly surprising that psychologists have elaborated quite varied hypotheses around sexual motivation. The chief of these is of course the personality theory of Sigmund Freud, which has been such a potent influence on modern psychology that it is treated separately in the following chapter.

Pain. Pain, likewise, is not a deficit motive, but it does relate directly to the survival of the individual and the preservation of tissues from harm. Almost any form of intense stimulation, light, sound, heat, cold, etc., can induce the sensation and the drive state of pain. Tension is quickly induced either by present pain or by the anticipation of pain (Chapter 5). Since methods of socialization of the child often involve physical pain, threats of pain, and vague warnings of possible future pain, pain and its derivatives have played a major role in theorizing about personality development.

The American behaviorists have made extensive use of pain and anticipated pain in their analyses of motivation. Mowrer (1939b) and Miller (1948b) have been particularly influential in this connection. Sketchily, their thesis runs like this: it is rather easy to establish the expectancy that a cue will be followed by pain. In the future, the presence of this cue will ensure mobilization of energy to avoid the cue (see the discussion of secondary motivation, below). Following such experiences, the child may acquire expectancies of danger from whole categories of stimuli; he may fear women, or loneliness, or public appearances, or economic success.

Exploratory Drive. Pain can fit fairly easily into the same kind of homeostatic framework which has been used in connection with hunger and thirst. Sex is more difficult, since it is not essential for the survival of the individual, but can be interpreted as homeostatic if we consider the possibility of a built-in mechanism for the survival of the race. The third of the nondeficit drives, the exploratory or curiosity drive, is extremely difficult to fit into a homeostatic framework.

By the exploratory drive we mean the dynamic tendency to explore the environment, to investigate new sources of stimulation, and to seek some variety in life. Babies and other young animals show a great deal of curiosity. Harlow et al. (1950), Berlyne (1955), and other investigators have shown that animals will do work simply to get additional sensory stimulation, e.g., in the form of looking out of a window. The importance of a curiosity drive in the area of personality is obvious. If such a drive is innate, then it would presumably account for differences in persons, such as tolerance for monotony, pioneering behavior, scientific investigation, and so on.

The actual status of the exploratory drive is controversial. Many psychologists, especially those who like homeostasis as a basic concept in human behavior, would prefer not to have anything to do with an exploratory drive. It is awkward to figure out how disturbance of an inner equilibrium can set off exploratory movements not directed to some other goal such as food. Exploration is more likely to upset equilibrium than to restore it!

Since exploratory behavior increases after a few hours in a very restricted environment, and decreases upon repeated exposure to the same situation even if this is complex (Berlyne, 1955), it follows the laws of deprivation and satiation which apply to hunger, thirst, and sex. This suggests that perhaps there is some kind of *cortical equilibrium* which requires an optimum amount of exteroceptive stimulation to maintain it. Decline in this stimulation gradually leads to disturbance of this equilibrium, with consequent tension and action which increases sensory stimulation. If this is so, the behavior becomes compatible with the homeostatic model.

Some behaviorists have preferred to treat curiosity as a secondary drive. This view holds that the animal originally is aroused by equilibrium disturbance such as deficit of food or water. Action and exploring new stimuli are necessary for homeostatic restoration. By the principle of secondary reinforcement (see below), moving around and exploring novel stimuli come to be valued because they are useful in satisfying basic drives. This view is not widely held but it is preferred by some psychologists who dislike to postulate the inheritance of a wide variety of drive states.

Individual Differences. The same sources of individual differences exist for the nondeficit as for the deficit motives: heredity and environment. Persons differ from one another in the extent of sex hormone production, and probably in the threshold for painful sensation. It is often assumed, without clearcut evidence, that such hereditary differences make for variation in personality. The assumption comes into question when we observe that differences in the pain threshold in the skin seem not to predict variations in observed traits which might plausibly have been affected by pain sensitivity. Indeed, Mowrer (1950b) has reported on the case of a girl apparently born with no pain sensitivity whatever in her skin. She manifested as much anxiety, concern about parental scolding, etc., as normal children, although she could hardly have acquired such patterns through the conditioning of pain reactions.

This does not mean that we can ignore the role of environment in influencing the pain responses of normal children. Certainly the occasions on which a person encounters pain will dependably affect his motivation in later situations.

Personality: Socialization of Biogenic Drives. Those psychologists who have most emphatically stressed the biogenic drives hold that personality formation is essentially a process of socializing these drives. The child demands food, but he must learn to conform to social patterns as to time, place, and manner of eating. He has sexual needs, but these are coerced, inhibited, and modified by social pressures and punishments. According to this view, personality is an interaction product, an outcome of biological tensions pushing against and being molded by social frustrations and opportunities for gratification.

A major difficulty encountered in this kind of approach has already been noted: it is that, in the adult person, few actions are directly motivated by the biogenic drives. It is thus necessary to devise some kind of theoretical bridge from the raw strivings of biology to the civilized motives of the mature personality. This bridge is built on two concepts, secondary drive and secondary reward.

SECONDARY DRIVE AND REWARD

The application of the biogenic drives to adult motivation must lean heavily upon the assumed attachment of these drives, or their attendant phenomena, to stimuli other than the deficits (or cues) which set off the drive inherently. That is, we cannot get very far with the adult personality by assuming that the hunger drive in its crude form is a major motive, but we could propose (as some have) that the mother is valued because she is a source of food, that the child comes to enjoy certain kinds of home surroundings, music, and similar stimuli because they are associated with food. The behaviorists in particular have made a great deal of the concepts of secondary drive and secondary reward.

Secondary Drive. The concept of secondary drive seems to have been first developed by Hull (see, e.g., Hull, 1951, p. 21). Dollard and Miller (1950) speak of "learned drive" or "secondary drive" as important determinants of adult motivation. "These learned drives are acquired on the basis of the primary drives, represent elaborations of them, and serve as a façade behind which the functions of the underlying innate drives are hidden" [pp. 31–32]. This implies that "previously neutral cues gain the capacity to play the same functional role in the learning and performance of new responses as do primary drives" [p. 78]. So, presumably, when one is placed in a situation where he has previously been hungry, he will at once experience hunger and be motivated to search for food.

Experiments on pain are cited to support the concept of secondary drive. It has been most difficult, on the other hand, to demonstrate experimentally a secondary drive based on hunger or thirst. Most psychologists therefore have substantial reservations regarding the utility of the secondary drive concept.

Secondary Reward. The counterpart of secondary drive is secondary reward, i.e., the notion that cues associated with food can have reward value even if they do not satisfy the hunger need. Dollard and Miller (1950) and Whiting and Child (1953) make extensive use of this concept in explaining personality development. Thus, the former authors note that "to a hungry infant, the sudden appearance of the mother with the bottle would be expected to function as a learned reinforcement; it also seems to soothe the infant and temporarily reduce crying and other signs of high drive" [p. 81]. From this, the authors conclude, we can infer that many objects and social relationships acquire drive-reducing attributes.

Perhaps the classic experiment on acquisition of secondary reward is that of Wolfe (1936), who trained chimpanzees to do work for poker chips. First the ape learned that poker chips could be exchanged for grapes. Then the chips were placed on a little cart loaded with bricks, and the animal had to pull on a rope to get it close enough to obtain the chips. The animals would hoard chips when grapes were not available; and when they had a goodly supply, would refuse to pull the bricks up to the cage to obtain more. Thus they manifested behavior typical of human responses to money and other incentives. These effects, indeed, have been duplicated in learning studies with children.

Valence. It will be noted that this is no more than the phenomenon referred to earlier in this volume as valence. If the person associates a cue with some pleasurable experience, such as food or comfort, the cue acquires positive valence; if the cue signals pain or frustration, it acquires negative valence. There seems to be considerable gain, on the side of simplicity, from using the valence terminology. The concept of secondary drive, aside from those phenomena based on pain, seems quite dubious; and the "reward" value of secondary reward is severely limited in many experiments. Secondary rewards lose their effectiveness quickly, especially in animal studies. Among human beings, a situation associated with food (e.g., clean linen, silver, etc.) may look very attractive but may have only slight reward value.

Single-drive and Multidrive Theories. We have stated that valence is always associated with tension. Positive valences tend to set up approaching responses, and negative valences, avoiding responses. By assuming that the tension in all drives is basically the same, Hull (1951) was able to develop a theory in terms of which there would be only a single drive, which he called D, and which would correspond to what Duffy (1957) calls arousal or energy mobilization. The direction, positive or negative, Hull sought to explain by stimuli associated with the drive states. Thus hunger might involve both tension and some visceral stimuli which direct behavior toward food. Love would include tension and also a positive orientation toward some person, and so on.

Freud, in his extensive theorizing which will be summarized in the following chapter, sometimes seemed to endorse a single-drive theory. Lewin, with his stress on tension as basically the same with either positive or negative valences, might likewise be classified in this group. The behaviorists, however, are most prone to adopt this view [2] and even they often lean to recognition of a number of specific drives rather than accepting a single-drive concept.

Multidrive Theories. The instinct theorists, such as McDougall and James, postulated inheritance of a variety of specific drives, or instincts. For reasons already noted, most psychologists abandoned the instinct view in the early twentieth century. The majority then adopted a theory of a few specific biogenic drives, including hunger, thirst, sex, etc., and sought to explain all motivated behavior by building on these. Hull's development of a single-drive theory grew out of this stage in the conception of motivation. In recent years there has been some dissatisfaction with the single-drive theory, and also with the stress on deficit motivation. Many psychologists feel that such simple views do an injustice to the complexity of human behavior. Cattell (1950) and Maslow (1954) have braved the climate of opinion to offer new theories of multiple "instincts" which seek to avoid some of the earlier pitfalls.

---

[2] Other authors adopting a single-drive view include Morgan (1957) and Beach (1942). Little has been done on integrating their theories with data at the complex level of personality.

Physiological evidence can be cited on both sides of this argument. Certainly most arousal states lead to similar physiological consequences: the changes in blood pressure, heart rate, electrical conductivity of the skin, and respiration are likely to be quite similar. Even emotions which are phenomenally so different as anger and fear give similar physiological effects, and they can be distinguished only by rather complex measures which must be treated separately for each individual being studied (Ax, 1953).

When the importance of the reticular system (a tiny but potent structure in the midbrain) was first recognized, it appeared that the activation of this system corresponded to Hull's *D*, i.e., this was the neural underpinning of a single tension system for all motivated states. Later, however, evidence was published (Olds and Milner, 1954; Delgado, Roberts, and Miller, 1954) pointing to two arousal systems, one of which seems to correspond to reward effects and one to punishment effects. It would be tempting to say that these verify the basic role of a dichotomy of valences, positive and negative. However, it should be noted that while behavior is limited to approach and avoidance, there may be accessory structures which are inherited and which determine specific patterns or occasions of approach and avoidance. If research verifies the existence of such structures, more complex than the simple reward and punishment centers, then we may be back in an era of multiple instincts.[3]

Significance for Personality Differences. The single-drive and multidrive theories obviously lead to different predictions about personality. The single-drive theory can be interpreted as indicating that a person who is vigorously motivated in one area will be similarly energetic in other activities. Exceptions would be explained on the basis of learning to inhibit vigorous effort in certain stimulating contexts. Guilford and Zimmerman (1956) report evidence along this line; their factor analysis of personality inventory data led to identifying a dimension of activity or energy level, along which their subjects were distributed from low to high activity.

Unfortunately, other observations cast doubt on this conclusion. We have cited Sheldon (1942), who asserted that his mesomorphs showed general vigor and aggression, but endomorphs were specifically motivated toward conditions of comfort and visceral gratification, while ectomorphs were more likely to channel effort toward ideational goals. Everyday observation indicates that the man who works very hard on professional problems may be lazy around the house, and the apathetic factory worker may mobilize tremendous energy on a deer hunt. There is, on the other hand, no evidence whatever to support the notion that these latter individuals vary either as regards the innate intensity of some biogenic drive or as regards learned gratifications of one or another drive. We cannot, therefore, offer any final

---

[3] It should be added that P. T. Young (1936) proposed an explanation of drive based on the assumption of two innate patterns of positive and negative affective tone. The neurological findings cited above seem to give some support to his views.

conclusion concerning the relevance of single-drive and multidrive concepts for personality. Each will have to rely heavily on learning and other processes to explain the motivated behavior of specific individuals.

SOCIOLOGICAL VIEWS OF MOTIVATION

The problem of personality has also been of extensive concern to sociologists, who, not unnaturally, have placed heavy emphasis on the environment, especially culture, as the determining influence. In dealing with problems of motivation, consequently, they tend to emphasize *acquired motives*. Conceptually, these closely resemble the secondary drives and secondary rewards described in the preceding paragraphs. To the extent that formal recognition is given to the question, it seems to be assumed that biogenic drives become transformed into social motives. Thus, Parsons and Shils (1952) say: "The orientation of action to objects entails selection, and possibly choice. Selection is made possible by *cognitive* discriminations, the location and characterization of the objects, which are simultaneously or successively experienced as having positive or negative value to the actor, in terms of their relevance to satisfaction of drives and their organization in motivation" [p. 5].[4] This view is clearly compatible with the view which has been set forth in earlier chapters of this volume, i.e., that objects acquire positive or negative valence in terms of a person's experience; and that a major determinant of valence is the extent to which the object has led to tension reduction, or gratification of biogenic drives.

Honigmann (1954), an anthropologist, bases his discussion of personality on a similar approach. Of motives he has this to say: "A motive may be defined as a condition *within* the organism that impels behavior toward personally desirable goals. Illustrative of a learned and socially shared motive is the Kaska Indian's dependency or longing for care and affection. The eagerness of the Plains Indian to accumulate war honors, the intention of a Kwakiutl chief to overcome his rivals in gift giving and gift destruction, the desire of a Samoan girl to win approval through non-presumption all depend on the operation of socially standardized life goals" [p. 35].

The stress here clearly is on acquired or secondary motives. However, in a later passage, Honigmann makes it clear that these develop from the biogenic drives. "Physiologically rooted drives constitute the ground plan on which many of the tensions or motives come to be structured. The secondary drives or motives represent learned ways of satisfying, experiencing, or interpreting the primary drive" [p. 186].[5]

It would thus appear that the sociologists and the psychologists who emphasize biogenic drives as motivation are not far apart in their views. The dif-

[4] Reprinted by permission of Harvard University Press.
[5] Quotations by permission of Harper and Brothers.

ference lies in the fact that the biology-oriented psychologists keep the focus rather clearly on the inherent drive states; the culture-oriented social scientists concede that the biogenic drives are operative somewhere in the background, but place the spotlight on the secondary motives which are acquired as the individual becomes socialized. In this respect, the sociological approach is very similar to the treatment of motivation as goal seeking which will be presented in Chapter 15.

THE NEW INSTINCT THEORIES

Our treatment of the biological side of motivation would be incomplete if we did not give some space to the new proponents of instinct theory. The approach of the behaviorists, with its very heavy stress on cultural environment and learning as the source of adult motivation, has proved unsatisfactory to many psychologists. Two examples of new instinct theories will be briefly mentioned here: R. B. Cattell (1950) and A. H. Maslow (1954).

Cattell's Ergic Theory. Cattell is essentially a follower of McDougall. He is, however, aware of the devastating criticisms encountered by the latter, and his theory of inherent dynamic patterns avoids most of these. He has, for example, used the term *erg* instead of "instinct" to identify these inborn needs. An erg, he notes, is a dynamic unity; it will be relatively stronger in one person, weaker in another; likewise within a single individual, it may wax or wane in strength, but if so, all its manifestations will increase or decrease together. Each erg or instinct has three attributes: the person tends to perceive more promptly certain classes of objects related to that erg; he tends to experience certain emotions in relation to these objects; and he starts on a course of action which ceases when a specific goal activity is achieved. Thus the sexual instinct would imply selective perception of appropriate sex objects, sexual emotion (and its derivatives, such as tender love) for a member of the opposite sex, and the release of effortful behavior which ceases with some kind of consummatory sexual behavior.

The exact number of human ergs is not precisely specified by Cattell (1950) and it may be that such a precise listing would depend on empirical research rather than on any theoretical analysis. He offers a listing of 14 ergs, in the order of their relative strength, which is reproduced here as Table 13.1. The estimate of strength is derived from measures such as: memory for words and pictures relating to the erg; galvanic skin response to such words or pictures; reported interest in this class of stimuli; reported time and money expenditures on a class of stimuli, and so on. The ranking in Table 13.1 is based chiefly on measures of attention to and memory for words and pictures.

The crucial question, with Cattell as with McDougall, is this: Can we demonstrate that such dynamic tendencies are in fact chiefly determined by heredity? Cattell proposed several criteria: (1) a similar pattern in mammals, especially primates, indicating a biological basis for the erg; (2) a universal pattern, appearing in a wide diversity of cultures; (3) the pattern of attention, emotion, and response mentioned above, despite environmental variations; (4) an accompanying unlearned facial and visceral pattern of expression; (5) pres-

Table 13.1

Cattell's List of "Ergs" Arranged in Order of Relative Strength

Erg	Colman and McRae's method *	Cattell's method
Mating	1	1
Self-assertion	6	2
Pugnacity	5	3
Repugnance	9	4
Appeal	Not included	5
Hunting	Not included	6
Laughter	Not included	7
Self-abasement	2	8
Construction	Not included	9
Flight	3	10
Curiosity	7	11
Protection	4	12
Gregariousness	8	13
Acquisition	10	14

* Colman and McRae, according to Cattell (1950), used the magnitude of the GSR to a variety of stimuli to obtain relative indices of strength of mobilization in these various areas. Cattell's ranking is a composite based on attention to and memory for activities, words, and pictures in each area.

SOURCE: Cattell (1950), p. 192. Reprinted by permission of McGraw-Hill Book Company, Inc.

ence at birth; (6) powerlessness of training to eliminate this propensity. It is not implied, of course, that any given erg must be supported by all of these. And Cattell seems to agree that we may never have incontrovertible proof on most ergs; we are likely at best to increase the probability that a given need is innately determined or a product of environment.

Space does not permit a detailed analysis of Cattell's list of ergs. It is fair to state that most American psychologists, at present, would reject his view that all these are chiefly determined by heredity. However, it is also important to observe that dissatisfaction with the biogenic drive theory and its sociological parallel, the theory that all motives are learned from the culture, is increasing. Thus there is likely to be an increase of interest in the instinct type of theory within the foreseeable future. Cattell's view may become important because of the extensive data he has gathered which links his theory with the observable aspects of personality (see, for example, Cattell, 1957).

Maslow's "Instinctoid" Theory. Like Cattell, Maslow's interest is primarily in personality, but he feels the necessity of grappling with the motivational problem because of its basic position in relation to personality. Maslow differs from Cattell in two important respects. First, his theory asserts a hierarchy of needs; the physiological needs (which have been labeled in preceding pages the biogenic drives) must be satiated before the "higher" needs can manifest themselves. Second, his theory adheres to more general categories and hence avoids the critical reaction elicited by some of Cattell's highly specific ergs.

Maslow proposes several groups of innately determined needs. He does not care to call them "instincts" but refers to them as "instinctoid," i.e., innate but not so specifically focused as the instincts. His theory proposes that there are five groups of basic needs: (1) The physiological needs, which he identifies with the biogenic drives or homeostatic needs. He notes, as we have, that it is impossible to make a definitive listing of these needs, since we do not know all the requirements of protoplasm. (2) When the physiological needs are relatively satiated, they are weakened and this makes possible the appearance of the safety needs. These include freedom from pain, discomfort, threat, and unfamiliar, disturbing stimuli. These, in other words, represent the pain-anxiety motives. (3) When the safety needs are satiated, and thus weakened, the belongingness and love needs appear. For Maslow this category includes sex and its various derivatives, love, friendship, desire for children, acceptance in a group. (4) Following the love needs Maslow lists the esteem needs. The individual is said to need both self-esteem and the esteem of others. He may come to seek prestige, recognition, fame, etc. (5) At the top of the hierarchy, and hence presumably manifested only when all the others have been relatively satisfied, is the need for self-actualization. Maslow never clearly defines this; he refers to it as "man's desire for self-fulfillment" or "the desire to become more and more what one is, to become everything that one is capable of becoming" [pp. 91–92]. In addition to these five, which he clearly considers the kernel of his theory, he also lists (6) the desire to know and understand, and (7) the aesthetic needs. These last two seem to be added somewhat as an afterthought.

Maslow's emphasis upon the hierarchy of needs is important. While each person has a variety of wants, he usually has no great difficulty in deciding which is the most urgent, and guiding his behavior accordingly. [When he cannot reach such a decision, he is in a state of conflict (cf. Chapter 6), but this conflict may result as much from inadequate perception of the goals and pathways open to him as from inability to decide about motivational importance.] The view that the satisfaction of the "lower" needs is a precondition to the appearance of other motives has been widely expressed. Claude Bernard, the French physiologist who coined the term "homeostasis," is credited with the statement that homeostatic equilibrium of inner states (blood chemistry, etc.) is "the true condition of the free life"—in other words, a person is not free to choose among objects and actions as long as he is driven by biogenic emergencies. Similarly, Lewis Mumford (1956) comments: "To live in the highest sense is to be freed from the pressure to survive" [p. 75].

It is, however, possible to treat these various kinds of needs (for physical security, belongingness, love) as products of a learning sequence based on physiological homeostasis (Chapter 4). The crucial question as regards Maslow's hierarchy, then, is that of justifying his emphasis on heredity. What arguments can be adduced to support the view that these "basic needs" are innately determined? Maslow offers some of the arguments listed by Cattell. He has, however, some ingenious variations. Cattell stressed continuity from mammal through primates to man; Maslow suggests that man, being a distinct species, may have his own unique instincts; or he may have instincts, such as altruism, in common with the higher apes, but not with white rats. Maslow agrees with Cattell about the importance of demonstrating that training is helpless to abolish some of these propensities; but he argues that a need *may* be innate and yet abolished by culture. He even argues whimsically that "we ought to protect the weak, subtle, and tender instinctoid needs if they are not to be overwhelmed by the tougher, more powerful culture" [p. 129]. He does not explain just how this point relates to his argument that personality breakdown results if the basic needs are frustrated.

Perhaps the chief inadequacy of Maslow's theory is that it has so little empirical support. We do not know, for example, precisely what observations he would call evidence for the "safety needs"; nor do we know that these needs show the functional unity which logic would require in order to group them together as Maslow does. We have little evidence with respect to the hierarchy as he arranges it; certainly there are individuals who do not fit his sequence, although in general it looks like the sequence worked out on a homeostatic basis in Chapter 4.

On the theoretical side, perhaps most criticism attaches to his tendency to get ethical considerations mixed up with his logic. For instance, he says, apparently to prove the instinctoid nature of the basic needs, that "the gratification of basic needs leads to consequences that may be called variously desirable, good, healthy . . ." [p. 142]. He fails to note that these same needs may lead to crime, violence, and war. But neither consequence proves anything about heredity.

Maslow's concept of self-actualization would seem to provide an excellent dynamic basis for the well-demonstrated importance of the self-image (Chapter 9). A major problem arises from the fact that each individual has multiple potentialities and can hardly "actualize" all of them (cf. page 206). His answer presumably would be that the person has learned a scale of values, places one or a few potentialities high in this scale, and thus concentrates energy rather than diffusing his efforts too widely. A number of other authors (Goldstein, 1947; Lecky, 1945; Rogers, 1951) have proposed theories which suggest an innate drive towards self-realization and self-consistency which is something more than mere egocentrism. While space does not permit us to review the specific suggestions they have offered, we must note that this building up of support for such a theory is impressive. It seems reasonable to anticipate the further clarification and consolidation of a theory of a "self-actualization" instinct.

Implications for Personality Differences. As with the other views of motivation described earlier, both the Cattell and Maslow approaches assume that the personality as observed is an interactional product, an outcome of inner motives pressing against an external environment, with consequent gratifications and frustrations. It would appear that Cattell leans farthest in the direction of emphasizing these innate impulses as personality determinants; Maslow even suggested that some "instinctoid" needs might be completely suppressed by cultural pressures, hence implying a relative preponderance of environment over heredity. Cattell has followed through on his theoretical speculations; some of his research on hereditary determination of manifest personality traits will be summarized in Chapter 16. Cattell (1957) has also attempted to demonstrate functional unities in motivated behavior which would confirm his theory with respect to the importance of particular inherited ergs. Most of the data cited have been collected by Cattell and his students; they naturally have interpreted the findings as supporting the theory, but other psychologists reviewing the research have questioned the conclusion. It is unfortunately true that research on personality, a complicated matter at best, often leads to ambiguous findings. In such a case the author of a theory is disposed to perceive confirmation of his views, whereas other psychologists remain unconvinced.

Somewhat the same situation holds for Maslow. His theory would imply that some individuals should show a relatively high focusing of motivation around the physiological needs; others, around the need for safety; others, around the self-esteem needs; and so on. On the basis of clinical interviews, Maslow claims that he does in fact observe such unities in the behavior of individuals. The interview as a research method, however, is subject to the criticisms noted in Chapter 2. Other clinical interviewers come out with quite different reports about the unities of individual behavior, notably the Freudians, whose theory is summarized in the following chapter. It should be feasible to devise fairly objective research which would tend to confirm or reject Maslow's theory, and such investigations may be available in the near future.

MOTIVATION THEORY AND PERSONALITY

In the foregoing pages we have cited some of the different approaches to motivation from the biological side. It is apparent that there are substantial differences of expert opinion with regard to such issues as instincts versus biogenic drives, and single versus multiple drives. Although the resolution of such differences may open up new understandings of differences in personality, we cannot be optimistic that they will be resolved in the immediate future.

It has been noted repeatedly in these discussions that motivation has two aspects: energy mobilization and energy channeling. People differ with respect to the amount of effort they mobilize, and also with respect to how well they focus it. They differ as regards kinds of satisfaction sought, specific goal objects perceived as potential gratifications, and so on. The problems raised in this chapter deal mostly with energy mobilization. The phenomena of personality, on the other hand, relate mostly to the area of energy distribution—preferred classes of goals, shifting of energy from one goal to another, persistence of specific goal striving, and so on. Thus it seems proper to pay more attention to this matter of the direction of behavior rather than to the problem of the ultimate energy sources. For this reason the following two chapters are devoted to different views with regard to the channeling of motivational energy.

SUMMARY

Man is a biological organism before he is a social entity. It is therefore not surprising that many psychologists have sought to build an understanding of personality on the biogenic drives: hunger, thirst, pain, etc. Since adult behavior does not show these drives in clear form, it has been necessary to assume the development through learning of secondary drives (cues setting off tension states within the individual) and secondary rewards (cues reducing tension).

According to this view, personality is a product of interaction between biology and social environment. Sociologists and anthropologists, while stressing the importance of the social milieu, generally accept the biological needs as basic to the development of social motives.

Instinct theories, such as those of McDougall and James, were criticized because they postulated the inheritance of complex functions which, it appeared, were probably learned. More recently, Cattell, Maslow, and others have been proposing instinct theories of a somewhat more sophisticated character.

For all the points of view presented, differences in personality may be considered to result from either heredity or environment. Inheritance may bring about differences in intensity of all drives, or of specific needs, or instincts; environment may inhibit some drives, or restrict the range of possible goals. Thus personalities reflect differences in the amount of energy mobilized and in the channeling of this energy toward desired objects, roles, and social situations.

SUGGESTIONS FOR READING

The biological approach to motivation is well summarized by P. T. Young in his *Motivation of behavior*. Instinct theory is persuasively presented by McDougall in his *Introduction to social psychology*, and pungently criticized by L. L. Bernard in *Instinct*. A modern behavioristic view, written with a focus on personality (abnormal), is Dollard and Miller: *Personality and psychotherapy*. In addition to presenting his own theory, Maslow, in *Motivation and personality*, offers stimulating comments about many other views of motivation.

CHAPTER 14

Psychoanalytic Theories of Motivation

The approach to motivation based upon visceral tensions, which was stressed in the preceding chapter, has had a preponderant influence upon American thought in the field of experimental psychology. As regards the psychology of personality, however, contributions in terms of drive theory have been relatively slight; and the revival of instinct theory, noted in the preceding pages, has been due chiefly to the dissatisfaction felt by personality theorists with the concept of drive.

Vastly greater influence upon the psychology of personality must be credited to a particular elaboration of instinct theory which is associated with the name of Sigmund Freud. For this reason the present chapter is devoted to Freud's theory and some of the important variants which have been developed.

To summarize Freud's massive contributions in a few pages is a difficult task, partly because the ideas are novel and intricately developed, partly because Freud changed his mind several times about major components of the theory. The task is not simplified by the amount of interpreting, modifying, and revising which has gone on since his death. Psychoanalysts have published many volumes elaborating Freud's notions, explaining what he "really" meant. Schools have split off from the main Freudian group, and vigorous controversies have ensued. Despite these complications, it is safe to assert that Freud's motivational theory has colored virtually every major contribution to personality research in the last fifty years.

It is worth noting that Freud, like the authors cited in Chapter 13, started with a strong biological bias. It is, after all, clear that every personality begins as a biological unit, and—within the range of scientific study, at any rate—can never be separated from that biological base. Freud also recognized, naturally, that the truly human aspects of personality develop as this biological fragment becomes socialized; and his final theory virtually buries the innate components of motivation under an elaborate superstructure of learned percepts and responses. His early writings even speculated about a biochemical basis for the sexual instinct, with presumed increases and decreases of some substance correlated with deprivation and satiation. However, such ideas gradually disappeared as the role of experience received constantly greater emphasis.

Basic Concepts. Freud at different times postulated the inheritance of different instincts. In all cases he laid heavy stress upon the sexual instinct, using this concept in a broad sense to refer to the pleasure-seeking tendencies of the individual. In an early version he held that personality develops out of the conflicts between the sex instinct and the ego instincts (hunger, pain, etc.). Later he developed the concept of a death instinct (impulse toward destruction); and in opposition to this he set a team composed of the sex and ego instincts (life instinct). While the concept of a death instinct has won little acceptance, the notion of personality as essentially a development out of conflict is not only basic in Freud but is also virtually unquestioned in all of psychology (cf. Chapter 6).

The Libido Theory. Freud proposed that we conceptualize all the energy available to the personality as *libido* or drive energy. The libido at first is entirely id energy, but later some of it becomes detached and is available for the functions of the ego and the superego. For modern followers of Freud, this libido is very similar to the biogenic energies already described, and differs only in that the use of a single concept (libido) implies that all these energies are interchangeable. About this many American psychologists would have considerable doubt.[1] It is true, of course, that all one's energy derives from a single source, namely, the food he eats. But in the functioning of the organism it is not clear that one biogenic drive can be substituted freely for another.

Cathexis. We are interested, however, in the Freudian theory. According to this view, libido is a kind of pleasure-seeking, life-maintaining energy which becomes focused on certain objects or goals. (We have used the term "valence" to identify objects which have acquired these energy-arousing properties.)

Freud held that the libido is highly mobile; it can be attached to an object and then withdrawn, like the pseudopod of an amoeba. In the newborn, the libido is supposed to be cathected diffusely to the body as a whole, and especially to the skin (cf. the child's desire to be fondled and the alleged deleterious results of lack of adequate stimulation, page 95). Later, however, the child attaches libido to objects, especially persons, and perceives them as sources of pleasure. If the person hurts him, physically or mentally, the libido may be withdrawn, and may again become narcissistic, i.e., self-love; or it may be displaced to another person who is perceived as distinctively different. Characteristically the first external object of libido attachment is a dependency relationship—the mother or other person who takes care of him.

The notion of cathexis can perhaps be made most clear by a humorous analogy offered by Bellak (1956). Suppose—he suggests—that baby John has

---

[1] It will be recalled that C. L. Hull (1951) used the concept of *D* or general drive in a way somewhat reminiscent of libido. His theory, however, focused on responses, whereas the Freudians have used the libido concept mostly in relation to perception of objects.

cathected

a total narcissistic libido of 100,000 Freudian units. (Freud assumed that there was some kind of total, and the diversion of libido to a new object meant withdrawing it from some prior object.) He may "invest" 20,000 units in his mother as an early love object. Likewise he may invest 5,000 in his father, 2,000 in an older brother, and so on. As he progresses through the various stages of psychosexual development (pages 106–110), he invests libido in his oral zone and objects related thereto, withdraws some but not all as he progresses through the anal and phallic to the genital stage. (The amount of libido left behind with each of these infantile love objects will determine the extent to which he remains infantile in limited aspects of personality.)

At the time of the Oedipus crisis, he may withdraw libido from his father and concentrate heavily on his mother to a dangerous degree. If the conflict is successfully resolved, i.e., he abandons the hope of possessing his mother completely and accepts identification with his father as the best way of keeping the affection of both parents, he will again withdraw very substantially from his mother's account. Much of this returns to the self, to narcissism. The latency stage is characterized by less love for others and more for the self. Finally, at the time of puberty, he may mobilize a great deal of libido, withdrawing it from his parents, his male friends, and even from himself, to endow richly some member of the opposite sex.

This whimsical version of cathexis serves to illustrate the basic point of the theory, namely, that in varying stages of development and with varying environmental experiences, the child focuses his energies on different persons, objects, and roles. It conforms to the view set forth in Chapters 5 and 6, that personality development is largely a process of learning to perceive these external objects as attractive or as threatening. It is also clear that the theory can be expanded to incorporate phenomena such as stimulus generalization— i.e., when libido is attached to one object, it will tend to spread to similar and related objects.

The libido theory assumes that negative valences (expectancy of threat) derive from fear of loss of a libidinal object. Thus, comments Bellak, we could assume that the boy at the time of the Oedipus crisis values his penis at 30,000 units and fears he might lose it (the castration complex) if he does not give up his demands for possession of the mother. Thus he withdraws libido from the mother in order to avoid the greater loss.[2]

Personality, then, is defined largely as the pattern of cathected libido characterizing an individual. This amounts to little more than saying that your personality is revealed by your likes and loves, your preferred activities, your love for yourself, and so on. (Through the concept of *countercathexis*, energy mobilized to oppose a desired act, the Freudian view can also embrace hos-

---

[2] We should not need to add that there is no way quantitatively of measuring libido, and that the figures cited are purely imaginary.

tilities, inhibitions, and prejudices.) Thus this conception is very closely parallel to that presented earlier (Chapter 5), in which personality is conceived as a pattern of positive and negative valences.

Libidinal Zones. The very earliest libidinal investment is thought to be a kind of diffuse cathexis of the infant's entire body. There is, however, a maturational process, appropriate to an instinct theory, in which the cathexis becomes relatively focused on parts of the body. Another way to state this is to say that there is *"an orderly maturational sequence of preferred loci of stimulation"* (Bellak, 1956). Thus, the suckling infant seems to derive maximum pleasure from stimulation of the lips; but with bodily development, the greatest enjoyment may seem to be in stimulation of the anal region, or of the genitals. Observations regarding the successive stages of personality development, as this sequence proceeds, have been cited in Chapter 5.

The Pleasure Principle. Freud's over-all view of how the organism relates to its environment is remarkably similar to the homeostatic conception utilized in Chapters 4 to 6 of this volume. He assumed that an instinct manifests itself by an arousal of tension, and that the organism seeks objects and actions by which the tension can be removed and the equilibrium restored. He tended to emphasize conscious pleasure in defining this concept, but it is obvious that he also included the possibility of unconscious pleasure, or the avoidance of pain.

Impetus, Aim, and Object. The tension which develops when any instinct is aroused is referred to as the *impetus* for any particular reaction; the physiological system which alone can release the tension has been called the *aim* and the outside situation, the *object* of this drive. Thus, in hunger, the inner tension furnishes the impetus; the alimentary mechanism is the aim, and food is the object. In such a case, the object may be specific (desire for a particular food) or general; the aim, however, cannot be changed. In the case of other desires, the aim also may be subject to variation if the tension is not specific.

Freud's view of these tensions is that they are innate, but capable of attachment to a diversity of stimuli through learning; thus the importance of heredity is recognized without being overstressed. We shall find, however, that he considers some aims and objects to be innately determined, which on critical inspection appear to be more correctly explained on the basis of learning.

Freud treats these tensions as basic states which are associated with, or represented in consciousness by, a feeling of unpleasantness, and as running a course which leads to pleasure: [3]

In the psychoanalytical theory of the mind we take it for granted that the course of mental processes is automatically regulated by the "pleasure-principle"; that is to say, we believe that any given process originates in an unpleasant state

[3] Freud (1922), p. 1.

of tension and thereupon determines for itself such a path that its ultimate issue coincides with a relaxation of this tension, *i.e.*, with avoidance of "pain" or with production of pleasure.

The pleasure principle, then, is conceived as an innate tendency of the organism which determines the manner in which psychic tensions are released. Forms of behavior which would lead in the direction of increased tension are inhibited, while those which lead to decrease of tension are facilitated. In the life of the infant, the pleasure principle dominates all behavior. He is a flagrant egotist, seeking his own ends at all times. He demands food, comfort, attention. Some adults likewise show no willingness to inhibit a demand for immediate satisfaction of their desires. We speak of them as "childish" or "infantile."

The Reality Principle. It is obvious that adult behavior in general is not governed exclusively by the pleasure principle. The generalized formula which distinguishes adult from infantile behavior, according to Freud, is the reality principle, which may be stated as follows: Immediate pleasure or release from pain may be dispensed with, in order to obtain greater pleasure or freedom from pain on a future occasion: [4]

The first case of such a check on the pleasure-principle is perfectly familiar to us in the regularity of its occurrence. We know that the pleasure-principle is adjusted to a primary mode of operation on the part of the psychic apparatus, and that for the preservation of the organism amid the difficulties of the external world it is *ab initio* useless and indeed extremely dangerous. Under the influence of the instinct of the ego for self-preservation, it is replaced by the "reality-principle," which without giving up the intention of ultimately attaining pleasure yet demands and enforces the postponement of satisfaction, the renunciation of manifold possibilities of it, and the temporary endurance of "pain" on the long and circuitous road to pleasure. The pleasure-principle however remains for a long time the method of operation of the sex impulses, which are not so easily educable, and it happens over and over again that whether acting through these impulses or operating in the ego itself it prevails over the reality-principle to the detriment of the whole organism.

It is not assumed that the reality principle can completely inhibit, for any length of time, the manifestation of a drive. Hendrick (1934), whose discussion of Freudian theory is considered authoritative, makes an analogy of hydraulics in which he suggests that behavior following the pleasure principle can be represented as in Figure 14.1: Here we see a source of motivational energy or pressure, the pump. The pressure (tension) in the system is prevented from rising above a certain level by the outlet at C. This is the consummatory response of food getting, pleasurable contact, or whatever is called for. If, in an organism controlled by the pleasure principle exclusively, blocking of the activity occurred as a result of interference (the valve at D), the result undoubtedly would be breakage of the system (as at X) to give an outlet for the pressure.

[4] *Ibid.,* p. 5.

The reality principle, according to this hydraulic analogy, can be interpreted as a way of diffusing and sustaining the tensions for a certain period of time or until a given level of pressure (much higher than the pleasure principle can tolerate) is reached. This is represented in Figure 14.2. Here we find the reality principle represented in function by a reservoir,

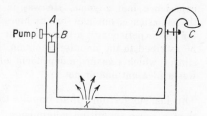

Fig. 14.1 The pleasure principle illustrated as a hydraulic system. (From Hendrick, 1934.)

in which tensions interfered with by social restrictions (the valve at D) may rise to the point E before rupture of the system occurs. The outlet at C' represents acts which will give more or less adequate outlet to the accumulated tension—acts which are controlled by social precepts—the valve at D'.

Freudianism, then, conceives the pleasure principle and the reality principle as dynamic laws governing the behavior of organisms. The simple, direct demands for gratification of innate desires characterize the infant's behavior, and these may be described by the pleasure principle. The ability to delay pleasures, to undergo discomfort in order to reach future gains, to satisfy desires by socially approved substitute activities—all these are characteristic of adult behavior and illustrate the reality principle. Almost all forms of behavior can be interpreted as cases of one or the other of these.

The Repetition Compulsion. There seem to be a few instances of behavior not in accord with either the pleasure principle or the reality principle. Small children are often overheard in verbal play or spoken fantasy, repeating an *unpleasant* experience, such as having a tooth pulled. The same sort of repetition occurs in episodic neuroses, in which an unpleasant scene is reenacted with all its harrowing emotions. We should be inclined to interpret this merely as habit, a manifestation of the general tendency of acts to be repeated when associated stimuli are present. However, Freud takes the view that there is a definite impulse to such forms of behavior: [5]

On impartial consideration one gains the impression that it is from another motive [than the pleasure-principle] that the child has turned the [unpleasant]

[5] *Ibid.*, p. 14.

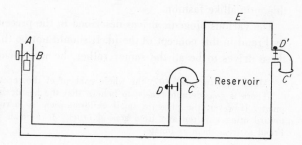

Fig. 14.2 The reality principle illustrated as a hydraulic system. (From Hendrick, 1934.)

experience into a game. He was in the first place passive, was overtaken by the experience, but now brings himself in as playing an active part, by repeating the experience as a game in spite of its unpleasing nature. This effort might be ascribed to the impulse to obtain the mastery of a situation (the "power" instinct) which remains independent of any question of whether the recollection was a pleasant one or not.

This last suggestion (of an impulse to master a situation) seems more plausible than a mere repetition compulsion.[6] Again, there is a question whether this form of behavior occurs spontaneously or whether it is derived from learning and observation of others.

Classification of Motivated Behavior. It is manifestly impossible to study a drive directly. We infer a sex drive from sexual behavior, a food drive from food-seeking activity, and so on. Classifying the impulses in this way, Hendrick (following Freud) finds three main groups of "instinctual" activities: the sexual impulses, those whose objects are pleasurable sensations of all kinds (not in the narrow sense of sex as such); the ego impulses, whose objects are nutrition and self-preservation in general; and the hostile impulses, those which are manifested in aggression toward others.[7]

Organization of Drives. For purposes of theoretical systematization, as well as for the explanation of results of analysis and treatment, Freud discusses the drives as organized into three generalized systems, the id, the ego and the superego. (The use of "ego" here must not be confused with the ego impulses.)

The Id. This is the collective term for impulses which are described as primitive and animallike. The raw, uncontrolled desire for food, for sexual satisfaction, or for attack and injury to someone else are characteristic of the id. We do not accept the id as part of our personalities; we refer to it in the third person: "*It* made me furious," "I was not myself," etc. The impulses of this group are governed by the pleasure principle exclusively. Morality, fear of consequences, discipline, and so on, are not part of this level of personality organization. Naturally the normal adult shows few reactions which are characteristic of the id. In the case of sadistic and overtly sexual crimes, Freud would say, id impulses have been directly expressed in action. The horror felt by the observer at such crimes is said to be due in substantial part to the vigor with which the id impulses have been repressed by parental training, and the person's fear that some day they might escape and cause him to act in this animallike fashion.

The various biogenic drives described in the preceding chapter are grouped by Freud in this concept of the id. It should not be thought that he considered these drives to be all the same; rather, he was creating a collective term to

---

[6] Many analysts now reject the whole concept of the repetition compulsion.

[7] There is considerable reason to believe that the hostile impulses are derived and not innate. However, the pleasure small children seem to derive from aggressive behavior toward other children and from acts of cruelty to animals and insects, as well, caused Freud to treat them as innate.

identify these atomistic, physiological needs. Freudians sometimes speak loosely of "the id striving" for some goal, but this is logically unsound. The id is not a functional entity; the elicitation of one biogenic drive occurs quite independently of the others. The striving, therefore, is of the total personality; but it is triggered and maintained by a specific need, one of those classified as belonging to the id.

The Ego. Even when the person is operating on the very primitive level of the pleasure principle, he must have contact with reality in order to locate objects which will satisfy the instinctual need, reduce tension, and restore pleasure (see Figure 14.4). As he moves to the reality principle, he develops a system of awareness of objects, expectancy of punishment, inhibition of action, and tolerance of continued tension. These perceptual and response patterns collectively make up what Freud (1936) called the ego:

> It seems to me that the ego obtains this influence [over various organic functions] in virtue of its intimate connections with the perceptual system; connections which, as we know, constitute its essence and provide the basis of its differentiation from the Id. In its function the perceptual system which we have called perceptual-conscious is bound up with the phenomenon of consciousness. It receives excitations not only from outside but from within, and endeavors, by means of the pleasure-unpleasure sensations which reach it from these directions, to direct the course of every mental event in accordance with the pleasure principle. We are very apt to think of the Ego as powerless against the Id, but when it is opposed to an instinctual process, it has only to give a "signal of unpleasure" in order to obtain its object with the aid of that almost omnipotent institution, the pleasure principle [pp. 21–22].

Divested of the anthropomorphic terms, this passage simply says that through perception we become aware both of objects which promise pleasure and of threats and potential punishments. If the perceptual system is working satisfactorily, these are balanced judgmentally and a decision is reached as to whether the amount of pleasure to be gotten is worth the pain involved.

In traditional Freudian theory, all energy derives from the id. The ego has none of its own. However, since it can evoke anxiety (which derives its potency from the id), the ego can actually control behavior by turning the energy of the id against itself; this is what we have called approach-avoidance conflict (Chapter 6). The functional effectiveness of the ego depends on the accuracy with which objects are identified and the consequences of dealing with such objects represented in awareness. Thus perceptual vigilance and defense, by inaccurately representing the objects of the external world, weaken the ego; just as repression, by distorting the content of memory, induces erroneous evaluation of consequences and so weakens the ego. Ego weakness, therefore, is closely related to neuroticism and emotional disturbance (cf. page 168).

The ego, consequently, corresponds to a major part of what has been described in earlier chapters of this book. A given personality is composed of the percepts which attract him (promise pleasure), the objects which threaten

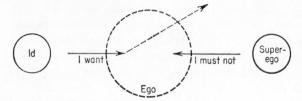

Fig. 14.3 The ego as mediator between id and superego. Various devices, such as repression and rationalization, are utilized by the ego to evade superego control and obtain gratification of desires.

him (arouse anxiety or fear of punishment), and the activities by which he approaches the one and avoids the other. The ego thus corresponds to the area which most students of personality have found particularly important.

It would be interesting to speculate on the reason why Freud relegated the ego to such a minor place in his theory. The ego was, of course, the locus of the defense mechanisms (see Chapter 6) by which the individual worked out compromises between the demands of his id and the pressures of the environment or the superego (Figure 14.3). But Freud seems to have been much more concerned with outlining a broad theory which would apply to everyone than with developing an approach which would account for the unique person. Later psychoanalysts have been far more interested in ego problems, and interest in perceptual-motor developments among children is characteristic of contemporary psychoanalysis, quite otherwise than in Freud's day.

The Superego. In his earliest formulations Freud described the dynamics of personality solely in terms of ego and id. Later he concluded that another element would have to be added. People sometimes inhibit biogenic drives not solely for fear of punishment, but simply because their inner standards oppose such drives. The aspect of personality which is composed of these inhibitory and command impulses, socially oriented but independent of social reward or punishment, he called the superego. This system develops as a result of introjection of social demands and prohibitions (cf. Figure 14.4*b*). In early childhood the parents and others threaten discomfort or disapproval if certain id impulses are expressed; gradually the child learns to forbid himself such gratifications and may punish himself (feel guilty) if he transgresses. The child also learns that he should manifest "good" character traits, such as honesty and integrity.

This analysis indicates that in considerable degree the superego corresponds to what we have called "character" (Chapter 10) or what is popularly designated as "conscience." The crucial role of superego development in the normal personality is indicated by the fact that an "infantile person" is one who is constantly acting at the id level, without consideration for social requirements.

It is important, consequently, in examining Freud's concept of the superego, to remember our comments on the problem of generalized versus specific views of character. Freud clearly implied that the superego becomes a generalized attribute of the individual; he speaks of some persons being "superego dominated" and the like. Popular psychology, with its concept of "will power"

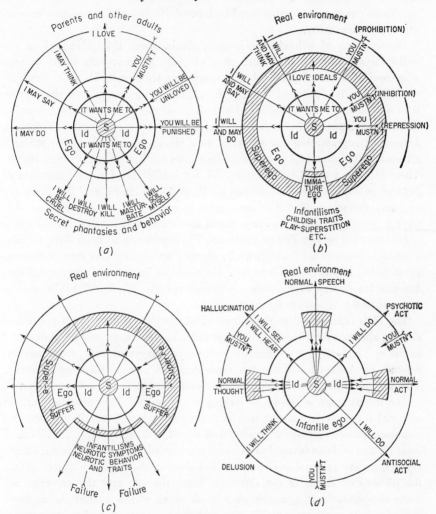

Fig. 14.4 Diagrammatic illustration of relations of id, ego, and superego. (*a*) In infancy there is no superego, and the ego tends to carry out the demands of the id unless the environment interferes (denoted by arrows pointing inward). (*b*) In normal adults, the superego forbids certain acts and thoughts. Almost every superego, however, has some gaps which permit childish reactions on occasion. (*c*) The neurotic adult has much wider gaps in the superego, but may also have excessively severe superego controls. (*d*) In the psychotic, the superego is fragmentary, and the ego poorly developed, so that the id is relatively unrestrained. Hence delusions, hallucinations, and dissociated acts characterize the psychotic. (From Hendrick, 1934.)

(or "won't power," as some wit has labeled it) likewise assumes a general aspect of personality.

Observations of behavior raise more doubt about this. Many of us are well-inhibited with regard to one class of goals, and not with others. A man who would not touch his neighbor's money may try to steal his wife; the businessman who is a pillar of the church on Sunday may engage in sharp practices on Monday; the politician who rants about embezzlement of labor union funds is undisturbed by embezzlement of funds by a corporation executive. Instead of representing the superego as a closed circle of uniform strength all around (Figure 14.4), it should be shown as having many weak points. There may be a trend (cf. Chapter 10) for inhibition of asocial impulses to become generalized, so that we can speak of "good character," but there are so many exceptions that it seems unwise to speak of "the superego" as if it were a functional unit. (To some extent this caution also holds for the ego.)

Interaction of the Three Systems. The interaction of these three impulse systems is represented graphically by another set of diagrams from Hendrick, presented in Figure 14.4. These four diagrams are intended to represent differences in interaction of the three systems in infants, in normal adults, and in neurotic and psychotic (insane) adults.

The id is represented as the source of all instinctual energy, all needs and desires, shown by arrows pointing outward. These desires are communicated to the ego and some are executed (arrows pointing outward). Some are inhibited by influences from the environment (arrows pointing inward). Thought, feeling, and behavior are represented as functions of the ego level.

The infant stage is shown as lacking the superego. This develops until at maturity it represents a strong barrier to the expression of socially disapproved impulses. Actions are now represented by "I will and may . . . ," i.e., I want to, and to do so is not disapproved. Some inhibitions, on the mature level, come from the external environment, but most of them now originate within the personality itself, in the superego. Since the ego and the superego are never complete, the diagram shows a break which allows infantile behavior of some kinds to reappear. Love is now directed to ideals, as well as to persons, but one may still have infantile attachments. Likewise destructive impulses may be directed against social conditions, instead of exclusively against things and people, but most personalities continue to show some infantile annoyances and rages.

With the neurotic and psychotic personalities this volume is not particularly concerned. It will suffice to point out that in these cases the ego and the superego are inadequately developed, or are broken by some traumatic experience which makes normal control of id impulses difficult or impossible. In the case of insanity, the ego (executive) function is not adequately adjusted to the requirements of the social environment imposed through the superego. Thus we have the individual experiencing thoughts and perceptions which are not in accordance with reality, but with the demands of the id (delusions, hallucinations).

Conscious and Unconscious Impulses. Freudian influence has been great with respect to the importance of unconscious drives. Since we have already pointed out that an unconscious drive is not unique, but is merely a drive for which the subject lacks adequate symbolic expression, we need not spend much time on this point. Its importance can be appreciated only if the student has some notion of the highly abstract, intellectualized, academic psychology of the nineteenth century, which limited itself to the study of conscious processes. Consciousness gives representation to only a very limited portion of human activity, and the vast majority of our desires, impulses, and emotional responses are inaccessible to introspective observation.

In calling attention to this very important fact, Freud unfortunately used a metaphorical expression, *"the* unconscious." Many psychologists took this expression literally and accused Freud of trying to set up entities within the mind, as faculty psychology had spoken of "the reason" and "the will." Actually "the unconscious" is to be taken only as a collective term for those phases of psychological activity which cannot be consciously observed. The relation of conscious to unconscious phenomena has been compared to the iceberg which is 90 per cent submerged and only 10 per cent visible. Figure 14.5, taken from Healy, Bronner, and Bowers (1931), gives an illustration of the possible relations of conscious, preconscious (accessible to memory, imagination, etc.) and unconscious (inaccessible) material.

Figure 14.5 also serves to point out that the conscious-unconscious division does not correspond to the divisions of id, ego, and superego which we have described. Originally Freud thought of the id as the unconscious and the ego as conscious. Later experience convinced him that parts of ego and superego were unconscious. The superego, for example, which is made up of the individual's identification of himself with his social controls, becomes largely composed of unconscious material. It is obvious, for instance, that these limitations and taboos begin to be acquired during the first year of life, and much of this childish learning occurs at a preverbal level. This material (the demand that certain desires be repressed) probably never is clearly conscious in the child's mind and quickly becomes completely unconscious. According to this view, the id is never conscious—a view which seems incorrect. The raw feelings, such as sexual desire, destructive hatred, and so on, seem to be conscious manifestations of impulses belonging to the id category. It is, however, clear that the vast majority of our "savage" impulses have been so completely repressed that they never reach the light of consciousness.

Development of Psychosexuality. According to Freudian theory, then, libido becomes attached to pleasure-giving objects, which are sometimes consciously perceived as desirable and sometimes sought without a conscious awareness that they are attractive. Anxiety becomes attached to threatening

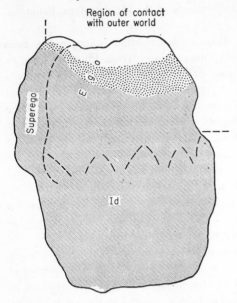

Region of contact
with outer world

Fig. 14.5 The "iceberg" analogy of conscious-unconscious relationships. The id is represented as entirely unconscious (heavy shading), while even ego and superego are mainly unconscious. The ego, in its function of carrying out demands of id and superego, represents most of the conscious and most of the region of contact with the outer world. (From Healy, Bronner, and Bowers, 1931.)

stimuli; while the energy of anxiety is drawn from the reservoir of libido, the person does not feel pleasure when anxiety is the prevailing mental state (but he may feel pleasure when the anxiety is reduced). The organization of libido and anxiety with various percepts and responses into the systems of ego and superego constitutes the process of personality development.

Another way of looking at this process was sketched in Chapter 5, where we summarized Freud's conception of oral, anal, phallic, and genital stages of psychosexual development. These stages involve the cathexis of libido to certain parts of the body, and to objects associated with the functioning of these parts. The discussion was presented in Chapter 5 for two reasons: (1) our emphasis at that point was on development, and the Freudian theory has profoundly affected our notions as to how personality development proceeds; and (2) as research cited at the point indicated, there is enough empirical support for this phase of Freud's theory to justify presenting it as an account of development. Our focus in the present chapter is on motivation and personality, and most of the material here is highly inferential, difficult to relate to empirical observation.

It would not be appropriate to review here the development of psychosexuality through the oral, anal, phallic, and genital stages.[8] There are, on the other hand, certain points about the formation of the mature personality, and especially about the motivation of relationships such as love and marriage, which merit consideration at this point. To place these ideas in their proper setting, we must restate some observations about infantile sexuality.

[8] It may, however, be wise for the student to reread pp. 106–110.

Infantile Sexuality. One of the facts about which the Freudian school builds its system is the observation that sex, as adults conceive it, is only a differentiated aspect of a generalized set of reactions present from birth onward. The infant manifests pleasure to stimulation of the lips, the nipples, and the genitals. Later he shows pleasure in his excretory functions, and may cause no end of trouble to the adults who are trying to teach him proper habits. When he learns that people are divided into two classes, he manifests great interest in sex differences and asks questions which cause inhibited adults a great deal of embarrassment. He expresses the wish that his father would die so that he could marry his mother and live with her forever after, and have children with her. All of these reactions are common; in fact, a child who did not manifest most of them during the first five years of life would seem peculiar.

It is, however, a tradition in our culture that all children are pure and "innocent." Wordsworth wrote, "Heaven lies about us in our infancy," giving expression to this view of the infant's relation to an adult ideal of perfection. Hence adults become quite angry when psychologists make the statement that children have sexual impulses. Actually, the amount of emotion produced in adults is proof of the importance of infantile sexuality. If infantile sexuality did not exist, it would be a matter of indifference to the individual, and he would not become angry when it was mentioned. But, having been forced to give up these pleasures in infancy by the stern process of training, we now become emotionally disturbed at being reminded of them—just as a salesman will become angry when reminded of the big sale that got away.

Love Relationships. Instead of speaking of the sexual development of the child, it may be clearer to speak of the development of love relationships. Most of the child's love is turned inward upon himself. He is primarily interested in his own pleasure, and much of his behavior is autoerotic, i.e., self-stimulation of erogenous zones. However, we find early in life evidence of strong attachments to specific individuals and the anticipation of pleasurable stimulation from them. This affective response we have already labeled "love." The child is positively conditioned to his parents, because both of them have ministered to his comfort and are by their presence associated with almost all of his pleasures. But it is clear that, during the first months of life, the preferred parent for children of both sexes is the mother. Later, the girl child is likely to shift to a preference for her father, while the boy continues a strong preference for his mother.

This unequal love is repressed by social training. A typical incident is the following, quoted from a college girl's autobiography:

I recall plainly an incident that occurred before I was four years old, since it happened in my first home. I had learned the baby trick of measuring love with my hands. My parents asked me one evening how much I loved my father, and I stretched my arms so far that they almost touched in back of me. Then, when they asked how much I loved my mother, I measured a tiny distance with my forefingers. Immediately I saw I was wrong, after one glance at my mother's face. So after that I tried very hard to keep them more nearly alike, though as I recall it, a little more preference was always shown in his favor. I never liked to sit close to my mother after I passed the baby stage, but there was nothing I liked better than to sit on my father's knee, and tell him secrets, and have him talk to me.

The significance of this unequal attachment for the parents, and the repression of the preference for one parent, is said by Freudians to lie in the development of the Oedipus complex, which we shall describe in a later paragraph.

Hate Relationships. Although Freud eventually decided that impulses of hostility were separate from the sexual impulses, his treatment of hate and attempts to injure others indicates that he considers these activities intimately related to love and sexual behavior. The young child loves his parents, but he hates each of them for monopolizing the attention of the other when it might be granted to him alone. These hate impulses are sometimes given overt expression, as when the little boy says, "I wish daddy would die so I could marry you," but usually they are repressed and obtain expression through substitute activities.

In most cases, the child develops ambivalent love-hate attitudes because of this fact. He loves his parents for the pleasure they give him, but hates them when they interfere with the pleasure he might get from someone else. This ambivalence often leads to personality problems in later life.

The Oedipus Complex. The developing love-hate reactions to one's parents are said to reach a climax at about the fifth year of life. At this time resistant, negativistic behavior has been found by various observers to be very high. The love need for the opposite-sex parent is expressed more or less openly, and the rivalry toward the other parent and toward other children in the family may be very keen. General emotional upset is commonly observed. The child shows a pronounced increase in fantasy, and expresses a desire to have children, etc. This period of emotional disturbance is described by analysts as the period of the Oedipus complex.

Failure successfully to resolve the Oedipus situation leads to various problems. Frequently we find a grown man who successively falls in love with women who are much older than he and who resemble (in one way or another) his mother. Again we find individuals who revolt blindly against any authority, and learn that to them authority is but a symbol of the parent whom they hated in childhood.

Parent Identification. The normal outcome of the Oedipus situation, if no traumatic conditions intervene, will be the abandonment of the child's open demand for the opposite-sex parent, and its replacement by an attempt at identification with the like-sex parent. This identification has been prepared usually by fantasies going on during the preceding stage, when the child has dreamed of himself as taking the place of one parent and marrying the other. Now, giving up hope of directly satisfying his desires, he begins to imitate the like-sex parent and thus by strategy gain the affection of the other parent. As we have frequently remarked, one of the fundamental facts in human behavior is that we behave toward symbols as though they were real and, by placing ourselves in substitute situations, obtain almost as much pleasure as from the originally desired condition.

The resolution of the Oedipus complex and the identification with the like-sex parent marks the end of the infantile sexual period. The child now progresses into a latency period, during which his interests are directed away from his own body and the possibilities of pleasure from contact with his parents, onto pleasures with friends. Because of his identification, his friends at this stage will be mostly of the same sex, and this is sometimes called the normal homosexual period.

Normal Adult Sexuality. After the latency stage—roughly from the fifth year of life until puberty—the individual regains the normal interest in the opposite sex. This renewed interest is determined by social and biological conditions. If no major interferences with the course of sexual development have occurred, the person now enters a stage of normal adult sexuality in which his quest for pleasurable activity follows a definite course, pretty well prescribed for him by the social group of which he is a member.

Relation of Infantile and Adult Sexuality. In many manifestations of adult sexuality we find hang-overs or vestiges of infantile sexuality. As examples we might mention the pleasures associated with the lips, the breasts, and other nongenital erogenous zones; perversions in which sexual and excretory structures are interchanged; and so on. Some of these persistent infantilisms are so common as not to be considered abnormal; others, more rare and subject to greater social disapproval in our particular group, are considered perverted. But it will help the student to keep a calm, scientific attitude toward problems of both normal and abnormal behavior if he remembers that these so-called "perversions" are perfectly normal in infants.

Various kinds of interferences with normal development of this series from infancy to maturity may result in personality abnormality. Infantile fixation on the mother or the father, of course, is seen in some adults. Homosexuality is considered a failure to develop to the normal heterosexuality of maturity. Unpleasant experiences with members of the opposite sex about the time of puberty may frighten the youth back to the homosexual mode of pleasure seeking. Any regression or failure to advance is a personality problem.

Individual Differences in Personality. Freud was never especially interested in the phenomena of individual differences in personality. His focus was either on universal principles of human development, or on the specific individual case with its conflicts, complexes, and cathexes.

The Freudian view, however, is entirely compatible with the emphasis developed in this book on traits as the major units of personality description. One factor is, of course, heredity. Freud speculated that some persons are born with a stronger id than others. This would lead to greater activity, stronger affectional relationships with people, and perhaps to more intense anxieties and depressions when these are aroused. It would mean that such a person, encountering a conflict situation, would react with more intense emotion and hence would show more symptoms of maladjustment than a person of weak id. (It will be remembered that we considered emotional maladjustment to be the converse of ego strength. Obviously, as outlined in Figure 14.4, a strong id is going to hamper the development of an integrated ego, as this term is used by Freud.)

The major variables determining trait development in psychoanalytic thinking would be environmental. In Freud's early writing, trauma was emphasized especially. Many of his neurotic patients showed a whole complex of symptoms (a trait, in our vocabulary) which apparently traced back to one or a series of painful experiences, usually sexual in character. Analysts generally are now more receptive to the idea of a long-continued series of minor frustrations, and also to overgratification, as sources of traits. Since these traits are localized in the ego, and the ego is the facet of personality which governs organism-environment relations, there are no problems here. Our analysis in terms of perception and the development of positive and negative valences (Chapter 5) would be entirely compatible with the usual Freudian presentation.

The psychoanalytic point of view has been of particular value in connection with certain special kinds of traits and value systems. To take a single example, some individuals show an excessively severe superego; they are ridden by a rigid and unyielding conscience. This condition can develop because of the death of a parent at an age when social taboos are just being taught, but the child has not yet learned when they can be relaxed and when kept firm. The death of the authority figure interrupts the learning process and the severe standards, which tolerate no exceptions, continue in force. (For a sample case of this type, see Erickson and Kubie, 1941.)

Critique of Freud. We have offered in passing some critical comments about Freud's theory. One of these merits considerable attention: It is the fact that id, ego, and superego do not behave like functional units. With respect to all three there is evidence that different components may vary substantially, one strong, another weak; hence, to speak of these as if they were unified is misleading. Somewhat related to this is the criticism that Freudians tend to personify these components; some of the writing about id-superego conflicts has all the qualities of a TV western, with the "good guy" battling the "bad guy" all over the place. Such a view is not in accord with the intentions of Freudian analysts, yet the habit of writing in this vein persists. This confuses not only students of psychology, but also laymen who encounter either Freud or his popularizers and acquire this oversimplified view of inner conflict. It would be helpful for the student to remember that the conflict is between components of himself, not between two little men off in a corner of his brain somewhere.

A second criticism is related to his stress on the maturational process, on the "unfolding" of the personality as it goes through the developmental stages. Inadequate attention is given to the role of the environment in determining whether a stage is observable, and what impact it has on personality.

Closely related to this is perhaps the major question raised about the psychoanalytic theory of personality. Today most psychologists hold that society, the cultural context within which the child grows, has a profound influence upon the motives which develop, as well as the channels for satisfying these motives. The alleged universality of the Oedipus complex has been challenged by the anthropologists, who find many primitive cultures in which the phenomenon is not observable. (This does not lessen the validity of the complex in our own culture, but it affects the theoretical structure.)

Finally, many psychologists are disturbed over what is neglected in Freudian theory. There is no consideration of such infantile needs as the need for stimulation and for movement, and virtually no attention given to such rather obvious biological drives as hunger and pain. The Freudians also reject the idea that adult motives may become independent of their infantile sources. The emphasis is upon fragments of infantile motivation persisting unchanged, or sublimated, into the mature personality; no attention is paid to the kind of self-enhancement motivation which was mentioned in Chapter 9 and will be considered more carefully in Chapter 15. Freudianism has inescapably a "backward look" in the sense that no explanation of adult behavior is accepted unless it ties firmly to an infantile motive of some kind. The importance of considering an adult's ambitions, his aspirations, and his current goal has been stated often in this volume. Failure to allow adequately for such motivation is probably the chief weakness of the Freudian view.

Acceptance of Freud. These comments do not indicate that Freud's view on motivation is rejected by American psychologists. On the contrary, a survey by Myerson (1939) showed the typical attitude to be "favorable but somewhat skeptical." Not more than 25 per cent of those responding could be counted as wholeheartedly endorsing Freud's views; on the other hand, less than 10 per cent completely rejected this approach to personality and motivation. The psychoanalytic doctrine, with all its shortcomings, has been a tremendous factor in the growth of a psychology of personality. And the genius of Freud was to a surprising extent responsible for the major theoretical structure, despite the fact that he has had many able students and disciples.

ALFRED ADLER

Not all of Freud's students became disciples. In some instances the dynamic cycle of rejection and reformulation was manifest. Alfred Adler, one of Freud's earliest pupils, rejected important aspects of the theory and proposed alternative formulations. We can only summarize a few of his ideas which have been widely influential in thinking about personality.

The essential postulate of Adlerian psychology, in terms of which the rest of it takes on meaning, is his insistence on the "life plan" of the individual, or the purpose, the goal, the "end in view" which determines reactions. Adler's psychology, therefore, is a purposive psychology, in contrast to the views of Hull and Freud, who deny purpose as a significant factor (except in the sense that past experiences may direct our behavior along lines which eventually prove to be useful).

According to this view, circumstances early in life focus attention on certain relationships between the individual and his physical-social environment. An individual who is small, physically inferior, and feels unnoticed may shape his whole life in terms of this relationship. A voice defect, a facial blemish, or some other characteristic may be the feature determining his reaction to his environment. The important matter, from Adler's viewpoint, is that the individual, usually unconsciously, sets up a certain "life plan," which is directed in such a way as either to overcome the defect or to compensate for it. The setting up of this goal or direction in life gives meaning to events which might otherwise fail to make sense. We have commented in previous chapters on such processes as imitation, identification, etc. It is apparent that while these processes are sufficient to explain the fact that a child adopts the characteristics of someone in his real or imaginary environment, they do not explain the selection of one rather than another person as the object of such an imitation or identification. Some selective process is at work. Adler believes that this is the unconscious "life plan" determined by felt inferiority in some physical or social relationship.

The Will-to-power. The driving force which impels the individual along his life plan is known as the will-to-power. In its nature this seems to be largely a matter of available psychophysiological energy, like Freud's libido. The difference is largely in the aims or objects to which it becomes selectively attached.

This may best be illustrated by an example. Starting on the physiological level, Adler found that in the case of paired or related organs, deficiency of one was often compensated by increased activity of the other. Thus a defective kidney on one side was found to result in hypertrophy of the other.

The same observation on other organ systems convinced him that there is a general principle in physiology of compensation for inferiority.

Now this principle of compensation for inferiority can be demonstrated on the implicit level as well. A person who is physically handicapped will be found to daydream of great athletic prowess. Boys who are sexually underdeveloped are often found to boast of their virility, their conquests, etc. These examples show implicit ("mental") compensation for physical or social inferiority. Compensations of one sort or another for feelings of intellectual inferiority are also common.

Adler believed, therefore, that the will-to-power was a fundamental drive, and that it was thwarted by some inferiority (in his early writing, a *real* inferiority; in later volumes, a *real or imagined* inferiority). This thwarting focused the attention of the individual upon his defective organ system, and a life plan was laid down to compensate for the defect. Sometimes, he concluded, this compensation might be direct (cf. Demosthenes's alleged cure of his tendency to stammer) or it might be indirect (as when a boy who is crippled physically prepares himself for a literary career). The important thing is that the will-to-power must be satisfied, and the life plan is determined with this end in view.

Complete Masculinity. According to Adler (1924), the ultimate goal of every individual is the attainment of what he calls complete masculinity. This assumption was based on studies mainly of neurotics who showed behavior of this sort. The weak, inadequate man strives for full and complete virility. The woman, however adequate she is as woman, feels inferior or deprived of something (the male organ) and strives to overcome her fate of being feminine. This striving Adler calls "the masculine protest." In illustration one thinks easily of many women who show by their behavior that they are seeking a masculine, rather than a feminine, goal. Since men have a favored position in our economic and political structure, it is not surprising that this often happens. We believe, however, that Adler exaggerates both its frequency and the extent to which biological factors are involved. The social and economic advantages of being a male, at least in Western culture, speedily come to the attention of most girls. It seems safe to predict that, as these handicaps to women are gradually abolished, the "masculine protest" will likewise become rare.

The Inadequacy of Childhood. One field in which Adler's contribution has been of real value is the treatment of certain problems of childhood. Adler emphasizes, in his treatment of child behavior, the feeling of inferiority and inadequacy which oppresses even the normal child. Physically insignificant and intellectually weak as compared with adults, the child has no outlet for his will-to-power. Thus he may show timidity, withdrawing, and seclusiveness; or, making a desperate effort to assert his individuality, he may resort to rebellion, exhibitionism, bullying smaller children, or even delinquency. Some adults fail to resolve this conflict and continue to show these infantile reactions.

The Adlerian approach to such problems is to provide suitable outlets in real situations for the child's will-to-power. These must, of course, be within his physical and intellectual scope. They can gradually be widened to provide compensations or sublimations of a sort appropriate to his age and social development.

The Importance of Social Climate. A major criticism of Adler is found in his excessive emphasis on organic factors. Thus he writes of feminine psychology as though all women desired biological equality with males, ignoring the social, political, and economic factors involved in "masculine-protest" behavior.

Similarly, his discussion of the effects of crippling and physical handicaps generally reads as if personality distortion were an inevitable accompaniment of such conditions. Actually, as Barker and others (1946) have shown, the effect of a physical handicap varies according to social attitudes. If the child and his parents interpret his handicap as a hopeless barrier to normal life, psychological stunting will result. In families where the handicapped child is encouraged to take an optimistic view and develop the resources remaining to him, very satisfactory personalities result. The same observation has been made with many physically disabled adults. Much depends on the way the injury is perceived and the extent to which the environment encourages constructive, independent ways of behaving.

Positive View of Dominance. While Adler seems to consider the will-to-power an innate need, his discussion of its operation is couched almost entirely in negative terms, i.e., as a reaction against inferiority or inadequacy. He posits some defective organ system or psychological function, about which the will-to-power is mobilized to deny or disprove the inferiority.

Several psychologists have reported experimental and observational data which suggest that there is a positive dominance drive, an innate tendency to achieve a status superior to others of the same species. Murchison (1935) and Schjelderup-Ebbe (1935) have studied the fighting behavior of chickens, which continues until a stable dominance status, or "pecking order," is evolved. This need to establish dominance seems independent of food, sex, and other drives, although it is intensified by injections of male sex hormone, and roosters so treated will actually achieve higher dominance status in the group of males.

Maslow (1936) has shown that monkeys and anthropoid apes manifest a dominance drive; and he feels certain that it is not a derivative from the hunger, sex, or other needs. Projecting his work into the human field, he has published a number of studies (1939, 1942) on the dominance drive at this level. While human material is inevitably more complex than that obtained by observing animals, he believes that the same generalizations hold for both investigations.

These contributions do not detract from the value of Adler's theory, but simply expand it as to field of application, while modifying it as to theoretical emphasis. In dealing with normal personalities, the psychologist constantly encounters behavior which illustrates the importance of dominance or the will-to-power as a major form of human motivation.

HORNEY AND FROMM

Adler initiated the battle against the heavily biological, hereditarian emphasis in Freudian theory. His views undoubtedly influenced many analysts who did not actually break away from the Freudian tradition. He also had an impact on the thinking of individuals who broke off and formed new centers of psychodynamic thought related to the Freudian school in some ways, but differing particularly in concern with the environment. Two important figures in this latter group are Karen Horney and Erich Fromm. Their similarity (and difference from the Freudians) resides in the emphasis they place upon interpersonal relations, the helplessness of the infant, the dependency of the child, and the exploitive nature of many parent-child relations.

Horney (1945), for example, finds the root of personality abnormality to lie in a *basic anxiety*. By this term she means "the feeling a child has of being isolated and helpless in a potentially hostile world" [p. 41]. That the child has good reason for feeling helpless under certain circumstances no one can doubt. Horney indicates that, given adequate care, this basic anxiety is not elicited (or perhaps becomes associated with so few situations that it does not crop up as a handicap in later life).

Where Adler stressed the fear of inferiority, and the compensatory drive for power, for superiority, Horney places her emphasis on the need for security. Some concern with security is normal (cf. Maslow's view in the preceding chapter). But if an individual is obsessed with security to the exclusion of self-development, his personality clearly is abnormal.

Horney rejects the theory of instinctive aggression, as for example in Freud's death instinct. She does, on the other hand, consider hostility an important dynamic factor in the organization of personality. Apparently it is learned from the social environment, perhaps in the manner suggested in Chapter 5.

On the positive side, Horney is concerned with the need for self-esteem. Apparently this is an innate need, although she is not very specific about it. Presumably not valuing oneself highly will evoke basic anxiety. An important source of maladjustment, to her way of thinking, is the conflict between the individual's ideal and real selves (cf. Chapter 9).

Erich Fromm. In some respects Fromm seems closer to Freud than does Horney. He recognizes the importance of biological needs, such as sex, but, like Horney, seems to feel that these are merely a kind of animal nature underlying human nature and human personality. The main positive drives in personality, he holds, are the desire for security and the desire for freedom. Security has some elements in common with the notion of homeostasis presented earlier. Fromm feels that when the individual is threatened, he is likely to overvalue security and resist any kind of change because change inevitably brings some insecurity. (In what is probably his most brilliant book, *Escape from Freedom*, he examines the flight of the German people into a totalitarian dictatorship as a device for increasing security and avoiding the perils of a democratic freedom which could not be understood or controlled.)

Because of the conditions of infancy, one comes to feel the necessity for belongingness, for being related to other human beings. Thus isolation and aloneness are major threats; in this respect Horney and Fromm are in close agreement. The young child needs a great deal of security, needs to feel that it belongs in a family. But as it matures, it is impelled by an inner motive (the desire for freedom) to escape from the very restrictions that provide this security. From this arise the conflicts of parents and children over dependence and independence. We shall have more to say on this point in Chapter 17.

Space does not permit a more extensive commentary on the social-psychoanalytic views on motivation, of which Horney and Fromm provide samples. In the following chapter we shall present a point of view on motivation, now widely held in the United States, which goes somewhat further than do Horney and Fromm in dropping the problem of instincts from consideration. Their contribution to this trend was substantial. Since they pointed out the hazards of Freud's overconcern with the instincts and his lack of interest in the social environment, they encouraged the formulation of personality problems in terms of social goals and aspirations, as opposed to innate needs and tensions.

SUMMARY

Freud's theory of motivation has been the most important single influence on our thinking about psychodynamics. His views emphasize instinct and maturation. In place of the biogenic drives, he uses the concept of the id as the raw animal base for personality. Libido, the only psychic energy, is released in the service of the id, but anxiety can block expression of id impulses. The ego develops as the organism becomes aware of objects and the social milieu, and identifies need-gratifying and threatening situations. The superego is formed as the child accepts into himself the commands and taboos imposed upon him by his parents; these provide the basis for character and conscience.

Adler's break with Freud was essentially over the importance of the environment. He proposed an innate need to avoid inferiority, and as its counterpart, a compensatory need to achieve superiority. Various kinds of parent-child relations can establish deep, unconscious feelings of inferiority which may provide the dynamic base for lifelong neurotic symptoms.

Horney and Fromm agree with Adler in his objection to Freud's emphasis on heredity, instinct, and maturation. Each has a strong emphasis on the child's relatedness to his environment, with resulting feelings of security or of threat. Their views are highly similar and are fairly close to the goal-seeking view of motivation to be presented in the following chapter.

SUGGESTIONS FOR READING

A selection of Freud's own writings which offers a variety of interesting material will be found in *The basic writings of Sigmund Freud* (Modern Library). Calvin S. Hall has written *A primer of Freudian psychology* which presents, many would say in oversimplified form, Freud's fundamental ideas. An authoritative but technical treatment of Freud is given by Hendrick, *Facts and theories of psychoanalysis*. Alfred Adler is best represented by his *Neurotic constitution;* and in *Understanding human nature* he has provided his own popularization. For Horney we recommend *Our inner conflicts* or *The neurotic personality of our time*. Fromm's best work is probably *Escape from freedom; Man for himself* gives more applications of his ideas to social situations. Excellent comparative analyses of all the theories deriving from Freud's are now available in Blum's *Psychoanalytic theories of personality* and Munroe's *Schools of psychoanalytic thought*.

CHAPTER 15

Motivation as Goal Seeking

In the two preceding chapters we have presented two widely held views with regard to the dynamic factors underlying personality. Biogenic drives and instincts have been stressed in this connection because personality must obviously have some basis in the inborn structure of the organism. Severe criticism has, however, been offered with respect to both the fairly simple behavioristic view and the subtle complications of psychoanalysis.

Many psychologists have recognized the inadequacy for personality of a motivational theory based on biogenic drives or instincts. Allport (1937) offers a cogent criticism of both the Freudians' and McDougall's instinct theory, and asserts the importance of treating personality in terms of the goals sought by the mature individual. Murphy (1947) has pointed out the great importance of goals in the integration of personality. Seward (1953) comments that "human activities seem to be largely instigated by goals that have little to do with bodily needs." And Harlow (1953) has carefully elaborated the role of external stimuli in mobilizing energy, in contrast to "inner states" as would be suggested by the drive and instinct theorists.

In what respects would it be more appropriate for a psychology of personality to concentrate on motivation as goal seeking instead of viewing motivation as an expression of inner drives and instincts? At least four points merit our consideration: (1) Phenomenally, each of us is likely to feel that he is pursuing goals rather than responding to inner tensions; although it is apparent that a subjective report like this often does not give reliable data, there is a possibility that the report is valid. (2) The temporal cycle of behavior based on biogenic drives is usually rather short, whereas adult human behavior shows long-term persistence directed toward a specific goal. (3) The processes of satiation and deprivation, as studied in connection with biogenic drives, do not seem to apply well to much motivated behavior of adults. (4) Contrary to homeostatic principles, much adult behavior tends to disturb equilibrium rather than to restore it. Let us consider these points as they bear on the problem of personality dynamics.

Goals in the Phenomenal Field. When a person is asked to explain why he did something, he answers in terms of goals, not in terms of drives or instincts. If a student is asked why he took a certain course, he replies in terms of a professional plan, a major requirement, or something of that sort. He does not rely on his acquisitive instinct, his anxiety about future hunger, or an anal-erotic fixation. This is not to say that the student's naïve answer is correct. We should, nonetheless, try to deal with motivation in terms that relate in some way to what the person perceives as his motives.

When either the drive theory or the libido theory is applied to the behavior of a specific individual, the discussion goes on in terms of goals, not in terms of visceral tensions or instincts. The individual fears a dominating mother, or he associates anxiety with tests of his ability, or he is intensely competitive in regard to social status. The theorist then tries to relate these observations on goals to his preferred theory of motivation. Perhaps it will be wiser to deal with personality in terms of goals and leave to other psychologists the problem of explaining goals by relating them to these basic biological factors.

The Time Cycle in Motivated Behavior. Another important argument favoring a stress on goals as opposed to drives lies in the temporal factor. We know that the energy mobilization dependent on hunger is a relatively short-term phenomenon; deprivation leads to activity, food is located, satiation leads to inactivity. The same is true to some extent for thirst, sex, and exploratory impulses; and even for pain, although secondary drive founded on pain can become a reasonably permanent energy source. Secondary drives or secondary rewards based on the other impulses seem feeble and short-lived.

Adult behavior, by contrast, shows persistent goal orientation lasting over years. The quest for a profession, political ambition, and many other kinds of life patterns illustrate this enduring characteristic. It seems much more realistic, therefore, to describe human behavior, particularly at the level of enduring organizations which make up personality, as a goal-seeking process rather than as a response to biogenic drives.[1]

The Problem of Nonsatiating Motives. Closely related to the foregoing is the problem of the effects of satiation. The short time cycle of the biogenic drives depends on the alternation of deprivation and satiation. Perhaps the long time cycle of goal-seeking behavior depends on the fact that such behavior appears not to be weakened by goal attainment.

We can observe this constantly in the people around us. A man who seeks prestige, or affection, or self-actualization may seem to continue investing

---

[1] In defense of a biologically oriented theory it may be observed that the above argument juggles time scales. The cycle for hunger and thirst is a matter of only a few hours; whereas the statements cited above about ambition, etc., usually relate to much longer units. It may be that an ambitious man actually does relax for hours or days after a coup; his seeming nonsatiation may be only a function of the fact that short time intervals are ignored in these observations.

just as much energy in his quest, even though he has achieved his goal in some considerable measure. Thus the head of a big corporation may work hard to make it larger, the politically successful man may seek higher office, the perpetual Don Juan may seek one amorous conquest after another. This is one of the major reasons for dissatisfaction with a theory of personality built around biogenic drives. Many of the important motivations of a specific person do not show this cyclic character such as is observed for hunger and thirst.

Sanford (1952) points up the problem with a clinical case. A young man becomes an obstetrician, spends appallingly long hours on his job, always berates himself for not doing enough for the mothers under his care, etc. Clinical study indicates that he has guilt feelings about not having helped his mother in her later years while he was getting his training. He is symbolically "helping mother" by his professional work, but since he cannot help his real mother in this way, his efforts never reduce the underlying tension.

Here we would suggest that the autonomous, nonsatiating motive is a quest for a goal which is incorrectly perceived. P. T. Young's rats will eat saccharine instead of protein; this does not reduce their hunger, so they go on compulsively taking in whatever is available. They are misled by the sweet taste of the saccharine, and presumably identify it with sugar. So, if a person misperceives the object or action which will reduce his inner tension, he may very well go on pursuing a course which leads only to a temporary and fleeting satisfaction, followed by the compulsive need to go on searching. This is especially likely if the correct goal object possesses both positive and negative valence (cf. Chapter 6), and he defends himself against the conflict by refusing to perceive clearly the nature of the object.

Deprivation and Weakening. Associated with the problem of satiation which does not weaken the motive (in contrast to the effects on biogenic drives) is its converse. Deprivation tends to strengthen drives; the longer a rat has gone without food, the harder he strives to attain it. But deprivation, if continued, weakens goal-seeking behavior.

Allison Davis (1946) has aptly described an instance of this sort in his analysis of the problems of the underprivileged worker (mainly, the Negro urban worker). The young Negro, Davis points out, may accept the middle-class value system in which education is a desirable goal, a nice house in the suburbs is attractive, and saving money is a valuable means to success. He takes a job, saves some money, signs up for technical training; but when a recession comes, he is laid off, and his money is used up for bare living expenses. If he gets his training, he finds higher-level jobs barred to him; he can't buy a house in the suburbs because of real estate restrictions; he has difficulty associating with white persons of similar interests. Eventually he comes to perceive all these middle-class goals as completely unattainable, and rejects them. He places high value on food, drink, and sex, because these are gratifications which the dominant culture cannot snatch away from him.

This process is by no means limited to Negroes and other minority groups. It is, indeed, common in a competitive society. Automobile workers (Chinoy, 1952) start out with aspirations to higher jobs; as they are repeatedly frustrated, they abandon these ambitions, perhaps developing rationalizations about not wanting responsibility, perhaps building hopes for their sons. In a society in which power positions are few, the average person must abandon such goals. If he does not, he will be repeatedly frustrated, tense, and hostile; since these states are unpleasant, he is likely to find a better solution in denying that he has such elevated aspirations.

The key concept in the weakening of social goals by deprivation, therefore, is the *perceived probability of success*. As this approaches zero, most persons stop responding to the goal in question. Only the rare individual keeps trying; and it seems likely that his final position will be in a mental hospital, not at the peak of a social pyramid (cf. Fig. 13.1, page 293).

Similarly, the nonsatiating character of success may be attributed to strengthening an expectancy rather than (as in the biological schema) to lowering of tension. A young man whose exhibitionistic need impels him into becoming an actor does not lose this need when he achieves status as a star; on the contrary, his exhibitionism often seems stronger. The would-be dictator craves power more and more as he obtains more. When Lord Acton wrote, "Power corrupts, and absolute power corrupts absolutely," he emphasized—perhaps not intentionally—the fact that these appetites grow stronger with satisfaction.

Goal Seeking Disturbs Equilibrium. Another argument in favor of a shift from drives to goals is based on the criticism of homeostasis which has been cited earlier. Much human behavior, we have noted, is only with difficulty described as directed to restoration of equilibrium. Often it is upsetting to one or more established equilibria. It was suggested elsewhere that a hierarchy of equilibria exists, and to preserve one of high value, the person may upset those of less importance. A somewhat less involved explanation would be that much of the individual's effort is not directed to equilibrium at all, except in the sense that when the person attains a goal, he may relax. The striving, however, is directed toward goal attainment, not toward the equilibrium in itself.

Some individuals manifestly seek goals which are upsetting to both social and biological equilibria. Allport (1955) uses the example of the famous polar explorer, Amundsen, who was constantly leaving his friends and pleasant surroundings to get into situations of extreme physical discomfort, hunger, and peril of death. Even in other, less extreme cases, we observe that men subject themselves to substantial discomfort and some danger to go hunting—and certainly the food brought home is not the goal involved. The young man who postpones marriage to obtain professional education is tolerating a condition of continued disequilibrium in order to pursue a goal. These examples should serve to illustrate the point. Much human behavior is far more adequately described as goal-seeking than as equilibrium-restoring.

Personality as an Autonomous Goal System. For the foregoing reasons, we propose in the present chapter to deal with personality as a system of goal strivings rather than as an organized pattern of drives or instincts. The presentation will consequently emphasize the external objects, persons, situations, and roles toward which the individual's behavior is oriented.

In thus shifting our focus from inner tensions to external goals, we do not intend to endorse the view that man is merely a puppet to his environment. While objects exist (presumably) in a real external world, they become goals only when so perceived by the person. There will be businessmen and admirals, lawyers and jet pilots, regardless of John; but when John perceives one of these social roles as desirable for himself, it functions as a goal. The determination of goals is consequently a bipolar process in which the person and the environment both participate.

The Importance of "Functional Autonomy." We are also assuming that there is some logical relationship between the data at the level of homeostasis and biological drive, or instinct, and the phenomena of goals. It seems, however, that this is a proper problem for experts on the psychology of motivation, and that an analysis of personality can be excused for avoiding it.

We are assuming, therefore, something like the principle of "functional autonomy" proposed by Allport (1937). A specific goal may have become important to the individual because it served a biological need; the sailor, for example, may have acquired his nautical skills in order to earn a living, but in the process he comes to love the sea and ships, and craves both when he has retired. Writing or reading of poetry, Allport notes, may in the first instance have reflected a sexual impulse; but with continuation, the individual may develop a fondness for poetry which is maintained long after the sexual impulse has been gratified, and even after it has waned with the aging process.

About the facts of functional autonomy there seems to be no question. It is similar to what the Freudian theory calls "cathexis of libido"; a certain amount of enjoyment has become connected to this object or action, and will be experienced whenever the stimulus occurs; or the person will actively seek the stimulus in order to get the pleasure involved. The baby does not love his mother solely when she is caring for him; his positive valence includes the mother as a total person. The pleasure the boy gets from baseball is not limited to the playing field; he can also take pleasure in his memories. In other words, we suggest that a positive or negative valence, once established, tends to endure unless some factor operates to eliminate it.

Experimental support for functional autonomy of some sort is extensive.

The behaviorists have attempted to incorporate the phenomena by their concepts of secondary drive and secondary reward (cf. Anderson, 1941; Zimmerman, 1957). Earl (1957) describes a study in which food-deprived mice had to dig through sand in order to obtain food. After the habit was firmly established, he began either feeding the mice before placing them in the sandbox, or giving them no food after digging. Despite these treatments (which should produce either satiation or extinction) the animals kept on digging, with no sign of extinction. "It was as if the very act of digging had become demanding or had developed 'invitational character,' " he comments.

There are, however, exceptions to the principle of functional autonomy if it is taken to apply to actions or motive sequences, and these exceptions support our emphasis on goal seeking. Consider the case of the infant; he is completely dependent on his mother, gets many need satisfactions and sensory pleasures from her, and might be expected to develop a deep dependency which would become autonomous. (Most children develop strong affection; but if this includes marked dependency, they are considered abnormal.)

Many learned expectancies are, of course, eliminated in the course of life. In infancy, the baby learns to expect help if he cries; later, he learns that this is "babyish" and he takes pride in controlling his tears. An ice-cream cone may look like a tremendous treat to him; later he finds it uninteresting. Girls, for several years, look dull or annoying; suddenly they become quite attractive. Hence, Allport's principle is not of universal applicability.

Perceiving an object in a changed context may cause it to change in valence. Chocolate candy may lose its pleasantness for a girl trying to keep a slender figure. It is now seen as a threat, not an attraction. Many a man has enjoyed reminiscing about "the old swimming hole" until he went back and took a look at it; then he wonders how he could ever have enjoyed swimming there. To some extent, perhaps, the functionally autonomous motives are those toward goals which have not lost their positive valence as a result of such experiences.

Functional autonomy probably holds most firmly for those goals which are associated with the self-image. One may learn to play golf to a modest level of skill, with considerable effort and after badgering from friends, but never come to perceive skill at golf as a significant accomplishment. The same man may perceive his professional skill as intimately ego-involved, and it may show all the features of functional autonomy. Szasz (1957) suggests that pleasure implies that "something has been added" (food is a good example) and pain that "something has been taken away." If someone criticizes my golf, I do not feel that anything has been taken away from my self-image; but a criticism of my professional efforts would represent considerable ego loss. We suggest, therefore, that a positive valence which becomes associated with the self-image will retain its potency for a long time (it has become autonomous); positive valences not so associated may readily be eliminated.

Partial Reinforcement. We have noted earlier (page 102) that stimuli associated with pleasure (or discomfort) will retain their motivating quality longer if the probability of the association is less than 100 per cent. This greater resistance to extinction on the part of stimulus-response units which have been developed with "partial reinforcement" has an interesting similarity to functional autonomy. It would seem that goals which have been regularly attained, and then become unattainable, are more likely to be abandoned as hopeless; whereas goals which have been attained often but not always will endure longer. The expectancy is, "If I keep on trying, I may reach the goal." This logic leads to the fairly obvious conclusion that parents must allow their children some frustrations and failures, trying to assure that repeated effort will be followed by success. Such a technique will implant goals of maximum durability in the face of disappointment.

Perceptual Constancy. Actually, if we deal with personality dynamics in terms of goals, we do not need the concept of functional autonomy. All goals are in a sense autonomous. The individual learns to perceive an object, person, situation, or social role as promising pleasurable stimulation and perhaps need reduction. Such percepts, once established, tend to persist in terms of perceptual constancy. They may be modified by associating new sensory consequences with them; e.g., the mother is an intensely desirable goal object in the first two or three years of life, but as she becomes a disciplinarian or as the father becomes an important figure for the child, some modification of perception occurs.

The charm of the "old swimming hole," the wonderful taste of "grandma's doughnuts," and other goals of childhood persist in part because we have left the scene and this modification has not occurred. In the case of persons with marked perceptual rigidity, even remaining on the scene may not bring changes. One suspects that the Freudian emphasis on persistence of childhood fixations may have resulted from the fact that marked rigidity is maladaptive, hence such individuals were more likely to become neurotic and seek therapy.

Perceptual Definition of Goal. The term "goal" seems simple enough. When a football team is trying to push the ball over the goal line for a touchdown, the "goal" is clear enough. Yet, for some of the men on the team, the desired outcome may be to please the coach, to get better publicity than a competitor on the team, to impress a girl friend, or to get a financial offer. The goal is a function of the individual's perceptions.

Actually this is true even on simpler levels. The goal as defined in animal experimentation is determined by the perceptions of the experimenter. If a rat is deprived of food for twenty-four hours, and then placed in a maze, he will restlessly explore until he comes upon the food; he eats and then engages in some other activity. We have no knowledge of what the rat was thinking about or whether he anticipated food; we simply observe and decide from his actions that food was the animal's goal. Similarly, an adolescent boy may begin to wash up and dress more neatly, stay where he can watch girls, offer to buy a girl a soda, etc. The observer concludes that "sex" is the "goal"— although the youth may deny this vigorously. When a man repeatedly irritates his employer, thus getting himself fired from one job after another, we may conclude that the goal is "punishment," or perhaps "independence from authority." Such goal-directed activity is commonly observed in abnormal personalities, and often enough in those considered normal.

We may, then, define a goal in terms of the person's perception, or in terms of an observer's perception. Usually, in the following pages, we shall imply that these two agree. Most adults correctly perceive most of the time the goal toward which they are striving. In many cases, however, the consciously perceived goal is only a symbol for some other goal, recognized vaguely or not at all. This means that we must consider the existence of unconscious goals.

Conscious and Unconscious Goals. When we speak of an individual as pursuing a certain goal, there is a certain tendency to think of this as a goal of which he is consciously aware. Such an assumption is unjustified.

Even if we deal with goals in terms of the portions of the person's phenomenal field which appear attractive to him, this need not imply that the goal itself is clearly recognized as such. We have cited extensive evidence on this point in earlier chapters. In connection with perception we noted that a change in background might cause a change in figure even though the perceiver never became aware of the ground. In the case of perceptual vigilance and defense it was shown that objects may look larger and brighter (or vice versa) under pressure of relevant motives. Subliminal conditioning experiments indicate that a person may respond to a cue without knowing that the cue is present. And hypnotic studies provide many instances in which an individual may try to execute some act without being able to explain why he wishes to do this.

The theoretical interpretation of unconscious goals varies, of course, from one school of psychology to another. The psychoanalysts assume that some aspect of the goal arouses feelings of anxiety, which lead to repression; the repression prevents the goal from entering consciousness, but does not keep it from influencing behavior. The behaviorists prefer to treat the unconscious event as something for which suitable verbal habits do not exist; thus, adolescents cannot talk about their sexual tensions because they have never learned verbal responses appropriate to describe the inner tensions they experience at this time.

On one point both schools agree; as long as potent goals are unconscious, it is difficult for the person to apply intelligence in attaining or abandoning them. When a goal is conscious, one can look at it more or less realistically, and decide: Is it worth the effort? How do I go about getting it? No such rational decisions can be made as regards unconscious goals; the person acts as if compelled in spite of himself—i.e., without regard to how this fits with his self-image and traits and values—and he cannot even use intelligence effectively to attain the goal, because he does not see clearly what it is he is trying to attain.

Suppose we consider the case of a woman, a professional, who repeatedly does things to interfere with her husband's career or takes advantage of circumstances to make it appear that she is more successful than he. Consciously she may deny that her goal is to outdo him, but the observer readily concludes that this is her major goal. When this is made conscious (e.g., through psychotherapy), it becomes possible for her to decide (1) whether she really wants a career, or whether she just wants to be superior to her husband; and, (2) to what extent she can attain all or part of her ambition without ruining her marriage. The role of consciousness, then, is no more than the role we have been ascribing all along to perception; i.e., if you can perceive clearly the attributes of an object or situation, you can respond more adaptively to it. A goal consciously pursued is less likely to lead one into a pitfall than one which is sought as if wandering blindfolded in a dark room.

Goals as Energy Mobilizers. One of the problems which personality theory has inherited from experimental psychology needs to be pointed out here. The concept of "goal" as commonly employed in studies of learning usually refers to a reinforcer, a substance which will release tension and end the behavior sequence being studied. Thus food at the end of a maze is spoken of as a goal for the rat.

We cannot reject this concept out of hand as regards personality. Certainly goals do have such functions for adult human beings. But the goal concept here must be expanded considerably. In the example cited above, the tension underlying a continuing behavior sequence was aroused by deprivation, and the goal merely reduced tension. In adult personalities a goal often serves the function of *increasing tension*, of mobilizing energy. The use of specific goals in learning (e.g., in industrial training) is primarily to increase effort. An athletic team works harder when oriented toward defeating a specific competitor—especially an old rival. The "goal" of a college degree serves to mobilize energy within the student. A professional goal activates the graduate.

This distinction is exceptionally important in relation to personality because we are concerned so much with patterns of energy mobilization. What makes Sammy run? Our understandings of our friends focus particularly on their energy systems. We know of this man that he will work hard when the goal is political; of another, that charitable enterprises will elicit more effort. Some persons focus sharply on one goal or class of goals; others diffuse their efforts over many goals. (This idea will be elaborated in later pages.) This is not to deny that personalities are also characterized by the kinds of objects which lead to relaxation and enjoyment, but—let us be honest—life involves much more striving toward goals than it does relaxation after goal attainment. Hence we stress that personality is a pattern of *goal seeking*.

The point made earlier about the nonsatiating motive is relevant here. Though a person asserts that he is striving for a certain goal, he does not relax when he achieves it. It is obvious, then, that he has not correctly perceived his own goal. The process of psychotherapy is often a long, drawn-out task of modifying the individual's awareness of goals and dangers, so that his percepts become more realistic.

Identification of Goals. How do we go about determining the goals which are directing the activity of a specific person? We may, of course, rely on phenomenal data; if he states that he desires a certain object, a given status or relationship, this is indicative—but not conclusive—evidence. Somewhat more valid is evidence derived from observation; if his activity level increases when he is moving toward the object, and diminishes when the object is unavailable, we suspect that this is his goal, even if he denies it consciously. We may also use various kinds of indirect evidence, such as projective testing, in which his fantasies may reveal a deep concern with a certain goal even though direct observation finds no activity directed toward it.

Studies of motivation in personality rely on all three kinds of evidence. A person may frankly say that his goal is to acquire money, honestly if possible. Or his behavior may indicate that he craves power, even though he cautiously avoids admitting this in his conversation with others. And finally, his fantasy life may reveal a strong desire for a dependency relationship, to lean on someone else and be relieved of responsibility, when his overt behavior shows nothing of this and when he consciously denies such a trend. Obviously, in analyzing a person, the psychologist considers all three levels.

PERSONALITY AS GOAL SEEKING

The foregoing considerations suggest that personality may be easier to understand as a dynamic, organized process of searching for goals rather than as a set of hunger, thirst, and sexual motives. Freud, of course, laid down principles which seem to have universal validity in his "pleasure principle" and "reality principle." But these relate just as comfortably to a discussion of goals as to a discussion of a sexual instinct; in fact, people every day encounter conflicts between short-range and long-range goals, although these are often remote from sexual interests.

A motivational theory of personality which relies primarily upon goal seeking has a certain attraction because of the complex problems it evades. If we simply say that we treat dynamics in terms of goals sought after, regardless of how the person acquired these goals, we have left behind some of the knottiest problems in motivation theory. Such a statement, indeed, opens the way for a pluralistic concept of motivation, in the sense that some goals may derive directly from biological gratifications, some may be desired because of symbolic value, and some may be accepted because a parent or other admired adult valued these goals.

A theory of motivation as goal seeking also has its practical aspects. One rarely tries to influence a friend, a wife, an employee, or a customer by appealing directly to biogenic drives. By contrast, we regularly try to modify personalities (or manipulate personalities) by offering and withholding goals. This approach, in other words, is more realistic in its integration with daily life.

The major gain, however, which accrues from this shift in emphasis lies in the fact that all the principles of perception become applicable to problems of dynamics. The development of expectancies, the problem of rigidity and constancy, the phenomena of stimulus generalization, and those relating to frames of reference, to mention a few, can be related to goal-seeking processes.

Goal Tenacity. In thinking about motivation and personality we seek to identify the important respects in which persons differ. One such aspect is the tenacity with which a given individual clings to a defined goal and pursues it despite all sorts of obstacles. We can readily observe such differences in people and recognize their importance in personality.

A major question with regard to the concept of goal tenacity is one we have met often in examining problems of personality: Is goal tenacity general or specific? Does a person show his typical level of tenacity all the time, or would it be incorrect to speak of a person as having a typical level? Clinical observers agree that it is proper to label some persons as highly goal-persistent, since they seem to cling to an ambition, once established, for a long time. It is apparent, nonetheless, that much depends on the perceived importance of the goal; it is in the nature of reality that a person obsessed with a goal, such as exploration, must abandon other goals, e.g., home, family, economic security.

Experimental evidence supporting the generalized nature of goal tenacity is offered by Ausubel and Schiff (1955). They find that each individual has developed a characteristic way of responding to success or failure in setting his level of aspiration. Some maintain high aspirations even in the face of repeated failure. These individuals may be (cf. Chapter 9) those who maintain the self-image by "trying for the stars." Through identification or through early learning such a person has come to perceive "setting high goals" as a valued aspect of self; and he prefers to maintain the constancy of this attribute even though it means repeated failure experiences.

Perceptual *rigidity* is almost certainly a component of such goal-oriented behavior. We suspect that the individual is incapable of modifying a percept, once established, regardless of the receipt of changing information.

Sublimation. A related problem is that of ease of sublimation, or the extent to which an individual can channel his energies into a search for substitute goals. Freud suggested that libido could be shifted from one goal object to another, almost in the manner of plugging an electric power line into one or another circuit. He recognized, however, that some individuals seem relatively incapable of sublimation whereas others make such shifts fairly easily.

Ease of sublimation almost certainly depends on the perceptual style called "leveling-sharpening." The leveler, the person who sees a great many objects as equivalent, would find sublimation easy because he could find many goal objects which looked comparable to the unattainable one. Thus, his affection for his mother (to take a typical Freudian example) could easily be displaced onto other women; the "sharpener," especially if he also tended to cling rigidly to past percepts, would remain bound to his mother by these affectional ties.

If the leveling tendency is extreme, the individual is likely to be accused of fickleness or inconsistency; he will see so little difference within a class of goal objects—members of the opposite sex, careers, religious ideals, or other values—that he transfers his enthusiasm all too readily from one to another.

Focusing. A second dynamic attribute of personality which is illumined by this approach is that of focusing. Some individuals scatter their energies over a wide variety of goal objects, whereas others restrict themselves to a limited number. This has some connection with the problem of sublimation, mentioned above, since substitute goals may appear to represent a scattering of effort. We are referring here, however, simply to the phenomenon of concentration on specific objectives versus trying to accomplish everything at once.

The relative attractiveness of goal objects is, of course, one component here. If the individual has not achieved a stable hierarchy of values in terms of which he can decide that one is more important than another, then many goals are seen as equally attractive and decisions are impossible.

A second element to be considered here is the field-analytical mode of perceiving, or ego autonomy (page 203). To the extent that a person is capable of concentrating on figure and ignoring the effects of variations in ground, he should be able to select one goal object and keep this in the center of the phenomenal field, ignoring other cues which are present.[2]

---

[2] Here, and elsewhere, we imply that this is the most adaptive mode of behavior, corresponding to what has been called "ego strength." It should be noted that focusing may be carried too far, with the effect of ignoring changes in context which should be recognized; hence, the individual who is extreme on ego autonomy may encounter some problems of adjustment by failing to note an external change which does really modify the significance of the goal object.

Focusing may imply an increase in the phenomenal magnitude of a given goal object. We have already noted (page 120) that some persons are subject to a decided distortion of the size and brightness of attractive objects. It may be that focusing is associated with such changes, and that this mechanism helps the individual keep his course of action in the specified direction.

Finally, we may note a difference among individuals with respect to whether the focus is on a class of objects or on a specific case. To take a very simple example, two young men may both show high interest in sexual goals; one finds it easy to substitute one woman for another, but the second is fixated on one woman and cannot accept anyone else.

Goal Seeking and Personality Organization. Categories of goal objects are defined by frames of reference. The child early learns to classify things, and he tends to associate positive or negative valence with a whole category in many instances. He sets up a hierarchy of values (cf. Chapter 11) in terms of which he makes choices among different goals. Thus, he may seek economic gain, political power, scientific prestige, security, etc., and when faced with a conflict among these, he is capable of making a decision. As noted in the preceding paragraphs, he may focus on a class or on a specific goal object; and he may concentrate or diffuse his energies.

The individual personality becomes identifiable, therefore, not only by his traits and attitudes but by his goals and their organization into hierarchies. The salesman and the political propagandist attempt to slant their messages, not merely to relate them to goals highly valued by everyone, but if possible to tap the strongest goals of a specific person. We observe this process especially in face-to-face persuasion, where an awareness of the major goals of the other person gives a tremendous advantage in phrasing appeals.

The Search for Underlying Motives. A popular guessing game is that of trying to figure out "what does he *really* want?" The psychologist's search for a theory of motivation is only a more complex form of this same activity. But, we may also ask, why is this search so popular? Why does everyone observe his associates and attempt to infer underlying motives?

The answer seems to be that motives are known to be relatively dependable guides to prediction. We have noted earlier (Chapter 8) that one seeks to identify traits of personality in order better to predict the behavior of one's friends. In the same way, we look for motives behind actions. Psychoanalytic theory developed in just this fashion. Freud was not satisfied with observing that a young man was constantly becoming enamored of women but always escaping prospects of marriage. He wanted to know what was behind this behavior. The inference of an unconscious fixation on the mother is one hypothesis. If this can be confirmed by other evidence, then it provides a guide for predicting future actions. More important, from Freud's viewpoint, it pinpoints the basic emotional response which must be modified if the individual is to make a normal adjustment.

The theorist may use subtle and unobservable constructs, such as those of libido and superego, as tools in his quest for these underlying consistencies in personality. The lay observer is more likely to look for goals which a person strives to attain, and use these as his unifying principles to predict future behavior. There are advantages to each approach.

CLASSIFYING HUMAN GOALS

It would be tempting, in the light of what has just been said about the unique motivations of each individual, to conclude that we cannot make broad classifications of goals which apply to everyone. One of the criticisms of instinct theory was that some persons show little or none of the motive implied for a specific instinct. Certainly there would be advantages in knowing the value hierarchies for each individual in practical dealings with him, but only in psychotherapy is such detailed knowledge likely to be acquired. It is indispensable, therefore, to work up classifications of goals which are relevant for the entire human race or for cultures or other subgroups.

To some extent this is what has already been done by the instinct theorists, although they believed they were cataloguing innate motives. Each instinct (cf. Cattell's list of ergs, page 302) is hypothesized because observation of human behavior indicated that considerable effort was expended along this line. Theorists emphasizing goals rather than inborn tendencies simply look for the external object or situation sought, instead of postulating an inner need. Among these we may note the list of four "wishes" espoused by W. I. Thomas, a major American sociologist: the wish for security, the wish for recognition, the wish for intimate response, and the wish for new experience. Roughly these refer to: the desire to be accepted into membership in important groups and to feel secure in such a relationship; the quest for higher standing, for prestige within the group; the desire for affectionate response (sexual in the broad Freudian sense) from others; and curiosity, the desire to explore, to have novel experiences and encounter new ideas and persons. Although we may find substantial areas of goal seeking which these do not cover, they represent a major segment of our motivational life.

Other writers have tried to draw all goal seeking into a single category by seeking some common denominator. Alfred Adler (1924) used the phrase "will-to-power" to identify what he considered the essential component of all goal seeking. The individual seeks power over his environment, over objects and people. If this formulation is taken flexibly, it covers virtually all kinds of behavior; we may note a certain similarity to the use of homeostasis, the notion that energy is mobilized to protect or restore equilibrium, in this volume.

Self-enhancement as Goal. Another monistic formulation is that of Snygg and Combs (1949) who have asserted that the "basic human need" should be defined as "the preservation and enhancement of the phenomenal self" [p. 58]. We have already shown (Chapter 9) how the self can be perceived as a tool. Just as one may satisfy inner needs more efficiently with better tools, and so may come to value them, likewise one can derive pleasure from enhancing the self-image, elevating the perceived value of the self.

Adler's "will-to-power" included mastery over both objects and persons, and in effect differs very little from the conception offered by Snygg and Combs. For them, a failure to deal effectively with objects or persons is likely to be perceived as devaluing to the ego of the individual involved—hence, it is a threat to be avoided. Conversely, the person will mobilize energy to accomplish those things which make the ego appear more valuable, even though the immediate outcome of the action is not especially desirable. Thus, a soldier will take risks in combat to preserve his standing in the eyes of his fellows; and a loyal member of a political party will do an unpleasant job to keep the approval of the party leaders. Some people put forth a lot of energy to do something merely for the sake of self-respect, i.e., so that the individual's percept of himself will not be devalued. This is roughly what we mean by "will power" in common speech. Will power is not an additional source of energy which can be tapped to help finish a job. But if the person has committed himself to do a job, and then finds it more difficult or unpleasant than anticipated, he feels compelled to finish it in order to maintain his position with others, or even in his own eyes. The defense of the ego, therefore, is often a source of energy.[3]

Murray's List of Needs. It is probably a futile effort either to compile a comprehensive list of all categories of goals important to human beings, or to reduce all goal seeking to a single category. The cultural anthropologists have made it clear that goals differ in substantial ways from one culture to another, and the sociologists have found that goals accepted in one portion of Western culture are not potent in other segments. Indeed, as was implied above, there are probably some organizations of goals which are distinctive and unique for a specific person, hence inherently incapable of inclusion within one of these lists.

As a simple and practical affair, on the other hand, we need some kind of working list or classification of goals. Such a list enables us to do research on such problems as the relative strength of some common goals (e.g., will-to-power) in different persons. It facilitates research on how goals are acquired, and what determinants are important for particular categories.

A list which has served exactly this purpose in American psychology is that prepared by H. A. Murray. Murray's inspiration is essentially Freudian, but his list was prepared in an effort to identify those goal-seeking patterns

---

[3] Conversely, the quitter, the person who leaves tasks unfinished with no apparent qualms, is the one who perceives his ego as not being involved in the task. He makes it clear that such failure does not lower his status in his own eyes, and—according to him—should not affect his standing with others.

which are relatively common in American culture. He sought to penetrate to observable human behavior and find out in what classes of situations, and for what purposes, adult humans mobilize energy. He lists some twenty different "needs," as follows: [4]

n Dominance	n Affiliation
n Achievement	n Nurturance
n Exhibition	n Succorance
n Autonomy	n Defendance
n Counteraction	n Harmavoidance
n Aggression	n Rejection
n Deference	n Abasement
n Order	n Infavoidance
n Sentience	n Heterosexuality
n Play	n Understanding

Murray says that a need is a hypothetical construct, but that we get evidence of it in many ways. A need X, he observes, is evidenced when a person searches for X, attends to X, imagines X, says he wants X, feels badly in absence of X, feels happy when in contact with X, and, most of all, when contact with X leads to cessation of an active behavior sequence.

This descriptive passage actually would apply better to a goal than to a need. One does not search for a need; he searches for a goal. One does not feel badly in the absence of a need; on the contrary, he feels relaxed when no need is pushing him into action. But the statements in the preceding paragraph do apply to goals, such as the goal of achievement.

What Murray has to offer, then, is a set of classes of goal objects and goal relationships which should be useful in comparing individuals. We know, for example, that one man shows a strong push toward achievement or toward dominance, while another seems more oriented toward affiliation (friendship, group acceptance); even though we do not know what people need, it is possible to observe what they strive for, and to fit them into Murray's categories in terms of the goals toward which they are motivated.

Implicit in Murray's scheme is the notion of a range of intensities of these motives. In one person need dominance is quite low; in another, it may be the main dynamic factor. Murray and his students have been fairly ingenious at devising methods for estimating the strength of these tendencies. McClelland et al. (1953) describe a variety of researches on need achievement, probably the most intensively studied of Murray's list. It will be instructive to examine some of these investigations.

Achievement. In the United States, with its mythology of success through hard work, no one should be surprised that people often show a kind of

. [4] The word "need" here implies only that the individual will exert effort on behalf of the kind of goal implied by the name of the need; it has nothing to do with biogenic needs, as described in Chap. 13. This list is taken from Murray (1938), pp. 144–145. The prefix n means need.

348   *Dynamics*

functionally autonomous "hard work" motive, a tendency to work hard even if there seems to be no reward in sight. Equally it is not surprising that psychologists should have spent a good deal of effort on the study of the achievement motive.

While Murray (1938) invented the concept of need achievement, McClelland (1953) and Atkinson (1954) have worked hard to study the "hard work" motive. At a common-sense level, need achievement refers to behavior which shows effort to accomplish something, to do one's best, to excel over others in performance. It is to be differentiated from exhibitionism (showing off without doing anything useful) and from dominance (desire to boss others around), although it is sometimes difficult to decide in a specific act which label to apply.

The devices used by McClelland and Atkinson in the study of need achievement are mainly projective devices since, as we noted earlier, overt behavior is influenced by too many factors. Vigorous study by a student may indicate an achievement goal, but it may also indicate economic motivation (expectancy that more will be earned), pressure from parents, etc. The projective test, since it gets away from such realistic factors, is thought to permit a more nearly "pure" expression of any motive.

The commonest measure employed is that of pictures from the TAT, and the quantitative score obtained is based on the frequency of stories containing an achievement theme. This score is validated chiefly by experiments such as the following: Martire (1956) had Ss write stories under relaxed conditions, and again just after taking a test which (they were told) had an important bearing on their educational future. The amount of achievement imagery increased sharply under the latter condition. If we assume that persons who show high achievement imagery under relaxed conditions are in fact under achievement tension all the time, as the entire group was when concerned about failing an important test, then we can argue that differences among persons in such imagery indicate differences in need achievement.[5] A number of studies have been published, comparing persons with high and low degrees of this goal-seeking tendency as shown by the TAT measure.

This means, in effect, that need achievement cannot be distinguished from a trait as defined in Chapter 8. It represents an intervening variable, not directly observed but inferred from specific indicators; it is defined by reference to a class of situations, not to a single concrete occurrence; it is assumed to show consistency across situations and over time. Consistency across different sets of pictures is low (Birney, 1959), averaging around +.29. The matter of consistency over time was an object of research by Kagan and Moss (1959), who analyzed records of 86 children taken during the eighth, eleventh, and fourteenth years of life. The consistency of achievement motivation is indicated by correlations of +.32, +.22, and +.16—barely enough to indicate some

[5] Many psychologists are dubious about the validity of this inference. However, it is being used in the absence of a better rationale for measurement of these important personal goals.

reliability, but not enough to make us feel that need achievement is a stable feature of the personality.

Need achievement has some substantial significance in the child's personality, however, as is indicated by further data from the Kagan and Moss research. Children who, at age eight, show clear-cut evidence of achievement motivation also reveal a greater gain in IQ than others showing fewer indicators of need achievement. The authors also report some relationship between achievement motivation at age eight and school marks for grades 2 to 5. (This relationship holds even when intelligence is held constant; it thus tends to validate the concept of achievement motivation.)

Other studies have indicated that need achievement is a factor in a person's adjustment to various life situations, and conversely, that various family and social-class indexes have some impact on need achievement. Further references will be made to some of these investigations in later chapters.

Affiliation. Like need achievement, need affiliation has been studied chiefly by the TAT technique. The basic validation procedure has subjects of some fairly close-knit group, such as a college fraternity, write stories under relaxed conditions, and later under conditions where social acceptability to their fellows has been questioned. From an analysis of the changes in stories, certain kinds of themes can be identified (concern about friendship, about rejection, etc.). These can later be used in scoring the stories of others (cf. Lansing and Heyns, 1959).

Both Shipley and Veroff (1952) and Atkinson, Heyns, and Veroff (1954) have reported a negative correlation between need affiliation and popularity in the group. This would seem to indicate that deprivation (lack of acceptance) increases the strength of need affiliation. We have pointed out earlier, however, that deprivation and satiation do not act in the same manner with social goals as with biogenic goals such as food and water. The occurrence of imagery about friendship, for example, can increase as a consequence of *habit* (repetition of such events) and not simply as a result of deprivation. The importance of habit in this connection increases the difficulty of distinguishing such goal-seeking tendencies from traits, which partake of the quality of generalized habits.

The affiliation motive must be assumed to underlie a considerable amount of socially significant behavior, such as choosing work partners, joining groups, and cooperating within a group. Most of the research findings so far are relatively inconclusive and will not be further reviewed here.

We may repeat here a point already made elsewhere, namely, that the significance of such goal orientations as achievement and affiliation will depend on other variables, particularly perceptual style. An individual who finds many goal objects or situations to be substantially equivalent will generalize his seeking activities fairly widely. Another may focus his energies more sharply. To one, achievement may be satisfying even if it is no more than catching the biggest fish in the local creek; to another, achievement must be sought in virtually all fields of endeavor; to a third, only a single class of achievement seems important and all others will be ignored. The same holds for affiliation: one person may be desirous of having friends everywhere, even if they are superficial; a second may want only one or two friends, but on a very intimate basis. (We are reminded here of Freud's concept of libido, and his notion that it could be focused or spread widely; one might be deeply fixated on one object or slightly attached to a number of objects.)

We also note, at this point, that studies of important goal-seeking tendencies, such as these, appear likely to throw much-needed light on the dynamics of personality. Biogenic drives, for all their obvious importance in early childhood, clearly do not motivate much of adult behavior. The Freudian theory has not lent itself handily to studies of normal motivation, especially in any quantitative form. Consequently, the locating of categories of goals, and grouping them where people show consistency in their dynamics, would appear to be a promising line of approach to personality. As we learn to identify the major goal orientations, and to get quantitative indexes of them, we shall progress more rapidly toward our own scientific goal of understanding personality.

A Note on Homeostasis. Any linkage of such goals as achievement and affiliation to biogenic equilibria and the doctrine of homeostasis must necessarily be speculative. The approach would have to be along the lines sketched in Chapter 4, namely, that the individual comes to value friendship and achievement because these are instrumental to the protection of the basic biological constancies.

Such an interpretation would imply that these goals become important as a result of early learning. In opposition, Maslow (1954) would undoubtedly argue that human beings are born with dynamic tendencies which are easily shaped into need achievement and need affiliation—his need for self-esteem and for security. Atkinson (1954) suggests that we can avoid a final answer to this question at this time, but the context indicates that he believes environment to be a more effective determinant than heredity. Proof that this is the case would not, of course, verify the homeostatic hypothesis; indeed, it is likely that this will be solely a matter of speculation for a long time.

THE CULTURAL DETERMINATION OF GOALS

The individual acquires his goals in a variety of ways. In Chapter 5 we noted some of the factors giving rise to positive valences for objects and persons. Generally speaking, such an event comes to have goal value for an individual as a consequence of need satisfaction, pleasurable sensory concomitants, or social definition as a goal. The first two of these are already familiar. Let us consider the third.

We have noted elsewhere that each child spontaneously develops a hierarchy of goal objects within a class, so that he knows he prefers ice cream to spinach, cake to dry bread, and so on. He learns, in other words, to rank things according to their desirability for some specific purpose. The parents and other adults cooperate with this process, telling him that some objects are "good" and others "bad"—clean foods versus dirty items, for example. He is also rewarded for actions which are labeled "good" and punished for those which are "bad." He finds that if he expresses certain opinions, he is scolded; for other statements, he receives praise.

The process of social determination of goals, then, is a many-pronged process in which adults tell the child what is good, reward him for agreeing, punish him when he fails to accept the social norm. The social milieu also makes him aware of some of the gratifying consequences of pursuing a certain goal. (He will also learn of the negative valences involved, but in many instances he learns little of these negative aspects until it is too late. Apparently some persons become so well socialized that they are not even aware of the undesirable aspects of some officially approved goals.)

Certainly the significance of this kind of determinant of motivation must be recognized. We are aware of the Frenchman's pride in France, his willingness to exert effort or endure pain for his nation's welfare, his hostility to Germans, and his readiness to attack them. Conversely, we observe the German's patriotic feeling for his country and his traditional distrust of the French. The competitive strivings of the Americans still contrast with the security orientation of the European, although this dichotomy has apparently been glossed over by developments on both sides of the Atlantic. In any event, we must find a place for a cultural factor in determining the goals men strive for.

Cultural Determination as Learning. There seems to be no real reason for feeling that this aspect of the problem is difficult. If we think in terms of learning to value objects which are associated with need satisfaction, we can readily see how the culture would determine what associations would be learned. The Italian child must learn to like pasta as a source of nourishment; packaged breakfast foods are not available. He must slake his thirst with wine and soon acquires a fondness for it, which his second cousin in the United States will not. The baby in Calcutta is compelled to develop a taste for rice, but in Bali it will be bananas.

Furthermore, the kinds of preferred familial relationships, the types of housing, the rhythms of daily life which are so enjoyable can be conceptualized as outcomes of learning. Rats can learn to like a goal box which is all white, and to be anxious when placed in one with zebra stripes. Human children can acquire not only such obvious cues, but also much subtler percepts and endow them with attractive or repelling attributes.

Parents may also build up tensions and may define certain actions as "good" or "bad." When these terms are given dynamic properties by rewards, by pain, by anxiety, by affection, and security, then the child is likely to pursue courses of action defined as good, while inhibiting those defined as bad. He may even accept this cultural directive so deeply that he tolerates homeostatic disturbances in order to cling to the "good" pattern,[6] as is suggested by Freud's assertion that the superego may dominate the id.

As we have noted elsewhere, it is not appropriate to try to work out here the details of how goals are acquired. It seems nevertheless important to show how cultural determination applies to some motivational tendencies which are of exceptional importance for personality. We shall comment on how the cultural approach relates to Freud's emphasis on sex and Adler's concept of the will-to-power.

SEX AND CIVILIZATION

No one would deny that biology has something to do with the potency of the sexual motive. But the work of the anthropologists indicates that the importance of sexual goals varies rather sharply from one culture to another. Since biology is not a variable in these comparisons, it is obvious that learning must be important. Let us consider how the individual may learn sexual goals and how he may be influenced to place them high in his scale of values.

Sex as a Conditioned Motive. Freud often writes as if the attachment of the child for his mother were an early manifestation of an innate sexual impulse. The processes of conditioning, however, can easily be invoked to explain this relationship. Kimball Young offers the following presentation of this view: [7]

> The first object of attachment for the infant is the mother. His reactions to her begin with nursing and with maternal care. . . . The fixation on the mother's breast is one of the first forms of conditioning. The Freudian psychologists have made a good deal of this early habit as the basis of sexual attachment and later sexual activity. There is much clinical evidence to connect the sucking and nursing act with later conditioning toward the sexual organs. Yet, at the beginning, the fixation appears dependent upon hunger and thirst more than upon sexual demands. Probably the tactile sensations of the lips upon the breast and the

---

[6] This overruling of basic drives by cultural goals should not be overestimated. In emergencies there is a tendency for the animal impulses to predominate; even "civilized" people have been known to resort to cannibalism in order to survive. Furthermore, the "good" pattern is often backed up by many other pressures. The patriotism of the soldier is by no means the only dynamic involved in his combat behavior. He faces punishment if he refuses service, if he retreats from danger, if he disobeys orders. Even more potent, in many cases, is the fact that he realizes that his combat behavior is a factor in the safety of his buddies. Thus there may be multiple valences operating to hold him in the danger spot. Even so, every army has its deserters, and also its psychiatric casualties—those who break down because of the intolerable pressure of culturally approved motives against biological drives.

[7] From Young (1930), p. 239. By permission of F. S. Crofts & Co., publishers.

sucking response itself are pleasurable, but that they are, for the child, sexual in any narrow sense is doubtful. On the other hand, so far as the mother is concerned, there may be a distinct erotic sensation from nursing the child. This, in turn, may lead the mother to fondle or pet the child while nursing and set up in him secondary reactions to sensitive and erogenous zone stimulations that will later become associated with his sexual activities.

The psychologists who adhere to one form or another of the position here stated by Young feel that Freud was not justified in his assumption that adult sexuality is in any real sense latent in the child, and that the infantile reactions which Freud correctly described may more properly be explained on this simpler basis. Young's point becomes even more emphatic when we consider the number of cases in which the child's attachment is to the nurse (or any adult who is a source of positive gratifications) rather than to the mother.

Suppression and Motivation. Even if there is a biological need present, the extent to which it becomes a major feature of personality will depend upon the extent to which the culture singles it out for special attention, e.g., by suppression. We may, as an illustration, consider the oxygen drive. This is a powerful drive when interfered with, but there are no social restrictions upon its satisfaction, and consequently we find no socially significant behavior resulting from it. But if someone devised a scheme by which oxygen could be made private property and sold at a profit, it would become an object of crime; and if to indulge in oxygen publicly were considered shameful, we should undoubtedly have some peculiarities of personality focused around the oxygen-seeking motive. The importance of a given need in personality development is rather definitely related to the cultural taboos and standards for the satisfaction of this impulse.

Mead (1939) has graphically depicted the difference in sex taboos and the cultural focus on sex for various primitive cultures. She finds substantial evidence that the amount of personality deviation which seems attributable to sex, and in general the intensity of sexual motivation, is much less where the culture is relatively indifferent to sex. Thus in Samoa, where sexual indulgence by adolescents was taken for granted and only married couples were expected to observe taboos on infidelity, she found no exaggerated interest in sex and little evidence of perversions, neuroses, or insanity which could be traced to sexual motivation. This was quite in contrast to other cultures that she had studied. This conclusion appears to be generally confirmed by other anthropologists working with a variety of primitive societies.

The imposition of cultural standards upon particular needs inevitably focuses the child's attention upon these tensions and their corresponding valences. When a child, in the course of his random exploration of his body, discovers that touching his sexual organs is pleasing, there is no necessary implication of greater importance than his discovery that candy is pleasant to taste. If adults find him engaged in sexual play, however, he will be scolded and punished—with more than the usual fervor. Such treatment serves to underscore the importance of this particular activity.

As Lewin's students have shown, the interruption of any activity does not end the tension underlying that activity. Unless a suitable substitute is provided, the child will resume the forbidden action as soon as opportunity allows. Thus the attempt to impose cultural taboos is likely to serve only to emphasize sex as an important phase of life.

Inhibition and Enhancement. Punishment not only underscores the importance of sex, but it may make sexual gratifications seem more pleasant than would otherwise be the case. Wright (1937) discovered that the interposition of a barrier caused a valence to function more powerfully. Taboos against sexual indulgence serve to make such gratifications more attractive.

In the course of his training for life in our culture, the child is regularly denied certain pleasures until he has performed certain set tasks. He may not have his dessert until he has eaten his spinach. He may not go to the movie until he has swept the cellar. He may have some candy if he wipes the dishes.

Upon encountering the sex taboo, however, he finds a pleasure which cannot be earned by any extra effort. It is not surprising that he treats this as a challenge, a situation calling for unusual exertion to achieve an extraordinarily attractive goal.

Introjection, Suggestion, and Motive. The potency of positive sexual valences is constantly being enhanced through movies, magazines, newspapers, advertising, and radio. America worships the cult of the young female figure. Girls identify themselves with movie stars and seek to be sexually alluring by every device known to modern advertising. Men are stimulated to desire and pursue these young women. Social evaluations of success and failure are closely linked with sex. The man who uses the right soap, hair tonic, or shaving lotion will win a beautiful bride and get a job in her father's firm. Girls saturate themselves in pulp magazines idealizing a kind of sybaritic prostitution sanctified by a marriage ceremony. While the physical aspects of sex are intriguingly censored in most romances, advertising has apparently dropped about six of the traditional seven veils already.

The child identifies himself with an adult, either in reality or in fiction. When it is suggested to him by this adult or by some spokesman (e.g., the advertising man) that sexual pleasures are more intense than any others, he is likely to accept this suggestion. As he introjects movies and fictional situations, the positive valence of sex is magnified more and more.

Social Premium upon Sexual Sophistication. As we come to consider the sexual impulses of older individuals, we find other social factors cooperating with those which we have already enumerated. There is considerable social pressure, particularly upon the adolescent, to become sexually sophisticated, i.e., to have (and be able to talk about) sexual experiences. This is a general phenomenon, but is particularly true in situations where a large number of unmarried young people are gathered together, as in an army barracks or a college dormitory and other comparable conditions. One of the main amusements of such groups consists of sitting in smoke-filled rooms telling stories of sexual conquest. But the unfortunate youth who cannot tell such stories or does not even know the vocabulary involved is subject to an extraordinary amount of ridicule and teasing. Under these circumstances, his early moral training, fears, etc., may break down and he will seek such experiences in order to avoid criticism. The conflict between the fear of transgressing the codes of moral behavior implanted in childhood and the positive valence of social conformity precipitates many personality disorders. Corson writes of the sexual factors in a group of psychotic cases among college men as follows: [8]

Most of the group had reached an age where success, or the lack of it, with girls, was important to the patient in securing the esteem of his associates. . . . M. I. C. found his "iron will" of no avail when it came to sharing a sleeping bag with a French widow. Keen was his disillusionment when he discovered the existence not only of a husband, but of other lovers as well. This experience followed closely the shattering of a romance by his mother, and constituted an added mental burden from which he has not completely recovered, although he has once more assumed a place in society. P. E. R. in his manic periods did what he considered "the manly thing" although at other times he shrank from association with women. . . . A. N. D. had continued to be "mother's pure pearl" but at a tremendous price. . . . C. O. U. was never able to raise his affections above the prostitute class. M. A. C. found that a wife added much to his load, and a return to his home shortly after marriage occurred early in the mental breakdown. . . . R. U. S. talked much of "women" and had many friendships with girls, overemphasizing the sexual distress that he caused in them, but never reaching the point of actual relations.

All of these boys wanted to do "the accepted thing." All had difficulty because sex was presented to them in a biased, unintelligent fashion. Neither did they find any aid in the old Puritanical standards with lurid ideas about masturbation and strict continence, nor a better solution in the opposite point of view. . . .

The whole social situation is so arranged as to keep sex constantly in the foreground of the adolescent's attention, and to place premiums of various kinds upon sexual sophistication as well as penalties upon ignorance.

Other Aspects of Freudian Theory. We have been concerned chiefly to establish the generalization that the Freudian emphasis upon sexual motivation as the prime mover in personality development is compatible with a culturally oriented viewpoint. Space does not permit a detailed analysis of other phases of Freudian theory, such as the development of psychosexuality. It would appear, however, that a straightforward treatment of parent-child relationships in terms of learning theory would provide an account which would explain about as much as the Freudians do of these stages.

The only one of the various phenomena emphasized by Freud which does

[8] From Corson (1927). Reprinted by permission of National Committee on Mental Hygiene, publishers.

not readily lend itself to the cultural approach is the Oedipus complex. The universality of the complex is rejected, however, by various anthropologists, who find it missing in cultures where the father-mother-child triangle is recognizably different from that of Western civilization.

The basic correctness of the Oedipus complex as a psychological feature of our own culture seems firmly established. Not only are clinicians almost unanimous in reporting such phenomena (not necessarily in Freudian language), but various statistical studies (cf. Stagner and Krout, 1940; Meltzer, 1941) confirm the idea in general. There are fragments of evidence which suggest that the occurrence of the Oedipus reaction is determined by the behavior of the parents, not of the child. Fathers seem to be by custom more severe with their sons, more indulgent with their daughters. Mothers often reverse this relationship. Thus the sex differential, which is the cornerstone of the Oedipus complex, may be a function of the behavior of the adults, which in turn is conditioned by cultural expectations. The rivalry and hostility associated with the Oedipus reaction would follow quite naturally, in any event.

CULTURE AND THE WILL-TO-POWER

If we turn from Freud to Adler, we find it even easier to formulate a cultural interpretation of the observed facts of motivation. The power drive, or the struggle against inferiority, as Adler presented it, is found to be a markedly different phenomenon in societies of different socioeconomic structure. Charles Darwin, who wrote down many things which had nothing to do with the theory of evolution, records the following interesting comparison of nineteenth-century inhabitants of Argentina and Chile: [9]

> The Guasos of Chile, who correspond to the Gauchos of the Pampas, are, however, a very different set of beings. Chile is the more civilized of the two countries, and the inhabitants, in consequence, have lost much individual character. Gradations in rank are much more strongly marked; the Guaso does not by any means consider every man his equal; and I was quite surprised to find that my companions did not like to eat at the same time with myself. This feeling of inequality is a necessary consequence of the existence of an aristocracy of wealth.

Numerous other observers have commented on the fact that the introduction of capitalist economy, with its sharp inequalities of financial and social standing, changes the "collective personality," i.e., the average personality, of the group members. An illustration similar to that cited by Darwin is the case of some American Indians before and after being "civilized." Other authors have given us descriptions of the South Sea Polynesians and other groups who have come under the sway of Western civilization.

In all these cases it is rather clearly indicated that, while distinctions of

[9] Darwin (1931).

rank were present, they were neither as clear cut nor as bitterly insisted upon before the introduction of the new social order. There seems to be a new attitude of arrogance on the part of those in the superior position (usually the white man on his mission of "civilizing" the barbarian, as in the case of the English in India) and new attitudes of envy, hate, and distrust in the suppressed group. Many of the more intelligent members of the Negro race show personality disturbances as a result of the inferior socioeconomic position they have been forced to take in America, and the traditional persecution of the Jews has left its mark in the traditions of this religious group, as well as upon the personalities of many of the current generation. Thus, while dominance (in the positive sense, as described by Maslow) probably exists in all human societies, *the sense of inferiority, and the will-to-power, develop out of a particular kind of social structure.*

Training for Inferiority. The fact that a child is small, weak, and intellectually handicapped as compared with his adult surroundings is inevitable. The fact that he is taught to bow down before the authority and omnipotence of adults is not. Some progress has been made, but it is still true that the dictatorial authority of the Roman paterfamilias is the basis of most family organization. The child is denied freedom of opinion or action. His hours are ordered and his very thoughts censored by adults. Under these circumstances, Adler's observation that the child suffers from feelings of inadequacy is the reverse of surprising.

The child's attention is focused on competition and on getting ahead of others. His mother, who wants him to grow bigger and learn faster than neighboring children, puts pressure on him to eat his spinach, to outdo his friends at games, and to excel at school. Social differentiations are indoctrinated by subtle, often unconscious, devices. If the family is economically handicapped, aspirations are likely to be painfully in the foreground; and more fortunate children are likely to make the poorer boy keenly conscious of his inferiority.

Adults are under constant pressure to achieve, to raise their status. In a factory community a foreman is a person of great prestige; to quote one small boy, "Muggsy thinks he's a big shot because his uncle used to be a foreman." Job hierarchies make for subtle social distinctions; in a railroad town, the husband's job determines the social circle in which the wife moves. Status pressure is not limited to Army and Navy posts.

A Pattern of Inequality. As Darwin noted, the existence of extreme variations in wealth induces awareness of social gradations, with concomitant concern for superiority and inferiority. American culture exalts power as a positive goal, second only to sex. Money is in many cases only a means to power and status. The successful executive who gives up a six-figure income to become an ambassador at a financial loss is showing the significance of status as a positive valence. The rapid expansion of unions in the decade after 1933 was in part a revolt of factory workers against a regime in which they had no status. The union tended to equalize the power of worker and executive.

Adler's treatment of women's inferiority complexes in terms of "masculine protest" could more satisfactorily be represented in terms of the cultural advantages attached to being a male. The foregoing analysis seems to indicate that all of Adler's theory revolves around culturally determined valences, that in a different culture the personality phenomena he has emphasized would disappear.

TRAITS AND GOAL ORIENTATIONS

Adler's "will-to-power" is closely related to Murray's need dominance. But it is also involved in what, in Chapter 8, we called a trait of dominance, or dominance behavior. Similarly, need affiliation is necessarily integrated with the trait of sociability. This suggests the importance of relating our discussion of goal seeking to the concept of trait.

Two points merit particular attention. One is the obvious conclusion that need, or motive, or goal, in this sense, is hardly different from our earlier usage of "trait." The similarity of need affiliation to what we have earlier called sociability is obvious. By his behavior, as by his daydreams, the individual reveals a desire to be with people, to have friendly contacts, to establish group membership. Although we have not described any trait exactly analogous to need achievement, it is clear that the evidence accumulated could apply just as well to a trait as to a need or goal orientation.

The second point is that the concept of trait should be reevaluated as having dynamic implications. Whereas some of the traits described in Chapter 8 are merely summaries of expressive patterns or response styles, others could just as well be listed here as motivational patterns: egotism versus modesty, suspiciousness, thriftiness, perseverance, curiosity, comfort loving. Such terms may be considered simply as descriptions of observable acts or of inferred mental states; but they may also be considered as predictions that energy will be mobilized on behalf of defined goals.

This tendency for the descriptive phase of personality study to get mixed with the dynamic phase has been recognized by many other psychologists. Bindra (1959) asserts of such concepts as instincts and needs that "such hypothetical constructs . . . provide merely redundant descriptions, not systematic interpretations" [p. 288]. He argues that we identify such a "need" as "the exploratory drive" by the observed fact that animals explore novel surroundings; does the hypothetical "drive" explain, or just add a new term? Similarly, we may ask whether having two terms, sociability and need affiliation, to describe an individual really adds anything.

Opinions among psychologists on this point are most diverse. McClelland (1951), agreeing that trait and motive are parallel and intimately related, seems to feel, however, that there is justification for keeping them apart. All-port (1955), after having earlier accepted the separation, seems to have shifted and accepted the notion of identity of trait and motive.

On the following points all students of personality are rather well agreed: (1) Neither a trait nor a complex goal orientation (such as achievement or affiliation) can be observed directly; each can be identified only through overt behavior or fantasy; in other words both trait and need are *hypothetical constructs*. (2) Whereas the terms "trait" and "need" are employed in different contexts for slightly different purposes, any difference in meaning is likely to depend upon an arbitrary position adopted by the user for his own reasons. (3) Thus, almost every trait has a dynamic implication of energy being mobilized to achieve some status or expectancy, whereas every goal orientation involves an organized perceptual pattern comparable to a trait.

To justify this virtual identification of trait with an organized goal-seeking tendency, we must return to our fundamental concept of personality development. In Chapter 5 it was shown that the young child begins developing by acquiring positive and negative valences, and by learning percepts and responses which were instrumental in getting him to positive valences, away from negative valences. Techniques in dealing with persons, social roles, conflicts, etc., involved these valences, percepts, and responses. In Chapter 8 we analyzed traits from the point of view of perception and behavior, without developing the significance of valences. But the valence is the dynamic side of the process; the person strives to reach positive valences and to evade negative valences.

In the case of Murray's need achievement we merely assert that the individual shows a pattern of mobilizing energy to reach certain situations which are socially defined as achievements (passing examinations, finishing a job, winning approval for performance). Similarly, need affiliation refers to a pattern of positive valences (friends, group membership, emotional security) and negative valences (loneliness, rejection, ostracism). At least for practical purposes, then, we can now extend our concept of trait. *A trait is a consistent pattern of perception, response, and goal striving.* When we describe any individual as manifesting a certain trait, we are at least implying that this shows on all three levels.

Determinants of Traits. Traits, considered in this threefold manner as perception, response, and motivation, make up the observable aspects of personality. How did they get that way? In our rather brief sketch of the developmental process, we made it clear that variations in the physiology of the organism and in the social environment could affect the traits of any single individual.

Biology can readily modify perception, motivation, and action through the structure of sense organs, the functioning of endocrine glands, inherited organic attributes, and so on. The child's traits can also vary as a result of differences in the family milieu, schooling, the culture pattern within which he grows up, and similar environmental variables. In the following chapters we round out our examination of the psychology of personality by looking at the data with regard to some of these influences.

SUMMARY

Theories which explain the dynamics of personality in terms of instinct or biogenic drive are not entirely satisfactory. Many psychologists prefer to concentrate on personality as a pattern of goal seeking, and disregard the problem of how goals are acquired. Such an approach has numerous advantages: It corresponds more closely to daily life; it avoids complications due to the fact that satiation and deprivation function differently as regards social and biological goals; and it makes use of the extensive material on perception which has proved useful in analyzing other aspects of personality.

The energy which man expends is biological, but it is channeled toward goals which are largely culturally determined. In the perception of goals, the individual may reveal rigidity (by clinging to infantile goals), wide stimulus generalization (by treating various objects as equivalent goals), and focusing (concentration or diffusion of energy). His frames of reference determine a hierarchy of importance of goals which is a distinctive feature of his personality.

The major determinant of goals appears to be culture. An examination of some important aspects of American civilization suggests that both Freud's stress on sexuality and Adler's emphasis on striving for power may be considered at least in part to be culturally determined. Such tendencies as need achievement and need affiliation are even more obviously outcomes of cultural influences.

When the concept of trait is reexamined in this light, it seems obvious that traits in general have dynamic as well as descriptive attributes. This means that most traits are organized patterns involving perception, response, and goal seeking.

SUGGESTIONS FOR READING

An excellent recent book on motivation, written from quite a different point of view, as compared with this chapter, is Bindra's *Motivation: a systematic reinterpretation.* Allport's *Becoming* and Murphy's *Personality: a biosocial approach to origins and structure* discuss in various chapters the concept of motivation sketched here.

DETERMINANTS

The personality is an effortful, striving, seeking unity. Whether we conceptualize it in terms of pushes from within, or of pulls from without, is not important. The individual is a dynamic pattern, seeking goals and need satisfactions in a manner which defines him as a person.

These motives are not satisfied in a vacuum. The outcome of the developmental sequence depends on the barriers encountered and the person's way of dealing with them. It depends on the threats to equilibrium and the kind of forestalling or restorative tactics utilized. Thus, to round out our picture of personality, we must give due consideration to the individual as a product of his environment.

For convenience we have included in this section the researches on the body itself as a personality variable. It is confusing to think of the body as a part of the environment, yet most of us have had the experience of treating a finger, a hand, or a foot as if it were an object, not a segment of the self. Cold-numbed fingers seem to be an obstacle to the satisfaction of an impulse, just as a bolted door may be. Thus we begin with physical variables as determinants of personality differences.

The child matures within a family setting. A generalized view of this development was given in early chapters. But not all families are alike; and such variations induce personality differences. This is also true of the play group, the school, the job, and marriage. Substantial research has been done on all these factors, showing how they may determine the personalities of individuals in particular social settings.

The individual, however, is not completely at the mercy of his environment. He is not purely passive, to be shaped by circumstances. To some extent he can change his environment on behalf of his personal integrity. Man can modify society. Thus we trace the full circle, from the child, molded by his social milieu, to the adult—a product of his culture—who may in a limited way shape the future of his society.

Biological Factors

Much of our discussion, so far, has implicitly assumed the existence of biological and social factors making for *differences* in personality, as well as those common to all personalities. In these concluding chapters, we shall bring together the major facts regarding the specific biological and social factors which determine a particular kind of personality.

Before entering upon a consideration of the available data on biological characteristics related to differences in personality traits, we should emphasize one note of caution. This is that every personality is a product of many interacting factors. The desire to find large and significant correlations between specific biological measurements and specific psychological characteristics is understandable. A realistic approach, however, suggests that personality is shaped by a great many small influences, not by a few very potent factors. If the student keeps this point in mind, he will realize that, although the relationships between biology and personality are small, they are nonetheless significant.

"Human Nature" Begins with Biology. Some psychologists like to stress the fact that human nature is essentially social—that the biological basis for action is ours commonly with the infrahuman animals. It is only proper to recognize, however, that social influences can operate only upon a biological organism. Differences in the quality of this physical structure will make for differences in the reaction to social conditions. Thus even the social psychologist cannot ignore biological mechanisms.

There are a number of different approaches which reveal the significance of biological factors. First, there is the investigation of heredity. Individuals differ as a result of innate conditions, irrespective of environmental influences. The technical problem of demonstrating that a given variation is hereditary and not acquired offers numerous difficulties, but it is worth some attention.

Second, we may study different organ systems and correlate variations in their functioning with personality patterns. Such internal differences may be determined by heredity or by earlier environment. In a few cases, we can relate the data on personality to specific variations in the organism, such as size and weight of endocrine glands.

Third, we may study the conditions of the body fluids, the biochemistry and hormonal constitution of the individual. Such functional differences may prove more enlightening than studies of glandular structure and size.

HEREDITY

Heredity is a common scapegoat, and persons who wish to avoid a sense of guilt over their sins of omission and commission in child rearing are prone to blame the youngster's incorrigible disposition upon his ancestors. As the ancestors are generally in no position to protest, the procedure seems safe, if not particularly helpful.

The evidence as regards the true importance of heredity does not render much support to this type of rationalization. Whereas most psychologists are convinced that heredity is a major determinant of intelligence (the common estimate being that heredity is about four times as important as environment in that area), they are by no means satisfied that personality is so rigidly limited by hereditary possibilities.

To some extent, one's evaluation of the nature-nurture ratio in personality will depend upon the definition of personality chosen. We have espoused the view that personality is basically an inner pattern of beliefs and expectancies about the self in relation to its environment. Such a definition stacks the cards in favor of an environmental emphasis. An approach which stressed temperament—breadth and intensity of emotional reactions, for example—would probably favor the inheritance hypothesis, although even here the evidence is somewhat ambiguous.

Technical Problems. The collection of satisfactory evidence on human heredity is intrinsically difficult. Geneticists find that the only decisive proof of the inheritance of a specific factor and its Mendelian ratio rests upon selective crossbreeding. Human beings are likely to object strenuously to proposals that biologists or psychologists select their mates and determine how many offspring they shall have.

Family biographies are notoriously unreliable as evidence of the inheritance of desirable or undesirable traits. The data are highly subjective in most cases. The extent to which family "pull" helped some members attain success is unknown, and the existence of favorable or unfavorable environments paralleling the presumptive hereditary strains is only too clear.

The best sources of evidence at present come from two types of studies: comparisons of identical and fraternal twins, and of identical twins separated in early life; and animal investigations. In the former group we can make comparisons with heredity controlled and environment the sole variable. In the latter type of research we can actually make crucial experiments on inbreeding and crossbreeding. Although the interpretation of animal data has in the past been dubious, recent work has advanced technically to the point that scarcely any debate can arise.

Identical versus Fraternal Twins. Identical (monozygotic) twins represent the sole instance in human biology of two individuals having exactly the same hereditary constitution. Fraternal (dizygotic) twins develop from separate fertilized egg cells, whereas identicals result from the accidental splitting of a single fertilized ovum. Thus the gene pattern is exactly alike in identical twins, whereas it may differ markedly in fraternals.

This means that if we compare the degree of resemblance of a pair of monozygotic twins with the degree of resemblance of a pair of dizygotic twins, we get an indication of the relative weight to be attached to heredity and to environment. Eysenck (1956b), for example, reports a study of such twin pairs in terms of the correlations of factor scores derived from measures of intelligence, measures of introversion-extraversion, and measures of autonomic reactivity, as shown in Table 16.1. This table says, in effect, that identical twins get scores on intelligence and autonomic measures which are about as much alike as if the same person took the test twice; the reliability coefficients for the measures are not much above the similarity coefficients. For fraternal twins, on the other hand, similarity is markedly less. On the personality trait data (extraversion), heredity clearly brings about some similarity, but not nearly so much as for the other measures. (Eysenck finds it necessary to apologize for the −.33 reported for fraternal twins on this measure; it is almost certainly due to a sampling error, as such correlations are usually positive but small.) The great weight attaching to heredity in determining autonomic reactivity should also be noted here, since autonomic "response style" has already been shown to be important in determining other personality traits (see, e.g., page 147). Other investigators have shown that identical twins are more alike than fraternal twins on occupational interests,

Table 16.1

Similarities of Fraternal and Identical Twins *

	Identical twins	Fraternal twins
Resemblance on intelligence (correlation)	+.82	+.38
Resemblance on extraversion	+.50	−.33
Resemblance on autonomic measures	+.93	+.72

* $p < .05$ in all differences.

SOURCE: Eysenck (1956b). Reprinted by permission of North-Holland Publishing Co.

personal tempo, patterns of free association, and other personality indexes. It thus appears clear that hereditary differences do play a substantial role in the determination of personality.

Cattell's Variance Study. Instead of studying similarities by correlation technique, as in the Eysenck research, it is possible to study the distribution of differences (variance technique). An elaborate study of this type is reported by Cattell, Blewett, and Beloff (1955).[1] In this research, 52 pairs of identical twins were compared with 32 pairs of fraternal twins, 91 pairs of siblings reared together, 36 pairs of unrelated children reared together, and 540 children drawn from the general population (neither related nor reared in the same environment). Given these samples, it is possible to examine the variances within groups having:

↗ The same heredity and similar environment (identicals)

↗ Related heredity and similar environment (fraternals)

↗ Related heredity and somewhat similar environment (siblings)

↗ Unrelated heredity and somewhat similar environment (adoptive children)

↗ Unrelated heredity with unrelated environment (children from the general population)

If there is significantly less variation (more similarity) within one of these groups than across groups, interpretations can be drawn as to the relative weights of heredity and environment.

The main conclusions of this investigation run as follows: (1) heredity weighs more heavily than environment in determining such traits as cyclothymia (easygoing, warmhearted, expressive) versus schizothymia (inflexible, cool, reserved); (2) heredity is also more influential as regards what Cattell calls "adventurous cyclothymia" (liking to meet people, kindly, impulsive) versus "withdrawn schizothymia" (shy, timid, hostile, secretive, inhibited); and (3) heredity is more potent in determining intelligence. This last comes as no surprise; it would have cast doubt on the method had the result been otherwise.

Environment is found to be more effective as regards such traits as tendermindedness, general neuroticism, will control, bodily anxiety, and surgency (cheerful, energetic, resourceful, adaptable). A relatively balanced determination (equal importance to heredity and environment) is reported for dominance, socialized morale, and "energetic conformity."

It is difficult to derive a general conclusion from these data, partly because of the somewhat confusing trait designations applied by Cattell. In terms of his method, each of the 12 personality traits is supposed to be independent of the

[1] For obvious reasons we shall not try to explain the logic or mathematics of their method, and its differences from correlation method. The authors admit some weaknesses in the procedure; they provide a series of answers to each question about heredity, based on different assumed answers to some unknown facts. We mention in the text only their "most probable" value for each item.

others; the overlapping of names, and of descriptive adjectives, is consequently hard to understand. On logical grounds we might expect that traits involving energy mobilization, emotional responsiveness, etc., would show maximum hereditary influence; sociability, morale, and similar patterns would be more affected by experience. Some of the Cattell data fit this simplification, but in some cases there appears to be a contradiction. A great deal more research is needed to clarify this question of the relative weights of heredity and environment.

Animal Investigations. The crucial test of a theory regarding the inheritance of personality will come from selective breeding experiments. Since these are impossible at the human level, investigators have turned to animals for such data. For reasons of space, we limit ourselves to two long-continued and carefully controlled studies of rats. Data are also available on dogs and other species, but they will not be reviewed here.

Hall's Study of Selective Breeding. Calvin S. Hall carried on, over a period of years, studies on selective breeding of rats for emotionality. The results are shown graphically in Figure 16.1. The procedure goes as follows: Rats were tested in an open-field situation; defecation, urination, and other signs of upset were taken as an index of emotionality. From the parent generation, only those animals showing relatively high scores were bred with each other to start an "emotional" strain; and animals from the lower end of the distribution were bred to start a nonemotional variety. In each successive generation the same procedure was followed; i.e., in the emotional group, low scorers were culled out, and in the nonemotionals, high scorers were not permitted to reproduce. As the graph shows, by the ninth generation the two strains had stabilized, the emotionals at a score level of about ten, their opposites at a level just above one.

To test for the hypothesis that the differences may have been due to factors other than heredity, Hall (1951) crossbred his two strains, beginning with the tenth generation. As is readily seen, the scores of these crosses resembled those of the original parent generation.

Hall was naturally interested in the mechanisms involved. The stepwise change in the emotional group (Figure 16.1) suggested that different organ systems might be involved, and that continuous experimentation had been necessary to get a strain with all of these loaded toward emotionality. Yeakel and Rhoades (1941), studying some of these animals, found that the emotional strain possessed larger endocrine glands—adrenals, pituitaries, and thyroids. Martin and Hall (1941) reported that the emotional group was *less* susceptible to convulsions when stimulated by an air blast.[2] It is to be hoped

---

[2] At first glance this seems confusing. Hall offers the hypothesis that the nonemotionals have an underactive ANS, that the air blast builds up tension which is not discharged and explodes in the seizure. The emotional strain, he suggests, releases tension quickly in visceral or skeletal activity and hence never builds up to a convulsion.

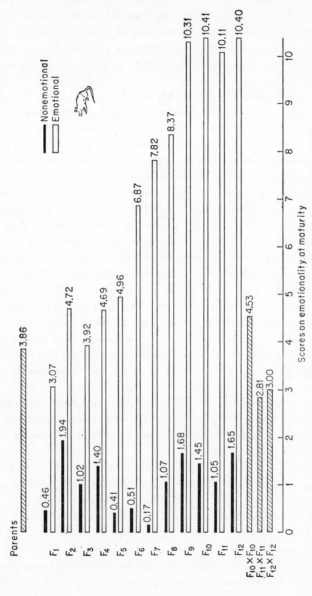

Fig. 16.1 Evidence for inheritance of emotionality in rats. The black bars represent emotionality scores of the low strain; white, of the very reactive strain. Crosshatched bars: parent generation and crossbreedings of the two selected strains. (Data from Hall, 1941; Hall, 1951.)

that studies of other physiological functions will be carried on with these rats, thus throwing light on some of the organ systems to be discussed later in this chapter.

The Tryon-Searle Study. An unexpected but valuable finding relevant for personality differences came from a series of breeding experiments by Tryon (1940) on maze-learning ability in rats. The study is particularly valuable because we have been accustomed to think of ability and personality as somewhat divorced from each other; the findings remind us that the organism is still a unit. Tryon's procedure required rats to learn a maze for hunger motivation, bred those which learned quickly to develop a bright strain, and those which learned slowly to obtain a dull strain. The strains bred true, i.e., the offspring of the first group were consistently quick learners and those in the second were slow in the maze. Searle (1949) then collected a large number of measures on members of both strains, intercorrelated and factor-analyzed them. The results showed, among other things, that the "brights" were considerably more responsive to food motivation than were the "dulls"; in other words, a substantial portion of the hereditary difference in "ability" was probably a difference in motivation. (This is not to deny that ability differences can be inherited; such differences do show in Searle's data, but not in quantity adequately to explain the strain differences in performance. On some problems, for example, the "dull" animals did as well as the "bright" group.) We shall have more to say about temperamental factors affecting use of ability in Chapter 19.

Genetic Constitution. Geneticists would especially like to learn whether given factors affecting personality are inherited as unitary dominant or recessive genes, multiple genes, etc. The data are not clear; many possibilities seem to exist. With regard to his crossbreeding experiments, Hall (1951) suggests that nonemotionality apparently is dominant over emotionality (the mean for the hybrids is closer to the low end of the scale), but probably not based on a single gene (note also the stepwise increase in scores of the emotional group).[3]

To the extent that this conclusion has any bearing on human genetics, we may optimistically suggest that determinants of ego strength—if hereditary— are dominant over those for neuroticism and emotionality. Some support for this is provided by data on human families (cf. Kallman, 1952). But we know that animal studies are only suggestive for human heredity.

Mode of Operation of Heredity. How can hereditary influences mold personality traits? A variety of such possibilities will be explored in this chapter. One such is through the inheritance of somatotype (Sheldon, 1942), which in turn may imply inheritance of differing muscular systems, visceral

---

[3] The multiple possibilities are suggested by an examination of data on audiogenic seizures in mice (Hall, 1951). In one genus of mouse, seizures seem related to a single dominant gene, in another genus, to a single recessive gene. For further comments on the improbability of arriving at a neat solution of this problem, see Kallman (1956), p. 371.

sensitivity, autonomic nervous system (ANS) irritability, and so on. We anticipate that, in time, the mode of operation of genetic attributes will be found to involve determination of perceptual and response styles (Chapter 7) as well as ease of formation of expectancies and conditioned responses (Chapter 6). It would not be surprising to find that sensory thresholds, for example, predisposed some individuals to attend more to external cues, others to internal. One is intrigued by the casual comment (Williams, 1956, p. 123) that out of 97 pugilists tested, only 10 showed normal responses to pain stimuli. Yet studies of persons competely lacking in pain sensitivity showed no special personality deviations!

We must also anticipate differences in strength and coordination of response, which will be perceived and be incorporated in the self-image. The boy who is stronger and more skillful than his fellows will develop a feeling of self-confidence; if he lives in a slum culture, he will find that a policy of fighting leads to success (cf. page 228). Differences in ANS reactivity and glandular responsiveness may cause some youngsters to picture themselves as highly emotional, going to pieces in stress situations, because this is exactly what happens.

In addition to these hereditary features which get incorporated directly in the self-image, we must recognize also that innate characteristics may act upon the environment in such a way as to elicit changed stimulation. Suppose we take, as a hypothetical example, the variable which Fries and Woolf (1954) call "congenital activity type," referring to the fact that infants within the first few hours after birth show wide variation in activity level. This may well be due to differences in ANS excitability and central nervous system (CNS) control, although no proof of this is available. Babies varying in activity level will get different kinds of information from the environment; the active infant will bump into objects, touch and handle, chew and taste; the passive baby will get some (not all) of the same visual and auditory cues, but not the tactual and proprioceptive inputs. The percepts developed by the active child will have strong kinesthetic components, which may have some significance in the development of perceptual style, and also in the nature of the self-image. Response style will almost certainly be quite different. Further, the active child will stimulate and perhaps provoke the parents, thus changing his social milieu. On the other hand, the quiet child is probably predisposed to a dependency relation on the parents, and to development of defense mechanisms such as withdrawal and fantasy. Although these predictions so far are verified only for a few cases, there seems little doubt that these are some of the consequences deriving from innate differences in activity level.

The Mechanism of Heredity and the Unique Personality. It can even be argued that there is a unique hereditary pattern for each of us, an innate basis for that unique adult personality of which we have spoken so frequently. Kallman (1956), who has written extensively on the subject of psychological heredity, offers the following remarks on this question: [4]

The effect of a gene expresses itself through the control of a specific enzyme which spurs on the production of a unit difference in development or function. The outcome of this action is subject either to reinforcement or interference by nonallelic genes, that is, other genes which are not located at the same point of a chromosome. . . . The aggregate of gene-specific personality constituents is so vast, and the number of interactive variables in the shaping of a behavior pattern so infinite, that every individual can count on being unique—identical twins excepted.

The modern view regarding genetic influences, therefore, is that they may determine universal, group, or unique individual attributes. We are all human because of our heredity; we are blonds or brunets, tall or short because of heredity; and we have distinctive faces, voices, and other features, also as a consequence of hereditary determinants. Such a statement does not exclude the important role for environment which is implied by our extensive discussions of learning and social influences in Chapters 5 to 11. As was indicated above, even identical twins show some differences. And as functions become more complex, the differences due to environment increase. The tendency to frighten easily may be innate; but the number of fears experienced, the number of cues which elicit anxiety, and the frequency of withdrawal from normal situations will be profoundly influenced by the learning process.

The Concept of Stress Tolerance. It is possible, then, that a major mode of operation of hereditary influences is through the variable which has been used, more or less incidentally, in earlier pages, of stress tolerance. As is perfectly obvious, individuals differ extensively in the amount of stress they can tolerate. Some persons become markedly upset by situations which are seen by others as relatively unimportant. It has often been supposed that there may be some kind of physiological basis for these differences. Freeman (1948), for example, proposed the concept of a "psychiatric Plimsoll mark" (referring to the mark on the side of a ship to show the maximum load it can carry). Operationally he suggested that success in discharging aroused tension was an index of this load limit. If an individual becomes very tense, as a result of some disturbing stimulus, and cannot work off this tension in the form of activity of some sort, he builds up increasing "residual load." Eventually he will build up so much tension that he will collapse.

Freeman seems to imply a hereditary tendency to discharge tension freely or to build up residual load. However, he is not very clear about this. Sheldon (1942), of course, holds that his somatotypes provide hereditary bases for such individual differences; particularly he indicates that the ectomorphic body type is likely to be associated with inadequate discharge of tension.

---

[4] Pp. 496–497. Reprinted by permission of the *American Journal of Psychiatry*.

Such a view, in one form or another, is common among European psychologists. Davidson et al. (1955) studied a group of Oxford University students and reported evidence that somatotype was important in determining "psychological vulnerability" to stress situations. Corman (1954), in France, and diTullio (1954), in Italy, hold a similar view, although they are more concerned with bodily types as related to differences in kind of mental disorder.

Stress tolerance may involve variations in functioning of the autonomic nervous system or the central nervous system, striped muscles and smooth muscles, the endocrine glands, and miscellaneous biochemical processes not included in these categories. The range of possible determinants of personality deviations, including mental disease, is indicated by *The Biology of Mental Health and Disease,*[5] a report of a 1950 conference at which experts reported on work involving variations in the chemical constituents of the brain, the blood-brain barrier, brain metabolism, electrical activity of the brain, endocrine factors, infantile anoxia of the brain, lack of vitamins, and assorted subtle physiological variables alleged to be significantly related to personality.

This volume, while promising, in the sense of pointing out intriguing hunches for research, offers little in the way of established fact as regards the identifiable differences in personality which have been reported in preceding chapters under the headings of style, traits, attitudes, and values. At best it identifies certain factors which have been shown to produce phenomena of marked emotional or motivational significance; at worst it notes cases in which abnormal personalities were found to deviate in some fashion from normal physiological functions. It must be recognized that the latter kind of evidence is very thin. If patients diagnosed as schizophrenics show chronic oxygen deficiency (p. 352), is this a cause or a consequence of the psychological abnormality? Certainly many abnormal personalities show behavioral changes which could lead to variations in oxygen consumption, nitrogen excretion, and so on. The other variety of evidence (that experimental induction of a deficiency leads to personality modification) is somewhat more convincing, and a few such studies will be cited in the following pages.

AUTONOMIC NERVOUS SYSTEM FUNCTIONS

Because of the intimate relation between the autonomic nervous system (ANS) and the phenomena of emotion and motivation, most writers on hereditary determination of personality have speculated on the importance of ANS functions. This system, composed of two more or less reciprocal portions —the sympathetic, or adrenergic, and the parasympathetic, or cholinergic— has a profound impact on the homeostatic processes and hence upon tempera-

[5] *The biology of mental health and disease: the Twenty-seventh Annual Conference of the Milbank Memorial Fund.* New York: Paul B. Hoeber, Inc., 1952.

ment and other aspects of personality. Kuntz writes as follows about the involvement of the ANS in homeostatic functions: [6]

Homeostasis, which implies the constancy and the stability of the internal environment of the organism, depends on the normal functional balance of the adrenergic and the cholinergic components of the visceral nerves, but it is mediated mainly through the sympathetic nerves. The discharge through these nerves of impulses which emanate from the higher visceral centers, particularly the hypothalamus, is diffuse and influences all the viscera, including the vascular system. They are, consequently, highly efficient in bringing about adjustments to external and internal environmental factors.

Because of the well-known relationship between ANS activity and emotion, psychologists began years ago the search for links between autonomic responses and temperamental traits. An early volume by Kempf (1919) proposed that a relationship existed but offered only remotely relevant data. Somewhat more promising was the work of Darrow (1932), who correlated a wide variety of autonomic indexes with responses on a personality inventory. Although Darrow himself found his results disappointing, others were encouraged by his occasionally significant data to continue the search. Notable among these is Freeman, whose *Energetics of Human Behavior* (1948) has already been cited (pages 145–146).

The body's response to frustration and the homeostatic recovery curve are obviously important to personality. Freeman (1939) imposed experimental frustrations on his subjects and then measured recovery through ANS activity. He found evidence for two processes, interacting but not mirror images of each other, which he called "drive arousal" and "discharge control." Persons high on the first would quickly mobilize energy in response to presence of a threat (and, presumably, of a positive goal, although Freeman did not study this). Those high on the second would prevent the expression of this energy arousal in overt action until the probability of success had been ascertained.

Freeman's Theory of Temperament. This finding led, naturally, to the development of a view about temperament set forth by Freeman (1948) in which people could be classified as to temperament in accordance with their position on three variables: drive arousal, discharge control, and discriminative capacity. (This third is obviously necessary to take care of the fact that the individual uses information about the environment; arousal depends on perception of significant stimuli, and control involves evaluation of consequences of action.) Figure 16.2 shows a three-dimensional scheme for locating persons in such a framework.

It would thus be possible to predict that there will be persons who have strong drive arousal and weak control, and who will thus be likely to commit crimes and generally make poor adjustments (the psychopath). Similarly, there will be persons of weak arousal and strong control, who seem to want

[6] Kuntz (1951), p. 68. Reprinted by permission of Charles C Thomas, publisher.

nothing and are afraid to try anything; they probably wind up in hospitals with a diagnosis of "inadequate personality." An individual high on both arousal and control should be very successful, because he would exert energy but not wastefully; something would depend, of course, on his discriminative capacity (intelligence). Since the foregoing predictions are highly obvious, they cannot be said to support Freeman; at best they say that his theory seems reasonable.

Empirical Data. Because Freeman assumes that his temperamental variables are expressions of ANS activity, studies which reveal significant correlations of data at the personality level with autonomic indexes may be considered as giving some support to his view. A number of such investigations are available. Wishner (1953) found that a pooled index of emotional disturbance on the Rorschach gave a significant correlation with a pooled measure of ANS disturbance. However, most investigators indicate that the problem is considerably more intricate than would be suggested by this simple relationship.

Freeman's theory seems to imply a balancing of sympathetic and parasympathetic innervation. Wenger (1941) developed a battery of tests of such activity and in later work (Wenger and Wellington, 1943) showed that

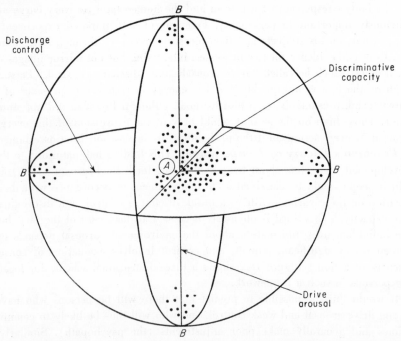

Fig. 16.2 The personality sphere according to Freeman. The three axes are at right angles to one another; this means that individuals vary independently on the three variables. (From Freeman, 1948, p. 267, by permission of Cornell University Press.)

children remain fairly constant on this index of balance from one year to the next (correlation about .70). Wenger (1947) followed this with a study of the personality attributes of persons high and low on this index. "Children with autonomic scores indicative of functionally parasympathetic predominance were found," he writes, "to manifest more emotional inhibition, less emotional excitability, and a lower frequency of activity with less fatigue; and proved to be more patient and neat than those children with autonomic scores indicative of functional predominance of the sympathetic system" [pp. 308–309]. These differences in overtly visible aspects of personality correspond rather well to the known functions of the sympathetic and parasympathetic systems, and also to the pattern to be expected on the basis of Freeman's formulation. More or less in support of this finding is that of Block (1957), who tested college students in a pseudo lie-detector situation. He found that Ss who had strong reactions of the sympathetic nervous system were rated as dependent, suggestible, dreamy, and idealistic. Those giving few sympathetic reactions (presumably parasympathetic dominated) were judged to be cool, evasive, opportunistic, and independent. These are at least compatible with Freeman's theory and with Wenger's data.

Autonomic Response Specificity. The rather unsatisfactory results obtained by studies of over-all indexes of autonomic balance led Lacey and Van Lehn (1952) to search for and find evidence of specific response patterns characterizing different persons. In effect this means that John may respond to threat situations mainly by changes in heart rate, Tom with blood-pressure changes, and Harry with changes in galvanic skin response (GSR) (all of these being sympathetic nervous system functions). The evidence collected by Lacey and Van Lehn indicates that, even though all of us have similar ANS mechanisms and over-all response functions, each individual tends to develop his own consistent pattern of responding to a stimulus which elicits ANS arousal.[7]

This should not have been so surprising. After all, everyone has a similar speech mechanism and yet our verbal habits are very different and quite characteristic for individuals. So the finding by Lacey and Van Lehn that these individual patterns of autonomic responses are quite consistent from one situation to another is plausible.

Once these individual patterns had been identified, it was possible to use them in relationship with conventional measures of personality. Lacey, Bateman, and Van Lehn (1952) found that they got very poor correlations between Rorschach scores and over-all ANS function, but when they took

---

[7] We have foreshadowed this possibility earlier (p. 93) in referring to the work of Ax (1953) on the unique physiological patterns shown by different individuals in states of fear and anger. The evidence reported by Berger (1958) suggests that groups may also differ as regards these relationships. He found a number of significant correlations of ANS measures and temperament traits in a group of hospitalized neurotics, but these could not be discovered when the same tests were tried on college students.

account of the person's preferred way of responding (in effect, taking his most extreme reaction regardless of which physiological function was involved), they got correlations as high as $+.43$. This seems to indicate that, while everyone shows emotional reactivity, the way in which this will be manifest is something of an individual matter.

Heredity or Environment? There is a certain implicit tendency to assume that emphasis on ANS function implies hereditary determination of personality, since the ANS is obviously inherited, and differences in function may be assumed likewise to be innate. This gets some support from the fact that Jost and Sontag (1944) correlated autonomic index scores for pairs of children and found higher resemblances for twins than for ordinary siblings.

There is some reason, on the other hand, to suspect that early learning may influence the consistent pattern of ANS responses; indeed, it would seem likely that the specificity found by Lacey and his associates may be due to learning. Thus we can only conclude that these findings show some support for a hereditarian point of view, but they are by no means conclusive.

CENTRAL NERVOUS SYSTEM

While it is easy to become fascinated with the ANS because of its immediate involvement in emotional and drive-arousal phenomena, one must not forget that the ANS is stirred into activity by messages from the central nervous system (CNS) and may likewise be denied overt expression by CNS inhibition. This may account for the inconclusive results of the ANS studies, and—we anticipate—for the even less clear outcomes of studies on CNS functioning in relation to personality traits.

Pavlov, the great Russian physiologist and psychologist, outlined over thirty years ago a theory of cortical excitation and inhibition from which he derived a scheme of personality types. Since his work was done entirely with dogs, it has little interest value for us, but it has stimulated some work on humans. Eysenck (1955, 1956a) has offered a theory of introversion-extraversion based on the assumption that people differ in cortical inhibition.

Eysenck's key concept, as was noted in Chapter 12, is that of reactive inhibition. Most of us, when asked to do the same simple task over and over, quickly build up resistance. However, there are individual differences in the speed and strength of the resistance, and on this basis Eysenck has formulated a theory to account for certain personality trends. Since the evidence so far published is favorable, we can say that the theory merits attention. Literally nothing, however, is known about the assumed physiological basis.

EEG Studies. In the quest for data about cortical functioning in relation to personality, the electroencephalogram (EEG) offers a tempting field for exploration. The results prior to 1950 were rather discouraging; EEG measures were not only unreliable (Hadley, 1940) but also seemed unrelated to personality. There were even arguments among the experts as to whether a given record was "abnormal" or not.

In recent years more positive results have been forthcoming. Mundy-Castle (1955) reports that the resting alpha rhythm correlates +.46 with ratings on temperament. People with high alpha frequency (cycles per second) get ratings higher on "primary functioning"—they are more likely to be considered impulsive and lacking in control. Subjects whose alpha frequencies are lower get ratings on the deliberate, cautious, inhibited side. Shipton and Walter (1957) and Werre (1957) both report that Ss with different kinds of EEG responses show different overt behavior, but the data on the personality side are quite vague. Ulett and others (1953) say they can pick out anxiety-prone air-crew members by measuring the response of the EEG to a flickering stimulus. Perhaps this indicates that the strong ego (resistant to modification by environmental pressure) rests on a cortex which resists interference with its normal rhythm. Since their finding has not been duplicated, it should not receive extended interpretation.

McAdam and Orme (1954) used an interview technique to estimate personality attributes, and related these to various features of the EEG. They also applied a group Rorschach device. Their chief findings were that extraversion seems to go with high-frequency EEG patterns, while introverts were more likely to show a preponderance of slower rhythms (alpha pattern). As would be expected, given this finding, they also got a positive correlation (+.41) of neuroticism on the Rorschach with per cent alpha; this is expected because introversion and neuroticism are generally correlated.

Somewhat similar findings are reported by Saul, Davis, and Davis (1949). They first classified their EEG records as relatively slow or fast waves, and as relatively regular or irregular. Then they sought for personality attributes common to these patterns. "Passive" personalities were found to fall mostly in the slow-regular group, and fairly aggressive, masculine women in a fast group. Demanding, hostile women patients showed a variable or mixed pattern. The classifications held up moderately well with a new group of patients, although the authors imply some disappointment in this connection.

Since alpha is the typical rhythm of the resting brain, which almost everyone develops when completely relaxed, and faster wave patterns develop when external stimulation is introduced, the above findings probaby indicate typical orientation or scanning patterns. The active, extraverted person will be very responsive to even slight external stimuli, and hence will show many fast waves. The quiet, passive, introverted person will withdraw his attention easily from external matters, and hence will show the slow alpha pattern. It is not clear that this statement is appropriate to Mundy-Castle's data, but it seems to fit the other studies cited.

Preferential patterns in scanning may also help to account for the somewhat confused data on ANS functioning and personality, cited in preceding pages. If we are correct in suggesting that some individuals scan more intensively from interoceptive inputs, it may follow that these individuals are more affected by ANS responses than the person who scans more the external inputs (vision and hearing). A logical deduction would be that a person acquires a self-image which includes attributes such as "highly emotional, easily upset" only if he (1) has strong ANS reactivity, and (2) scans the afferent impulses resulting from these visceral responses.

At present the evidence on this point is extremely sketchy. We call attention only to a study by Mandler and Kremen (1958), in which data were gathered on loss of efficiency in complex mental activity when ANS responses occurred. They found no correlation between extent of ANS response (measured instrumentally) and interference with thinking; but they did obtain a significant correlation between *awareness* of visceral response and loss of efficiency. "It appears," they say, "that interference is more a function of perceived rather than of actually present autonomic discharge" [p. 395]. Relations between ANS functioning and personality thus may be indirect, by way of perception, rather than direct.

THE ENDOCRINE GLANDS

Another prolific source of theorizing about personality lies in the rapidly expanding science of endocrinology. The study of persons suffering from abnormal glandular conditions provides conclusive proof that the hormones have an impact upon personality. From this finding, some popularizers have evolved elaborate and often highly imaginative theories in which the normal personality is also a product of glandular secretions.

Among those who have exaggerated the importance of endocrine glands in the determination of personality is Louis Berman. In two books, *The Glands Regulating Personality* (1928) and *New Creations in Human Beings* (1938), he has made claims for endocrinology far beyond any reasonable factual basis. With almost no evidence, he argues that "the neurotic and the deteriorated, the insane and the criminal" are victims of glandular derangements and can be cured by glandular therapy; he speaks of the "profound control of the entire process of maturation of the personality" which can be attained through endocrine measures. Quite in contrast is the sober conclusion of Hoskins: "Before psychology, sociology and criminology can be convincingly rewritten as merely special aspects of endocrinology, many more facts than are now available will have to be collected and integrated." [8]

Studies of the relationships between endocrine function and personality have taken several forms. The earliest was the clinical observation of individuals with glandular insufficiency. Later came studies of persons from whom glands had to be removed for medical reasons. More recently we have had

[8] Hoskins (1941), p. 348.

experimental studies in which hormones are administered under controlled
conditions and the effects recorded; and in animals, experimental removal
of glands when no disease process is apparent. Thus we get increasingly
precise evidence about the nature of the consequences to be expected when
either a deficit or a surplus of a given hormone exists.

Unfortunately, these studies have not led to any clear pattern of effects on
personality. The situation is complicated and confused. As Cleghorn (1952)
has commented, "We cannot isolate the influence of changes in the internal
chemical environment from genetic endowment and previous experience."
To date, therefore, we have mostly suggestive and somewhat vague statements about possible relationships. The amount of firm knowledge in the area
is quite small. The following comments are thus necessarily tentative.

The Thyroid. One of the simplest and most carefully studied of the
endocrine glands is the thyroid. Located near the larynx, it is more accessible to investigation than are the others; it also, in many instances, manifests
abnormality by an obvious swelling.

The one basic function of thyroxin, the thyroid hormone, is to regulate
oxygen consumption and, hence, energy output. The basal metabolic rate,
while not solely determined by the thyroid, is ordinarily considered an excellent index of the production of thyroxin. Persons suffering from hypothyroidism (subnormal production of the hormone) thus are characterized by sluggishness, inertia, and dullness. In children the condition is
associated with a marked drop in intelligence; glandular therapy thus can
cure some—but by no means all—cases of subnormal IQ.

On the personality side, hypothyroids are likely to be lethargic and unresponsive, but sometimes they show a truculent irritability. Some observers
have described them as depressed, dissatisfied, and distrustful—a picture
reminiscent of Kretschmer's schizoid temperament. In line with this is the
report that some cases of schizophrenia—though not very many—show decided improvement as a result of thyroid medication.

On the hyperthyroid side (cases of excessive hormone production), we
find the symptoms to be increased nervous tension, excitement, and anxiety.
The reactivity of the autonomic nervous system is exaggerated. The patient
is characteristically jumpy, overactive, and restless.

The symptoms of the hyperthyroid patient seem to be directly related
to energy level, and may be presumed to be an immediate outcome of the
excessive glandular secretion. In the case of hypothyroidism, however, many
clinicians suspect that the personality changes are, in part, products of learning and social influence. The individual is aware of and resents his sluggishness; thus he may occasionally flare up, displacing his hostility onto others.
That he would feel depressed and dissatisfied, in view of his handicap, is also
easily understood without referring to hormonal influences as such.

Various students have tried to tie up these clinical findings with observations of normal people. Typical is the report of Dispensa (1938), who correlated basal metabolic rate with scores on the Bernreuter and Humm-Wadsworth personality inventories. In no case was there a significant relationship obtained. The same conclusion is justified by numbers of other investigations. Intelligence is also unrelated to metabolic rate, within normal populations. Thus we are forced to reject the notion that normal variations in activity, energy level, nervousness, or intelligence should be traced to individual differences in thyroid function.

The Adrenals. The adrenal glands, located over the kidneys, have two functional portions, the cortex and the medulla. There are several important hormones secreted by this gland, epinephrine and nor-epinephrine from the medulla, and perhaps a number of others from the cortex.

The Adrenal Cortex. The complexity of the interrelationships of the adrenal cortex with various other functions is suggested by Figure 16.3. Actually, this diagram is oversimplified too, in that it does not show the involvement of the ANS. It should be apparent, nonetheless, that the adrenal cortical hormones,

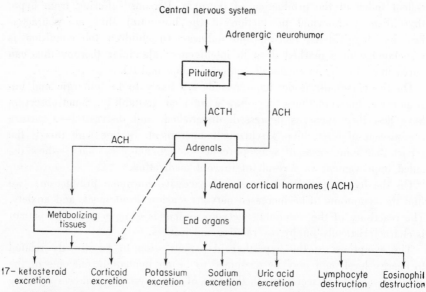

PITUITARY–ADRENAL MECHANISM

Fig. 16.3 Schema showing pituitary-adrenal response system. Adrenocorticotrophin (ACTH) stimulates the adrenal cortex to synthesize and release adrenal cortical hormones (ACH). Cortical steroid hormones exert negative feedback to control the ACTH release. ACH are metabolized and act upon target organs to modify the amounts of excreted urinary substances and blood-cell levels listed at the bottom of the figure. End organs are tissues of the body, the metabolism of which is affected by adrenal steroids. These include the lymphatic system, kidney, muscle, and brain. (Reprinted by permission from Pincus and Hoagland, *Amer. J. Psychiat.*, 1950, **106**, p. 644.)

which are not yet firmly identified and are not subject to direct measurement at this time, have far-reaching significance for bodily activities.

The chief significance of the adrenal cortical hormones for personality—so far as we know it today—lies in the emergency or stress reaction. While epinephrine (see below) has been known for a long time to be a glandular component of the emergency "fight or flight" pattern, the role of the adrenal cortex has been discovered more recently. As Hoagland (1952) commented, the technical problems were great. The pituitary releases adrenocorticotrophic hormone (ACTH), which acts upon the adrenal cortex to produce at least 15 steroid substances. Hoagland has used mostly a quantitative measure of the 17-ketosteroids as an index of this phase of stress response. His work indicates that normal persons show a decided increase in these steroids when under cold stress, when taking test flights in an airplane, and when under failure frustration and stress. Schizophrenics give steroid values in the normal range when relaxed (a little above control subjects) but they fail to respond to stress with an increase in steroid output. Hoagland thinks this may be due to the fact that their hormone output is unnaturally elevated (in terms of glandular capacity) all the time, hence there is no reserve capacity for stress situations. This, he thinks, may account for the schizophrenic's inability to deal with life's problems.

Within the normal range of personalities, Gerard and Phillips (1953) have shown that persons of high status (on an index of educational and occupational achievement) show less adrenocortical response to stress than do persons of low status. Since other studies of the same group of subjects showed that the high-status group had fewer emotional disturbances and more "ego strength," they concluded that there was some functional connection between adrenocortical function and these personality aspects. Unfortunately, as is almost always true with studies of this sort, we cannot tell which is cause and which is effect. If the high-status persons are more sure of themselves, and undisturbed by laboratory test situations, they may experience less stress and show lower hormone activity. On the other hand, the excessive response of the low-status group may have been a factor preventing them from achieving more highly. (Strong bodily response to emotion may interfere with efficient adjustment.)

Epinephrine and Nor-epinephrine. It appears that the resting adrenal medulla secretes nor-epinephrine, but upon appearance of an emergency (fear or anger) or stress stimulus, epinephrine is secreted. The physiological response to epinephrine (sometimes called adrenalin) is very similar to that elicited by stimulation of the sympathetic nervous system, and it is usually found that both the hormonal and the neural components are involved in a given emotional response. The epinephrine reaction includes a rise in blood pressure, pulse rate, and cardiac output, with a decreased peripheral vascular resistance. Nor-epinephrine also gives a rise in blood pressure (but without increase in heart rate or heart output) as a result of an increase in peripheral resistance.

Since these patterns had been found to differentiate certain groups of mental disease patients, Funkenstein et al. (1957) decided to utilize them in an intensive study of bodily reaction correlated with personality variables. Their concern was with two aspects of visceral reactivity: (1) the immediate response to a frustrating situation; and (2) the changing response pattern as the subject tried, on repeated occasions, to master the frustration. Two kinds of stress situations were employed: one, arithmetic problems of considerable difficulty, with heckling by the experimenter; the other, a "delayed speech feedback" or sonic confuser apparatus, in which the individual hears his own spoken voice with a delay of about 0.2 second. This apparatus, which seems harmless, produces severe upset in virtually every subject.

In brief, the findings were as follows: First, the subjects (college men) reacted in ways quite similar to those reported by their roommates for non-laboratory situations; second, the physiological reactions could typically be grouped into patterns; and third, the circulatory responses were consistently associated with broad personality trends. Our interest, of course, is in this last category of results.

Most striking was the fact that some personality estimates correlated well with the initial or emergency response to frustration, whereas others correlated well with improvement over repeated exposures. Table 16.2 shows the pattern of correlations. The groups involved are as follows: for the immediate stress reaction, Ss could be classified on the basis of interview data as those expressing mostly anger directed outward, at the experiment or experimenter; those directing anger inward, at the self; and those experiencing anxiety without anger. The anger-out group consistently showed the physiological pattern associated with nor-epinephrine; the other two groups, equally consistently, showed the epinephrine pattern. For the repeated stress situation, Ss were classified as follows: mastery (e.g., changing from anger to no emotion and showing decrease of physiological response); delayed mastery (e.g., changing from anxiety to anger-out to no emotion); unchanged (those showing no improvement in three experiments); and deteriorate (those whose emotional disturbance increased in successive trials, with corresponding increase in physiological disturbance).[9]

As Table 16.2 indicates, the reaction of the individual to an immediate stress (emergency phase) is significantly related to such aspects of personality as his self-image, his perception of his parents, his punitive and aggressive fantasies on TAT, perceived social discrepancy, etc. None of these measures

[9] It seems unfortunate that no groups were set up based exclusively on physiological responses. All comparisons were based on the above categories, which used verbal responses as criteria. However, it will be noted that the results are consistent; this suggests that the categorization used was appropriate.

is significantly related to the development of mastery of stress over time. Mastery of stress, on the other hand, is significantly associated with a measure of personality integration, with perceptions of other people, and with "assessment of reality." Let us break down some of these a little more specifically.

The anger-out group had a low intensity of physiological response, with evidence of secretion of nor-epinephrine. Anger-in subjects had a higher intensity of response, with evidence of epinephrine secretion. Severe-anxiety sub-

Table 16.2

Differences in Physiological Stress Reactions and Personality Variables

	Reactions to immediate stress			Reactions to repeated stress			
	Anger out	Anger in	Anxiety	Mastery	Delayed mastery	Un- changed	Deteri- orate
Internal concept of self (best minus worse)	High	Low	Low	*	*	*	*
Perception of parents (authority)	Father	Father	Mother	*	*	*	*
Fantasies of aggression	Low	High	Medium	*	*	*	*
Interpersonal relations (agreement of self-image with assumed rating by others)	*	*	*	Medium	High	Medium	Low
Assessment of reality (description of own behavior)	*	*	*	High	High	Low	Low
Integration of personality: Positive emotions	*	*	*	Medium	Mixed	High	Low
Negative emotions	*	*	*	Medium	Mixed	Low	High

* No significant differences reported (or an occasional significant ratio not supported by other related comparisons).

SOURCE: Funkenstein et al. (1957). The comparisons summarized here are taken from a variety of tables in the original.

jects were like anger-in, but more extreme. Some Ss showed no particular upset in the experiment, particularly in the later stages, and were scored "no emotion."

Anger-in and anxiety cases involve the presence of conflict and inhibitory impulses, whereas the anger-out group reacts in a more primitive fashion. On the Brownfain test of "stability" of self-image (cf. page 193) the anger-out group showed a wide difference between "best" and "worst" selves, whereas the others showed little difference (presumably reflecting self-criticism). The groups reporting anger perceived the father as the source of authority; for anxiety, the mother was more authoritative. Some comments on the role of the parent in socializing the child's emotions will be offered in Chapter 17.

In terms of ability to master stresses when repeated, the significant differences run as follows: the delayed mastery group showed high insight (agreement of self-rating with assumed rating by others, high) whereas the group getting worse with repetition showed low insight; the two mastery groups gave realistic descriptions of their own stress behavior; and in terms of balance of positive and negative emotions, the unchanged group showed a surplus of positive, the deteriorate group of negative emotions. We may infer that ego strength was lowest in the deteriorate group (perceived themselves as failing to master stresses), with the mastery and unchanged groups not clearly different.

There are many other aspects of the Funkenstein research which would merit exploration if space permitted. The major conclusion to be derived from it is that both immediate stress response and delayed mastery of physiological reactions to stress have personality correlates; these are different, but fall into meaningful patterns.

The Gonads. Biologically, all human beings are somewhat bisexual. The embryonic sex structures of male and female embryos are virtually indistinguishable, and it is not especially uncommon to find some male hormone produced by adult ovaries and some female hormone production in adult males. There are numerous lines of evidence which indicate that at least a few "male" and "female" personality traits are related to the balance existing between these male and female hormones in the blood stream.

The effects of castrating males are well known—at least, in the animal kingdom. Castrated horses, bulls, and hogs are more docile, less aggressive, and less active than their unoperated fellows. Studies of castrated human males seem to agree that there is a parallel reduction in energy level and emotional responsiveness. Many observers, however, report a certain cold intensity of emotion, particularly hate, which leads to premeditated violence under suitable conditions. Much of this, one hazards, may be due to resentment for the handicap and denial of a normal love life, displaced onto any person who is perceived as a source of frustration.

In animals, hyperactivity of the male sex glands leads to an increase in sex drive and to somewhat increased dominance. After roosters have formed a "pecking order," injection of a submissive cock with male hormone will cause him to move up in the hierarchy. Some personality effects have been reported from injections of human beings with male hormone, but the results are confusing. Benedetti (1957) warns us that hormonal injections may have diametrically opposite effects in different persons; there may be an interaction either with other glands or with the preexisting psychological equilibrium.

Early and Late Maturation. Nature gives us an opportunity to study differences related to male sex hormone. Some boys mature early in sexual hormone production, whereas others are delayed. There is evidence that this has some impact on personality. We all know, of course, that at a certain age boys begin to perceive girls as attractive instead of annoying. There are also changes in other interests, and in behavior, as well as change in voice, and growth of pubic hair.

Are the changes in personality which appear at this time due primarily to endocrine factors or to social stimulation? Jones (1957) offers arguments to favor the latter view. In a longitudinal study, a number of boys twelve to seventeen years old were followed up when about thirty-three years of age. Some of the boys had been early in sexual and physical maturing, whereas others were late in maturing. Observations of them as adolescents indicated the following differences: "Early-maturing boys were . . . more relaxed, poised and matter-of-fact. Consistent differences in other characteristics, such as interest in the opposite sex and 'good-naturedness,' were obtained over nine semesters of observation. Late-maturing boys were described as more expressive, active, talkative, eager, attention-getting" [p. 127].

The differences, in subdued form, were still present at age thirty-three. On adult personality tests the "early maturers" made significantly higher scores on desire to make a good impression, on responsibility, and on "socialization," lower scores on impulsivity. On Edwards's PPS they earned high scores for need dominance, low for need succorance. Jones believes that these differences were at least in part due to the fact that the early maturers were treated as adults more readily and at a younger age; they were allowed to take on responsibility with less supervision. The late maturers, on the other hand, continued to be treated as children, although chronologically they were as old as the other group. Some evidence was obtained of frustration and damage to self-image in the late-maturing group.

Somewhat similar results are reported by Smith and Lebo (1956). They compared boys twelve to fifteen, using alternately chronological age and maturity as indicated by growth of pubic hair. The latter index correlated well with maturity as shown by reports of activities engaged in, while CA correlated poorly. On the other hand, attitudes toward girls and toward parents seemed related to CA, not to sexual maturity. Using a more precise measure of sex hormone excreted in the urine, Sollenberger (1940) also found maturity of interest going with increased hormonal output.

Benedek and Rubenstein (1939) have shown an interesting parallel between the ovarian hormone cycle and emotional attitudes. Independently one of these investigators studied vaginal smears from a group of women patients who were being psychoanalyzed by the other. It was shown that, when the glands were producing a surplus of follicular hormone, the emotions were directed outward and there was a heightened interest in social contacts, especially with men; when progestin was the chief hormone produced, the psychic orientation was inward and personal. At the transition there was likely to be some flightiness and irritability. Although this is a long way from proving that feminine extraverts and introverts are determined by permanent excesses of one or the other hormone, it is suggestive of what future researches may bring forth.

Summary on Endocrines and Personality. Such studies as those cited in the preceding pages leave little doubt that endocrine functions and personality traits are interrelated; however, the experts caution us against assuming that a specific personality trait is related to a specific endocrine product. Cleghorn (1952) notes that "there is little, if any, specificity of reaction in the abnormality which occurs" from endocrine deviations. He further states that "the same disease state or hormonal agent may produce different disturbances in different individuals, e.g., ACTH may produce mania or depression" [p. 270]. As we have suggested in connection with the ANS, each person may develop his own specific response pattern. The outcome of a glandular change, then, will vary according to the pattern upon which it is imposed.[10]

Further, we must allow ample room for the operation of perceptual variables. A glandular deviation may produce a peculiar personality not because of any physiological function but because the individual perceives himself as peculiar and therefore as abnormal. Similarly the effect of social perception must not be ignored. If others perceive a boy as mature (as suggested by Jones, above), he is likely to behave accordingly—what we called the "looking-glass" effect. Because of these and similar variables, few endocrinologists (or psychologists) would care to assert that effects of glandular conditions on personality follow any simple pattern.

---

[10] This conclusion is reached also by Marzi and Teodori (1955), who show that the psychological disturbances associated with endocrine abnormalities often seem to vary depending on the personality prior to the onset of physical symptoms. They also note that correction of a hormonal condition may not lead to modification of a personality deviation, even though the evidence indicates that the glandular problem occurred first. Perhaps perceptual and response patterns which were adjustive for the endocrine pathology persist after the need for them has disappeared.

BIOCHEMICAL INDIVIDUALITY

Most of our discussion, above, of endocrine and biochemical effects on personality has assumed that we need consider only universal, general relationships; the usual investigation has sought for evidence that when *x* occurs on the biochemical level, *y* occurs on the psychological plane. We can hardly work without some such assumption. But an eminent biochemist, Roger J. Williams, has suggested that every individual is in some respects unique with respect to his biochemistry. This raises the alarming possibility that a chemical change which often produces effect *y* may on occasion fail to do so because of the unique make-up of the person affected (see also Kallman on heredity, cited on page 371).

In a way, Williams is adopting the same position taken by psychologists who assume that everyone is a little maladjusted. He states that *"practically every human being is a deviate in some respects."* [11] He shows, for example, that in a group of ten "normal" young men, one was consistently below the acceptable level on blood sugar, another high on blood uric acid, and a third always showed serum amylase values below the normal range. A fourth was uniformly high on alkaline phosphatase, and a fifth on acetylcholinesterase. Some showed high variability from day to day, others very little. These data support a hypothesis of biochemical individuality, just as we have argued earlier that psychological data justify the conclusion that every personality is unique.

The variety of patterns discovered by Williams is shown by Figure 16.4, which summarizes the findings for several young men of an intensive process of bioassay. Figure 16.4a shows the hypothetical normal pattern, if an individual were average in all of his biochemical functions. (It should be noted that only 31 measures were obtained; the actual number of chemical functions which are susceptible of measurement is vastly greater than this.) Figure 16.4b to g shows patterns obtained for six of the subjects. It is obvious that millions of patterns, each different, can be obtained using only these 31 measures. It thus appears that Williams has provided us with a biological base for the concept of the unique personality with which psychologists have so often been concerned.

Williams develops his data in such a way as to show that each person may have unique glandular functioning, and unique nutritional needs. It seems that what constitutes an adequate diet for some people is by no means satisfactory for others. Deficiencies and drive states may thus arise in persons who are apparently receiving adequate supplies. This does not support a conclusion that maladjustments and breakdowns can be attributed to these

[11] Williams (1956), p. 3; italics in original. The reference, of course, is to being a deviate in some biochemical dimension.

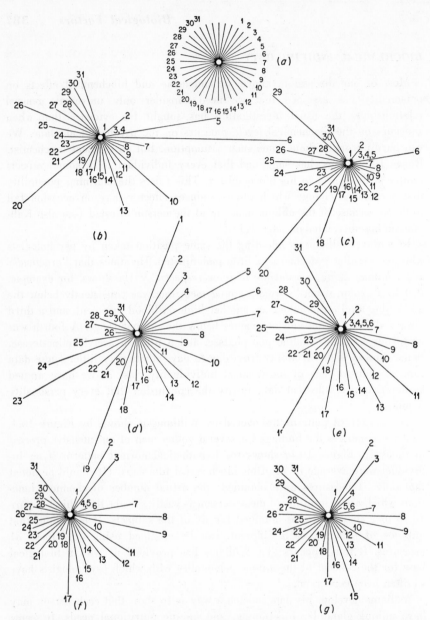

Fig. 16.4 Unique biochemical patterns: (*a*) hypothetical normal individual; (*b*)–(*g*) obtained patterns. Variables tested are taste sensitivity (1, creatinine; 2, sucrose; 3, KCl; 4, NaCl; 5, HCl), salivary constituents (6, uric acid; 7, glucose; 8, leucine; 9, valine; 10, citrulline; 11, alanine; 12, lysine; 13, taurine; 14, glycine; 15, serine; 16, glutamic acid; 17, aspartic acid), and urinary constituents (18, citrate; 19, base rf. 28; 20, acid rf. 32; 21, gonadotropin; 22, pH; 23, pigment/creatinine; 24, chloride/creatinine; 25, hippuric acid/creatinine; 26, creatinine; 27, taurine; 28, glycine; 29, serine; 30, citrulline; 31, alanine). (From Williams, 1958, Figs. 1–13, pp. 6–7; reprinted by permission of author and publishers.)

deficiencies, but it opens up interesting vistas for further research. Perhaps, in the long run, we shall find that the differential sensitivity which causes one boy to react badly to a family stress, while his brother is unaffected, stems from biochemical differences.

The major contribution of Williams's work to psychology lies in his systematic undermining of the concept of the average man. There is no such thing, he points out, as the "typical individual." As Figure 16.4 shows, no one of his subjects shows a pattern of biochemistry even faintly resembling the hypothetical normal (*a*). Some individuals show uniformity within a cluster of measures (for example, *c*, measures 7-17) but other persons do not reveal clustering of these measures. Only two persons have similar patterns (*f* and *g*); these happen to be identical twins. (This is one of the instances Williams cites to support his stress on heredity.)

The simple fact—well known to psychologists—is that too much emphasis has been placed on the norm or average. The early psychologists studied general laws of perception, but in recent years we have found important differences in perceptual style (Chapter 7). More recently there has been a great deal published on general laws of learning, but the experiments on selective learning show that the individual has his own variations in the way he obeys these general "laws." Similarly, some treatments of motivation (Chapters 13 and 14) tend to stress uniformities, whereas an awareness of the diversity of human goals (Chapter 15) leads us to a recognition of the individuality of motivation. It behooves students of personality, therefore, to spend less time thinking about the stages of psychosexual development and more about variations in these sequences, less time on uniformity of perceiving, more on the person's distinctive way of perceiving. In later chapters we shall note the coercive effect of culture in making people more alike. Just now it is appropriate to observe that biology provides a base for uniqueness in that people are differently equipped to select and reject items from this cultural environment.

EXTERNALLY IMPOSED BIOLOGICAL CONDITIONS

Most of the foregoing comments on biological factors in personality determination have related to mechanisms, presumably inherited, which function in a deviant manner and seem involved in related personality deviations. This emphasis was intentional, in that we were looking for possible variables which might support the conclusions on heredity presented at the very beginning of the chapter. Obviously, heredity may influence ANS, CNS, glands, and other biochemical functions.

We have found it important to note, however, in several connections that these relations may be reciprocal. Not only do the glands influence personality; established personality patterns affect glandular function. The same holds for other biological variables.

Before concluding this chapter it seems appropriate to pay some attention to variables, essentially biological in character, which are not hereditary. The bodily mechanism may be affected by illness, by hunger (both as to calories and as to specific chemicals), by drugs, etc. It is a tribute to the stability of the personality that it is unmodified by minor variations of this type. However, prolonged biological stress imposed by the environment can clearly bring about personality modifications.

Prolonged Hunger and Personality. Evidence of personality breakdown has been reported for observations of famine victims, inmates of concentration camps, and other persons forcibly subjected to semistarvation for considerable periods of time. It is difficult, however, to get objective data on the nature of these changes. The extensive studies of Keys, Brozek, and collaborators (1950) are therefore particularly interesting. In this series of investigations, data were collected on 36 young men, conscientious objectors during World War II, who received a semistarvation diet for 24 weeks and lost about 25 per cent of their normal body weight.

Diaries kept by the men, ratings by observers, and objective tests indi-

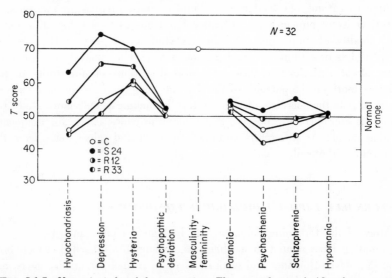

Fig. 16.5 Neurosis induced by starvation. The control record (C) shows average MMPI profile for 20 young men prior to the experiment; S24, profile after 24 weeks of semistarvation, weight loss 25 per cent; R12, after 12 weeks of rehabilitation diet; R33, after 33 weeks of rehabilitation. For S24, note high scores on hypochondriasis, depression, and hysteria, the "neurotic triad," with virtually no change in paranoia or schizophrenia scores. Note also close return of R33 to C profile. (From Keys et al., 1950, by permission of University of Minnesota Press.)

cated that trait changes of great magnitude accompanied the body changes. Figure 16.5 shows the changes in mean profile on MMPI after twenty-four weeks of the inadequate diet, and again after thirty-three weeks of a rehabilitation diet. There is a sharp elevation of the "neurotic triad," hysteria, hypochondriasis, and depression, in the profile taken after twenty-four weeks of hunger. Item analysis revealed that this shift could not be attributed to the reports of symptoms such as weakness, fatigue, and dizziness, which would be directly attributable to the starvation.

The extent of the changes in motivational pattern, in fantasy life, and in other aspects of personality can be judged from some of the following excerpts from Brozek (1953), describing one of the subjects in the semistarvation experiment: "He resented the hold, the compelling nature of his deprivation and struggled to deny the sway which so purely 'animal' a drive could exert over his life. Yet he was inevitably drawn toward food and discussions of food. . . . About this time his interests had undergo(ne?) a radical change. The egocentric effects of the semistarvation, added to a new realization of the importance of personal security, led to dropping of all relief study and training" [p. 114]. The subject spoke of his girl friend's weekend visit as a "considerable strain" (all of his sexual motivation had disappeared) ; when he thumbed through magazines, "pictures of food were most appealing" (vigilance) ; he experienced food dreams and felt guilty when he dreamed of eating! The analogy to the sexual obsessions of some young men is almost startling!

Such evidence tends to support the view of Brozek that the starvation experience, involving as it does prolonged frustration of a basic drive (disturbance of an essential constancy, blocking of approved pathways for restoring it) led to a true neurosis. Although the symptoms disappeared after a long period of dietary rehabilitation, it seems entirely possible that the changes would have proved irreversible had the hunger continued for a longer period.

Vitamin Intake. Experimental induction of symptoms of abnormal personality has been reported by Wilder (1952) to be achieved through sharp reduction in vitamin B intake. "With moderate restriction of thiamine," he writes, "the abnormalities came on slowly . . . faculties involving attention, interest, ambition, and sociability were unmistakably affected. . . . With more severe restriction of thiamine mental changes appeared more rapidly and were unmistakable; in some instances explosive episodes, tantrums, furors, and even rages occurred" [p. 534]. These changes disappeared when adequate supplies of vitamin B were added to the diet.

In the case of the conscientious objectors, the starvation was quantitative and the men were acutely conscious of it. They knew quite well what their frustrations were. A vitamin deficiency is another matter. The subjects in

Wilder's research did not know anything was wrong with their diet. Yet they also showed neurotic symptoms. Two interpretations are possible: (1) that a dietary inadequacy like this causes frustration even though the individual cannot be conscious of it; or (2) that such a deficiency causes physical effects, e.g., weakness, inaccuracy, which are frustrating, and the neurotic traits derive indirectly therefore from the diet. Since we know each of these possibilities to be applicable in other instances, we cannot arbitrarily decide which is correct.

Do such studies indicate that explosive, irritable personalities developed because of a chronic vitamin deficiency? A study of the same persons, over time, would be necessary to confirm such a view. That it may be at least a contributing factor is indicated by the following well-known facts: (1) that children are more susceptible to various kinds of dietary deficiencies than adults, i.e., damage results more promptly and may be irreversible; and (2) that daily requirements of vitamins differ, so that an adequate amount for the average person is not necessarily sufficient for some individuals with deviant biochemistry. Hence we must agree that a vitamin deficiency may have an adverse effect on personality development in some children.

Does this indicate that children or adults will be helped to adjust, with respect to personality, by vitamin supplements? The evidence here is not encouraging. Studies in institutions, where conditions can be well controlled, indicate that abnormal personalities do not as a rule benefit from vitamin feeding beyond the minimum required. Where such benefits have been reported, the suspicion often arises that the patient enjoyed the extra attention he was getting during the experiment and so became more genial, more sociable, and more cooperative. There are many pitfalls in this kind of complex personality research.

It should not be assumed that either semistarvation or vitamin deficiency can be treated as an important causal factor with respect to normal differences in personality. Deviations of the extent cited above would be rare in Western countries, although they are deplorably frequent in Asia and Africa (and may very well account for some social problems in those areas). But they do remind us of the close link between "the body" and "the personality," that the two are really one. They also lend some credibility to the notion that at least minimum gratification of basic biological needs is a prerequisite to a personality which is "normal" as we now understand that term.

Tolerance for Physical Stress. The Air Force, looking for men who can stand the physical stresses likely to be encountered in space exploration, has sought data on the personality traits and physical attributes of men who can stand high acceleration stress. One such study, by Silverman et al. (1957) dealt with TAT performances of men who black out at moderate accelerations versus those who can tolerate high acceleration. The group with high stress tolerance gave indications of traits of stubbornness, aggression, and impulsiveness. Those with low stress tolerance seemed more dependent, inhibited, and subject to control by others.

This would seem to indicate that high stress tolerance goes with what we have earlier called the "strong ego." At this point we cannot guess whether this relationship is due to early experience (learning to bear discomfort in order to achieve a goal), or whether it represents an innate physiological factor (sturdy mechanism favors developing self-confidence and other attributes of the strong ego).

Reaction to Drugs. Space does not permit us to analyze the interesting research set off by the discovery that certain drugs mimic the effects of a psychotic personality breakdown—hallucinations, loss of a sense of personal identity, disorientation in space and time, etc. So far these studies have not uncovered anything which seemed to have important implications for the normal, intact, nondrugged personality.

One curious observation deserves mention. In the exploratory work of Abramson et al. (1955) on the effects of LSD-25, one of these drugs, it was necessary to use a placebo (a harmless tablet) with the control group. As a result of suggestion, the members of this group also reported some sensory disturbances and other symptoms. Later the groups were rotated, experimental Ss receiving the placebo and control Ss getting the real drug. When all the reported symptoms were tallied, a rather surprising fact appeared: a person who reported numerous symptoms under LSD also reported a number when receiving the placebo; and a person who reported few symptoms under the drug reported proportionately few with the placebo. The absolute *number* of symptoms increased with LSD; but the ranking of persons in the total group, as to frequency of symptoms, remained relatively constant, so that the correlation of number of symptoms in the two conditions was +.60.

This is probably a sensory or perceptual phenomenon. Each of us has many unconscious processes going on all the time: heartbeat, breathing, digestion, etc. Under special conditions we become aware of these and can describe them. Apparently this sensitivity is a characteristic individual phenomenon; the person gets a sugar pill, and reports 10 kinds of inner sensory effects; if he gets LSD, he reports 25. Another person, less sensitive, may report only 5 with placebo, and 15 with the drug. That this suggestibility has something to do with changing one's personality to fit the environment seems plausible. It may even be related to acquiescent response set and to field-dependent perception. Further work is needed to determine just how it relates to personality formation.

Resistance to Infection. We mention here, for what it is worth, another curious observation. Greenfield et al. (1959) studied patients with infectious mononucleosis, a disease for which there is no known chemotherapy; the patient simply has to rest and recover on his own resources. The authors noted that recovery time ranged from about a week to four or six weeks.

When they gave Barron's ego-strength scale to their patients, they found that persons making a relatively fast recovery—less than twelve days' illness —were significantly higher on ego strength than the slow recovery group.

Such a finding may be another obscure clue to the theory of general organismic superiority of persons with high ego strength. Or it may mean that persons with highly efficient physiological mechanisms get a variety of sensory feedback which fosters the formation of what we have called the strong ego. The authors even suggest that persons who do not accurately perceive their own inner states are handicapped in dealing with illness! One does not see how such percepts would aid in dealing with mononucleosis— but the idea is appealing.

It would seem that such a physiological attribute as ability to deal with infection would not itself be a result of emotional or other psychological factors. Such, however, is not the case. There is every reason to believe that some "infectious" illnesses are due to emotional stress, in the sense that the person would have been able to resist infection but for the interference of stress effects. A striking bit of evidence to support this view is provided by Riess, Spain, and Molomut (1955), who studied ability to heal wounds follow· ing stress. Physical injury was used because it is easier to control than bac· teriological infection. Mice were subjected to convulsive seizures by auditory stimulation, then tested for wound repair. Healing was slower in the seizure animals than in control mice not subjected to stress. This could lead us to theorize that among Greenfield's mononucleosis patients, those who had suf· fered severe emotional trauma had lost the ability to resist infection.

These investigations on externally imposed biological conditions, such as health, drugs, hunger, and injuries, suggest one generalization more than any other. This is that desirable attributes go together: efficient homeostasis seems to go with what we have called "ego strength." Poor tolerance for stress goes with manifestations of neuroticism and emotional maladjustment. This is quite plausible. However, we know more about the functional unity of the psychological variables in this equation than we do about the physio-logical side. As we obtain more information about the extent to which the various biological indexes of adaptation to stress correlate with one an-other, we shall be on firmer ground in generalizing about the biological deter-minants of personality.

BIOLOGY AND PERSONALITY

The nature of the intricate interrelationship between the biological and the phenomenal level of data regarding personality is only partially understood. It is at present generally conceived as a two-way relationship in which changes at either level modify processes on the other. For example, it is easy to demonstrate that with maturation of the sex glands, organisms of the opposite sex are perceived as more attractive than before. Here a biochemical change induces a phenomenal change. But conversely, if a person sees some object approaching, and suddenly recognizes it as a dangerous animal, his phenomenal field changes immediately, and a vast array of physiological changes follow rapidly. (Selye's general adaptation syndrome includes hormonal, visceral, and muscular components, which can readily be elicited by a purely emotional experience.)

It follows from this that causation is not a unidirectional process as regards the determination of observable personality traits. Physiological variables, such as subnormal thyroid or supernormal adrenal secretion, may modify perceptions regularly and so bring about expectancies, uniform percepts of self, or of environmental stimuli. Conversely, regular exposure to traumatic stimuli (what Selye calls *stressors*) may induce irreversible changes in the endocrine glands, in the circulatory system, and in some visceral organs such as the stomach.

These facts point to the importance of unifying concepts, such as stress and homeostasis, which cut across the artificial boundary between the "physical" and the "mental." Strictly speaking, we do not care about whether a given event in a person's biography is "physical" or "mental" except when we want to know what variables to manipulate in order to produce the event again. A stressor may be a change within the organism, or it may be an environmental event. All stressors have in common the fact that they disturb some steady state. The corrective and protective activities of the organism follow the principle of homeostasis, but these responses may be primarily on a biological level (metabolic changes, biochemical modifications) or primarily on a psychological level (adaptive habits, defense mechanisms, personality traits).

In a sense it is obvious that all personality has a biological base. But it is more appropriate to think of personality as a biophysical and biosocial unity. The total individual is an organized pattern of biological and psychological mechanisms for maintaining his integrity as a living organism and as a product of social experience.

SUMMARY

The human personality originates within and, for scientific purposes, can never be separated from a biological organism. The innate attributes of this structure obviously will have substantial influence on the inner personality pattern which develops. To some extent the evidence indicates that hereditary attributes are reflected directly in aspects of emotion and energy mobilization: the glands, the ANS, and even some CNS functions may be involved here.

The role of the sex hormones and of the adrenal hormones in determining certain patterns of adjustment has been demonstrated. It is not absolutely clear, however, that these glandular secretion levels are not themselves determined by earlier experiences on a psychological level; in other words, though the role of a biological process is undebatable, its status as an independent variable is not certain. The fact that each individual seems to have a unique biochemical pattern may perhaps give us some biological basis for our frequent assertion that every personality is unique; the absence of correlations between biochemical measures and psychological measures renders the evidence less satisfying than might otherwise be the case.

The body responds to various biological stresses, such as prolonged hunger, vitamin deficiency, acceleration stress, drugs, etc., in its own characteristic fashion. These stress reactions are also correlated with personality variations. In general, persons who deal adequately with stress on the biological level seem to be those who manifest "desirable" attributes on the psychological level. This is both plausible and encouraging, but a great deal more evidence is needed before it can be considered an established fact.

SUGGESTIONS FOR READING

The literature on biological factors in personality has not been collected and evaluated in recent years. *The anatomy of personality*, by Fry and Haggard, argues for a hereditary view of personality, but the evidence cited is open to other interpretations. G. L. Freeman's *Energetics of human behavior* recognizes the role of environment but outlines a good biological basis for personality. Unfortunately, many of his conclusions go beyond his evidence, too. A symposium which deals with biological factors mostly in abnormal personalities is *The biology of mental health and disease*, report of the Twenty-seventh Annual Conference of the Milbank Memorial Fund; some of the articles mention studies of personalities within the normal range. Several chapters of Murphy's *Personality: a biosocial approach to origins and structure* give stimulating comments on biological research relevant to the psychology of personality.

CHAPTER 17

The Family: Childhood

Personality is an interaction product, the resultant of heredity and environment. As we noted in Chapters 5 and 6, the environment puts certain pressures on the organism; perception and learning operate to develop techniques for dealing with the environment, and these techniques become generalized as traits, values, and persistent motives.

The study of personality is thus a constant interweaving of organismic and environmental factors. We have touched on considerations of instinct, glandular conditions, the autonomic nervous system; we have also noted the importance of rewards, trauma, goals, and barriers. The personality of a specific individual is molded by all these factors.

Running through all our discussions of perception and learning, of goals and values, is the implied importance of the social environment; but we have written as if this environment were uniform for all children. This was a compromise imposed by practical necessity; it was impossible to write about the process of personality development in general, and at the same time give recognition to the variations in parental behavior, the range of culture patterns, the differences among authority figures, the economic and social class influences which differ so much and have so great an impact on the growing child. It is now necessary to examine these variable influences.

We have stressed the child's imitation of his parents, his acquisition of pictures of social roles, and his tendency to act out, in later relationships, the emotions first associated with his parents. But not all parents are alike; indeed, parental behavior shows virtually the extreme range which would be implied by our frequent assertion that every personality is unique. Since both father and mother are adult personalities of great complexity, it must be expected that they will act out their parental roles in quite varying fashions. This chapter will explore some of the variations in the ways parents treat the child and consequent effects of such treatment in inducing variations in the child's developing personality. Later chapters will pay attention to the impact of other social variables, such as the school system, economic conditions, etc.

Special Importance of Family Conditions. All schools of psychology are in agreement that the impact of the family on the child's personality is of

397

preeminent importance, even though many experts in this field would object to the specific formulation of the Freudians (see Chapter 14 and pages 106–110). The logic supporting this emphasis on early childhood runs as follows:

1. The child must necessarily acquire expectancies and responses in the family situation. Since his opportunities to observe at this time are severely limited, he will acquire mainly likes and dislikes, stereotypes about people, expectancies of security or of danger, and conditioned emotional responses based on his family milieu.

2. Once these have been acquired, the principle of selective learning will operate. New experiences will be accepted as confirming early beliefs, or rejected as atypical. The so-called "law of primacy" may be interpreted as meaning that if expectancy A has been first acquired, any conflicting expectancy B will be doubly difficult to establish, since A must first be broken up.

Empirical evidence also gives ample support to an emphasis on infancy and early childhood as decisive determinants of personality. In later pages we shall mention such lines of investigation as those of imprinting (fixation of first perceptual experiences) in animals, infantile trauma in animals, separation of human babies from their mothers, and patterns of parental behavior correlated with later observations of the child's personality. All these studies confirm the prediction that the experiences of the first few years (some would say, the first year) mold the personality in such wise that later possibilities for development are severely limited.

Interaction of Organic and Social Factors. In connection with each of these investigations of social factors it is proper to repeat a caution: the organic variables described in the preceding chapter interact with the social influences in the development of any specific personality. Since it would be awkward to keep repeating this warning, we place it here at the beginning of the discussion.

One such basic variable which must be taken into consideration is the emotional response style of the child. As was noted in the preceding chapter, the work of Sheldon gives support to the view that some children are inherently more responsive, more vigorous in their emotional behavior, than others. In line with this, it is interesting to consider the comment by Stoke (1950) based on his observations of young children: "Given parents who reject a child, the response of the child will be determined in considerable part by its own temperament. Vigorous children . . . react aggressively toward those who reject them. Less vigorous, outgoing children may attempt to hide their hurts and simply withdraw from the reality of the situation as far as is compatible with other conditions" [p. 179]. Of course the child's innate tendencies will affect his response to any treatment, not just to rejection. Even at an early age, we must consider not only the family pattern but also the organic attributes of the child.

We do not know much about the inheritance of perceptual styles, but obviously these, if innate, will influence the child's reaction to parental treatment. The child may, for example, transfer his attitudes toward his father to other authority figures; but he may not. The significant variable here probably is perceptual style; if he tends to generalize freely, this transfer will occur; if he tends to accentuate differences, the transfer is less likely.

Personality is a product of interacting heredity and environment. Emphasis in the following pages on the importance of social factors does not justify us in ignoring the innate aspect. It must be remembered at all times that the child is a biological organism and that his biological attributes impose limits on the effectiveness of the social pattern.

STUDIES OF EARLY INFANCY

The psychological theorist is likely to place special stress on the importance of the very first events in the child's life: those of the first few days or weeks. But experimentation on human infants at this age is sharply limited by ethical considerations; damage could be inflicted very easily. Hence it is necessary to use evidence from animal infants in some cases and attempt to extrapolate to human development.

Imprinting. One intriguing phenomenon which has been observed in infant animals of certain species is known as "imprinting." Ethologists (students of animal behavior), such as Lorenz and Tinbergen, have observed this phenomenon particularly in birds emerging from the egg: the first moving object seen acquires a perceptually distinctive character for the young bird, and he will follow it devotedly (cf. Jaynes, 1956). Lorenz, for example, reports that ducklings became quite attached to him, followed him around, and showed distress when prevented from doing so. Hebb [1] comments that "if the eggs of the graylag goose are . . . hatched in an incubator, the young geese attach themselves socially to the species to which they are first exposed on leaving the incubator. *At maturity the courting behavior . . . is directed toward the foster species.* The foster species, also, need not always be another kind of bird, but might be a dog or a man."

The occurrence of such phenomena is not easy to demonstrate in primates and human beings because of the helplessness of the infant. It is at least an interesting speculation that the human infant "imprints" the mother and is thus psychologically ready to develop the close attachment and dependency relationship which so often is observable, and that his later tendency to fall in love with a girl just like mother is based on a similar process.

Infantile Deprivation. Hunt (1941) showed that if infant rats were subjected to fairly severe hunger frustration at weaning time, they would later show more intense hoarding of food pellets than litter-mate controls. This can be interpreted as indicating the formation of a kind of expectancy ("the food

[1] Hebb (1958), p. 124. Reprinted by permission of W. B. Saunders Co.

supply is undependable") such that, when the adult rats were rendered hungry, this expectancy was reactivated and the animals began to hoard when food was available to them. This resembles, of course, the protective homeostatic action described in Chapter 4.

Sensory deprivation in early infancy also produces striking variations in adult behavior. Riesen (1947) studied chimpanzees reared in darkness as compared with normal controls. The normal animal, seeing a new object and getting an electric shock when it approaches him, will quickly learn to avoid it. The chimp reared in darkness, on the other hand, when brought into the light, takes weeks of repetition and many shocks before he becomes capable of utilizing the visual cue to avoid the unpleasant stimulus. In other words, an environment which is lacking in a certain kind of stimulation may seriously handicap the organism when later it encounters such stimuli; and this handicap apparently is never completely eliminated.

Even more startling is the report by Melzack and Scott (1957) on dogs reared in isolation from birth. These dogs, confined in small cages with no objects to explore and no chance to acquire pain expectancies, proved remarkably stupid at learning to avoid pain when released at maturity. For example, the dog would explore a lighted match by putting his nose to the flame; this masochistic behavior was repeated day after day, with no evidence of avoidance conditioning. For the normal dog, one such incident was enough. Similarly, Melzack and Thompson (1956) reared puppies in perceptual and social isolation. When released at maturity, the dogs could not acquire normal social interactions either with other dogs or with human beings.

Many other such experiments could be cited, but these will serve to establish our point. Animals deprived of certain classes of stimulation in infancy are permanently modified as regards their capacity to deal with such stimuli. To the extent that we can generalize from such subjects to human beings, we must conclude that some very fundamental features of personality may be determined (within limits) by opportunity to learn, or by denial of such opportunity. Thus, lack of affectionate handling in infancy may affect the child's expectancies, and his behavior, as regards manifestations of affection in later life. As will be noted later, some evidence supports this prediction.

The Mother as Secondary Reward. Another kind of study which would be difficult to conduct with human beings relates to the sensory attributes of the mother. We have implied in earlier chapters that love of mother may be a secondary reward function; the mother is a source of food for the hungry infant, hence her mere presence acquires positive valence. Thus Dollard and Miller (1950) write: "When the hungry infant is fed, some of the wonderful relaxation responses which it experiences can be conditioned to the stimuli of those persons who are caring for the child. Thereafter the mere appearance of the mother can produce a momentary feeling of well-being" [p. 133]. There is, of course, a considerable discrepancy between the "momentary feeling" they describe and the long-enduring affectionate responses seen in human beings. For rats the secondary reward value of a stimulus associated with a goal does fade rapidly; with the human child and mother this result seems not to follow.

Harlow's Study on Pseudomothers. The oversimplified behavioristic view that love of mother is simply a response to a source of food has been rather thoroughly demolished by some ingenious experiments reported by Harlow (1958). In these investigations infant monkeys were fed on forms vaguely resembling a female adult monkey. One series used a form made of hard wire mesh; the other used a form made of foam rubber covered with terry cloth. The difference in responsiveness to this "pseudomother" figure after a few weeks was astonishing. To the soft pseudomother, the baby monkeys would run for security when frightened, would bring objects as if to show them off, and would show behavior described by the observers as "affectionate." To the hard pseudomother, no such behavior occurred. The absence of this figure caused no distress, and its presence, when the monkey was frightened, brought no apparent security.

These observations lead to the conclusion that love of mother, at the primate level, cannot be identified with a secondary reward value based on feeding. As an absolute minimum Harlow's work indicates that the sensory cues induced by the mother's contact with the child are important factors in the development of positive valence. The work of Brody (1956) on "patterns of mothering" suggests that smooth or rough movements, soft or loud voice, and similar cues provided by the mother also become part of the mother image and play a role in determining how the child perceives his mother. Chodorkoff (1960) has extended and confirmed Brody's research.

In later years the child learns something of social expectancies and objects if his mother doesn't act the way mothers are supposed to behave. But this comes late and is undoubtedly of minor importance. The child's picture of his mother, and the positive or negative valence built into this image, are determined within the first year or two of life. And it is the whole pattern of sensory gratification and equilibrium restoration, experienced by the child in the presence of the mother, which enters into this process. Feeding no doubt is important, but its significance has been grossly exaggerated.

Infantile Deprivation in Humans. Ethical considerations prevent experimentation on human infants by depriving them of light, sound, food, or comfort. Society, however, is ruthless enough in its own way, and so we get experimental deprivation of infants as a result of war, death of the mother, or institutionalization of the infant. We can also observe relative deprivation in the intact family, since some mothers give far less attention and stimulation to the baby than do others.

Major credit goes to Margaret Ribble (1944) and René Spitz (1945) for initiating a series of investigations on the effect of severe psychological deprivation in infancy. Reporting on a study of 600 infants, Ribble asserts that lack of adequate cuddling, stroking, and other close physical contacts with some friendly adult can impose serious handicaps on the growing infant (cf. the animal studies cited above). Some of the infants so deprived, she notes, react with exaggerated negativism, others with exaggerated regression. The negativistic symptoms include refusal to suck, vomiting, breath holding, and constipation. The regressive reaction is often even more alarming: A kind of stupor develops, peripheral circulation is poor, and nutrition is very unsatisfactory. Without a change of diet, this condition can be improved by introducing a foster mother who regularly fondles, strokes, and caresses the child.

A related study is that of Goldfarb (1943, 1944). He compared two groups of adolescents: one group had been orphaned and placed in institutions prior to the age of eighteen months; the other was composed of children who had not been institutionalized until a later age. The early-orphaned group showed marked symptoms of emotional deprivation; as adolescents they were relatively apathetic and immature. They showed expectancies that people would be cold, indifferent, and unloving. It seems plausible to suspect that, once such attitudes are firmly established in the early years, no amount of later emotional security will completely eradicate them. (As will be noted in Chapter 18, some individuals even in marriage seem unable to feel loved and accepted; they probably belong in this category.) Edmiston and Baird (1949) confirm Goldfarb's conclusions in general, if not in all details.

Ribble's point of view has not gone unchallenged. One critic (Orlansky, 1949) has referred to her articles as "hysterical" and says it is impossible to separate her empirical observations from her dogmatic opinions. Pinneau (1950) has taken exception both to her logic and to her empirical data. Dennis (1941) and Dennis and Najarian (1957) have cited observations which at least place in question the accuracy of her predictions as to the consequences for personality of limited mothering in infancy. Orlansky notes that studies of primitive cultures also cast some doubt at least on the generality of Ribble's conclusions, inasmuch as some primitive societies normally seem to provide the kind of care which she considers fatal to the child. Survival of these societies casts some doubt upon the general conclusion.

This is not to suggest that, in general, manifestations of interest and affection are not good for the child. As we shall show later, comparisons of different mothering practices lead to a conclusion not markedly different, except in intensity, from that expressed by Ribble. Mothering is important, but its significance can be exaggerated.

The Critical-period Hypothesis. Ribble was quite emphatic in her view that the drastic effects to be expected from lack of mothering were related to a specific time period. If the child gets a feeling of security for the first year, detrimental consequences are less noticeable. This calls to mind William James's doctrine of the transitory nature of instincts, the view that if an instinct were not exercised at the crucial stage in individual development, it would wither and disappear. The animal studies (e.g., on imprinting) confirm the notion that critical periods exist for some functions, and the studies of infant deprivation indicate that if some functions are not acquired early, they will be acquired with great difficulty or not at all.

The subject of critical periods in human development has been of particular interest to the Freudians. It will be remembered that Freud postulated certain stages of psychosexual development, through focusing on oral, to anal, then phallic, and later genital functions. According to this view, frustration at the oral stage will have certain definitive effects on personality; frustration at the early or late anal stage, other effects, and so on. Although much has been published on this problem, little controlled research can be found. An exception is the work of Goldman-Eisler, who studied early-weaned children and compared them with children weaned at later ages (Goldman, 1948; Goldman-Eisler, 1951). She found evidence for the pessimism, expectancy of deprivation, and other traits predicted by the theory.

A careful analysis of the evidence on critical periods in human infancy has been published by Stendler (1952). Her judgment is that the data favor a critical-period theory. For example, with respect to the dependency of the child on the mother, she observed that such dependency is essential to survival in the early months of life. Later, however, the child characteristically begins efforts to become independent. Frustration of these strivings can readily lead to overdependency, whereas similar treatment at other age levels does not have this effect.

Stendler does not propose that a timetable be set up for the establishment of specified personality traits at definite ages. Not only do children have different hereditary potentialities (cf. Chapter 16) and mature at different rates, but there may be effects deriving from prior learning which interact with the critical period in development. Parents and child-guidance personnel who wish to use this phenomenon in a practical way will thus be required, it appears, to chart the development of the individual child and identify significant stages by behavior sequences rather than by chronological age alone.

STUDIES OF SPECIFIC PARENTAL PRACTICES

It will be more instructive if we turn our attention from general theoretical questions to studies of specific behavior of parents toward their children. Implicit in our treatment of personality development has been the notion that the child acquires percepts, positive and negative valences, habits, and a self-image from his interactions with his environment. This view can be validated only if we can show some consistent relations between parental treatment and child personality.

The best procedure for such investigations would be to observe the parent-child interaction, then wait a year or so and gather data on the child's personality. Longitudinal studies of this kind are being conducted, but the returns are not yet clear enough to interpret. A second method is to gather independently data on the parent's behavior and the child's personality. This technique encounters the difficulty that some of the parental behavior may be determined by the child, not the other way round. A third method, used in early researches (Stagner, 1938; Stagner and Krout, 1940) and still useful within limits, involves asking the child or adolescent to describe how his parents treated him, and correlate these reports with personality data. The obvious weakness here is that we do not get "real" parent behavior, but only the child's view of it, which may be quite misleading.

Patterns of Mothering. A first task, in this frame of reference, is to find the dimensions along which parental behavior differs. A good beginning in this respect is the work of Brody (1956) on *Patterns of Mothering.* She studied very intensively 32 young mothers with their babies, paying particular attention to methods of feeding, cleaning, handling, offering objects to, and speaking to the baby. She found that she could divide the mothers into "types"; one was composed of the mothers who were most sensitive to the infant's needs, most consistent in their treatment, and most attentive. The other groups deviated from this ideal in being insensitive to the child, inconsistent in behavior, overactive, overattentive, or excessively sensitive. (Brody objects to classifying her mothers as "accepting" or "rejecting," because such terms imply more than the behavior she observed.) There were also important differences among the groups in their attitudes toward motherhood, toward methods of child care, and so on.

Brody notes that we cannot identify the affectionate relationship with the mothering relationship. Several mothers were obviously very fond of their babies, yet succeeded in disrupting the normal rhythm of the child's activity by failing to observe or perhaps by lack of understanding. For example, one very affectionate mother "stimulated him almost incessantly and actively prevented him from going to sleep. She fed him, off and on, for over a two-hour period. . . . She shook the rattle in his hand when he lay relaxed, and she repeatedly gave him a teething ring and then immediately withdrew it from his mouth to feed him." [2] It is tempting to speculate that this child will expect such constant stimulation from his later environment.

It might be thought that the activity of feeding the child would be the single component of the mother's activity which would be most important in terms of effects on the child's personality. Brody concurs in this judgment, as regards the behavior of her 32 mothers at most age levels. However, she notes that with the youngest infants (four weeks), it was the activity designated as moving (hugging, rocking, bouncing, standing) which seemed best to identify mothers as belonging to one or another type. This may be plausible in view

[2] Brody (1956), pp. 200–201. Reprinted by permission of International Universities Press.

of the importance ascribed earlier to the child's somesthetic sensations—from muscles, joints, viscera—in molding personality traits. It seems clear (cf. Aldrich and others, 1946) that the application of pleasurable stimulation to the infant's body is an important component of early conditioning. Perhaps the foundations of a broad perceptual pattern which may be characterized as an expectation of pleasure are laid down at this time.

Brody's data do not give us much information about specific effects on the children. To the extent that ratings are available, they seem to indicate that mothers could deviate from an optimal way of treating the child in the direction of doing either too much or too little, and either was likely to be somewhat detrimental.

The Sears Study. Less intensive, but covering much more behavior and more cases, is the study by Sears, Maccoby, and Levin (1957), which deals with child-rearing practices of over three hundred young mothers in the Boston area. Their interview schedule included questions about feeding habits, toilet training, sex and modesty training, restrictions on aggression by the child, handling the child's dependency attitudes, use of physical punishment, and threats to withdraw love. As this list shows, the mother is constantly interacting with the child during his first few years, providing sensory stimuli and also meanings, as he grows older, which will become merged in his perception of her.

A factor analysis of the ratings made by interviewers in the homes led to the conclusion that specific situations, such as feeding or toilet training, had less significance than the mother's personality and attitudes toward the child. Mothers who demanded neat table manners were severe in toilet training and were restrictive with regard to active play in the house. Thus, one concludes, the molding of the child's personality is not limited to one particular biological function (or even stages, as Freud suggested), but depends on the mother's attitudes in general, and upon other concepts of family life. The significant dimensions along which mothers differed one from another were as follows:

1. *Permissiveness-Strictness*. Mothers varied from highly permissive to quite restrictive, and this attitude came out in a wide variety of behaviors. As will be noted later, it played a substantial role in determining certain aspects of the child's personality. Obviously it determined the frequency of frustrations, and conversely, of gratifications, in a number of areas.

2. *General Family Adjustment*. Mothers who perceived themselves as worthwhile, who gave high evaluations of their husbands, and who were satisfied with their current life situations could be said to possess high morale in their mother role. Such a home situation obviously gives the child a chance to develop generalized images of adult human beings as happy, secure, and friendly; a home with low mother morale presents images quite different from these. As other studies show, many of the child's traits can be related quite directly to this aspect of home life.

3. *Warmth of Mother-child Relationship.* A mother may care for her child with statistical precision, but without communicating affection and warmth. The warm-cold dimension was revealed in time spent playing with the child, affectionate interactions with him, use of praise, etc. This factor seems to have particular importance in determining how the child will perceive other actions of the mother; e.g., use of physical punishment by a "warm" mother may have desirable social effects, whereas such punishment by a "cold" mother leads to antisocial aggression.

Parents of Problem Children. The Sears data dealt exclusively with parents of "normal" children—none of them had manifest problems. Would the same factors show up in a study of parents of problem children? Becker et al. (1959) studied 57 families, about half of whom had children being treated at a psychological clinic. The data collected were quite different from those obtained in the Sears study. Consequently, it is interesting to note that some factors are clearly identical in the two investigations. Becker's factors are: (1) general family maladjustment, similar to Sears's factor *B*; (2) a factor defined mainly by the difference between clinic and nonclinic families; (3) a parent personality factor, mainly ego strength versus emotionality; (4) protectiveness toward the child; (5) democracy in family policy; and (6) permissiveness. Of these, (4) is somewhat similar to Sears's factor *C*, and (6) close to Sears's factor *A*. Factor (5) contains items which in the Sears data were distributed among the three main factors. Thus there seems fair agreement on the importance of these patterns.

The Becker study merits mention on another ground. Most research in this area has concentrated on mothers. (The Sears data are based entirely on mothers' reports; the behavior of the father is represented only as the mother observed it.) The Becker investigation indicates that the behavior of the father may be of substantial importance in determining whether or not the child becomes a behavior problem; on factor (2), there were significant loadings on *four* aspects of father's behavior and *none* for the mother. It seems safe to conclude that psychologists must put more emphasis on fathers as influences on the child's personality.

Effects of These Variations. What are the effects of variations in these aspects of parental treatment of the child? We do not as yet have follow-up studies which will give satisfactory answers. In the Sears data a number of relationships are reported, of which we shall mention only a few.

1. *Strictness and Warmth.* If we take strictness in toilet training (which was a good index of factor *A*, the permissive-strict dimension) as an example, we find that the child's emotional upset during training is directly related to severity. Only 11 per cent of those receiving "slight pressure" showed disturbance, whereas 55 per cent of those receiving "quite severe pressure" were upset. A cross-comparison with the dimension of warmth of affection, however, revealed that severity is upsetting primarily where the mother is

relatively cold toward the child. Thus it is not a single aspect, but a complex of aspects, which determines how the child will respond.

Feeding problems are generally agreed to be indicative of a personality getting off to a poor start. In the Sears data, the two items most closely related to occurrence of feeding problems were: mother's warmth to child, and use of physical punishment. As warmth of affection *decreased*, feeding problems became more frequent; and as physical punishment was used more often, feeding problems occurred more often.

Extensive data on permissiveness were gathered by Watson (1957) for a large number of children. He found that permissive child-rearing practices were associated with better socialization and cooperation, more friendly feelings toward other children, higher degrees of initiative and independence. Permissive practices resulted in children who had less hostility and showed more spontaneity, originality, and creativity. These desirable consequences are generally described also by Mummery (1954) who suggests that permissive rearing helps develop "assertiveness" and leadership qualities. We can judge that giving the child some freedom to try out his own judgment and make decisions without parental controls helps strengthen the ego; we may suspect, from some of Mummery's comments, that such children also may present some problems to the parents by being too self-assertive. Children need some controls, some awareness of limits to permissible behavior; without these controls, children become egocentric and socially thoughtless.

2. *Rejection and Dependency.* Dependency as a trait in small children (clinging to mother, crying when she leaves, demanding attention) is an important facet of personality. The Sears data indicate that if the mother seems to reject the child, he is more dependent than if he feels accepted. Punishment for aggression toward the parents produces more dependency, although punishment in general is not related. The data thus do not seem to support the conclusion by Stendler (1954) that the overdependent child gets that way because the mother rewards him for behaving in this fashion. There are, of course, differences in the data (age of children, for example) which make comparisons difficult. However, the Sears data seem to point toward an anxiety about helplessness, which is intensified by continued separation from or rebuff by the mother, and reduced when the mother gives affection and encouragement (cf. the discussion of Horney, page 329).

3. *Rejection and Aggression.* Sears found that the effect of permissive or severe attitudes toward aggressive behavior differed depending on the warmth of the mother's affection. Generally, severe attitudes and punishment increased the level of the child's aggressive behavior, and this effect was exaggerated if the mother was relatively cold toward the child.

Somewhat similar results were found in a study by Eron (1959), who used a different approach. School children were nominated by their fellows (the Guess Who technique) for various kinds of aggressive behavior. Such aggressiveness correlated with interview ratings of the family as follows: with rejection by parents, and with punishment for aggression by father, but— surprisingly—not with aggression as shown by either parent. This seems to indicate that it is the child's feeling of *being unloved*, rather than his seeing an aggressive model, which sets off his aggressive acts at school.

Lesser's work on mothers' approaches to socializing aggressive behavior throws light on a tricky problem in research on personality. As we noted in Chapter 3, some studies of tests such as TAT indicate that fantasied hostility predicts real aggressive behavior (see also page 113), whereas other studies find no relation or even a negative correlation between the two expressions of hostility. Lesser (1957) hypothesized that if the mother permits or encourages aggressive behavior, the overt and projective scores for aggression will agree closely; if the mother discourages overt aggression, then the projective score may be quite different. His results confirmed the hypothesis neatly; overt aggression was scored by the Guess Who method and fantasied aggression by TAT. If the mother encouraged overt aggressive expression, the correlation of the two scores was $+.43$; if she *discouraged* it, the correlation was $-.41$. Thus, for the first group, either measure would indicate about how much tension was felt; but in the second group, the overt score has obviously been lowered by maternal training.[3]

Rejection, Aggression, and Delinquency. Jenkins (1957) proposed that delinquents should be divided into two categories: motivation- or goal-oriented, and frustration-oriented, following Maier (1949). Hewitt and Jenkins (1946) had earlier published extensive data using the classifications "socialized delinquent" (for motivation-oriented) and "unsocialized aggressive" (for frustration-oriented). The former category is associated with gang activities, stealing, etc.; the latter, with destruction of property and generalized hostility.

When we look at the study of mothers' behavior in relation to delinquency (Table 17.1), we realize that the data fit Jenkins's theory. Mothers who reject their offspring from birth are likely to produce unsocialized delinquents. These youngsters are deeply insecure, have no faith in anyone, and often engage in seemingly irrational destruction. On the other hand, mothers who care for their infants when young, but later neglect them, are more likely to produce socialized delinquents. The boy in this case has acquired some positive orientations toward the human race and is capable of enjoying contacts with other youngsters, as in a gang. He fights mainly for some sensible reason, destroys property only when some gang code is involved, steals for group pleasures.

---

[3] Such studies may help the student to understand also why many clinical psychologists have faith in projective tests despite the moderate to poor validities reported in Chap. 3. It may be that many of the "validation" studies have failed to take just such variables into consideration.

Table 17.1

Intercorrelations of Family Situation and Problem Behavior Patterns

Situational pattern *	Frequency in 500 cases	Correlation with behavior pattern		
		Unsocialized aggressive	Socialized delinquent	Overinhibited
Parental rejection	101	.48	.02	−.20
Negligence and exposure	78	.12	.63	−.17
Family repression	106	.10	−.12	.52

* Cases were classified as illustrating a given family situational pattern when it was clearly defined. Hence the frequency does not add up to 500.
SOURCE: Hewitt and Jenkins (1946).

As Sears et al. noted in their study of mothering, true rejection of an infant in our culture is rare. The following case description is therefore cited, both to give a clearer picture of what is meant by maternal rejection and to illustrate the kind of behavior Jenkins calls frustration-oriented: [4]

Robert is a fourteen-year-old white boy of illegitimate birth. . . . The chief complaint was made by the mother who states that "Robert is the meanest devil God ever gave any mother for a son." Robert has been known to the juvenile court authorities since the age of nine years. At that time his mother filed a complaint, stating that he had removed the clothing from his smaller sister on two occasions. He had frequently displayed temper tantrums and fits of jealousy of this baby sister seven years younger than himself. . . . Since the age of eight years he had been openly antagonistic toward his mother, even kicking and striking her. . . . Robert . . . was also caught smoking and called his mother numerous vulgar insulting names. . . . He broke a window, ran upstairs, and asserted he was going to jump out and kill himself. When his mother grabbed him, he choked the baby. Two weeks later he ran away again, but returned home without being noticed and took $3.50 from his mother's purse and a dollar bill from his father's suit. . . .
The mother has said that she hunted for things that would hurt her husband's feelings, and finally felt most successful in using Robert. The father and his sister both state that the mother hated Robert from the first, never complimented or praised him, never kept her promises to him. At Christmas time she showed a great partiality toward the other children in the gifts she purchased, and when the father gave things to Robert, he had to conceal their real value from her. For the past six years the mother has taunted Robert and told the relatives that her husband is not the boy's father.

Rejection of Parent by Child. No one would be surprised if the boy just described rejected his mother; indeed, it is obvious that he has done so.

[4] Hewitt and Jenkins (1946), pp. 37–41. Reprinted by permission.

Probably the typical outcome of rejection by the parent is rejection by the child, and this too can have important significance for rebellious, aggressive, delinquent behavior. In a study bearing directly on this issue, Nye (1958) comments that "through intimate and continuous contacts parents become the most crucial agents in the internalization of the mores. If the child rejects the agent it appears unlikely that the internalization process would be effective" [p. 71]. Conditions which may lead to rejection of the parent by the child, he suggests, may include: children of immigrant parents who wish to assert their identification with the majority culture; upward-mobile youngsters who are "ashamed" of their parents, having adopted middle-class standards; and parents who deviate in any substantial way from the norms of other parents in the community.

We have indicated above that rejection by the parents is not only a desperate threat to the child, but also a source of frustration and aggression. Such aggression may to some extent be controlled by inhibitory responses, and by awareness of social norms. But if the child has also rejected the parent,

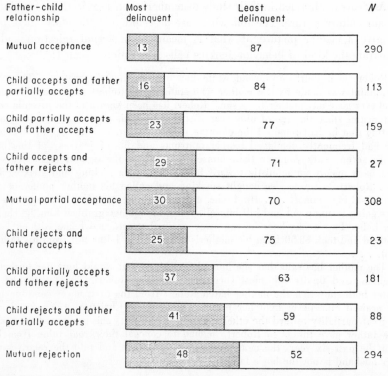

Fig. 17.1 Father-child rejection and delinquency. Degrees of mutual acceptance or rejection are shown on the left; percentages reporting delinquent behavior are given within the bars. (From Nye, 1958, Table 8.6, p. 76, by permission of John Wiley and Sons, publishers.)

then he probably rejects the norms which are symbolized by the parent. In such cases we are especially likely to observe delinquent acts to get even with the parents, to hurt them, or to assert his independence.

Nye's data indicate that, in a group of high school students, rejection by the parent goes with more delinquent acts; and rejection of the parent by the child also goes with such behavior. Combined, they give a sharply increased frequency of delinquent acts. As Figure 17.1 shows, the proportion of youngsters falling into Nye's "most delinquent" category increases rapidly with degrees of mutual rejection.

Control of Aggression by Punishment. The control of aggression through punishment is especially tricky because of the dual role played by punishment. As has been stressed several times, we conceive of aggressive behavior as being set off by frustration. When the child acts aggressively, he frequently encounters parental punishment; but this punishment is also a frustration, and hence a stimulus to further aggression. It is easy to recognize here the possibility of a vicious circle. The environment triggers aggression, the parents punish the aggression, and this sets off more aggression. The so-called "incorrigible" delinquent is often if not always an example of such a cycle (see page 114).

To support this analysis Sears (1950) conducted a careful study of 42 preschool children on whom observational data of home treatment were available. Sears predicted that home punishment would relate differently to overt aggression (attacks on other children in the preschool) and to fantasy aggression (attacks on dolls in a play situation). Severely punished children, he thought, would be more frustrated and hence would be tempted to behave aggressively; but the beginning of such an act would set off anxiety, and so overt aggression would be inhibited. In the doll-play situation, no anxiety would be aroused, and hence this group should show maximum aggression.

The results nicely confirmed Sears's reasoning. When the children were classified into three groups by severity of home punishment, the most punished group was at maximum in the doll-play aggression, but the middle group was at maximum in the overt aggression measures.[5] The least-punished group was lowest in both respects.

The Development of Conscience. Few would question that a superior approach to the problem of delinquency lies in the development of character. The work of Sears et al. throws light on this process and on the varying family situations which contribute to it.

Conservatives, those who advocate "spare the rod and spoil the child," will be disappointed with the findings as regards the role of physical punishment. Contrary to the view held by such punitive individuals, the evidence is

---

[5] It is assumed that the middle group has more frustration, hence more instigation to aggression, than the least-punished children; and, having less anxiety than the severely punished group, vents aggression in overt acts more freely.

Table 17.2
Development of Conscience and Techniques of Discipline

	Percentage of children rated "high" on conscience
Mothers are:	
High in use of praise	32
Low in use of praise	17
High in use of reasoning	30
Low in use of reasoning	16
High in use of tangible rewards	20
Low in use of tangible rewards	28
High in use of physical punishment	15
Low in use of physical punishment	32
Mother is relatively warm, and:	
Uses withdrawal of love fairly often	42
Uses little or no withdrawal of love	24
Mother is relatively cold, and:	
Uses withdrawal of love fairly often	18
Uses little or no withdrawal of love	25

SOURCE: Adapted from Tables X:3 and X:4, pp. 386 and 388, Sears et al. (1957). Used by permission of Row, Peterson & Co., publishers.

that there is a *negative* relationship between physical punishment and the development of conscience. As indicated in Table 17.2, in families where use of physical punishment is relatively high, the child is *less* likely to be rated high on conscience. (It will be recalled—cf. page 232—that juvenile delinquents were subjected to physical punishment more than matched nondelinquent controls.)

According to Freudian theory, the child develops a superego (conscience) as he comes to identify with his parents, particularly the like-sex parent, and commands himself to behave as his parents would wish to have him. This suggests that an atmosphere of emotional warmth will favor identification, and hence development of conscience; it may also be interpreted as indicating that disciplinary techniques, such as *withholding love*, will foster identification more rapidly than techniques of physical punishment. Both these predictions are supported by the Sears data. The greatest concentration of children high on ratings for conscience is found in those families where the mother shows emotional warmth to the child, but uses the withdrawal of love as a disciplinary technique.[6]

[6] The difference between the warm, affectionate mothers and those who are relatively cold, as seen in the table, is instructive. The mother must give affection, so that

Some psychologists have said that almost any technique for socializing children will work if the children feel loved. There is a good deal of support for this view, though we must recognize that some techniques are ruled out by the fact that children will not feel loved if these are employed. The basic learning, in relation to character and conscience, is that of values; and these are transmitted primarily through identification of the child with the parent. Such identification is impossible if the parent is perceived as a source of frustration and denial; it is feasible only if the parent is perceived as a source of gratification, affection, and security. Under these latter circumstances, the child can adopt the viewpoint of the parent, see things as the parent sees them, and accept as good the values of the parent. This process, the Sears data indicate, is more effective when the child must try to win the mother's love, i.e., identify the behavior which she disapproves, and inhibit such behavior. As these inhibitions become firmly established, conscience and character are built into the personality.

Development of Ego Strength. The extensive effects of a democratic home atmosphere (explanation of rules, opportunity for child to express opinion, absence of arbitrary domination) upon the child's personality can be well illustrated by referring to a study by Baldwin (1948). In this case the proportionate effect of a given home practice was computed for 45 different aspects of child behavior. Although many of the results were nonsignificant, quite a few were clearly not chance outcomes. Among these were the following; children from highly democratic homes are more likely to show:

- High social interaction
- Friendly play
- Success in approaching other children
- Success in aggression
- Success in bossing others
- Seeking attention and receiving attention
- Protesting against inferiority
- Constructiveness
- Dramatic play

These attributes suggest that the democratic home, by its practices, aids the child in developing those perceptions of himself and others which contribute to formation of a "strong ego." He is low on anxiety and withdrawing tendencies, feels self-confident, is dominant but not unfriendly. These characteristics fit our description of ego strength (page 200).

In this and other studies Baldwin has shown that the effects of democratic home treatment interact with other aspects of the home, such as warmth of

---

the child comes to expect it, before its withdrawal can make any impression. In those families where the child receives little affection, withdrawal is not effective because the child feels he has already lost; there will be no reward for him even if he does try to win his mother's love.

affection and indulgence. The outcome of a specific type of discipline or training program, then, will vary accordingly as such factors are involved.

Family Morale and Child Personality. It will be remembered that both the Sears study and the Becker study indicated one major dimension of family life to be a kind of general morale pattern, including satisfaction of the parents with each other and with the home situation, but likely to involve also inconsistency of discipline, differing standards held by the parents, quarrels between parents, etc. Since we have stressed the notion that the child acquires role models from his family, it is obvious that a low-morale home does not start him off on a favorable path. Either a boy or a girl will find samples of behavior to imitate and will acquire expectancies about family roles, which will have strong unpleasant components. This, of course, is the basis for the pattern of "neuroticism" or "ego weakness."

One of the best attempts to measure family morale and relate it to specific personality traits of adolescents seems to be that of Stott (1939, 1941). He administered to some 1,800 Nebraska adolescents a questionnaire covering parent-child relationships and a personality inventory. The family-life questionnaire was intercorrelated and subjected to factor analysis, from which three "patterns" emerged: a group of families characterized by mutual confidence, affection, and companionability between parents and children; a "family-discord" pattern; and a "nervous-tension" pattern. Special analysis was made of the first two factors. The results were as expected: Children com-

Table 17.3

Correlations between Desirable Parent-Adolescent Relationship and Desirable Traits of Personality

California personality score	*Correlation*
Total adjustment	.62
I. Self-adjustment	.50
a. Self-reliance	.27
b. Sense of personal worth	.32
c. Sense of personal freedom	.55
d. Feeling of belonging	.44
e. Freedom from withdrawing tendencies	.46
f. Freedom from nervous symptoms	.33
II. Social adjustment	.62
a. Social standards	.27
b. Social skills	.42
c. Freedom from antisocial tendencies	.44
d. Family relations	.65
e. School relations	.43
f. Community relations	.36

SOURCE: Stott (1941). Reprinted by permission of Duke University Press, publishers.

ing from homes where the "good-morale" pattern predominated were better adjusted, more independent, and more satisfactorily related to their parents than were the average of the group. Similarly, those coming from homes where the second pattern was manifest were, in general, poorly adjusted. As Table 17.3 shows, this effect is more clearly observable in social adjustment, but in every respect the correlations favor the conclusion that good family morale is productive of desirable personality traits. In the Becker study, it will be remembered, occurrence of conduct problems was especially associated with poor family morale; the occurrence of withdrawn, unhappy problem children had no relationship to this kind of family pattern.

If we take a look at several of these studies (Baldwin; Becker et al.; Stott; Watson), it begins to appear that permissiveness and democracy provide the atmosphere for ego strength to develop; severe punishment, strict rules, and authoritarianism prevent the child from developing self-confidence or assurance in relating himself to others. It seems clear, therefore, that the strict, punitive parent produces children with personality problems.

PARENT PERSONALITIES AND CHILD PERSONALITY

The role of being a parent calls for certain kinds of behavior on the part of the individual who finds himself in this role. Some of the kinds of behavior have been cited above: feeding, toilet training, sex training, control of aggression. In executing the role, parents differ in ways such as strict to permissive, warm and affectionate to cool and withdrawn, anxious or nonanxious about the role, and so on.

It is inevitable that a major set of determinants of how the role is executed will fall in the category of "parent's personality." An individual who is high on "schizoid tendency," withdrawn, unable to express affection, distant with everyone, is likely to show the same pattern with a newborn baby. One who has a strong sex drive, and a great deal of anxiety about keeping it under control, is likely to be especially severe when the child shows sexual exploratory behavior.

Mother's Adjustment and Child's Adjustment. Behrens (1954) collected detailed observations on 25 preschool children with clinical problems, and obtained a variety of data on their mothers. The extent of the child's adjustment problem was most closely related to a measure of mother's behavior (rejection, overprotection, disciplinary practices, toilet training). However, there was no particular kind of action most likely to produce child problems. Rather, any deviation from an optimal way of treating the child was found to increase the probability that the child would have difficulty, and mothers with the highest deviation score had the most severe problems in their children [7] (correlation of +.93).

---

[7] A closely parallel result was reported by Klatskin, Jackson, and Wilkin (1956).

Similarly, she found a correlation of $+.80$ between child's behavior and *weakness* of ego structure (the mother had a poor self-image, lacked impulse control, was emotional, etc.). This seems to indicate that people who have developed severely maladjusted personalities just cannot take the strain of child rearing and probably should avoid the parental role. Women who are contented in the maternal role (Altman, 1958) have children who are judged as having desirable personalities.

An encouraging aspect of the Behrens study is that the closest correlation is not child personality with adult personality, but child personality with adult behavior. This is optimistic because it is difficult to change a person's total character structure, but it is feasible to teach specific modes of child-rearing behavior. Unfortunately, in most instances mothers do not receive training in this role; society assumes that all females instinctively know how to rear children, and, as our data show, such an assumption is completely inaccurate.

[*Authoritarianism and Discipline.*] The data of various studies indicate that rigidity and severity of discipline lead to undesirable personalities in children. Hart (1957) finds evidence to indicate that style of discipline is a function of "authoritarian" characteristics. Mothers scoring high on the F scale (see page 250) tended to use more physical punishment, ridicule, and threats.[8] Mothers low on the F scale used withdrawal of love, denial of rewards, and ostracism. This pattern seems to relate plausibly to the differences described earlier (page 411) on the basis of the study by Sears and associates. It would also support some of the statements on behavior of the parents of authoritarians (cf. page 251), if we assume that these mothers were repeating the treatment they had received as children.

Such an assumption receives support from the work of Mussen and Kagan (1958), who used the Asch conformity experiment with children. Extreme conformists and nonconformists were queried about their relations with their parents. The conforming group gave a picture of parents as cold, punitive, and rejecting. If the parents "really" show such characteristics, it would follow that they are handing down their personality patterns to their children.

Motives for Maternal Rejection. An important question, in the light of our discussion of rejection and aggression, is this: What kind of maternal personality is associated with rejection of her child? Ackerman believes it useful to classify rejections as being specific to this particular child, or non-specific, i.e., any child would have been rejected. Among the former he

---

[8] Hart's study inevitably raises some doubt as to the correctness of our emphasis (Chap. 11) on response set (acquiescence) as the main determinant of scores on the F scale. The behavior of the mothers here certainly fits the general meaning of "authoritarian" more than "acquiescent." Perhaps the two can be harmonized by suggesting that the authoritarian mothers, as little girls, had been subjected to just such dominative discipline; that they became acquiescent to avoid the unpleasant controls, and also acquired a picture of the mother role which they practice with their own offspring.

mentions, "A mother rejects a hairy child because she has had a life-long anxiety about excess hair on her legs and breasts . . . then there is the mother, very vain about her figure, who never forgives the child for the change after birth in the contour of her breasts." [9] In other words, to the extent that the child symbolizes negative valences in the phenomenal world of the mother, he is likely to be rejected either consciously or unconsciously.

Among the nonspecific motives for rejection he suggests such items as: the woman who wants to divorce her husband, finds she is pregnant, and is unconsciously hostile to the child for binding her to an unpleasant situation; the child who is born just after the family finances suffer a bad blow; the child who interferes with her professional career; and so on.

We are not, in this volume, concerned either with a detailed catalogue of such motives, or with practical measures for dealing with them. These points are considered here to make concrete the notion that the mother's personality determines her treatment of the child; and this treatment determines the child's personality development. This is the law of the transmission of personality traits; some influence comes from heredity and a great deal of influence comes from environment, especially the family.

PARENTS AS MODELS

The mechanism of identification, to which reference has been made frequently, implies that the child will accept one parent as a model and imitate his or her behavior. We assume that this begins as wishful thinking: "I wish I were big and strong and athletic like Daddy." Imitation of the parent's actions gives some semblance of reality to the fantasy; acts perceived as quite different from the parent will be inhibited. The self-image is patterned on the perceived personality of the parent.

This process has its negative counterpart, of course, in rejection of the parent by the child. Where the emotional relationship is one of hostility, the child may deny any similarity to the parent, and may practice actions which assert a difference. Methods of depth psychology sometimes uncover a secret similarity, as in the case of the unconscious self-image (see page 210), but at the conscious level, the child's personality is quite unlike that of the parent.

We must anticipate that each of these processes will be represented in any sizable population of persons studied; therefore we cannot predict a high degree of similarity of parent personality and child personality. Since emotional warmth and identification are undoubtedly more common, we would predict that on the average correlations will be positive, but not high. This is exactly what we find. Studies by Sopchak (1958), Patterson (1943), Sward and Friedman (1935), and Hoffeditz (1934) agree in reporting low positive

---

[9] From *Psychodynamics of family life*, p. 168. By Nathan W. Ackerman, copyright 1958, Basic Books, Inc., publishers.

Table 17.4

Parent-child Similarities on the Bernreuter Inventory

Scale		Mothers	Sons	Daughters
N (emotionality)	Fathers	.16	.06	.23
	Mothers	..	.01	.27
S (self-sufficiency)	Fathers	.09	.20	.09
	Mothers	..	.05	.16
D (dominance)	Fathers	.15	.19	.20
	Mothers	..	.02	.28

correlations on specific traits. Table 17.4 shows the results reported by Hoffeditz, using the Bernreuter inventory for emotionality, self-sufficiency, and dominance. The correlations are all positive but nonsignificant.

Table 17.4 summarizes the individual parent-child correlations. It indicates only very low relationships on these traits. However, it is notable that the father-son correlation is each time higher than the mother-son correlation; the mother-daughter coefficient similarly is greater than that for fathers and daughters. The same general tendency is reported by Sward and Friedman, who found that children correlated with like-sex parents .29, .31, .31, and .11,[10] while opposite-sex parents correlated .16, .24, .27, and .05. These findings seem to support our general view on the importance of identification.

Hoffeditz computed the correlation of the average of the parents with the average of the children for the 100 families studied. These correlations for the three trait measures, N, S, and D, were respectively .28, .21, and .29. Each of these is higher than any of the coefficients reported in Table 17.4 for the corresponding trait measure. This suggests that a more definite relationship is predictable when the uniqueness of each parent and each child is to some extent canceled out, leaving the "family pattern" of common elements visible. A similar observation has been made of intrafamily similarities in height, weight, etc.

Resemblance of parent and child may, of course, depend upon heredity and common experiences as well as upon identification. Hauer (1955) reports that he ran frustration tolerance tests on newborn infants and their parents. There was a significant positive correlation with the mother's frustration tolerance, but not with the father's. This suggests the possibility of prenatal learning (demonstrated by Marquis, 1931), since heredity would be determined equally by father and mother. Or it may mean that mothers of low

[10] For groups respectively of Jewish boys, Jewish girls, gentile boys, and gentile girls.

tolerance may secrete hormones (see page 382) which affect the infant and induce a similar response pattern.

Models in Child-rearing Techniques. One of the most important areas in which the parent is assumed to function as a role model for the child is the field of child-rearing techniques. It seems to be a matter of common sense that the child will acquire a picture of the proper way to treat children, and so will duplicate his parents' tactics when he takes on the same role.

Although this theory seems quite plausible, doubt has been cast upon its validity by the research of Bronson, Katten, and Livson (1959). These authors compared the present behavior of a group of young parents with what they said regarding the behavior of their own parents. Three comparisons are reported: what the present father (or mother) said about the grandparents (his own mother or father); what the present mother and father are observed to do in the home; and what the present child says about his mother and father.

The major conclusion by the authors is that there seems to be no particular connection between the reported behavior of grandmother (or grandfather) and the present behavior of mother or father as observed by the psychologist. Only two trends seem worth noting: Mothers tend to repeat the authority pattern (if grandmother had major authority in the home, mother tends to adopt a similar role); and fathers tend to imitate the affectional behavior of grandfather (if he was more affectionate than average to his son, the latter, on becoming a father, shows decidedly affectionate behavior to a son). Actually, the reader may conclude that these two findings are rather important; even if more had been hoped for, these trends confirm the expectancy that the parental role is in some respects handed down from one generation to another. (If the authors had tried to identify cases of rejection of the grandparents, and adoption of an opposite role pattern, the significance of the findings might have been substantially increased.)

Family Relationships in Attitudes and Values. The most extensive study of similarities within the family on attitudes and values is probably that of Fisher (1948). She reports correlations of something over two hundred college students with one or both parents, including economic attitudes, attitudes on moral and religious questions, and the six Allport-Vernon values. Probably her most interesting finding is that all the correlations are positive, i.e., children tend to resemble their parents on all these assorted issues.

In the light of the emphasis placed on identification with the like-sex parent, it is interesting to observe Fisher's median correlations. In every case the highest degree of similarity is found for mother and daughter, and the lowest for mother and son. The daughter-father correlations range slightly above those for son with father; this may indicate greater independence of sons from family influences generally, since such independence is a more socially approved trait for boys than for girls.

Fisher's data also indicate that intrafamily resemblance is likely to be especially high for religious values, somewhat less for economic (practical) values, and low for the other four scales in the Allport-Vernon test. We may easily infer that these similarities are functions of the amount of discussion or joint family behavior related to each area. Churchgoing and religious participation become matters of verbal and other kinds of behavior in most families fairly early and often. Questions of practicality, especially as regards family finances, are also likely to be threshed out with the whole group or with individual children. On the other hand, not much discussion of "love of truth" or aesthetic standards is likely to occur in the typical American home. It is plausible, then, to suspect that parental attitudes are transmitted to children if and when the child effectively learns to perceive correctly his parents' position. This will not hold if there is emotional rejection of the parent by the child, but it may be assumed that such rejection is infrequent enough not to confuse these data unduly. Rejection may be a factor in reducing the correlations from higher values which might have been anticipated.

Parents Not the Only Determinants. In interpreting the foregoing studies on the effect of parental practices and characteristics upon the personality of the child, we must keep in mind that the parents are by no means the sole determiners of the child's behavior. These studies were made on adolescents. During the years, they have been influenced by companions, schoolteachers, and other individuals, institutions, reading matter, motion pictures, and so on. If their social and emotional reactions were identical with those of their parents, it would be a matter for surprise. Aside from the question of primacy, it is doubtful that the parents have much advantage in imposing their ideas on children beyond the preschool age.

SIBLING RELATIONSHIPS

So far we have dealt with the child in the family as if he were an only child. The presence of siblings naturally makes life more complicated. For the first-born, who has dominated the scene and enjoyed extensive attention from both parents, it is a bitter blow to have a new baby born into the family. Regressive behavior (loss of toilet habits, even loss of speech skills) is often observed at this point. One explanation is that the older child is imitating the baby, trying to get the attention the baby is receiving; another is that the emotional upset causes loss of coordination and control as well as poorer discrimination of situations.

The child readily comes to perceive a baby brother or sister as a rival for parental affection and consequently as a threat to security. The intensity of the jealousy so evoked is well known. Sears et al. (1957) comment that quarreling between siblings is a major problem for mothers, although it is difficult to know just how important it is as compared with the food, sex, and other problems discussed earlier. In terms of their categories, sibling rivalry is a phase of training the child's aggressive behavior, and it is interesting to observe that the same mothers who are permissive as regards feeding and sex habits are also permissive in this area.

Cooperative and Competitive Behavior. Interaction among siblings provides the earliest models for cooperative and for competitive activities. This is particularly true if the children are of similar ages. If a first-born child reaches the age of five or six before another child comes into the family, he will of course have begun to acquire such habits in interacting with his peer group, in play situations, and in nursery school.

Adler (1924) placed heavy emphasis on the importance of sibling rivalry in establishing competitive, hostile attitudes toward persons in the environment. It will be remembered that, for Adler, a striving for superiority, a will-to-power, was the major motive of the personality. Since the child feels helpless in the face of the superior size, strength, and wisdom of adults, he gets his first chance to satisfy this motive in relation to his sibling. Such strivings, once well established in the personality, determine a life style of competing with others, constantly trying to attain a superior position.

Birth Order and Personality. Closely related to problems of jealousy and rivalry among siblings is the matter of birth order. Many students of personality, notably Adler, have developed rather elaborate hypotheses about the personality implications of being the first-born, the middle child, the youngest child, and so on. It is obvious, for example, that the first-born receives the full attention of his parents for perhaps a year or two, then is dispossessed by a new infant. The shock of this experience often induces regression to more infantile behavior.

Attempts to verify these effects with personality inventories have not been successful (cf. Stagner and Katzoff, 1936). Differences between children in different sequences have generally been found to be small, and not always in accordance with the theory.

A study using teachers' ratings of children obtained more significant results, generally supporting the notion that birth order does constitute a significant determinant of some attributes of personality. Koch (1955) studied a large number of elementary school children, carefully selected to fit certain combinations of boy-and-girl groupings and age differences in the family. One of her most striking findings is that the age at which a new sibling arrives is of great importance. First-born boys who have a sib two to four years younger are rated very high on hostility, jealousy, and other anger-related traits; whereas boys whose sib is less than two years or more than four years younger do not rate nearly so high on these attributes. This suggests what we referred to above as the "critical-period" hypothesis; at the age of two the little boy has developed enough self-awareness to react with anger to the intruder, but by the age of four he has begun to achieve some independence of his parents and so is less frustrated by the new baby.

Koch notes that the child's ability to relate to his peers, others of his own age group, is a function to some extent of this family constellation. If two sibs are very close in age, they may become "involved" with each other, both in fun and in quarrels, and have few contacts with outsiders. A wide age disparity, on the other hand, seems to favor (for the older child) a self-confident, friendly, gregarious pattern with leadership potential. However, these and the other conclusions reached by Koch must always be qualified; they may hold statistically, but there will be many exceptions.

ADOLESCENCE

Many parents would agree that the most difficult of all phases of personality development is that of adolescence. During the early teen-age period, there is a decided shift from acceptance of parental norms, ideals, and patterns to conformity to the peer group. Often a marked increase in negativism and hostility to the parents goes along with this. Emotional instability seems exaggerated. Both the parent and the adolescent himself are often puzzled at his behavior.

The Search for Independence. Adolescence does not reflect the quarrels of sibling rivalry, apparently because the youth does not perceive other members of his peer group as rivals for any major goals, such as the affection of his parents. The main theme of adolescence seems to be found in another dynamic aspect of childhood, the striving for independence. We have noted in other connections that the child is torn between his desire to retain security, to protect an established equilibrium, and his desire for autonomy and independence. Security says to the child, "Don't explore; you don't know what may happen." Independence says, "Let's investigate; it may be exciting." It was partly on this basis that authors such as Maslow, Cattell, and Harlow endorsed the view that curiosity was an instinct.

Independence, however, is far more than curiosity. It involves the need to test one's own capacities, to arrive at decisions without assistance. In an early form children show it when they refuse aid in dressing themselves, want to go to the store alone, and so on. (It is probable that some of this derives from observation of adults and from the expectancy, "If I do this, I shall be more grown-up.") In any event, whether innate or due to experience, this striving toward independence is shown in vigorous form by most children.

Some parents encourage independent activity by the child. Others, whether fearful that the child may be injured or preferring to keep him under close observation, prevent such practice in making decisions, taking chances, and perhaps getting hurt. Overprotective mothers may especially interfere with the development of self-reliance and independent judgment.

Sherman (1948) reports that "emancipated" college women, those who have been encouraged to develop independence of thought and action, show desirable personality traits: They are more emotionally stable and more self-sufficient, although somewhat less sociable. Interestingly enough, it would appear from the data of Warnath (1955) that the adolescent is more likely to get this kind of training in a cohesive rather than a loosely organized family. He reports that close-knit families seem to produce children with more self-confidence and more independence; youngsters having these characteristics were likewise usually chosen by their classmates as having attractive personalities.

Adolescence as Discontinuity. The adolescent in the United States is particularly a victim of what Benedict (1949) has called a discontinuity in cultural conditioning. She refers to the fact that in our culture the young child is expected to be submissive and dependent, rely upon adults rather than upon his own decisions; and conversely, the adult is expected to be authoritative, independent, dominant, and decisive. But at what point does the child move from one set of expectancies to the other? [11]

The lack of a clear-cut set of expectancies at this age level accounts for much of the adolescent's unpredictable behavior and emotional sensitivity. As Lewin (1935) has commented, lack of such role definition creates insecurity, and insecurity readily leads to both vacillation and emotional disturbance.

Independence Training. Krebs (1958) asked college students about their training for independence. He included such questions as: "At what age were you expected to show pride in your ability to do things well?" "When were you expected to try hard things for yourself without asking for help?" He found a wide range of differences with respect to such training—which, incidentally, could as well be called training for need achievement as for independence. He found, rather interestingly, that adolescents who had received early encouragement to develop independence were less conforming (in the Asch experiment) than those who received such training late or not at all. It would appear that, if parents keep the child dependent, he later transfers this dependence to his peer group; whereas, if he develops independence, he is able to stand up against both adult pressure and peer group pressure.

Peer Evaluations. The importance of peer evaluations has, in one way or another, appeared often in this volume. Such ratings of a personality may be used to validate personality tests, or to explore the effect of some experimental variable, or to predict future success, e.g., as a military officer. The validity of such ratings depends on the fact that persons at the same level as the subject have excellent opportunities to observe and are not biased in the way that outsiders may be.

[11] By her use of the terms "conditioning" and "habit," Benedict implies that specific responses are involved. For the reasons stated in connection with the discussion of traits, see pp. 160–162, we have restated her point of view in terms of expectancies. The decisive issue in child rearing is not what specific movements the child makes, but whether he behaves in such wise that adults see him as meeting these role requirements.

Peer evaluations, however, are important in another way: as determiners of personality. We stressed, in Chapter 9, the "looking-glass" theory of the self—the notion that the self-image tends to pick up and incorporate evaluations from others. In the case of the young child, the most significant evaluations come from the parents. For the adolescent, on the other hand, the peer evaluations seem to be of greater importance (cf. Manis, 1955; Mannheim, 1957). Even at earlier ages, it is pointed out by Koch (1956), the mother is not the only determinant of the child's expectancies and values; siblings and playmates soon become important.

The exaggerated importance of peer evaluations in adolescence, as illustrated by fads in clothing, in amusements, in speech, and the like, may derive from the increasing conflicts with parents at this age. The adolescent may very well perceive himself as an adult and demand the privileges pertaining to that status. The parent may still perceive him as a child (perceptual constancy). This sets off conflicts about the use of the family car, the hours the child keeps, proper recreation, and other topics. Rejecting the parental standards on these issues, the adolescent may simply go all the way and reject all adult norms in favor of teen-age standards. He will then respond favorably to peer group pressures and ignore pressure from the parents or other adults.

The general consensus among psychologists is that the basic traits of personality have been laid down long before adolescence and that changes occurring at this period are likely to be both superficial and transitory. There is, nonetheless, some opportunity for fundamental modification of traits and self-image under these pressures. As we shall point out in the following chapter, even in adult life there is some evidence for change in personality in response to environmental stimulation.

SUMMARY

The major determinants of personality operate during the earliest years of life. This means that the child is a creation primarily of his family—at first, perhaps, of the mother, but the evidence indicates that fathers too are important. Families differ in the rewards, frustrations, punishments, and threats imposed upon the children; they differ also in the kinds of models offered by parents for imitation and for the formation of role expectancies.

Studies of animals and of human infants confirm the importance of the first year of life. It may well be that the basic pattern of the individual personality can never be changed after the first year; this is not easily subjected to test. Certainly serious deprivation of affection and care during that year has extensive repercussions.

Permissiveness and affection seem to lead to more desirable attributes of personality than strictness and rejection. Punishment is not important if the child feels secure in the family; but without a feeling of being loved, it leads to hostility and delinquency.

It is assumed that parents tend to reenact the methods of child rearing experienced in their own childhood; the evidence is somewhat contradictory. The cultural trend seems to be away from the patriarchal authoritarian family toward a more democratic, equalitarian structure; there is some evidence that this type produces children of greater ego strength than the traditional pattern.

The child's personality is also affected by his relations with siblings and peers. Most psychologists do not consider these influences important enough to outweigh the decisive effects of parent-child relations.

Adolescence is peculiarly a time of transition; the child is moving from one role to another and lacks clear-cut expectancies to guide him. This insecurity fosters rebelliousness, exaggerated demands for independence, emotional instability—in interacting with parents—and an excessive conformity in relating to the peer group. Most observers suspect that the personality changes of adolescence are superficial and temporary, that the patterns laid down in early childhood will structure the adult personality. This does not mean, of course, that adolescent disturbance should be ignored by parents or by other adults.

SUGGESTIONS FOR READING

Miller and Swanson, *The changing American parent*, and Sears, Maccoby, and Levin, *Patterns of child rearing*, offer valuable information with regard to the behavior of parents. Neither volume goes carefully into implications for child personality. Jersild's *The psychology of adolescence* summarizes research and offers sound interpretation regarding personality problems at this "difficult" age. Martin and Stendler, in their *Child development*, discuss the effect of family pressures on personality. Whiting and Child's *Child training and personality* gives a good theoretical analysis of parental treatment and child response, but the illustrative material is taken almost exclusively from primitive cultures. Lois B. Murphy's *Personality in young children* focuses primarily on methods of studying the child personality, with not very much attention to family determinants. *Personality and the cultural pattern*, by J. S. Plant, provides stimulating insights into the relation between large-scale sociological variables and aspects of individual personality, as does Chap. 2 of *Family, socialization and interaction process*, by Parsons and Bales.

The Family: Maturity

As Wordsworth once wrote, "The child is father of the man." The preceding chapter elaborated on this theme, indicating ways in which childhood pressures led to adult traits and ego patterns. But it must be apparent that personality does not stop changing at age sixteen, or eighteen, or twenty-one: True, the principles of habit and perceptual constancy make change more difficult, but it is not impossible. The conditions of adult living play their part in this continuing interaction of organism and environment. The present chapter will explore some of the aspects of family life as personality influences; by definition, it will be limited to adults in their roles as husband and wife, father and mother. Later chapters will at least sketch some of the extrafamilial influences which may also play a part in the shaping of personality.

The relation of the child to his family is, as has been demonstrated, not a simple matter of being passively molded into a pattern. It is rather an interaction in which biological factors and early learning place limits on the environmental effects. Such a conception must be emphasized even more strongly as we come, in this and the following chapters, to consider the personality of the adult being influenced by and interacting with other pressures. Consequently there will be more attention paid to the reciprocal effect of personality upon the environment, at least in the sense of modifying the pattern of influence, than was manifest in the preceding chapter.[1]

The Adult in the Family Role System. Any institution, such as marriage, can be defined as a system of roles. Each role carries with it certain role expectations; i.e., people in a culture expect husbands to behave in a certain way, wives to do certain things, etc. For some purposes, it is sufficient to know the generalized cultural expectancies; however, if we are dealing with a specific husband and wife, we need to know the expectancies brought by each

---

[1] No attempt will be made, however, even to touch on the extensive literature relating to the significance of personality for occupational success, leadership, political influence, and so on. The primary concern will be with the effect of environment on the individual; secondarily, with the way in which previously established traits interact with and modify these influences.

Fig. 18.1 Differing expectancies about marriage. The cartoonist cleverly suggests the egocentric expectancies each spouse may bring to marriage. Conflict will result from the situation pictured; harmony ensues if the expectancies fit together. (Drawings by Ted Key. Reprinted by permission from *How to develop your thinking ability*, by Kenneth S. Keyes, Jr., Copyright, 1950, McGraw-Hill Book Company, Inc.)

to the marriage. Figure 18.1 whimsically shows how contradictory these may be.

In terms of the analysis of individual personalities and the demands of the role system, then, we can identify the significant questions to be asked about any marriage or similar social relationship. For what goals is the individual striving? How does he perceive the role (what expectancies has he?) and himself in the role? How does he perceive the person in the reciprocal role? Does he find satisfaction in the role? And how does he attempt to control specific situations to increase his satisfaction? [2]

We must anticipate, consequently, the following possibilities with regard to how the person fits into his role: (1) either or both individuals ignore the role expectations and continue egocentrically; (2) either or both subordinate individual demands to the expectations of the marital role; (3) either or both subordinate themselves to demands of the parental role; or (4) either or both subordinate personal goals to the cultural pattern of the community. Obviously, in practice, we find one spouse showing one of these and the other a different pattern. Many variations are thus possible as regards the kinds of role conflicts and personal conflicts occurring within the marital relationship. Since this book is about personality and not about marriage in general, we shall confine ourselves to noting investigations of two types: those in which the role execu-

[2] The questions are modified slightly from Ackerman and Behrens (1956).

tion reflects personality traits of the partners; and those in which individual personalities are modified by the interaction of roles.

A marriage, it must be noted, involves other roles than those of husband and wife. Especially the birth of children leads to assumption of the roles of parents. The preceding chapter stressed the impact of parents on children; we may well consider the effect of children on parents, and the effect of marital adjustment on execution of the parental role.

MARITAL SELECTION

Entry upon the role of husband or wife depends upon being selected as a mate (or upon selecting one and successfully engineering a marriage). We must therefore concern ourselves with the personality traits relevant to marital selection.

The "Attraction of Opposites." A popular theory has it that opposites are attracted to each other; e.g., blonds fall in love with brunets, tall men love short women, talkative girls are drawn to quiet men. It is always easy to find a couple who dramatically illustrate this notion. Statistically, however, the odds favor the marriage of persons who are similar.

Kelly (1955) reports on a follow-up study of 300 couples whom he had studied in 1934, when they were only engaged. Even at this early stage of mutual attraction, similarities were preponderant over differences. On a variety of personality characteristics, the couple correlations ranged from $-.02$ to $+.58$, with a median of near $+.30$. The restudy twenty years later indicated that (for those who had married) the range of correlations was similar. He notes, however, that a few changes did occur; curiously enough, these were in the direction of decreased similarity!

Many other studies support the view that "like attracts like" rather than the reverse. On some sociocultural variables, such as religion, very high degrees of similarity are reported. Burgess and Wallin (1944) found a correlation of $+.54$ for religion. Even on purely physical variables such as height and complexion, homogamy (selection of similar mates) is the rule.

The Hypothesis of Complementary Needs. The evidence indicates that like tends to marry like. Young people choose as mates persons of similar economic background, similar religion, physique, and personality. There are, however, many exceptions to this rule; and furthermore, this observation tells us nothing about the choice of mates within such a large group.

Winch (1952) has proposed what he calls the "hypothesis of complementary needs" as a device for filling this gap. Briefly, this hypothesis states that "each individual seeks within his or her field of eligibles for that person who gives the greatest promise of providing him or her with maximum need gratification" [p. 406]. This sounds much too calculating; Winch means, of course, that the person will perceive as attractive, and will seek to marry, that eligible individual whose attributes evoke expectancies of need gratification. Thus, he suggests, a girl with a need to feel protected will be selectively attracted to men with a need to be dominant and protecting. A man with a need for a mother substitute will be attracted to motherly women, and so on. Such selections would be within a "field of eligibles," however; i.e., they would be chosen from the same church group or the same nationality group, the same neighborhood, etc. Winch tries in this way to avoid coming into conflict with the data on similarity in surface personality. He is talking about deeper needs and goals.

Evidence favoring this theory has been reported by Winch, Ktsanes, and Ktsanes (1954), and against it, by Bowerman and Day (1956). More appropriate, unquestionably, would be research to determine *under what conditions* people choose similar mates, and when they choose those with complementary patterns.

Part of the difficulty arises from the phenomena of perceptual distortion on which we have laid so much emphasis. A girl may be attracted to a man on the basis of cues which have little validity for revealing inner personality patterns; she may be influenced much more by a physical similarity to her father than by evidence of motivations and temperament. Further, we must recognize the operation of needs at different levels of consciousness; a girl may say that she wants a husband who will let her work and treat her as an equal, when unconsciously she prefers to be dominated and protected. Thus, lacking insight into her own deeper impulses, she may think she is choosing a "complementary" mate when in fact she is not. And finally we must recognize that, even if she has correctly diagnosed her own inner motives, she may be in error about him.[3] Thus, even if we assume a tendency for Winch's hypothesis to operate in mate selection, we cannot expect to get very satisfactory verification from empirical data because of the numerous sources of error in making these choices.

Role of the Oedipus Complex. The problems mentioned in testing Winch's theory are also present when we attempt to investigate Freud's concept of the Oedipus complex as a factor in marital selection. The nature of this complex has been described earlier (cf. pages 108, 322). It involves a preponderant fixation of love on the parent of the opposite sex. Margaret Mead (1939) suggests that our family pattern, with only two significant adults, leads to this focusing. In any event, substantial evidence indicates that the occurrence of such a complex is common, if not universal, in Western families.

It is natural to suppose that this will have some bearing on the choice of a

---

[3] A variant of the theory of complementary needs is that of the individual who marries someone else to reform him or to help him get over personal difficulties. LeMasters (1957) comments that success in a marriage of this kind is theoretically possible, but the chances are heavily against it. He might have added that the person who most needs a warning on this point is the least likely to pay attention to it!

mate. If a boy successfully resolves his Oedipus problem, he identifies with his father and ceases to be the father's rival. He can then go on to fall in love with a girl who is perceived as similar to his mother. Failure to resolve the Oedipus problem leaves the boy attached to his real mother and hence blocked from falling in love with a person his own age.

This line of reasoning prompted Winch (1950) to explore the attitudes toward parents of a rather large sample of college students, who were first classified as to their "courtship status." High status was defined as being already married, engaged, or informally committed. Low status included no dating, some dating, and going steady without marital intent. Winch found that among men, low courtship status was associated significantly with being attached to the mother, and with feeling that mother was more affectionate. This finding would fit the prediction that a persistence of the Oedipus reaction would interfere with heterosexual adjustment. Young women, however, gave answers indicating that high courtship status went with continued preference for the father; in other words, their tendency is opposed to the Freudian prediction. Winch believes that the apparent contradiction in results can be explained on a cultural basis; young men, to take on the role laid out for them by society, must loosen the Oedipus ties to the mother; and the persistence of this relationship is a handicap. Young women, by contrast, are not impelled to achieve independence; they can fit into a sex role in modern society merely by transferring dependency from father to husband. There is some evidence from studies of happiness in marriage which is compatible with this interpretation.

Another hypothesis derived from Freudian theory suggests that dependent men will prefer to marry "motherly" women, and some writers have interpreted this as meaning that large-breasted women, symbolizing ample capacity for mothering, will be preferred as mates by such men. Scodel (1957) devised an elaborate paired-comparisons method for identifying men with such preferences, using photographs as stimuli, and then compared the extreme cases on a TAT measure of need dependency. His results are contrary to Freudian theory. The more dependent men choose small-breasted women as more sexually attractive. Scodel offers what he calls a "learning theory" interpretation of this, viz., that male babies receiving ample gratification at the breast grow up to prefer the same physique in a mate. Unfortunately, this—like the psychoanalytic view—is rather imaginative, since there is no evidence that breast size is correlated with nursing gratification; and Scodel has no data to indicate that the two groups of men actually had mothers of differing dimensions. The study is thus interesting for the questions it raises rather than for the answers it provides.

Significance of Popular Stereotypes. The parents are only one of the diverse sources from which an individual acquires a mental image of "an appropriate mate." Other sources include friends, the movies, romantic novels, etc. Sociology-oriented psychologists would emphasize also the cultural norm of beauty—e.g., the flat-chested female of the 1920s has given way to the bosomy beauties of the 1950s. Finally, the student of personality is likely to observe that accidents of an individual's biography may cause him to cling to a percept which fits neither of these patterns. His own self-image, for example, plays a role in determining to what kind of mate he will be attracted.

An interesting demonstration of this last point is found in a study by Beigel (1957). In a public opinion type of study, Beigel asked several hundred persons "what characteristics are most desirable" in a male and in a female. About 90 per cent immediately assumed that he meant for love or marriage, since this apparently was the meaning of "desirable" in the context of sex differences. He cites particularly the attribute of intelligence as an illustration of the findings. Of the men questioned about two-thirds spontaneously mentioned intelligence (or some synonym) as important; some wanted a woman of equal intelligence, some preferred the mate to be brighter than himself, others the reverse. The largest single group felt that average intelligence, *less than the man possessed*, made a woman desirable. Next largest was the group voting for equal intelligence; and only a handful wanted a woman "brighter than myself." The unconscious motives revealed in the accompanying remarks were striking. Some wanted the woman to be able to make friends easily and impress them favorably, and this almost invariably revealed anxiety about social inadequacy on the man's part. Some wanted an intelligent wife to supplement the family income, probably also suggestive of felt inadequacy in the economic sphere. Most of these wanted the wife to be equal or inferior in intelligence; they feared the domination of the wife, or her independence. A curious stereotype about sex motivation was also revealed; a large proportion of men who wanted a "dumb" wife held that such women were "more sexy." The anticipated sexual enjoyment, therefore, may have been as important as the motif of male dominance.

Finally, it is interesting to comment that, in the small group of men wanting brighter wives, frank dependency motives were indicated. When a man says that his mother always helped him make decisions and that he would want a wife capable of doing this, his desire for a substitute mother becomes rather obvious.

Childhood experiences, then, determine percepts of mother, of teacher, of female relatives and friends of the family. But the boy finds attraction (positive valence) in such percepts in accordance with a variety of factors. Does he identify with his father? If so, and if the parental marriage is happy, the mother image becomes dominant. But if he rejects his father, he may or may not cling to his mother. And if he rejects his mother, he is likely to go to the opposite extreme and be drawn to females who are at opposite poles to her salient traits. (Obviously, these generalizations apply to girls just as much as to boys.)

MARITAL ADJUSTMENT

After an individual has assumed the role of husband or wife, there is still the problem of role execution. How adequately does the personality fit the role requirements? Marital adjustment occurs as people learn to conform to each other's expectancies, satisfy each other's needs, and adapt to each other's habits. Burgess and Wallin (1953) present evidence that most of this adjusting, in so far as it involves modification of behavior and expectancy, is done by the wife. This may be a reflection of the patriarchal tradition, still visible in American culture; or—perhaps this is really the same idea—the role of wife is central to the personality, and hence carries great weight in perceptions, whereas the husband is likely also to have occupational, political, and other roles outside the home. This multiplicity of male roles may mean that the husband feels less pressure to modify his egocentric behavior to fit role requirements at home.

Response Conflicts. Mowrer (1935) labels one class of marital conflict as "response conflict," referring to W. I. Thomas's "wish for intimate response." A better term might utilize the notion of an expectancy and need for tender affection. Because of differences in childhood background, men and women may have quite diverse expectancies as to what is proper in the way of affectionate gestures. Ackerman offers an interesting illustration: [4]

The young wife, married only six months, . . . consulted a psychiatrist because she was considering a separation. Initially, the psychiatrist was hard put to discover the reason. He felt puzzled because it proved so difficult to uncover the significant area of conflict. In many ways she seemed satisfied with the relationship. Finally, he asked this young woman if she had a sexual problem with her husband. She said: "Oh, no! Sexual intercourse is perfect; it couldn't be better." "Then what in the world is really the trouble?" asked the psychiatrist. The woman then blurted out her true complaint. "When we have sex, there's just no verbal intercourse at all." Her basic unhappiness was simply that her husband didn't talk enough.

In a study by Ktsanes (1955), designed to support Winch's theory of complementary needs, it was found that "nurturance" was one of the attributes which seemed to follow the complementary pattern. Nurturance, it will be remembered, is Murray's term for the desire to take care of, assist, and support another person. It seems likely that, if one spouse desires such a relationship and the other does not wish to be "mothered" in this way, difficulties will arise.

In some families, children rarely see any manifestations of affection between their parents. They may thus grow up with an unconscious assumption that this is the proper way to behave in marriage. Differences in such expectancies lead to response conflicts.

[4] Ackerman (1958), p. 153. Reprinted by permission.

Dominance Conflicts. A second common variety of role conflict in marriage can best be described as conflict over dominance. Whenever two persons enter into a social interaction, questions arise as to leadership and followership. Commonly in Western culture the male is designated as the dominant mate, but there is an increasing trend toward equalitarian marriages. If the husband is unwilling to go along with this, serious difficulties can result.

Another case of Ackerman's, too long to quote in full, is illustrative: [5]

A couple, each professionally successful, had been comfortably married for nine years. Then, as the husband put it, "All hell broke loose." The previous relationship was based on male dominance and apparent submissive acceptance by the wife. She was, however, afflicted with a severe ulcerative colitis and finally went into psychotherapy. After some years of therapy she suddenly rebelled against his dominative behavior, defiantly altered their domestic routines, denied him sexual gratification, and so on. Although her colitis improved sharply, her marital adjustment disappeared completely.

This case is not cited to support the popular myth that many marriages are destroyed by therapeutic treatment of one member. On the contrary, far more marriages are saved by aiding the neurotic individual to live comfortably with himself and to stop making impossible demands on his mate. It does, however, indicate the importance of dominance relationships in the adjustment process.

Ackerman refers to the family as a homeostatic relation. Mother and child achieve an equilibrium, but this is affected by the interaction of mother and father. Husband and wife achieve equilibrium, but this may be upset by economic factors, by changes in the community, by therapy, as cited above, and by many other influences. If homeostasis holds here, it means that people change their behavior to try to restore the preexisting balance. But we must remember that the person also has important internal equilibria which he must defend—as the wife in the preceding example had to defend her physical survival in the face of a serious illness. The family is not, then, an automatically self-repairing mechanism, at least not in every instance. It does, nevertheless, have homeostatic properties and tends toward the development of stable adjustment. This amounts only to saying that, given the original motivations toward marriage, individuals learn adjustive behavior and so remove many sources of friction.

Dominance and Divorce. We can readily recognize three alternatives for the marriage relationship: dominance by the husband (the traditional pat-

---

[5] It appears from Ackerman's description that the colitis predated the marriage and may have resulted from her suppression of intense emotions in relation to her parents. It is common knowledge that strong emotions can cause diarrhea and irritation of the colon, with bleeding and ulceration. The husband was attracted to her because of her submissiveness (cf. Winch's theory) and the basis for marital adjustment was upset by her discovery that she had to express her emotions outwardly to relieve her psychosomatic illness.

tern), equality as regards decision making (the rising trend, at least in the United States), and dominance by the wife. Jacobson (1952) devised an inventory to measure attitudes toward these dominance relationships. His findings confirm the prediction that conflicts over dominance are a potent source of marital difficulty.

Jacobson compared two large groups, one of couples which had fairly recently been divorced, the other of couples still married. No measure of marital happiness was included, but we can safely assume that, on the average, the married group was doing better than those who had resorted to divorce. The most interesting findings were: (1) The mean difference in attitudes on dominance in the family was only 6.6 points for the married couples, but was 27.7 points for the divorced cases; in other words, if husband and wife had similar attitudes toward distribution of authority, conflict was less. (2) Examination of group means indicated that the divorced males were strong for husband dominance, and divorced females leaned toward dominance by the wife, as the proper way to run a household. Among the married couples, the trend was more toward equality of dominance.[6] The statistics suggest that there may have been a number of cases in the latter group where both parties endorsed male authority, and even some favoring female authority; as long as the partners agreed, no serious conflict seemed to emerge.

Prediction of Dominance. It may be possible to predict marital dominance by using childhood background data. Lu (1952) used material later published in Burgess and Wallin (1953). The data allowed identification of male-dominated, equal, and female-dominated couples in engagement. Later many of these couples were studied after marriage. Lu found biographical items which distinguished the three groups at engagement, then used these items to predict marital dominance. Although his accuracy was far from perfect, it indicated substantial consistency in couple behavior.

An example will illustrate the findings. Items which predicted a wife-dominant marriage included the following: Husband reports no conflict with his mother as a boy, but wife reports conflict with hers; wife got her own way as a child; husband didn't mind parental discipline, wife did; husband was not rebellious toward parental authority, wife was. It seems plausible that a girl child with a strong ego and resistance to parental control techniques will grow up to dominate her mate. And, as the statistics above indicate, her chances of a happy marriage are poor.

Sex Conflicts. The importance of sexual gratification as a basic goal anticipated from marriage should not be underestimated. Consequently, conflicts about sex must be expected to have important effects on marriage. On

---

[6] It is worth noting here that Locke and Karlsson (1952) studied a large number of marriages in both the United States and Sweden, and found equalitarian attitudes on authority favoring adjustment in both nations.

the other hand, as noted in preceding paragraphs, sex may be merely a tool in conflicts based on other goals; for instance, either husband or wife may utilize withdrawal from sexual relations as a device for punishing the partner.

The data on sexual behavior in males and females collected by Kinsey and his coworkers (1948, 1953) support the hypothesis that, on the average, males experience stronger sex urges and are more upset by sexual deprivation or frustration than are females. This does not, however, justify the conclusion that for any particular couple the difference will be in this direction. It is worth mentioning that the individual with the most active sex life, in either Kinsey study, *was a woman.* In the various investigations of marital adjustment, many cases turn up where the stronger motivation of the wife contributes to maladjustment. This quickly gets mixed up with other considerations, however; e.g., the husband begins to doubt his masculine virility under such circumstances and may become defensively hostile to the wife.

Premarital Sex Experience and Adjustment. There is an extensive folklore on premarital sexual experience and the occurrence of sex conflicts in marriage. Some theories hold that such experience helps adjustment by correcting ignorance, others that it interferes by building up guilt feelings. The studies of Terman (1938) and Locke (1951) are in agreement on two conclusions with respect to this controversy: (1) such experience *with future spouse only* is neither a help nor a hindrance to adjustment; and (2) such experience with a variety of persons is definitely a handicap.

We suspect that the explanation here lies in personality, not in sexual behavior. The kind of individual who is incapable of forming an enduring emotional attachment to a particular person flits from affair to affair; and if he enters into a marriage, he will continue to flit. Premarital sex, in other words, probably does not in itself contribute to a higher incidence of marital conflict for such individuals.

Marital Conflicts and Personal Conflicts. The basic problem in a marital difficulty often lies fairly definitely within a single person—though this is not true as often as disgruntled wives and husbands tend to claim. Sometimes the individual has within himself conflicting values and expectancies which disrupt the marriage. Levy and Munroe (1938) describe an interesting case of this kind:

A young woman encouraged her husband to belong to several clubs, plan for golf, squash, and tennis at frequent intervals, etc. Yet she managed regularly, quite "accidentally," to prevent him from attending affairs at his clubs and from keeping his engagements for sports. It quickly became apparent that she was suffering from a conflict between her desire to help him get ahead in his career and her desire to have him at home. She felt some jealousy because of his greater freedom of activity. Her discreet sabotage of his social life outside the family was entirely unconscious, but nonetheless effective. And it precipitated marital conflict which was fully conscious.

There are many such examples. A husband may consciously want his wife to have a career and personal freedom; unconsciously his picture of a proper wife is one who stays home and minds the baby. Differences in expectancies, as we have noted earlier, readily set off marital difficulties; and it is particularly exasperating to one member of the family when another engages in such contradictory behaviors as those noted.

The marital role can be played by an individual only within the limits defined by his already-crystallized personality. If this personality lacks integration (incorporates contradictory expectancies and values), his enactment of the role is going to be erratic and disturbing to the family. Marital and family conflict, therefore, is often an expression of personality disturbance. And this need not be at the extreme level of mental illness to be a serious problem for the spouse and children.

MEASUREMENT OF MARITAL ADJUSTMENT

Studies of the types cited in the preceding pages represent the early tradition in marriage research. The emphasis was on examination of particular marriages, clinically or by interview, and identification of a problem or series of problems. In more recent years there has grown up a great interest in developing measures of marital adjustment, happiness, or satisfaction (the terms have been used more or less interchangeably) and correlating the measures with various possible determinants. The concept of marital adjustment has much in common with the idea of emotional adjustment, as this was used in Chapters 8 and 9.

Terman's Measure of Happiness. Terman notes that in many cultures the question of marital happiness would seem odd. Where marriage is merely a means of sexual gratification for the male, or a device for begetting sons known to be his own, no one would bother to measure marital happiness. But in Western culture the individual is considered important, and the pursuit of happiness is considered acceptable for both wife and husband.

To get a quantitative score for marital happiness, Terman used answers to a series of items such as: engaging in outside interests together; agreeing on how to handle finances; agreeing on religion, on show of affection, on recreation; do you ever regret getting married; how happy would you judge your marriage to be; etc. In addition a list of complaints was presented, and these (if checked) were added into the score. The result was a score which (although subject to criticism) gave at least rough quantification to the idea of marital adjustment.

Evidence of validity was obtained in various ways. All the items cited above intercorrelated positively, the average being $+.57$; thus marital adjustment seems to be a unitary process. The individual's judgment of his happiness in marriage correlated well with score on the remaining items.

Husband-wife correlation was +.67 for rating of the happiness of the marriage. Since Terman worked anonymously, he could not get outside judgments of validity of the scores, but later studies have shown that divorced couples get scores far below the mean of happily married groups. Thus it appears that the marital adjustment score has practical validity.

The major application of this type of score has been in determining factors which predict marital conflict. This kind of knowledge may potentially enable marriage counselors to aid in minimizing conflicts, either by preventing unwise marriages or by providing counseling which will modify the impact of specific variables (LeMasters, 1957). The most significant of these variables, not unnaturally, have been found in the childhood backgrounds of the spouses.

The Importance of Family Background. One of Terman's goals was to prepare a predictive scale which would estimate, from family background data, the probabilities of a successful marriage. He found the following items to have high predictive value in relation to scores on his marital happiness scale:[7]

1. Superior happiness of parents
2. Childhood happiness
3. Lack of conflict with mother
4. Home discipline that was firm, not harsh
5. Strong attachment to mother
6. Strong attachment to father
7. Lack of conflict with father
8. Parental frankness about matters of sex
9. Infrequency and mildness of childhood punishment
10. Premarital attitude toward sex that was free from disgust or aversion

The reader will note that these are precisely the kinds of variables which were pinpointed in the preceding chapter as significant for the development of ego strength and freedom from excessive emotionality. This fits with the observation (see below) that individuals rated as emotionally well adjusted have high marital adjustment scores. The individual growing up in the kind of home indicated by Terman's ten items will acquire favorable images of marriage and of the appropriate sex role, will be able to accept the sexual aspect of marriage, and will not develop unconscious hostilities toward the opposite-sex role which will interfere with cooperation in running a household.

In Locke's study of happily married versus divorced couples, some (but not all) of Terman's findings were confirmed. Locke's data (1951) support Terman as regards: happiness of parents (for men but not for women); happiness as child (for women, not for men); lack of conflict with both mother and father; and discipline in the parental home. (In the latter connection it

[7] From Terman (1938), p. 372. Reprinted by permission of McGraw-Hill Book Company, Inc.

is interesting to note that either too severe or too permissive an arrangement proved undesirable, with severity having more damaging effects.) Some of Locke's findings give indirect support to the importance of childhood sex training, but the question was not asked directly.

The Importance of Personality Traits. Terman (1938) compared happily and unhappily married husbands and wives on a number of items taken from the Bernreuter Personality Inventory and the Strong Vocational Interest Inventory. In general, the former discriminated the happiness groups, while the latter did not. The general procedure is illustrated by Table 18.1. It is clear from this tabulation that happily married husbands differ from the unhappy, and the happily married wives from those less fortunate, on items such as those shown.

Personality differences may precede, and participate in causing, marital difficulties, or they may result from such conflicts. We have used one item of each type in Table 18.1. Experiencing feelings of loneliness may be a consequence of marital troubles, whereas trying to get one's own way even if fighting ensues, we may suspect, is likely to precipitate marital problems. In setting up his prediction measure, Terman reduced the weight allotted to items which seemed to reflect prior marital troubles.

Terman found personality variables to be even more successful in predicting total marital adjustment than were his background factors. This is plausi-

Table 18.1

Personality Items Related to Marital Happiness

Item	Husbands			Wives		
	Happy per cent	*Unhappy per cent*	*C.R.**	*Happy per cent*	*Unhappy per cent*	*C.R.**
Do you try to get your own way even if you have to fight for it?						
Yes	35	45	−2.0	25	43	−3.8
No	55	45	+2.1	66	47	+4.0
Do you often experience feelings of loneliness?						
Yes	16	46	−6.5	22	49	−5.7
No	81	49	+6.9	75	50	+5.3

* Critical ratio, an index of significance. All of those shown exceed the .05 level.
SOURCE: Terman (1938). Modified from Table 27, pp. 122–123. Reprinted by permission of McGraw-Hill Book Company, Inc.

ble. Background factors operate on a marriage only to the extent that these influences have modified habits, perceptions, and goals of the individual. Since some persons are surprisingly resistant to specific kinds of environmental influences, a measure based on the resultant personality will be more valid than one based on the influences expected to modify the personality.

Husbands. Happily married men in the Terman sample indicate even, stable emotions. They tend to enjoy social gatherings and are somewhat extraverted, lacking in self-consciousness. They describe themselves as being more ready to take on responsibility, having more initiative, liking methodical procedures, and liking people. From these attributes we get at least some reason to suppose that these men are higher on ego strength than the unhappily married men. As might be expected, the unhappily married group report more neurotic symptoms: useless thoughts, more frequent states of excitement, more alternations of mood. However, these may reflect the impact of the marital tensions. If continued, it must be assumed that they will become permanent attributes of the personality.

Wives. The happy wives show evidence of security feelings. They report kindly attitudes toward others and expectancies of kindness in return. They do not easily take offense and allege that they are not excessively concerned about the impressions they make upon others. As in the case of the husbands, their self-descriptions give some indication of superior ego strength. According to expectation, unhappy wives report many emotional tensions, fluctuations of mood, inferiority feelings, irritability, and anxiety. In the absence of further data, we cannot tell whether these attributes preceded the marital troubles (as they may well have) or resulted from conflict with the husbands.

The importance of emotional maladjustment ("neuroticism") in marital satisfaction is underscored by a rather extensive study reported by Burchinal et al. (1957). Testing four sizable samples of couples in four states, they find an average correlation of considerable size between lack of neurotic symptoms and marital satisfaction (Table 18.2). As an interesting sidelight they computed the correlation of one mate's emotional adjustment with the other's satisfaction; as the table shows, the wife's personality does not materially affect the husband's satisfaction, but neuroticism on the part of the husband evidently has a substantial detrimental effect on the wife. Perhaps husbands ignore emotionality of their spouses, whereas wives find it difficult to follow this tactic.

Locke's study (1951) utilized a simple rating scale as opposed to the inventory type of question. His data suggest that happily married persons are likely to rate themselves as ready to assume responsibility, strict in dealing with children, taking leadership roles in the community, making decisions quickly, slow in getting angry (and quick in recovering), sociable, and affectionate. The divorced persons were significantly lower on these items. Here

Table 18.2

Emotional Adjustment and Marital Satisfaction

	No. of cases	Average r	Range of r's
Husband's emotional adjustment and his satisfaction	242	+.39	.31 to .54
Wife's emotional adjustment and her satisfaction	246	+.42	.34 to .62
Husband's satisfaction and wife's emotional adjustment	242	+.11	−.06 to +.38
Wife's satisfaction and husband's emotional adjustment	245	+.37	+.28 to +.52

SOURCE: Burchinal et al. (1957).

again we get implications of ego strength as a variable making for success in marriage.

Similarity of Personality. We have noted in earlier pages that engaged couples resemble each other more than random pairs in the population, and that married couples likewise are similar. More importance attaches to this finding in the light of Terman's report that agreement of husband and wife on certain inventory items gives a prognosis of happiness in marriage. Out of a total of 140 points in his prediction scale, 28 points (20 per cent) are based on agreement on certain items: e.g., "Do you want someone to be with you when you receive bad news?" One can imagine that similarity in such matters would aid adjustment. Conversely, there were a few items in which disagreement actually favored adjustment; they are not easy to interpret, but they suggest that happiness is sometimes aided by having one partner dominant and one somewhat submissive. This is as close as Terman's data come to Winch's theory of complementary needs, and Locke's materials are not analyzed in such a way as to throw light on the predictive value of such differences.

Preston et al. (1952) analyzed several hundred personality ratings of clients at a marital counseling center. They confirm the typical finding (that husbands and wives resemble each other in many specific traits) and also find some evidence that a happier marriage is associated with greater reported similarity. In both groups, interestingly enough, they found that *assumed* similarity (self-ratings correlated with predictions for the spouse) was substantially higher than *real* similarity; and this assumed similarity was greater for the happier group. Degree of assumed similarity correlated significantly with judged happiness of the marriage.

At the moment it seems safe to assert that both real similarity and assumed similarity foster happiness in marriage; and if this is combined with mutual understanding, that is still better. We can hardly recommend that young people at or before marriage exchange Rorschach, TAT, and MMPI protocols, but there might be some benefits derived. Certainly any devices which increase accuracy of perception of the self and of the partner should decrease errors of expectancy and, hence, disappointments and frustrations.

A Multiple-predictor Study. Corsini (1956a) applied the multiple-correlation technique, often used in predicting success of employees on jobs, to the prediction of marital happiness. He combined the three factors cited above: biographical items from childhood, personality items such as those found effective by Terman, and a Q-sort measure of personal similarity. As can quickly be seen in Table 18.3, the multiple-predictor technique gives surprisingly high accuracy. By the use of the three sets of prediction items, he reduces predictive errors almost to zero.

Sexual Factors in Marital Adjustment. We noted in the preceding chapter that permissiveness was a major variable in mother-child relations, and that absence of a punitive attitude regarding sex play was a significant indicator of this variable. It was further indicated that permissiveness at this early age seemed favorable to good personality development. We note also that Terman found an important background factor aiding marital adjustment to be "parental frankness about matters of sex." Davis (1929) noted that marital happiness was favored by receiving some sex instruction prior to marriage. Such data suggest that premarital sex training has an important place in marital happiness. More significance, of course, attaches to actual sexual behavior as a determinant of marital adjustment.

Table 18.3

Improving Prediction of Marital Happiness
with Additional Measures

Predictive measure	Happiness of	
	Husband	Wife
Personality	.65	.68
Early background	.65	.43
Similarity of mates	.61	.75
Background + similarity	.76	.78
Personality + similarity	.78	.73
Personality + background	.68	.76
Personality + background + similarity	.82	.87

SOURCE: Corsini (1956a). Table 1, p. 241. Reprinted by permission of the author and *Marriage and Family Living*.

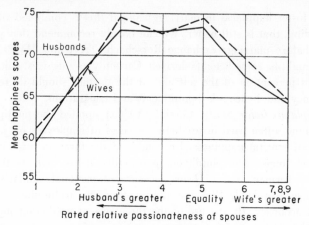

Fig. 18.2   Sex drive and marital happiness. Relative equality of sex motivation makes for highest happiness scores. (From Terman, 1938.)

The Importance of Sexual Adjustment. The success of a marriage is a matter of total personality, not merely the sex impulse. Few people, however, will deny that sexual gratification is one of the major goals expected in the marital relationship; it must be assumed that frustration in this respect will have a disturbing effect. Thomason (1955) repeated the early investigation of Terman (1938). Thomason's conclusions are summed up as follows: (1) "The quality of total marital and sexual adjustment of both husbands and wives was decidedly increased if the wife always had a climax in sexual intercourse." (2) "The quality of total marital and sexual adjustment is significantly greater if both mates reach a climax together in intercourse." (3) "Both husbands and wives were significantly more likely to have both a better total marital happiness and sexual adjustment if their . . . mates were attractive sexually, sexual intercourse was by mutual desire, and their mates were willing and able to have intercourse as often as they wished it" [pp. 158, 159, 162].

The importance of similarity in strength of sex drive was emphasized by Terman's data. Figure 18.2 shows graphically how happiness in marriage is related to this variable. Deviation from a rating of equality in either direction lowers the mean happiness score, although a slightly greater drive on the husband's side seems to be a minor matter. Locke's data support this conclusion.

As Thomason concluded, the ability of the wife to reach sexual orgasm is also a significant factor in marital happiness. Figure 18.3 (from Terman's data) indicates that the mean happiness score, for both husbands and wives, increases rapidly as the wife's adequacy in this respect improves.[8]

[8] Terman had originally assumed that orgasm adequacy of wives was primarily a function of early sexual training, or perhaps of fear. After exhaustive study (Terman,

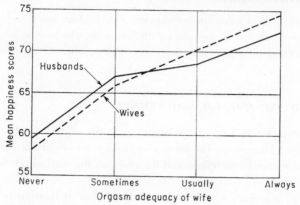

Fig. 18.3 Marital happiness and wife's sexual reaction. Happiness scores of both husband and wife increase with wife's ability to reach full gratification in the sexual relationship. (From Terman, 1938.)

Some interest attaches to sexual items which did *not* predict marital adjustment. Premarital sexual relations with the future spouse did not differentiate happily and unhappily married couples (Terman), but intercourse with others did tend to lower future marital adjustment. This may reflect a personality trait (restless seeking, inability to form a stable relationship with one person) rather than a simple sex problem. Terman's data show no effect of fear of pregnancy on adjustment; Locke, however, indicates that it lowers adjustment. Similarly, Terman found no relation of adjustment to birth-control measures employed; Locke indicates that use of contraceptives increases significantly the chances of a successful marriage. Differences in wording of questions, and in the sample studied, may account for these apparently contradictory findings.

Prediction of Divorce. Although the group involved is a rather special case, some interest attaches to a study of the predictive success of marital adjustment scores for occurrence of divorce in later years. Terman and Oden (1947) report results in a follow-up study of the "gifted children" first studied by Terman in the early 1920s. In 1940 marital prediction scales and marital happiness scales were given to more than 600 of these gifted subjects and their spouses. In 1947 it was found that 46 couples had been broken by divorce. It was then possible to ascertain how these subjects compared with the 90 per cent still married. The data show that both the prediction score (based on premarital attributes) and the happiness score predict divorce with significant accuracy.[9] Both men and women who later divorced scored

---

1951), he was forced to admit that the incapacity of some women to reach sexual climax was a real mystery; he even speculated that it might be a constitutional trait.

[9] Interestingly enough, sexual adjustment in 1940 was considerably less accurate at predicting divorce than either the 1940 happiness score or the 1940 childhood background material.

well below the group mean on both scales. This finding tends to validate both the happiness score itself, and the prediction scale which, it is hoped, will be useful in premarital counseling to reduce the number of unsuccessful marriages.

THE CHILD AND MARITAL ADJUSTMENT

It is appropriate to pay special attention to the impact of children on the husband-wife relationship. The birth of a child is a normal but not always expected consequence of marriage, and the effect on the marital relationship may be substantial.

Even when a woman wishes to bear a child, her motivation may be other than a simple love for children. Ackerman (1958) lists a number of motives which turn up in psychiatric practice: to neutralize anxiety about sterility or frigidity; to please the husband (sometimes, to punish the husband); to hold the husband; to win approval of her own parents and friends; to meet the cultural stereotype of a proper family life; or to provide a symbol through which she can live her childhood over again. The way each parent will perceive the new infant, and will respond to it, is naturally modified by circumstances such as those here implied.

Children and Marital Stability. Sometimes a woman, fearing that her husband is about to leave her, decides to get pregnant so that he will keep the family together for the child's sake. Although this no doubt works well at times, one wonders how much damage it does to the child, and whether the wife is happier in the long run for having adopted this maneuver.

The first pregnancy may interfere somewhat with sexual adjustment. Landis, Poffenberger, and Poffenberger (1950) found that about one-fourth of married college couples studied considered the pregnancy to have been an unfavorable influence in this respect. (However, about 17 per cent said the effect was favorable, so the trend, if any, is not substantial.)

Children may represent the fulfillment of wishes of both marital partners, or they may represent blockages to other goals. In the case of young people attending college, the unexpected birth of a child into a marriage may introduce serious strains. Christensen and Philbrick (1952) studied several hundred student couples at Purdue University and found that, in general, marital difficulties were more acute in families with children, and became worse with increase from one to two children. There was a curious improvement in marital adjustment of couples with three children, but the number of couples in this category was (not surprisingly) a very small group, and may perhaps have been composed of those who wanted and could care adequately for three children. The authors asked if the children had been planned, and found a significantly higher marital adjustment where this was so. It is the unplanned baby which constitutes the upsetting factor.

Locke (1951) reports that the presence or absence of children does not seem to affect the frequency of divorce. If the conflict situation is too serious, divorce or separation occurs anyhow. Similarly, Terman (1938) reported that the presence of children did not significantly affect the marital adjustment scores of couples in his sample; and Locke and Karlsson (1952) agree. It seems improbable, therefore, that the simple statistical fact of parenthood influences marital adjustment in a single direction. Conversely, it seems safe to assume that at least the first child always has an important impact on the parents, but probably to strengthen a favorable situation or to accentuate a conflict situation.

The Shift in Parental Roles. Particularly at the birth of the first baby in a family, the parents are required to accept totally new roles. The mother is likely to find that she has taken on a 12- to 15-hour daily job, in addition to her former duties as housekeeper and wife. She may pay less attention to her husband's conversation, and to his sexual needs, under these conditions. The father finds that he has more responsibility, more anxieties. He has taken on an obligation, perhaps unintentionally. He may perceive the child as confirmation of his virility, but he may contrariwise feel that he is now hobbled. We cannot evaluate the shift in parental roles without recognizing the importance of such perceptual variations.

Both mother and father may find the new infant eliciting impulses toward dominance. Although the helplessness of the baby appeals to nurturant trends, there is a substantial likelihood that the person with strong dominance needs will seize this opportunity for self-assertion. As noted in the preceding chapter, this is often hard on the child.

Marital and Parental Adjustment. Just as sexual adjustment problems generalize to disturb all aspects of a marital relationship, so marital problems generalize to disturb parental relations. Porter (1955) finds a correlation of .41 (highly significant) between a measure of parental acceptance of children and a scale for marital adjustment. If the husband and wife are not happy in their marriage, it is a poor solution for them to become parents. The most probable outcome is that the child, too, will have a difficult time in this situation.

Children develop unfavorable attitudes toward their parents when the marriage is unhappy, according to Wallin and Vollmer (1953). This is hardly surprising, since each parent will probably supply plenty of arguments for disliking the other! Often the child is forced to take sides in the conflict, and this usually is resolved by favoring the mother (who is, after all, the primary symbol of security for children of both sexes). But this involves violating the cultural norm that the child should express equal affection for both parents. Furthermore, to the extent that the boy is thus prevented from identifying with the father, his emotional maturity is slowed down and his acceptance of the masculine role in life handicapped. In happy marriages, Wallin and

Vollmer comment, there are few conflicts with adolescent children. The happy parent has enough security to be permissive, to encourage developing independence and responsibility. Unhappy parents, on the other hand, may resolve various inner tensions by trying to impose controls on the children; a man frustrated in dominance may boss his son, and a woman denied affection or attention by her husband may become so demanding of demonstrations from the child as to seem to destroy all freedom for him to develop as an individual. This continuing dialectical relationship between group and personality holds, of course, elsewhere than in the family, but nowhere else is it so clear or so important.

THE PROCESS OF MARITAL ACCOMMODATION

The interaction of two individuals in a situation such as marriage may be characterized as a learning process (for each considered individually) or as a process of accommodation, in the sense that a new social group is being developed. Either term is appropriate. Accommodation has been used more commonly in group contexts (cf. Stagner, 1956), but the process seems identical when persons are taken as units.

Every accommodation process involves goals, norms, and techniques. Each of the parties to the marriage has certain goals which are sought through entering upon this venture. Each has certain norms, both as to these goals and as to the proper behavior of each party—expectancies, we have called them. And each has certain habits or ways of behaving, certain techniques for relating to other persons.

In marriage, accommodation may involve change of goals. The young man who marries for sexual gratification may find many other pleasant aspects of the relationship, and his conception of the goals obtainable through marriage will be modified. A girl who marries because "she doesn't want to be an old maid" may find sex, companionship, sympathy, and emotional support to be additional gains from the relationship. Conversely, in an unhappy marriage the original goal—sex, economic security, or something else—may come to appear very unimportant. The negative valence associated with the relationship may override these other aspects.

Similarly, norms tend to change in marriage. A girl who was brought up to believe that "sex is not nice" may find it possible to see things differently. The youth who assumed that he could run around freely after marriage, while his wife stayed home to mind the children, may learn differently. (If he does not, he may encounter very unpleasant consequences.) Visiting with other married couples changes the context of married life, gives people new ways of looking at things. The average young person who has seen only his parents at close range has only a single model of "what married people act like." As he acquires a wider range of experience, his norms and expectancies are modified.

Habits also change. Since, especially in the early stages of marriage, young people have certain important reward values for each other, we can assume that conditions are favorable for rewarding certain kinds of behavior and not reinforcing others. Tender, affectionate behavior leads to pleasant experiences; harsh, angry interchanges prevent pleasant contacts.

Theorizing along the above lines leads to the prediction that personality will change in marriage. The data as to actual changes are somewhat ambiguous. Kelly (1955) did not observe any increase in marital similarity in his twenty-year follow-up study. He finds "little tendency either for the husband to change toward the original score of his wife, or the wife to change toward that of her husband." However, it may be that learning in marriage leads not to similarity but to complementarity, as would be suggested by Winch. Farber and Blackman (1956) indicate that a measure of marital tensions at the end of the first three years of married life gives a good prediction of tensions after fourteen years. In the same vein is the observation by Stroup (1953) that premarital background predicts marital success just as accurately for persons married more than fifteen years as for those married less than five. If marriage produced much change in personality, this should not be true. These studies suggest the old adage, "The more things change, the more they remain the same." Personal rigidity and selective learning may prevent personality growth in marriage. This pessimistic view is supported by the studies of Terman and Oden (1947) and others which indicate that premarital measures of personality and developmental history predict not only marital success but also divorce.

These findings do not, however, preclude the possibility of a changing course of adjustment in marriage. We may, for example, speculate as follows: Marriage is a goal-seeking venture for both parties. Some of these goals are short-run matters, such as sexual gratification, economic security, dependency; others are long-time affairs. No doubt most marriages start off in a favorable context because some gratifications accrue to both parties in the early stages. With time, however, the background factors begin to operate: The husband begins to complain because his wife does not meet his expectations, or he modifies his expectations to conform to her behavior, or she changes to meet his demands. Should either of the latter possibilities develop, a favorable adjustment is in store. Since the personality tends to be pretty well crystallized by the age of matrimony, most people do not change, and so complaints are the rule if expectations do not fit. Over time, then, tensions may become exacerbated until divorce occurs.

One of the few investigators of marital problems who has given special attention to this problem is Locke, whose work has already been cited. Locke comments that "the alienation process (break-up of a marriage) is generally a slow cumulation of conflicts and disagreements. . . . If the course of the alienation process is far advanced, the spouses tend to express derogatory attitudes toward each other, tend to have many complaints about the mate and the marriage, and tend to exaggerate the deficiencies of the mate and the marriage." [10]

Such observations support our prediction that personality modification does occur in the course of the marriage. The studies of premarital personality indicate that couples resembling each other have a good chance of being happy; and since this pattern is rewarding, it seems that happy couples at least should become more alike. Since unhappy couples are more emotionally disturbed at marriage, they should become more disturbed over time. The evidence on these points is far from clear. What is needed is a longitudinal study, following up the same couples over a period of twenty to thirty years. As such data accumulate, we can feel more confident about the accommodation process as it goes on in the marital relationship.

SUMMARY

Merely as a result of the passing of time and physiological maturation, the child reaches the age of marriage. During the intervening years, his personality has been molded by his parents, by his friends, by his culture, by the accidents of his personal experiences. He has acquired an image of proper role behavior in marriage, as regards both himself and his mate. He has also a set of standards which determines the kind of opposite-sex person he will find attractive and marriageable.

The evidence indicates that at least for the manifest aspects of personality, including attitudes, interests, values, and traits, similarity makes for better marital prospects. The theory of complementary needs merits some consideration but may be relevant for only a small segment of personality dynamics. Especially important, it seems, is mutual understanding, something which is achievable more readily if the childhood backgrounds are similar. Some traits seem to have negative prediction value regardless of similarity, such as anxiety, depression, and other manifestations of emotional instability. The converse, which we have identified with ego strength, includes self-confidence, poise, tolerance of difference, and realistic perception of persons and situations; presence of this pattern in one (preferably both) partners gives a highly favorable prediction for the marriage.

Every marriage is a goal-seeking process. Goals may include dominance of another person, sexual gratification, economic security, tenderness, and emotional response. Conflicts in these areas seem especially likely to lead to unhappiness if not to divorce. However, most marriages involve accommodation, i.e., mutual modification of personality, and it is obvious that changes in goals may accompany successful marriages. Rigidity (inability to modify goal ex-

[10] Locke (1951), p. 358. Reprinted by permission of Henry Holt & Co.

pectancies) probably is associated with divorce, although the evidence on this point is vague.

Although psychologists are generally agreed that sex is not as important as is commonly believed, it does play a major role in marital adjustment. Sex techniques, however, seem to have no predictive value for success. Equality of sex drive seems to be more important than other aspects of the sexual relationship.

The distribution of authority in the marriage is likewise significant for success. Equalitarian marriages seem to be happier, and less likely to end in divorce, than those dominated by either partner. Dominance by the husband may go with success if it coincides with the wife's expectancies. Indeed, it seems likely that dominance by the wife could occur in a happy marriage if this fitted the husband's needs. Similarity of cultural background thus aids marriage by increasing the likelihood that the couple will have similar images as to proper role behavior in marriage.

Children seem to play no important role in keeping a marriage together or breaking it up. Some evidence indicates that unplanned children present a special source of tension.

Like every interpersonal relationship, marriage probably leads to modification of personality. The exact kinds of modification to be expected must be related to particular kinds of personalities in particular marriages; no predictions are possible as to the effects of marriage in general.

SUGGESTIONS FOR READING

The classic study of personality and marital adjustment is Terman's *Psychological factors in marital happiness*. The major findings of this study have now been confirmed several times. Locke's *Predicting adjustment in marriage* bears particularly upon factors leading to divorce. LeMasters, in his *Modern courtship and marriage*, gives abridged summaries of several important studies in this area and offers generally sage advice to young people, mostly based on the research data. A book which rejects the statistical, survey approach in favor of clinical insights into specific families is that of Ackerman, *The psychodynamics of family life*. Another clinical approach, somewhat more provocative than Ackerman's, will be found in Bergler, *Divorce won't help*.

ノ ノ ノ CHAPTER **19**

The School System

A significant part of the American child's life is spent in school. In most states he is required by law to spend several months each year, between the ages of six and sixteen, in an approved educational institution. Here he continues the process—which has gone on in the family—of liking and disliking, conforming and rebelling, acquiring a conception of the world and of himself.

Obviously much of the child's personality is already shaped by the time he is six. Many of his reactions to the school situation will simply be transfers from family learning, as he perceives equivalent stimuli to be present. Hostility to parents, whether overt or latent, may appear as rebelliousness toward the teacher. Insecurity based on rejection may be manifest as aggressiveness, an excessive and insatiable demand for affection, or suspiciousness. Sibling rivalry is likely to take the form of competition with classmates.

No social situation, of course, ever completely duplicates another. Although the teacher may be perceived as a parent substitute, she is not the parent, and differences in her behavior are significant for the child's development. Perhaps even more important is the fact that the child is now faced by certain institutional rules and requirements which are new and frustrating. Further, the school poses certain tasks, rewards, and punishments, to which the child must adapt according to his ability and motivation. The school, therefore, poses new problems to be solved, new taboos to be accepted into the superego, and new models for imitation and identification, all of which contribute their share to the molding of personality.

Recognition of this aspect of the schools as personality agencies has, unfortunately, been formal rather than functional. We have educated our children in business and professional methods and in skilled trades; many nations have educated their children to glorify military heroes and accept war gladly; and some cultures stress the acquisition of fine manners and conformity to established ritual. It is doubtful, however, that any public school system has ever embraced the aim of personality development as its major purpose. Without formal intent, however, the American system of schools and colleges does function as an institutionalized force for the shaping of personality.

450

Our procedure in dealing with this material will resemble that adopted for Chapter 18. There are certain role requirements for teachers and for students which merit attention. There are, further, certain institutional rules which impose frustrations and permit gratifications of certain kinds. In addition, the personalities of individual teachers become important influences on the child (we omit as unmeasurable the harassing effect some children have on their teachers), whether through the treatment imposed by the teacher or through the mechanism of imitation. The content of the curriculum plays a role, perhaps minor, in shaping some aspects of personality. And finally, we shall take a brief look at the other side of the coin: the part played by the child's personality in determining the success with which he handles the problems facing him in the educational process.

THE INSTITUTIONAL PATTERN

Our educational system is an institution, a set of behaviors and expectancies as to proper roles. If we take the public schools as an example, we find decision-making power concentrated in the hands of the school board, usually an elective body including no one who has ever had teaching experience, often not even parents. Authority is delegated by the board to an administrative staff, which passes on instructions to the teachers. The teachers are expected to adopt an authoritarian role as regards the students.

Traditional education (prior to World War I) followed this hierarchical pattern closely. With the development of "progressive education," some efforts were made to democratize the system, but they were not always effective. And, in the new, post-Sputnik concern with better education, the traditional authoritarianism seems again on the rise.

Role of the Administrator. In theory the role of the administrator is to arrange things so that the teacher can do an optimum job of teaching without being bothered by problems of books, space, and equipment. In practice the administrator quite often functions as an autocrat, laying down not only curricula but also techniques; the ideal of some principals is to be able to look at a clock and say, "Right now Miss Smith's class is working at the top of page 173 in this textbook."

The importance of the administrator in determining the emotional tone of a school is well illustrated by Lyman (1949). In doing a testing survey in a city school system, he was impressed by the contrast between two schools from similar neighborhoods; in one school he had had excellent cooperation from the pupils, whereas in the other there had been much disorder and sabotage of the study. He tried out an inventory of attitudes toward the school and found that, in the disorderly school, attitudes were exceedingly unfavorable in general; however, they came to a focus in hostility toward the principal,

whose behavior apparently gave the pupils some justification for their feelings.
[It is to be expected that some administrators will be relatively more authoritarian, others more democratic.]Unfortunately, little has been found to identify the personality determinants of such actions. The F scale (page 250), for example, does not predict whether a principal will behave in an authoritarian fashion (Hines, 1956).

The Teacher's Role. A large proportion of classroom teaching is also authoritarian. This is true not only because the teacher presumably knows more than the students and is in a better position to decide what they need to know; it also follows because authoritarianism maintains the pattern, provides some substitute balm for the teacher's ego, and is less difficult than handling the class democratically. There is, consequently, a general sequence in which the teacher decides upon goals, makes assignments, requires certain performances, and evaluates these as satisfactory or unsatisfactory. The student gets considerable practice in submitting to arbitrary control, but relatively little in exploring new problems, developing independent thought, planning projects, and deciding when he has done a good job.

Analysis of Teacher Roles. The foregoing characterization of the teacher's behavior is obviously too sketchy and is biased in a critical direction.[Many teachers attempt to take the child's personal attributes into consideration, try to arouse motivation, and invite participation.] We noted in the preceding chapter that, in every social group, there seem to be at least two distinguishable roles: that of getting a job done (achievement), and that of expressing emotions (expression). In marriage the male role has usually stressed achievement, and the female role has provided for more emotional expression. Although we are not concerned in this volume with the behavior of industrial leaders, we may note that the task of supervision has at least two components: structuring (planning and directing a job) and consideration (improving human relations). These seem parallel to the roles in marriage.

Work on the role of the teacher has not, for the most part, picked up this idea. However, Ryan and Wandt (1952) did a factor analysis of teacher behaviors which points in the same direction.[They got evidence for five independent dimensions in assessments of secondary school teachers, as follows:]

A. Fair and democratic methods
B. Business-like, organized, responsible
C. Encourages student participation, challenging, interesting
D. Enthusiastic
E. Openminded

[In a similar study of college teachers, Gibb (1955) identified four dimensions, which he labeled as follows:]

I. Social distance: mixes easily, not dominative, friendly, democratic
II. Explanation, tells students how they are doing

III. Organization, initiative

IV. Production-domination, pressure for achievement

⌈It seems likely that these two studies have found substantially the same thing, and that these separate dimensions probably could be reduced to two: those concerned with putting across material, getting the job done; and those concerned with friendliness, good human relations, warm emotional responsiveness.⌉

It is worthwhile noting, in this connection, that studies of students' evaluations of teachers indicate that they can identify such variables in their teachers. Further, some students show a preference for teachers high on the warm, friendly, expressive dimension; others prefer one with "cognitive merit," one who knows the material and can put it across. Both these qualities, obviously, are desirable. Some thirty or forty years ago stress on the cognitive side was heavy; more recently, emphasis has been placed on the need for teachers with warm, democratic traits. As will be noted later in this chapter, there is some reason to think that the trend just now is back toward somewhat greater concern for accomplishment, with less urgency attached to making the child happy.

Teacher Role and "Social Climate." Obviously the manner in which the teacher carries out his role will determine the emotional atmosphere, or "social climate," in the classroom. An authoritarian teacher will establish an autocratic climate, while a democratic teacher will create a different kind of atmosphere. These differences will imply differences in the number of frustrations imposed upon the students, and in the kind of personality development encouraged.

The experiments of Lewin, Lippitt, and White (1939) made a pioneering contribution to the conceptualization of social climate, as well as defining significant variables which make it possible for us to apply the plan to an educational model. The experiments made use of boys' clubs in which leaders were carefully instructed in procedures to create definite kinds of climates. Three patterns were defined in advance: authoritarian, democratic, and laissez-faire. The operations used to distinguish these three are outlined in Table 19.1.

It will be clear at a glance that the correct analogue of a typical classroom situation is the authoritarian or autocratic group. Policy, in its broad forms, is dictated by the school board or by state law. Even within the limits so prescribed, the teacher is very unlikely to give students any chance to vote or to voice a preference as to procedure. Assignments are customarily given piecemeal, with little over-all perspective, and are subject to arbitrary modification at the whim of the teacher. Rules are so set that children cannot cooperate, must carry out a particular routine set by the teacher, and have no chance for self-expression or group identification. The rules usually prescribe that a certain number shall be adjudged as failing, no matter how good their performance or effort. Criticism is likely to be quite personal, and the teacher

Table 19.1

Patterns of Autocracy, Democracy, and Laissez Faire

Authoritarian	*Democratic*	*Laissez-faire*
All determination of policy was by the leader.	All policies were a matter of group discussion and decision, encouraged and assisted by leader.	Complete freedom existed for group or individual decision, without any leader participation.
Techniques and activity steps were dictated by the authority, one at a time, so that future steps were always uncertain to a large degree.	Activity perspective was gained during first discussion period. General steps to group goal were sketched, and, where technical advice was needed, the leader suggested two or three alternative procedures from which choice could be made.	Various materials were supplied by the leader, who made it clear that he would supply information when asked. He took no other part in work discussions.
The leader usually dictated the particular work task and work companions of each member.	The members were free to work with whomever they chose, and the division of tasks was left up to the group.	There was complete nonparticipation by leader.
The dominator was "personal" in his praise and criticism of the work of each member, but remained aloof from active group participation, except when demonstrating. He was friendly or impersonal rather than openly hostile.	The leader was "objective" or "fact-minded" in his praise and criticism, and tried to be a regular group member in spirit without doing too much of the work.	Very infrequent comments were made on member activities unless questioned, and there was no attempt to participate or interfere with the course of events.

SOURCE: Lewin, Lippitt, and White (1939).

very rarely accepts a status on a level with the pupils. The points of similarity between school procedure and the democratic pattern as experimentally defined are relatively uncommon.

Lewin and his associates found that the autocratic atmosphere tended to increase aggression and hostility; verbal comments and overt acts were more aggressive, either within the club or as soon as the club adjourned. Most of this hostility was directed upon club members; two boys were forced to drop out as they became "scapegoats" in turn. Although the same boys (and the same leaders) participated in democratic groups, no such incidents occurred in the democratic atmosphere. The democratic setup led to constructive, thoughtful, cooperative behavior. Generally the quality of work done seemed higher in the democratic group.

By and large, the boys liked the democratic procedure. A few, notably the son of an army officer, liked the autocratic leadership. Nobody liked the laissez-faire situation, in which students got no pleasure either from accomplishing something or from working closely with an interesting adult. The suggestion has since been made that some so-called "democratic" classroom procedures have led to the creation of a laissez-faire situation, unstructured, without leadership, and getting nowhere.

Dominative Techniques in Teaching. As we have noted above, the typical classroom resembles the autocratic atmosphere devised by Lewin. There has been an attempt, under the general label of "progressive education," to get away from the teacher-dominated, curriculum-centered pattern of teaching, to a child-centered approach. The studies of actual educational situations most closely related to Lewin's work stem from this kind of thinking about the school and its functions.

H. H. Anderson (1945) has published a number of studies of teaching procedure under the heading of *dominative* and *integrative* behavior. The concept of dominative behavior, as he employs it, is closely related to Lewin's autocratic atmosphere; integration, to Lewin's democracy. Examples of dominative acts by teachers are expressed in such instructions as these: "You will have to do it this way"; "Sit over here"; "You can't do that now." Criticism, threats, orders, and lectures come in this group. Integrative behavior, on the other hand, is flexible and child-centered. "Who would like to do this?" "What shall we do now?" Attempts by the teacher to help the child understand his problem, but without giving him the correct answer, come in this group. The integrative response seeks to understand the child's purposes and adapt the school activity to them, rather than forcing the child to accept the activity as stereotyped.

As could be predicted by any student of our educational system, the proportion of dominative to integrative contacts with children is high for virtually every teacher studied. It would appear that a psychologically "good" teacher would be one whose dominative acts were only twice as frequent as her integrative approaches.

It has been demonstrated in studies of pairs of children (Anderson, 1937) that domination by one child incites domination (resistance, counteraggression) by the other. It is safe to assert that many children react in the same way to teacher domination. It is also obvious that dominative techniques prevent the child from developing self-reliance, independent thought, and cooperative attitudes.

Most young children fit more or less normally into this scheme of things because they come from homes which, on the average, are also authoritarian.

However, the child who ventures to disagree with the teacher is speedily told his place. Woodworth (1935) quotes an incident from the life of Gene Stratton-Porter, who "came early into conflict with the teacher, who had written on the blackboard the sentence, 'Little birds in their nests agree,' and was pointing out the good example set by the birds, when Gene, from her intimate knowledge of bird households, interrupted: 'Oh, but they *don't* agree! They fight like anything. They pull feathers and peck at each other's eyes till they are all bloody.' She got the punishment to be expected. . . ."

Another incident is reported by a college student. "When I was in Mr. A's history class, I offered a suggestion about something—the American Revolution, I think. He said that it was very good, and asked where I got it. When I said it was my own opinion, he became quite indignant, and said that high school students were not allowed to have opinions of their own."

Superiority of Democratic Approach. In America it should not be necessary to argue that the democratic approach to education is superior to the dictatorial method. Unfortunately, attempts to modify rigid curricular requirements in favor of a child-centered approach often encounter belligerent opposition, and some other valuable experiments have been stopped entirely.

Mowrer (1939a) has described an experiment in the democratic management of a group of delinquent or problem children. When these children were shifted from autocratic to democratic control, with a great deal of self-government, the number of disciplinary problems decreased, children learned to cooperate and live in a civilized manner together, and emotional adjustments improved. Nevertheless, the plan ultimately had to be abandoned because of public opposition. The same thing has happened to many successful experiments in prison and reform-school management.

The work of Lewin, Anderson, Mowrer, and others who have studied this problem seems unanimous in indicating the democratic approach to be most successful. It permits maximum personality development for each child, prepares him for group living, prepares him to study questions and make his own decisions, and gives superior training in emotional self-control.

The typical school organization at present tends to create in children an attitude of yielding to authority, letting others do the planning, avoiding decisions. It unquestionably has a considerable responsibility for the number of infantile personalities that are met on every hand in adult life.

The Requirement of Failure. The experience of failure is bound to be painful, particularly when it is interpreted by parents and teachers as something of which one should be ashamed. Repeated painful contacts with any situation will cause fear or hatred of that situation. Yet we organize our schools in such a way that certain children are doomed to failure each year. Teachers rarely seem to perceive the irony of encouraging every child to strive for high marks, then giving grades on a distribution basis so that a fixed percentage is certain to fail. Even if a distribution curve is not employed, the setting of arbitrary subject-matter requirements dooms many to failure, since they simply are not endowed with the mental abilities essential to this kind of performance.

Sandin (1944) studied a group of 139 slow-progress children and 277 regular-progress children from grades 1 to 8. He found that those who failed more than once were uniformly rated by both teachers and classmates as having less desirable personalities. Boys in this group received significantly more ratings as unfriendly, cruel, and bullying; they were also characterized as unhappy and grouchy, quarrelsome and disagreeable, rude and impolite, inconsiderate, selfish, and boastful. The girls were rated as inattentive, daydreaming, and easily discouraged. Among the boys, clearly, we have an aggressive reaction to the unpleasantness and frustration of a school system not geared to their needs and abilities; the girls, on the other hand, attempt to withdraw. Neither reaction makes for a sound, well-adjusted personality.

The school can do justice to children of limited verbal capacity only by providing education of a type suited to their potentialities and providing rewards which will motivate them to continue trying. The number of juvenile delinquents whose antisocial behavior is basically traceable to an arbitrary school system has never been computed, but it must be large.

The institutional pattern of the arbitrary curriculum, which refuses to make allowance for individual differences in children, also works a hardship on the child of superior mental capacity. Held back to the pace of the average pupil, he readily becomes bored and often hostile to the school. Several studies which have plotted behavior problems against intelligence quotient have reported an excess as the IQ deviates in either direction from 100. Both the inferior and the superior suffer from the inflexible pattern. An interesting illustration of the kind of problem often manifested by the brighter child is given by Pressey and Robinson: [1]

In another instance a bright, nervous, high-strung third-grade child refused point-blank to read aloud a simple story about animals that talked because she regarded it as silly. The order was repeated, the stubbornness increased, and the exasperated young teacher told the child she could not leave school until she had read the story aloud. At five o'clock the deadlock was broken by the principal, who required merely that the girl read a passage from any book, whereupon the youngster proudly pulled from her desk a copy of *David Copperfield* and read a passage with gusto. . . . The work was far below the level of her interests and ability; the episode was the climax of an accumulated exasperation at work which she considered beneath her. And she craved the satisfaction of showing what difficult material she could and ordinarily did read.

Role Conflict and Teacher Personality. It is clear that there are two roles offered to the teacher: one, to be dominative and arbitrary, to adopt a strictly task-centered view and ignore problems of the individual child;

[1] Pressey and Robinson (1944), p. 188. Reprinted by permission of Harper & Brothers, publishers.

and the other, to be warm and sympathetic, to try to make children happy, without worrying much about achievement. Naturally the typical teacher tries to fill both roles. This is likely to lead to *role conflict,* to a situation in which tension is raised because no correct response is clearly visible.

There are obviously at least two ways in which personality is related to role conflicts:

1. If the individual encounters many role conflicts, his tension level will be raised, he will perceive many situations as unpleasant, and he may break down, lose ego control, and begin to perceive events unrealistically. Role conflicts, then, may have a deleterious effect on personality. We mentioned this possibility in connection with marriage (the wife, especially, finds herself in conflicting roles as housekeeper, mother, mistress, and social secretary).

2. Another possibility is that persons with certain personality trends will be conflict-prone, i.e., will be upset by role conflicts which do not disturb others. A person who does not perceive clean-cut differences, who has trouble making up his mind, will be unable to resolve his conflicts. Hamlet, his mind "sicklied o'er by the pale cast of thought," could not reach a decision; he was torn between the roles of devoted son and loyal subject. A different kind of personality would either have killed his stepfather promptly or decided to accept the situation.

Guba and Getzels (1955) propose the term "conflict-prone" to identify individuals who find it disturbing to be trapped by these contradictory demands. They studied role conflicts among instructors at Air University. Despite the hierarchical structure of the military, with decisions on a command basis, not by discussion and group decision, the instructors had been told to be democratic, to encourage participation, to permit disagreement with the instructor. Some men found the conflict between their roles as teachers and as officers quite painful. Others seemed unperturbed by these differences. The investigators identified two groups of instructors, respectively high and low on role conflict, and administered a variety of personality tests to them. The main conclusions were: The conflict-prone individual was less masculine, more socially introverted, more prone to depression, and displayed feelings of inferiority and nervousness—the pattern we have called the "weak-ego" personality. The conflict-prone group were also higher on prejudice and on the F scale (page 250), and tended to be extrapunitive as shown on the Rosenzweig Picture-frustration Test (page 113).

Although the evidence does not support generalization from this to other kinds of role conflicts, the "face validity" of the generalization seems high. The ego, as we have treated it, is a process of assessing the environment, identifying significant objects or cues, and deciding on action. Persons of strong ego, we have said, "keep the eye on the ball," pick out the essential elements of a situation, avoid distraction by irrelevant cues. Doing so, they succeed, and thus have a maximum number of successes and a minimum of frustrations. Their perceptions of the world and of other people are mainly pleasant. The weak ego, distracted by minor aspects of a problem, unable to adhere to a course of action, fails, is unhappy, acquires a lot of negative valences, and experiences a plethora of worries and hostilities. We observe an interacting process in which ego adequacy leads to success, which strengthens the ego; ego inadequacy leads to failure, with still further ego-weakening consequences.

PERSONALITIES OF TEACHERS

Personalities of teachers undoubtedly vary in many ways; the phenomenon of being conflict-prone is one of these, but others are also important. Conversely, it is likely that personalities of teachers are alike in certain ways, and different from the general run of the population. What kinds of persons go into teaching?

Manifest Needs of Teachers. We have referred earlier to the Edwards Personal Preference Schedule, an inventory which attempts to measure needs as defined by Murray (page 346). Adams, Blood, and Taylor (1959) report on a study of a substantial group of experienced women teachers, and of female students in a college of education, using the Edwards PPS. Their data are summarized in Figure 19.1.

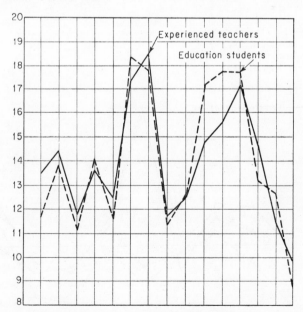

Fig. 19.1 Profiles on the Edwards PPS for experienced female teachers and female college of education students. (Data from Adams, Blood, and Taylor, 1959.)

The profile indicates needs substantially above expectancy for affiliation and intraception, change, nurturance, and abasement. Low scores are recorded for aggression and heterosexuality, with moderately low scores for succorance, autonomy, and order. Most of these are compatible with observable characteristics of women teachers. They want to be liked, to understand, to help others, and to stay in the background. They are inclined to deny tendencies such as fighting with others, and being attracted by the opposite sex. (Such attributes would have led to ejection from the profession twenty years ago; today they are tolerated more by parents and school boards, but are still likely to encounter disapproval.) They do not seek much in the way of independent decision-making power—and, in our regimented school system, could hardly get it in any event. Rather surprising is their low score on desire for order and the high score on change.

Especially impressive is the close parallel of the curve for teachers and for students. Evidently the selection system is working well, in the sense that students learn what kind of personality is likely to fit into the teaching profession.

MMPI Profile for College Professors. Appleby and Haner (1956) tested most of the faculty in a small college, and a sample of students planning for a teaching career. The comparative MMPI profiles are shown in Figure 19.2. The male professors are significantly above MMPI male norms on

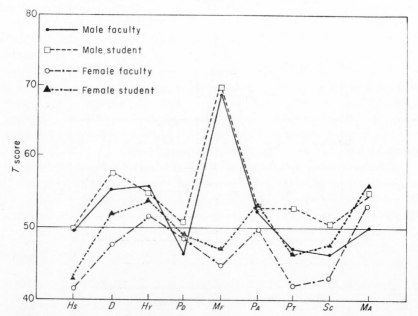

Fig. 19.2 MMPI profiles of college faculty and students. (From Appleby and Haner, 1956; reprinted by permission of the authors.)

depression, hysteria, and masculinity scales (the last is surprising); both male and female professors are significantly below the norm on the *Pd* and schizophrenic scales. It will be remembered that *Pd* measures rebellious tendencies; if professors have such (the late Senator McCarthy to the contrary notwithstanding), they are thoroughly repressed.[2] None of the mean scores, however, reaches the level which indicates abnormal personality.

The curves for male students and male faculty, and for female students and female faculty members, are closely parallel. As in the case of Figure 19.1, we can only comment that the selection system seems to pick students to go into teaching who resemble those already active in the profession.

Social Frustrations and Personality. These and other studies suggest that the popular stereotype of the teacher as a rather meek, anxious, and retiring individual has some accuracy. A consideration of the social context within which the teacher must operate will indicate that this kind of personality is needed to adapt to the role.

Not only do teachers characteristically find themselves bossed by an administrator (see above), but they are also likely to be hemmed in with restrictions and frustrations imposed by the community. Kimball Young (1930) made a tabulation of some of the bizarre rules laid down by school boards for the control of young women in the profession. They include abstention from dancing, card playing, and smoking, limitations as to type of dress, a taboo on being seen with a man between sunset and sunrise, etc. No doubt many of these have been eased substantially in recent years. It is nevertheless still true that an individual subjects himself to a substantial amount of frustration by going into teaching.

The rewards, furthermore, leave much to be desired. The typical starting salary for a teacher with a college degree is below the average pay of an assembly-line factory worker. A young Ph.D. going into college teaching in 1960 received about as much as a B.A. taking an industrial job. Nor is their prestige high enough to compensate much. The rewards have to come from helping children, from satisfying one's curiosity, from leading a quiet, secure life.

Attitudes toward Teaching. An important variable in role execution, of course, is the attitude of the individual as regards appropriate behavior in the role. Some teachers believe that "children should be seen and not heard." Others want to encourage children to feel that the teacher is a friend, that complaints are permitted, and that they will be praised for independent thought.

The Minnesota Teacher Attitude Inventory (MTAI) (see Cook et al., 1951;

[2] Riesman (1958) alleges that some professors were secretly pleased at the accusation that they dealt in dangerous ideas; he whimsically suggests that "an elderly man, doubtful of his attractiveness, might reap a certain comfort from a false accusation that he is having an affair with a pretty girl." Many professors would like to have ideas, if they only dared.

Cook and Medley, 1955) has been widely used to select new teachers, or to provide a basis for discussion of teaching methods. Embodying the newer ideas regarding teacher-child relationships, the MTAI gives high scores to those who invite discussion, permit the children some voice in procedures, and try to consider each pupil's individual needs. The focus is on the aspect of the teaching role which emphasizes human relations and emotional expression: Ryan and Wandt's factors *A, C, D* and *E*, Gibb's factor I. There is a great deal of evidence that most children prefer teachers who are high on the MTAI.[3] The data on amount learned under different teachers indicate that MTAI score is not an important variable. Children can learn, regardless of the teacher; they may, however, develop a great deal of hostility toward teacher or school, which may have significance for the future.

The makers of the MTAI assumed that the primary attribute of a good teacher was the ability to create a warm, friendly atmosphere in the classroom. This, of course, is desirable. Della Piana and Gage (1955), however, bring out another aspect of the problem. Teachers high on MTAI are apparently best for those students with high affective needs, i.e., needs for warmth and support. But students with high cognitive needs, those wishing to satisfy intellectual curiosity and to develop new skill, may not profit from this kind of teacher.

The discovery that the needs of students may be of varying kinds is important. The watchword of the progressive movement in education was always: Gear education to the needs of the child. But the conception of the child's needs may perhaps have been excessively childish. Some pupils, no doubt, need a continuation of maternal warmth; others, especially by the time they reach high school, have acquired a thirst for knowledge which is unrewarded if the teacher's efforts are limited to creating a favorable atmosphere.

Attitudes toward Child Behavior. Another important variable is the attitude of the teacher toward deviant child behavior. Mental hygienists feel that the detection of certain kinds of defense mechanisms and incipient traits of personality early in life can be a step toward helping the child improve his personality. Obviously this function depends on whether teachers agree with mental health experts as regards undesirable pupil behavior.

The classic research in this field is that of Wickman (1928), who asked teachers to check from a list of child behaviors those which were most disturbing. The teachers' judgments resembled those of conservative parents rather than those made by child psychologists. The most serious problems

---

[3] It should also be noted (Cook and Medley, 1955) that teachers scoring high on MTAI also make high scores on the *K* scale of MMPI. This scale usually indicates a desire to make a good impression, even to the extent of a little unconscious falsification. Teachers high on MTAI, consequently, are probably those with a strong need to make a good impression on the students, to be loved by them. That such a personality will have both advantages and disadvantages in the teaching roles outlined above is fairly obvious.

were those which upset the teacher, not those which psychiatrists consider prognostic of neurosis or psychosis.

Wickman has been criticized as unfair to the teachers on several grounds. The most important is that the instructions he gave the teachers were not identical with those given to the mental hygiene experts. However, it appears from the work of Sparks (1952) that the teachers would probably have differed from the experts anyhow. Sparks had teachers rate the Wickman problem list, using the instructions given the mental hygienists (on the basis of "seriousness for the future of the child"). The teachers picked out as most important the ethical problems, such as stealing, lying, bullying, heterosexual activity. Now perhaps these are serious in the sense that they might lead to jail; but this is not the same as considering the danger of a neurotic or psychotic personality. (A reasonable answer might be that we must consider both sets of dangers; but Sparks's data suggest that the teachers still do not manifest much concern for personality hazards.)

Teachers as Models. Like the parent, the teacher is often a model for imitation and identification. School situations may imprint certain pictures in the child's mind which serve as standards for the judgment of proper behavior in the future. Even when he resents the teacher's tactics, he may adopt them himself on a later occasion.

Boynton, Dugger, and Turner (1934) have shown that this effect is strong enough to be measured, even in a single school. A number of teachers and pupils in their classes filled out the Bernreuter Personal Inventory, which was scored for neurotic tendency. Although there was not perfect agreement, there was a perceptible trend for teachers who were emotionally unstable to have students scoring toward that end of the scale. This is easy to understand. Even though the child is in school for only five or six hours a day, a teacher who is fretful, explosive, irritable, and nagging will set up many emotional reverberations. Pupils would need a very favorable home life indeed to balance such a school situation.

Toward Better Teaching. The school system can never fit properly into a democratic society until it is reorganized on a democratic basis, with participation by pupils and teachers, as well as administrators and political executives. The teaching staff will not be of the proper caliber for molding future citizens until salaries are raised, arbitrary personal restrictions removed, and work loads lowered. In the meantime, various experiments have shown that better teaching is possible even under present conditions.

These experiments have centered around expanding the teacher's conception of her own personality and the factors determining pupil behavior. Thus Ojemann and Wilkinson (1939) devised procedures by which the teacher studied problem pupils in the context of home environment, economic problems, and play situations. Inevitably the teacher became more understanding and tolerant; quite amazingly, she also became more effective in getting across academic material, and the personalities of her pupils showed significant improvement. Baruch (1945) concentrated on instilling an attitude of acceptance of the child's emotional problem (as opposed to moralistic, disciplinary, rejecting attitudes). At the beginning of the study, almost all teachers showed these negative attitudes. Almost two-thirds improved in self-understanding and in understanding of children's problems; it is believed that the handling of pupils was materially changed for the better.

French (1944) has given a detailed account of the techniques of an autocratic group leader and the devices by which he was retrained in democratic methods. The specific instance is that of a scoutmaster, but the applicability to schoolteachers is plain. It is possible to get better results with young people without resorting to dictatorial procedures.

These studies indicate that sound application of psychology to the training of teachers can have beneficial effects upon the personality of the pupil. Obviously, the elements in the school situation which are destructive of the teacher's morale and personal integrity must also be eliminated if this training is to be effective.

THE CHILD'S PERSONALITY AND ACHIEVEMENT

School routines and teacher personalities are important elements to which the child must adjust. But his achievement is also going to be in part a function of his own personality, of his goals and percepts as these have been acquired over past years. And his achievement will in turn modify his personality. These remarks seem rather obvious, and they are supported by extensive research, but it is surprisingly difficult to reduce to orderly patterns the kinds of interactions which have been reported.

We find, for example, that academic marks correlate $+.66$ with ratings of personality by the teacher, and only $+.46$ with IQ, for several hundred junior high school students (Russell and Thalman, 1955). The partial correlation of personality with marks, holding IQ constant, is $+.56$.[4] Does this mean that students of superior personality achieve more, regardless of ability? Or does it mean that teachers give high marks to students with pleasant personalities, regardless of performance on examination? In other words, we are typically plagued here by our inability to determine which is the independent variable.

Because of this problem, it has seemed more fruitful to work with fairly specific performances rather than with marks in general. These studies in-

---

[4] A partial correlation is a device for estimating the size of the relationship between two variables if a third were held constant. In the example cited, we wished to know whether differences in intelligence might affect both personality ratings and grades, and thus spuriously raise the correlation of grades with personality. The figures cited give some support to the notion that a child received good marks from some teachers purely because the child had a likable personality.

clude investigations of particular kinds of educational disabilities, and inadequacies in certain kinds of test performance.

Specific Educational Disabilities. Teachers often encounter a child who has normal or superior academic aptitude, but because of an emotional difficulty does poorly in one or more subjects. Thus Vorhaus (1946) analyzed the Rorschach patterns of 25 children with reading disability, and found evidence that the failure to read was a form of unconscious hostility to the environment. Externally the children were submissive; they were not "behavior problems" as most teachers and parents understand this term. Their resistance to domination by outside influence had simply become canalized in the form of refusal to learn to read. A plausible explanation of the basis for this behavior is found in the report by Missildine (1946), who examined another group of children with reading trouble. One-third of the children had overtly hostile mothers and another third had mothers who were markedly tense, criticizing, and coercive in their attitudes toward the child. One infers that the child has found (by chance) that his failure to read successfully elicits concern and anxiety from his mother; [5] he then repeats this behavior as a means of "getting even" for the arbitrary or hostile treatment that he receives.

Morgan (1924) cites an interesting case of a boy with a specific spelling defect. He could do ordinary fourth-grade spelling, but persistently missed certain very simple words. The word "girl," for example, was spelled *gurl, gerl, girle, gyrl,* etc. It appeared that he was carefully refusing to give the correct spelling. The origin of this difficulty was found to lie in an intense antagonism to girls and women, which in turn depended on unresolved sex conflicts related to his mother. After some elementary sex education, he began to give the correct spellings for these words and his difficulty soon disappeared completely. Although such obvious cases of the relation of personality problems to educational disability are rare, one finds many illustrations in which the personality factor enters as an important determinant.

Reading and Arithmetic. One of the traditional problems of the teacher is the child who can read but can't do arithmetic. Most often this has been ascribed to specific painful experiences which have caused any number work to be seen as threatening. The possibility that there may be some poorly defined but rather general personality attribute involved is offered by the studies of Lynn (1957) and Altus (1952). Lynn found that children whose grade performance in reading was significantly above that for arith-metic were rated as more anxious than the opposite group. Altus compared women college students who earned high scores on language (*L*) of the American Council on Education Aptitude Test, but low scores on quantitative (*Q*), with a group low on *L*, high on *Q*. He found that a number of MMPI items differentiated the two groups: The women high on quantitative

---

[5] The mothers were generally competitive about the child's performance relative to other children (cf. Chap. 17).

ability gave signs of emotional immaturity, were very conventional, and had a good deal of anxiety. There is an obvious conflict with Lynn's data on the last point. Perhaps anxiety is associated with any specific kind of educational handicap, whether it be poor performance on languages or on numerical skills.[6]

On the other hand, there may be an innate ability or perceptual difference which sets off this particular sequence. Munroe (1946) comments that the college women she studied who were high on Q were "formbound and literal" in their intellectual approach, whereas those high on L were more subjective and literary. It may be that girls who find a literal, concrete, stimulus-bound approach natural or even unavoidable will in turn tend toward masculinity of interests and encounter some adjustment difficulties as a result. Pemberton (1951) has shown that, for men, a higher score on Q goes with an extraverted, conforming personality, with practical values, active, and impulsive; men higher on L, conversely, are said to be reflective, introverted, literary, and theoretical. There are enough similarities with the Munroe and Altus data here to suggest innate or early-acquired differences in way of perceiving reality. The difference favoring Q is compatible with masculine but not with feminine roles, or so it seems.

Granick (1955) finds that children judged to have mild emotional disturbances, as compared to children judged to have none, were handicapped on a widely used performance test of mental ability (Cornell-Coxe) but not on the Stanford-Binet, which is largely verbal. They were especially poor on reproducing complex visual designs from memory. This may tie in with field-analytical perception (cf. Chapter 7), absence of which is associated with ego weakness and emotional instability (Chapter 9).

Personality Traits and Use of Ability. It has long been observed that intelligence scores alone do not predict school success. Some students work harder, persevere, concentrate more effectively, and achieve relatively higher marks than their ability scores indicate. There are, apparently, personality factors involved in the student's use of his ability. In Table 19.2 we summarize correlations between ability and achievement for different groups of college freshmen selected on the basis of Bernreuter personality test scores.

Examination of this table indicates that persons possessing relatively desirable personality traits make better use of their intelligence. Low scores on Bernreuter's neurotic scale and high scores on his self-sufficiency and dominance scales are associated with well-adjusted personalities. In each in-

---

[6] An alternative explanation for the Altus data might have been that the high-Q females had identified with their fathers, developed masculine skills (including arithmetic), and showed the personality disturbance commonly observed in persons failing to adjust to their social role. However, Spilka and Kimble (1958) tried to replicate Altus's data on women, without success. It may be that populations at different colleges vary on this kind of relationship. Certainly it would be unwise to do much speculating until the data are clearer.

stance the correlation of intelligence with grade-point average is higher for students at the preferred end of the scale. It seems probable that students who are poorly adjusted to themselves or to their social environment may vary widely in their approach to their studies. One may plunge into his work as an escape from an unpleasant world, whereas a second becomes absorbed in extracurricular activities, and a third simply broods about his troubles. The effective use of intelligence, thus, is highly variable for these students.

Both Munroe (1945) and Montalto (1946) indicate that prediction of academic performance can be improved if Rorschach records are studied in addition to the usual academic aptitude test scores. Emotional disturbance

Table 19.2

**Ability-achievement Correlation
in Extreme Personality Groups**

Personality traits	r
High score on neuroticism	.45
Low score on neuroticism	.60
High score on self-sufficiency	.59
Low score on self-sufficiency	.37
High score on dominance	.71
Low score on dominance	.44
Entire group	.51

and various other factors detectable in the Rorschach performance seem to influence significantly the use made by the student of his mental ability.

A somewhat similar study, using MMPI, is reported by Hoyt and Norman (1954). They classified their students into three groups, and got the following correlations of aptitude with grades:

1. T score above 70 on two or more MMPI scales, $r = .31$
2. T score above 70 on one MMPI scale, $r = .51$
3. No T score above 60 on MMPI, $r = .62$.

Thus the persons who seem high on ego strength, or not handicapped by marked trends toward any kind of emotional deviation, get grades pretty much in proportion to ability.[7] Those with tendencies toward emotional problems may *underachieve* or *overachieve* in proportion to ability, depending on the kind of defense adopted.

The vexing problem of high school dropouts may also be illuminated by personality studies. Roessel (1954) reports that, on nine of ten MMPI scales used, dropouts were significantly higher (more abnormal) than students who stayed to graduate. (The exception was masculinity, which has no abnormal connotation.) In general, the higher the MMPI score, the lower the

---

[7] On the MMPI, a T score of 70 or more on any scale is considered a serious indication of an abnormal personality pattern.

grade at which the student quit. The dropouts were in many instances young-sters of high IQ.

A study of efficient mental work. Although it does not involve school marks, interest attaches to a study by Babcock (1940). In it 313 subjects, ranging from eighteen to thirty-six years of age—mental level from sixteen years to very superior—were given the Babcock-Levy examination, a measure of simple learning performance, substitution, and continuous mental work. It is a measure of efficiency, rather than ability as such. These subjects were also given the Bernreuter Personality Inventory.

Various comparisons were made within the results, all of them confirming the hypothesis that efficiency is a function of personality traits. In Table 19.3 are reproduced the average percentile scores on four personality traits for the top 10 per cent of the group, as compared with the bottom 10 per cent, in mental efficiency. It is apparent that the *less efficient* individuals tend to score high on neuroticism, introversion, and self-conscious-ness; low on dominance. As noted elsewhere, these are the scores which characterize generally maladjusted personalities.

Babcock also presents the average mental-efficiency score for persons scoring at the top or bottom of each personality scale. As Table 19.4 shows, persons who are high on neurotic tendency and introversion score below their proper level on the efficiency test, whereas those high on dominance score slightly above the expected point. All these differences are significant statistically. Thus, even if we rule out such factors as the interaction of teacher and pupil, the nature of material studied, social distractions and other environmental variables, the mental efficiency of the individual is a function of personality as well as of intelligence. Babcock seems to suggest that the neurotic personality is a result (in part) of low mental efficiency; it would seem equally plausible to hold that the various emotional conflicts,

Table 19.3

Personality Scores of Persons Showing Highest and Lowest Relative Efficiency on Babcock-Levy Examination

Bernreuter scale	*Highest decile efficiency*	*Lowest decile efficiency*	*Chances in 100 of true difference*
N (neuroticism)	48.8	71.5	100
I (introversion)	40.8	65.0	100
D (dominance)	58.1	38.7	100
C (self-consciousness)	50.6	76.3	100

SOURCE: Babcock (1940).

Table 19.4

**Relative Efficiency Rating of Persons Making Extreme
Scores on Bernreuter Personality Scales**

Bernreuter scale	Highest decile personality	Lowest decile personality	Chances in 100 of true difference
N (neuroticism)	−1.01	0.19	100
I (introversion)	−1.01	0.75	100
D (dominance)	0.21	−0.51	97

SOURCE: Babcock (1940).

inconsistencies, and instabilities which we have found to be characteristic of these personalities render impossible an effective use of their mental talents.

Differential Achievement. The real crux of the matter is this: Does a measure of personality add anything to our understanding of why some people use their intelligence and use it more effectively than others? For many years, educators have been identifying pupils as underachievers and overachievers; the former are those who accomplish less than is expected of persons with their ability; the latter accomplish more than is expected. Stagner (1933a) selected groups above or below the line of regression of grades on scholastic aptitude and showed that significant personality differences existed. In more recent studies a more sophisticated technique has been developed. The student's grade-point average is predicted from his aptitude test score, and this is subtracted from the grade-point average actually earned. If the difference is a positive value, he is an overachiever, if negative, an underachiever. In order to minimize chance variations, these studies generally use only persons showing several points difference.

The above method was used by Owens and Johnson (1949) on college students. Their data resemble those of Stagner (1933) in suggesting that underachievers are perhaps excessively sociable; they may use their energies on social affairs instead of educational enterprises. Owens and Johnson also find that underachievers show more evidence of hostility and changeable moods; they are somewhat overactive and rebellious.[8]

An effort to develop a scale which would predict underachievement di-

[8] This is the combination of high *Ma* and high *Pd* scores on MMPI, noted in Chap. 10 (p. 226) as a predictor of delinquency. Evidently there are many ways in which this combination can express itself other than getting into trouble with the police. On the basis of the study by Malloy (1955), we might speculate that at least some underachievers are punishing their parents for what is perceived as excessively strict control by refusing to achieve in school.

rectly is that of McQuary and Truax (1955). They followed the usual procedure of finding subjects whose achievements deviated from prediction, then analyzed responses to a personality inventory. They found a considerable number of items which significantly separated under- from overachievers. Underachievers were more likely to say "true" to items such as: using alcohol to excess, conformity to group, loyalty to group if it is in trouble, getting around the law if possible, enjoying social gatherings, having trouble in concentrating, and experiencing various obsessive symptoms. Here again we find evidence for group orientation, anxiety, and a desire for social as against isolated pleasures.[9] None of these studies, of course, prove that sociability leads to neglect of study, and hence to underachieving; it is at least possible that the anxiety and obsessive symptoms indicate inner conflicts which the person tries to escape by crowd activities. The net effect, of course, is the same. Taking all of them, including the Babcock study, into consideration, we must conclude that failures in emotional adjustment will, at the very least, tend to reduce the efficient use of innate ability.

As might reasonably be expected, need achievement has also been shown to be a factor in under- or overachievement. Applezweig et al. (1956) predicted grades for college women and separated them into under- and overachievers. On the TAT test for need achievement, the latter group made significantly higher scores, indicating stronger achievement motivation. A measure of need affiliation did not differentiate the two groups; however, it was found that this motive was involved indirectly. The girls were asked to name their best friends, and when the grade points of these friends were computed, it was found that the two groups differed significantly. Thus it appeared that the girls whose *friends* made high grades put greater effort into schoolwork (because of need affiliation) even if they were not strong on need achievement.

Family Values and Need Achievement. In an important study of the effect of family on overachievement or underachievement in high school, Strodtbeck (1955) made a careful analysis of attitudes of parents, attitudes of sons, and school performance. His first step was to prepare a scale for attitudes related to overachieving and underachieving (in relation to intelligence) in high school. The final scale included 8 out of 27 items, 6 of which are shown in Table 19.5. These items were identified by analysis of the answers of 600 students who were neither Jewish nor Italian. This was important because the Jewish and Italian groups were to be used to compare effects of family values.

From the Jewish and Italian groups of students Strodtbeck then selected 24 of each, stratified so that each group included equal proportions of over-

---

[9] Obviously the McQuary-Truax scale requires cross validation. The authors tried it out on another group, but of such different characteristics that the results are hard to interpret.

Table 19.5

Items Which Discriminate between Over- and Underachieving High School Students *

1. Planning only makes a person unhappy since your plans hardly ever work out anyhow.   (F)
2. When a man is born, the success he's going to have is already in the cards, so he might as well accept it and not fight against it.   (F)
3. The best kind of job to have is one where you are part of an organization all working together even if you don't get individual credit.   (F)
4. When the time comes for a boy to take a job, he should stay near his parents, even if it means giving up a good job opportunity.   (F)
5. It's silly for a teen-ager to put money into a car when the money could be used to get started in business or for an education.   (T)
6. Nowadays, with world conditions what they are, the wise person lives for today and lets tomorrow take care of itself.   (F)

* These are six of the eight items which distinguished over- from underachievers. Of the six shown, the first four were also more often answered in the achiever direction by Jewish children as compared to Italians. The answers of overachievers are shown in parentheses.

SOURCE: Strodtbeck (1955).

and underachievers, and equal proportions of families of high, medium, and low socioeconomic status. These 48 families were then interviewed and comparisons made as to achievement values. Among the main findings are: (1) fathers of higher socioeconomic status answer the questions in Table 19.5 as overachievers answer them; (2) fathers of overachievers answer as do overachievers; (3) Jewish and Italian fathers do not differ as groups, although subgroups show differences; but (4) Jewish mothers show answers typical of overachievers, Italian mothers, of underachievers. Since the over-all data indicate that Jewish boys were more often overachievers, this suggests the importance of the mother (in cutting family restraints on the son?—see item 4 in Table 19.5, for example). Even clearer evidence comes from correlations; sons' attitudes correlate $+.35$ with mothers, $-.02$ with fathers' attitudes on these items.

It might be inferred from this observation that mothers have more influence on the development of need achievement, which seems to underlie the answers to the key items and is implied by the nature of over- and underachievement as defined. This conclusion would be premature. Strodtbeck included in his interview a family discussion in which certain crucial decisions were proposed. He computed a "power" score in terms of the family member whose answer (previously ascertained) was accepted by the family in the home discussion. When the father's power score is correlated with the son's achievement value score, the resulting figure is $-.44$, a highly significant relationship. Thus, fathers with high power in the family tend to *deflate* achievement strivings in their sons! (Since the data also indicate that fathers of high economic status earn high power scores, it may be that these boys were held down by a feeling that they could not successfully compete with the father. The Freudians have argued that sons normally want to "best" the father, even if the Oedipus complex has ended in identification. If the father has very high status, the sons may well perceive such competition as hopeless, and hence make no effort to achieve.)

Training for Independent Thinking. It might be assumed that highly effective use of intelligence would be fostered by the permissive, indulgent parental tactics described in Chapter 17 as optimal for infant adjustment. Evidence collected by Drews and Teahan (1957) raises doubts about this. They identified children who were making good use of their ability (achievers) and those earning grades considerably below ability (underachievers). The mothers of these children answered a questionnaire about child-rearing policies; much to the authors' surprise, the mothers of achievers got scores indicating a "dominative" and "ignoring" policy. However, examination of the questionnaire raises a question as to the accuracy of the interpretation. Mothers of achievers answered "yes" to items such as: "Children should not interrupt adult conversation." "Children should have the opportunity to express their opinions to their parents." "Children should be allowed to manage their affairs with little supervision from adults." Although it may be that these can be called "ignoring," it seems just as possible that they indicate encouragement of early independence and responsibility.

It is somewhat amusing to note that the achievers' mothers deviate *away* from the ideal pattern postulated by a group of clinical psychologists for this questionnaire (Shoben, 1949). It seems possible that an ideal of permissiveness at early ages may need modification to impose some pressures for performance on the older child. We shall have further comments on this point later.

Personality and IQ Change. Another line of evidence bearing on the problem of mental efficiency comes from the work of Sontag, Baker, and Nelson (1958). These investigators followed a number of children from birth to the age of 10 years. The data included mental test scores, descriptions of home environment, personality ratings of children, and a variety of other items. The focus of the research was on the development of the child over a considerable time span, and our interest is in the changes in intelligence noted during this time.

The authors identified 35 children who increased in IQ between the ages of $4\frac{1}{2}$ and 6 years, and another 35 who decreased during the same period. They likewise identified 35 who increased from 6 to 10, and 35 who decreased. (Many of these were the same, but some children leveled out at age 6.) In both age periods, boys showed more accelerative trends than girls. This may be due to the earlier start of girls, or to the personality factors to be noted below, which are somewhat sex-linked.

When the personality ratings are compared for children who showed IQ changes between 4½ and 6 years, the following attributes are found to go with IQ acceleration: independence, aggressiveness, anticipation, and competitiveness. (By anticipation is meant ability to take a long-run view of rewards; the other terms are probably clear.) In every case, children who showed IQ acceleration were judged significantly higher than those showing IQ declines.

If we consider the changes in IQ from 6 to 10, the findings are essentially the same but more clearly defined, as might be expected with increasing personality individuation at the later age. Children showing IQ acceleration from age 6 to age 10 years were significantly higher on: independence, aggressiveness, self-initiation, problem solving,[10] anticipation, competitiveness, sibling rivalry, scholastic competitiveness, scholastic independence, and parental emphasis on school achievement.

Need Achievement. As before, if we look for a common factor running through these ratings, it is found to be what we have called need achievement Some parents have encouraged the child to solve problems on his own, to keep plugging away, and to feel proud of achievement (cf. Krebs, 1958). Others have either ignored achievement or provided so much assistance that no feeling of satisfaction has become associated with independent activity. Some parents actively discourage independent efforts to solve problems. In such cases the child perceives himself as inadequate, incompetent to deal with difficult tasks.

The interpretation of the study seems clear. The IQ, far from being a measure of innate capacity, is, as early as age 6, a composite of capacity and achievement. By the time the child has reached age 10, the achievement component is probably somewhat larger. Further data are needed to learn whether this process continues.

In terms of practical significance this investigation has even broader implications. Parents can foster independent thought and effort, can encourage initiative in problem solving, and can consequently make *possible* an increase in IQ. So, no doubt, can good teaching.

It may well be that an essential element in the process is the competitive attitude engendered by parents of the accelerative group. Whether or not there is an innate "instinct of competition," it is clear that competitive attitudes are easily acquired. The extra effort put into intellectual tasks by a competitive push may make a great deal of difference in measures of intelligence and achievement.[11]

---

[10] Ratings on problem solving were essentially ratings on effort to solve difficult problems, unwillingness to quit or to shift responsibility to others.

[11] There must be some pressure, whether competitive or otherwise. In a study of families of children with increasing IQs, Baldwin et al. (1945) comment, "The democratic environment is the one most conducive to mental development; when it is non-indulgent, it is conducive to intellectual growth in all its aspects. The least stimulating

Is an increase in IQ, and in scholastic performance, desirable under such conditions? This is a question of social value. As such, we shall return to it in Chapter 21. Let it only be noted here that the deprecation of competitive behavior, so sharp in the 1930s, seems to be on the wane. Concern is now rising for intellectual excellence, and many educators are willing to settle for cautious use of competitive motivation on behalf of maximum utilization of our available intellectual talents.

THE SCHOOLS AND PERSONALITY IMPROVEMENT

In this volume we have stayed scrupulously away from the vast literature on "personality improvement," most of which has only the most tenuous connection with scientific principles. We must, however, consider the possibility that the school system, as an institution, must be revised to function as an agency for this purpose.

The Child-centered School. Actually, this was the aim of a considerable proportion of the efforts loosely grouped under the ambiguous phrase, "the child-centered school" or "student-centered teaching." The point of view which led to the Minnesota Teacher Attitude Inventory as an approach to selecting teachers, and to the elimination of arbitrary standards in giving marks, was involved here. Children can be harmed by excessive rigidity of treatment, and those who are inept in a given subject readily develop hostility to school, inferiority feelings, anxiety, and depression subsequent to failure. It thus seemed plausible to propose that each child be graded on the extent to which he made use of his ability, and that teaching assignments be tailored to his ability. These experiments represented a marked shift from the arbitrary policies described on page 455.

Student-centered teaching has generally included efforts to reduce anxieties about learning, to involve the student in planning course activities, and to maximize interaction among students as opposed to student-teacher relations. A number of experiments have been conducted to assess the impact of such techniques on learning. As far as factual knowledge goes, the result generally has been a standoff—either the instructor-centered or student-centered method being slightly but not significantly superior. On personality changes most of the data indicate a slight but not significant superiority for the student-centered approach. Bovard (1951) finds some evidence to indicate that group-centered teaching increases the tendency of students toward conformity. This and similar attitudinal changes should receive further investigation. However, many psychologists are skeptical of the prospect that extensive changes in any phase of personality can be produced by a change in teach-

sorts of environment seem to be the highly indulgent or the highly restrictive ones" [p. 66]. Presumably a highly indulgent school would also be minimally stimulating; some demands are essential to growth.

ing techniques. After all, the child is only in school for a few hours each day, and a given experiment usually runs for only a few months. The entrenched attributes against which the teacher is working have been practiced and reinforced for years. Under the circumstances, it is surprising that modifications of classroom and teacher procedure have led to any measurable effects.

Certainly the most dramatic report of the effectiveness of a mental-health approach in the schools is that of Fleming (1951). In this case children were given a medical examination and records made of certain symptoms which seemed to be psychosomatic. Then a careful personality study was prepared on each child, which stressed his needs and frustrations. The teacher received help in planning treatment for each individual youngster. A control group received no such work-up or special guidance. The medical examiner studied the children again after several months and found clear improvement in 96 per cent of the counseled cases, only 50 per cent in the control group. (The physician was not told in which group a child had been.) This seems to indicate that illnesses of a psychosomatic nature can be aided by improved teacher techniques.[12]

Fleming makes no mention of whether any improvement in IQ resulted from the individual instructional programs for his experimental group. It has been shown, nonetheless (cf. Sarason, 1953; Chidester and Menninger, 1936), that steps to reduce anxiety and other emotional disturbances can lead to markedly higher performance on intelligence tests and to an improved functioning on tasks of an intellectual nature.[13]

Frustration and Catharsis. Teaching techniques, it has been implied earlier, often lead to frustration of the child's impulses. A minimum of this is of course inevitable. Two points merit consideration: (1) if frustration is perceived as arbitrary, the aggressive tension is higher; and (2) if suitable catharsis is provided, the detrimental effects of tension can be reduced. Horwitz (1956) and his collaborators tested these hypotheses in a classroom type of situation and verified their correctness. Action by a teacher perceived as simply imposition of her personal whim, not for good reason, elicited a high level of aggression; and this led to poorer performance on tests. Suitable

---

[12] Some readers will wonder about the 50 per cent of the control group which improved. This may have been due to a variety of factors: (1) teachers may have used better methods with all children, not just those on whom special plans were prepared; (2) symptoms of a psychosomatic type are so variable that a change of 50 per cent of the children may not be beyond chance; (3) there may have been a change in the atmosphere of the whole school favorable to child adjustment; (4) the first examinations may have been made at a time of physical or academic stress so that the number of children showing symptoms was unusually high.

[13] After this chapter was in final form, a special issue of the *Journal of Social Issues* (1959, **15**, No. 1) appeared in print with a number of valuable contributions on Mental Health in the Classroom. The research studies reported therein do not require any revision of the conclusions offered here, but they enrich our understanding of many of the problems involved.

outlets for complaints ("catharsis") reduced tension and improved performance.

An incidental finding of considerable importance is that student expectancies also play a role in aggressive feelings. If the pupils have been led to expect a democratic voice in decision making, and are then arbitrarily told what they must do, hostility is enhanced. There is, consequently, an implicit danger in "student-centered" programs and educational democracy; if the teachers fail to conform in practice to what the students expect, there will be an actual increase in friction instead of a decrease. Further, if some teachers hold out against the more flexible approach, they will have trouble and probably will cause some for other teachers.

If aggression is frequently elicited by school conditions, it will become habitual; and teachers will be perceived as objects of hostility. Other authority figures are likely to be perceived in the same way (stimulus equivalence). It is important, for example, that Hollander and Bair (1952) found the adjustment of recruits to Navy life (acceptance of the authority situation) to be related to the recruit's attitude toward his high school teachers. An attitude of rebellion toward leaders, if chronic, can undoubtedly create personality difficulties which will hamper later adjustment.

The wise use of catharsis can aid not only in dealing with frustrations, but also with anxiety. McKeachie et al. (1955) experimented with different devices for reducing examination anxiety. The specific techniques tried need not concern us here, but the general result was that such devices often led to higher grades and to better attitudes toward academic work.

In connection with the Moffitt-Stagner study of perception and anxiety (page 123), the speculation was offered that scanning of internal cues may reduce efficiency of scanning external sources of information. We know that anxiety, aggression, and other tension states increase the flow of cues from bodily organs to the central nervous system. Some inefficiency of intellectual functioning, consequently, may be anticipated in persons with high anxiety level, frequent changes of moods, depressions and daydreams.

The Flint Guidance Experiment. If unresolved emotional problems do in fact interfere with efficient use of ability, as the data indicate, then adequate testing, guidance, and counseling of students should aid materially in adjustment. Evidence that high school counseling can in fact bring about such beneficial effects is provided by an extensive study in Flint, Michigan. Cantoni (1953, 1955) has reported on an intensive guidance program begun in September, 1939, when a class of over four hundred students was randomly divided into experimental and control groups. All took certain tests, but from this point on, the controls received only the customary contacts with school personnel. For the experimental group of 234, many had weekly interviews with counselors, others somewhat less often; test scores and school records were discussed, also home problems and vocational plans. Speakers were brought in to discuss special occupations with the experimental group, whose members also made visits to many industrial establishments. It seems clear that every student had extensive contacts with the counseling program.

By graduation, June, 1943, the experimental group had only 140 members, and controls, 119. In a follow-up in 1952, Cantoni succeeded in obtaining retests on 121 experimental and 100 control students. These returns are considered excellent.[14]

The results are on the spectacular side. The experimental subjects had achieved significantly higher occupational status (despite initially equal IQs) and more advanced education than the controls. There was a slight tendency for the experimental group to be higher on "economic status" (housing and similar status indexes), and a significant tendency to have more books, musical instruments, and similar "cultural" possessions.

As regards personality attributes, with which we are especially concerned, the results are decidedly encouraging. On total adjustment score on the Bell inventory, experimental males were significantly superior to control males, and experimental females somewhat above control females. The men were especially different as regards "home adjustment" (to family, etc.), vocational adjustment, and social adjustment (to friends and social groups). They were also different, but less sharply, on health adjustment and emotional adjustment. (It should be remembered that the counseling program was somewhat loaded on the side of learning about jobs and problems associated with job adjustment.) Table 19.6 shows the differences in mean scores for the male subjects. There is certainly strong reason to accept Cantoni's conclusion that "the program of counseling and guidance which the experimental group members received during high school has favorably affected their later adjustment."

There are, of course, many other ways in which guidance and counseling can minimize the harmful effects of failure and maximize learning and personality development. A major problem today is that such services are expensive, and many taxpayers believe the cost is too high. Psychologists, in general, argue that the cost of *not* providing this kind of educational program is too high—too high in terms of lost scientists, engineers, artists, and writers, too high in terms of juvenile delinquency, too dangerous in face of international tensions. We shall have more to say on this point in Chapter 21.

Basic Mechanisms. How can we best think about the interaction of academic performance and personality? The mechanism of motivation seems to be fundamental. What are the effects of successes and failures in tasks upon perception of those tasks, and upon later energy mobilization when the task is presented?

---

[14] Statistical analysis showed that those located in the follow-up did not differ in any significant way from the original population; that is, there is no selective bias in returns.

Table 19.6

**Performance on the Bell Adjustment Inventory
of Students in the Flint Guidance Program**

	Experimental males	*Control males*
Ninth grade: total adjustment	35.07 *	34.65
Twelfth grade: total adjustment	26.82	31.78
Follow-up:		
Home adjustment	3.93	6.63
Health adjustment	3.65	4.95
Social adjustment	7.93	10.05
Emotional adjustment	4.46	5.83
Vocational adjustment	5.08	7.28
Total adjustment	23.46	36.15

* Lower scores indicate better adjustment; hence, the experimental
group started with a slight handicap. The experimentals improved
steadily through the twelfth grade and follow-up tests; controls
improved slightly at twelfth grade, then relapsed over the subsequent nine years.
SOURCE: Cantoni (1953).

It has already been implied, in preceding pages, that the underachiever and
the overachiever differ as regards distribution of energy. The former tends
to channel more effort into his social life and perhaps into rebellion against
academic rules; the latter puts energy into schoolwork, perhaps to the exclusion of normal interest in other affairs. Do we have any insights as to how this
distribution comes about?

Success and Failure. The major variable, it would seem, is the effect of success or of failure upon perception of a task. We have cited, in Chapter 6, evidence that people tend to block out awareness of cues which signal pain or
discomfort. Although there is no physical pain involved in academic failure,
there is a great deal of psychic tension associated with ego devaluation, loss
of approval from parents and authority figures, and perhaps other more direct
frustrations.

The effect on mental activity of success or failure in a nonintellectual task
was explored by Lantz (1945). She had children take one form of an intelligence test, then engage in a "ball-playing" game which was rigged so that
success or failure came arbitrarily. The game was interesting and the children
became quite involved in it. After the end of the game, the alternate form of
the test was administered. Success increased performance above the normal
practice gain, whereas failure caused a decline even below the level reached
in the first test. The loss in the latter group affected especially items requiring

reasoning and abstract thought; little damage was done to pure rote memory items. The failing group showed aggressive reactions toward themselves or the experiment, and tried to leave the room where it took place.[15]

The same kinds of effects can be demonstrated by using intellectual tasks instead of games. In this volume numerous experiments have been cited in which induced failure is used to build up tension, evoke aggression, etc. It seems safe to assume that failure on tasks attempted, even without vigorous motivation, will have some of these effects.

Now consider the situation of the child in school. Many children are deficient either in general intelligence or in certain special abilities needed for success. Those coming from poorer homes lack background information, experiences with books and magazines, an orientation toward key points in a problem; in short, they are inadequately prepared for school. If all children are faced with the same tasks, large numbers are going to fail. And, failing, they will develop hostility toward teacher and school, will do less well on tasks following failure, and will attempt to get away from the school, physically or in fantasy. Conversely, the child who succeeds will come to perceive school tasks as a way of obtaining satisfaction, will attach positive valence to intellectual skill, will do better on successive assignments, and so on.

This is the basic argument for the child-centered classroom, for providing the teacher with adequate information about the child's abilities, and for allowing success at different levels of performance. There can be little doubt that traditional education produced many youngsters who hated school and who dropped out at the earliest legal age. Many investigations have suggested that the school has been a potent cause of juvenile delinquency by its failure to take these factors into consideration. "Progressive" schools adopted a policy of promotion regardless of performance which had as its aim the avoidance of some of these detrimental consequences of failure. Whether the technique has been successful is debatable, but we must recognize the good intentions of those devising the routine.

Tactics of Delay. In addition to the fundamental fact of shift in energy as a result of success or failure in school, it has been suggested that poor achievers suffer from a kind of motivational inadequacy which might be called "activity delay" (Brown, Abeles, and Iscoe, 1954). The investigators took college students receiving high and low grades, but roughly equated for ability. In one experiment letters were sent out asking students to come to a meeting to fill out a questionnaire for a visiting investigator; 80 per cent of the high group and 13 per cent of the low group came in response to the first letter; even with direct telephone contact, some of the lows never came. In a second study the investigators sent letters, signed by the president of the university, asking students to come and participate in a project dealing with attitudes

---

[15] Similar results with young children are reported by Barker, Dembo, and Lewin (1941).

toward the Korean war and the draft, topics of general student concern at the time; the second letter "ordered" the student to report for this study; later direct phone contacts were made. Of 660 students, 220 responded to the first letter, and an additional 243 to the second, 81 to a phone call, and 63 promised but never appeared. The grade-point average of each group was successively lower. Since there was no reason to fear an intellectual failure by reporting, the authors assume that in many cases the nonresponders intended to come, but "forgot," were distracted by other interests, or delayed until it was too late to keep the appointment. Hostility to college authority may have been a factor. In any event, the hypothesis is that energy cannot be mobilized in time to meet deadlines. (Most college students can see a connection between such an attribute and the receipt of low grades.)

Ability being equal, then, differential aspects of experience may lead some children to perceive school tasks as pleasant challenges, others to see them as frustrations and threats. The one group will channel energy into intellectual endeavors, the others, away from schoolwork. Aside from this factor, it may be that some youngsters are "slow starters" and, in the typical school routine, never get assignments finished on time; hence they fail regardless of ability. Undoubtedly there are other variables which merit consideration, such as the attitude of the parents toward schoolwork (and the extent to which they have fostered need achievement—cf. page 471). These, however, lie outside the range of pupil-school interaction.

Educational Policy and Personality Development. We may then ask, is it possible to make reasonable suggestions as to sound educational policy which will be compatible with the development of desirable personality traits in children? Some hints have already been offered; we can now try to draw these together.

Reference was made earlier to Benedict's concept of discontinuities in cultural conditioning—e.g., in the failure to provide at adolescence for gradually increasing responsibility and independence. The same problem arises in relation to the schools.

What some authors have referred to as the Freudian revolution—only partly Freudian, but nonetheless stimulated by a concern for healthy personalities—in family patterns has led to greatly increased permissiveness and decidedly less harshness in the socializing of young children. The evidence favoring such a policy was and is overwhelming. It must be recognized, nonetheless, that permissiveness has an end, and the adult world must demand discipline, self-control, and respect for the rights of others. Spontaneity in young children is excellent, but the adolescent who makes up his own traffic rules as he drives a car is a menace.[16]

---

[16] Protests about indiscriminate permissiveness have even begun to come from the colleges of education. Balthazar (1955) gives an exhaustive analysis of the literature

Our goal, then, is to provide adequate permissiveness in the first few years so that the child develops a favorable view of his parents and a secure attitude toward the world. But following this we must help the child become aware of limits and restrictions. Frustration tolerance must be acquired. Not all jobs are delightful; indeed, it is fairly likely that every person will find himself faced with many chores which are as a minimum dull and uninteresting. Execution of role obligations as parents requires impulse control and adherence to a task once undertaken. At some point prior to maturity this training sequence must begin. It seems undebatable, therefore, that the school must stop insisting that children do only what they wish to do, and see that they get some practice in carrying out assignments even if these are somewhat unpleasant.

David Riesman (1958) suggests that perhaps the progressive educators have not only won their battle, but have overreached themselves. Where it once was essential to modify educational practice because the average child quickly learned to hate school, today it is important to remember that ignoramuses, no matter how happy they are, represent a major danger to Western civilization. The current trend, therefore, is for the schools to become somewhat more demanding as regards academic performance. It seems plausible that some shifting of public school policy may help to bridge the discontinuity which has developed between permissiveness and demands for effort. The child can, by stages, be introduced to firm requirements and limits of irresponsibility. This should facilitate adaptation to an adult world of obligations and laws.

The School's Duty to Be Upsetting. Commenting on a valuable study of personality changes in college women from their freshman to their senior year, Sanford (1956a) notes that the senior women showed evidence of being both more mature and more disturbed or upset. Perhaps, he reflects, colleges have an obligation to upset their students, to "bring on growing pains." No doubt, demanding that they behave independently, questioning some of their stereotyped beliefs, and proposing new ways of thinking can upset the student's equilibrium. "If we were interested in stability alone," writes Sanford, "we would do well to plan a program designed to keep freshmen as they are, rather than to try to increase their education, their maturity, and their flexibility" [p. 42].

We are, therefore, faced with another paradox. On the one hand, the psychologist is saying that the school should be concerned about hostilities and anxieties of pupils, try to avoid new ones and to reduce those already in

---

and concludes that the Dewey philosophy never did imply rampant permissiveness. To fit into society the child must encounter some frustrations, be required to solve problems when he would rather play. This is akin to Freud's dictum that we must forgo the pleasure principle in favor of the reality principle.

motion. On the other, he says that we must disrupt infantile or uninformed equilibria, and press the youngster to seek a new goal, a new stability on a more mature and better-educated level.

Obviously a sound educational philosophy must incorporate both horns of this dilemma. One help is found in the fact that security should be established early; pressure to break up low-level integrations should begin gradually and at a later age. Another is found in shifting emotional orientations from persons to ideas. Anxiety about the self is detrimental; anxiety about nuclear war can be channeled usefully. Hostility to the teacher blocks learning; hostility to poverty and exploitation may facilitate education.

Academic Excellence and Competitive Motivation. Somewhat similar considerations hold as regards the newly recognized importance of "academic excellence." In the 1930s the evils of competition, both economic and academic, came in for considerable attention; the desirability of cooperative effort was stressed. Even earlier, in the expensive private colleges, there had developed the notion that "a gentleman's grade was a C." For some years educators have deplored the notion of competition among students for marks, and have tended to devise marking systems which minimized such tendencies by eliminating rewards for outstanding academic achievement.

Today the social need is for maximum utilization of our pool of talent. This means that it is hazardous to lull many bright youngsters into quiet mediocrity. Parents and teachers will probably find it necessary to foster the development of what we have been calling need achievement.

One way of doing this, of course, is to reinstate a system of competitive motivation. It may prove unavoidable that some pressure for academic excellence will take the form of competition among students. This will be less harmful if the conditions of the competition are so arranged that differences in ability are not too large. It is cruel to the dull youngster to spur him on to compete with those of greater talent, just as it is hard on the seven-year-old boy who tries to equal the physical performance of his ten-year-old brother.

Identification with Superior Teachers. There is, however, an alternative route to academic excellence which merits consideration as a matter of policy. This is that superior teachers usually attract bright students who identify with the teacher, accept intellectual values, and channel energy into a quest for knowledge. Too many potentially superior teachers are today being lured by financial rewards into becoming soap salesmen and television comedians. Unless substantial increases are made in the relative economic return to teachers, this will continue.

Financial rewards are not, of course, the only considerations. There are many excellent teachers in our educational system today who could be earning far more elsewhere. The needs profile for teachers (Figure 19.1) indicates other appeals of importance, such as autonomy and affiliation. But need achievement is below the norm for both the teachers and students shown, and this should be changed. Increased prestige and respect to teachers would help; more opportunities for teachers to do research, write, and publish would be of great value. It is likely, then, that superior teachers will be drawn into the field, and have the desired effects on the next generation, only if economic and prestige rewards go up while teaching loads go down. Whether this will happen depends on whether citizens perceive the consequent values as urgent enough to bear the costs involved.

SUMMARY

The educational system ranks next to the family in terms of importance for personality. Our children typically spend a large portion of each day, week, and year within its range of influence. Sources of pressure upon the child may come from the institutional pattern of the school, the personality of the teacher, teachers' attitudes, and difficulties with specific subject-matter areas.

It is clearly unfair to demand equal performance of children with wide differences in ability; those low in intelligence suffer from chronic failure and become hostile to school; those high in intelligence become bored and may drop out. Permissiveness and modification of the school routine to fit the child are valuable, especially in the early grades. However, as the child matures he may develop more curiosity and feel frustrated by an excessively soft, permissive program. Furthermore, social needs indicate the importance of challenging superior students to strive for academic excellence.

The efficient use of ability is handicapped by emotional problems. Underachievers are usually more gregarious, but may also show excessive activity, rebellious attitudes toward the school, and moods or anxiety. Ego strength is associated with optimal use of ability.

Better methods of teaching, use of catharsis, guidance, and counseling can have favorable effects on children's personalities. Steps to attract superior teachers into the profession would also be valuable, since children often identify with and model themselves on teachers.

SUGGESTIONS FOR READING

The literature on educational psychology is so voluminous that any selection of a few books is highly arbitrary. The following will assist anyone beginning an exploration of the many investigations and opinions which have been published with regard to the problems discussed in this chapter: Blair, Jones, and Simpson, *Educational psychology* (particularly chaps. 11, 12, and 22); Lee J. Cronbach, *Educational psychology* (particularly chaps. 11, 15, and 18); and Pressey,

Robinson, and Horrocks, *Psychology in education* (particularly chaps. 7 and 14.) Special interest may attach to the work of an Adlerian psychiatrist on educational problems: Dreikurs, *Psychology in the classroom,* offers three good chapters on principles, followed by numerous interesting case studies. Another book which merits special mention is Murphy and Ladd, *Emotional factors in learning,* which deals mainly with emotional conditions interfering with learning at the college level.

CHAPTER 20

Economic Factors

The personality is shaped jointly by the physical and the social environment. Or, since most of the mediating agencies are social, we should say that some influences take the form of expectations held by others, whereas some derive from the actions of others. Thus, in the family, parental expectations mold the child in many important respects. If the father expects his son to be brave and vigorous, such actions will be rewarded, and the boy will be encouraged to develop a congruent self-image. But if the father punishes arbitrarily and inconsistently, this will have important consequences irrespective of the expectations held by the parents.

These two kinds of influence are well illustrated in the economic sphere. Some pressures take the form of expectations. (Parents expect a boy to rise higher than his father, teachers expect him to develop research or intellectual skills as opposed to money-gathering facility.) Other economic influences are imposed more directly; the lack of money leads directly to certain kinds of frustrations, which are often exaggerated by expectations held by the boy himself and by his fellows.

To some extent the personality is molded also by other institutional factors in our society, notably political and religious. Neither of these, however, is as constant or as potent as the economic. Furthermore, there are certain common misconceptions about the relation of the economic milieu to personality which merit demolition. This chapter will therefore be restricted to a consideration of the interaction of various economic factors with personality.

Economic conditions and expectations about economic role can be fractionated in various ways. We may consider, for their relation to personality, the occupational system, the income pyramid, and social expectancies.

THE OCCUPATIONAL SYSTEM

Western civilization is built around a differentiated system of occupations and some degree of free choice for the individual within this system. The degree is limited by a variety of factors: intelligence and special abilities, for example; educational opportunity; restrictions by employers; and the compatibility of the personality with the demands of the occupational role. If the individual achieves entry into an occupation, he may succeed or fail, and in the process, his personality will be substantially modified.

The various influence processes substantially take the form of those already enumerated. Certain expectancies (held by society in general, by parents, or by teachers) mold for the youth a picture which he is likely to use as a guide. Barriers block the execution of motivated acts which are contrary to occupational roles. Rewards are handed out for conformity to "company ideology" or to professional standards. Punishments, likewise, are meted out. The young person perceives prestige figures within his chosen field and tends to identify with, to imitate them. He adopts a frame of reference which is appropriate to his reference group, the persons successful in this occupation.

The structure of American economic society is divided not only horizontally into occupations, but vertically in terms of status. Since occupations differ as regards various rewards—income, security, prestige—individuals will achieve need satisfaction and pleasurable consequences, or frustration and discomfort, according to the kind of vocation they enter. Further, within each occupation there are vertical distinctions in terms of relative status, income, and power. Thus observations of personality-occupation relations are likely to reflect both horizontal and vertical influences. Since the research data do not demonstrate neat separations of these two, the discussion in the following pages will simply present some of the personality-occupation relations.

Interest and Occupation. In our discussion of methods of studying personality no mention was made of a type of instrument widely used in advising students with respect to occupational choice. This is the vocational interest inventory; the most widely used is that developed by E. K. Strong, which consists of some four hundred items, sampling a person's interests in objects, activities, and social relationships. Keys are available to show how a given person scores in comparison to people who are now actively engaged in a given vocation. Thurstone (1931) did a factor-analytic study of Strong's scores for 18 professions and concluded that the results indicated four broad interest patterns: scientific, linguistic, business, and "interest in people." Other studies suggest that interest in business may be broken down into interest in detail (e.g., accounting) and interest in contact (e.g., selling).

It seems clear that there are several sources of relationship between interests and occupational success. (1) If a person likes certain situations, he will seek these, and so will be exposed to some occupations but not others. An easy example is the preference for outdoor work versus desk work. (2) Interest leads to exploratory manipulations, hence to early acquisition of skill and presumably to improved chances of success. This is known to be true of scientific and musical careers, and may well hold for others. (3) If pursuit of an occupation forces one into disliked situations, he will be disposed to quit and seek a more congenial location. (4) If a person is doing what he likes, he will probably exert more effort and hence be more successful.

Follow-up studies of persons twenty years or more after taking the Strong test indicate clearly that a person's chance of success is definitely related to his interest pattern. Strong (1955) has demonstrated that interest patterns in college have a high predictive value for later occupation. For instance, if a student obtained an *A* score on the engineer scale in 1930, he had an 83 to 17 chance of being an engineer in 1948; whereas, if he obtained a *C* score for engineer, the chances are 97 to 3 that he will *not* be an engineer in 1948. These expectancy ratios give the most eloquent testimony to the predictive value of the test as regards occupational behavior.

Perhaps even more important, from the point of view of the student choosing a career, is the question, "Will I be satisfied in this occupation?" In the follow-up of 1949, Strong included questions on job satisfaction. He found that interest scores as of 1930 had a low but significant correlation with satisfaction in 1949. Subjects also took the interest test again in 1949; these scores correlated somewhat higher with satisfaction. It would appear, therefore, that: (1) interest pattern in college predicts the *probable* occupation at a highly significant level; (2) if the person enters an occupation for which he has a high interest score, his chances of being satisfied are *increased* by a modest amount; and (3) if his interests *change* to fit the occupational pattern more closely, he will be still better satisfied. All these findings are to be expected; the data confirming them will make vocational counselors and parents happier, since they provide reassurance as to the wisdom of taking interest scores into consideration in making choices.

Values. Since, as the Thurstone factor analysis suggests, the fundamental dimensions of the Strong test may be quite similar to the six values covered by the Allport-Vernon-Lindzey scale (cf. page 259), we are not surprised that occupations differ in the modal pattern of values. A sample profile, for a group of psychologists, was given in Figure 11.1. Distinctive value patterns have been reported for research scientists, social workers, nurses, and other groups. The interpretation would be the same as for the interest data.

Focusing of Interest. An intriguing finding, in this connection, is that the individual whose interests focus pretty well on one or a few occupational categories seems to have greater personality integration than persons whose interests scatter over a large number of occupations. Helper and McQuitty (1953) applied McQuitty's technique of agreement analysis to college students with focused and unfocused interests. The results indicated higher integration in the former group. Although there is a possibility of a statistical artifact in the method, it appears reasonable that the person who is attracted to varying occupational roles might have acquired percepts and habits which are relatively inconsistent. This is a promising area for further study.

Temperament. Beyond the rather obvious areas of interest and value, there are many other aspects of personality which might plausibly be related to occupation in one or another respect. Enough data have been collected to show that temperamental traits have some relevance; and the individual's self-image can also be shown to vary, at least with occupational status. Some of these findings may actually show effects upon the person of being in a given role; but most research so far has related to the task of finding persons who will fit into a given occupation or position.

Temperament Patterns in Various Occupations. This process of getting the individual into an appropriate occupation has been extraordinarily haphazard in the past; and while the success of Russia's Sputnik has suddenly focused more attention on the task of getting potential scientists and engineers into proper educational channels, it is not yet clear that much more effective placement is occurring. The trouble, as Cattell has pointed out pungently, is that nobody has ever bothered to ascertain the optimum temperament patterns for various kinds of occupations. The result has been "guidance by guess" rather than with objective data to assist in making a choice.

Cattell and his associates (1956) have made a small start toward supplying the needed data. Using his 16 PF Questionnaire, they provide normative profiles for various occupations, ranging from "clerks, female" to "executives and directors." However, as the investigators have noted, it would be desirable to match a student's profile not merely with people in an occupation, but with those who are successful. Thus they break down the "psychiatric technician" category into successful and unsuccessful (by supervisor's ratings) and show that certain factor scores are predictive of success in this job. Obviously every occupation has to be studied in this manner before the matching of personality to occupation will attain maximum utility.

Profile for Research Scientists. As an example of the method, the temperament profile for "research scientists" has been plotted in Figure 20.1 (the data are from Cattell and Drevdahl, 1955). The profile suggests that outstanding traits of research scientists, aside from intelligence, are: withdrawn; depressed; independent of group standards; low on anxiety, but somewhat sensitive emotionally, and somewhat paranoid (suspicious of others). They are also rather adventurous, self-sufficient, and high on superego control. Most, if not all, of these are plausible in terms of the kinds of tasks undertaken and the working conditions of the group. Except for the score on depression, all the extreme scores suggest temperamental attributes necessary for working on novel problems independently of what others think. The importance of the Cattell contribution, of course, is to put these ideas into objective form so that students may be compared quantitatively with this pattern to help predict adaptation to the occupation.

Other examples have been shown in this text of how profiles can be used to identify the salient traits of an occupational group. Figure 19.2 showed the MMPI profile of most of the members of a college faculty, compared with the profile of the students; and Figure 11.1 showed the Allport-Vernon values profile for a group of psychology professors, superimposed on the profile for their students. As such information becomes more generally available, the process of guidance should function more effectively.

Effects of Occupation on Personality. Our primary concern, however, is not with personality as a determinant of occupational choice; our interest is more in the occupation as a determinant of personality characteristics. Unfortunately, we found it necessary to consider the possibility that any association of personality with occupation might be due to selection of cases, not to the effects of working under the conditions of that career pattern.

Studies of occupation as a determinant are virtually nonexistent. The appropriate technique will be to gather data on persons entering a vocation, and then follow them up after several years. With the increasing use of

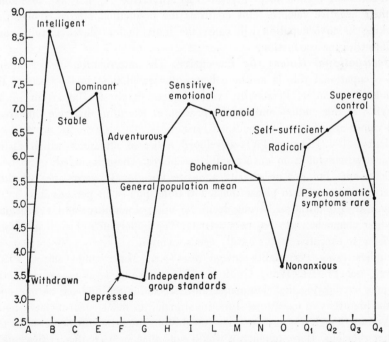

Fig. 20.1 Temperament profile for research scientists. (Data from Cattell and Drev-aahl, 1955.)

personality evaluations in student guidance, as cited above, and with exten-sive testing by employers, such studies are now fairly easy to execute and will probably appear in considerable numbers as time goes by.

The Tannenbaum Study. One study merits mention in this connection, even though it does not cover the precise point of the preceding paragraphs. It does show that working under certain conditions for a year induces changes in responses to items such as those on personality inventories. Tannenbaum (1957) was in a position to test certain clerical employees before a change was made in their working conditions. Part of the group was switched to a more democratic type of supervision, in which each clerk had more individual freedom of action than before. Another part was changed to a more firmly structured type of supervision, with a more clearly defined hierarchy of responsibility. Certain predictions were made as to the direction of change of likes and dislikes as a consequence of working under these conditions. A retest, conducted after a year, confirmed the predictions. People who work under conditions of autonomy come to prefer autonomy; those who work under hierarchical control accept (or even like) such control.

This study is relevant for our topic because it appears that the process identified as "functional autonomy" is at work here. Activities which lead to need satisfaction come to be perceived as attractive—or, at worst, lose some of their negative valence. This confirms the prediction, offered above, that working in an occupation will cause the individual to develop traits com-patible with the occupation.

Occupational Roles: the Executive. The interrelation of personality and occupational role is nowhere better illustrated than in the case of the high-level executive. Personality variables are manifestly important in his arriving at this status; and, in the process of executing his role, his traits and values are likely to be modified further.

Henry (1949), using TAT, developed a list of attributes which distin-guished successful from unsuccessful executives. These included: high need achievement (but not necessarily a desire for glory); acceptance of their superiors and desire to please them, but little interest in persons inferior to them in the organization; strong desire for upward mobility; and a great deal of vigor channeled into business activity. The importance of such attributes in rising to executive status hardly needs mention.

Studies using personality inventories (e.g., Miner and Culver, 1955; Meyer and Pressel, 1954; Guilford, 1952) have generally confirmed the obvious by showing that dominance and self-confidence increase as one goes up the hierarchy of executives. Emotional maladjustment (neuroticism) tends to decline, though less consistently. Sociability shows a slight decrease in the higher echelons. Here, again, we would note that such characteristics might both facilitate the achievement of executive status, and be reinforced by the conditions of life at that level. Required by his role to give orders, the executive must behave in a dominant fashion; if he does not already place a high value on himself and his judgment, others will soon convince him that he should do so. Because of the "looking-glass effect," his self-confidence will increase. He will be spared many blockages and frustrations which cause others to become irritable; he will escape many threats and anxieties which might cause him to worry and brood. There is, then, a reciprocal relation between person and role which is of considerable significance for the psychology of personality.

The Young Executive. Another group of considerable interest is composed of the young men rising in the management hierarchy, the so-called "junior executives." Interest in this group has been extensive since World War II; W. H. Whyte's *The Organization Man* and Vance Packard's *The Status Seekers* are two recent books discussing some features of life at this level. The major stress, of course, has been on the tremendous pressure for conformity and the acceptance of the values of top management.

The importance of the Asch experiments on conforming behavior must be noted here. The young man coming into a management group will inevitably encounter many ambiguous situations where he does not clearly perceive the desirable course of action. Naturally he accepts the majority judgment as a guide in structuring such situations. Further, if he happens to have a clear view of a given event and if his conclusion differs from the majority, he will quickly be made to feel embarrassed and uncomfortable. He is subject to continuous "merit rating" by his superior, and one of the major factors determining a good rating is acceptance of company ideology, the profit system, opposition to unions, and criticism of the "welfare state." Thus a variety of rewards and punishments converge to push him in the direction of a uniform mode of thinking. If he continues to resist, he is dropped from the organization.

An interesting corollary to this sequence has been asserted by some observers; this is that the young executive learns to play it safe, to avoid sharp competitiveness with his fellows, to seek to be a good team member rather than an outstanding individual. This argument holds that the era of the "robber barons," in which ruthless individualism ran rampant, has been replaced by the era of the "grey flannel suit," in which the values of individualism have been lost completely. Probably neither of these extremes is correct; however, it is likely that the pendulum has swung away from the excesses of individualism so far that we have now trained out of our bright young men some desirable aspects of this value system. Some further speculations on this point are offered in the following chapter.

Occupational Roles: the Union Leader. Of growing importance in American society is another occupational role, that of the union leader. Because of the differences in structure of industry and union, it must be expected that some traits will differentiate union executives from company executives. In the typical corporation, power is explicitly concentrated at the top and is delegated downward; in the union, power is, theoretically at least, held by the membership and delegated upward. One can then anticipate that company officials will be characterized by a vertical orientation, striving to move up a ladder, whereas union leaders will have more of a horizontal orientation, looking to the group for support and evidence of success. At least some evidence has been collected to support this prediction (Stagner, 1956, p. 246).

Here again an interaction of original personality and role requirements must be expected. A man is not likely to accept a post in a union unless he accepts the ideology, but he becomes more intensely involved as he functions in this task. Similarly, he must be more concerned about group acceptance and group approval than he is with the boss's praise, or he would not have become active in the union. As he works for the union, his main source of strength and rewards is the membership group or some select portion of it. Thus he puts a still higher value on group approval.

A few studies reveal that union leaders share with company executives some of the generalized traits mentioned above. For example, a study by Rosen and Rosen (1957) utilized 21 business agents in a large metropolitan union. Interviews indicated that their roles required heavy investments of time and energy; they also had to be somewhat cautious and skeptical in their dealings both with management and with union members. They felt pressure to be tactful even in the face of hostility and aggression.

The MMPI was used as a personality measure. The business agents were high on hypochondriasis and conversion hysteria; each of these characteristics probably indicates emotional stress and concern with implications for health. They were also high on the *Pd* scale, which involves rebellion against authority and disregard of social norms—attributes essential in the early days of the union movement, but perhaps less important today. Finally, they were high on the *Ma* scale, indicating the high activity level at which they operated.

It will be recalled that a combination of high *Ma* and high *Pd* scores predicted juvenile delinquency in the Hathaway-Monachesi study (page 226). However, only about 20 per cent of the boys with such scores actually became delinquent. Perhaps another fraction gets drawn into union work. (Contrary to popular news stories, the number of unionists who are delinquents is quite small.) The selection of unionism as a channel for satisfying motives may be a function of the particular needs felt by these individuals. To illustrate this possibility we turn to another investigation.

Belgrad (1957) also studied the personality attributes of union officials, using the Edwards PPS, an inventory based on the system of needs developed by Murray (see page 347). His study differs from that of Rosen and Rosen in that he distinguished between 23 officials who had to deal with management and union members frequently, whom he called "interactors," and a second group of 21 who handled primarily paper work for the union, labeled "enactors." The former group corresponds to the cases in the Rosen research.

It would appear from Figure 20.2 that both groups differ from Edwards's norm in being high on dominance, nurturance, and intraception, low in succorance and exhibition. Edwards defines these traits as follows (these are abbreviations of Edwards's sketches):

Dominance: to argue for one's point of view, to be a leader in groups to which one belongs, to make group decisions, to tell others how to do their jobs. Nurturance: to help friends when they are in trouble, to assist others less fortunate, to do small favors for others. Intraception: to analyze one's motives and feelings, to observe others, to understand how others feel about problems, to predict how others will act. Succorance: to have others provide help when in trouble, to seek encouragement from others, to have others be kindly, to have a fuss made over one when hurt. Exhibition: to say witty and clever things, to tell amusing jokes and stories, to talk about personal achievements, to be the center of attention.

It is easy to see why these union leaders should be high on dominance and nurturance, and low on succorance. They could scarcely function in their social roles without such traits. Some observers of union activity will doubt the typicality of the findings on intraception and exhibitionism; we shall know more on this point only after further studies.

Significant differences were found within the union group on a number

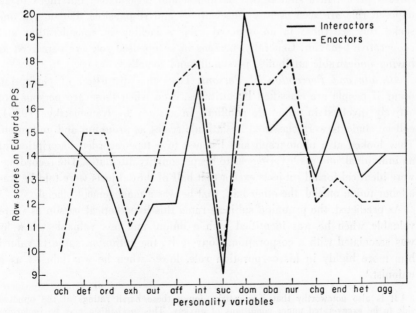

Fig. 20.2 The Edwards PPS profile for union officials. (From Belgrad, 1957.)

of variables. The interactors were significantly higher on need achievement and lower on affiliation; they were also higher on endurance. To anyone who knows the kind of life led by the typical union organizer, this last item needs no explanation. Clearly, the union bargainers and executives tend to be like company executives in having a high dominance score and high need achievement, whereas the enactors, those handling records, etc., do not show this.

These studies are particularly significant in that they show the interpenetration of social role and personality. No personality develops by itself alone; and individuals are not interchangeable units to be fitted into social roles arbitrarily. For effective performance, the personality must be appropriate to the role; and behaving in a role tends to modify the individual to increase this congruence.

Social Role and Person Perception. When an individual takes on a social role, certain modifications of personality must be expected to occur. A social role also modifies perception of persons in associated roles. Haire (1955) obtained such evidence from 76 members of a central labor council and 108 company executives. They were shown photographs of men, with accompanying biographical material, and asked to judge the personalities of these men. All data were identical except that for half of each group of subjects, a given photograph was labeled as "local manager of a small factory" or as "secretary-treasurer of his union."

The major conclusions were as follows: Persons in one social role perceive a person in a similar role as honest and dependable, but those in an opposed role are seen as less conscientious and responsible. Persons in one social role see those in an opposed role as lacking in consideration and cooperative behavior. Generally, persons in an opposed role are perceived as having undesirable attributes, personally and socially.

Attitude and Perception of Persons. Does this distortion of perception occur if people are classified by attitudes, even when these are persons not actively involved in economic conflict? In a study by Kamenetzky (1955), college students were classified by attitude scales as prounion and antiunion. They looked at a photograph and listened to a tape-recorded description of an individual, and made ratings as to his personality attributes. The recordings were identical for all subjects except that half of the subjects were told he was a labor union official, the other half, that he was a management official.

As predicted, the prounion subjects rated this hypothetical person as more valuable when he was identified with a union, and less valuable when he was associated with a corporation. Conversely, the antiunion subjects valued him more highly in his corporation role, lower when he was labeled as a unionist.[1]

---

[1] It is also noteworthy that Kamenetzky found these harsh ratings of the opposed side to be exaggerated under conditions of anxiety. This mechanism may be important

This confirmation of the Haire study suggests that attitudes play an important part in perceptual distortions even if the person under consideration is only an observer of the political, economic, or religious group which is the attitude object. If the Russians, having anti-American attitudes, are doomed to misperceive us as unfair, cruel, and worthless, the chances of persuading them to join in a cooperative program seem small. More will be offered on this point in Chapter 21.

Goals and Job Satisfaction. A study which has used Murray's scheme for classifying goals is that of Schaffer (1953) on job satisfaction. He asked employed men to indicate their relative desire to attain goals, such as creativity, achievement, pay, dependency—not using these terms, of course. Later they were asked how well these needs were satisfied on the job, and finally, they were asked how well satisfied they were with their jobs. As Schaffer had predicted, the goals which were perceived by the person as most important to him were those which predicted low job satisfaction when they were frustrated. Blocking attainment of a goal which does not look important to a person has little effect on his satisfaction, according to this study.

With this general conclusion one can hardly quarrel. Only if we took the generalized D, or single-drive, theory in a very literal form could we expect blockages of all goals to be equally significant for personality. If we assume that there is a hierarchy of major and minor goals, as Maslow, for example, proposed a hierarchy of instinctive impulses, then it must follow that perceiving a major goal as unattainable is a severe threat to the person's self-valuation, whereas his inability to attain a trivial goal has no effect on his self-image. This prediction has been verified by Diggory and Magaziner (1959) using imposed failure. College men who had rated themselves on several abilities (self-valuation) were led to believe that success on a certain task would have an important bearing on their future careers. A control group was given the same task, but without this suggestion. Both were told that they had failed, and then repeated the self-valuation procedure. The first group devalued themselves not only on over-all adequacy but also on several specific abilities. The second group showed no change in self-value. The effect of failure to reach a goal, then, is a function of perceived importance of the goal.

Selection of an occupation, and the effects of being in such an occupation upon the person, will depend on the goals he seeks. As is suggested in Figure 20.3, multiple goals, with both positive and negative valences, are usually involved with occupational role. Selection of a career involves solution of an approach-avoidance conflict; and if this selection has ignored important aspects of the role, whether for emotional reasons or as a result of ignorance,

in explaining the bitterness of strikes, problems in settling international crises, and even some of the exacerbations of marital conflict.

the conflict will become more severe with time. Obviously, this is a matter of the perceived importance of the goals which are not being attained. If they are seen as trivial, no disturbance results. But if the unattained goals are highly valued, then the person experiences failure.

Failure and Ego Defense. Repeated punishment and criticism for failure may have two kinds of consequences. First, as the Diggory-Magaziner study indicates, the individual may devalue himself. But this is painful, and as the perceived value of the self gets lower and lower, acute anxiety is aroused. This may elicit a perceptual defense mechanism, which most characteristically takes the form of denying any evidence that the self is inadequate. To explain the failure, therefore, the person criticizes the environment—the task, the instructor, the boss, the army, the government.

This process is probably involved in the personality pattern described by Rosenzweig (1945) as ego-defensive behavior. Rosenzweig pointed out that a person placed in a frustrating situation may react by ego defense or need persistence. The latter involves a continued insistence upon the importance of satisfying the need, whereas the former implies shifting to a maintenance of self-esteem, even if this means abandoning the original goal. There is some question as to the success of Rosenzweig's Picture-frustration Test in identifying individuals who consistently choose one or the other of these alternatives, but it is clear that specific instances of behavior can be classified in these categories. Thus, a student receiving a poor mark on an examination can respond with need persistence (by asking for help, by studying more, or even by cheating on the next examination), whereas a second student responds by arguing that his answers were right or that the professor was prejudiced. Generally it would appear that need persistence is associated with a more realistic orientation and a strong ego (cf. Chapter 9); ego defensiveness occurs when the person must keep face at all costs.

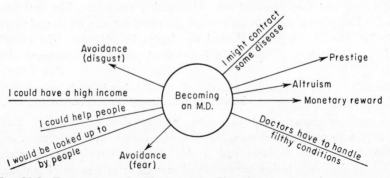

Fig. 20.3 Expectancy, goal, and occupation. The selection of an occupation imposes an approach-avoidance conflict. If selection is unwise, the conflict becomes more severe as the person continues in his occupation.

The extent to which such motivational trends are molded by early child-hood experiences is unknown. It is generally assumed that the child who has succeeded and been rewarded for persistence along a given track will show need persistence; and that he who has been subjected to sharp criticism for failures will become defensive. The work of Solley and Stagner (1956) indicated that subjects who became ego defensive in a failure situation were less efficient than those who remained focused on the task at hand.

Goals of the Underprivileged Worker. The effects of employment conditions in inculcating motives, values, and attitudes toward work can be well illustrated by the observations cited by Davis (1946) on underprivileged workers—uneducated, unskilled Negro and white workers (see page 334). Executives take for granted such values as punctuality, responsibility, and achievement—getting ahead. The underprivileged worker instead clings to basic biological goals, such as food, liquor, and sex. Davis notes that many businessmen casually ascribe these differences to heredity instead of inquiring as to the effects of the work environment [2] and the home environment.

Davis cites illustrations of workers who decide to try to get a technical education and rise in the work hierarchy. They save their money, get training, and then are denied employment because of race. The sacrifice has been in vain. Or, being only partially literate, they cannot deal with work orders, blueprints, and other written accompaniments of the higher-status job. Or, being last on, they are first to be laid off when business declines. Hence this group of workers is very likely to conclude—from personal experience and from watching their friends—that the middle-class values of saving, better training, etc., are delusions and mirages.

Another important demoralizing factor, he notes, is the fact that the Negro worker, even if he has a fairly good income, cannot buy a decent house. Thus one of the major rewards of sobriety, steady work, and responsible behavior —a pleasant place in which to rear one's children—is denied him.

The key principle here is what we have called the perceived probability of goal attainment (page 293). When the probability of achieving any particular goal is perceived as zero, that goal no longer influences the individual's behavior. If the minority-group worker sees no hope of earning good housing, a respected status on the job, and a stable income, he will inevitably reject the middle-class behavior patterns which are presumed to lead to these goals. He will orient his efforts toward food, liquor, and sex, the attain-

---

[2] Distressingly little has been done by psychologists on this problem. Roe (1956) has prepared an extensive discussion of the psychological attributes differentiating persons in one occupation from those in another. She has, however, included virtually nothing on the effects of the occupational environment on personality, family life, and other activities outside the task itself. Dyer (1956) studied families in relation to the father's job satisfaction, but did not consider such variables as marital conflict, parent-child conflict, or personality effects.

ment of which is fairly easy and, once enjoyed, cannot be snatched away by an arbitrary employment system.[3]

This picture of the effect of working conditions on personality cuts across occupations, of course, and relates primarily to persons handicapped by race, nationality, illiteracy, and similar factors. The example nonetheless will serve to verify our point, namely, that adult work environments can lead to substantial modifications in major aspects of personality. One can hardly doubt that the violence associated with coal miners, lumberjacks, and longshoremen is a function as much of their life conditions as it is of the kind of men attracted into these jobs. The constant presence of physical danger at work must lead to a lack of concern with physical safety or pain.

Job Frustrations and Child Rearing. Not only is the job important in terms of modifying the personalities of adults; it has far-reaching implications for the behavior of parents toward their children. We have noted in Chapter 17 the significance of affection for the child, of patience and sympathy, of some freedom to explore—and, above all, of a model with which the child can identify. What impact will job frustrations have on the way parents bring up their children?

Knowing the close association of frustration with aggression, we must predict that parents whose working lives are full of blockages and dissatisfactions will be more aggressive with their children, less affectionate and sympathetic. The father may feel that because of the children, he must stay on a dirty, irritating job; but in the process, he may unconsciously blame them and treat them with less affection than would otherwise be the case. Or he may simply build up tensions on the job which he cannot express for fear of discharge, and so these are vented on noisy, active youngsters when he comes home.

The literature on the effects on children of living in economically underprivileged homes is now extensive. We do not have much data which specifically relate treatment of children to job frustrations of parents, but we do know that workers in poorly paid jobs are consistently more dissatisfied and show lower morale than those in the higher brackets. In the following pages, therefore, we shall indicate some of the effects of poverty on the developing child personality.

SOCIAL-CLASS INFLUENCES ON PERSONALITY

Since the effects of income, kinds of housing, father's occupation, and other economic conditions upon the child's personality can conveniently be lumped

[3] It would appear from the data of LeShan (1952) that working-class children live within a narrower time span than middle-class pupils. This seems to be related to Davis's observations on goals, and perhaps also to our comments on the learning of impulse control (page 117).

under the heading of social-class influences, we are adopting this course. Two points need to be made in justification of this procedure. The first is that, when such influences have been studied separately, the various kinds of economic factors have similar results. The second relates to the existence of classes in American society. Like the Russians, we are prone to claim that ours is a classless society; and the evidence indicates that neither assertion is justified. At least, if we do not have social classes, people behave as if we did; and we shall therefore assume that there are true class stratifications in American society.[4] In the main we shall be comparing the so-called "middle class" (including people of somewhat above average income, professional-managerial occupations, preferred residential housing, etc.) with the "working class" (including manual workers, incomes average and below, inferior housing).

The prediction that children of lower economic status will experience more frustrations and more personality problems has been verified by Drucker and Remmers (1952) in a survey type of study of 1,000 junior high school students. The subjects were asked to check, from a list of 101 items, the problems they had experienced. These items had been validated by clinicians as indicative of potential personality maladjustment.

In Table 20.1 are shown the mean number of problems checked by children of varying status. The first comparison, of low versus high economic status, was based on the child's report of housing, appliance ownership, etc. Comparisons based on father's education and mother's education—each of which has been demonstrated to serve as an index of status—are also given. In all three cases, children from less-privileged families report more personality problems. The differences are not only statistically significant; they indicate that the poorer child may have as many as 50 per cent more problems than his more fortunate classmate.

Social-class identification is also related to problems of adjustment. Sims (1954) asked high school and college students whether they came from "middle-class" or "working-class" families. The latter group showed substantial handicaps in social adjustment and some handicap in home adjustment. The occupational status of the father can also be used as an index of class status, with parallel results. Springer (1938) classified grade school children in this way and found less emotional stability in the poorer group. Handicaps are observed as early as nursery school (Gesell and Lord, 1927).

Data from Personality Inventories. Numerous studies have applied personality inventories to sample populations and then ascertained differences between middle-class and working-class respondents. This kind of research, unfortunately, encounters many methodological complications, the correct

[4] The evidence on the psychological reality of social classes in the United States is too extensive for discussion here. For a brief analysis, see Stagner (1956), chap. 9; for a more extended treatment, see Centers (1949).

Table 20.1

Social-class Groupings and Personality Problems of Adolescents

	N	Mean	p
Low economic status	723	18.1	
High economic status	277	13.2	.01
Father's education:			
Grade school only	573	18.9	
High school graduate	221	13.8	*
Attended college	206	13.9	.01 *
Mother's education:			
Grade school only	519	19.2	
High school graduate	294	14.8	
Attended college	187	12.8	.01 *

* Grade school vs. college.

SOURCE: Drucker and Remmers (1952). Reprinted by permission of the American Psychological Association, Inc.

solutions to which are not at present matters of agreement among psychologists. For example: Education and class status are highly correlated. If we are trying to measure the effect of class status on personality, do we match the groups from the two classes on education? If we do, we study rather unrealistic samples from each group. This problem of matching cases from different classes so as to eliminate the effect of undesired variables thus merges into the problem of interpreting differences when they are located. This question will be discussed later.

MMPI Studies. When we consider the extensive use of MMPI, it is surprising that so few studies report on class differences. Gough (1946) offers data from a study of over two hundred high school seniors. He found that his "high social status" or middle-class groups were characterized by the following: positive literary and aesthetic attitudes; social poise and self-confidence; denial of fears and anxieties; broad-minded attitudes on sex and religion, and some excess of dogmatic, self-righteous opinions. The first three will surprise no one. Lower-class youngsters probably have not been exposed to literary and aesthetic stimuli; they have been hampered by their class origin as regards development of poise and self-confidence; and they have been subjected to more threats, more insecurities. Some would have predicted that working-class youth would be more broad-minded on sex; but in fact, the Freudian revolution, with its encouragement to parents to talk freely about sex to children, is still largely a middle-class phenomenon.

In a correlational analysis using the same inventory responses, Gough showed that low-status subjects in general receive unfavorable scores on MMPI. The working-class youngsters had more complaints of bodily symptoms (*Hs*), which may have been a reflection of poorer medical care; they were somewhat more rebellious (*Pd*), a point of significance in relation to delinquency (see page 226), and a little more schizophrenic in some respects; and they were inclined to depression and emotional disturbance more than the higher-status subjects. The benefits of poverty, it would appear, are hard to identify. The handicaps of poverty are pretty obvious.

California Test of Personality. Another inventory which gives numerous scores is the California Test of Personality. Stott (1945a, 1945b) administered this test to some eight hundred adolescents living on farms and in small towns. The farm children showed somewhat better self-adjustment (better self-image, fewer worries, etc.) than did the nonfarm children. Social adjustment was equal for the two groups. Within the nonfarm cases, there was a tendency for those of lower economic status to be handicapped as to both self-adjustment and social adjustment.

Within the farm group it was possible to distinguish status levels (value of farm, cultural level of parents). The correlations here were compatible with the others mentioned, i.e., young people from wealthier, better-educated families made higher scores on both self-adjustment and social adjustment.

Bernreuter Personality Inventory. Several studies have reported class differences on the Bernreuter inventory: e.g., Hoffeditz (1934), Mintzer and Sargent (1939), and Patterson (1943). All are in agreement that lower-class status is associated with the less desirable ends of the scales: poorer subjects had more worries, less self-sufficiency, more introversion, less dominance.

Bias in Construction of Inventories. It has been suggested that these inventories contain a built-in bias, in that the psychologist, typically middle-class himself, may unintentionally construct items which assume that middle-class values are the right ones. A well-designed study to test this hypothesis, by Hoffman and Albizu-Miranda (1955), confirms the suggestion in part. The authors took the "neurotic-tendency" items from the Bernreuter inventory and asked judges to rate them for class bias. A biased item was defined as one which favored the middle class without having any theoretical relevance to mental health or neuroticism. Forty items were found in which five judges agreed on bias; thirty-nine were agreed upon as unbiased; and forty-six were unclassified (because of disagreements).

The kinds of items chosen as biased can be illustrated as follows: "Have you organized any clubs, teams, or other groups on your own initiative?" This is much more a middle-class than a working-class pattern, and it seems to have no clear relation to "neurotic tendency." Other biased items indicate that one is not "talkative at social gatherings," "finds it difficult to speak in public," and so on. Suppression of emotions, self-confidence, orderliness, industriousness, and conformity to convention and authority are implied by the biased items. Desirable though these traits may be, it seems dubious to treat lack of them as evidence of "neurotic tendency."

The Bernreuter scale was given to several hundred high school students, from among whom were selected 75 who identified themselves as "working class" and whose fathers did manual work; also 75 who identified themselves as "middle class" and whose fathers did nonmanual work. The results on the biased and unbiased items are shown in Table 20.2.

Hoffman and Albizu-Miranda had predicted that the working-class youngsters would make undesirable scores on the biased items, as compared with their middle-class schoolmates, but they would not differ on the unbiased items. The prediction was only half-supported; the working-class mean is on the undesirable side on both biased and unbiased items. It is worth noting, however, that the difference between the two class groups is 12 points (male) and 28 points (female) on the biased items, but only 7 points (male) and 14 points (female) on the unbiased items. The alleged difference is thus reduced, but definitely not eliminated, by excluding items on which judges detect a class bias.

This study leaves us with two alternatives: (1) that maladjustment or "neurotic tendency" is in fact increased by working-class hazards, frustrations, and cultural expectancies; or (2) that the significance of items as indicators of such traits as this one cannot be evaluated without reference to answers of a group of persons from the working class. This point will come up for discussion later.

It is interesting to note that while class differences continue significant even with the "unbiased" items, sex differences do not. Evidently some of the alleged sex difference in neuroticism may be due to the failure of females

Table 20.2

Scores on Bernreuter Inventory for Working-class and Middle-class High School Students

	Working class		Middle class	
	Male	*Female*	*Male*	*Female*
Total score	−43.45	17.58	−64.76	−42.05
Biased items	−14.38	10.18	−26.34	−18.85
Unbiased items	−12.58	−2.46	−19.86	−16.69

SOURCE: Hoffman and Albizu-Miranda (1955), Table 1, p. 151. Reprinted by permission of American Psychological Association, Inc.

to accept certain "middle-class" values such as suppression of emotions, orderliness, and self-confidence.

Comparison with Stereotyped Expectancies. The above studies show that we can anticipate some consistent differences in traits and self-image of persons divided by economic status. It is interesting to compare these with the stereotyped expectancies held by college students with regard to men differing in income. Luft (1957) asked students to answer the California Test of Personality as they imagined a person (described to them) would fill it out. The facts given about this person were quite vague—name, age, level of education, home town, etc. Half of the group was told that this man earned $250 a week; the other half heard that he earned $42.50 a week (somewhat below the national average for manual workers at that time). It was assumed that the students would project their own preconceptions about wealth differences into the test situation.

This prediction was amply confirmed. The "rich man" was seen as being more self-reliant, perceiving himself as more valuable, having somewhat more personal freedom and feeling of belonging; he rated higher on social standards and social skills, on family, occupational, and community relations. These findings suggest that the student stereotype was not especially unrealistic, except as follows: When the answers for the "poor man" were compared with actual responses of a small group of local laborers, it was apparent that the students had projected much more of an inferiority feeling than these workers revealed.

Another interesting sidelight of this study was that students at an expensive private university "upgraded" the rich man more than students at a state college. The university group may have had personal contacts with very wealthy, very successful (and probably very self-assured) men. This may have moved their judgments further along the scale we assume to exist, as compared with the judgments made by the state college students.[5]

Projective Test Data. It is difficult to find projective test data on large enough samples of the population to justify comments on the socioeconomic implications. Even in the group of almost one thousand boys studied by Glueck and Glueck (1950), there is no control group of higher economic status. (Of necessity the majority of both delinquents and controls came from the bottom stratum, economically speaking, of the population.) The authors feel impelled, nevertheless, to comment on some trends in the Rorschach data which are present for both groups, and hence presumably reflect the economic frustrations common at this level: "general vague or unconscious feelings

[5] The relative accuracy of this particular stereotype should not encourage the reader to assume that all stereotypes have some modicum of truth in them. In many instances people develop stereotypes with no basis in personal observation. Hence, students will describe Russians, Chinese, Turks, etc., and reveal stereotyped expectancies about such nationalities, without ever having met a person belonging to one of these groups. Luft's "rich man, poor man" study at least stays within the range of probable experience.

of insecurity and/or anxiety"; "the feeling of not being wanted or loved"; *absence* of "an attitude of kindliness and trust." Although these trends depend on the judgment of the Rorschach experts, in the sense that no controls of higher economic status were tested, the figures are sufficiently extreme to warrant attention. Thus, 89 per cent of delinquents and 96 per cent of nondelinquents were judged to show feelings of insecurity, 96 per cent and 93 per cent, lack of kindliness and trust, and so on. Unless we assume that the test is hopelessly biased (an assumption denied by other studies), we must concede that boys in low economic homes are likely to suffer from these types of personality distortion.

Auld (1952b) compared a group of middle-class boys studied by Hertz (1942) with nondelinquent working-class boys studied by Glueck and Glueck (1950). The typical profiles would suggest that the middle-class boy is more imaginative and intelligent, is more mature, has better control of his emotions, is more responsive to his environment, and has more emotional warmth.

But, asks Auld, "are middle-class boys *actually* richer in inner life, more mature, emotionally warmer, and better controlled?" Such a conclusion, he indicates, would be at least premature. This cautious attitude is not shown by all investigators; Fine, Fulkerson, and Phillips (1955) correlated a measure of Rorschach maladjustment indexes with what they call social attainment (education, occupation level, etc.). Men of higher attainments showed significantly better emotional adjustment according to the Rorschach. They concluded, "Within a normal group, *maladjustment is significantly related to the level of social attainment* and its constituent parts, such as occupation-educational level" [p. 35]. Our preference is for the suspension of judgment expressed by Auld. The data collected by Fine, Fulkerson, and Phillips could be interpreted as indicating that our norms for maladjustment need to be computed separately for different occupational and educational levels.

A Study of Upper-class Personalities. The majority of the data available on class differences involves a comparison of middle-class and working-class subjects. This is inevitable because the two groups make up a preponderance of the American population. There is, however, a small group which the social anthropologists call "upper class," and McArthur (1955) has tried to identify some respects in which they differ from middle-class persons. His subjects were Harvard freshmen; among these, many come from wealthy, long-established families and have usually attended private schools, while others come from the public schools and in general represent managerial and newly wealthy families. He arbitrarily decided to treat private school graduates as upper class and public school graduates as middle class. There were 90 freshmen in the former group and 111 in the latter. TAT stories were used to determine differences in motives and values.

The results indicate that there are psychologically consistent differences between the two groups. The value of work (need achievement) is perhaps the key factor. In the upper-class stories, work is accepted only when it leads to certain kinds of interesting experiences. In the middle-class group, work is perceived as a means to glory, to money, to autonomy; attending college is a way to reach these ends. For the middle-class group the mother appears to be a pressure agent; domination by the parents is a more frequent theme for them. For the upper-class subjects parents seem less significant; one wonders if this reflects less actual contact of children with parents in this subculture.

It is necessary to conclude here, as with other class studies, that we are only on the fringe of the problem. Certainly it would be proper to have a better class criterion than simply attendance at private schools; and if possible, it would be desirable to learn something about the differences in parent-child relations before concluding that such data as these reflect true class differences in personality.

MECHANISMS OF SOCIAL-CLASS INFLUENCE

The studies cited indicate that substantial differences are found on personality assessment devices when children of one social-class grouping are compared with those from another. Certain kinds of response patterns occur more frequently among working-class than among middle-class children. Leaving aside the technical questions raised earlier, let us assume that these do represent true personality variables, and then ask: What are some possible explanations for these findings? Two major hypotheses have been offered: (1) that families of differing social class have different child-rearing practices which elicit these personality findings; and (2) that the actual experiences of the individual, as a result of economic frustrations, housing conditions, access to recreational facilities, and educational opportunities, shape his personality.

Social Class and Child-rearing Practices. For a considerable time cultural anthropologists have been studying the relation of approved child-rearing techniques within a culture to the "modal personality" of that culture (cf. Kardiner, 1939; Whiting and Child, 1953). On occasions this has gone to ridiculous extremes, such as the suggestion that the Russian predilection for dictatorial governments arises from the practice of swaddling infants. Disregarding such eccentricities, we find substantial evidence to support the view that a culture possesses a certain inner unity, so that adult personality and infant training seem plausibly consistent with one another. It must be noted, however, that this does not verify a causal relationship. The infant not only is subjected to a certain regimen in socialization; he also grows up in a cultural milieu in which men do certain things and women do others, in which certain beliefs about illness are virtually universal, in which suspicion of others is encountered everywhere. The mere processes of acquiring expectancies, imitating role models, and identifying with prestige figures consequently could account for the molding of the child to the modal adult pattern. His earliest experiences are not necessarily crucial, although of course they may be.

A test of the importance of child-rearing practices for personality development is consequently more decisive in a situation such as that in the United States, where multiple role models are available, diverse prestige figures are observed, both gregarious and withdrawn social patterns are acceptable, both trust and suspicion are often encountered (cf. Chapter 21), and so on. What this means is that a significant relation between child rearing and adult personality can less readily be ascribed to learning in later childhood and maturity, as was possible in the more homogeneous primitive societies.

The Chicago Study of Class Differences. It would appear that the first careful research on class differences in child rearing was that of Davis and Havighurst (1946). Using white and Negro middle-class and lower-class mothers, they found decided class differences in breast feeding, severity of toilet training, etc. Some of the items included are shown in Table 20.3. These differences might be expected to induce class differences in later personality traits, although one may question whether they would predict the kinds of differences we have noted in the preceding pages.

The exploration of this question is unnecessary because several later studies contradict the Davis-Havighurst report. Miller and Swanson (1958) studied a considerably larger sample of mothers in the Detroit area, and used a more reliable sampling procedure which may be assumed to have minimized the chance that the class differences are mixed in with other, irrelevant differences (as may have happened in the Chicago study). Their findings are sharply at variance with the Davis-Havighurst conclusions. As can be seen from Table 20.3, of 28 possible confirmations, Miller and Swanson report only six, three at a level of confidence not generally acceptable; and one group showed a significant contradiction of the Chicago conclusion.

The situation is not made any clearer by a comparison of the Detroit study with the Sears-Maccoby-Levin research in the Boston area, which was mentioned earlier (page 405). The Boston data not only do not confirm the Chicago results; they also contradict significantly several of the Detroit conclusions. (It might be noted that Boston and Detroit agree on one fairly important point, which is the greater use of physical punishment by lower-class mothers, and this may be compatible with some of the data on aggression and delinquency cited above.)

As a consequence of this situation, it seems clear that we cannot support the theory that differences in child-rearing practice account for class differences in later personality. However, two further points should be made. It is at least conceivable that *deviations* from accepted patterns of child rearing, such as those described in Chapter 17, are quite important, but that class dif-

Table 20.3

Comparison of the Chicago and Detroit Findings on Social-class Differences in Child-rearing Practices *

Chicago finding	*Detroit finding*			
	Entre-preneurial middles vs. Entre-preneurial lowers	*Entre-preneurial middles vs. Bureau-cratic lowers*	*Bureau-cratic middles vs. Bureau-cratic lowers*	*Bureau-cratic middles vs. Entre-preneurial lowers*
More lower-class children are fed only at the breast	0	0	0	0
More lower-class children are fed on demand	+(.20)	+(.05)	0	0
Middle-class children are weaned earlier	0	0	+(.10)	0
Bowel training is begun earlier with middle-class children	+(.05)	+(.01)	0	0
Bladder training is begun earlier with middle-class children	0	+(.10)	0	−(.02)
More lower-class parents complete bladder training by 18 months	0	0	0	0
Middle class expects higher occupational status for children	0	0	0	0

* A plus (+) sign means that the Detroit findings agree with those stated in the left margin for the Chicago study. The number in parentheses indicates the confidence level for the significance of the differences in the two Detroit groups being compared. A minus (−) sign indicates a finding opposite to the Chicago study. A zero (0) means that the *p* value for the Detroit groups was .50 or larger, i.e., no group differences worth listing.

ferences are not. And we should again note that the child's *perception* of how he is treated counts for more than what physically occurs.

Social Class and Individual Frustrations. Inability to accept the explanation based on class differences in child rearing impels us to examine the second alternative, namely, that differences in the child's later environment, and differences in the family milieu other than those of ordinary child-rearing routines, determine the findings on personality traits.

Unpleasant Expectancies. Many of the traits ascribed to lower-status youth in the preceding pages can be characterized as indicating a surplus of unpleasant expectancies. When we say that lower-class adolescents have more fears, worries, and anxieties, this is certainly clear. Is this another case (cf. Chapter 4) in which the perceptual field comes to reflect, not perfectly but with some faithfulness, the external environment?

We must expect income differences to be associated with some greater incidence of *biological frustrations:* less food, less palatable food, less comfortable clothing, less adequate housing. Differences in the father's occupation have decided effects on such satisfactions. The assembly-line worker who is laid off for a month or more each year at model change-over time has more difficulty providing for his children than has the clerical employee whose job is considerably more secure. Construction workers may receive high incomes for a part of the year and nothing in another part. Both the actual impact of such layoffs and the anxiety of the adults about such threats will affect the child's perception of the world in which he lives.

Also important are the *social frustrations* likely to be associated with class status. In commenting earlier on inventory bias we cited questions about group activities, school clubs, etc. Numerous studies show that middle-class and upper-class children dominate school activities, achieve leadership roles, and generally receive the gratifications involved. Other social frustrations may derive from ridicule (for clothing, type of housing), ineptness in dealing with middle-class situations, lack of verbal facility in schoolwork, and similar problems. The cruelty of young children is notorious; in a predominantly working-class school a middle-class youngster may be physically mistreated, and in a middle-class group the poorer child is subject to social mistreatment. The domination of the school by middle-class values is a part of this picture (cf. Chapter 19).

Family Disorganization. We must keep in mind the demoralizing effects of economic insecurity and of actual hardship on the parents as well as on the children, because the physical punishment inflicted and the emotional buffeting from the parents will reflect adult tensions. The laid-off steelworker does not consciously displace his aggressions onto his son, but the son's misbehavior at this time precipitates a storm out of proportion to its seriousness. Further, as was mentioned in Chapter 17, "family morale," the harmonious functioning of parent and child roles, is important for the child's personality development.

Hayward (1935) reports on studies in which several hundred children were asked a large number of questions regarding family harmony and peace. On this basis a "family disorganization score" was computed. Table 20.4 shows the average score for normal groups of high, medium, and low economic status, and for a delinquent group corresponding to the low group in economic level.

This table shows a rapid increase in family disorganization as the economic status decreases. The delinquent group is characterized by considerably greater internal difficulty than the normal group of similar status, but the difference does not meet a statistical criterion for a "significant difference." The most probable explanation is that economic group III includes some families which can stand the shock of hardship without complete disintegration, whereas others cannot. Those families which break down to a greater extent produce more delinquents. However, in any case, a family which has a score of 40 or more on such a questionnaire as Hayward's is a decidedly unwholesome place for a child to live. The data suggest that one of the major causes is economic status. Thus, even though overt acts of delinquency may not occur in some families, personality difficulties and long-time problems undoubtedly develop.

Table 20.4

Economic Status and Family Disorganization

Economic status *	Mean	S.D.	N.
I	23.8	13.6	21
II	32.6	18.1	55
III	45.0	21.0	22
Del. III	57.4	24.9	103

* Critical ratios: I–II, 2.37; II–III, 2.43; I–III, 4.0; III–Del. III, 2.48.

SOURCE: Hayward (1935).

This observation of Hayward's on family disruption is given interesting confirmation by Hamilton's findings on the relationship between financial status and marital happiness. It is reported (Hamilton and McGowan, 1929) that the wife of a man earning $5,000 or more yearly has 54 chances in 100 of being content with her marriage, whereas those whose husbands earn less than this amount have only 36 chances in 100 of attaining such satisfaction. Since (at the time the data were collected) less than one family in ten had such an income, the importance of such a finding for prospective marital stability is considerable. It is clear from divorce statistics that broken homes are far more common in poorer than in well-to-do strata of society. The effect of a broken home upon children is well known. Even if the marriage continues, friction about money, housing, and similar questions must necessarily be detrimental to the child's mental health.

INTERPRETATION OF CLASS DIFFERENCES

It is now appropriate to return to the problem raised earlier: Do the class differences in personality reflect true personality variables, or do they represent a middle-class bias on the part of the test developers?

The argument of the immediately preceding paragraphs would suggest that children of lower economic status do indeed develop a surplus of fears, worries, anxieties, and aggressions, as compared with more fortunate youngsters. At least the circumstances are such that it would be indeed surprising not to find such a difference. But this does not resolve our problem. We have, throughout this entire book, taken the position that personality is a pattern of perceptions. Implicitly, however, there has been a theme that personality is reflected in *distorted* perceptions, those not supported by consensual agreement. If a woman says she sees a tree outside her window, no one interprets this as evidence of a personality problem; but if she sees dozens of cuddly little babies nestled in its branches, we immediately diagnose a personality disturbance. How does this bear on the problem of class differences?

Consider the case of the working-class boy whose answers indicate that he sees little or no chance of becoming a leader in school clubs, Scouts, and other groups. Does this mean lack of self-confidence, or accurate perception of the situation? Statistics indicate that his response is rather accurate. Can we then interpret it as evidence for an inner variable, a personality trait? We are not on very safe ground in doing so.

Everyone has some worries. We have, in Chapter 8 and elsewhere, dealt with evidence of ego weakness or emotional instability in comparative terms: Some individuals show more worries, more depressions, more avoidance of reality than the average, and we interpret this deviation as evidence of a personality problem. But realistically, the working-class child has more to worry about. Further, he will often be handicapped in school, and will fail. He will not get hired for the best jobs because of his family background, lack of manners, and lesser education, so he will experience severe ego devaluation. Can we then judge his personality against a standard of the entire population, or solely against persons of similar socioeconomic status? As long as we adhere to a detached counting of emotions, this is not important; but as soon as we use terms like "emotional maladjustment," "ego strength," and "impulse control," we are implying a standard of normality. Class differences in environment clearly result in some differences in perception and behavior. But when we attempt to apply an evaluative label to these—when we try to say whether the effect of the difference is beneficial or harmful—we must have a relevant standard. It is this standard which we do not have.

The commonest solution, of course, has been for the psychologist to use his own standard, i.e., a middle-class perception of the appropriate behavior. By this criterion lower-class children are likely to be handicapped. And since employment, political preferment, and prestige status are likely to be parceled out by middle-class standards, perhaps this conclusion is justified. But a lower-class view might well be that the additional toughness, aggressiveness, and realism of the lower-class youth could be considered evidence of his superiority. (During the war, many youngsters from underprivileged areas earned medals because of their readiness for combat, aggressiveness, and willingness to risk bodily harm.) Thus, the traits which we consider "adjustive" in a college-suburban culture may be maladjustive in a different cultural setting.

It is difficult to draw a sharp distinction between those kinds of responses which can be called realistic adjustments to working-class problems, and those which represent emotional disturbance because of these real frustrations. We have an alternative of two kinds of interpretations: (1) that working-class children are not really handicapped as to personality development, but should be judged on completely independent norms; or (2) that the "maladjusted" responses reported do in fact represent blocks to a full, normal personality. Our best guess is that the truth involves both of these. Probably some of the class difference in response reflects only realistic perception of difficulties; the remainder represents a true handicap imposed by the unequal distribution of rewards and barriers in our society.

ECONOMIC FACTORS AND ATTITUDES

The scapegoat theory of prejudice, as outlined in Chapter 11, holds that hostility to minority groups represents aggression displaced from other, more fundamental frustrations. Freudians, for example, have often suggested that the hostility involved in such attitudes was originally directed to the parents, has been repressed, and is now deflected onto Negroes, Jews, Catholics, or other locally available out-groups. Somewhat greater attention has been given, in recent years, to the theory that *economic frustrations* lie at the root of such hostile attitudes.

This theory has been used in explaining the rise of fascism in Italy and Germany after World War I. It has been applied to instances of social aggression in the United States. Hovland and Sears (1940) found evidence that the rate of lynching of Negroes in the Southern states was related to the value of the cotton crop prior to World War II; in good years there were fewer such murders, in years of economic hardship for the white farmers, lynching increased. The assumption was that economic frustration evoked aggression, which, having no rational target, was focused onto the helpless minority group.

Bird and Monachesi (1954) attempted to get at hostile attitudes in residential areas which had been all white, and into which Negro families were moving. This transition involved both economic and ego frustrations for the whites, and of course an economic decline had preceded the change. The evidence indicated that those persons who disliked the neighborhood showed more prejudice against Negroes; and among these, those who were dissatisfied with their jobs were especially so. Since the Negroes can scarcely have influenced the job situation, the authors interpret this as evidence favoring the displacement hypothesis.

In efforts to test the theory in the laboratory, experimental frustrations were introduced by Miller and Bugelski (1948) and Cowen, Landes, and Schaet (1959); tests of attitude toward minority groups before and after the frustration indicated an increase in prejudice. On the other hand, Congdon (1954) used a very similar method and failed to obtain evidence of displaced aggression.

In support of the theory is the work of Bettelheim and Janowitz (1950) in which they interviewed veterans of World War II regarding attitudes toward Jews and Negroes. They found a significant relationship between a loss of economic and social status from prewar to postwar years and presence of decided hostility to both minorities (Table 20.5).

Attitudes are admittedly complex phenomena, involving both perceptual and motivational aspects (cf. Chapter 11). It is thus not entirely surprising that there have been contradictory findings in these investigations. Realistic frustrations are hard to establish in the laboratory; college students are notoriously skeptical of what is being done to them in this situation, and thus may perceive an event not as frustrating but merely as an item for curiosity. Economic frustrations, by contrast, cannot be controlled, and many irrelevant variables get involved. In the Bettelheim-Janowitz data, for example, we do not know

Table 20.5

Social Mobility and Prejudiced Attitudes of Veterans *

	Downward † mobility, per cent	No mobility, per cent	Upward mobility, per cent
Attitudes to Negroes:			
Tolerant and stereotyped	28	26	50
Outspoken and intense	72	74	50
Attitudes to Jews:			
Tolerant and stereotyped	28	75	68
Outspoken and intense	72	25	32

* Mobility = shift in socioeconomic position from immediate prewar position to that at time of interview; a shift of 1 or more grades on the Edwards scale was treated as evidence of mobility.

† Only 18 men in downward group.

SOURCE: Bettelheim and Janowitz (1950). Derived from Table 4 (IV), p. 59, and Table 2 (VIII), p. 150. Reprinted by permission.

what the prewar attitudes of the veterans may have been; in the Bird-Monachesi study, intelligence and other confusing differences may have affected the attitudinal results.

Despite these complications, the preponderance of the evidence seems to support a displacement theory of prejudice and an interpretation of social movements based on aggression as having their roots in major socioeconomic frustrations.[6] As will be noted in the final chapter of this book, such psychological findings merit serious consideration by persons engaged in social planning.

Authoritarianism, Income, and Occupation. The studies of *The Authoritarian Personality* led to the conclusion, disappointing to its authors, that working-class men were more "authoritarian" than middle-class men. This disappointment is clearly suggested by an uncalled-for statement interpolated into the discussion of differences in scores: "It is true, of course, as a matter of economic and social fact, that the crucial role in the struggle against increasing concentration of economic power will have to be played by the working people, acting in accordance with their self-interest, but it is foolhardy to underestimate the susceptibility to fascist propaganda within these masses themselves" [p. 267]. The naïve conception of "economic and social fact" is amusing; the sudden switch from parent-child relations (cf. Chapter 17) to "fascist propaganda" as the explanation of group differences is distressing.

Remembering that the *F* scale is subject to the "acquiescence" response set (page 253), and that educated persons are likely to be somewhat more critical of glittering generalizations than are persons with less verbal training, we can predict that education will have a negative correlation with *F* score. This is amply confirmed by Table 20.6, giving results for an adult sample collected by Roberts and Rokeach (1956). Whereas income is also negatively related (thus supporting the finding of the Adorno group that middle-class men are more "liberal"), the education effect is substantially larger. Also interesting, in the Roberts-Rokeach data, is the fact that all three attitude scales are subject to the acquiescent response set, and the pattern of correlations is virtually identical. "Anomie" here refers to an attitude of "normlessness," of loss of faith in society; the individual must look out for himself, the law will not help him. Ethnocentrism, of course, is anti-Negro, anti-Jewish prejudice in this case. The upper-income, better-educated cases, then, appear to be less preju-

[6] Since communism, in contrast to fascism, is not involved directly in ethnic prejudice, we have not incorporated relevant research regarding communist attitudes in the above section. It is worth noting, however, that procommunist ideology is an aggressive manifestation and may in some cases reflect displaced hostility. A study of Italian trade unionists (Stagner, 1959) indicated that those most vigorously dissatisfied with their jobs were most belligerently procommunist. However, this is not clearly an evidence of displacement, since the employer (source of job frustration) is part of the group to be attacked by the Communists. Pure displacement occurs only when there is no rational connection between the original frustration and the target of the attack.

Table 20.6

**Relation of Education and Income
to Authoritarian Attitudes ***

	Educa-tion	Income
Anomie (Srole scale) †	−.51	−.41
Authoritarianism (*F* scale)	−.45	−.24
Ethnocentrism (*E* scale)	−.50	−.23

* All items on all scales are phrased so that an answer high on anomie, authoritarianism, or ethnocentrism is the yes answer.
† Anomie = normlessness, otherwise, a kind of loss of faith in society, every man for himself.
SOURCE: Roberts and Rokeach (1956).

diced, less anarchistic, and less authoritarian [7]—but it is possible that all these results are spurious because of the acquiescence problem.

We can hardly criticize the average worker, of limited education, not overly intelligent, who has encountered many failures in his attempts to get ahead and who must habitually take orders from various persons placed in charge of him by economic circumstance. His acquiescence may be thought of as an adjustment mechanism; when he has tried to oppose his own opinion to that of "the higher-ups," he has usually come off second-best. He may not actually be more authoritarian or more prejudiced; in the Bettelheim-Janowitz study, where prejudice was assessed from free comments, economic status did not predict either anti-Jewish or anti-Negro feeling. It was necessary to bring downward social mobility into consideration with its implication of especially severe frustration, before a clear-cut relation of economic factors to prejudice could be demonstrated.

SUMMARY

The individual must live within the economic system; he is thus affected by it in many ways. He must accept certain kinds of economic roles, and conform to working conditions prescribed for these roles. He achieves (or fails to achieve) rewards, such as income and prestige; the incidence of these gratifications determines how well he can care for his children, the social reception the youngsters will encounter, and even to some extent his relations with

[7] MacKinnon and Centers (1956) likewise found a sample of manual workers substantially more "authoritarian" than nonmanuals. The same acquiescence problem is involved in their data.

his wife and the probabilities of a harmonious home life. The traits and self-image, the motives and values, of both parent and child will be modified by these economic pressures.

A major controversy has centered around the extent to which the apparently undesirable effects of poverty on personality might be a function of child-rearing practices. Early data had indicated consistent class differences in child rearing, but later studies have contradicted this. The interpretation is thus offered that class differences in income and satisfaction account for the surplus of unpleasant expectancies found in working-class children and adults. Whether this represents a true maladjustment of personality or an improper imposition of middle-class norms on people for whom these norms are inappropriate cannot be answered decisively.

Attitudinal differences related to income seem to follow the scapegoat principle, i.e., persons of lower-class status show more prejudices and may be assumed to displace hostility from other, unperceived sources. Social changes and revolutionary movements may reflect the focusing of aggression upon the symbols of the established order as a consequence of economic frustrations.

SUGGESTIONS FOR READING

Nothing has been said in this chapter about the extensive use of personality measures in business and industry. Good accounts of such applications will be found in Ghiselli and Brown, *Personnel and industrial psychology*, Smith's *Psychology of industrial behavior*, and similar texts. Some observations on personality and union-management relations are presented in Stagner, *Psychology of industrial conflict*. Personality needs and occupational choice are discussed by Anne Roe in *The psychology of occupations*.

The most recent studies on economic factors affecting the family and especially child-rearing practices are Miller and Swanson, *The changing American parent*, and Sears, Maccoby, and Levin, *Patterns of child rearing*.

CHAPTER 21

Personality and Social Values

The individual human personality is the product of a learning sequence. Driven by inner tensions and guided by external valences, the child conforms to social pressures, introjects cultural norms, and imitates the behavior of leading figures in his milieu. While recognizing the importance of accidents in the individual biography, we feel nonetheless impelled to conclude that personality is in the main a mirror of the culture.[1]

The corollary of this principle is that the culture is a mirror of personality. A culture has no existence apart from the individuals who comprise it. Feudalism died in Western Europe when individuals in large numbers rejected the basic value standards involved. The noticeable changes in American culture of the twentieth century have evolved as individuals proposed and accepted new norms, set up new frames of reference, and imitated new models. Unfortunately, social scientists have given a great deal of attention to the principle that culture is the major determinant of personality, while giving relatively little to the thesis that culture is a summation of individual personalities.

Concept of the Sick Society. Given this reciprocal relationship of personality and culture, it becomes obvious that we can think of the society as the determiner of personality breakdown and mental illness; hence, that the society itself is, in a sense, pathological. This point has been argued effectively by Frank (1936), Halliday (1948), Fromm (1955), and others. Many people, of course, refuse to see defects in the social system; as Frank comments, "At present we cherish a belief in a normal, intact society against which we see these criminals, those psychopaths, these warring husbands and wives, these recalcitrant adolescents, these shameless prostitutes and vicious sex offenders,

---

[1] This point is made even more clear if consideration is given to the data of cultural anthropology, which limitations of space have forced us to exclude from this volume. As Maslow has pointed out, psychologists are guilty of a tremendous "sampling error" if they base their conclusions only on personalities developing within Western culture. There are primitive cultures in which aggressiveness, suspiciousness, autistic thinking, masochism, and other patterns are grossly overemphasized or rigorously suppressed, as compared with our civilization. The "normal" individual in many of these cultures would seem insane when judged by our norms, and the reverse would also be true in many instances.

as so many rebels who threaten society and so must be punished, disciplined or otherwise individually treated."

Against this denial of social responsibility Frank poses the analysis of personality by scientific psychology. Character is a product of experience; the superego, the individual's conscience, is molded by social taboos, commands, and obligations. The delinquent is the plausible outcome of social conflicts and frustrations (Chapter 10); his environment has failed to supply suitable role models and value systems (Chapter 11). Thus, Frank asserts, "When the culture no longer provides for a superego that is integrated and wholesome, but by its many conflicts and ambiguities makes the superego socially ineffective if not self-destructive, we must recognize the necessity of revising our ethical and moral ideas."

Conflicts within the Value System. Is it really true that American culture offers to our young people a set of values in conflict with one another, values which lead to conflicting social expectancies and suggest incompatible responses? Consider the following list of beliefs which are common in American culture: [2]

1. This is a world in which it is "every man for himself and the devil take the hindmost."

But: no man lives to himself alone; you should love your neighbor as yourself; we should all work together as good Americans.

2. Democracy is the best form of social organization ever developed; all men are created free and equal.

But: most of the people are too dumb, or shiftless, or both, to be trusted with a voice in the handling of industrial problems and probably in government, too.

3. Doing your own job well, wherever you are, is more important than trying to make a lot of money.

But: money makes the world go round.

4. Religion and the "finer things of life" are what we value most highly.

But: religion and business don't mix.

5. It is smart to have the newest model automobile, the most modern industrial processes, and the latest technical equipment.

But: anybody who proposes tampering with our fundamental institutions of government or industry is a dangerous radical and should be shipped back where he came from.

6. Poverty is deplorable, and we should take steps to eliminate it from America.

But: the poor you have always with you.

7. Hard work and thrift are signs of sound character; they are the dependable roads to success.

[2] Many such listings have been published; this one is more or less directly adapted from pp. 60–62 of R. S. Lynd's *Knowledge for what?*

But: the smart boys know how to make money and go places without working.

It would be possible to increase this list substantially, and to show that we impose contradictory expectations upon our children by rearing them in this kind of culture. Like Norman Maier's rats or Pavlov's dogs, the human being finds himself in a conflict situation and tends to develop an "experimental neurosis," except that this is no experiment.

In connection with our discussions of home, school, and industry we have emphasized the contradictions between authority and democracy, between submissiveness and independence, between domination and cooperation. It is only when we take the larger social framework into consideration that this picture becomes understandable. It is not enough to ascribe a child's personality distortion to a domineering mother. Why does the mother become dominative, and why does the child resist? Many labor conflicts arise because of the will-to-power of business executives and union leaders; but some workers develop neurotic symptoms in this same situation. Neither the social nor the personal conflict can be considered desirable in a broad humanitarian frame of reference.

The Sane Society. Fromm (1955) points out that there are ample grounds for diagnosing Western civilization as suffering from an analogue of paranoid schizophrenia; we see on all sides delusions of national grandeur or divine mission, delusions of persecution, blind destructiveness in war, sadistic fantasies on our television screens, distorted perceptions in which huge surpluses of food represent economic disasters. Is it surprising that, in such a context, personalities break down and juvenile delinquency mounts?

Fromm's view implies that a society may be sane or not sane. He would reject cultural relativism (which argues that people can adapt to any culture, and that psychological abnormality must always be judged relative to the person's culture; this point was discussed in the preceding chapter). There are, he says, "universal criteria for mental health which are valid for the human race as such." Given these criteria, it becomes possible to define a sane society and to plan for social therapy. "A sane society," he writes, "is that which corresponds to the needs of man—not necessarily to what he *feels* to be his needs, because even the most pathological aims can be felt subjectively as that which the person wants most; but to what his needs are *objectively*, as they can be ascertained by the study of man." [3]

VALUES AND THE HOMEOSTATIC MODEL

In many respects, we have shown, personalities follow the pattern of homeostasis. The individual establishes a favorable equilibrium and exerts effort to

---

[3] Fromm (1955), p. 20. Reprinted by permission of Rinehart & Co., publishers.

maintain it, resists pressures to change. Habit, perceptual constancy, and rigidity are some of the processes contributing to this resistance to change.

Society also seems to follow a homeostatic model. Once an equilibrium has been established, strong forces resist disturbing it. The pressure for conformity, which has been described earlier, tends to interfere with efforts by individuals to change the existing pattern. As we saw during the McCarthy era of 1952–1956, punishments can also be applied to persons who have deviant ideas. Thus the forces making for stability and security, within both the individual and his society, are quite potent.

The Paradox of Social Change. It is this set of circumstances which has given rise to the familiar paradox: "You can't change the individual unless you first change society" and "You can't change society unless you first change human nature." Since the individual is molded by his early environment, the argument goes, you must first modify the environment; but since the environment can't be changed until you change people's personalities, the prospects are hopeless. Naturally the conservative, the person who wants no change, likes this point of view.

Perhaps, if man were limited to the simple reflex level of homeostasis, this barrier to advancement might hold. Highly stereotyped cultures, isolated from contact with others, have been perpetuated for hundreds of years with little apparent change. It is, however, clear that when individuals experience frustration as a result of culture patterns, they are capable of imagining a different social order and of taking action to break up the old equilibrium in favor of a new system. Every revolution is proof that society can be changed; history tells us that some important social modifications have been achieved without violence, as in the United States from 1933 to 1940.

Social Change Is Necessary. Fromm defined the sane society as one providing adequate gratification for human needs. The society which is not sane, by the same token, is one which offers a surplus of deprivations and frustrations. But it is exactly such conditions which lead to personality breakdown, to scapegoating, to delinquency, and to war. Thus, in sheer self-preservation, to protect the valued aspects of our individual and social existences, we must seek to create a sane society.

It is a sign of maladjustment, not of realism, when psychologists and psychiatrists argue that they must help their patients to become adjusted to *established* conditions and values. Adjustment calls for clear perception of all important aspects of reality. As we noted in a preceding chapter, education must at times disturb equilibria; the task of the school is to turn out mature citizens, not happy morons. The colleges likewise have an obligation to make young people aware of the frustrations, inconsistencies, and conflicts within existing society, so that they can choose intelligently among various possible courses of action.

The philosophy of cultural relativity has been useful in breaking down the false conception of an unchanging, unmodifiable human nature. But it may have, in turn, proved a block to progressive thinking by instilling the unconscious principle that the individual could achieve adequate happiness and self-development in any cultural framework. As Murphy has pointed out: [4]

There is surely little sense in continuing to speak as if man could adapt himself equally well to any environment. Here the concept of cultural relativism has done immense damage, indeed as great damage, I believe, as the concept of unchanging human nature. Both notions are blatantly at variance with the findings of cultural sciences. If man is to be moulded to society, society must also be moulded to man.

Personality, it was argued in Chapter 15, is not purely a homeostatic mechanism. The individual strives for goals, and he is capable of abandoning a comfortable berth in favor of exploration, social reform, and the realization of ideals.

The primary group (family and close friendships) lays down certain patterns which transfer to secondary-group relationships: thus, the child's attitude toward authority transfers from parents to school, industry, and government. His craving for security and his demand for recognition will also determine much of his behavior in the larger group situation.

It appears likely that the reverse of this equation holds true to some extent, i.e., that activities on the larger social level may have adjustive value for relieving primary-group tensions. In summing up a study of the personality development of young radicals, Krout and Stagner wrote as follows: [5]

In a world in which secondary-group contacts have assumed a dominant role, adjustment of primary-group tensions may now be satisfactorily accomplished in this fashion (*i.e.*, through secondary-group activities). The day in which such tensions expressed themselves in primary-group relationships is perhaps passing. Henceforth, it may be expected that economic tensions will cause more maladjustments than before, and, conversely, that the substitutive value of socioeconomic integration may be greater than previously.

Certainly we have adequate evidence to indicate that social reforms may reduce the frequency of primary-group conflicts. Even if the larger cultural changes have no immediate adjustment value, therefore, they are amply justified; but it seems likely that the individual, by adopting a positive program of attempting to modify social values, adds something to his own life which benefits his personality integration.

Resistance to Social Change. In the face of these considerations, why is it that many individuals, even those facing social catastrophe, make no effort to modify the environment and so to avert disaster? An excellent analysis of this question has been made by Allport, Bruner, and Jandorf (1941), who analyzed 90 detailed autobiographies of victims of Nazi persecution. "Several lines of evidence," they write, "force us to the conclusion that our subjects

---

[4] Murphy (1939), p. 111. Reprinted by permission of the *Journal of Social Psychology.*
[5] Krout and Stagner (1939), p. 44. Reprinted by permission.

actively resisted recognition of the seriousness of the situation, or in cases where the seriousness was realized, failed at first to make a realistic adjustment to it." [6]

These lines of evidence converge on four psychological mechanisms which prevented attempts to deal adaptively with the situation: (1) *persistent goal striving* (the desire to continue in quest of the culturally established goals, family security, education of children, business success); (2) *need to retain a structured field* (adoption of a new course of action threatened insecurity, upsetting established ways of behavior, adapting to strange customs); (3) the *pull of the familiar* exerted a positive attraction; and (4) *unconscious defense mechanisms,* such as denial of danger, rationalization of the situation, fantasy, and temporary isolation, cooperated to prevent realistic action.

All these processes can readily be identified in the thinking and behavior even of persons who are not endangered by so paralyzing a threat as that of the Nazi terror. In America today, many individuals who are threatened with economic insecurity, racial and religious prejudice, industrial autocracy, and atomic war, show the same concentration on traditional goals, the same clinging to familiar patterns, and repression of any awareness of danger. From our viewpoint, such individuals seem as maladjusted as adults who cling to infantile gratifications and repress their strivings for sexual and social maturity. The ultimate result may be social disaster, rather than individual psychosis; it is nonetheless tragic.

The Individual's Obligation to Society. A psychologist can scarcely endorse any except an individual-centered culture. Being constantly impressed with the importance of the unique personality, he inevitably rejects a totalitarian doctrine which seeks to set the nation, the race, or any other group above the welfare of the individual. To him, the social organization is a means to personality development, not an end in itself.

Nevertheless, there are circumstances under which a concern for social conditions is self-preservative as well as race-preservative. When the Nazi menace loomed over Germany, many intelligent liberals avoided taking action, feeling no personal responsibility. In the dictatorship which ensued, these individuals suffered terrific frustrations and maladjustments; often they resisted and died when it was too late. The achievement of a social order in which each person has a fair chance to develop his own capacities to the optimum, in which personality frustrations and maladjustments are minimized, is a task to which each of us owes certain obligations. Otherwise, we, like those Germans who thought Hitler no personal menace to them, may find ourselves losing both liberty and life.

But this social order, with its opportunity for individual self-expression and the pursuit of goals free from undue state domination, is both an end and a

---

[6] The italics are mine.

means. It is desirable to the educated man because of his culturally derived needs and the functionally autonomous character of his activities. But it is, if preserved, improved, and extended in scope, also a preventive of dictatorship and war.

The rise of fascism, of communism, and of similar totalitarian movements, must be traced to roots in the individual personality. Fascists are frustrated people who have turned to group action as a tentative solution to their problems. They are joined together by common delusions, common hatreds, and common aspirations. The extent to which economic catastrophe and, even more, threats of disaster contributed to the rise of the Nazi organization has been described by various authors. The role of frustrated desires for ego expansion, dominance, and grandeur must have been equal or greater (cf. Abel, 1938). The identification of each individual Nazi with Hitler and with Greater Germany was a satisfaction of a deep personal need. Persecution of Jews and radicals was a means of release for pent-up aggressions. The feeling of superiority to Jews and to all non-Germans served a dynamic purpose for many. Hitler's propaganda was effective not because of any personal gifts that he possessed, and not because of the technical competence of Goebbels, but because it provided substitute goals for deep-seated strivings of many Germans.

Similarly, the Communist typically shows his craving for superiority in his belief in the mystical infallibility of the Party; he displaces hostility onto capitalists instead of onto racial minorities; he obtains a feeling of power by introjecting the might of the U.S.S.R. The amount of perceptual distortion required to accept the conquest of Hungary and of Tibet as evidence of brotherly love indicates an intense emotional involvement in the communist ideology. And it is just this powerful motivation, in the Communist and in the Fascist, which makes them so dangerous. The amount of energy they can mobilize, and the damage they can do, are tremendous.

Prevention. It is not common sense to leave a mountain road without a guardrail, while building a hospital at the foot to care for survivors of accidents. It is not good judgment to become so fascinated with our color television sets, our chromium-trimmed chariots, and our foam-rubber mattresses that we cannot act to protect more basic values.

It is important that we learn more about the personalities of the men in the Kremlin. But it is even more important that we look at the internal inconsistencies of our own society, the frustrations and conflicts which breed fascist and communist fanatics.

PSYCHOLOGICAL DETERMINISM AND SOCIAL CHOICE

We must now face up to still another dilemma, this one in part a creation of modern psychology. The foregoing discussion implies that individuals are free to choose new social values. But the whole tenor of this book has been that the individual personality today is *determined* by what it was yesterday. In other words, scientific psychology takes the position that the person's behavior, thoughts, desires, and emotions are predictable outcomes of his experiences. If this is so, how can we talk about choice? How can we say to the individual that he *should* adopt one course of action rather than another? Isn't his choice of values already determined for him?

The situation is not so bad as it looks. Let us consider the following points: (1) Freedom versus determinism is not a clear-cut choice. The advocates of "creative spontaneity" for the individual do not propose that he make up his own traffic rules as he drives. Such a course necessarily leads either to incarceration or to extermination. Freedom, consequently, is always freedom within a frame of reference. (2) Practice in making intelligent choices needs to begin in childhood, within well-chosen limits. In the traditional family of authoritarian control, unquestioning conformity to past precedents, and severe anxiety and guilt for deviant choices, the child did not learn to choose wisely. His choices were unconsciously determined and consciously rationalized. (3) The process of choice is a perceptual process. There is no psychological mystery about the discrimination of objects with different attributes; and there is no theoretical problem involved in extending this to include intelligent differentiation of long-range courses of action, either for the individual or for the social group. And this, after all, is precisely what the social philosophers mean by freedom of the will. It is pure sophistry to argue that free will implies that people may jump out of windows without the presence of any deterministic factor. Actually, most people are free to jump out of windows; but free choice, based upon perception of alternative consequences, determines that they do not act in this fashion. Determinism, then, is involved only in the sense that past experiences determine the individual's percept, the attributes of the situation as seen by him.

Such a conception of determinism is in fact compatible with the kind of human freedom our democratic philosophy endorses. The intelligent democrat is assumed to look at proposed courses of action, assess the attributes of the perceived consequences, and choose that policy which leads to desirable results. There is nothing more mysterious here than in the case of the rat who learns to choose between a long and a short pathway to a foodbox. The crucial question is: Can our intelligent democrat see the difference between paths leading to maximum long-range gratification, and those leading to destruction?

Psychologists, intentionally or not, have been making modest contributions toward developing such skills. Parents have for twenty years now been receiving advice favoring more freedom, less rigid discipline for children; more affection, and punishment based on loss of love rather than pain; and frank discussion of many formerly tabooed subjects. Such training should have some value in reducing trends toward blind conformity, rejection of new ideas, and inability to choose an alternative not favored by current authority. Similarly, the schools have shifted toward less rote learning, more insistence on insight and accurate detection or analysis of problems. Teachers are learning to maintain their status more by superior knowledge, poise, and understanding, less by authoritarian techniques. Even in industry, foremen are learning to consider the wishes and points of view of workers, rather than demanding blind obedience; and where they do not learn this in management training courses, labor unions are providing negative reinforcements which aid in restructuring the foreman's perceptual field.

These signs justify a prediction that democratic man is on the road to improving his capacity for wise choice among social policies, given access to essential information about the attributes of these policies. Even a rat will fail to learn a maze if he is prevented from obtaining the necessary cues; and human beings will behave like robots if their channels of communication input are restricted to the robot level.

Let us now return to our speculations about homeostasis and goal seeking. The processes we have lumped under the rubric of homeostasis are essential to survival. Without them, freedom is an irrelevant topic; indeed, it is a dead issue, along with the man about whose freedom we are concerned. But the individual regularly moves from one homeostatic level to another. The infant learns to abandon sucking in favor of chewing, but only after he receives information indicating that solid nourishment has greater value. Adolescents learn to develop independence of parents, but not if the information received is such as to make independent choice seem frightening. Adults have some freedom to move in the scale of social classes, but many working-class men are afraid of the possible consequences of such a shift. To them the threat involved appears larger than the potential reward.

The baby's behavior is deterministic in the sense that one cannot argue about biochemistry, calories, and types of food. The baby will never be free to decide that he can get all his minerals, vitamins, etc., from milk. An attempt to reject determinism at this level is stupid. The adolescent's behavior is mostly determined by that of his parents; if they are sufficiently severe, he can be conditioned to such complete dependency that he will be incapable of developing free choice. The industrial worker's behavior is determined by his job experiences, the stories he hears from others, and mass communications. Whether he will act on security considerations (protecting an established equilibrium) or seek to establish a new equilibrium depends on his perception of alternatives. Determinism operates, then, if one has access only to a biased sample of information. In either event his behavior can legitimately be called homeostatic.

Free Choice and Social Policy. We assert, therefore, that there is no conflict between a psychological theory which says that people learn to discriminate between alternative goal objects, and a social theory which says that man must be free to choose between democracy and dictatorship. Man must, indeed, be free to choose dictatorship; and we must rely on clear perception of the threats and frustrations involved to induce a rejection of this alternative. Perceptual defense, unconscious blocking, repression—any psychological process which prevents clear perception of all parts of the phenomenal field—will increase the chances that he will choose unwisely. Allport (1955) refers poetically to the "marshland of unreason in human nature whose seepage clouds man's judgment at the ballot box" [p. 99]. A major task of psychology, then, is to foster those techniques of child training, education, and mental hygiene which will maximize clear awareness of all attributes of himself and his environment.

Free choice must also include freedom to choose alternatives not approved by current authorities. Our brush with McCarthyism indicates that even in a democracy, authoritarian techniques may be used to punish individuals who question conventional wisdom. It is impossible to move to a new and higher level of equilibrium without exploring new ideas and doubting established policies. Since some people are obtaining high gratification from the established equilibrium, one should not be surprised if they attempt to crush the upstart who wishes to disturb their comfortable status. (Cf. the problems of military officers who have advocated strange concepts—Billy Mitchell, Rickover, and others.) This holds in politics and economics just as much as in the military.

Again, it is possible to discern some optimistic signs in this respect. Contrary to the experience of Nazi Germany and Soviet Russia, the United States has managed to tolerate social disturbance without establishing authoritarian control to prevent deviant ideas. Many college professors are intimidated and fear to mention any facts critical of our existent institutions; but the data of Lazarsfeld and Thielens (1958) point to a rebirth of intellectual curiosity among scholars. If intelligent social thinkers are capable of devising new alternatives for social action, and if they are permitted to inform our people about these alternatives, then free choice becomes a meaningful phrase and democracy a functioning social philosophy.

TOWARD MATURE SOCIAL VALUES

A mature society assumes the existence of mature personalities. Dictatorship and war are made possible by emotional infantilism on the part of both leaders and followers, and the conditions they create are such as to block the adequate personality development either of adults or of children. A mature society must be democratic; i.e., it must provide freedom for each unique personality to develop to its maximum potentialities, restricted only by the requirement that this development imposes no barriers on other personalities.

A first approximation to a program for achieving mature personalities in a free society is found in the data collected by Stagner (1945). In this case, 52 prominent American social psychologists gave their views on various proposals, presented formally as a program for the long-term prevention of war, but in essence a plan for the relief of human frustration and the development of well-adjusted personalities. In Table 21.1 are reproduced those items which received a high degree of approval from virtually every psychologist polled. It will be valuable to analyze briefly the implications of this program.

Authority and Discipline. The desire to dominate may be innate, if we apply Maslow's data on apes and Murchison's on chickens to the human species. Whether innate or acquired through cultural assimilation, the wish for power and authority finds its complete and uninhibited expression only in infantile personalities. The mature individual is willing to grant to others the same rights that he demands—i.e., he will not attempt to force them into submission for the sake of satisfying his own impulse to dominate.

In the democratic system we have worked out a rough application of this principle to governmental institutions. Infantile, power-seeking individuals who impose unnecessary frustrations upon the citizenry can be ejected from positions of authority by peaceful means. Unfortunately, the educational and the economic systems are relatively unaffected by this democratic point of

Table 21.1

Toward a Psychologically Oriented Social Order *

Proposal	Average rating
1. Give workers more self-expression through increasing the trend toward industrial democracy	1.24
2. Guarantee a minimum standard of living to every family (in relation to economic resources of nation, etc.)	1.26
3. Educate for scientific thinking in human relations, trying to achieve insight into animistic "scapegoat" reactions	1.28
4. Increase opportunities for higher education for youth in the lower economic strata	1.50
5. Decrease concentration of wealth through government-financed cooperatives, consumer and producer	1.53
6. Reduce emphasis on competition and getting ahead in our culture	1.70
7. Provide widespread mental-hygiene clinics for adults and expecially for children	1.81
8. Give increased opportunities for individual prestige and recognition through hobbies, contests, etc., not connected with the economic system	1.88

* These proposals were presented with the following instructions:
"A great many planners believe that permanent peace can be achieved only on the basis of the alleviation of aggressive tensions within the individual. This includes both the arousal and the dispersal of such tensions. Please rate the following proposals on a 5-point scale."
The results are based on the replies of 52 prominent American social psychologists. Maximum approval would be indicated by a rating of 1.00; maximum disapproval by 5.00. Items receiving mean ratings beyond 2.00 are not reproduced here.
SOURCE: Stagner (1945).

view. As was noted in Chapter 20, a great many personality maladjustments seem traceable to the autocratic form of our industrial organization, and certainly a great deal of labor strife has its roots in this power relationship. The frustrations, moreover, which the adult receives in connection with his job may have repercussions upon his wife, children, and neighbors. He may join an organization persecuting minority groups, as an outlet for his own aggressions; or he may become a belligerent nationalist and thus contribute in a minor way to the occurrence of international war. McGranahan (1946) notes that Nazi youth differ most markedly from American young people in their high value placed on authority and the submission of the individual. This value is appropriate to a totalitarian society, with its ruthless frustration of many citizens.

Industrial democracy, therefore, merits its high rank among the new social values which need to be inculcated if a mature culture, favorable to mature personalities, is to be developed. Industrial democracy need not connote anarchy, any more than political democracy eliminates authority and discipline from the governmental process. It should imply the establishment of rules to protect the integrity and self-respect of the worker, treating him as a valued human personality and not as an extension of a machine. It should allow the worker some voice in his working conditions—an opportunity to make positive suggestions, as well as to reject those which are painful or frustrating to him. Every employee of an industrial enterprise should have an opportunity to feel that the product is in some degree an extension of his own personality. Industrial democracy would bring to psychological maturity the last great stronghold of arbitrary authority and infantile domination: our economic system.

Economic Frustrations. Preceding chapters have presented data to show that economic frustrations have seriously detrimental effects upon personalities of both adults and children. These effects may be either direct, as through discomfort and deprivation of needed care, or indirect, through depriving the child of emotional security and affection from his parents.

In view of these facts, it is not surprising that two items (see Table 21.1) relating to economic frustrations rate highly with the psychologists. Item 2 (guaranteed minimum standard of living) and item 5 (decreased concentration of wealth) would each tend in the direction of reducing biological frustrations in the poorer levels of our society. They would also tend to relieve stress, worry, and uncertainty over impending economic disasters. Over a period of time it may be assumed that item 5 would lead to a narrowing of the extreme difference now existing between wealthy and poor; this would reduce jealousy and hostility based on that perceived difference.

As Davis (1946) has pointed out in his perceptive article on the psychology of the underprivileged worker, these economic reforms could safely be expected to bring about major changes in the personalities of many individuals.

The marginal worker (marginal, by virtue of race, physical or educational handicap, so that he is the last hired and the first fired) has learned not to accept the goals of our culture. Economic security would give him protection and make possible acceptance of the educational and other goals approved by our society.

Economic insecurity is also a major factor in anti-Semitism, persecution of racial groups, and other "scapegoat" reactions. Frenkel-Brunswik and Sanford (1945) conclude that overt anti-Semitic activity is likely to be set off by economic worries. Hovland and Sears (1940) found that lynchings of Negroes in the South tended to increase as the value of cotton decreased. Aggression based on economic frustration is displaced onto minority groups, with drastic effects upon freedom for personality development in these groups.

Competition and Prestige. Like the Kwakiutl and the Mundugumor,[7] American culture places a high value on competitiveness and prestige. While competition has undoubtedly had beneficial effects in economic and other aspects of our society, it can, if exaggerated, have very harmful consequences. Even the business-minded advocates of "free competition" quickly indicate that competition should in their opinion be not entirely free. "Unfair competition" (usually "That which hurts my business") should be barred.

Competition as between individuals may have benign or malignant effects, depending on how it is perceived. Good-natured competitiveness, with no intense emotional reaction set off either by success or by failure, is stimulating and pleasant. Tense rivalry, with keen elation for the victor and black depression for the loser, is not.

Many individuals are handicapped by heredity or environment for the competitions in our modern culture. Low intelligence dooms the child to chronic failure in a one-track school. Lack of educational advantages denies him promotion in business. An environment which has not inculcated certain personality traits may mean failure in professional affairs.

The economic proposals, particularly item 5, would tend to reduce the bitterness of competition in that realm. Item 6 proposes a general diminution of emphasis on "getting ahead." This would presumably be implemented through the schools and through parent-education classes, in which specific suggestions would be offered as to ways of reducing this competitive pressure. Item 8 implies that sublimation of many competitive tendencies into noneconomic channels would provide the individual with ego gratification and increase his self-esteem.

Is this compatible with the need for increased motivation of bright young people, with pressure for "academic excellence," as suggested in Chapter 19? It is feasible if we can build into students the kind of intrinsic motivation which is gratified by achievement without regard to competition. William

[7] For a description of Kwakiutl culture, see Benedict (1934); for the Mundugumor, Mead (1935).

James once suggested that the struggle against nature could be a "moral equivalent for war." Perhaps achievement and prestige could be moral equivalents for competition.

Changing Perceptions and Expectancies. Finally, we come to a group of three proposals which, while nominally cultural in character, actually relate directly to personality modification. It must be assumed that there will be many misfits and maladjustments, even under an improved social order; that people will feel jealous, suspicious, resentful, and hostile toward their neighbors; that unique person-to-person interactions will produce some emotional problems.

Such emotions can do little damage to the individual or to his surroundings if he has insight into himself and perceives clearly the nature of his situation. Anti-Semitism, prejudice against Negroes, totalitarianism, and warmongering are social attitudes displacing emotional tensions from personal to group goals. Vindictive and destructive attitudes are most common in frustrated groups, according to a variety of public-opinion polls. Warmaking attitudes are displacements of personal aggressions (Brown, 1942). There is every reason to suppose that if individuals had clearer insight into their own motives and emotions, they could resolve their problems without resorting to social aggression. The social psychologists, therefore, gave high approval to item 3, which seeks to eliminate animistic thinking and scapegoat reactions. A general expansion of higher education (item 4) was also approved, for reasons which may have included economic advantage to the young persons concerned, as well as broader insights. Finally, expert care in the early years for children developing emotional maladjustments (item 7) is endorsed as a procedure for nipping neuroses "in the bud."

The individual who perceives other human beings as threatening and dangerous to himself is not only a maladjusted personality who needs therapy; he is also a potential menace to others. Conceiving his ego, or even his life, to be in danger, he may take aggressive action against the person or the group which he considers responsible. If he succeeds in focusing the hostilities of others upon the same persons or symbols that he hates and fears, he may bring great frustration and psychological harm to many human beings. Thus it is no mere academic proposition that conditions making for neurosis are conditions which endanger persons far beyond the immediate impact of the situation.

The economist Kenneth Galbraith, in his book, *The Affluent Society*, asserts that the American economic system is capable of vast increases in social services, such as education, health programs, and social insurance. The "conventional wisdom" of conservative economics, he says, is not questioned because people do not want to upset the existing equilibrium. In long-range terms, however, it may be homeostatic to make some minor changes now rather than suffer catastrophic disturbances later.

Fromm, in *The Sane Society*, examines the implications for mental health of totalitarianism (fascist and communist), of a profit-sharing program (which he calls, for some reason, supercapitalism), and of various forms of socialism. He holds that the only healthy kind of economic system will be one in which "*every working person would be an active and responsible partici-pant, where work would be attractive and meaningful, where capital would not employ labor, but labor would employ capital.*" [8]

As Fromm points out, there may be a variety of institutional forms through which such a society could be achieved. What is important is that we set up such a goal and seek for paths by which it can be attained. It is futile to talk about a mature society, in which the psychologically adjusted man is the ideal, without considering the economic aspects of such a society. Unnecessary bar-riers to free personality development must be broken down; biological and ego frustrations must be reduced to a minimum. Within such a framework mature personalities can become the rule rather than the exception.

EDUCATIONAL ACTION

The proposals which have been set forth also call for positive action in the sphere of education. It is held that our educational institutions could function (1) in correcting distorted thinking and in improving personality adjustment within the existing patterns; and (2) in teaching social values basic to democracy, implanting attitudes which would facilitate the adoption of the eco-nomic, political, and social reforms which would aim toward the goal of mature personalities in a free society.

What are the values which correlate highly with a basic belief in democracy? What are the accessory perceptual patterns, over and above a mere stereo-typed approval of democracy as such, which will support and strengthen democratic practices?

The publications of Harding (1944a, 1944b) offer some valuable clues at this point. Harding has shown that a belief in democracy, placing a high value upon democratic institutions, is positively related to the following values:

- Naturalism (a scientific view of man in the universe)
- Socialization (all classes are equal)
- Progress (it is good to try new ideas)
- Activism (we should encourage critical thinking)

Doubt or rejection of democracy was found to be associated with the follow-ing values:

- Authoritarianism (my government, right or wrong)
- Transcendentalism (powers outside of and higher than man)

[8] Fromm (1955), pp. 283–284. Reprinted by permission of Rinehart & Co., publishers.

⁄ Personal security (limited to the upper classes)

⁄ Status quo (don't disturb existing balances)

⁄ Passivism (students should accept what teachers say)

Thus we have some very concrete suggestions as to the kind of values children should be encouraged to adopt.

Whether parents, schoolteachers, and employers will cheerfully give up the pleasures that they enjoy as a result of authoritarian, status quo, and passivist values is not so clear. Certainly the means developed to achieve these democratic values must themselves be democratic. The U.S.S.R. seems to prove conclusively that autocratic methods do not provide a short cut to democracy. The principle of functional autonomy operates: Those who give orders enjoy doing so and want to continue; those who submit to domination may not enjoy it, but they certainly do not develop attitudes and skills suitable to democracy.

Education for democratic values must, therefore, be channeled through democratic procedures. Adult education classes, child-guidance clinics, nursery schools, parent training, the public schools, and the colleges must all be used as mediums for spreading these ideas. If we have faith in the superiority of democratic ideals, we should believe that such education will ultimately succeed. Nevertheless, it is a form of self-protection to hasten the process as much as possible.

The Individual and Social Resistance. It may appear that we have forgotten the point, made early in this chapter, that society also defends equilibria, hence, that persons who propose fundamental changes in institutions are likely to encounter disapproval, pressure toward conformity, even punishment. Let us consider the implications of this point for the individual. Can he maintain any reasonable kind of psychological adjustment while advocating such a program?

We should note, first of all, that the individual who endorses social reform is usually frustrated and dissatisfied with some aspect of the social order. If he is not personally injured, he feels pain because he identifies with persons who are harmed by undesirable social conditions. The energy to overcome some social opposition is derived from these sources. There are, in addition, protective measures he can take.

Adjustment to Subcultures. The culture is not a homogeneous structure. Patterns appropriate to the wealthy are not suitable for the working class. Professional men and teachers are expected to show less aggressiveness than businessmen do. The individual who finds himself in conflict with the culture on one plane may be able to move to another, in which the standards and expectancies are closer to his needs. As more individuals develop and rear children within this subculture, the particular deviations fostered there become widespread and gradually affect the remainder of the culture. Such an example is the urbanization of America, with its marked effect even upon those persons remaining in rural areas.

Forming Mutually Supporting Groups. Even though there may be no sub-culture exemplifying the values espoused by a nonconforming individual, he may find it possible to draw together a few other personalities of similar de-viation, and the members of the group may thus render mutual support. Such an instance occurs in the development of a new religion or a radical political party. Because of personal frustrations, one or more persons reject the cul-tural norms in a given regard and project a new norm based on fantasy. If they can locate others who are sensitized to this same modification of social value, they may succeed in organizing a group within which they obtain social approval, prestige, and even protection against the wrath of the larger culture. Eventually this may lead to the evolution of a new subculture and so to the modification or even the overthrow of the major culture.

Encapsulation. The individual may reject the norms of his society, but he may not seek (or may fail to find) supporters for his proposed new values. In such a case he may simply encapsulate himself, withdraw from social contacts, and perhaps write or propagandize for his new ideals. Although this pathway leads to much psychic pain, we must presume, in terms of Freud's reality prin-ciple, that the total pain is less than that which would result from enforced conformity to established values.

PERSONALITY AND SOCIETY

We have defined personality as the individual's conception of himself in relation to his environment. The adjusted personality is one in which these conceptions bear a realistic relation to physical and social facts. The self-image is normal when the individual perceives realistically his own strong and weak points, his abilities and handicaps. The orientation to society is normal when the individual correctly perceives the positive and negative valences, the bar-riers and pathways in his field.

A maladjusted or neurotic personality may deviate from this norm in various ways. The self-image, for example, may be distorted to exaggerate one's beauty, intelligence, or talent. On the contrary, of course, the distortion may be in the denial of ability or overemphasis on weakness. Similarly, the view of society may be neurotically optimistic, involving a denial of real problems and usually a rejection of responsibilities; or it may be neurotically pessimistic, leading to a paralysis of action in the face of unreal but terrifying dangers.

It is clear that a program calling for well-adjusted personalities must rec-ognize in some degree the adaptation of the individual to social reality here and now. If, however, the person achieves insight into his own emotions and his relations with society, he may realistically decide to reject social conformity in favor of education for a new social ideal. Even if he develops a superficial adaptation to established social norms, he may still cling to a fantasied perception of a new society, and may in numerous ways help to bring that fantasy into being on the level of reality.

In the long run, however, personality and society must continue in their relationships as virtual mirror images of each other; and this means that there must be continual progress toward the goal of mature personalities in a mature society. Human intelligence must be freed from emotional bonds within the personality if it is to be effective in working for a better society; it must be freed from irrational environmental frustrations if it is to achieve a well-rounded personality. Progress along one line will facilitate gains on the other. Ultimately we can anticipate our goal—free personalities in a free society.

SUMMARY

The individual personality is, in the main, a mirror of the culture; and the culture is, in essence, a composite of the personalities which exist within it. Excessive environmental frustrations can distort personality, and frustrated personalities may accept ideals, such as those of dictatorship, which perpetuate and aggravate individual problems.

It is proposed that the optimum personality development can be achieved only in an individual-centered culture, and that such a culture can be attained. Specific suggestions include the extension of democracy to economic activities, the reduction of biological frustrations, and other devices for alleviation of aggressive tensions; also, educational policies aimed at ending the emotional persecution of scapegoats and developing mature personalities, immune to propaganda fostering hate and fear.

Although individuals run certain risks in endorsing such proposals in contradiction to cultural norms, the risks may well be evaluated as smaller than those inherent in following a course which may lead to atomic war. Psychology offers the possibility of modifying individual values, with the ultimate aim of modifying the culture to provide greater freedom for all individuals. The task is to free intelligence from the bonds of emotional and cultural distortion. The goal is the development of mature personalities in a truly democratic society.

SUGGESTIONS FOR READING

There are many excellent books dealing with the relation of individual, personal attributes to broad social values. By Erich Fromm we would mention

Escape from freedom and *The sane society*; by Gardner Murphy, *Human potentialities*; by Lewis Mumford, *In the name of sanity* and *The transformations of man*. On the specific problem of war, Gardner Murphy's *Human nature and enduring peace* is valuable. On democratic freedoms, James Marshall's *Freedom to be free* is still fresh and stimulating. On communist appeals and tactics a sound analysis is that of Jules Monnerot: *Psychology and sociology of communism*. The general viewpoint of cultural anthropology with respect to individual-group interaction is well stated by Kardiner, *The individual and his society*.

Bibliography and Author Index*

Abramson, H. A., et al. 1955. Lysergic acid diethylamide (LSD-25): I. Physiological and perceptual responses. *J. Psychol.*, **39**, 3–60. [393]

Abt, L. E., and Leopold Bellak. 1950. *Projective psychology.* New York: Knopf. [61, 65]

Ackerman, Nathan W. 1958. *The psychodynamics of family life.* New York: Basic Books. [417, 432, 444, 449]

——— and Marjorie L. Behrens. 1956. A study of family diagnosis. *Amer. J. Orthopsychiat.*, **26**, 66–78. [427]

Adams, Donald K. 1954. Conflict and integration. *J. Pers.*, **22**, 548–556. [116]

Adams, Henry L., Don F. Blood, and Herbert C. Taylor. 1959. Personality differences among arts and sciences students, education students, and experienced teachers. *Amer. Psychologist*, **14**, 371. [459]

Adler, Alfred. 1917. The neurotic constitution. New York: Moffat, Yard. [331]

———. 1924. *Practice and theory of individual psychology.* New York: Harcourt, Brace. [345, 421]

———. 1927. *Understanding human nature.* New York: Greenberg. [331]

Adorno, T. W., Else Frenkel-Brunswik, Daniel J. Levinson, and R. Nevitt Sanford. 1950. *The authoritarian personality.* New York: Harper. [152, 249, 251, 252, 263, 513]

Albino, Ronald C. 1948. The stable and labile personality types of Luria in clinically normal individuals. *Brit. J. Psychol.*, **39**, 54–60. [145]

Aldrich, C. A., M. Norval, C. Knop, and F. Venegas. 1946. The crying of newly born babies: IV. Follow-up study after additional nursing care had been provided. *J. Pediat.*, **28**, 665–670. [405]

Allen, Robert M. 1958. *Personality assessment procedures.* New York: Harper. [33, 41, 57, 59, 63, 65]

Allport, Floyd H. 1924. Social psychology. Boston: Houghton Mifflin. [5]

Allport, Gordon W. 1935. Attitudes. In C. Murchison (Ed.), *Handbook of social psychology.* Worcester, Mass.: Clark Univer. Press. [216]

———. 1937. *Personality: a psychological interpretation.* New York: Holt. [7, 26, 134, 181, 182, 194, 216, 217, 332, 336]

---

* Books and articles cited in the text are included in this Bibliography, with an indication of the pages on which references to them will be found. When reducing the length of the text, it has been necessary to delete some citations, but the references are retained here, with a notation of the pages to which they are relevant. In some cases, citations may disagree with the conclusions offered in the text; a reference here indicates only that I considered the material published, not that I interpret it as supporting my conclusions on the specific issue involved.

Allport, Gordon W. 1953. The trend in motivational theory. *Amer. J. Orthopsychiat.*, **23**, 107–119. [333]

———. 1955. *Becoming: basic considerations for a psychology of personality.* New Haven, Conn.: Yale Univer. Press. [26, 70, 185, 213, 335, 359, 360, 525]

——— and Floyd H. Allport. 1928. The A-S reaction study. Boston: Houghton Mifflin. [199]

———, Jerome S. Bruner, and E. M. Jandorf. 1941. Personality under social catastrophe: Ninety life histories of the Nazi revolution. *Charact. & Pers.*, **10**, 1–22. [520]

——— and H. S. Odbert. 1936. Trait-names: a psycholexical study. *Psychol. Monogr.*, **47**, No. 211. [163, 166]

——— and P. E. Vernon. 1932. *Studies in expressive movement.* New York: Macmillan. [147, 148, 155]

———, ———, and Gardner Lindzey. 1951. *Manual: a study of values.* (Rev. ed.) Boston: Houghton Mifflin. [178, 259, 487]

Alpert, Augusta, Peter B. Neubauer, and Annemarie Weil. 1956. Unusual variations in drive endowment. *Psychoanal. Stud. Child*, **11**, 125–163. [292]

Altman, C. H. 1958. Relationships between maternal attitudes and child personality structure. *Amer. J. Orthopsychiat.*, **28**, 160–169. [416]

Altus, William D. 1952. Personality correlates of Q-L variability on the ACE. *J. consult. Psychol.*, **16**, 284–291. [465]

———. 1958. Q-L variability, MMPI responses, and college males. *J. consult. Psychol.*, **22**, 367–371. [465]

Ancona, Leonardo. 1954. Indagine sulla natura psichica del "response set." La "motivazione al successo." *Arch. Psicol. Neur. Psich.*, **15**, 23–72 [254]

Anderson, E. E. 1941. The externalization of drive: III. Maze learning by non-rewarded and by satiated rats. *J. genet. Psychol.*, **59**, 397–426. [337]

Anderson, H. H. 1937. Domination and integration in the social behavior of young children in an experimental situation. *Genet. Psychol. Monogr.*, **19**, 341–408. [455]

———. 1945. Studies in dominative and socially integrative behavior. *Amer. J. Orthopsychiat.*, **15**, 133–139. [455]

——— and Gladys L. Anderson. 1951. *Introduction to projective techniques.* Englewood Cliffs, N.J.: Prentice-Hall. [61, 65]

——— and J. E. Brewer. 1946. Studies of teachers' classroom personalities: II. Effects of teachers' dominative and integrative contacts on children's classroom behavior. *Appl. Psychol. Monogr.* No. 8. [455]

Angyal, A. 1941. Foundations for a science of personality. New York: Commonwealth Fund. [15]

Ansbacher, Heinz L. 1937. Perception of number as affected by monetary value of objects. *Arch. Psychol., N.Y.* No. 215. [120]

Appleby, Thomas L., and Charles F. Haner. 1956. MMPI profiles of a college faculty. *Proc. Iowa Acad. Sci.*, **53**, 605–609. [460]

Applezweig, M. H., G. Moeller, and H. Burdick. 1956. Multimotive prediction of academic success. *Psychol. Rep.*, **2**, 489–496. [470]

Asch, S. E. 1952. Social psychology. Englewood Cliffs, N.J.: Prentice-Hall. [152, 258, 491]

Asher, E. J., and R. S. Ort. 1951. Eye movement as a complex indicator. *J. gen. Psychol.*, **45**, 209–217. [122]

Atkinson, John W. 1953. The achievement motive and recall of interrupted and completed tasks. *J. exp. Psychol.*, **46**, 381–390. [348]

———. 1954. Explorations using imaginative thought to assess the strength of human motives. In *Nebraska symposium on motivation.* Lincoln, Neb.: Univer. of Nebraska Press. [348, 350]

Atkinson, John W., R. W. Heyns, and J. Veroff. 1954. The effect of experimental arousal of the affiliation motive on thematic apperception. *J. abnorm. soc. Psychol.,* **49,** 405–410. [349]

Auld, Frank, Jr. 1952a. Influence of social class on personality test responses. *Psychol. Bull.,* **49,** 318–332. [502]

———. 1952b. Influence of social class on tests of personality. *Drew Univer. Stud.* No. 5, Dec., 1952. [504]

Ausubel, David P. 1956. Introduction to a threshold concept of primary drives. *J. gen. Psychol.,* **54,** 209–229. [291]

———, Earl E. Balthazar, Irene Rosenthal, Leonard S. Blackman, Seymour H. Schpoont, and Joan Welkowitz. 1954. Perceived parent attitudes as determinants of children's ego structure. *Child Develpm.,* **25,** 173–183. [408]

——— and Herbert M. Schiff. 1955. A level of aspiration approach to the measurement of goal tenacity. *J. gen. Psychol.,* **52,** 97–110. [342]

———, ———, and Marjorie P. Zeleny. 1953. "Real-life" measures of academic and vocational aspiration in adolescents: relation to laboratory measures and to adjustment. *Child Develpm.,* **24,** 155–168. [208]

Ax, Albert. 1953. The physiological differentiation between fear and anger in humans. *Psychosom. Med.,* **15,** 433–442. [93, 130, 299, 375]

Babcock, H. 1940. Personality and efficiency of mental functioning. *Amer. J. Orthopsychiat.,* **10,** 527–532. [468–469]

Baker, L. E. 1938. The pupillary response conditioned to subliminal auditory stimuli. *Psychol. Monogr.,* **50,** No. 223. [98]

Baker, Lawrence M., and Jane S. Harris. 1949. The validation of Rorschach test results against laboratory behavior. *J. clin. Psychol.,* **5,** 161–164. [56]

Baldwin, Alfred L. 1948. Socialization and the parent-child relationship. *Child Develpm.,* **19,** 127–136. [413, 415]

———, Urie Bronfenbrenner, and F. L. Strodtbeck. 1958. *Talent and society.* Princeton, N.J.: Van Nostrand. [470]

———, Joan Kalhorn, and Fay Huffman Breese. 1945. Patterns of parent behavior. *Psychol. Monogr.,* **58,** No. 3 (Whole No. 268). [473]

Balthazar, Earl Edward. 1955. The influence of permissive child rearing practices on personality development. *Dissertation Abstr.,* **15,** 82. [480]

Barahona Fernandes, H. J. 1955. La sensibilité intérieure et le moi. *Evolut. psychiat.,* **4,** 597–620. [278, 279]

Barker, Edwin N. 1958. Authoritarianism of the political right, center, and left. Unpublished doctoral dissertation, Teachers College, Columbia Univer. [252]

Barker, Roger G., T. Dembo, and K. Lewin. 1941. Frustration and regression. *Univer. Iowa Stud. Child Welf.,* **18,** No. 1. [479]

———, Beatrice A. Wright, and Mollie R. Gonick. 1946. Adjustment to physical handicap and illness: a survey of the social psychology of physique and disability. *Soc. Sci. Res. Coun. Bull.,* No. 55. [328]

——— and Herbert F. Wright. 1951. *One boy's day.* New York: Harper. [38]

——— and ———. 1954. *Midwest and its children.* Evanston, Ill.: Row, Petersen. [38]

Barlow, John A. 1956. Secondary motivation through classical conditioning: a reconsideration of the nature of backward conditioning. *Psychol. Rev.,* **63,** 406–408. [98]

Barnes, Charles A. 1952. A statistical study of the Freudian theory of levels of psychosexual development. *Genet. Psychol. Monogr.,* **45,** 105–174. [110]

Barnes, Eugene H. 1956. Factors, response bias, and the MMPI. *J. consult. Psychol.,* **20,** 419–421. [154]

Barron, Frank. 1953. An ego-strength scale which predicts response to psychotherapy. *J. consult. Psychol.,* **17,** 327–333. [200]

Barry, Herbert, III, Margaret K. Bacon, and Irvin L. Child. 1957. A cross-cultural survey of some sex differences in socialization. *J. abnorm. soc. Psychol.,* **55,** 327–332. [180]

Bartlett, F. C. 1932. *Remembering.* New York: Macmillan. [173]

Baruch, Dorothy W. 1945. Procedures in training teachers to prevent and reduce mental hygiene problems. *J. genet. Psychol.,* **67,** 143–178. [464]

Basowitz, Harold, Sheldon J. Korchin, and Roy R. Grinker. 1954. Anxiety in life stress. *J. Psychol.,* **38,** 503–510. [123]

———, Harold Persky, Sheldon J. Korchin, and Roy R. Grinker. 1955. *Anxiety and stress.* New York: McGraw-Hill. [115–120]

Bass, Bernard. 1955. Authoritarianism or acquiescence? *J. abnorm. soc. Psychol.,* **51,** 611–623. [254]

Baughman, Emmett E. 1951. Rorschach scores as a function of examiner difference. *J. proj. Tech.,* **15,** 243–249. [56]

Beach, Frank A. 1942. Sexual behavior of prepuberal male and female rats treated with gonadal hormones. *J. comp. Psychol.,* **34,** 285–292. [298]

——— and Julian Jaynes. 1954. Effects of early experience upon the behavior of animals. *Psychol. Bull.,* **51,** 239–263. [399]

Beams, Howard L. 1954. Affectivity as a factor in the apparent size of pictured food objects. *J. exp. Psychol.,* **47,** 197–200. [120]

Beck, Samuel J. 1953. The science of personality—nomothetic or idiographic? *Psychol. Rev.,* **60,** 353–359. [7, 16]

Becker, Howard S., and James W. Carper. 1956. Identification with an occupation. *Amer. J. Sociol.,* **61,** 289–298. [485]

Becker, Wesley C., Donald R. Peterson, Leo A. Hellmer, Donald J. Shoemaker, and Herbert C. Quay. 1959. Factors in parental behavior and personality as related to problem behavior in children. *J. consult. Psychol.,* **23,** 107–118. [406, 415]

Behrens, Marjorie L. 1954. Child rearing and the character structure of the mother. *Child Develpm.,* **25,** 225–238. [415]

Beigel, Hugo G. 1957. Evaluation of intelligence in the heterosexual relationship. *J. soc. Psychol.,* **46,** 65–80. [431]

Belgrad, Herbert J. 1957. The union leader: psychodynamics of a social role. Unpublished master's thesis, Univer. of Illinois. [492–493]

Belk, W. P., and F. W. Sunderman. 1947. A survey of the accuracy of chemical analysis in clinical laboratories. *Am. J. clin. Path.,* **17,** 853. [34]

Bellak, Leopold. 1948. The TAT blank, analysis sheets, and guide to interpretation of the TAT. New York: Psychological Corp. [59]

———. 1956. Psychoanalytic theory of personality. In J. L. McCary (Ed.), *Psychology of Personality,* New York: Logos Press. Pp. 1–62. [86, 202, 309, 311]

Bender, Irving E. 1958. Changes in religious interest: a retest after 15 years. *J. abnorm. soc. Psychol.,* **57,** 41–46. [248, 261]

Bendig, A. W. 1954. Factor analysis of student ratings of psychology instructors on the Purdue scale. *J. educ. Psychol.,* **45,** 385–393. [452]

———. 1958. Manifest anxiety and projective and objective measures of need achievement. *J. consult. Psychol.,* **21,** 354. [348]

Benedek, T., and B. B. Rubenstein. 1939. Correlations between ovarian activity and psychodynamic processes: I. The ovulative phase. *Psychosom. Med.,* **1,** 245–270. [386]

Benedetti. G. 1957. Die Bedeutung der Persönlichkeitsforschung für die endokrinologische Forschung. *Z. Psychother. med. Psychol.,* **7,** 1–9. [385]

Benedict, Ruth. 1934. *Patterns of culture.* Boston: Houghton Mifflin. [528]

Benedict, Ruth. 1949. Continuities and discontinuities in cultural conditioning. In Patrick Mullahy (Ed.), *A study of interpersonal relations*. New York: Hermitage House, Inc. [423, 480]

Benjamin, J. D., and F. G. Ebaugh. 1938. Diagnostic validity of Rorschach test. *Amer. J. Psychiat.*, **94**, 1163–1178. [56]

Berg, Irwin A. 1955. Response bias and personality: the deviation hypothesis. *J. Psychol.*, **40**, 61–72. [153]

Berger, Leslie. 1958. Interrelationships of autonomic and personality variables. Unpublished doctoral dissertation, Univer. of Michigan. [375]

Bergeron, M., and J. C. Benoit. 1954. Biotypologie et psychiatrie. *Evolut. psychiat.*, **3**, 341–375. [278]

Bergler, Edmund. 1948. *Divorce won't help*. New York: Harper. [449]

Berlyne, D. E. 1954. An experimental study of human curiosity. *Brit. J. Psychol.*, **45**, 256–265. [295]

——. 1955. The arousal and satiation of perceptual curiosity in the rat. *J. comp. physiol. Psychol.*, **48**, 238–246. [295]

—— and J. Slater. 1957. Perceptual curiosity, exploratory behavior, and maze learning. *J. comp. physiol. Psychol.*, **50**, 228–232. [295]

Berman, L. 1928. *The glands regulating personality*. (2nd ed.) New York: Macmillan. [378]

——. 1938. *New creations in human beings*. New York: Doubleday. [378]

Bernard, Luther L. 1924. *Instinct: a study in social psychology*. New York: Holt.

Bernreuter, Robert G. 1933a. The theory and construction of the Personality Inventory. *J. soc. Psychol.*, **4**, 383–405. [199]

——. 1933b. Validity of the Personality Inventory. *Personnel J.*, **11**, 383–386. [50]

Bernstein, Arnold. 1955. Some relations between techniques of feeding and training during infancy and certain behavior in childhood. *Genet. Psychol. Monogr.*, **51**, 3–44. [403]

Bettelheim, Bruno, and Morris Janowitz. 1950. *Dynamics of prejudice*. New York: Harper. [263, 512]

Bexton, W. H., W. Heron, and T. H. Scott. 1954. Effects of decreased variation in the sensory environment. *Canad. J. Psychol.*, **8**, 70–76. [400]

Bieri, James, and Edward Blacker. 1956. External and internal stimulus factors in Rorschach performance. *J. consult. Psychol.*, **20**, 1–7. [81]

Bieshuevel, S., and D. R. Pitt. 1955. Relationship between secondary function and some aspects of speed and tempo of behavior. *Acta Psychol.*, **11**, 373–396. [148]

Billingslea, Fred Y., and Herbert Bloom. 1950. Comparative effect of frustration and success on goal-directed behavior in the classroom. *J. abnorm. soc. Psychol.*, **45**, 510–515. [478]

Bills, Robert E. 1956. Personality changes during student-centered teaching. *J. educ. Res.*, **50**, 121–126. [475]

Bindra, Dalbir. 1959. *Motivation: a systematic reinterpretation*. New York: Ronald. [358, 360]

Bird, Charles, and Elio D. Monachesi. 1954. Prejudice and discontent. *J. abnorm. soc. Psychol.*, **49**, 29–35. [511]

Birkelo, C. C., W. E. Chamberlain, P. S. Phelps, P. E. Schools, D. Zacks, and J. Yerushalmy. 1947. Tuberculosis case finding: a comparison of the effectiveness of various roentgenographic and photofluorographic methods. *J. Amer. Med. Ass.*, **133**, 359. [34]

Birney, Robert C. 1959. The reliability of the achievement motive. *J. abnorm. soc. Psychol.*, **58**, 266–267 [348]

Birren, J. E. 1944. Psychological examinations of children who later became psychotic. *J. abnorm. soc. Psychol.*, **39**, 84–95. [177]

Blair, Glenn M., Stuart R. Jones, and Ray H. Simpson. 1954. *Educational psychology.* New York: Macmillan. [483]

Blake, Robert R. 1948. Ocular activity during administration of the Rorschach test. *J. clin. Psychol.*, **4**, 159–169. [123]

——— and W. Dennis. 1943. Development of stereotypes concerning the Negro. *J. abnorm. soc. Psychol.*, **38**, 525–531. [246]

———, H. Helson, and Jane Srygley Mouton. 1957. The generality of conformity behavior as a function of factual anchorage, difficulty of task, and amount of social pressure. *J. Pers.*, **25**, 294–305. [40, 153]

——— and Glenn Ramsey. (Eds.). 1951. *Perception: an approach to personality.* New York: Ronald. [86, 141]

Bliss, Eugene, L., Claude J. Migeon, C. H. Harden Branch, and Leo T. Samuels. 1956. Reaction of the adrenal cortex to emotional stress. *Psychosom. Med.*, **18**, 56–76. [380]

Block, Jack. 1955. Personality characteristics associated with fathers' attitudes toward child-rearing. *Child Develpm.*, **26**, 41–48. [406]

———. 1957. A study of affective responsiveness in a lie-detection situation. *J. abnorm. soc. Psychol.*, **55**, 11–15. [375]

Blood, Robert O., Jr. 1954. Consequences of permissiveness for parents of young children. *Marriage Fam. Living*, **15**, 209–212. [407]

Blum, Gerald S. 1955a. *Psychoanalytic theories of personality.* New York: McGraw-Hill. [286, 331]

———. 1955b. Perceptual defense revisited. *J. abnorm. soc. Psychol.*, **51**, 24–29. [122]

——— and Daniel R. Miller. 1952. Exploring the psychoanalytic theory of the oral character. *J. Pers.*, **20**, 287–304. [282]

Bovard, Everett W. 1951. Psychology of classroom interaction. *J. educ. Res.*, **45**, 215–224. [474]

Bowerman, Charles E., and Barbara R. Day. 1956. Test of the theory of complementary needs as applied to couples during courtship. *Amer. soc. Rev.*, **21**, 602–605. [429]

Boynton, P. L., H. Dugger, and M. Turner. 1934. Emotional stability of teachers and pupils. *J. juv. Res.*, **18**, 223–232. [463]

Brody, Sylvia. 1956. *Patterns of mothering: maternal influence during infancy.* New York: International Universities. [95, 401, 404]

Bronson, Wanda C., Edith S. Katton, and Norman Livson. 1959. Patterns of authority and affection in two generations. *J. abnorm. soc. Psychol.*, **58**, 143–152. [419]

Brown, Junius F. 1940. *Psychodynamics of abnormal behavior.* New York: McGraw-Hill. [282]

———. 1942. The theory of the aggressive urges and war-time behavior. *J. soc. Psychol.*, **15**, 355–380. [529]

Brown, William F., Norman Abeles, and Ira Iscoe. 1954. Motivational differences between high and low scholarship college students. *J. educ. Psychol.*, **45**, 215–223. [479]

Brownfain, John J. 1952. Stability of the self-concept as a dimension of personality. *J. abnorm. soc. Psychol.*, **47**, 597–606. [193, 384]

Brozek, Josef. 1953. Semi-starvation and nutritional rehabilitation: a qualitative case study, with emphasis on behavior. *J. clin. Nutrition*, **1**, 107–118. [391]

———. 1955. Personality changes with age: an item analysis of the Minnesota Multi-Phasic Personality Inventory. *J. Geront.*, **10**, 194–206. [178]

Bruner, Jerome S., and C. C. Goodman. 1947. Value and need as organizing factors in perception. *J. abnorm. soc. Psychol.*, **42**, 33–43. [120]

Brunswik, Egon. 1947. *Systematic and representative design of psychological experiments.* Berkeley, Calif.: Univer. of California Press. [37]

Burchinal, Lee G., Glenn R. Hawkes, and Bruce Gardner. 1957. Personality characteristics and marital satisfaction. *Soc. Forces,* **35,** 218–222. [439, 440]

Burgess, Ernest W., and Leonard S. Cottrell, Jr. 1939. *Predicting success or failure in marriage.* Englewood Cliffs, N.J.: Prentice-Hall. [435]

—— and Paul Wallin. 1944. Homogamy in personality characteristics. *J. abnorm. soc. Psychol.,* **39,** 475–481. [428]

—— and ——. 1953. *Engagement and marriage.* Philadelphia: Lippincott. [432, 434]

Burt, Cyril. 1948. Factorial study of temperamental traits. *Brit. J. Psychol.* (Stat. Sec.), **1,** 178–203. [96]

Burwen, Leroy S., and Donald T. Campbell. 1957. The generality of attitudes toward authority and non-authority figures. *J. abnorm. soc. Psychol.,* **54,** 24–31. [247]

Bush, Robert R., and J. W. M. Whiting. 1953. On the theory of psychoanalytic displacement. *J. abnorm. soc. Psychol.,* **48,** 261–272. [114]

Butler, Robert A. 1957. The effect of deprivation of visual incentives on visual exploration motivation in monkeys. *J. comp. physiol. Psychol.,* **50,** 177–179. [295]

Callis, Robert. 1953. Efficiency of Minnesota Teachers Attitude Inventory for predicting interpersonal relations in classroom. *J. appl. Psychol.,* **37,** 82–85. [462]

Calvin, A. D., and Wayne H. Holtzman. 1953. Adjustment and the discrepancy between self concept and inferred self. *J. consult. Psychol.,* **17,** 39–44. [191]

Cameron, D. E. 1941. *Objective and experimental psychiatry.* New York: Macmillan. [49]

Cannon, W. B. 1928. *Bodily changes in hunger, pain, fear, and rage.* New York: Appleton-Century. [69–71]

Cantoni, Louis J. 1953. A follow-up study of the personal adjustment of the subjects who participated in the 1939–1943 Flint, Michigan, guidance demonstration. Unpublished doctoral dissertation, Univer. of Michigan. [476, 478]

——. 1955. Long-term effects of the Flint, Michigan guidance experiment. *Psychol. Rep.,* **1,** 359–362. [476]

Capwell, Dora F. 1945. Personality patterns of adolescent girls: II. Delinquents and non-delinquents. *J. appl. Psychol.,* **29,** 289–297. [225]

Carlson, Virgil R., and Richard S. Lazarus. 1953. A repetition of Meyer Williams' study of intellectual control under stress and associated Rorschach factors. *J. consult. Psychol.,* **17,** 247–253. [56]

Carter, H. D. 1935. Twin similarities in emotional traits. *Charact. and Pers.,* **4,** 61–78. [365]

Cason, Hulsey. 1930. Common annoyances. *Psychol. Monogr.,* **40,** No. 182. [161]

Cass, Loretta K. 1952. Parent-child relationships and delinquency. *J. abnorm. soc. Psychol.,* **47,** 101–104. [410]

Cattell, Raymond B. 1945. Principal trait clusters for describing personality. *Psychol. Bull.,* **42,** 129–161. [163–165]

——. 1950. Personality: a systematic theoretical and factual study. New York: McGraw-Hill. [26, 37, 137, 158, 159, 181, 190, 298, 301, 302]

——. 1955. The principal replicated factors discovered in objective personality tests. *J. abnorm. soc. Psychol.,* **50,** 291–314. [46]

——. 1956. Validation and intensification of the Sixteen Personality Factor Questionnaire. *J. clin. Psychol.,* **12,** 205–214. [46]

——. 1957. *Personality and motivation structure and measurement.* Yonkers, N.Y.: World. [37, 39, 46, 164, 168, 181, 200, 303, 305]

Cattell, Raymond B., Duncan B. Blewett, and John R. Beloff. 1955. The inheritance of personality: a multiple variance analysis determination of approximate nature-nurture ratios for primary personality factors in Q-data. *Amer. J. hum. Genet.*, **7**, 122–146. [366]

———, M. Day, and Tor Meeland. 1956. Occupational profiles on the Sixteen Personality Factor Questionnaire. *Occup. Psychol.*, **30**, 10–19. [488]

——— and J. E. Drevdahl. 1955. A comparison of the personality profile (16 PF) of eminent researchers with that of eminent teachers and administrators, and of the general population. *Brit. J. Psychol.*, **46**, 248–261. [488, 489]

——— and Walter Gruen. 1953. The personality factor structure of 11 year old children in terms of behavior rating data. *J. clin. Psychol.*, **9**, 256–266. [46]

——— and Ivan H. Scheier. 1958. Clinical validities by analyzing the psychiatrist exemplified in relation to anxiety diagnoses. *Amer. J. Orthopsychiat.*, **28**, 699–713. [62]

Centers, Richard, 1949. *Psychology of social classes.* Princeton, N.J.: Princeton Univer. Press. [499]

Cesa-Bianchi, M., G. Jacono, and A. Perugia. 1953. Il disegno come mezzo diagnostico della personalità. *Arch. Psicol. Neurol. Psichiat.*, **14**, 207–208. [147]

Chein, I. 1943. Personality and typology. *J. soc. Psychol.*, **18**, 89–109. [266]

Chidester, L., and Karl Menninger. 1936. The application of psychoanalytic methods to the study of mental retardation. *Amer. J. Orthopsychiat.*, **6**, 616–625. [475]

Child, Irvin L. 1950. Relation of somatotype to self-ratings on Sheldon's temperamental traits. *J. Pers.*, **18**, 440–453. [277, 278]

——— and Margaret K. Bacon. 1954. Cultural pressures and achievement motivation. In P. H. Hoch and J. Zubin (Eds.), *Psychopathology of childhood.* New York: Grune & Stratton. Pp. 166–176. [470]

——— and L. W. Doob. 1943. Factors determining national stereotypes. *J. soc. Psychol.*, **17**, 203–219. [242]

———, Kitty F. Frank, and Thomas Storm. 1956. Self-ratings and TAT: their relations to each other and to childhood background. *J. Pers.*, **25**, 96–114. [61]

Chinoy, Ely. 1952. Tradition of opportunity and the aspirations of automobile workers. *Amer. J. Sociol.*, **57**, 453–459. [335]

Chisholm, G. Brock. 1948. The individual's responsibility for world peace. *Bull. Menninger Clin.*, **12**, 73–80. [525]

Chodorkoff, Bernard. 1954a. Self-perception, perceptual defense, and adjustment. *J. abnorm. soc. Psychol.*, **49**, 508–512. [191]

———. 1954b. Adjustment and the discrepancy between the perceived and ideal self. *J. clin. Psychol.*, **10**, 266–268. [191]

Chodorkoff, Joan. 1960. Infant development as a function of mother-child interaction. Unpublished doctoral dissertation, Wayne State Univer. [401]

Christenson, Harold T., and Robert E. Philbrick. 1952. Family size as a factor in the marital adjustment of college couples. *Amer. soc. Rev.*, **17**, 306–312. [444]

Christie, Richard, and Marie Jahoda. 1954. *Studies in the scope and method of "The authoritarian personality."* Glencoe, Ill.: Free Press. [263]

Clark, G., and H. G. Birch. 1945. Hormonal modifications of social behavior: I. The effect of sex-hormone administration on the social status of a male-castrate chimpanzee. *Psychosom. Med.*, **7**, 321–329. [386]

Clark, James W., and Dalbir Bindra. 1956. Individual differences in pain thresholds. *Canad. J. Psychol.*, **10**, 69–76. [370]

Cleghorn, Robert A. 1952. Endocrine influence on personality and behavior. In Milbank Memorial Fund, *Biology of mental health and disease.* New York: Hoeber-Harper. Pp. 265–273. [379, 386]

Cline, Victor B. 1955. Ability to judge personality assessed with a stress interview and sound-film technique. *J. abnorm. soc. Psychol.*, **50**, 183–187. [37]

Cochrane, A. L., P. J. Chapman, and P. D. Oldham. 1951. Observer's errors in taking medical histories. *Lancet*, **260**, 1007–1009. [34]

Cohen, Arthur R. 1955. Social norms, arbitrariness of frustration, and status of the agent of frustration in the frustration-aggression hypothesis. *J. abnorm. soc. Psychol.*, **51**, 222–226. [113]

——, Ezra Stotland, and Donald M. Wolfe. 1955. An experimental investigation of need for cognition. *J. abnorm. soc. Psychol.*, **51**, 291–294. [303]

Cohen, Louis D. 1954. Level of aspiration behavior and feelings of adequacy and self-acceptance. *J. abnorm. soc. Psychol.*, **49**, 84–86. [209]

Cohn, Thomas S. 1953. Factors related to scores on F (predisposition to fascism) scale. *Dissertation Abst.*, **13**, 863–864. [254]

——. 1956. Relation of the F scale to a response set to answer positively. *J. soc. Psychol.*, **44**, 129–133. [152]

Combs, Arthur W., and Donald Snygg. 1959. *Individual behavior.* (Rev. ed.) New York: Harper. [292, 345]

Comroe, B. J. 1936. Follow-up study of 100 patients diagnosed as "neurosis." *J. nerv. ment. Dis.*, **83**, 679–684. [49]

Congdon, Clyde S. 1954. Effects on attitudes resulting from experimental frustration. Unpublished master's thesis, Univer. of Illinois. [512]

Cook, W. W., C. H. Leeds, and R. Callis. 1951. *The Minnesota Teacher Attitude Inventory.* New York: Psychological Corp. [461]

—— and Donald M. Medley. 1955. Relationship between Minnesota Teacher Attitude Inventory scores and scores on certain scales of the Minnesota Multiphasic Personality Inventory. *J. appl. Psychol.*, **39**, 123–129. [462]

Cooley, Charles H. 1902. *Human nature and social order.* New York: Scribner. [185]

Corman, Louis. 1954. La morpho-psychologie en psychiatrie. *Evolut. psychiat.*, **3**, 433–454. [278, 372]

Corsini, Raymond J. 1956a. Multiple predictors of marital happiness. *Marriage Fam. Living*, **18**, 240–242. [441]

——. 1956b. Understanding and similarity in marriage. *J. abnorm. soc. Psychol.*, **52**, 327–332. [428]

Corson, H. F. 1927. Factors in development of psychoses in college men. *Ment. Hyg., N.Y.*, **11**, 496–518. [355]

Cowen, Emory L., Fred Heilizer, and Howard S. Axelrod. 1955. Self-concept conflict indicators and learning. *J. abnorm. soc. Psychol.*, **51**, 242–245. [245]

——, Judah Landes, and Donald E. Schaet. 1959. Effects of mild frustration on the expression of prejudiced attitudes. *J. abnorm. soc. Psychol.*, **58**, 33–38. [512]

Crandall, Vaughn J., and Ursula Bellugi. 1954. Some relationships of interpersonal and intrapersonal conceptualizations to personal-social adjustment. *J. Pers.*, **23**, 224–232. [198]

Cronbach, Lee J. 1954. *Educational psychology.* New York: Harcourt, Brace. [483]

——. 1955. Processes affecting scores on "understanding others" and "assumed similarity." *Psychol. Bull.*, **52**, 177–194. [140]

—— and Goldine C. Gleser. 1953. Assessing similarity between profiles. *Psychol. Bull.*, **50**, 456–473. [271]

—— and Paul E. Meehl. 1955. Construct validity in psychological tests. *Psychol. Bull.*, **52**, 281–302. [51]

Crook, M. N. 1941. Retest correlations in neuroticism. *J. gen. Psychol.*, **24**, 173–182. [177]

Crook, M. N. 1943. Retest with the Thurstone Personality Schedule after 6½ years. *J. gen. Psychol.*, **28**, 111–120. [175]

Crutchfield, Richard S. 1951. Assessment of persons through a quasi group-interaction technique. *J. abnorm. soc. Psychol.*, **46**, 577–588. [39]

———. 1955. Conformity and character. *Amer. Psychologist*, **10**, 191–198. [255]

———, Donald C. Woodworth, and Ruth S. Albrecht. 1958. *Perceptual performance and the effective person.* Wright Air Development Center, Pers. Lab., Lackland A.F.B., Texas. (WADC-TN-58-60). [221]

Culler, Elmer. 1938. Recent advances in some concepts of conditioning. *Psychol. Rev.*, **45**, 134–153. [99]

Dailey, Charles A. 1952. Effects of premature conclusion upon the acquisition of understanding of a person. *J. Psychol.*, **33**, 133–152. [36, 83]

Darling, R. P. 1940. Autonomic action in relation to personality traits of children. *J. abnorm. soc. Psychol.*, **35**, 246–260. [373]

——— and C. W. Darrow. 1938. Determining activity of the autonomic nervous system from measurements of autonomic change. *J. Psychol.*, **5**, 85–89. [373]

Darrow, C. W. 1932. Reaction tendencies relating to personality. In K. S. Lashley, *Studies in the dynamics of behavior.* Chicago: Univer. of Chicago Press. [373]

———. 1953. The relation of cerebral to autonomic activity in the conditioned emotional reactions of children. *Ann. N. Y. Acad. Sci.*, **56**, 289–301. [373]

Darwin, Charles. 1931. Voyage of the Beagle. Philadelphia: Lippincott. [356]

Das, Rhea S. 1955. An investigation of attitude structure and some hypothesized personality correlates. Unpublished doctoral dissertation, Univer. of Illinois. [192]

Davids, Anthony. 1955. Generality and consistency of relations between the alienation syndrome and cognitive processes. *J. abnorm. soc. Psychol.*, **51**, 61–67. [189, 254, 255]

———. 1956. Past experience and present personality dispositions as determinants of selective auditory memory. *J. Pers.*, **25**, 19–32. [123]

——— and Henry Pildner, Jr. 1958. Comparison of direct and projective methods of personality assessment under different conditions of motivation. *Psychol. Monogr.*, **72**, (11), 1–30. (Whole No. 464). [48]

Davidson, H. H. 1943. *Personality and economic background.* New York: King's Crown. [501]

Davidson, May A., D. Lee, R. W. Parnell, and S. J. G. Spencer. 1955. The detection of psychological vulnerability in students. *J. ment. Sci.*, **101**, 810–825. [372]

———, R. G. McInness, and R. W. Parnell. 1957. Distribution of personality traits in seven-year-old children: a combined psychological, psychiatric, and somatotype study. *Brit. J. educ. Psychol.*, **27**, 48–61. [278]

Davis, Allison. 1946. Motivation of the underprivileged worker. In W. F. Whyte, *Industry and society.* New York: McGraw-Hill. [293, 334, 497, 527]

——— and Robert J. Havighurst. 1946. Social class and color differences in child-rearing. *Amer. soc. Rev.*, **11**, 698–710. [506]

Davis, Katharine B. 1929. *Factors in the sex life of 2,200 women.* New York: Harper. [441]

Davitz, Joel R., and Donald J. Mason. 1955. Socially facilitated reduction of a fear response in rats. *J. comp. physiol. Psychol.*, **48**, 149–151. [131]

Delgado, J. M. R., W. W. Roberts, and Neal E. Miller. 1954. Learning motivated by electrical stimulation of the brain. *Amer. J. Physiol.*, **179**, 587–593. [90, 299]

Della Piana, G. M., and N. L. Gage. 1955. Pupils' values and the validity of the Minnesota Teacher Attitude Inventory. *J. educ. Psychol.*, **46**, 167–178. [462]

DeLucia, Joseph J. 1953. Emotional vs. frequency factors in word-recognition time and association time. Unpublished doctoral dissertation, Univer. of Illinois. [144]

—— and Ross Stagner. 1954. Emotional vs. frequency factors in word-recognition time and association time. *J. Pers.*, **22**, 299–309. [122]

Denker, P. G. 1939. Prognosis of insured neurotics. *N.Y. St. J. Med.*, **39**, 238–247.

Dennis, Wayne. 1941. Infant development under conditions of restricted practice and of minimum social stimulation. *Genet. Psychol. Monogr.*, **23**, 143–189. [402]

—— and Pergrouhi Najarian. 1957. Infant development under environmental handicap. *Psychol. Monogr.*, **71** (7) (Whole No. 436). [402]

Denny, M. R. 1957. Learning through stimulus satiation. *J. exp. Psychol.*, **54**, 62–64. [295]

Deutscher, Clifford. 1955. Leveling and sharpening as manifested in discrimination learning, threshold and problem solving behavior. *Dissertation Abstr.*, **15**, 1656. [139]

DeWit, Fred. 1955. The measurement of values by means of analysis of judgments. Unpublished doctoral dissertation, Univer. of Illinois. [252]

Diamond, Solomon. 1957. *Personality and temperament.* New York: Harper. [26, 92, 110, 157, 158, 168, 181, 267]

Dice, L. R. 1935. Inheritance of waltzing and epilepsy in mice of the genus *Peromyscus. J. Mammalogy.*, **16**, 25–35. [369]

Dickinson, R. L., and L. Beam. 1931. *A thousand marriages: a medical study of sex adjustment.* Baltimore: Williams & Wilkins. [442]

Diggory, James C., and Daniel E. Magaziner. 1959. Self-evaluation as a function of instrumentally relevant capacities. *Bull. de l'Assoc. Int. de Psychol. Appliq.*, **8**, 46–63. [495, 496]

Diller, Leonard. 1954. Conscious and unconscious self-attitudes after success and failure. *J. Pers.*, **23**, 1–12. [211]

Dispensa, J. 1938. Relationship of the thyroid with intelligence and personality. *J. Psychol.*, **6**, 181–186. [380]

DiTullio, B. 1954. Biotypologie et criminologie. *Evolut. psychiat.*, **3**, 421–431. [372]

Doctor, R. F., and C. L. Winder. 1954. Delinquent performance on the Porteus Maze Test. *J. consult. Psychol.*, **18**, 71–83. [230]

Dollard, John, et al. 1939. *Frustration and aggression.* New Haven, Conn.: Yale Univer. Press. [113]

—— and Neal E. Miller. 1950. *Personality and psychotherapy.* New York: McGraw-Hill. [99, 185, 297, 307]

Donceel, Joseph F., Benjamin S. Alimena, and Catherine M. Birch. 1949. Influence of prestige suggestion on the answers of a personality inventory. *J. appl. Psychol.*, **33**, 352–355. [101]

Douvan, Elizabeth. 1956. Social status and success strivings. *J. abnorm. soc. Psychol.*, **52**, 219–223. [502]

—— and Joseph Adelson. 1958. Psychodynamics of social mobility in adolescent boys. *J. abnorm. soc. Psychol.*, **56**, 31–44. [502]

Drake, L. E., and Eugene R. Oetting. 1957. An MMPI pattern and a suppressor variable predictive of academic achievement. *J. counsel. Psychol.*, **4**, 245–247. [469]

Drews, Elizabeth, and John E. Teahan. 1957. Parental attitudes and academic achievement. *J. clin. Psychol.*, **13**, 328–332. [472]

Dreikurs, Rudolf. 1957. *Psychology in the classroom.* New York: Harper. [484]

Drucker, A. J., and H. H. Remmers. 1952. Environmental determinants of basic difficulty problems. *J. abnorm. soc. Psychol.*, **47**, 379–381. [499, 500]

Dublineau, J. 1954. Esquisse d'une typologïe évolutive et fonctionnelle. *Evolut. psychiat.*, **3**, 473–505. [278]

Duffy, Elizabeth. 1957. The psychological significance of the concept of "arousal" or "activation." *Psychol. Rev.*, **64**, 265–275. [147, 298]

Dukes, William F. 1955. Psychological studies of values. *Psychol. Bull.*, **52**, 24–50. [259]

——— and William Bevan, Jr. 1952a. Accentuation and response variability in the perception of personally relevant objects. *J. Pers.*, **20**, 457–465. [120]

——— and ———. 1952b. Size estimation and monetary value: a correlation. *J. Psychol.*, **34**, 43–54. [121]

Dulany, Don. E., Jr. 1955. Avoidance learning of perceptual defense and vigilance. *J. abnorm. soc. Psychol.*, **55**, 333–338. [122]

Duncan, Glen M., S. H. Frazier, E. M. Litin, A. M. Johnson, and A. J. Barron. 1958. Etiological factors in first-degree murder. *J. Amer. Med. Assn.*, **168**, 1755–1758. [233]

Dyer, William G. 1956. A comparison of families of high and low job satisfaction. *Marriage Fam. Living*, **18**, 58–60. [497]

Dymond, Rosalind. 1954. Inter-personal perception and marital happiness. *Canad. J. Psychol.*, **8**, 164–171. [440]

Earl, Robert W. 1957. Motivation, performance and extinction. *J. comp. physiol. Psychol.*, **50**, 248–251. [337]

Edmiston, R. W., and Frances Baird. 1949. The adjustment of orphanage children. *J. educ. Psychol.*, **40**, 482–488. [402]

Edwards, Allen L. 1941. Political frames of reference as a factor influencing recognition. *J. abnorm. soc. Psychol.*, **36**, 35–40. [172, 245]

———. 1953. The relationship between the judged desirability of a trait and the probability that the trait will be endorsed. *J. appl. Psychol.*, **37**, 90–93. [47]

———. 1954. *Personal preference schedule manual.* New York: Psychological Corp. [47, 459, 492]

Ellis, Albert. 1953. Recent research with personality inventories. *J. consult. Psychol.*, **17**, 45–49. [50, 51]

———. 1957. Sex problems of couples seen for marriage counseling. *J. Fam. Welf.*, **3**, 81–84. [442]

Ellson, D. G. 1941. Hallucinations produced by sensory conditioning. *J. exp. Psychol.*, **28**, 1–20. [75]

Enke, W. 1927. Die Konstitutionstypen im Rorschach'shen Experimente. *Z. f. Ges. Neurol. u. Psychiat.*, **108**, 643–674. [274]

Epstein, Seymour. 1955. Unconscious self-evaluation in a normal and a schizophrenic group. *J. abnorm. soc. Psychol.*, **50**, 65–70. [210]

Erickson, M. H., and L. S. Kubie. 1941. Successful treatment of a case of acute hysterical depression by a return under hypnosis to a critical phase of childhood. *Psychoanal. Quart.*, **10**, 583–609. [324]

Eriksen, Charles W. 1952. Defense against ego-threat in memory and perception. *J. abnorm. soc. Psychol.*, **47**, 230–235. [144]

———. 1954a. Psychological defenses and "ego strength" in the recall of completed and incompleted tasks. *J. abnorm. soc. Psychol.*, **49**, 45–50. [200]

———. 1954b. Some personality correlates of stimulus generalization under stress. *J. abnorm. soc. Psychol.*, **49**, 561–565. [129]

——— and Thayer Browne. 1956. An experimental and theoretical analysis of perceptual defense. *J. abnorm. soc. Psychol.*, **52**, 224–230. [122]

Erikson, Erik H. 1950. *The child and society.* New York: Norton. [109]

Eron, Leonard. 1950. A normative study of the Thematic Apperception Test. *Psychol. Monogr.*, **64** (9), 1–48. [60]

———. 1959. Psychosocial development of aggressive behavior. Lecture given at Wayne State Univer., Detroit, Mich., April 30, 1959. [407]

Eysenck, Hans J. 1948. "Neuroticism" and handwriting. *J. abnorm. soc. Psychol.*, **43**, 94–96. [149]

———. 1951. Neuroticism in twins. *Eugenics Rev.*, **43**, 79–82. [365]

———. 1953. *The structure of human personality.* London: Methuen. [167, 181, 267, 268, 269, 286]

———. 1954. The science of personality: nomothetic! *Psychol. Rev.*, **61**, 339–342. [7, 16]

———. 1955. Cortical inhibition: figural after-effect, and theory of personality. *J. abnorm. soc. Psychol.*, **51**, 94–106. [270, 376]

———. 1956a. Reminiscence, drive and personality theory. *J. abnorm. soc. Psychol.*, **53**, 328–333. [376]

———. 1956b. The inheritance of extroversion-introversion. *Acta Psychol.*, **12**, 95–110. [365]

——— and D. B. Prell. 1951. The inheritance of neuroticism: an experimental study. *J. ment. Sci.*, **97**, 441–465. [365]

Faigin, H. 1958. Case report: social behavior of young children in the kibbutz. *J. abnorm. soc. Psychol.*, **56**, 117–129. [402]

Falk, John L. 1956. Issues distinguishing idiographic from nomothetic approaches to personality theory. *Psychol. Rev.*, **63**, 53–62. [7, 16]

Farber, Bernard, and Leonard S. Blackman. 1956. Marital role tensions and number and sex of children. *Amer. soc. Rev.*, **21**, 596–601. [447]

Farber, M. L. 1955. The anal character and political aggression. *J. abnorm. soc. Psychol.*, **51**, 486–489. [281]

Fearing, Franklin. 1957. Values east, west, and in between. (Review of Morris's *Varieties of human value.*) *Contemp. Psychol.*, **2**, 157–159. [262]

Feffer, Melvin, and Leslie Phillips. 1953. Social attainment and performance under stress. *J. Pers.*, **22**, 284–297. [380]

Ferguson, L. W. 1952. *Personality measurement.* New York: McGraw-Hill. [33, 41, 43, 65, 263]

Feshbach, Seymour, and Robert D. Singer. 1957. Effects of fear arousal and suppression of fear upon social perception. *J. abnorm. soc. Psychol.*, **55**, 283–288. [95]

Festinger, Leon. 1942. Wish, expectation, and group standards as factors influencing level of aspiration. *J. abnorm. soc. Psychol.*, **37**, 184–200. [208]

Fey, William F. 1955. Acceptance by others and its relation to acceptance of self and others: a revaluation. *J. abnorm. soc. Psychol.*, **50**, 274–276. [198]

Fiedler, Fred E. 1958. *Leader attitudes and group effectiveness.* Urbana, Ill.: Univer. of Illinois Press. [140]

Fiedler, Miriam Foster, and Joseph L. Stone. 1956. The Rorschachs of selected groups of children in comparison with published norms: II. The effect of socio-economic status on Rorschach performance. *J. proj. Tech.*, **20**, 273–279. [504]

Filer, Robert J. 1952. Frustration, satisfaction, and other factors affecting the attractiveness of goal objects. *J. abnorm. soc. Psychol.*, **47**, 203–212. [121]

Fine, Harold J., Samuel C. Fulkerson, and Leslie Phillips. 1955. Maladjustment and social attainment. *J. abnorm. soc. Psychol.*, **50**, 33–35. [504]

Fisher, Sarah Carolyn. 1948. Relationship of attitudes, opinions, and values among family members. Berkeley, Calif.: Univer. of California Press. [248, 419]

Fisher, Seymour, and Sidney E. Cleveland. 1955. The role of body image in psychosomatic symptom choice. *Psychol. Monogr.*, **69**, No. 17 (Whole No. 402). [187]

——— and ———. 1956. Body image boundaries and style of life. *J. abnorm. soc. Psychol.*, **52**, 373–379. [187]

——— and ———. 1957. An approach to physiological reactivity in terms of a body-image schema. *Psychol. Rev.*, **64**, 26–37. [187]

Fiske, Donald W. 1949. Consistency of the factorial structures of personality ratings from different sources. *J. abnorm. soc. Psychol.*, **44**, 329–344. [164]

Fleming, Robert S. 1951. Psychosomatic illness and emotional needs. *Educ. Leadership*, **9**, 119–123. [475]

Fooks, Gilbert, and Ross R. Thomas. 1957. Differential qualitative performance of delinquents on the Porteus maze. *J. consult. Psychol.*, **21**, 351–353. [230]

Foote, Nelson N. 1956. Parsonian theory of family process. *Sociometry*, **19**, 40–46. [426]

Forer, B. R. 1949. The fallacy of personal validation: a classroom demonstration of gullibility. *J. abnorm. soc. Psychol.*, **44**, 118–123. [50]

Fosberg, I. A. 1941. An experimental study of the reliability of the Rorschach psychodiagnostic technique. *Rorschach Res. Exch.*, **5**, 72–84. [55]

Frank, J. D. 1935. Some psychological determinants of level of aspiration. *Amer. J. Psychol.*, **47**, 285–293. [208]

Frank, L. K. 1936. Society as the patient. *Amer. J. Sociol.*, **42**, 335–344. [516]

Freedman, L. Z., and A. B. Hollingshead. 1957. Neurosis and social class. *Amer. J. Psychiat.*, **113**, 769–775. [501]

Freeman, G. L. 1939. Toward a psychiatric Plimsoll mark; physiological recovery quotients in experimentally induced frustration. *J. Psychol.*, **8**, 247–252. [373]

———. 1948. *Energetics of human behavior.* Ithaca, N.Y.: Cornell Univer. Press. [22, 70, 145, 171, 223, 292, 371, 373, 374, 396]

French, Elizabeth G., and Irene Chadwick. 1956. Some characteristics in affiliation motivation. *J. abnorm. soc. Psychol.*, **52**, 296–300. [349]

French, J. R. P., Jr. 1944. Retraining an autocratic leader. *J. abnorm. soc. Psychol.*, **39**, 224–237. [464]

Frenkel-Brunswik, Else. 1948. A study of prejudice in children. *Hum. Relat.*, **1**, 295–306. [258]

———. 1949. Intolerance of ambiguity as an emotional and perceptual personality variable. *J. Pers.*, **18**, 108–143. [255]

———. 1951. Personality theory and perception. In Blake, R. R., and G. V. Ramsey (Eds.) *Perception: an approach to personality.* New York: Ronald. Pp. 356–420. [141]

———, and R. Nevitt Sanford. 1945. Some personality factors in anti-Semitism. *J. Psychol.*, **20**, 271–291. [198, 528]

Freud, S. 1920. *General introduction to psychoanalysis.* New York: Boni & Liveright. [17, 185]

———. 1922. *Beyond the pleasure principle.* London: International Psychoanalytic Press. [311, 313]

———. 1924. *Collected papers.* London: International Psychoanalytic Press. [112, 186, 281]

———. 1936. *The problem of anxiety.* New York: Norton. [315]

———. 1938. *Basic writings of . . . .* (Trans. by A. A. Brill.) New York: Modern Library. [331]

Frick, J. W. 1955. Improving prediction of academic achievement by use of MMPI. *J. appl. Psychol.*, **39**, 49–52. [467]

——— and Helen E. Kenner. 1956. A validation study of the prediction of college achievement. *J. appl. Psychol.*, **40**, 251–252. [467]

Friedman, Ira. 1955. Phenomenal, ideal and projected conceptions of self. *J. abnorm. soc. Psychol.*, **51**, 611–615. [191]

———. 1957. Characteristics of the Thematic Apperception Test heroes of normal, psychoneurotic, and paranoid schizophrenic subjects. *J. proj. Tech.*, **21**, 272–276. [60]

Friedman, Stanley M. 1952. An empirical study of the castration and Oedipus complexes. *Genet. Psychol. Monogr.*, **46**, 61–130. [110]

Fries, Margaret E. 1954. Some hypotheses on the role of congenital activity type in personality development. *Int. J. Psychoanal.*, **35**, 206–207. [370]

—— and Paul J. Woolf. 1954. Some hypotheses on the role of the congenital activity type in personality development. *Psychoanal. Stud. Child*, **8**, 48–64. [370]

Fromm, Erich. 1941. *Escape from freedom.* New York: Rinehart. [330, 331, 533]

——. 1947. *Man for himself.* New York: Rinehart. [331]

——. 1955. *The sane society.* New York: Rinehart. [516, 518, 530]

Fromm-Reichman, Frieda. 1950. *Principles of intensive psychotherapy.* Chicago: Univer. of Chicago Press. [100]

Fry, C. C., and H. W. Haggard. 1936. *Anatomy of personality.* New York: Harper. [396]

Funkenstein, Daniel H., Stanley H. King, and Margaret E. Drolette. 1957. *Mastery of stress.* Cambridge, Mass.: Harvard Univer. Press. [193, 204, 382–383]

Gage, Nathaniel L., and Lee J. Cronbach. 1955. Conceptual and methodological problems in interpersonal perception. *Psychol. Rev.*, **62**, 411–423. [36]

——, George S. Leavitt, and George C. Stone. 1957. The psychological meaning of acquiescence set for authoritarianism. *J. abnorm. soc. Psychol.*, **55**, 98–103. [254]

Gaier, E. L., and Marilyn C. Lee. 1953. Pattern analysis: the configural approach to predictive measurement. *Psychol. Bull.*, **50**, 140–148. [270]

Galbraith, J. K. 1958. *The affluent society.* Boston: Houghton Mifflin. [529]

Gantt, W. H. 1942. Origin and development of nervous disturbances experimentally produced. *Amer. J. Psychiat.*, **98**, 475–481. [131]

Gardner, Riley W. 1953. Cognitive styles in categorizing behavior. *J. Pers.*, **22**, 214–233. [140]

Gerard, Donald L., and Leslie Phillips. 1953. Relation of social attainment to psychological and adrenocortical reactions to stress. *A.M.A. Arch. Neurol. Psychiat.*, **69**, 350–354. [381]

Gesell, Arnold, and E. E. Lord. 1927. Psychological comparison of nursery school children from homes of low and high economic status. *J. genet. Psychol.*, **34**, 554–557. [499]

Getzels, J. W., and E. G. Guba. 1954. Role, role conflict, and effectiveness: an empirical study. *Amer. sociol. Rev.*, **19**, 164–175. [458]

—— and ——. 1955. Role conflict and personality. *J. Pers.*, **24**, 74–85. [458]

Ghent, Lila. 1951. The relation of experience to the development of hunger. *Canad. J. Psychol.*, **5**, 77–81. [291]

Ghiselli, Edwin E., and Clarence W. Brown. 1955. *Personnel and industrial psychology.* (2nd ed.) New York: McGraw-Hill. [515]

Gibb, Cecil A. 1955. Classroom behavior of the college teacher. *Educ. Psychol. Measmt.*, **15**, 254–263. [452, 462]

Gilchrist, J. C., and L. S. Nesberg. 1952. Need and perceptual change in need-related objects. *J. exp. Psychol.*, **44**, 369–376. [121]

Glueck, Sheldon, and Eleanor Glueck. 1950. *Unraveling juvenile delinquency.* New York: Commonwealth Fund. [227, 228, 231, 232, 236, 503, 504]

—— and ——. 1956. *Physique and delinquency.* New York: Harper. [230, 236]

Goldfarb, W. 1943. Effects of early institutional care on adolescent personality. *J. exp. Educ.*, **12**, 106–129. [402]

——. 1944. Effects of early institutional care on adolescent personality: Rorschach data. *Amer. J. Orthopsychiat.*, **14**, 441–447. [402]

Goldman, Frieda. 1948. Breast feeding and character formation. *J. Pers.*, **17**, 83–103. [403]

Goldman-Eisler, Frieda. 1951. The problem of "orality" and of its origin in early childhood. *J. ment. Sci.*, **97**, 765–782. [107, 403]

Goldstein, Kurt. 1935. *The organism.* New York: American Book. [206, 305]

Gollin, Eugene S., and Alan Baron. 1954. Response consistency in perception and retention. *J. exp. Psychol.*, **47**, 259–262. [144]

Goode, William J. 1951. Economic factors and marital stability. *Amer. soc. Rev.*, **16**, 802–812. [509]

Goodenough, Florence L. 1931. *Anger in young children.* Minneapolis: Univer. of Minnesota Press. [180]

Gordon, Jesse E. 1957. Interpersonal predictions of repressors and sensitizers. *J. Pers.*, **25**, 686–698. [144]

Gordon, Leonard V., and Ernest S. Stapleton. 1956. Fakability of a forced-choice personality test under realistic high school employment conditions. *J. appl. Psychol.*, **40**, 258–262. [48]

Gottschaldt, K. 1926. Ueber den Einfluss der Erfahrung auf die Wahrnehmung von Figuren. *Psychol. Forsch.*, **8**, 261–317. [140]

Gough, Harrison G. 1946. The relationship of socio-economic status to personality inventory and achievement test scores. *J. educ. Psychol.*, **37**, 527–540. [500]

———, Herbert McClosky, and Paul Meehl. 1952. A personality scale for social responsibility. *J. abnorm. soc. Psychol.*, **47**, 73–80. [220, 221]

Gould, Rosalind. 1939. An experimental analysis of "level of aspiration." *Genet. Psychol. Monogr.*, **21**, 31–115. [208]

Granger, G. W. 1953. Personality and visual perception: a review. *J. ment. Sci.*, **99**, 8–43. [143]

Granick, Samuel. 1955. Intellectual performance as related to emotional instability in children. *J. abnorm. soc. Psychol.*, **51**, 653–656. [466]

Grant, David A., and Jerome J. Schiller. 1953. Generalization of the conditioned galvanic skin response to visual stimuli. *J. exp. Psychol.*, **46**, 309–313. [97]

Grant, Marguerite Q., Virginia Ives, and Jane H. Ranzoni. 1952. Reliability and validity of judges' ratings of adjustment on the Rorschach. *Psychol. Monogr.*, **66** (2). [55, 57]

Green, A. W. 1946. Middle class male child and neurosis. *Amer. sociol. Rev.*, **11**, 31–41. [501]

Greenfield, Norman S., Robert Roessler, and Archer P. Crosley. 1959. Ego strength and length of recovery from infectious mononucleosis. *J. nerv. ment. Dis.*, **128**, 125–128. [393]

Gruen, E. W. 1945. Level of aspiration in relation to personality factors in adolescents. *Child Develpm.*, **16**, 181–188. [209]

Grygier, T. G. 1957. Psychometric aspects of homosexuality. *J. ment. Sci.*, **103**, 514–526. [47, 282]

Guba, E. G., and G. W. Getzels. 1955. Personality and teacher effectiveness: a problem in theoretical research. *J. educ. Psychol.*, **46**, 330–344. [458]

Guilford, Joan S. 1952. Temperament traits of executives and supervisors measured by the Guilford personality inventories. *J. appl. Psychol.*, **36**, 228–233. [490]

Guilford, Joy Paul. 1948. The Guilford Personality Inventories. In O. Kaplan (Ed.), *Encyclopedia of vocational guidance.* New York: Philosophical Library. Pp. 1007–1010. [13, 164]

———. 1959. *Personality.* New York: McGraw-Hill. [158, 181]

——— and Wayne S. Zimmerman. 1956. Fourteen dimensions of temperament. *Psychol. Monogr.*, **70** (10) (No. 417). [166, 299]

Guthrie, E. R. 1944. Personality in terms of associative learning. In J. McV. Hunt, *Personality and the behavior disorders.* New York: Ronald. [6, 160]

Guttman, Louis. 1950. The basis for scalogram analysis. In S. A. Stouffer et al., *Measurement and prediction.* Princeton, N.J.: Princeton Univer. Press. [240]

Hadley, J. M. 1940. Some relationships between electrical signs of central and peripheral activity: I. During rest. *J. exp. Psychol.*, **27**, 640–656. [376]

Haire, Mason. 1955. Role-perceptions in labor-management relations: an experimental approach. *Industr. Lab. Rel. Rev.*, **8**, 204–216. [242, 494]

—— and Florence Morrison. 1957. School children's perceptions of labor and management. *J. soc. Psychol.*, **46**, 179–197. [242]

Hall, Calvin S. 1941. Temperament: a survey of animal studies. *Psychol. Bull.*, **38**, 909–943. [368]

——. 1951. The genetics of behavior. In S. S. Stevens (Ed.), *Handbook of experimental psychology*. New York: Wiley. Pp. 304–329. [367, 369]

——. 1954. *A primer of Freudian psychology*. Cleveland: World Publishing. [331]

—— and S. J. Klein. 1942. Individual differences in aggressiveness in rats. *J. comp. Psychol.*, **33**, 371–383. [367]

—— and Gardner Lindzey. 1957. *Theories of personality*. New York: Wiley. [286]

Halliday, James L. 1948. *Psychosocial medicine*. New York: Norton. [516]

Hamilton, G. V., and K. McGowan. 1929. What is wrong with marriage? New York: Boni. [559]

Hamilton, Vernon. 1957. Perceptual and personality dynamics in reactions to ambiguity. *Brit. J. Psychol.*, **48**, 200–215. [119]

Hammer, E. F., and Z. Piotrowski. 1953. Hostility as a factor in the clinician's personality. *J. proj. Tech.*, **17**, 210–216. [62]

Hammond, Kenneth R., and Lawrence I. O'Kelly. 1955. A note on adjustment as achievement. *J. abnorm. soc. Psychol.*, **51**, 171–174. [128]

Harding, L. W. 1944a. A value-type generalization test. *J. soc. Psychol.*, **19**, 53–79. [530]

——. 1944b. The value-type problemmaire. *J. soc. Psychol.*, **19**, 115–144. [530]

Harlow, Harry F. 1953. Motivation as a factor in new responses. In Marshall R. Jones (Ed.), *Nebraska symposium on motivation*. Lincoln, Neb.: Univer. of Nebraska Press. [332]

——. 1958. The nature of love. *Amer. Psychologist*, **13**, 673–685. [94, 401]

—— and Ross Stagner. 1932. Psychology of feelings and emotions: I. Theory of feelings. *Psychol. Rev.*, **39**, 570–589. [90, 91]

—— and ——. 1933. Psychology of feelings and emotions: II. Theory of emotions. *Psychol. Rev.*, **40**, 184–195. [93]

——, Margaret K. Harlow, and D. R. Meyer. 1950. Learning motivated by a manipulation drive. *J. exp. Psychol.*, **40**, 228–234. [295]

Harris, Dale B., Harrison G. Gough, and William E. Martin. 1950. Children's ethnic attitudes: II. Relationship to parental beliefs concerning child training. *Child Develpm.*, **21**, 169–181. [258]

——, A. M. Rose, K. E. Clark, and F. Valasek. 1955. Personality differences between responsible and less responsible children. *J. genet. Psychol.*, **87**, 103–109. [221]

Harrison, R. 1940. Studies in the use and validity of the Thematic Apperception Test with mentally disordered patients: II. A qualitative validity study. *Charact. & Pers.*, **9**, 122–133. [60]

—— and J. B. Rotter. 1945. A note on the reliability of the Thematic Apperception Test. *J. abnorm. soc. Psychol.*, **40**, 97–99. [60]

Harrower, Molly R. 1950. Group techniques for the Rorschach test. In L. E. Abt and L. Bellak (Eds.), *Projective psychology*. New York: Knopf. [57, 58]

Hart, I. 1957. Maternal child-rearing practices and authoritarian ideology. *J. abnorm. soc. Psychol.*, **55**, 232–237. [416]

Hartmann, Heinz. 1939. Ego psychology and the problem of adaptation. Trans. in D. Rapaport, *Organization and pathology of thought.* New York: Columbia Univer. Press, 1951. [203]

Hartshorne, H., and M. A. May. 1928. *Studies in deceit.* New York: Macmillan. [31, 215, 236]

—— and J. B. Maller. 1929. *Studies in service and self-control.* New York: Macmillan. [215, 236]

——, M. A. May, and F. K. Shuttleworth. 1930. *Studies in the organization of character.* New York: Macmillan. [215, 236]

Hastings, Philip K. 1952. A relationship between visual perception and level of personality security. *J. abnorm. soc. Psychol.,* **47,** 552–560. [202]

Hathaway, S. R., and J. C. McKinley. 1940. A multiphasic personality schedule: I. Construction of the schedule. *J. Psychol.,* **10,** 249–254. [44, 167]

—— and Paul E. Meehl. 1951. *An atlas for the clinical use of MMPI.* Minneapolis: Univer. of Minnesota Press. [190]

—— and Elio D. Monachesi. 1952. The Minnesota Multiphasic Personality Inventory in the study of juvenile delinquents. *Amer. sociol. Rev.,* **17,** 704–710. [226, 492]

—— and ——. 1953. *Analyzing and predicting juvenile delinquency with the MMPI.* Minneapolis: Univer. of Minnesota Press. [226, 230, 231]

Hauer, Herbert J. 1955. Frustration in neonates: an investigation of the relationship between frustration tolerance of neonates and frustration tolerance of their parents. *Dissertation Abstr.,* **15,** 1914. [418]

Havighurst, Robert J., and Hilda Taba. 1949. *Adolescent character and personality.* New York: Wiley. [218, 236, 265]

Havron, M. D., and C. N. Cofer. 1957. On the learning of material congruent and incongruent with attitudes. *J. soc. Psychol.,* **46,** 91–98. [245]

Hawkes, Glenn R., Lee G. Burchinal, and Bruce Gardner. 1956. Marital satisfaction, personality characteristics, and parental acceptance of children. *J. counsel. Psychol.,* **3,** 216–221. [439]

Hayward, R. S. 1935. Child's report of psychological factors in the family. *Arch. Psychol., N.Y.,* **28,** No. 189. [508]

Healy, William, Augusta F. Bronner, and Anna M. Bowers. 1931. *The structure and meaning of psychoanalysis.* New York: Knopf. [319, 320]

Hebb, D. O. 1949. *The organization of behavior.* New York: Wiley. [75, 89, 223, 292]

——. 1958. *A textbook of psychology.* Philadelphia: Saunders. [399]

Heider, F. 1944. Social perception and phenomenal causality. *Psychol. Rev.,* **51,** 358–374. [76]

Heine, Ralph W. 1953. A comparison of patients' reports on psychotherapeutic experience with psychoanalytic, nondirective, and Adlerian therapists. *Amer. J. Psychoth.,* **7,** (1), 16–23. [102]

Heinicke, Christoph M. 1956. Some effects of separating two-year-old children from their parents: a comparative study. *Hum. Relat.,* **9,** 105–176. [401]

Helfant, K. 1952. Parents' attitudes vs. adolescent hostility in the determination of adolescents' socio-political attitudes. *Psychol. Monogr.,* **66,** No. 13. [424]

Helper, Malcolm M. 1955. Learning theory and the self concept. *J. abnorm. soc. Psychol.,* **51,** 184–194. [189]

—— and Louis L. McQuitty. 1953. Some relations of personality integration to occupational interests. *J. soc. Psychol.,* **38,** 219–231. [487]

Helson, Harry. 1947. Adaptation level as a frame of reference for prediction of psychophysical data. *Amer. J. Psychol.,* **60,** 1–29. [78, 243]

——, R. R. Blake, Jane S. Mouton, and Joseph A. Olmstead. 1956. Attitudes as adjustments to stimulus, background and residual factors. *J. abnorm. soc. Psychol.*, **52**, 314–322. [243]

Hendrick, I. 1934. *Facts and theories of psychoanalysis.* New York: Knopf. [312, 317, 331]

Henry, William E. 1949. The business executive: psychodynamics of a social role. *Amer. J. Sociol.*, **54**, 286–291. [60, 490]

———. 1956. *The analysis of fantasy: the thematic apperception technique in the study of personality.* New York: Wiley. [60]

Hernández-Peón, Raúl, Harald Scherrer, and Michel Jouvet. 1955. Modification of electrical activity of cochlear nucleus during "attention" in unanesthetized cats. *Science*, **123**, 331–332. [82]

Heron, Alastair. 1956. The effects of real-life motivation on questionnaire response. *J. appl. Psychol.*, **40**, 65–68. [48]

Heron, W., B. K. Doan, and T. H. Scott. 1956. Visual disturbances after prolonged perceptual isolation. *Canad. J. Psychol.*, **10**, 13–18. [400]

Hertz, Marguerite R. 1934. Reliability of Rorschach ink-blot test. *J. appl. Psychol.*, **18**, 461–477. [55]

———. 1942. Personality patterns in adolescents as portrayed by Rorschach ink-blot method. *J. gen. Psychol.*, **27**, 119–188. [504]

Hess, Robert D., and Gerald Handel. 1956. Patterns of aggression in parents and their children. *J. genet. Psychol.*, **89**, 199–212. [408]

Hewitt, L. E., and R. L. Jenkins. 1946. *Fundamental patterns of maladjustment: dynamics of their origin.* Springfield, Ill.: State of Illinois. [408, 409]

Heymans, G. 1908. Ueber einige psychische Korrelationen. *Z. f. angew. Psychol.*, **1**, 313–381. [138]

Hilton, Andrew C., S. F. Bolin, J. W. Parker, Jr., E. K. Taylor, and W. B. Walker. 1955. The validity of personnel assessments by professional psychologists. *J. appl. Psychol.*, **39**, 287–293. [63]

Himelhoch, Jerome, and Sylvia Fava (Eds.). 1955. *Sexual behavior in American society.* New York: Norton. [442]

Himelstein, Philip, Arthur E. Eschenbach, and A. Carp. 1958. Interrelationships among three measures of need-achievement. *J. consult. Psychol.*, **22**, 451–452. [348]

Hines, Vynce A. 1956. F scale, GAMIN, and public school principal behavior. *J. educ. Psychol.*, **47**, 321–328. [452]

Hirsch, J., and J. C. Boudreau. 1958. Studies in experimental behavior genetics: I. The heritability of phototaxis in a population of *Drosophila melanogaster*. *J. comp. physiol. Psychol.*, **51**, 647–651. [367]

Hoagland, Hudson. 1952. Metabolic and physiologic disturbances in the psychoses. In Milbank Memorial Fund. *Biology of mental health and disease.* New York: Hoeber-Harper. Pp. 434–449. [381]

Hoch, Paul H., and Joseph Zubin (Eds.). 1954. *Anxiety.* New York: Grune & Stratton. [370]

——— and ——— (Eds.). 1955. *Psychopathology of childhood.* New York: Grune & Stratton. [470]

Hochbaum, Godfrey M. 1954. The relation between group members' self-confidence and their reactions to group pressures to uniformity. *Amer. sociol. Rev.*, **19**, 678–687. [204]

Hochberg, J. E., S. L. Haber, and T. A. Ryan. 1955. "Perceptual defense" as an interference phenomenon. *Percep. mot. Skills*, **5**, 15–17. [123]

Hoehn, Arthur J., and Eli Saltz. 1956. Effect of teacher-student interviews on classroom achievement. *J. educ. Psychol.*, **47**, 424–435. [476]

Hoffeditz, Louise E. 1934. Family resemblances in personality traits. *J. soc. Psychol.*, **5**, 214–227. [417, 418, 501]

Hoffman, Martin L. 1953. Some psychodynamic factors in compulsive conformity. *J. abnorm. soc. Psychol.*, **48**, 383–393. [204]

—— and C. Albizu-Miranda. 1955. Middle class bias in personality testing. *J. abnorm. soc. Psychol.*, **51**, 150–152. [501, 502]

Hollander, E. P. 1954. Authoritarianism and leadership choice in a military setting. *J. abnorm. soc. Psychol.*, **49**, 365–370. [476]

—— and John T. Bair. 1952. Pretraining attitudes toward authority-figures as predictors of inadequate motivation among naval aviation cadets. J. S. Naval Sch. Aviat., Med., *Res. Rep.*, Proj. No. NM. 001 058.05.05,5. [476]

—— and ——. 1954. Attitudes toward authority-figures as correlates of motivation among naval aviation cadets. *J. appl. Psychol.*, **38**, 21–25. [476]

Hollingworth, H. L. 1920. *Psychology of functional neuroses.* New York: Appleton-Century. [42, 167]

Holmberg, Allan R. 1950. *Nomads of the long bow.* Smithsonian Institute of Social Anthropology. Publ. 10, Washington: U.S. Government Printing Office. [291]

Holzberg, Jules D., and Fred Hahn. 1952. The picture-frustration technique as a measure of hostility and guilt in adolescent psychopaths. *Amer. J. Orthopsychiat.*, **22**, 776–797. [226]

Holzman, Philip S. 1954. The relation of assimilation tendencies in visual, auditory, and kinesthetic time-error to cognitive attitudes of leveling and sharpening. *J. Pers.*, **22**, 375–394. [139]

—— and George S. Klein. 1956. Motive and style in reality contact. *Bull. Menninger Clin.*, **20** (4), 181–191. [139]

Honigman, John J. 1954. *Culture and personality.* New York: Harper. [300]

Horney, Karen. 1937. *The neurotic personality of our time.* New York: Norton. [331]

——. 1945. *Our inner conflicts.* New York: Norton. [329, 331]

Horowitz, Eugene L. 1935. Spatial localization of the self. *J. soc. Psychol.*, **6**, 379–387. [183]

——. 1936. Development of attitude toward the Negro. *Arch. Psychol.*, *N.Y.*, **28**, No. 194. [246]

—— and Ruth E. Horowitz. 1938. Development of social attitudes in children. *Sociometry*, **1**, 301–338. [246]

Horwitz, Murray. 1956. Psychological needs as a function of social environments. In Leonard D. White (Ed.), *State of the social sciences.* Chicago: Univer. of Chicago Press. Pp. 162–183. [475]

Hoskins, R. G. 1941. *Endocrinology.* New York: Norton. [378]

Hovland, C. I., and R. R. Sears. 1940. Correlation of economic indices with lynchings. *J. Psychol.*, **9**, 301–310. [511, 528]

Hoyt, Donald P., and Warren T. Norman. 1954. Adjustment and academic predictability. *J. counsel. Psychol.*, **1**, 96–99. [467]

Hudson, Bradford B. 1954. Anxiety in response to the unfamiliar. *J. soc. Issues*, **10** (3), 53–60. [255]

Hull, Clark L. 1951. *Essentials of behavior.* New Haven, Conn.: Yale Univer. Press. [297, 298, 309]

——. 1952. *A behavior system.* New Haven, Conn.: Yale Univer. Press. [297]

Humphreys, Lloyd G. 1957. Characteristics of type concepts with special reference to Sheldon's typology: *Psychol. Bull.*, **54**, 218–228. [278]

Hunt, J. McV. 1941. Effects of infant feeding-frustration upon adult hoarding in the albino rat. *J. abnorm. soc. Psychol.*, **36**, 338–360. [399]

——. 1944. *Personality and the behavior disorders.* New York: Ronald. 2 vols. [28, 272, 401, 496]

Huntley, C. W. 1940. Judgments of self based upon records of expressive behavior. *J. abnorm. soc. Psychol.*, **35**, 398–427. [210, 211]

Ingersoll, Hazel L. 1948. A study of the transmission of authority patterns in the family. *Genet. Psychol. Monogr.*, **38**, 225–302. [419]

Jackson, Douglas N. 1954. A further examination of the role of autism in a visual figure-ground relationship. *J. Psychol.*, **38**, 339–357. [81]

——, S. J. Messick, and Charles M. Solley. 1957a. A multidimensional scaling approach to the perception of personality. *J. Psychol.*, **44**, 311–318. [32]

——, ——, and ——. 1957b. How "rigid" is the "authoritarian?" *J. abnorm. soc. Psychol.*, **54**, 137–140. [152, 253, 254]

Jackson, Lydia. 1950. Emotional attitudes toward the family of normal, neurotic, and delinquent children. Part II. *Brit. J. Psychol.*, **41**, 173–185. [410]

Jacobson, Alver H. 1952. Conflict of attitudes toward the roles of husband and wife in marriage. *Amer. soc. Rev.*, **17**, 146–150. [434]

Jaensch, E. R. 1930. *Eidetic imagery.* New York: Harcourt, Brace. [272]

Janis, Irving L. 1954. Personality correlates of susceptibility to persuasion. *J. Pers.*, **22**, 504–518. [153]

—— and Peter B. Fields. 1956. A behavioral assessment of persuasibility: consistency of individual indifferences. *Sociometry*, **19**, 241–259. [153]

Jansen, Luther R. 1952. Measuring family solidarity. *Amer. soc. Rev.*, **17**, 727–733. [414]

Jaynes, Julian. 1956. Imprinting: the interaction of learned and innate behavior: I. Development and generalization. *J. comp. physiol. Psychol.*, **49**, 201–206. [399]

Jenkins, Richard L. 1957. Motivation and frustration in delinquency. *Amer. J. Orthopsychiat.*, **27**, 528–537. [408]

Jennings, L. Sherman. 1948. Minnesota Multiphasic Personality Inventory: differentiation of psychologically good and poor combat risks among flying personnel. *J. Aviat. Med.*, **19**, 222–226; 237. [50]

Jensen, Arthur R. 1957. Aggression in fantasy and overt behavior. *Psychol. Monogr.*, **71** (16), No. 445. [411]

Jersild, Arthur T. 1957. *The psychology of adolescence.* New York: Macmillan. [425]

Jessor, Richard. 1956. Social values and psychotherapy. *J. consult. Psychol.*, **20**, 264–266. [523]

Jones, Marshall B. 1957. The Pensacola Z Survey: a study in the measurement of authoritarian tendency. *Psychol. Monogr.*, **71**, No. 23 (Whole No. 452). [255]

Jones, Mary Cover. 1924. The elimination of children's fears. *J. exp. Psychol.*, **7**, 382–390 [131]

——. 1957. The later career of boys who were early or late-maturing. *Child Develpm.*, **28**, 113–128. [385]

—— and Nancy Bayley. 1950. Physical maturing among boys as related to behavior. *J. educ. Psychol.*, **41**, 129–148. [385]

Jost, H. 1941. Some physiological changes during frustration. *Child Develpm.*, **12**, 9–15. [130]

—— and L. W. Sontag. 1944. The genetic factor in autonomic nervous system function. *Psychosom. Med.*, **6**, 308–310. [376]

Jourard, Sidney M. Identification, parent-cathexis, and self-esteem. *J. consult. Psychol.*, **21**, 375–380. [199]

—— and Richard M. Remy. 1955. Perceived parental attitudes, the self, and security. *J. consult. Psychol.*, **19**, 364–366. [188, 195]

—— and Paul F. Secord. 1955a. Body-cathexis and personality. *Brit. J. Psychol.*, **46**, 130–138. [187]

Jourard, Sidney M., and Paul F. Secord. 1955b. Body-cathexis and the ideal female figure. *J. abnorm. soc. Psychol.*, **50**, 243–246. [187]

Jung, C. G. 1923. *Psychological types.* New York: Harcourt, Brace. [266, 268, 272, 286]

Kaden, S. E., and H. Lipton. 1960. Rorschach developmental scores and post-hospital adjustment of married male schizophrenics. *J. proj. Tech.*, **24**, 144–147. [202]

Kagan, Jerome, and Howard A. Moss. 1959. Stability and validity of achievement fantasy. *J. abnorm. soc. Psychol.*, **58**, 357–364. [348]

——— and Paul H. Mussen. 1956. Dependency themes on the TAT and group conformity. *J. consult. Psychol.*, **20**, 29–32. [258]

Kalis, Betty L. 1957. Some relationships between size perception and ego adequacy. *J. Pers.*, **25**, 439–450. [200]

Kallman, Franz J. 1952. Genetic aspects of psychoses. In *Biology of mental health and disease.* New York: Hoeber-Harper. Pp. 283–298. [369]

———. 1956. The genetics of human behavior. *Amer. J. Psychiat.*, **113**, 496–501. [369, 371]

Kamenetzky, Joseph. 1955. Anxiety and attitude as variables affecting perception of persons. Unpublished doctoral dissertation, Univer. of Illinois. [142, 494]

Kardiner, A. 1939. *The individual and his society.* New York: Columbia Univer. Press. [505, 534]

Karson, Samuel, and Kenneth B. Pool. 1957. Construct validity of the Sixteen Personality Factors Test. *J. clin. Psychol.*, **13**, 245–252. [46]

Keeley, Benjamin J. 1955. Value convergence and marital relations. *Marriage Fam. Living*, **17**, 342–345. [428]

Kelly, E. L. 1955. Consistency of the adult personality. *Amer. Psychologist*, **10**, 659–681. [176, 178, 428, 447]

——— and D. W. Fiske. 1951. Prediction of performance in clinical psychology. Ann Arbor, Mich.: Univer. of Michigan Press. [60]

Kelly, George A. 1955. *Psychology of personal constructs.* New York: Norton. 2 vols. [74]

Kempf, E. J. 1919. Autonomic functions and the personality. *Nerv. ment. Dis. Monogr. Ser.*, No. 28. [4, 373]

Kerr, M. 1936. Temperamental differences in twins. *Brit. J. Psychol.*, **27**, 51–59. [365]

Keys, Ancel. 1952. Experimental induction of psychoneuroses by starvation. In Milbank Memorial Fund. *Biology of mental health and disease.* New York: Hoeber-Harper. Pp. 515–525. [390]

———, Jozef Brozek, Austin Henschel, Olaf Mickelsen, and H. L. Taylor. 1950. *The biology of human starvation.* Minneapolis: Univer. of Minnesota Press. 2 vols. [85, 390]

King, Stanley H., and Andrew F. Henry. 1955. Aggression and cardiovascular reactions related to parental control over behavior. *J. abnorm. soc. Psychol.*, **50**, 206–210. [382]

Kinsey, Alfred C., W. B. Pomeroy, and C. E. Martin. 1948. *Sexual behavior in the human male.* Philadelphia: Saunders. [435]

———, ———, ———, and P. H. Gebhard. 1953. *Sexual behavior in the human female.* Philadelphia: Saunders. [435]

Kirkpatrick, Clifford, and Charles Hobart. 1954. Disagreement, disagreement estimate, and non-empathetic imputations for intimacy groups varying from favorite date to married. *Amer. sociol. Rev.*, **19**, 10–19. [428]

Klatskin, Ethelyn H., Edith B. Jackson, and Louise C. Wilkin. 1956. Influence of degree of flexibility in maternal child care practices on early child behavior. *Amer. J. Orthopsychiat.*, **26**, 79–93. [415]

Klausner, Samuel Z. 1953. Social class and self-concept. *J. soc. Psychol.*, **38**, 201–205. [502]

Klein, George S. 1951. The personal world through perception. In Robert R. Blake and Glen Ramsey (Eds.), *Perception: an approach to personality*. New York: Ronald. Pp. 328–355. [138, 155, 267]

——. 1956. Perception, motives and personality. In J. L. McCary (Ed.), *Psychology of personality*. New York: Logos Press. Pp. 121–200. [138]

——. 1958. Cognitive control and motivation. In Gardner Lindzey (Ed.), *Assessment of motives*. New York: Rinehart. Pp. 87–118. [155]

——, Ann D. Salomon, J. W. Gudmund Smith, et al. 1959. Studies in cognitive style and the regulation of need. Unpublished manuscript. [121]

—— and H. J. Schlesinger. 1949. Where is the perceiver in perceptual theory? *J. Pers.*, **18**, 32–47. [138]

—— and ——. 1951. Perceptual attitudes toward instability: I. Prediction of apparent movement experiences from Rorschach responses. *J. Pers.*, **19**, 289–302. [141]

——, ——, and David E. Meister. 1951. The effect of personal values on perception: an experimental critique. *Psychol. Rev.*, **58**, 96–112. [121]

Klopfer, B., and D. M. Kelley. 1942. *The Rorschach technique*. Yonkers, N.Y.: World Book. [54]

Kluckhohn, Clyde, and Henry A. Murray. 1948. *Personality in nature, society and culture*. New York: Alfred A. Knopf. [280, 398]

Koch, Helen L. 1955. Some personality correlates of sex, sibling position, and sex of sibling among five- and six-year children. *Genet. Psychol. Monogr.*, **52**, 3–50. [421]

——. 1956. Attitudes of young children toward their peers as related to certain characteristics of their siblings. *Psychol. Monogr.*, **70**, No. 19. [424]

Köhler, Wolfgang. 1948. *Gestalt psychology*. (Rev. ed.) New York: Liveright. [75]

Koffka, K. 1935. *Principles of gestalt psychology*. New York: Harcourt, Brace. [183]

Korchin, Sheldon J., and Harold Basowitz. 1954. Perceptual adequacy in a life stress. *J. Psychol.*, **38**, 495–502. [123, 142]

Korner, Ija N. 1956. Of values, value lag, and mental health. *Amer. Psychologist*, **11**, 543–546 [523]

Kornhauser, Arthur W. 1945. Replies of psychologists to a short questionnaire on mental test developments, personality inventories, and the Rorschach test. *Educ. psychol. Measmt*, **5**, 3–15. [63]

Korobow, Norman. 1955. Reactions to stress: a reflection of personality trait organization. *J. abnorm. soc. Psychol.*, **51**, 464–468. [200]

Korzybski, Alfred. 1933. *Science and sanity*. Lancaster, Pa.: International Non-Aristotelian Press. [83]

Kragh, Ulf. 1955. *The actual-genetic model of perception-personality*. Lund, Sweden: C. W. K. Gleerup. [97]

Krebs, Allen M. 1958. Two determinants of conformity: age of independence, training and achievement. *J. abnorm. soc. Psychol.*, **56**, 130–131. [423, 473]

Kretschmer, E. 1925. *Physique and character*. New York: Harcourt, Brace. [274]

Kretschmer, Wolfgang, Jr. 1954. La signification de la constitution dans les troubles psychiques. *Evolut. psychiat.*, **3**, 409–419. [278]

Krout, Maurice H. 1935. Autistic gestures. *Psychol. Monogr.*, **46**, No. 208. [151]

—— and Ross Stagner. 1939. Personality development in radicals: a comparative study. *Sociometry*, **2**, 31–46. [247, 520]

—— and Johanna K. Tabin. 1954. Measuring personality in developmental terms: the personal preference scale. *Genet. Psychol. Monogr.*, **50**, 289–335. [47, 106, 282]

Krugman, J. I. 1942. A clinical validation of the Rorschach with problem children. *Rorschach. Res. Exch.*, **6**, 61–70. [56]

Krumboltz, John D. 1957. Measuring achievement motivation: a review. *J. counsel. Psychol.*, **4**, 191–198. [348]

—— and W. W. Farquhar. 1957. Reliability and validity of n-achievement. *J. consult. Psychol.*, **21**, 226–231. [348]

Ktsanes, Thomas. 1955. Mate selection on the basis of personality type: an empirical typology of personality. *Amer. soc. Rev.*, **20**, 547–551. [432]

Kubie, L. S. 1948. Instincts and homeostasis. *Psychosom. Med.*, **10**, 15–30. [304]

Kuhlen, R. G., 1945. Age differences in personality during adult years. *Psychol. Bull.*, **42**, 333–358. [178]

Kuntz, Albert. 1951. *Visceral innervation and its relation to personality.* Springfield, Ill.: Charles C Thomas. [373]

Kurtz, Albert K. 1948. A research test of the Rorschach test. *Person. Psychol.*, **1**, 41–51. [58]

Kurtz, Paul W. 1956. Human nature, homeostasis, and value. *Phil. phenomenol. Res.*, **17**, 36–55. [83–85]

Kutner, Bernard. 1958. Patterns of mental functioning associated with prejudice in children. *Psychol. Monogr.*, **72**, No. 7 (Whole No. 460). [255]

Lacey, John I. 1950. Individual differences in somatic response patterns. *J. comp. physiol. Psychol.*, **43**, 338–350. [375]

——, Dorothy E. Bateman, and Ruth Van Lehn. 1952. Autonomic response specificity and Rorschach color responses. *Psychosom. Med.*, **14**, 256–260. [375]

—— and Ruth Van Lehn. 1952. Differential emphasis in somatic response to stress. *Psychosom. Med.*, **14**, 71–81. [375]

LaForge, Rolfe, Timothy F. Leary, Herbert Naboisek, H. S. Coffey, and Mervin B. Freedman. 1954. The interpersonal dimension of personality: II. An objective study of repression. *J. Pers.*, **23**, 129–153. [166]

Lambert, William H., and Elizabeth C. Lambert. 1953. Some indirect effects of reward on children's size estimation. *J. abnorm. soc. Psychol.*, **48**, 507–510. [120]

——, R. L. Solomon, and P. Watson. 1949. Reinforcement and extinction as factor in size estimation. *J. exp. Psychol.*, **39**, 637–641. [120]

Landis, Judson T., Thomas Poffenberger, and Shirley Poffenberger. 1950. The effects of first pregnancy upon the sexual adjustment of 212 couples. *Amer. sociol. Rev.*, **15**, 766–772. [444]

Lane, R. E. 1955. Political personality and electoral choice. *Amer. pol. sci. Rev.*, **49**, 173–190. [255]

Lansing, John B., and Roger W. Heyns. 1959. Need affiliation and frequency of four types of communication. *J. abnorm. soc. Psychol.*, **58**, 365–372. [349]

Lantz, Beatrice. 1945. Some dynamic aspects of success and failure. *Psychol. Monogr.*, **59**, No. 1. [478]

Layton, Wilbur L. 1954. The variability of individuals' scores upon successive testings on the Minnesota Multiphasic Personality Inventory. *Educ. psychol. Measmt*, **14**, 634–640. [48]

Lazarsfeld, Paul F., and Wagner Thielens, Jr. 1958. *The academic mind.* Glencoe, Ill.: Free Press. [525]

Lazarus, R. S., C. W. Eriksen, and C. P. Fonda. 1951. Personality dynamics and auditory perceptual recognition. *J. Pers.*, **19**, 471–482. [123]

—— and Nicholas Longo. 1953. The consistency of psychological defenses against threat. *J. abnorm. soc. Psychol.*, **48**, 495–499. [144]

—— and R. A. McCleary. 1950. Autonomic discrimination without awareness: an interim report. *J. Pers.*, **18**, 171–179. [123]

——, Herbert Yousem, and David Arenberg. 1953. Hunger and perception. *J. Pers.*, **21**, 312–328. [121]

Leary, Timothy. 1955. The theory and measurement methodology of interpersonal communication. *Psychiatry*, **18**, 147–161. [166]

———. 1956. *Interpersonal diagnosis of personality*. New York: Ronald Press. [166]

——— and Hubert S. Coffey. 1955. Interpersonal diagnosis: some problems of methodology and validation. *J. abnorm. soc. Psychol.*, **50**, 110–124. [167]

Leavy, Stanley A., and L. Z. Freedman. 1956. Psychoneurosis and economic life. *Soc. Probl.*, **4**, 55–66. [501]

Lecky, Prescott. 1945. *Self-consistency: a theory of personality*. New York: Island Press Co-operative, Inc. [213, 305]

Leeds, Carroll H. 1950. A scale for measuring teacher-pupil attitudes and teacher-pupil rapport. *Psychol. Monogr.*, **64**, No. 6 (Whole No. 312). [461]

———. 1956. Teacher attitudes and temperament as a measure of teacher-pupil rapport. *J. appl. Psychol.*, **40**, 333–337. [461]

Leeper, Robert W. 1935. Study of a neglected portion of the field of learning—the development of sensory organization. *J. genet. Psychol.*, **46**, 41–75. [80]

———. 1953. What contributions might cognitive learning theory make to our understanding of personality? *J. Pers.*, **22**, 32–40. [76]

Leitsch, Mary, and Sibylle Escalona. 1949. The reactions of infants to stress. *Psychoanal. Stud. Child*, **3/4**, 121–140. [404]

LeMasters, E. E. 1957. *Modern courtship and marriage*. New York: Macmillan. [429, 437, 449]

LeShan, Lawrence L. 1952. Time orientation and social class. *J. abnorm. soc. Psychol.*, **47**, 589–592. [498]

Lesser, Gerald S. 1957. Relationship between overt and fantasy aggression as a function of maternal response to aggression. *J. abnorm. soc. Psychol.*, **55**, 218–221. [408]

Levine, J. M., and Gardner Murphy. 1943. Learning and forgetting of controversial material. *J. abnorm. soc. Psychol.*, **38**, 507–517. [245]

Levine, Seymour, J. A. Chevalier, and S. J. Korchin. 1956. Effects of early shock and handling on later avoidance learning. *J. Pers.*, **24**, 475–493. [95]

Levinson, Daniel J. 1949. An approach to the theory and measurement of ethnocentric ideology. *J. Psychol.*, **28**, 19–39. [152]

———. 1957. Authoritarian personality and foreign policy. *Conflict Resolution*, **1**, 37–47. [255]

——— and Phyllis Huffman. 1954. Traditional family ideology and its relation to personality. *J. Pers.*, **23**, 251–273. [416]

Levy, J., and Ruth Munroe. 1938. *The happy family*. New York: Knopf. [435]

Levy, Leon H. 1956. The meaning and generality of perceived actual-ideal discrepancies. *J. consult. Psychol.*, **20**, 396–398. [191]

Lewin, Kurt. 1935. *Dynamic theory of personality*. New York: McGraw-Hill. [284, 292]

———. 1938. Conceptual representation and measurement of psychological forces. *Contr. psychol. Theor.*, **1**, No. 4. Durham, N.C.: Duke Univer. Press. [115–117]

———. 1943. Defining the field at a given time. *Psychol. Rev.*, **50**, 292–310. [105]

———, R. Lippitt, and R. K. White. 1939. Patterns of aggressive behavior in experimentally created "social climates." *J. soc. Psychol.*, **10**, 271–300. [453, 454]

Lewinsohn, Peter M. 1956. Some individual differences in physiological reactivity to stress. *J. comp. physiol. Psychol.*, **49**, 271–277. [375]

Liddell, H. S. 1956. *Emotional hazards in animals and men*. Springfield, Ill.: Charles C Thomas. [95]

Likert, Rensis. 1932. A technique for the measurement of attitudes. *Arch. Psychol., N.Y.*, No. 140. [240]

Lindner, Harold. 1955. Psychology of the adult criminal. In G. J. Dudycha, *Psychology for law enforcement officers*. Springfield, Ill.: Charles C Thomas. [234]

Lindner, Robert M. 1944. *Rebel without a cause*. New York: Grune & Stratton. [233]

Lindzey, Gardner (Ed.). 1958. *Assessment of human motives*. New York: Rinehart. [155]

—— and Peter S. Herman. 1955. Thematic Apperception Test: a note on reliability and situational validity. *J. proj. Tech.*, **19**, 36–42. [60]

Linton, Harriet B. 1955. Dependence on external influence: correlates in perception, attitudes, and judgment. *J. abnorm. soc. Psychol.*, **51**, 502–507. [152, 258]

Lippitt, Ronald, Norman Polansky, and Sidney Rosen. 1952. The dynamics of power: a field study of social influence in groups of children. *Hum. Relat.*, **5**, 37–64. [127]

Lisansky, Edith S. 1956. The inter-examiner reliability of the Rorschach test. *J. proj. Tech.*, **20**, 310–317. [55]

Little, Kenneth B., and Edwin S. Shneidman. 1955. The validity of thematic projective technique interpretations. *J. Pers.*, **23**, 285–294. [60]

—— and ——. 1959. Congruencies among interpretations of psychological test and anamnestic data. *Psychol. Monogr.*, **73**, No. 6 (Whole No. 476). [60]

Littman, Richard A. 1956. Infantile experience and adult behavior in the white rat. *J. genet. Psychol.*, **88**, 11–24. [400]

——, R. C. A. Moore, and John Pierce-Jones. 1957. Social class differences in child rearing: a third community for comparison with Chicago and Newton. *Amer. soc. Rev.*, **22**, 694–704. [505]

Locke, Harvey J. 1951. *Predicting adjustment in marriage*. New York: Holt. [435, 437, 439, 442, 443, 445, 447, 448, 449]

—— and Georg Karlsson. 1952. Marital adjustment and prediction in Sweden and the United States. *Amer. soc. Rev.*, **17**, 10–17. [434, 445]

Loevinger, Jane. 1955. Some principles of personality measurement. *Educ. psychol. Measmt*, **15**, 3–17. [62]

Lofchie, Stanley H. 1955. The performance of adults under distraction stress: a developmental approach. *J. Psychol.*, **39**, 109–116. [130]

Lorr, Maurice, and Victor Fields. 1954. A factorial study of body types. *J. clin. Psychol.*, **10**, 182–185. [277]

Lovell, C. 1945. Study of the factor structure of thirteen personality variables. *Educ. psychol. Measmt*, **5**, 335–350. [166]

Lowenfeld, John, Seymour Rubenfeld, and George M. Guthrie. 1956. Verbal inhibition in subception. *J. gen. Psychol.*, **54**, 171–176. [123]

Lowrey, I. G. 1940. Personality distortion and early institutional care. *Amer. J. Orthopsychiat.*, **10**, 576–586. [401]

Lu, Yi-Chuang. 1952. Predicting roles in marriage. *Amer. J. Sociol.*, **58**, 51–55. [434]

Luchins, A. S. 1951. On recent usage of the einstellung-effect as a test of rigidity. *J. consult. Psychol.*, **4**, 89–94. [140]

Luft, Joseph. 1950. Implicit hypotheses and clinical prediction. *J. abnorm. soc. Psychol.*, **45**, 756–759. [36]

——. 1957. Monetary value and the perception of persons. *J. soc. Psychol.*, **46**, 245–251. [503]

Lundervold, Arne. 1952. An electromyographic investigation of tense and relaxed subjects. *J. nerv. ment. Dis.*, **115**, 512–525. [147]

Luria, A. R. 1932. *Nature of human conflicts*. New York: Liveright. [145]

Lyle, William H., Jr., and Eugene E. Levitt. 1955. Punitiveness, authoritarianism, and parental discipline of grade school children. *J. abnorm. soc. Psychol.*, **51**, 42–46. [416]

Lyman, Howard B. 1949. Differentiating attitudes of students at two high schools by use of a school attitude inventory. *Educ. psychol. Measmt*, **9**, 227–232. [451]

Lynd, R. S. 1939. *Knowledge for what?* Princeton, N.J.: Princeton Univer. Press. [517]

Lynn, R. 1957. Temperamental characteristics related to disparity of attainment in reading and arithmetic. *Brit. J. educ. Psychol.*, **27**, 62–67. [465]

Macfarlane, Jean W., Lucile Allen, and Marjorie P. Honzik. 1954. *A developmental study of the behavior problems of normal children between twenty-one months and fourteen years.* Berkeley, Calif.: Univer. of California Press. Pp. vii, 221. [176, 177]

MacKinnon, Donald W. 1944. The structure of personality. In J. McV. Hunt, *Personality and behavior disorders.* New York: Ronald. [272]

———. 1958. *An assessment study of air force officers. Part V. Summary and applications.* Wright Air Development Center, Personnel Laboratory, Lackland Air Force Base, Texas. [221]

MacKinnon, William J., and Richard Centers. 1956. Authoritarianism and urban stratification. *Amer. J. Sociol.*, **61**, 610–620. [514]

MacLeod, Robert B. 1949. Perceptual constancy and the problem of motivation. *Canad. J. Psychol.*, **3**, 57–66. [333]

Maddy, Nancy Ruth. 1943. Comparison of children's personality traits, attitudes, and intelligence with parental occupation. *Genet. Psychol. Monogr.*, **27**, 3–65. [501]

Maier, Norman R. F. 1949. *Frustration: the study of behavior without a goal.* New York: McGraw-Hill. [408]

———. 1956. Frustration theory: restatement and extension. *Psychol. Rev.*, **63**, 370–388. [408]

Mailloux, Noel. 1956. Determinismo psichico, libertá e sviluppo della personalitá. *Arch. Psicol. Neur. Psich.*, **17**, 853–865. [522]

Malinowski, B. 1927. *Sex and repression in savage society.* New York: Harcourt, Brace. [352]

Malloy, John. 1955. Prediction of college achievement with the life experience inventory. *Educ. psychol. Measmt*, **15**, 170–180. [469]

Malmo, Robert B., A. Arthur Smith, and Werner A. Kohlmeyer. 1956. Motor manifestation of conflict in interview: a case study. *J. abnorm. soc. Psychol.*, **52**, 268–271. [147]

——— and Harvey Wallerstein. 1955. Rigidity and reactive inhibition. *J. abnorm. soc. Psychol.*, **50**, 345–348. [376]

———, ———, and Charles Shagass. 1953. Headache proneness and mechanisms of motor conflict in psychiatric patients. *J. Pers.*, **22**, 163–187. [147]

Mandler, George, and Irwin Kremen. 1958. Autonomic feedback: a correlational study. *J. Pers.*, **26**, 388–399. [378]

———, Jean M. Mandler, and Ellen T. Uviller. 1958. Autonomic feedback: the perception of autonomic activity. *J. abnorm. soc. Psychol.*, **56**, 367–373. [79]

Manis, Melvin. 1955. Social interaction and the self concept. *J. abnorm. soc. Psychol.*, **51**, 362–370. [189, 195, 424]

Mannheim, Betty F. 1957. Influence of reference groups and membership groups on the self-image. Urbana, Ill.: Group Effectiveness Res. Lab., Univer. of Illinois. [189, 424]

Marquis, Dorothy P. 1931. Can conditioned responses be established in the newborn infant? *J. genet. Psychol.*, **39**, 479–492. [418]

Marshall, James. 1943. *The freedom to be free.* New York: John Day. [534]

Martin, R. F., and C. S. Hall. 1941. Emotional behavior in the rat. V. Incidence of behavior derangements resulting from air-blast stimulation in emotional and nonemotional strains of rats. *J. comp. Psychol.*, **32**, 191–204. [367]

Martin, William E., and Celia Stendler. 1953. *Child development.* New York: Harcourt, Brace. [425]

Martire, John G. 1956. Relationships between the self concept and differences in the strength and generality of achievement motivation. *J. Pers.*, **24**, 364–375. [348]

Marzi, A., and U. Teodori. 1955. Ricerche sulla personalità in alcune endocrinopatie. *Rassegna di Neurologia vegetativa*, **11**, 87–161. [386]

Masling, Joseph M. 1957. The effects of warm and cold interaction on the interpretation of a projective protocol. *J. proj. Tech.*, **21**, 377–383. [62]

Maslow, A. H. 1936. Role of dominance in social and sexual behavior of infra-human primates. III. *J. genet. Psychol.*, **48**, 310–338. [328]

———. 1939. Dominance, personality, and social behavior in women. *J. soc. Psychol.*, **10**, 3–39. [199, 328]

———. 1942. Self-esteem (dominance-feeling) and sexuality in women. *J. soc. Psychol.*, **16**, 259–294. [328]

———, E. Hirsch, M. Stein, and I. Honigmann. 1945. A clinically derived test for measuring psychological security-insecurity. *J. genet. Psychol.*, **33**, 21–41. [197]

———. 1954. *Motivation and personality*. New York: Harper. [104, 206, 298, 301, 307, 350]

Masserman, J. H., and H. T. Carmichael. 1938. Diagnosis and prognosis in psychiatry. *J. ment. Sci.*, **84**, 893–946. [49]

Matthews, Ravenna, Curtis Hardyck, and Theodore R. Sarbin. 1953. Self-organization as a factor in the performance of selected cognitive tasks. *J. abnorm. soc. Psychol.*, **48**, 500–502. [202]

May, Mark A. 1929. The adult in the community. In C. Murchison, *Foundations of experimental psychology*. Worcester, Mass.: Clark Univer. Press. [5]

May, Rollo, et al. 1958. *Existence: a new dimension in psychiatry and psychology*. New York: Basic Books. [185]

May, W. T., and W. S. Wells. 1955. Manifest anxiety as related to some perceptual modes. *Percept. mot. Skills*, **5**, 127–131. [142]

Mead, G. H. 1934. *Mind, self and society*. Chicago: Univer. of Chicago Press. [185]

Mead, Margaret. 1935. *Sex and temperament in three primitive societies*. New York: Morrow. [22, 528]

———. 1939. *From the South Seas*. New York: Morrow. [353, 429]

Mehlman, Benjamin. 1952. The reliability of psychiatric diagnoses. *J. abnorm. soc. Psychol.*, **47**, 577–578. [49]

——— and Stephen Lee Whiteman. 1955. The relationship between certain pictures of the Rosenzweig picture-frustration study and corresponding behavioral situations. *J. clin. Psychol.*, **11**, 15–19. [60]

Meltzer, H. 1936. Economic security and children's attitudes to parents. *Amer. J. Orthopsychiat.*, **6**, 590–608. [501]

———. 1941. Sex differences in parental preference patterns. *Charact. & Pers.*, **10**, 114–128. [356]

Melzack, Ronald. 1954. Genesis of emotional behavior: an experimental study of the dog. *J. comp. physiol. Psychol.*, **47**, 166–168. [95]

——— and T. H. Scott. 1957. The effects of early experience on the response to pain. *J. comp. physiol. Psychol.*, **50**, 155–161. [400]

——— and William R. Thompson. 1956. Effects of early experience on social behavior. *Canad. J. Psychol.*, **10**, 82–90. [400]

Menninger, Karl A. 1954. Homeostatic regulatory function of the ego. Part II. Regulatory device of the ego under stress. *J. Amer. Psychoanal. Ass.*, **2**, 280–310. [70]

Menzies, R. 1941. Further studies of conditioned vasomotor responses in human subjects. *J. exp. Psychol.*, **29**, 457–482. [98]

Meyer, Henry D., and Glenn L. Pressel. 1954. Personality test scores in the management hierarchy. *J. appl. Psychol.*, **38**, 73–80. [490]

Meyer, Mortimer M., and Ruth S. Tolman. 1955. Correspondence between attitudes and images of parental figures in TAT stories and in therapeutic interviews. *J. consult. Psychol.*, **19**, 79–82. [61]

Michael, Archer. 1955. A conflict interpretation of certain perceptual dynamics. Unpublished doctoral dissertation, Univer. of Illinois. [121]

Milbank Memorial Fund. 1952. *Biology of mental health and disease.* New York: Hoeber-Harper. [372, 379, 386, 396]

Miller, Christine. 1954. Consistency of cognitive behavior as a function of personality characteristics. *J. Pers.,* **23,** 233–249. [144]

Miller, Daniel R., and Guy E. Swanson. 1958. *The changing American parent: a study in the Detroit area.* New York: Wiley. [425, 506, 515]

Miller, James G. 1940. Role of motivation in learning without awareness. *Amer. J. Psychol.,* **53,** 229–239. [123]

Miller, N. E. 1948a. Theory and experiment relating psychoanalytic displacement to stimulus-response generalization. *J. abnorm. soc. Psychol.,* **43,** 155–178. [114]

———. 1948b. Studies of fear as an acquirable drive: I. Fear as motivation and fear-reduction as reinforcement in the learning of new responses. *J. exp. Psychol.,* **38,** 89–101. [295]

——— and R. Bugelski. 1948. Minor studies of aggression: II. The influence of frustration imposed by the in-group on attitudes expressed toward out-groups. *J. Psychol.,* **25,** 437–442. [247, 512]

——— and J. Dollard. 1941. *Social learning and imitation.* New Haven, Conn.: Yale Univer. Press. [126]

Miner, John B., and John E. Culver. 1955. Some aspects of the executive personality. *J. appl. Psychol.,* **39,** 348–353. [490]

Mintz, Elizabeth E. 1957. Personal problems and diagnostic errors of clinical psychologists. *J. proj. Tech.,* **21,** 123–128. [62]

Mintzer, S., and S. S. Sargent. 1939. The relationship between family economic status and some personality traits of college students. *Sch. and Soc.,* **49,** 322–324. [501]

Mira, E. 1940. Myokinetic psychodiagnosis. *Proc. Roy. Soc. Med.,* **33,** 173–194. [149]

Missildine, W. H. 1946. The emotional background of thirty children with reading disabilities with emphasis on its coercive elements. *Nerv. Child,* **5,** 263–272. [465]

Mitchell, James V. 1955. Factor analysis of a "Guess Who" questionnaire designed to identify significant behavior patterns in children. *J. Pers.,* **24,** 376–386. [31]

Miyamoto, Frank S., and Sanford M. Dornbusch. 1956. A test of interactionist hypotheses of self-conception. *Amer. J. Sociol.,* **61,** 399–403. [189]

Moeller, George, and Mortimer H. Applezweig. 1957. A motivational factor in conformity. *J. abnorm. soc. Psychol.,* **55,** 114–120. [152]

Moffitt, J. Weldon. 1953. Perceptual variables as influenced by manifest and threat-induced anxiety. Unpublished doctoral dissertation, Univer. of Illinois. [142]

——— and Ross Stagner. 1955. Perceptual rigidity and closure as functions of anxiety. *J. abnorm. soc. Psychol.,* **52,** 354–357. [83, 123, 476]

Monnerot, Jules. 1953. *Sociology and psychology of communism.* Boston: Beacon Press. [534]

Monro, A. B. 1955. Psychiatric types: a Q-technique study of 200 patients. *J. ment. Sci.,* **101,** 330–343. [271]

Montalto, F. D. 1946. Application of group Rorschach technique to problems of achievement in college. *J. clin. Psychol.,* **2,** 254–260. [467]

Mooney, C. M. 1954. A factorial study of closure. *Canad. J. Psychol.,* **8,** 51–60. [83]

Moreno, Florence B. 1942. Sociometric status of children in nursery school group. *Sociometry,* **5,** 395–411. [31]

Moreno, J. L. 1934. Who shall survive? *Nerv. ment. Dis. Monogr. Ser.,* No. 58. [31]

Morgan, Clifford T. 1957. Physiological mechanisms of motivation. In Marshall R. Jones (Ed.), *Nebraska symposium on motivation.* Lincoln, Neb.: Univer. of Nebraska Press. [292, 298]

Morgan, John J. B. 1924. *Psychology of the unadjusted school child.* New York: Macmillan. [465]

Morris, Charles. 1948. Physique and cultural patterns. In Clyde Kluckhohn and Henry A. Murray, *Personality in nature, society and culture.* New York: Knopf. [280]

———. 1956. *Varieties of human value.* Chicago: Univer. of Chicago Press. [261, 262, 263]

——— and Lyle V. Jones. 1955. Value scales and dimensions. *J. abnorm. soc. Psychol.,* **51,** 523–535. [262]

Moustakas, Clark E. 1955. Frequency and intensity of negative attitudes expressed in play therapy: a comparison of well-adjusted and disturbed young children. *J. genet. Psychol.,* **86,** 309–325. [167]

Mouton, Jane Srygley, Robert R. Blake, and Benjamin Fruchter. 1955. The validity of sociometric responses. *Sociometry,* **18,** 181–206. [31]

Mowrer, Harriet E. 1935. *Personality adjustment and domestic discord.* New York: American Book. [432]

Mowrer, O. H. 1939a. Authoritarianism vs. "self-government" in the management of children's aggressive (anti-social) reactions as a preparation for citizenship in a democracy. *J. soc. Psychol.,* **10,** 121–126. [456]

———. 1939b. A stimulus-response analysis of anxiety and its role as a reinforcing agent. *Psychol. Rev.,* **46,** 553–566. [295]

———. 1950a. *Learning theory and personality dynamics.* New York: Ronald. [99]

———. 1950b. Pain, punishment, guilt and anxiety. In P. Hoch and J. Zubin, *Anxiety.* New York: Grune & Stratton. [370]

——— and C. Kluckhohn. 1944. Dynamic theory of personality. In J. McV. Hunt, *Personality and behavior disorders.* New York: Ronald. [28]

Mumford, Lewis. 1954. *In the name of sanity.* New York: Harcourt, Brace. [534]

———. 1956. *The transformations of man.* New York: Harper. [304, 534]

Mummery, Dorothy V. 1954. Family backgrounds of assertive and non-assertive children. *Child Develpm.,* **25,** 63–80. [407]

Mundy-Castle, A. C. 1955. The electro-encephalogram in relation to temperament. *Acta Psychol.,* **11,** 397–411. [377]

Munroe, Ruth L. 1945. Prediction of the adjustment and academic performance of college students by a modification of the Rorschach method. *Appl. Psychol. Monogr.,* No. 7. [467]

———. 1946. Rorschach findings on college students showing different constellations of subscores on A.C.E. *J. consult. Psychol.,* **10,** 301–316. [466]

———. 1955. *Schools of psychoanalytic thought.* New York: Dryden. [106, 331]

Murchison, Carl. 1935. Experimental measurement of a social hierarchy in *Gallus domesticus. J. gen. Psychol.,* **12,** 3–39. [328]

Murphy, Gardner. 1939. The research task of social psychology. *J. soc. Psychol.,* **10,** 107–120. [520]

———. 1945. *Human nature and enduring peace.* Boston: Houghton Mifflin. [534]

———. 1947. *Personality: a biosocial approach to origins and structure.* New York: Harper. [26, 110, 134, 185, 213, 322, 360, 396]

———. 1956. Affect and perceptual learning. *Psychol. Rev.,* **63,** 1–15. [80]

———. 1958. *Human potentialities.* New York: Basic Books. [534]

——— and F. Jensen. 1932. *Approaches to personality.* New York: Coward-McCann. [272, 283, 286]

Murphy, J. V., and R. E. Miller. 1956. The manipulation of dominance in monkeys with conditioned fear. *J. abnorm. soc. Psychol.,* **53,** 244–248. [95]

Murphy, Lois B. 1937. *Social behavior and child personality.* New York: Columbia Univer. Press. [299]

———. 1956. *Personality in young children.* Vol. I. *Methods for the study of personality in young children.* New York: Basic Books. [425]

Murphy, Lois B. and Henry Ladd. 1944. *Emotional factors in learning.* New York: Columbia Univer. Press. [484]

Murray, Henry A. 1933. Effect of fear upon estimates of maliciousness of other personalities. *J. soc. Psychol.,* **4,** 310–329. [121]

———. 1938. *Explorations in personality.* New York: Oxford Univer. Press. [35, 53, 58, 347, 348, 459, 495]

Mussen, Paul Henry, and Mary C. Jones. 1957. Self-conceptions, motivations, and interpersonal attitudes of late- and early-maturing boys. *Child Develpm.,* **28,** 243–256. [385]

——— and J. Kagan. 1958. Group conformity and perceptions of parents. *Child Develpm.,* **29,** 57–60. [416]

——— and Anne B. Wyszynski. 1952. Personality and political participation. *Hum. Relat.,* **5,** 65–82. [255]

Myerson, A. 1939. The attitude of neurologists, psychiatrists, and psychologists toward psychoanalysis. *Amer. J. Psychiat.,* **96,** 623–641. [325]

McAdam, W., and J. E. Orme. 1954. Personality traits and the normal electro-encephalogram. *J. ment. Sci.,* **100,** 913–921. [377]

McArthur, Charles. 1955. Personality differences between middle and upper classes. *J. abnorm. soc. Psychol.,* **50,** 247–254. [504]

McCandless, Boyd, and Harold D. Holloway. 1955. Race prejudice and intolerance of ambiguity in children. *J. abnorm. soc. Psychol.,* **51,** 692–693. [255]

McCary, J. L. (Ed.) 1956. *Psychology of personality: six modern approaches.* New York: Logos Press. [86, 202, 309, 311]

McClelland, David C. 1951. *Personality.* New York: Sloane. [28, 279, 358]

——— (Ed.) 1955. *Studies in motivation.* New York: Appleton-Century-Crofts. [348]

——— and J. W. Atkinson. 1948. The projective expression of needs: I. The effect of different intensities of the hunger drive on perception. *J. Psychol.,* **25,** 205–232. [121]

———, ———, R. A. Clark, and E. L. Lowell. 1953. *The achievement motive.* New York: Appleton-Century-Crofts. [347, 348]

McClosky, Herbert. Conservatism and personality. 1958. *Amer. Pol. Sci. Rev.,* **52,** 27–45. [255–257]

McDougall, William. 1908. *Introduction to social psychology.* London: Methuen. [289, 298, 307]

McIntyre, Charles J. 1952. Acceptance by others and its relation to acceptance of self and others. *J. abnorm. soc. Psychol.,* **47,** 624–625. [198]

McKeachie, W. J., Donald Pollie, and Joseph Speisman. 1955. Relieving anxiety in classroom examinations. *J. abnorm. soc. Psychol.,* **50,** 93–98. [476]

McKinney, Fred. 1958. *Counseling for personality adjustment in schools and colleges.* Boston: Houghton Mifflin. [26]

McKinnon, Kathern Mae. 1942. Consistency and change in behavior manifestations. *Child Develpm. Monogr.,* No. 30. New York: Teachers College. [176, 177]

McQuary, John P., and W. E. Truax. 1955. An under-achievement scale. *J. educ. Res.,* **48,** 393–399. [469]

McQuitty, Louis L. 1949. Diversity of self-endorsements as a measure of individual differences in personality. *Educ. psychol. Measmt,* **9,** 3–14. [192]

———. 1950. A measure of personality integration in relation to the concept of the self. *J. Pers.,* **18,** 461–482. [192, 271]

———. 1956. Agreement analysis: classifying persons by predominant patterns of responses. *Brit. J. stat. Psychol.,* **9,** 5–16. [271]

———. 1957. Elementary linkage analysis for isolating orthogonal and oblique types and typal relevances. *Educ. psychol. Measmt,* **17,** 207–229. [270]

Neilon, Patricia. 1948. Shirley's babies after 15 years: a personality study. *J. genet. Psychol.*, **73**, 175–186. [176]

Nelson, Erland N. P. 1954. Persistence of attitudes of college students fourteen years later. *Psychol. Monogr.*, **68**, No. 2 (Whole No. 373). [248, 249]

Nettler, Gwynn. 1957. A measure of alienation. *Amer. sociol. Rev.*, **22**, 670–677. [189]

Newcomb, Theodore M. 1943. *Personality and social change.* New York: Dryden. [250]

―――― and G. Svehla. 1937. Intra-family relationships in attitude. *Sociometry*, **1**, 180–205. [248]

Newman, S. H., J. M. Bobbitt, and D. C. Cameron. 1946. The reliability of the interview method in an officer candidate evaluation program. *Amer. Psychologist*, **1**, 103–109. [33]

Norman, Ralph D. 1953. Interrelationships among acceptance-rejection, self-other-identity, insight into self, and realistic perceptions of others. *J. soc. Psychol.*, **37**, 205–235. [198]

Northway, Mary L. 1940. The concept of "schema." *Brit. J. Psychol.*, **30**, 316–325; **31**, 22–36. [77]

Nunnally, J. C. 1955. An investigation of some propositions of self-conception: the case of Miss Sun. *J. abnorm. soc. Psychol.*, **50**, 87–92. [190]

Nuthman, Anne M. 1957. Conditioning of a response class on a personality test. *J. abnorm. soc. Psychol.*, **54**, 19–23. [101]

Nye, Ivan F. 1958. *Family relationships and delinquent behavior.* New York: Wiley. [410]

Ojemann, R. H., and F. R. Wilkinson. 1939. Effect on pupil growth of an increase in teachers' understanding of pupil behavior. *J. exp. Educ.*, **8**, 143–147. [463]

Olds, James, and Peter Milner. 1954. Positive reinforcement produced by electrical stimulation of septal area and other regions of rat brain. *J. comp. physiol. Psychol.*, **47**, 419–427. [90, 299]

Orlansky, H. 1949. Infant care and personality. *Psychol. Bull.*, **46**, 1–48. [402]

Osgood, Charles E., and George Suci. 1952. A measure of relation determined by both mean difference and profile information. *Psychol. Bull.*, **49**, 251–262. [271]

―――, ―――, and Percy W. Tannenbaum. 1957. *Measurement of meaning.* Urbana, Ill.: Univer. of Illinois Press. [47, 238, 241, 244]

OSS Assessment Staff. 1948. *Assessment of men.* New York: Rinehart. [39]

Otis, Jack. 1954. Some problems in the provision of psychotherapeutic services in institutions of higher learning. *Bulletin, Amer. Assn. Univer. Profs.*, **40** (3), 456–471. [49]

Owens, William A., and Wilma C. Johnson. 1949. Some measured personality traits of collegiate underachievers. *J. educ. Psychol.*, **40**, 41–46. [469]

Packard, Vance. 1959. *The status seekers.* New York: McKay. [491]

Page, H., J. Thurston, C. Nuthman, G. Calden, and T. Lorenz. 1955. An empirical study of the relationship of four classes of body habitus to responses on the MMPI. *Psychol. Rep.*, **1**, 159–165. [277]

Parsons, Talcott, and R. F. Bales. 1955. *Family, socialization and interaction process.* Glencoe, Ill.: Free Press. [425]

―――― and Edward A. Shils. 1952. Values, motives and systems of action. In Parsons and Shils (Eds.), *Toward a general theory of action.* Cambridge, Mass.: Harvard Univer. Press. [300]

Pastore, Nicholas. 1952. Role of arbitrariness in the frustration-aggression hypothesis. *J. abnorm. soc. Psychol.*, **47**, 728–731. [113]

Patterson, C. H. 1943. Note on Bernreuter personality of mothers and some measures of child personality. *J. soc. Psychol.*, **17**, 89–92. [417, 501]

Pemberton, Carol L. 1951. Personality inventory data related to ACE subscores. *J. consult. Psychol.*, **15**, 160–162. [466]

Perlmutter, Howard V. 1954. Some characteristics of the xenophilic personality. *J. Psychol.*, **38**, 291–300. [250]

Peters, James S. 1957. Socio-economic egocentrism in delinquents and non-delinquents. *Purdue Univer. Stud. Higher Educ.*, No. 85. [226]

Peterson, T. D. 1936. The relationship between certain attitudes of parents and children. Bull. Purdue Univer., **37**, 127–144. [248]

Philip, B. R. 1949. The frame of reference concept. *Canad. J. Psychol.*, **3**, 73–79. [78]

Phillips, E. Lakin. 1951. Parent-child similarities in personality disturbances. *J. clin. Psychol.*, **7**, 188–190. [417]

Pincus, Gregory, and Hudson Hoagland. 1950. Adrenal cortical responses to stress in normal men and in those with personality disorders. *Amer. J. Psychiat.*, **106**, 641–650. [380]

Pinneau, Samuel R. 1950. A critique of the articles by Margaret Ribble. *Child Develpm.*, **21**, 203–228. [402]

Plant, J. S. 1937. *Personality and the cultural pattern.* New York: Commonwealth Fund. [425]

Porter, Blaine M. 1955. The relationship between marital adjustment and parental acceptance of children. *J. Home Econ.*, **47**, 157–164. [445]

Porteus, Stanley D. 1945. Q-scores, temperament and delinquency. *J. soc. Psychol.*, **21**, 81–103. [230]

Pressey, Sidney L., and Francis Robinson. 1944. *Psychology and the new education.* New York: Harper [457]

———, ———, and John E. Horrocks. 1959. *Psychology in education.* New York: Harper. [483]

Preston, Malcolm G., and J. A. Bayton. 1941. Differential effect of a social variable upon three levels of aspiration. *J. exp. Psychol.*, **29**, 351–369. [209]

———, William L. Peltz, Emily Hartshorne Mudd, and Hazel B. Froscher. 1952. Impressions of personality as a function of marital conflict. *J. abnorm. soc. Psychol.*, **47**, 326–336. [440]

Prince, Morton. 1924. *The unconscious.* (2nd ed.) New York: Macmillan. [4]

Proshansky, H. M. 1943. Projective method for the study of attitudes. *J. abnorm. soc. Psychol.*, **38**, 393–395. [242]

Pullen, Maxwell S. 1952. Rigidity in adult male psychotics and its modification by convulsive shock therapy. Unpublished doctoral dissertation, Univer. of Illinois. [139]

Purcell, Kenneth. 1956. The TAT and anti-social behavior. *J. consult. Psychol.*, **20**, 449–456. [60]

Rabin, A. I. 1957. Personality maturity of kibbutz (Israeli collective settlement) children and non-kibbutz children as reflected in Rorschach findings. *J. proj. Tech.*, **21**, 148–153. [402]

Raines, G. N., and J. H. Rohrer. 1955. The operational matrix of psychiatric practice: I. Consistency and variability in interview impressions of different psychiatrists. *Amer. J. Psychiat.*, **111**, 721–733. [49]

Rank, O. 1929. *The trauma of birth.* London: Routledge & Kegan Paul, Ltd. [87]

Raskin, Allen. 1954. A learning theory paradigm for perceptual vigilance and perceptual defense phenomena. *Dissertation Abst.*, **14**, 2130. [122]

Ray, Oakley S. 1959. Personality factors in motor learning and reminiscence. *J. abnorm. soc. Psychol.*, **59**, 199–203. [270]

Reece, Michael M. 1954. The effect of shock on recognition thresholds. *J. abnorm. soc. Psychol.*, **49**, 165–172. [122]

Reich, Wilhelm. 1949. *Character analysis.* New York: Orgone Press. [147]

Remmers, H. H. 1933. Generalized attitude scaling technique. *Psychol. Bull.*, **30**, 719–720. [239]

Ribble, Margaret. 1944. Infantile experience in relation to personality development. In J. McV. Hunt, *Personality and behavior disorders.* New York: Ronald. [401]

Riesen, Austin H. 1947. The development of visual perception in man and chimpanzee. *Sci.* **106,** 107–108. [400]

Riesman, David. 1958. *Constraint and variety in American education.* New York: Doubleday. [461, 481]

Riess, Bernard F., David M. Spain, and Norman Molomut. 1955. Effect of sub-convulsive audiogenic stress on recovery from physiological damage. *Psych. Rep.,* **1,** 267–275. [394]

Rimoldi, Horacio J. A. 1951. Personal tempo. *J. abnorm. soc. Psychol.,* **46,** 283–303. [148]

Roback, A. A. 1957. *Freudiana.* Cambridge: Science-Art Publ. [149]

Roberts, Alan H., and Milton Rokeach. 1956. Anomie, authoritarianism, and prejudice: a replication. *Amer. J. Sociol.,* **61,** 355–358. [513, 514]

Roe, Anne. 1956. *Psychology of occupations.* New York: Wiley. [497, 515]

Roessel, Fred P. 1954. Minnesota Multiphasic Personality Inventory results for high school drop-outs and graduates. *Dissertation Abst.,* **14,** 942–943. [467]

Rogers, Carl R. 1942. *Counseling and psychotherapy.* Boston: Houghton Mifflin. [17]

———. 1951. *Client-centered therapy.* Boston: Houghton Mifflin. [305]

Rokeach, Milton. 1954. The nature and meaning of dogmatism. *Psychol. Rev.,* **61,** 194–204. [251, 252]

Rorschach, Herman. 1921. *Psychodiagnostik.* Leipzig: Ernst Bircher Verlag. [52]

———. 1942. *Psychodiagnostics.* (Trans. by Paul Lemkau and Bernard Kronenberg.) Berne, Switzerland: Huber Verlag. [56]

Rosen, Alexander C. 1954. Change in perceptual threshold as a protective function of the organism. *J. Pers.,* **23,** 182–194. [122]

Rosen, Hjalmar, and Ruth A. H. Rosen. 1957. Personality variables and role in a union business agent group. *J. appl. Psychol.,* **41,** 131–136. [492]

Rosenzweig, Saul. 1943. An experimental study of "repression" with special reference to need-persistive and ego-defensive reactions to frustration. *J. exp. Psychol.,* **32,** 64–74. [496]

———. 1944a. An outline of frustration theory. In J. McV. Hunt, *Personality and behavior disorders.* New York: Ronald. [496]

———. 1944b. Converging approaches to personality. *Psychol. Rev.,* **51,** 248–256. [330]

———. 1945. The picture-association method and its application in a study of reactions to frustration. *J. Pers.,* **14,** 3–23. [61, 496]

———. 1950. Levels of behavior in psychodiagnosis with special reference to the picture frustration study. *Amer. J. Orthopsychiat.,* **20,** 63–72. [341]

Rudin, Stanley A. 1955. Influence of context on the perception of complex stimuli. Unpublished doctoral dissertation, Univer. of Illinois. [203]

——— and Ross Stagner. 1958. Figure-ground phenomena in the perception of physical and social stimuli. *J. Psychol.,* **45,** 213–225. [203]

Russell, Ivan L., and W. A. Thalman. 1955. Personality: does it influence teachers' marks? *J. educ. Res.,* **48,** 561–564. [464]

Ryan, D. G., and E. Wandt. 1952. Factor analysis of observed teacher behaviors in secondary school: a study of criterion data. *Educ. psychol. Measmt,* **12,** 574–586. [452, 462]

Sandin, A. A. 1944. Social and emotional adjustments of regularly promoted and non-promoted pupils. *Child Develpm. Monogr.,* No. 32. New York: Teachers College. [457]

Sanford, Nevitt R. 1937. Effects of abstinence from food upon imaginal processes: a further study. *J. Psychol.,* **3,** 145–159. [121]

Sanford, Nevitt R. 1952. Family impact on personality: the point of view of a psychoanalyst. In J. E. Hulett, Jr. and Ross Stagner (Eds.), *Problems of social psychology*. Urbana, Ill.: Univer. of Illinois Press. [334]

———. 1956a. Personality development during the college years. *J. soc. Issues*, **12** (4), 3–69. [481]

———. 1956b. Surface and depth in the individual personality. *Psychol. Rev.*, **63**, 349–359. [163]

Sappenfield, Bert R. 1954. *Personality dynamics: an integrative psychology of adjustment*. New York: Knopf. [126]

Sarason, Seymour B. 1953. *Psychological problems in mental deficiency*. (2nd ed.) New York: Harper. [475]

Saul, Leon J., H. Davis, and P. A. Davis. 1949. Psychologic correlations with the electroencephalogram. *Psychosom. Med.*, **11**, 361–376. [377]

Schaffer, Robert H. 1953. Job satisfaction as related to need satisfaction in work. *Psychol. Monogr.*, **67**, No. 14 (Whole No. 364). [495]

Scheerer, Martin. 1953. Personality functioning and cognitive psychology. *J. Pers.*, **22**, 1–16. [333]

Schiller, L. 1942. Ganzheitliche Auffassung und Persönlichkeitstypus. *Z. Psychol.*, **153**, 43–80. [138]

Schjelderup-Ebbe, T. 1935. Social behavior of birds. In C. Murchison, *Handbook of social psychology*. Worcester, Mass.: Clark Univer. Press. [328]

Schützenberger, M. P. 1954. A tentative classification of goal-seeking behaviours. *J. ment. Sci.*, **100**, 97–102. [345]

Schwilck, Gene L. 1956. An experimental study of the effectiveness of direct and indirect methods of character education. *Union Coll. Stud. Char. Res.*, **1**, (14), 201–229. [217]

Scodel, Alvin. 1957. Heterosexual somatic preference and fantasy dependency. *J. consult. Psychol.*, **21**, 371–374. [430]

Searle, Lloyd V. 1949. The organization of hereditary maze-brightness and maze-dullness. *Genet. Psychol. Monogr.*, **39**, 279–325. [369]

Sears, Pauline S. 1940. Levels of aspiration in academically successful and unsuccessful children. *J. abnorm. soc. Psychol.*, **35**, 498–536. [478]

Sears, Robert R. 1936. Experimental studies of projection: I. Attribution of traits. *J. soc. Psychol.*, **7**, 151–163. [125]

———. 1950. Relation of fantasy aggression to interpersonal aggression. *Child Develpm.*, **21**, 5–6. [411]

———, Eleanor E. Maccoby, and Harry Levin. 1957. *Patterns of child rearing*. Evanston, Ill.: Row, Peterson. [405, 412, 425, 506, 515]

Selye, Hans. 1956. *The stress of life*. New York: McGraw-Hill. [86, 111, 129, 134, 395]

Sen, Amya. 1953. A preliminary study of the Thematic Apperception Test. *Brit. J. stat. Psychol.*, **6**, 91–100. [60]

Seward, John P. 1953. How are motives learned? *Psychol. Rev.*, **60**, 99–110. [332]

———. 1956. Drive, incentive, and reinforcement. *Psychol. Rev.*, **63**, 195–203. [332]

Sewell, William H., and Archie O. Haller. 1956. Social status and personality adjustment of the child. *Sociometry*, **19**, 114–125. [501]

Shaffer, Laurance F., and Edward J. Shoben. 1956. *The psychology of adjustment*. (2nd ed.) Boston: Houghton Mifflin. [26, 126, 134]

Shaw, Franklin J., and Robert S. Ort. 1953. *Personal adjustment in the American culture*. New York: Harper. [126]

Sheffield, Fred D., J. J. Wulff, and R. Backer. 1951. Reward value of copulation without sex drive reduction. *J. comp. physiol. Psychol.*, **44**, 3–8. [294]

Sheldon, William H. 1940. *Varieties of human physique*. New York: Harper. [275]

Sheldon, William H. 1942. Varieties of temperament. New York: Harper. [91, 223, 275, 286, 293, 299, 369, 371]

———. 1944. Constitutional factors in personality. In J. McV. Hunt, *Personality and the behavior disorders.* New York: Ronald. [274, 277]

———. 1949. *Varieties of delinquent youth.* New York: Harper. [228, 229]

Sherman, Arthur W., Jr. 1948. Personality factors in the psychological weaning of college women. *Educ. psychol. Measmt,* **8,** 249–256. [423]

Sherman, Mandel. 1927. The differentiation of emotional responses in infants: I. Judgments of emotional responses from motion picture views and from actual observations. *J. comp. Psychol.,* **7,** 265–284. [93]

Shils, Edward A. 1954. Authoritarianism: "right" and "left." In Richard Christie and Marie Jahoda (Eds.), *Studies in scope and method of "The authoritarian personality."* Glencoe, Ill.: Free Press. Pp. 24–49. [251]

Shipley, T. E., Jr., and J. Veroff. 1952. A projective measure of need for affiliation. *J. exp. Psychol.,* **43,** 349–356. [349]

Shipton, Janet, and Walter W. Grey. 1957. Les relations entre les activités alpha, les modes de pensée et les affinités sociales. *EEG clin. Neurophysiol.,* Suppl. 6, pp. 183–202. [377]

Shirley, M. M. 1933. *The first two years of life.* Minneapolis: Univer. of Minnesota Press. [176]

Shneidman, Edwin S. 1947. The Make-A-Picture-Story (MAPS) projective personality test: a preliminary report. *J. consult. Psychol.,* **11,** 315–325. [53]

Shoben, Edward J., Jr. 1949. The assessment of parental attitudes in relation to child adjustment. *Genet. Psychol. Monogr.,* **39,** 101–148. [472]

Silverman, A. J., S. I. Cohen, G. D. Zuidema, and C. S. Lazar. 1957. Prediction of physiological stress tolerance from projective tests: "The Focused Thematic Test." *J. proj. Tech.,* **21,** 189–193. [392]

Silverman, Lloyd H. 1958. A Q-sort study of the validity of evaluations made from projective techniques. Unpublished doctoral dissertation, New York Univer. [190]

Simpson, James E. 1956. The influence of auditory stimulation on aniseikonic perception: I. A. preliminary study. *J. Psychol.,* **41,** 235–241. [121, 123]

Sims, Verner M. 1954. Relations between the social-class identification and personality adjustment of a group of high school and college students. *J. soc. Psychol.,* **40,** 323–327. [499]

Skinner, B. F. 1953. *Science and behavior.* New York: Macmillan. [102]

Smith, George Horsley. 1954. Personality scores and the personal distance effect. *J. soc. Psychol.,* **39,** 57–62. [202]

Smith, Henry C. 1949. Psychometric checks on hypotheses derived from Sheldon's work on physique and temperament. *J. Pers.,* **17,** 310–320. [280]

———. 1955. *Psychology of industrial behavior.* McGraw-Hill. [515]

Smith, M. Brewster, Jerome S. Bruner, and Robert W. White. 1956. *Opinions and personality.* New York: Wiley. [263]

Smith, Walter D., and Dell Lebo. 1956. Some changing aspects of the self-concept of pubescent males. *J. genet. Psychol.,* **88,** 61–75. [385]

Smith, William M. 1952. Past experience and the perception of visual size. *Amer. J. Psychol.,* **65,** 389–403. [121]

Snygg, Donald, and Arthur W. Combs. 1949. *Individual behavior.* New York: Harper. [292, 345]

——— and ———. 1950. The phenomenological approach and the problem of "unconscious" behavior: a reply to Dr. Smith. *J. abnorm. soc. Psychol.,* **45,** 523–528. [339]

Sollenberger, R. T. 1940. Some relationships between the urinary excretion of male hormone by maturing boys and their expressed interests and attitudes. *J. Psychol.*, **9**, 170–190. [386]

Solley, Charles M., Jr. 1954. Drive, barrier conditions, and personality variables affecting problem-solving behavior. Unpublished doctoral dissertation, Univer. of Illinois. [202]

———— and J. Long. 1960. Affect, fantasy, and figure-ground organization. *J. gen. Psychol.*, **62**, 75–82. [81]

———— and Robert Sommer. 1957. Perceptual autism in children. *J. gen. Psychol.*, **56**, 3–11. [80, 81, 120]

———— and Ross Stagner. 1956. Effects of magnitude of temporal barriers, type of goal, and perception of self. *J. exp. Psychol.*, **51**, 62–70. [497]

Sontag, Lester W., Charles T. Baker, and Virginia L. Nelson. 1958. Mental growth and personality development: a longitudinal study. *Monogr. Soc. Res. Child Develpm.*, **23**, No. 2 (Whole No. 68). [472]

Sopchak, Andrew L. 1958. Spearman correlations between MMPI scores of college students and their parents. *J. consult. Psychol.*, **22**, 207–209. [417]

Sparks, Jack Norman. 1952. Teachers' attitudes toward the behavior problems of children. *J. educ. Psychol.*, **43**, 284–291. [463]

Spilka, B., and Gloria Kimble. 1958. Personality correlates of Q-L differentials on the ACE. *J. consult. Psychol.*, **22**, 142. [466]

Spitz, René A. 1945. Hospitalism. *Psychoanal. Stud. Child*, **1**, 53–74. [92, 95, 401]

————. 1950. Anxiety in infancy: a study of its manifestations in the first year of life. *Int. J. Psychoanal.*, **31**, 138–143. [95]

Spranger, E. 1928. *Types of men.* (Tr. by P. J. W. Pigors.) Halle: Niemyer. [268]

Springer, N. N. 1938. The influence of general social status on the emotional stability of children. *J. genet. Psychol.*, **53**, 321–328. [499]

Srole, Leo. 1951. Social dysfunction, personality and social distance attitudes. Paper read at American Sociological Society, December. [514]

Stagner, Ross. 1933a. Relation of personality to academic aptitude and achievement. *J. educ. Res.*, **26**, 648–660. [469]

————. 1933b. Improved norms for four personality tests. *Amer. J. Psychol.*, **45**, 303–307. [179]

————. 1935. Economic status and personality. *Sch. & Soc.*, **42**, 551–552. [501]

————. 1936a. Fascist attitudes: an exploratory study. *J. soc. Psychol.*, **7**, 309–319. [250]

————. 1936b. Fascist attitudes: determining conditions. *J. soc. Psychol.*, **7**, 438–454. [250]

————. 1937. Wisconsin Scale of Personality Traits. *J. abnorm. soc. Psychol.*, **31**, 463–472. [199]

————. 1938. Role of parents in development of emotional instability. *Amer. J. Orthopsychiat.*, **8**, 122–129. [404]

————. 1944. Studies of aggressive social attitudes: III. Role of personal and family scores. *J. soc. Psychol.*, **20**, 129–140. [247]

————. 1945. Opinions of psychologists on peace planning. *J. Psychol.*, **19**, 3–16. [525, 526]

————. 1950. Stereotypes of workers and executives among college men. *J. abnorm. soc. Psychol.*, **45**, 743–748. [242]

————. 1951. Homeostasis as a unifying concept in personality theory. *Psychol. Rev.*, **58**, 5–17. [19, 69–71]

————. 1952. Personality development. *Rev. educ. Res.*, **22**, 459–474. [8, 93]

————. 1954. Attitude toward authority: an exploratory study. *J. soc. Psychol.*, **40**, 197–210. [247]

————. 1956. *Psychology of industrial conflict.* New York: Wiley. [263, 446, 492, 499, 515]

Stagner, Ross. 1958. Gullibility of personnel managers. *Pers. Psychol.*, **11**, 347–352. [50, 149]

———. 1959. Note on communist attitudes and job satisfaction. *Pers. Psychol.*, **11**, 509–514. [513]

——— and Clyde S. Congdon. 1955. Another failure to demonstrate displacement of aggression. *J. abnorm. soc. Psychol.*, **51**, 695–696. [247]

——— and E. T. Katzoff. 1936. Personality as related to birth order and family size. *J. appl. Psychol.*, **20**, 340–346. [421]

——— and Maurice H. Krout. 1940. Correlational study of personality development and structure. *J. abnorm. soc. Psychol.*, **35**, 339–355. [281, 356, 404]

———, Edwin D. Lawson, and J. Weldon Moffitt. 1955. The Krout Personal Preference Scale: a factor-analytic study. *J. clin. Psychol.*, **11**, 103–113. [282]

——— and Weldon J. Moffitt. 1956. A statistical study of Freud's theory of personality types. *J. clin. Psychol.*, **12**, 72–74. [282]

——— and C. E. Osgood. 1941. Experimental analysis of a nationalistic frame of reference. *J. soc. Psychol.*, **14**, 389–401. [241]

——— and ———. 1946. Impact of war on a nationalistic frame of reference. *J. soc. Psychol.*, **24**, 187–215. [241]

Stendler, Celia. 1952. Critical periods in socialization and overdependency. *Child Develpm.*, **23**, 3–12. [403]

———. 1954. Possible causes of overdependency in young children. *Child Develpm.*, **25**, 125–146. [407]

Stephenson, William. 1950. A statistical approach to typology: the study of trait universes. *J. clin. Psychol.*, **6**, 26–38. [271]

———. 1953. *The study of behavior: Q-technique and its methodology.* Chicago: Univer. of Chicago Press. [181, 190, 265, 267, 286]

Stern, George G., Morris I. Stein, and Benjamin S. Bloom. 1956. *Methods in personality assessment.* Glencoe, Ill.: Free Press. [34]

Stewart, A., I. H. Weiland, A. R. Leider, C. A. Mangham, T. H. Holmes, and H. S. Ripley. 1954. Excessive infant crying (colic) in relation to parent behavior. *Amer. J. Psychiat.*, **110**, 687–694. [94, 95]

Stoke, Stuart M. 1950. An inquiry into the concept of identification. *J. genet. Psychol.*, **76**, 163–189. [398]

Stott, Leland H. 1939. Some family life patterns and their relation to personality development in children. *J. exp. Educ.*, **8**, 148–160. [414, 415]

———. 1941. Parent-adolescent adjustment: its measurement and significance. *Charact. and Pers.*, **10**, 140–150. [414, 415]

———. 1945a. Family prosperity in relation to the psychological adjustments of farm folk. *Rural Sociol.*, **10**, 256–263. [501]

———. 1945b. Some environmental factors in relation to the personality adjustments of rural children. *Rural Sociol.*, **10**, 394–403. [501]

Stouffer, Samuel. 1931. Experimental comparison of a statistical and a case history technique of attitude research. *Publ. Amer. Sociol. Soc.*, **25**, 154. [243]

Strodtbeck, Fred L. 1955. *Family interaction and achievement values.* Midwestern Psychological Assn. (See also Baldwin et al., 1958.) [470, 471]

Strong, Edward K. 1955. *Vocational interests 18 years after college.* Minneapolis: Univer. of Minnesota Press. [486, 487]

Stroup, Atlee L. 1953. Predicting marital success or failure in an urban population. *Amer. sociol. Rev.*, **18**, 558–562. [447]

Sullivan, Harry S. 1953. *The interpersonal theory of psychiatry.* New York: Norton. [185]

Sward, K., and M. B. Friedman. 1935. Family resemblance in temperament. *J. abnorm. soc. Psychol.*, **30**, 256–261. [417]

Symonds, Percival M. 1928. *The nature of conduct.* New York: Macmillan. [5]

———. 1931. *Diagnosing personality and conduct.* New York: Appleton-Century. [33, 41]

———. 1951. *The ego and the self.* New York: Appleton-Century-Crofts. [200, 213]

———. 1955. A contribution to our knowledge of the validity of the Rorschach. *J. proj. Tech.,* **19,** 152–162. [56]

Szasz, Thomas S. 1957. *Pain and pleasure.* New York: Basic Books. [337]

Talmadge, Max. 1958. Expressive graphic movements and their relationship to temperament factors. *Psychol. Monogr.,* **72,** No. 16 (Whole No. 469). [150]

Tannenbaum, Arnold S. 1957. Personality change as a result of an experimental change of environmental conditions. *J. abnorm. soc. Psychol.,* **55,** 404–406. [490]

Taylor, Irving A. 1960. Similarities in the structure of extreme social attitudes. *Psychol. Monogr.,* **74,** No. 2 (Whole No. 489). [255]

Taylor, Janet A. 1953. A personality scale of manifest anxiety. *J. abnorm. soc. Psychol.,* **48,** 285–290. [52]

——— and Allan Rechtschaffen. 1959. Manifest anxiety and reversed alphabet printing. *J. abnorm. soc. Psychol.,* **58,** 221–224. [52]

Terman, Lewis M. 1938. *Psychological factors in marital happiness.* New York: McGraw-Hill. [435–438, 440, 442, 443, 445, 449]

———. 1951. Correlates of orgasm adequacy in a group of 556 wives. *J. Psychol.,* **32,** 115–172. [442]

——— and M. H. Oden. 1947. *The gifted child grows up.* Stanford, Calif.: Stanford Univer. Press. [443, 447]

Thetford, William N. 1952. An objective measure of frustration tolerance in evaluating psychotherapy. In Werner Wolff and Joseph W. Precker (Eds.), *Success in psychotherapy.* New York: Grune & Stratton. [130, 131]

Thigpen, Corbett H., and H. M. Cleckley. 1957. *The three faces of Eve.* New York: McGraw-Hill. [196]

Thomason, Bruce. 1955. Marital sexual behavior and total marital adjustments: a research report. In J. Himelhoch and S. L. Fava (Eds.), *Sexual behavior in American society.* New York: Norton. Pp. 153–163. [442]

Thurstone, L. L. 1929. Theory of attitude measurement. *Psychol. Rev.,* **36,** 222–241. [239]

———. 1931. A multiple factor study of vocational interests. *Personnel J.,* **10,** 198–205. [486]

———. 1951. Experimental tests of temperament. In Gosta Ekman, Torsten Husén, Gunnar Johansson, and Carl I. Sandstrom (Eds.), *Essays in psychology: David Katz.* Uppsala: Almqvist and Wiksells. [138]

——— and Thelma G. Thurstone. 1930. A neurotic inventory. *J. soc. Psychol.,* **1,** 3–30. [167, 168]

Toch, Hans H. and Albert H. Hastorf. 1955. Homeostatis in psychology. *Psychiatry,* **18,** 81–92. [70]

Tolman, Edward C. 1932. *Purposive behavior in animals and men.* New York: Appleton-Century. [8]

Tolor, Alexander. 1955. Rigidity of self-concept as a mechanism in the maintenance of personality equilibrium, and as an expression of this equilibrium. *Dissertation Abstr.,* **15,** 1121–1122. [193]

Tryon, Caroline McC. 1939. Evaluation of adolescent personality by adolescents. *Monogr. Soc. Res. Child Develpm.,* **4,** No. 4. [178]

Tryon, R. C. 1940. Studies in individual differences in maze ability: VII. The specific components of maze ability, and a general theory of psychological components. *J. comp. Psychol.,* **30,** 283–335. [369]

Tucker, L. R. 1940. Role of correlated factors in factor analysis. *Psychometrika*, **5**, 141–152. [172]

Turney, A. H., and F. I. Collins. 1940. An experiment in improving the personality of high school seniors. *J. educ. Psychol.*, **31**, 550–553. [476]

Tyler, F. T. 1951. A factorial analysis of 15 MMPI scales. *J. consult. Psychol.*, **15**, 451–456. [44]

Ulett, George A., Goldine Gleser, George Winokur, and Ann Lawler. 1953. The EEG and reaction to photic stimulation as an index of anxiety-proneness. *EEG clin. Neurophysiol.*, **5**, 230–232. [377]

Vernon, P. E. 1933. The Rorschach ink-blot test. *Brit. J. med. Psychol.*, **13**, 89–118, 179–200, 271–291. [55]

———. 1935. Recent work on the Rorschach test. *J. ment. Sci.*, **81**, 849–920. [57]

——— and G. W. Allport. 1931. A test for personal values. *J. abnorm. soc. Psychol.*, **26**, 231–248. [259]

Verplanck, W. S. 1955. The operant from rat to man: an introduction to some recent experiments on human behavior. *Trans. N.Y. Acad. Sci.*, Ser. II, 17, 594–601. [101]

Voas, R. B., J. T. Bair, and R. K. Ambler. 1956. Relationship between behavior in a stress situation and later separation from flight training with expressed anxiety toward flying. *Psychol. Rep.*, **2**, 393–397. [39]

Vorhaus, P. G. 1946. Non-reading as an expression of resistance. *Rorschach Res. Exch.*, **10**, 60–69. [465]

Wallin, Paul. 1954. Marital happiness of parents and their children's attitude toward marriage. *Amer. sociol. Rev.*, **19**, 20–23. [439]

——— and Howard M. Vollmer. 1953. Marital happiness of parents and their children's attitudes to them. *Amer. soc. Rev.*, **18**, 424–431. [445]

Wallinga, Jack V. 1956. Variability of psychiatric diagnosis. *U.S. Armed Forces med. J.*, **7**, 1305–1312. [49]

Walters, James, Doris Pearce, and Lucille Dahms. 1957. Affectional and aggressive behavior of preschool children. *Child Develpm.*, **28**, 15–26. [407]

Warnath, Charles F. 1955. The relation of family cohesiveness and adolescent independence to social effectiveness. *Marriage Fam. Living*, **17**, 346–348. [423]

Warren, Anne Bonner, and David A. Grant. 1955. The relation of conditioned discrimination to the MMPI *Pd* personality variable. *J. exp. Psychol.*, **49**, 23–27. [226]

Watson, Goodwin. 1957. Some personality differences in children related to strict or permissive parental discipline. *J. Psychol.*, **44**, 227–249. [407, 415]

Watson, J. B. 1924. *Psychology from the standpoint of the behaviorist.* (2nd ed.) Philadelphia: Lippincott. [5, 93, 112]

Weber, Christian O. 1949. Homeostasis and servo-mechanisms for what? *Psychol. Rev.*, **56**, 234–239. [70]

Weisgerber, Charles A. 1954. The relationship of perseveration to a number of personality traits and to adjustment. *J. gen. Psychol.*, **50**, 3–13. [171]

Weiss, Walter, and Bernard J. Fine. 1955. Opinion change as a function of some intrapersonal attributes of the communicatees. *J. abnorm. soc. Psychol.*, **51**, 246–253. [231]

——— and ———. 1956. The effect of induced aggressiveness on opinion change. *J. abnorm. soc. Psychol.*, **52**, 109–114. [231]

Wenger, Marion A. 1941. The measurement of individual differences in autonomic balance. *Psychosom. Med.*, **3**, 427–434. [374]

———. 1947. Preliminary study of the significance of measures of autonomic balance. *Psychosom. Med.*, **9**, 301–309. [375]

——— and Margaret Wellington. 1943. The measurement of autonomic balance in children: method and normative data. *Psychosom. Med.*, **5**, 241–253. [374]

Werner, Heinz, and Seymour Wapner. 1955. Changes in psychological distance under conditions of danger. *J. Pers.*, **24**, 153–167. [82]

Werre, P. F. 1957. *Relationships between electroencephalographic and psychological data in normal adults.* Leiden: Universitaire Pers. [377]

White, Benjamin. 1954. Visual and auditory closure. *J. exp. Psychol.*, **48**, 234–240. [36]

————— and Eli Saltz. 1957. Measurement of reproducibility. *Psychol. Bull.*, **54**, 81–99. [168]

White, Leonard D. (Ed.) 1956. *The state of the social sciences.* Chicago: Univer. of Chicago Press. [475]

Whiting, John W. M., and Irvin L. Child. 1953. *Child training and personality.* New Haven, Conn.: Yale Univer. Press. [205, 297, 425, 505]

Whyte, W. H. 1956. *The organization man.* New York: Simon and Schuster. [491]

Wickes, Frances G. 1938. *The inner world of man.* New York: Rinehart. [286]

Wickman, E. 1928. *Children's behavior and teachers' attitudes.* New York: Commonwealth Fund. [462]

Wiersma, E. 1906. Die Sekundärfunktionen bei Psychosen. *J. f. Psychol. u. Neurol.*, **8**, 1–24. [138]

Wilder, Russell M. 1952. Experimental induction of psychoneuroses through restriction of intake of thiamin. In Milbank Memorial Fund. *Biology of mental health and disease.* New York: Hoeber-Harper. Pp. 531–539. [391]

Williams, Meyer. 1947. An experimental study of intellectual control under stress and associated Rorschach factors. *J. consult. Psychol.*, **11**, 21–29. [56]

Williams, Roger J. 1953. *Free and unequal.* Austin, Tex.: Univer. of Texas Press. [370]

—————. 1956. *Biochemical individuality.* New York: John Wiley. [370, 387]

—————. 1958. Chemical anthropology—an open door. *Amer. Scientist*, March, 1958, 1–23. [388]

Winch, Robert F. 1950. Some data bearing on the Oedipus complex. *J. abnorm. soc. Psychol.*, **45**, 481–490. [430]

—————. 1952. *The modern family.* New York: Holt. [428]

—————. 1958. *Mate-selection: a study of complementary needs.* New York: Harper. [429]

—————, Thomas Ktsanes, and Virginia Ktsanes. 1954. Theory of complementary needs in mate-selection. *Amer. soc. Rev.*, **19**, 241–249. [429]

Winthrop, Henry. 1957. The consistency of attitude patterns as a function of body type. *J. Pers.*, **25**, 372–382. [280]

Wishner, Julius. 1953. Neurosis and tension: an exploratory study of relationship of physiological and Rorschach measures. *J. abnorm. soc. Psychol.*, **48**, 253–260. [374]

Witkin, Herman A., Helen B. Lewis, Karen Machover, P. B. Meissner, and Seymour Wapner. 1954. *Personality through perception.* New York: Harper. [143, 203]

Wolfe, J. B. 1936. Effectiveness of token rewards for chimpanzees. *Comp. Psychol. Monogr.*, **13**, No. 60. [297]

Wolff, Werner. 1943. *The expression of personality: experimental depth psychology.* New York: Harper. [192, 210]

Woodworth, Donald G., Frank Barron, and Donald W. MacKinnon. 1957. *An analysis of life history interviewers' ratings for 100 Air Force captains.* AFPTRC-TN-57-129 (ASTIA Doc. No. Ad. 146 401). [221]

Woodworth, R. S. 1935. *Psychology.* (3rd ed.) New York: Holt. [436]

Wright, H. F. 1937. Influence of barriers upon strength of motivation. Duke Univer. *Contr. psychol. Theor.*, **1**, No. 3. Durham, N.C.: Duke Univer. Press. [354]

Yeakel, E. H., and R. P. Rhoades. 1941. Comparison of body and endocrine gland weights of emotional and non-emotional rats. *Endocrinology*, **28**, 337–340. [367]

Young, Kimball. 1930. *Social psychology.* New York: Crofts. [352, 461]

Young, Paul T. 1936. Motivation of behavior. New York: Wiley. [299, 307]

———. 1955. The role of hedonic processes in motivation. In Marshall R. Jones (Ed.), *Nebraska symposium on motivation.* Pp. 193–238. [100]

——— and E. H. Shuford, Jr. 1954. Intensity, duration, and repetition of hedonic processes as related to acquisition of motives. *J. comp. physiol. Psychol.,* **47,** 298–305. [100]

Zimmerman, Donald W. 1957. Durable secondary reinforcement: method and theory. *Psychol. Rev.,* **64,** 373–383. [100, 337]

Index

Ability, traits and use of, 466
Abstraction, personality as, 8
Academic achievement (see Achievement)
Academic excellence, 482, 528
Acceleration stress, 392
Acceptance of self, 198
Accommodation, marital, 446
Achievement, family values and, 470
   need, 347, 504
     and family values, 470
     training for, 472
   traits and, 464–470
Acquiescence, 151
   and authoritarianism, 253
   and self-confidence, 204
Active-motor type, 146
Activity level, 299, 370
Adaptation level, 78, 103, 243
Administrator, school, 451
Adolescence, 422
Adrenal cortex, 380
Adrenal medulla, 381
Aesthetic need, 303
Affective tone and motivation, 299
Affiliation, 349
   and sociability, 358
Affluent society, 529
Age differences, attitudes, 248
   traits, 178
Age role, 178
Aggression, 112, 407
   delinquency and, 408
   displacement of, 114
   expression of, 113
   intensity of, 113
Aim, 311
Aloneness, 330

Ambiguity, intolerance of, 119, 141
   and authoritarianism, 255
   as threat, 82
Anal stage, 107
Anal type, 281
Analysis of personality, 10
Anchoring point, type as, 273
Animistic versus realistic thinking, 17
Anomie, 513
Anti-Semitism, 528
Anxiety, 115–120, 315, 329
   authoritarianism and, 255
   closure and, 142
   examinations and, 476
   physiology of, 130
Apperceptive mass, 105
Approach-approach conflict, 116
Approach-avoidance conflict, 116, 315
   in occupational choice, 495
Areal factor, 148, 150
Arithmetic, 465
Aspiration and self-image, 189
Aspiration level, 207–209
   and ego weakness, 209
   and group norms, 208
   variability of, 208
Assumed similarity, 140
Attitude, 238
   age differences in, 248
   attributes of, 238
   economic factors in, 511
   family similarity, 419
   objective reference, 238
   perception of others and, 494
Attraction of opposites, 428
Authoritarianism, 152, 247, 249–258, 530
   acquired preference for, 490

577

Authoritarianism, childrearing and, 416
  conformity and, 258
  versus democratic policy, 457
  economic status and, 513
  of group leaders, 453
  parents and, 251
Authority figures, delinquency and, 233
  hostility to, 480, 526
  parents as, 127
Autobiography, 242
Autoerotic behavior, 321
Autonomic nervous system, 130, 367, 372–376
Autonomous motive, 334
Avoidance conflict, 116

Barrier, 111, 130
Behavior ratings, 37, 96
Behaviorism, 29, 295
Belongingness need, 303
Biochemical individuality, 387–389
Biogenic drives, 290–296
Birth order, 421
Birth trauma, 87
Blockage, 111, 130
Body image, 186
  and social norms, 187
Body type (*see* Somatotype)

Castration complex, 108, 310
Categorizing attitude, 140
Catharsis, 114
  in school, 475
Cathexis, 309, 336
Central nervous system, traits and, 376–378
Centrifugal factor, 148
Cerebrotonia, 275
Chance, 33, 38*n*., 57*n*., 174
Change and homeostasis, 22, 105, 109, 132
Character, 214, 316
  ego strength and, 219
  generality versus specificity, 216, 233
  inner organization, 220–224
  training, 217
Character Education Inquiry, 215–218
Child-centered school, 474
Childhood experience and marital adjustment, 437

Childrearing techniques, 419
  economic class and, 505–507
Class (*see* Social class)
Closure, 36, 83, 283
  and anxiety, 123, 142
  intolerance of ambiguity and, 259
Cognitive need, 303
  of pupils, 462
Color on Rorschach, 55
Common traits, 43
Communists, 522
Company officials, 242
Compensation for inferiority, 327
Competition, 357, 421, 482, 528
Complementary needs in marriage, 428
Conditioning, classical, 98
  instrumental, 99
Conflict, 110, 115–117
  school achievement and, 465
  solutions, 120–125
  types of, 115
Conformity, 39, 151
  authoritarianism and, 258
  ego strength, 204
  young executives, 491
Congenital activity type, 370
Conscience, 316, 411
Consensual validation, 9, 74, 77*n*.
Consistency, in defense mechanisms, 144
  of *F* scale, 250
  quest for, 194
  of ratings, 34
  of trait scores, 175–177
  (*See also* Reliability)
Constancies, perceptual, 82
  and homeostasis, 83–84
  of persons, 83
  as steady states, 83
Construct validity, 51
Context, 74
  added by memory, 75
Contrast in description, 11
Conventionalism, 250, 253
Cooperation, 421
Correlation, 34*n*., 96
Cortical equilibrium, 295
Cortical inhibition, 376
Counteraggression, 114
Countercathexis, 310
Criminals, 233

Criterion versus construct validity, 51
  delinquent groups, 224–231
  fallibility of, 49
  group, 44
Critical-period hypothesis, 402
Cross-validation, 49
Cultural climate, 248
Culture, as factor in motivation, 325
  influenced by personality, 23, 516

Death instinct, 112
Deficit drives, 292
Definition, of personality, 4–7
  of traits, errors in, 35
Delaying tactics and school failure, 479
Delinquents, body type of, 228, 278
  family influences on, 231
  MMPI scores, 225–227
  Rorschach data, 227–228
  self-image of, 226
Democracy, in childrearing, 406
  in industry, 527
  in school, 454
Dependency, 94, 407
  and marital selection, 430
Depression, 91
Deprivation, 291, 292, 334
  infantile, 399
  sensory, 400
Determinism, 18, 522
Deviant response style, 153–154
Dichotomy, of good-bad characters, 235
  of personality types, 266
Differentiation of social roles, 97
Dimensions of meaning, 239
Discharge control, 373
Discharge types, 145–146
Discipline, 416
Discontinuity, 423
Discrepancy of self-image from ideal, 191
Displacement, 114
  of aggression, 247, 512, 529
  of anxiety, 118
  of libido, 309
Distortion, memory, 120, 173
  perceptual, 120–122, 201–202, 244
Distribution, errors of, 35
Disturbance of equilibrium, 19, 69
  and developmental progress, 109
  duty of education in, 481

Divorce, 433
  prediction of, 443
Dominance, 328, 385
  conflicts over, 433
  physique and, 279
Dominative behavior in teaching, 455
Drive arousal, 373
Dropouts, 467
Drugs, 393

Economic factors, and attitudes, 511
  and traits, 498–504
Ectomorphy, 275
Edwards Personal Preference Schedule, 47,
    459, 493
Efficiency in mental work, 202, 468
Ego, 315
Ego autonomy, 203–205, 343
Ego defense, 496
Ego ideal, 190
Ego strength, 43, 164, 167, 200–202, 315
  and character, 219
  delinquency and, 233
  development of, 413
  guidance for, 477
  and marital adjustment, 439
  of mother and child, 415
  of parents, 406
  physiological correlates, 168, 381, 394
  of teachers, 458
    and pupils, 463
Egotism (see Self-esteem)
Electroencephalogram, 376–377
Embedded-figures task, 140
Emotional instability (see Ego strength)
Emotions, 93–97
Emphasis factor, 148, 150
Encapsulation, 532
Endocrine glands, 170, 367, 378–386
Endomorphy, 275, 299
Energy level, 299
Energy mobilization, 129, 340
Equilibrium (see Steady state)
Epinephrine, 381
Ergic theory, 301–303
Error in observing personality, 33–37
Esteem need, 303
Examinations, anxiety about, 476
Excitement, 90–91

Executive, social role, 490
  vertical orientation, 492
Expectancy, class differences in, 503
  economic deprivation and, 508
  elimination of, 337
  emotion and, 93
  family determination, 398
  frustration and, 114
  in marriage, 426
  need to modify, 529
  about occupations, 486
  personality as, 8
  about school, 451
Explanation, "field," 21
  historical, 21
  levels of reality in, 21
Exploratory drive, 295
Expressive movements, 15, 40, 147–151
Extrapunitive aggression, 113
Extraversion, 164
  and EEG, 377
  and scanning, 273
  as type, 272

F (fascism) scale, 152
  acquiescent response set, 253
  consistency of, 250
  left-wing bias, 252
  mothers, 416
  validity of, 251
Factor analysis, 31, 96, 158–159
  of teaching performance, 452
  "ways of life," 262
Fads, 424
Failure, effect on personality, 478
  required by school rules, 456
  and self-evaluation, 210
Family, and delinquency, 231
  and expectancy, 398
  impact of economic hardship on, 508
  influence on attitudes, 246
Family morale, 405, 414
Family values and need achievement, 470
Fantasy, 132
  and self-image, 196
Fascism, 511
Father role, in delinquency, 232
  in school achievement, 471
  in trait determination, 406

Fear, 93
  of pregnancy, 443
Feedback, 79, 91, 170
  negative, 79n.
  physiological, 79, 90
  positive, 79n., 114
  role in temperament, 279
  social, 79
Feelings, 88–93
  physiological bases for, 90
  role of feedback in, 90
  temperament and, 92
Field-analytical perception, 142
Field-dependent perception, 143, 203
Figure-ground organization, 81, 142
  modified by learning, 81
Focusing, 81, 123, 343
  of interests, 487
Forced-choice technique, 47
Forgetting, selective, 172
  trait change and, 177
Frame of reference, 78, 103, 243, 262, 273
Free will as perceptual problem, 523
Freudian theory, of motives, 308–326
  of stages, 106–110
  test based on, 46, 282
Frustration, 111
  and aggression, 112
  arbitrary, 113
  authority figures and, 113
  economic, 499, 508
  physiological effects of, 373
    and traits, 382, 391
  in social planning, 519
  of teachers, 461
    and pupils, 475
  and valence, 293
Frustration tolerance, 130, 197, 200, 481
  and partial reinforcement, 103
Functional autonomy, 336
Functional unity, 157
  of motives, 305

General adaptation syndrome, 129
Generalization, 97
Genetic continuity, 18, 105
Gestalt theory, 283
Gestures, 147–151
Glandular factors (*see* Endocrine glands)

Goals, classification of, 345
  conscious and unconscious, 339
  cultural determination of, 350
  as energy mobilizers, 340
  perceptual definition of, 338
  tenacity of, 342
Gonads, 384
  maturation, and traits, 385
Graphic response style, 147
Graphology, 149
Gratification, 293
Group approval, and delinquency, 234
  and self-image, 188
Group formation, 532
Guess Who test, 31
Guidance in schools, 476
Guilt, 201
  and authoritarianism, 255

Habit and aggressive behavior, 114
Halo effect, 36
Happiness in marriage, 436
Hate relationships, 322
Heredity, and biogenic drives, 292
  and ego strength, 366
  of temperament, 279
  of traits, 170, 364–372
  and unique personality, 370
Hierarchy, of needs, 303, 335
  of steady states, 85
  of values, 103–106, 223
Homeostasis, 19, 69–71, 291, 304, 350, 373
  atomistic, 20
  criminal behavior and, 234
  feelings and, 88–93
  holistic, 20
  and perceiving, 71
  and personality change, 22, 105, 109
  and social change, 518–522
  and valence, 71
  and values, 237
Homogamy, 428
Honesty, 216–217
Hostility, and authoritarianism, 250, 255
  and delinquency, 228
Human nature, biological foundation of,
  363
Hunger, prolonged, and traits, 390
Hyperthyroid, 379
Hypothetical construct, 359

Id, 314
Ideal self, 190
  of delinquents, 232
Identical twins, 365
Identification, 127, 310, 322, 417
  and delinquency, 232
  with parents, 108, 417
  with teachers, 482
Ideology as valued steady state, 84
Ideomotor discharge type, 146
Illusion, 74
Imitation, 126
Impetus, 311
Imprinting, 96, 399
Impulse control, 128, 168, 201, 232, 233,
  316
  character and, 223
  EEG and, 377
Independence, 422
  training for, 423, 472
Indicator, 169
Individual differences, 13, 88
Industrial democracy, 527
Infantile deprivation, 399, 401
Infantile experiences, 95, 104
Infantile sexuality, 321
Infection, resistance to, 393
Inferiority, 327, 328
  and social structure, 357
Inhibition, 128, 201
Ink-blot test (*see* Rorschach test)
Insight, 198
  and authoritarianism, 258
Instability, intolerance of, 141
Instinctoid theory, 303–306
Instincts, 289–290, 301–306
Institutional pattern in schools, 451
Integration, relation to occupation, 487
  of self-image, 192
Integrity, 221, 234
  and impulse control, 223
  and social expectancy, 222
Intelligence, 170
  and authoritarianism, 254
  influence in marital selection, 431
Intelligence quotient and personality vari-
  ables, 472
Interest and occupational success, 486
Interoceptive stimulation, 378
Intervening variable, 186
  personality as, 7

Introjection, 125, 316, 354
Intropunitive aggression, 113
Introversion, 164
  as anchoring point, 273
  and EEG, 377
  and scanning, 273
  as type, 272
Inventory, 42–52
  assumptions of, 43
  class bias in, 501
  qualities needed, 48
Isolation experiments, 95

Job satisfactions, 495
  and child rearing, 498

Krout Personal Preference Schedule, 47

Labile response type, 145
Laissez-faire climate, 455
Learning, 98–103
  and conflict adjustment, 125
  effect of attitude on, 245
Leveling, 138–139
Levels of consciousness, 339
Libidinal zones, 311
Libido, 309, 336
Lie score, MMPI, 45
Life plan, 326
Location on Rorschach, 54
Love of mother as secondary reward, 94,
  400
Love relationship, 321
Loyalty, 235
Lynching, 511

Malnutrition and personality, 85
Marital adjustment, 432–448
  and childhood experience, 437
  contraceptives, 443
  and dominance conflicts, 433
  measurement of, 436–444
  multiple predictor study, 441
  and parental adjustment, 445
  and response conflicts, 432
  role of children in, 444
  traits and, 438

Marital selection, 428
Martyr, 86, 237
Masculinity as goal, 327
Mask versus inner personality, 6, 53, 101,
  151
Matched-dependent behavior, 126
Mental-health approach in schools, 475
Mesomorphy, 228, 275
  and aggression, 299
Miniature situation, 39
Minnesota Multiphasic Personality Inventory (MMPI), 44–46
  delinquents, 226
  economic status and, 500
  school achievement and, 467
  teachers, profile, 460
Models, parents as, 417
  for personality, 127, 132
Monozygotic (identical) twins, 365
Moral behavior, 214–220
  generality versus specificity in, 216
  and reputation, 218
Mother country, 247
Mothering, patterns of, 404
Mothers, role in delinquency, 232
  and school achievement, 471
  in trait determination, 404
Motivation, biological approach to, 290
  as determiner of ability, 369, 473, 479
  sociological approach to, 300
Movement on Rorschach, 55
Multidrive theory, 298
Multiple causation, 18, 175
Multiple goals, 495
Murderers, 233
Myokinetic psychodiagnosis, 149

National differences in values, 262
Nazis, 522
Need achievement, 347, 504
Need affiliation, 349
Need persistence, 496
Needs, esteem, 104
  love, 104
  Maslow classification, 104
  Murray classification, 346
  physiological, 104
  safety, 104
  self-actualization, 104
  of teachers, 459

Negroes, attitudes toward, 246
Neuroticism (*see* Ego strength)
Nondeficit drives, 294
Nonsatiating motive, 333
Norepinephrine, 381
Normal curve, 13, 173
Norms, acquisition of social, 128
   and class differences, 510
Numerical measures, 12

Object of instinct, 311
Objectivity, and observer prejudice, 64
   of projectives, 62
Oedipus complex, 108, 119, 310, 322
   and marital selection, 429
Opinionaire, 239
   Guttman, 240
   Likert, 240
   Thurstone, 239
Oral stage, 106
Oral type, 281
Overachievers, 467, 469

Pain as drive, 294
Parasympathetic nervous system, 131
Parent image, 119
Parental role in marriage, 445
Part-whole relation to types, 283
Partial reinforcement, 102
   and frustration tolerance, 103, 338
Peace planning, 526
Peer ratings, 49, 423
Perceived probability of goal attainment,
   103, 113, 293, 335, 338
Percept, 15, 75
Perception, as basis of personality, 8, 70–
   83
   of others, and self-image, 198
      and social role, 494
   and problems of measurement, 63
   social versus physical, 76
Perceptual constancy, 338
Perceptual defense, 120–123, 315
   as personal style, 144
   and social change, 525
Perceptual style, 138–144, 202–204
   and ego autonomy, 203
   and motivation, 343
   and vigilance, 121

Permissiveness, 405
   in school, 480
Perspective, 212
Pessimism of conservatives, 256
Phenomenal field, 72–73, 105, 143, 333
Phobia, 118
Physiological needs (biogenic drives), 290–
   296
Physique, and delinquency, 278
   and dominance, 279
   and personality type, 274–280
   and ways of life, 280
   (*See also* Somatotype)
Picture-frustration test, 61
Pleasantness as sign of equilibrium, 88
Pleasure principle, 117, 311
Porteus maze and delinquency, 230
Power, valuation of, 250
Power figures, 127
Prejudice and economic frustration, 511–
   513
Premarital sex experience, 435
Primacy, law of, 398
Probability of goal attainment, 113, 293,
   335, 497
Process, personality as, 18
Profile correlation, 282
Profile method, 190
Profile types, 267
Projection, 125
Projective tests, of attitudes, 242
   and economic class, 503
   (*See also* Rorschach test; Thermatic
   Apperception Test)
Psychosexual development, 106–108, 319
Psychosomatic conditions, 130
Psychotherapy, 130
Punishment, and aggression, 411
   and delinquency, 231, 232
Pure case, type as, 284

Q sort, 190
Questionnaire (*see* Inventory; Opinionaire)

Rating scales, 32
Rationalization, 124
Reactive inhibition, 376
   as basis for types, 270
Reading disability, 465

Realistic percepts, 168
Realistic thinking, 17
Reality for each individual, 9, 72, 76
Reality principle, 117, 312
Reasoning, 132
Recording instruments, 28, 62
Reference group, 188, 243
Reinforcement, 99
    partial, 102, 105, 338
    secondary, 100
    verbal, 101
Rejection, 407
    and delinquency, 408
    motives for, 416
Reliability, 158, 175
    chance errors and, 64
    consistency, 34, 48
    of psychiatric diagnoses, 49*n*.
    of ratings, 33
    of Rorschach, 55
    stability, 34, 48
    of TAT, 60
Repetition compulsion, 313
Repression, 123–124
Research scientists, temperament profile,
    488
Resistance to social conformity, 531
Response, adaptive versus expressive as-
    pect, 15
    personality as, 6, 11, 37–40
    trait as, 160
Response conflicts and divorce, 433
Response set, 253
Response shaping, 101
Response style, 144–154
Responsibility, 220
    perceived, 242
Rigidity, 139, 201, 342
    and authoritarianism, 255, 256
Role and perception of others, 494
Role conflict and teacher personality, 457
Role system, in marriage, 426
    occupational, 485
    in schools, 452
Rorschach test, 53–58
    administration of, 54
    of delinquents, 227–228
    interpretation of, 54–55
    reliability of, 55
    school achievement and, 467
    validity of, 56

Safety needs, 303
Sampling, 122, 123
    perceptual, 75
Sampling error, 64, 516
Sane society, 518
Satiation, 71, 291, 292, 335
Scalogram, 240
Scanning, 76, 80, 140, 377, 476
Scapegoat, 246, 528
Schema, 77, 103
    (*See also* Stereotypes)
Secondary drive, 296, 300, 337
Secondary reinforcement, 100, 297, 300
    337
Security, 94, 196–198, 422
    and authoritarianism, 259
    expectancy and, 95
    and marital adjustment, 439
    need for, 329
Segmental selves, 196
Selective breeding, 367
Selective forgetting, 172, 245
    (*See also* Repression)
Selective learning, 245, 398
Selective perception, 120, 161, 172, 244
Self and self-image, 185, 205
Self-actualizing, 206
    need for, 303
Self-awareness, 183–184
Self-enhancement, 345
Self-esteem, 199, 329
    and efficient functioning, 202
Self-image, 168, 305, 337, 370, 532
    and attitudes, 242
    and delinquent behavior, 234
    unconscious, 209
Self-ratings, 50
Self-respect, 195
Semantic differential, 47, 202, 241, 252
Semantic space, 244
Sensory deprivation, 400
Sentence-completion test, 61
Sex, barriers to, 353
    as drive, 294, 309, 352
Sex role, 179
Sexual adjustment in marriage, 442
Sharpening, 139
Sibling relationships, 420
Similarity, in marriage, 428, 440
    parent-child, 417
Similarity scaling, 32

Single-drive theory, 298, 309, 495
16 PF Scale, 46
Sociability and affiliation, 358
Social change, 519–532
  resistance to, 520
Social class, and attitudes, 511
  and temperament, 498–504
Social climate, 328
  in schools, 453
Social expectancy, 180
Social roles, differentiation of, 97, 128
  (*See also* Role)
Socialism, 241, 530
Socialization, 115, 128, 180, 296
  and delinquency, 233
Society as the patient, 516
Sociological view of motivation, 300
Sociometry, 31
Somatic discharge type, 146
Somatotonia, 275
Somatotype, 228, 371
  and delinquency, 228
  and temperament, 274–280
Source trait, 163
Specificity of ANS responses, 375
Stability, of ratings, 34
  of self-image, 193
  of trait scores, 175
Stable response type, 145
Stages, Freudian theory of, 106–108
  anal, 107
  genital, 108
  infantile passive, 106
  latency, 108
  oral, 106
  phallic, 107
Standardization and sampling error, 64
Status, 486
Steady state, 19, 70, 84
  disturbed by goal seeking, 335
Stereotypes, 36, 238
  attributes of, 238
  in marital selection, 430
Stimulation, internal versus external, 80, 207
Stimulus, personality as, 5, 11, 30–37
Stimulus-bound personalities, 255
Stimulus generalization, 118
Stress, 111, 129–132, 381
  acceleration, 392
  and homeostasis, 129

Stress, mastery of, 383
  tolerance, 129, 200, 371
Strictness, 405
Structured test (*see* Inventory)
Study of values, stability, 261
  validity, 260
Style (*see* Perceptual style; Response style)
Subcultures, 531
Sublimation, 343
Suggestibility, 127
Suggestion, 126, 354
Superego, 232, 316, 412, 517
Supraordinate type, 267
Surface trait, 163
Symbolism, 118
Sympathetic nervous system, 131
  balance with parasympathetic system, 374

Temperament, 92
  and ANS, 373
  and glands, 378–386
  occupational choice and, 488
  role of heredity in, 279, 364–370
  social class and, 498
  traits of, 156
Tempo, personal, 148, 150
Tension, 71, 129, 291, 311, 340
Tension level as response style, 147
Thematic Apperception Test (TAT), 58–61
  administration of, 58
  scoring, 59
  and self-image, 192
  and therapy interviews, 61
Threat, 310
  ambiguity as, 82
Threshold, for homeostatic disturbance, 20, 211
  sensory, 75, 370
Thyroid, 379
Trait, 14, 156, 238
  as abstraction, 159
  age differences in, 178
  common, 43, 157
  consistency of, 175–177
  continuum, 162
  effect on marital adjustment, 438
  as frame of reference, 160
  and goal orientation, 358

Trait, higher-order habit, 160
  interpersonal definition of, 166
  as mental set, 160
  origin of, 169
  and personal style, 173
  quantitative nature of, 43
  sex differences in, 179
  subjective reference of, 160
  surface versus source, 163
  unique, 157
Transfer, positive, 97
Twins, identical versus fraternal, 365
Type, 265
  anal-erotic, 281
  as anchoring point, 285
  based on body type, 274
  based on mental functions, 271
  based on perception, 265
  introvert versus extravert, 271
  multivariate determination, 269
  oral-erotic, 281
  phallic, 282
  psychoanalytic theory of, 280–283
  as pure case, 284
  as qualitative grouping, 270

Unconscious goal, 339
  and marital conflict, 435
Unconscious impulse, 319
Unconscious self-judgment, 209
Underachievers, 467, 469
Underprivileged worker, 293, 334, 497, 527
Unequal units, errors due to, 35
Union leader, 242
  goals of, 493
  horizontal orientation, 492
  occupational role, 491

Unique person, 7, 186
  biochemical basis, 387
  heredity and, 370, 387–389
  as object of observation, 16
  and reward value, 100
Unity of personality, 19, 193
  perceived, 36
Unpleasantness as sign of disturbance, 89
Upper-class personality, 504

Valence, 71, 89, 104, 297, 310, 337
  negative, 71, 115, 118
  positive, 71, 119
  strengthened by barrier, 354
Validity, 34
  affected by situation, 48
  constant errors and, 63
  of F scale, 251
  of inventories, 48, 50
  of projectives, 56, 60, 81n.
  of ratings, 34
Value, 259, 261
  family similarity in, 419
Value system, conflicts within, 517
Vigilance, 120, 315
Visceral response, awareness of, 91, 378
Viscerotonia, 275
Vitamin intake, 391
Vocal discharge type, 146

War, prevention of, 526
Warmth of mother-child interaction, 406
Ways of life, 261–262
  and physique, 280
Whole personality, 14, 30
Will power, 224
Will-to-power, 326, 345, 356–358